Against Affective Formalism

Against Affective Formalism

MATISSE, BERGSON, MODERNISM

Todd Cronan

University of Minnesota Press
Minneapolis
London

MM

Publication of this book has been aided by a grant from the Millard Meiss Publication Fund of the College Art Association.

The University of Minnesota Press gratefully acknowledges financial assistance provided for the publication of this book from the College of Arts and Sciences and the Laney Graduate School at Emory University.

Published by the University of Minnesota Press
111 Third Avenue South, Suite 290
Minneapolis, MN 55401-2520
http://www.upress.umn.edu

Library of Congress Cataloging-in-Publication Data

Cronan, Todd.
Against affective formalism : Matisse, Bergson, modernism / Todd Cronan.
Includes bibliographical references and index.
ISBN 978-0-8166-7602-6 (hc)
ISBN 978-0-8166-7603-3 (pb)
1. Matisse, Henri, 1869–1954—Criticism and interpretation. 2. Bergson, Henri, 1859–1941. 3. Modernism (Aesthetics). 4. Representation (Philosophy). I. Title.
N6853.M33C76 2013
759.4—dc23

2013015888

Printed in the United States of America on acid-free paper

20 19 18 17 16 15 14 13   10 9 8 7 6 5 4 3 2 1

I think what we're missing is an idea, an idea to express outside painting. To push to its conclusion what we were discussing, that is to say no longer to do anything that represents anything. . . . Perhaps we are a happy generation in the sense that we might be the only one to have realized that stone, color, etc., no matter the material in which the human spirit finds pleasure, has its own life, independent of what we make it represent. . . . Do you understand? It is crucial!

—André Derain to Henri Matisse, 1906

The only thing one should ask of a painter is that he express his intentions clearly. . . . My goal is to render my emotion.

—Henri Matisse, 1929

Contents

List of Illustrations ix

INTRODUCTION Modernism against Representation 1

ONE Painting as Affect Machine 23

TWO Freedom and Memory: *Bergson's Theory of Hypnotic Agency* 65

THREE The Influence of Others: *Matisse and* Personnalité 109

FOUR Matisse and Mimesis 165

CONCLUSION From Art to Object: *The Case of Paul Valéry* 221

Acknowledgments 253

Notes 255

Index 311

List of Illustrations

Figure 1.1. Henri Matisse, *Harmony in Red,* 1908 25

Figure 1.2. Henri Matisse, interior of the Chapel of the Rosary, Vence, France, 1948–51 29

Figure 1.3. Eugène Delacroix, *The Massacre at Chios,* 1824 31

Figure 1.4. Henri Matisse, *Music,* 1910 33

Figure 1.5. Nicolas Poussin, *The Testament of Eudamidas,* 1644–48 40

Figure 1.6. Paul Gauguin, *Aha oe feii? (Are You Jealous?),* 1892 49

Figure 1.7. Paul Gauguin, *Manao tupapau (The Spirit of the Dead Watching),* 1892 50

Figure 1.8. Anonymous Flemish painter, *Lot and His Daughters,* ca. 1500 62

Figure 2.1. Henri Matisse, *Mademoiselle Yvonne Landsberg,* 1914 100

Figure 2.2. Henri Matisse, *Lagoon,* from *Jazz,* 1947 106

Figure 3.1. Paul Cézanne, *The Large Bathers,* 1906 118

Figure 3.2. Henri Matisse, *Self-Portrait,* 1906 125

Figure 3.3. Henri Matisse, sketch of a film set, ca. 1921–23 127

Figure 3.4. Henri Matisse, *Still Life with a Checked Tablecloth,* ca. 1903 131

Figure 3.5. Henri Matisse, *The Red Blouse,* 1936 132

Figure 3.6. Henri Matisse, *The Swimmer in the Aquarium,* from *Jazz,* 1947 133

Figure 3.7. Henri Matisse, *The Alps in Savoy,* ca. 1901 135

Figure 3.8. Henri Matisse, *Pine Trees,* ca. 1901 135

Figure 3.9. Paul Cézanne, *Standing Nude,* 1898–99 137

Figure 3.10. Henri Matisse, *Standing Nude,* ca. 1901 137

Figure 3.11. Henri Matisse, *Standing Nude,* ca. 1905 138

Figure 3.12. Henri Matisse, *The Model,* ca. 1900 139

Figure 3.13. Henri Matisse, *Nude Study in Blue,* ca. 1899–1900 139

Figure 3.14. Henri Matisse, *The Weeper,* 1900–1903 140

Figure 3.15. Henri Matisse, *Standing Nude, Arm Raised,* 1901–3 141

Figure 3.16. Paul Cézanne, *The Bather,* ca. 1885 143

Figure 3.17. Henri Matisse, *Interior with a Young Girl (Girl Reading),* 1905–6 144

Figure 3.18. Henri Matisse, *Auguste Pellerin II,* 1917 144

Figure 3.19. Henri Matisse, *Guitarist,* 1903 146

Figure 3.20. Édouard Manet, *Olympia,* 1863–65 147

Figure 3.21. Édouard Manet, *The Dead Toreador,* ca. 1864 148

Figure 3.22. Henri Matisse, *The Dead Christ, after Philippe de Champaigne,* 1895 149
Figure 3.23. Édouard Manet, *Monk in Prayer,* 1865 150
Figure 3.24. Jean-Baptiste-Camille Corot, *Seated Monk, Reading,* 1857 150
Figure 3.25. Henri Matisse, *Italian Man (Bevilacqua),* ca. 1902 151
Figure 3.26. Pablo Picasso, *Winter Landscape,* 1950 161
Figure 3.27. Hélène Adant, photograph of Matisse's bedroom at Hotel Régina, Nice, ca. 1952 162
Figure 4.1. Henri Matisse, *Jaguar Devouring a Hare (after Antoine-Louis Barye),* 1899–1901 173
Figure 4.2. Henri Matisse, *Portrait Medallion (II),* 1894 177
Figure 4.3. Henri Matisse, *Still Life with Fruits and Bottles,* 1896 179
Figure 4.4. Henri Matisse, *Still Life with Clay Pitcher and Black Knife,* 1896 179
Figure 4.5. Henri Matisse, *Still Life with Two Bottles,* 1897 180
Figure 4.6. Henri Matisse, *Still Life with Apples,* 1897 181
Figure 4.7. Henri Matisse, *Room at Ajaccio,* 1898 183
Figure 4.8. Henri Matisse, *Still Life with Black Knives,* 1898 184
Figure 4.9. Henri Matisse, *Still Life with an Oil Jug,* 1898 186
Figure 4.10. Henri Matisse, *Still Life with Pitcher,* ca. 1898 186
Figure 4.11. Henri Matisse, *The Rose,* ca. 1906 191
Figure 4.12. Henri Matisse, *Le Bonheur de vivre,* 1905–6 192
Figure 4.13. Henri Matisse, *Standing Nude,* 1906 193
Figure 4.14. Paul Cézanne, *Plaster Putto,* ca. 1895 197
Figure 4.15. Paul Cézanne, *The Peppermint Bottle,* 1893–95 198
Figure 4.16. Paul Cézanne, *Still Life with Statuette,* 1894–95 199
Figure 4.17. Paul Cézanne, *Stoneware Pitcher,* 1893–94 200
Figure 4.18. Henri Matisse, *Le Luxe I,* 1907 202
Figure 4.19. Henri Matisse, *Bathers with a Turtle,* 1908 204
Figure 4.20. Henri Matisse, *Still Life with African Sculpture,* 1908–9 205
Figure 4.21. Henri Matisse, *Still Life with Crab and Clay Pitcher,* 1896 207
Figure 4.22. Henri Matisse, *The Snail,* 1953 208
Figure 4.23. Henri Matisse, *Plate with Nude,* 1907 209
Figure 4.24. Henri Matisse, *Small Crouching Torso,* 1908 209
Figure 4.25. Henri Matisse with *Small Crouching Torso,* ca. 1950 210
Figure 4.26. Auguste Rodin, *The Crouching Woman,* conceived 1880–82; cast 1925 212
Figure 4.27. Aristide Joseph-Bonaventure Maillol, *Woman with Crab,* 1903 212
Figure 4.28. Henri Matisse, *Copy after Puget's Écorché,* 1903 216
Figure 4.29. Henri Matisse, *Still Life with Aubergines,* 1911 218
Figure 4.30. Henri Matisse, *The Painter in His Studio,* 1916 219
Figure 4.31. Henri Matisse, *Laurette in a Green Robe (Black Background),* 1916 219
Figure C.1. Paul Valéry with the sculptor Renée Vautier, 1934 237

Plate 1. Henri Matisse, *The Dance (II),* 1910
Plate 2. Henri Matisse, *Carmelina,* ca. 1903
Plate 3. Henri Matisse, *Standing Nude (Study in Blue),* ca. 1901
Plate 4. Henri Matisse, *The Monk,* 1903
Plate 5. Henri Matisse, *Woman Reading,* 1895
Plate 6. Henri Matisse, *Still Life with Self-Portrait,* 1895
Plate 7. Henri Matisse, *Still Life,* 1899
Plate 8. Henri Matisse, *Fruit and Coffee Pot,* 1899
Plate 9. Henri Matisse, *Café Table,* 1899
Plate 10. Henri Matisse, *Studio under the Eaves,* ca. 1903
Plate 11. Henri Matisse, *Bouquet on a Bamboo Table,* ca. 1903
Plate 12. Henri Matisse, *The Geranium,* 1906
Plate 13. Henri Matisse, *Pink Onions,* ca. 1906
Plate 14. Henri Matisse, *Dishes and Melon,* 1906
Plate 15. Henri Matisse, *Still Life with Plaster Figure,* 1906
Plate 16. Henri Matisse, *Flowers,* 1906
Plate 17. Henri Matisse, *The Red Rugs,* 1906
Plate 18. Henri Matisse, *Dishes and Fruit on a Red and Black Carpet,* 1906
Plate 19. Henri Matisse, *Le Luxe II,* 1907–8
Plate 20. Henri Matisse, *Interior with Aubergines,* 1911

INTRODUCTION

Modernism against Representation

> I affirmed: it's over. Basic colors. Every plane is a plane and there is to be no representation.
>
> —Alexander Rodchenko, "Working with Mayakovsky"

> Nothing here is representative; rather, it is all life and lived experience.
>
> —Gilles Deleuze and Félix Guattari, *Anti-Oedipus*

THIS IS A BOOK ABOUT MODERNISM'S DISSATISFACTIONS with representation. A central line of modernist thought turns on the effort to overcome representation in the name of something more direct, more immediate in its capacity to generate bodily or affective experience. Modernist alternatives to representation privilege materiality, the body, experience, presence, and sensation. Although this dissatisfaction with representation can be traced to the controversies prompted by the philosophy of Descartes, in which the self is terminally separated from the world by a screen of images, it became a central problem in avant-garde thought and practice at the beginning of the twentieth century.[1]

Alexander Rodchenko's dream of an art with "no representation" and Piet Mondrian's effort "to dispense with all the arts" and replace them with "concrete reality" are well-known instances of the antirepresentational impulse so central to the historical avant-gardes.[2] When these artists staked their claims against art, they were not staking them simply against figuration but in the name of something that would be more like reality. To understand this impulse we must return to the moment in modernism before it became commonplace. Focusing on that inaugural moment allows us to see not only the instability of avant-garde attacks on representation but also the depth of the fantasy of what Jacques Derrida called the "dream of the pure and simple absence of frame."[3]

Representation and Affect

This study centers on two key figures within the history of modernism: the painter Henri Matisse (1869–1954) and the philosopher Henri Bergson (1859–1941). Although Matisse and Bergson have been paired in art historical literature since the 1910s because of their shared commitment to an ontology of flux, becoming, and change, they also shared a more problematic and unexamined association in terms of their mutual dissatisfaction with representation itself. For Bergson, representation was necessary for practical communication, but it also filtered out the deeper strains of intuitive life. The "craving for symbolical representation," Bergson lamented, "deprives feelings in advance of every kind of living activity."[4] The suppression of intuitive life, for Bergson, could lead to madness. Similarly, for Matisse, representation frustrated the possibility of direct expressive connection between himself and the beholder. Matisse dreamed of a mode of artistic production—the creation of affective "machines"[5]—that could transfer expressive content into the soul of the viewer without representational mediation. In the ideal encounter, the "feelings and the soul of the painter travel without difficulty into the spirit of he who looks on."[6] Of course Matisse was not simply describing a psychological encounter; he also conceived of color as a mode of sensory contact. "For me, color is a force. My paintings . . . give sensations of energy."[7] Here, the picture dissolves into a pulsating field of forces, delivering up energetic sensations to the viewer's body. Whether Matisse believed in the direct delivery of "feelings" or "sensations of energy" to the beholder is not in question, however; rather, what is in question is the relevance of an unmediated affective contact between paint and viewer.[8]

As I will show, Matisse's work suggests something other than fantasies of expressive communion or affective transfer. Contrary to what Matisse sometimes said about the transparency of expression or the immediacy of affect, I will argue that his works reflect on the problems of representing oneself to another, of how it is that a set of marks on a canvas or a sheet of paper can be understood or misunderstood, felt or rejected, by a beholder or even by oneself. Matisse came to feel that any work that did not open itself up to the possibility of *failing* to mean to another was a work that failed to mean at all. Indeed, Matisse continually thematized the representational limits of his practice through strategies of framing (windows, thresholds, architecture, pictures within pictures, images of empty frames, decorative designs), through self-portraiture or depictions of himself at work, through persistent emphasis on the studio and the stage, and through a set of recurrent structural arrangements based on relationships between proximity and distance, clarity and ambiguity, intimacy and difference. It is the discovery of the limits of and potentials for representation that is the primary content of his oeuvre.

My emphasis on the representational foundations of Matisse's work stands against recent accounts that stress the effects produced by his works on the viewer. Yve-Alain Bois, for instance, in his influential writings on Matisse, describes the ways in which the artist developed a surefire "system" to produce violent sensations in the beholder's body (whether the sensations are violent or pleasant is immaterial from my perspective).[9] Matisse's works "affect us so much," Bois explains in "On Matisse: The Blinding," because they force the beholder into an awareness of the "principal nodes of psychic life."[10] These repressed psychic preconditions are forced into awareness by an even more basic bodily encounter with line and color. Through complex formal patterning, Bois argues, Matisse is able to set in motion the "rhythm of a pendulum at the core of our vision" (112). That Matisse's work can induce such an "irresolvable oscillation of our perception" (112) matches up exactly with Bergson's notion that certain works of art "cause our faculty of perception to oscillate,"[11] and for both authors this perceptual effect, while it emerges within a representational setting, is the condition for representation itself. For both Bois and Bergson this causal encounter with line and color produces traumatic effects, destabilizing putatively classical modes of representation and the normative selfhood that sustains it. What the traumatic experience of one's suppressed bodily setting reveals is the "intentional nature of the perceptual field."[12] The disoriented perceiver comes to know the constructed and ideological nature—that is what "intentional" means in Bois's phrase—of his seemingly transparent reality. Once again, it is not that Bois denies the status of representation—far from it; traumatic effects occur within a representational setting, disturbing it from within. Bois's mistake is to orient his accounts around these affective moments—perceptual contradictions tied to bodily effects—within representation that can never be open to dispute. Or rather, disagreements about cause and effect, what actually happens to the beholder, differ entirely from what a work means, or how we interpret what happens. Effects are evaluated through verification (Did the effect happen?); interpretations of a work's meaning are evaluated in terms of the persuasiveness of one's claims (Is the account convincing?). Put another way, we might ask what would it be like to disagree with an account that says an arrangement of lines and colors sets in play a "rhythm of the pendulum at the core of our vision." It is hard to imagine a set of arguments beyond the empirical analysis of the eye—a procedure Bois rejects (as do I, but for different reasons)—that would falsify the claim. Which is another way of saying that an assertion about the viewer's perceptual response is something wholly different from an interpretation of what a work might mean. The presumed value of adhering to perceptual responses is that it avoids any unverifiable assertion about the artist's intentions to produce those responses. But, as I will argue, this value becomes a liability when it comes to making sense of what a work means. Without an appeal to the artist—what the artist might have meant by the marks he or she made, unverifiable as that effort will be, but verifiability is not the point with meaning—one cannot differentiate between relevant and irrelevant sensations before a work.

But to truly dismantle the affective turn one must return to the sources of these claims within modernism itself. One can draw out, for instance, from Matisse's and Bergson's practices, a theory of affect that authorizes many of the concerns of contemporary critics such as Bois. That this account would be only a *partial* account of their aims (at best) will be one of the upshots of my analysis. What I aim to provide is a history of the derivation of a dominant mode of postmodern theory and practice from a set of failed modernist beliefs. What makes Matisse's and Bergson's cases so fascinating for current discussions about affect and form is the depth of their investment in antirepresentationalism and their ultimate refusal of its terms.

The primacy of beholder response and the inadequacy of artistic intention were major concerns for early theorizers of modernism. Roland Barthes could easily provide a genealogy for his account of the "death of the author" by citing modern masters such as Mallarmé, Valéry, and Proust. Literary critics, Barthes argued, were driven by the mistaken desire to "assign a 'secret,' an ultimate meaning" to a text.[13] But because "we can never know" for certain what an author meant, it followed for Barthes that the only sense we *could* know was the one supplied by the readers (142). To tie a work to a single author was, Barthes insisted, to "impose a limit on that text" (147). Because an author's intention was not available to scrutiny, Barthes reasoned that the unity of the text was not at its origin in the author "but in its destination," the audience (148). Once the text was stripped of its author, or it exceeded their capacity to secure their intentions through the public function of writing, meaning became meaning*s*: every reader was an author (whether he or she knew it or not). Then again, it is hard to see what "meaning" actually means for Barthes. If there is no "Author-God" "releasing a single 'theological' meaning" (146)—an instance of Barthesian overkill—then how is it that *any* reader's interpretation rises to the level of meaning? If there is not a single meaning to a text—whatever it might be—then how could any interpretation be said to be wrong? Wrong in terms of what? On what grounds could it be? What new readers have instead of new meanings are new affects attached to their various, and therefore differing, bodies. (Thus, as I will show, there is a clear homology to be drawn between the seemingly incongruous semiotics of Barthes and the affect theory of Deleuze.) Because making assertions about what an artist meant by his or her letters and marks was something that could never be verified, the alternative, looking at what *actually happened* to the beholder or what the reader did with a text, was a truly secure foundation for aesthetic inquiry. But that logic traded meaning for security, which is a higher price than we should accept.

Of course for Barthes, as for those who follow him, one well-known ground for disagreement is the work's public or institutional meaning. But that account immediately runs into trouble when it comes to conflicting public meanings (a word in the dictionary, for instance, that holds two contradictory meanings; a work that was understood by historical publics in conflicting ways). If there are two (or two hundred) contrary meanings for a word, work, or event, then both become part of its meaning. And when meaning becomes a matter of accumulating uses—what is called anthropology—then it is not really meaning we're after, but more like a set of facts. Facts, of course, provide grounds for dispute but are entirely different grounds for disputes about meaning. There would be no reason, or no grounds, for asserting the legitimacy of one reception over another, except if that assertion is to say it is one the artist could have intended.

That what actually happened to the beholder was a threat to art and aesthetics, and not its salvation, was one of the major concerns of both Kant's *Critique of Judgment* (1790) and Hegel's *Aesthetics* (1823–29) at the beginning of the modernist period. Although Kant and Hegel are frequently criticized (or celebrated) for being overly sensual or subjective in their approach to art, this does not accurately capture their aims. In section 9 of the *Critique of Judgment,* for instance, Kant writes that the "key" to the whole *Critique* is in establishing the priority of the "Feeling of Pleasure" versus "Judging of the object."[14] Which comes first? His answer is unequivocal: "Judging precedes the pleasure." Why? "If the pleasure in the given object came first," if the beholder's response was primary, then "that kind of pleasure would be none other than mere agreeableness in the sensation, so that by its very nature it could only have private validity."[15] The agreeable is defined by "private feeling," something that is "restricted to his own person." And as Kant suggests, "It would be folly to dispute the judgment of another that is different from our own in such a matter, with the aim of condemning it as incorrect." It is the *privacy* of the agreeable (what we now call affect, and whether it is pleasurable or not, beautiful or ugly, is beside the point) that renders it unavailable to disagreement from others.[16] "With the beautiful," on the other hand, or rather with art more generally, "it is entirely different" from the agreeable. Judging artworks beautiful is to "expect the very same satisfaction of others: he judges not merely for himself, but for everyone."[17] It is in the nature of an affect, of bodily response, that it is happening to a body, regardless of whether it happens to another. Alternately, when someone interprets a work he or she is asserting its shared validity, its meaning for everyone, even if that interpretation begins and ends in the viewer's "subjective" response. What makes those responses shareable is the assumption that they are the ones intended by the artist. The agreeable makes no assertion about what a work means, only about what it does.

Hegel offers a similarly influential voice for the problems raised in this book. What Hegel shows, following Kant on this point, is that from the beginning of modern writing on art, assigning primacy to response was a mistaken tendency that needed to be challenged continuously. Here is Hegel in the pages that follow his famous judgment about art as a "thing of the past." He is reflecting on the fashionable idea that "art is meant to arouse feeling":

> Feeling as such is an entirely empty form of subjective affection. . . . Consequently, the investigation of the feelings which art evokes, or is supposed to evoke, does not get beyond vagueness; it is a study which precisely abstracts from the content proper and its concrete essence and concept. For reflection on *feeling* is satisfied with observing subjective emotional reaction in its particular character, instead of immersing itself in the thing at issue i.e. in the work of art, plumbing its depths, and in addition relinquishing mere subjectivity and its states. But in the case of feeling it is precisely this empty subjectivity which is not only retained but is the chief thing, and this is why men are so fond of having feelings. But this too is why a study of this kind becomes wearisome on account of its indefiniteness and emptiness, and disagreeable by its concentration on tiny subjective peculiarities.[18]

Hegel clearly differentiates the beholder's "emotional reaction" from its vehicle, the "work of art." Of course affect theorists no longer talk about feelings at all but about *intensities*—nervous, optical, molecular, hydraulic, sensorial—and how they constitute the basic matter of human experience. But it is hard to see how that difference in language matters much here. Hegel's main point about the failure of feeling as a guide to art was that "differences between feelings are . . . not differences in the thing itself."[19] To describe what is happening to the beholder before a work of art is not the same as describing what is happening in the work. A report about what something makes one feel is not a belief about what it means.

Specularity, Mimesis, Literalism

As I have suggested above, my use of the word *representation* is broader than its customary usage in art history. Part of the problem with the term is that it is often construed in a too-narrow sense to designate illustration, depiction, or likeness. When it is defined this way, being against representation is the same as being against figuration. That is not the problem I am concerned with here. Moreover, it should be clear that when someone such as Rodchenko says there is "no representation" in his color panels, he does not mean that he has produced pure abstractions. In this instance Rodchenko is responding to Malevich's abstractions, which still suggested to him a mode of representational art. Rodchenko means that his works are not like artworks anymore; they are more like *objects.*[20] And it is this distinction—the one between artworks and objects, and not the one between abstraction and figuration—that is at stake in the following analysis. Representation, in my account, defines the ontological difference between the work of art and the world "outside" it. The effort to break down or eliminate that distinction between work and world is the subject of my history. This is crucial because once the work of art loses its "art" status and becomes like an object, it also becomes available to beholder response in the way that any object does. And one does not bring intentions to bear on the experience of objects in the way one does with artworks.

Part of what it means to defend representation is to defend it against its reduction to a monolithic entity. On the face of it, this effort hardly seems controversial. But as I will show, many of the leading approaches to representation in the humanities today see it as a mechanism that inevitably denies "lived experience" or falsifies reality through putatively naturalized signs. On this view, to represent is to flatten the world of experience, to reduce it to a lifeless image of itself. I refuse this kind of reduction that treats representation as a deadening form of communication—what a typical commentary describes as "frictionless conduits of verbal exchange"[21]—or as a detached object of contemplative mastery, either condemned or celebrated under the term *opticality.*[22] The fact that representation mediates our connection with the world renders our feelings for or against it beside the point. As I will suggest, there is no (coherent) position to be had on representation. To affirm representation does not require any claim about the transparency or opacity, naturalness or arbitrariness of signs. I will speak instead about the animate or dead, compelling or clichéd quality of a sign. Because we inevitably use signs to communicate, the problem becomes that of making them meaningful, or meaningful again, as though for the first time (never imagining they are really new).

The matter of representation under modernism is complicated because Matisse and Bergson, when they were not disparaging representation, could be seen as overly *embracing* it. Critics, for instance, frequently attacked Matisse for taking a detached attitude toward the world. André Gide described Matisse's work as the "exposition of theorems." His paintings are "products of theory," Gide explained, "everything in them can be deduced, explained; intuition plays no part."[23] Similarly, Jacques Rivière saw Matisse as someone who "stands *apart* from things when he paints." Looking at a Matisse, Rivière sighed, is like looking at a "theorem." One felt as though "nothing that breathes is part of it; it is a sparkling extract."[24]

Considered altogether, these issues present a conundrum. On one side are accounts of Matisse that see him as a precursor of those today who want to describe artworks in terms of affects or sensations that have nothing to do with meaning. On this view, Matisse's painted surfaces generate emotions or energies in the viewer's mind or body beyond any appeal to the artist's effort to do so. On the other side are accounts that see him as a detached observer of the world, standing apart from reality and living in a fictitious space of ideas. It is my aim to show that neither account provides adequate terms to understand Matisse's project. Neither bodily affect nor detached observation, neither dreamlike merger nor contemplative detachment, captures the mode of address exemplified by Matisse's work. Between affectivity and specularity lies a mode of representation that I describe as mimetic, immersive, or unconscious, a mode that speaks directly to Matisse's as well as Bergson's basic intentions.[25] That Matisse and Bergson found no way to access this mimetic mode of representation except *through* its detached and specular opposite was a fact that bred, alternately, psychic distress and virtuosic performance.

The challenge of this book, then, is twofold: first, to show the contradictions and oscillations between two modes of representation—what I will call the specular and the mimetic—in Matisse's and Bergson's work; and second, to show how these representational concerns also constituted a *refusal* of the terms of literalism and affect. For now, I will try to further unpack the relationship between specular and mimetic representation and then take up the question of the refusal of affect.

The German language distinguishes two senses of the word *representation* along the lines of *Vorstellung* and *Darstellung. Vorstellung* signifies an observational position, a standing apart from oneself and from the world;[26] *Darstellung* signifies an engaged activity such as that of an actor immersed in a role. In his account of the "Freudian subject," Mikkel Borch-Jacobsen carefully establishes the difference between these two modes of representation:

> Thus the subject either plays a part in the spectacle or is a spectator; either he merely sees or he sees *himself*, by presenting himself to himself, confronting himself, in the objectivity of the *Vor-stellung*; either he is in representation, here and now, *in* the scene on the stage, or he is representing himself there, *on* the stage. This dilemma is implacable, insurmountable. The lack of distinction between self and other—the mimesis—has to be acted out; yet no sooner is it represented to the subject in the specular mode than it is betrayed.[27]

Borch-Jacobsen helpfully captures the ontological bearing of the difference between seeing and seeing oneself, between *Vorstellung* and *Darstellung.* One cannot both fully act and watch oneself at the same time. Although the difference between the two modes of representation is irresolvable, it nonetheless produces a wide range of problems. For Matisse and Bergson the effort to overcome the difference was a source of both creative potential and psychic conflict.

Matisse typically described his working process along these two lines of representation, the mimetic and the specular, distinguishing between the immersive act of painting and the observational act of looking at his work as though he were its (first) public. He would sometimes describe the difference in temporal terms. As he wrote in the conclusion to his "Notes of a Painter": "An artist must realize, when he is reasoning, that his picture is an artifice, but when he paints, he must have the feeling that he has copied nature."[28] Matisse also conceived of the two impulses as simultaneous: "To give yourself completely to what you're doing while simultaneously watching yourself do it."[29] And at times he would make conscious observation the condition for any immersive connection with his medium: "An artist is an explorer. He should begin by seeking himself, seeing himself act. Then, he should not restrain himself."[30] To explore and observe, to lose oneself and stand apart, it is this oscillation and doubling that is insistently figured in Matisse's art.

Similarly, the distinction between these two modes of representation—performing an act and representing the act to oneself—appears throughout Bergson's philosophical writings. Bergson clarifies the distinction in *Creative Evolution*: "When we mechanically perform a habitual action, when the somnambulist automatically acts his dream, unconsciousness may be absolute; but this is merely due to the fact that the representation of the act is held in check by the performance of the act itself. . . . *Representation is stopped up by action.*"[31]

For Bergson, automaticity and habit are mechanical actions completely lacking in intentionality. Actions taken without one's active production of their significance—such as following a rule, a theory, an idea, or a habit—are not really actions at all. If an action is unmindfully pursued as a matter of routine, the action "no longer *represents* our past to us, it *acts* it" for us.[32] In Bergson's terms, habitual action is an effort to "repudiate" one's intention, signifying the effort of someone to "continually act his life instead of truly representing it to himself: a conscious automaton, he would follow the lead of useful habits."[33] Bergson's writings are saturated with extreme images of nonintentionality: automatons, somnambulism, hypnotism, and catatonic subjects dominate his oeuvre. As I will show, these pathologized subjects act as a switch point: they at once represent the denial of intentionality and an ideal mode of action beyond the limits of instrumental reason. To loosen the hold of practical reason while still remaining an active agent was Bergson's guiding ideal. Matisse shared this ideal but could nonetheless describe it in terms of unconscious or absorptive activity without the least suggestion of nonintentionality, a crucial distinction that will form the basis of my comparison—and ultimate contrast—of their practices. Bergson described habitual action as "animal" and defined an animal as something that "lived and acted, rather than represented." An animal actor "remains the captive of his perception"; animality is a mode of being that is "*acted* rather than *thought*."[34] A fully intentional agent, on the other hand, is "not limited to *playing* his past life again; he *represents* . . . it" to himself.[35] It was Bergson's aim to reveal how most of our actions are performed unconsciously but that a more reflective awareness of ourselves and what we do would lead to better kinds of knowledge about ourselves and the world. In "our normal life," he observed, "we speak rather than think; we 'are acted' rather than act ourselves." "To act freely," then, "is to recover possession of oneself."[36] Bergson described fully intentional or self-determined modes of action as being *"self-possessed,"* as a "coinciding of ourself with ourself." Only when an action is intended, when it is represented to oneself in the act, is it "truly free."[37]

Intentionality

These two modes of representation—"unconscious" versus conscious, mimetic versus specular—appear within the historical context of Matisse's and Bergson's practices as two modes of *hypnosis,* a mysterious altered state of consciousness or state of unconsciousness that gripped the imagination of their generation.[38] Hypnosis emerged as an enormously rich but fraught idea in the work of both Matisse and Bergson. On one hand, hypnosis suggested a mode of experiential and expressive connection between persons and others so powerful that the divisions between subject and object, self and world, were felt to be dissolved. On this view, hypnosis served as a model for the kind of immersive relationship between artist and artwork or artwork and beholder that Matisse aimed to achieve. On the other hand, hypnosis implied the existence of a detached separation between hypnotist and subject, hence by analogy a kind of observational relation between artist and audience, as the artist imagined having hypnotic mastery over the viewer, enabling the former to influence the latter and make the viewer do what the artist willed. On this model, the artist as hypnotist could manipulate lines and colors to produce specific, and frequently violent, affective states in the beholder. One unexpected and unsettling consequence of this view was that artists began to conceive of lines and colors as living lives of their own, acting beyond or without the artist's control. Indeed, lines and colors were increasingly thought to embody and generate affective results regardless of the artist's desire to express anything through them. So what began as a mode of hypnotic mastery over the beholder became a competition between two forms of agency: the artist's versus that of the materials. What the experience of hypnosis taught Matisse and Bergson (the latter with a set of experiments with hypnotized patients that used images) was that the effort to make the beholder think or feel whatever the artist wanted actually ended up making what the artist wanted completely irrelevant. The lines and colors that acted on beholders acted on them irrespective of the artist's intentions.

This leads me to one last, introductory point. What Matisse's and Bergson's encounter with hypnosis helps us see is the centrality of issues of intentionality in their work. It is as if their confrontation with the phenomenon of hypnosis brought to the fore, in complex and unexpected ways, questions concerning the artist's intentions that were entangled in all the other interpretive issues I have already adumbrated.

Intentionality was a beleaguered notion throughout the twentieth century and remains in bad repute today.[39] To say that the legal and philosophically nuanced accounts of intentionality have yet to enter into art historical discourse is a vast understatement.[40] Attitudes toward intention usually take one of two forms: either the denial that intention plays any determinative role in the meaning of a work because it is inaccessible or (more popularly) the assertion that intention is relevant but unreliable because the artist cannot control the way the work will be understood or experienced. While the latter claims are true—or truistic—they are true only insofar as we are talking about the work's effects and not their meaning or taking the effects of a work for its "meaning" (as I will show, on the latter account, the use of the word *meaning* is mistaken).

On a related point, it is clear that most available notions of what constitutes an intention are a little thin (to put it mildly) and usually involve some idea of complete conscious awareness or discursive availability. It is what Marcel Duchamp calls a matter of "conscious control, intellectual control,"[41] and it is hard to imagine what artist would subscribe to the idea. Duchamp's point in a talk such as "The Creative Act" (1957) is to reject the expressionist claim that there is a seamless "transference [of intentions] from the artist to the spectator." Rather than transference, Duchamp insists on the "difference between an intention and its realization." There is, he says, a missing "link, a gap representing the inability of the artist to express fully his intention."[42] I suspect no one would argue with him on the last point, nor should they. The point Duchamp is making here is about the problem of artistic communication, which is also to say, he is not talking about the problem of meaning. But the crucial move, the one that haunts most versions of anti-intentionalism, is that the possible or frequent failure of communication is supposed to tell us something about the nature of artistic meaning. The elision of effect into meaning occurs when Duchamp cartoonishly defines intention as something "fully self-conscious," a matter of complete "intellectual control."

Duchamp's point is to show how in the process of artistic creation the artist's preformed idea, or plan, is fundamentally altered in the encounter with a resistant medium. Duchamp describes this loss of intentionality as the transformation of a work of art into an "état brut," which in turn renders it available for the viewer's "creative act," one that necessarily implies the infinite production of significations. So what seemed to be a cogent point about artistic communication—that one's intentions change in the creative process—turns out to be about the insufficiency of intentionality as a category *altogether.*

In what follows I do not suggest that intentions can be "recovered" by an appeal to the artist's writings, statements, interviews, documents, or biography, or to the artist's conscious sense of his work's meaning, although all of these items may often provide important avenues for interpretation. The appeal to artistic intention is *not* an appeal to artistic *psychology,* to figuring out what is going on inside an artist's head or heart. My account is antipsychological in this sense. Indeed, the primary evidence to which I appeal in my account of Matisse are the visual characteristics of his work. And the characteristics that are relevant to my account are the ones I see as intended by the artist. Of course there is no capacity for me to verify which effects are intended and which ones are just mine. My interpretation, any interpretation, is not something that can be verified by some fact of the matter. One is either persuaded by the case or one is not. Furthermore, intentionality should be clearly separated from the question of quality or evaluation. Whether or not the artist succeeds in making his intentions known is not a question I am asking here. What does matter is that intentions make works of art different from other objects in the world where intentions do not matter or do not figure centrally.

For Matisse, intention was typically not a matter of a predetermined plan, conscious awareness, or a set of mental contents. On occasion Matisse spoke of his intention as an event separate from the act of making, speaking of his "conception." "For me all is in the conception [tout est dans la conception]. It is thus necessary to have a clear vision of the whole right from the beginning."[43] And again, nearly forty years later: "I have my conception in my head, and I want to realize it. . . . I know where I want to end up."[44] Far more often Matisse described his intentions as something that emerged with the making of the work. This is how he more typically described his practice: "No one is more surprised than I am at the results, for I can never tell what a work will reveal to me."[45] "When you work," Picasso similarly noted, "you don't know what is going to come out of it. It is not indecision, the fact is it changes while you are at work." "While I am working," Picasso went on to say, "I am not conscious of what I am putting on the canvas. . . . It is only later that I begin to estimate more exactly the effect of my work."[46] (Jackson Pollock similarly remarked, "It is only after a sort of 'get acquainted' period that I see what I have been about.")[47] For an anti-intentionalist these claims point to the limitations of any account of artistic control (or failed efforts at control made after the fact). For Duchamp, for instance, observing the difference between conscious plan and artistic result led him to theorize the insufficiency of intention as a category. "This gap . . . between what he intended to realize and did realize," Duchamp explains, opens up a space for the spectator to "create" the work in the absence of the artist's capacity to complete it.[48] Because the artist's intention is always different from (or lesser than), rather than evolving with, the actual work made, Duchamp insists that the spectator makes up the difference by giving the work meaning when the artist could not. Duchamp's approach is indicative of the most typical mistake of anti-intentionalism: the confusion of communication (or effect) with meaning.[49] But the truism that says no work fully communicates what an artist intends is logically unrelated to whether the work bears intentions. Just because an artist fails to express everything he or she meant in a work does not mean the work is not intended, only that it is a less than fully successful work. Whether one finds a work fully successful, or beautiful or expressive or meaningful, is a question unrelated to the one posed here: Is the work of art defined by what the author intended (again, even if the author could not discursively articulate that intention)?

A more nuanced notion of intention would show there is a wide range of actions that pass beyond or rise above "intellectual control" but that are still fully, perhaps especially, intended. This is what Picasso means when he says that the artist is "always calculating without knowing it." And again: "I consider a work of art as the product of calculations, calculations that are frequently unknown to the author himself." But no matter how unknown those actions feel, one doesn't "cease to be oneself on that account."[50] Sigmund Freud called those actions that are yours but that you do not fully understand *unconscious.* And to say that an act was made unconsciously did not signal for Freud that the act was unintended or a matter of bodily affect (at least after 1895). On the contrary, unconscious acts are the most fully intended ones.[51] The subject of Freud's *The Psychopathology of Everyday Life* (1901) is what he calls "unconscious intentions"—how to recognize them and interpret them—and critics such as William Empson built their careers on interpreting them in poetry and literature.[52] Put another way, to say that an artist did not know what a work meant until he made it is not to say that it was unintended; it might mean that what resulted was exactly what the artist intended, but it was something he could not articulate at the level of "intellectual control." If the artist could articulate it at the level of intellectual control, it is hard to see why he or she would make art to begin with.

In the majority but not all of the cases I will argue that Matisse's intentions did not exist before the encounter with his medium; rather, they emerged in and through the process of production. More often than not, Matisse came to know his intentions once they had been externalized for a beholder (even if it was himself), and that beholder could in turn come to know him- or herself in the encounter with the work. Rather than conscious awareness, I understand intentionality in Matisse's work as a set of recurrent structural patterns occurring so deeply, and emerging through so many layers of psychological tension, that they are best described as happening at the level of the "structural unconscious."[53]

Just to reiterate, because this point will likely go down the hardest: intentional analysis is not a matter of finally or ultimately knowing, recovering, or extracting what an artist meant when he or she made a work of art—an impossible task—but it is to say that an artist meant something by his or her work, and that is what the art historian aims to understand by whatever means available. There is no moment when the intention is fully captured or recovered by the interpreter. One makes a case for what one thinks an artist meant by his or her work, and one also assumes the account will be accepted or challenged by later writers. Trying to understand what someone, anyone, meant by something in the past is an ongoing challenge, but the challenge should not be forfeited on the grounds that one cannot have absolute certainty. (Barthes famously rejected the effort to extract "a single 'theological' meaning [the 'message' of the Author-God]" from a text, but he should have made this view of intention one of his mythologies.)[54]

Finally, intentionality has nothing to do with *method.* Saying that a work of art means whatever the artist intended it to mean (again, I assume the artist would not be able to articulate that meaning discursively) does not tell one how to get at what an artist means. All the traditional modes of inquiry stand. I happen to mobilize phenomenological and psychoanalytic terms to better understand Matisse's and Bergson's intentions, but that says nothing about other approaches. Any method that aims to understand what the artist meant, and not what happened to a work in its historical, institutional, or public reception, or what happens to the viewer regardless of what the artist might have meant, is intentionalist. My methods here are largely psychoanalytic and phenomenological, as I think these approaches best help us to see what Matisse and Bergson meant in and by their work, but that has no bearing on the more basic question of intention. Every interpreter appeals to intentionality in order to establish what a work is and what it is not; anyone committed to understanding what a work means rather than what it does appeals to intentionality.

Overview

Against the background of the issues I have just sketched, I shall proceed in the following way. Chapter 1, "Painting as Affect Machine," presents a history of what I call "affective formalism" and lays the theoretical and historical foundations for the book as a whole. Focusing on the denigration of representation by avant-garde artists from the French Symbolists of the late nineteenth century to the "theater of cruelty" of Antonin Artaud, this chapter considers the consequences and results of the affective turn in modern art (the second affective turn can be identified with postmodernism). For these writers and artists, the experience of an artwork was a highly charged physical encounter that involved sensations passing directly into the body of the viewer through qualities inherent in line and color. In its most extreme form, affective formalism denies both representation and intentionality (although it does not require that denial). The artist and the medium dissolve into material flows of sensory and affective currents. Line and color are held to work of their own accord and beyond any material embodiment to generate affective states in the viewer. The result of this antirepresentational impulse, the one I come to in my conclusion, is that the *viewer* becomes the primary agent of artistic significance, which is also to say the viewer comes to replace the artist as the primary locus of meaning.[55] (Bois fulfills his own logic when he shows how semiotic undecidability "makes the reader a creator.")[56] And once the viewer replaces the artist as the origin of meaning, the possibility of meaning itself is put in doubt: the work of art becomes a kind of object, one that is not interpreted but experienced. The reason I say this will become clear as we proceed.

Chapter 2, "Freedom and Memory: Bergson's Theory of Hypnotic Agency," examines the problem of freedom, action, and intentionality in Bergson's philosophy. While Bergson is committed to describing and celebrating modes of human freedom—what he called acts of "appropriation," "self-determination," and "self-possession"—he is part of a larger generational skepticism about the capacity of agents to decide actions for themselves. Bergson's dissatisfaction with human agency emerges with his theorization of "ontological memory," the nonhuman foundation of free action. The picture Bergson ends up producing is of competing "agencies": ontological memory versus human action. Bergson grounds his account of memory in clinical accounts of brain damage, personality disorders, and near-death experience. These pathologized bodies—bodies so physically and mentally abject that they have passed beyond the scope of representation—reveal the limits of Bergson's concept of freedom. Remarkably, Bergson articulates an alternative account of human agency in his writings on déjà vu and "psychical research." After establishing the limits of Bergson's theory of freedom, I show how his writings on hypnosis, including his earliest text, "Unconscious Simulation in the State of Hypnosis" of 1886, as well as *Time and Free Will* (1889), present a picture of *artistic* intentionality at odds with his more generalized theory of freedom. As I will show, Bergson literally could not imagine the work of art or its reception outside an intentionalist framework.

The chapter concludes with a consideration of the wide-ranging and increasingly dominant influence of the "New Bergsonism" on the interpretation of Matisse, including discussion of the writings of Bois, Alastair Wright, Mark Antliff, Catherine Bock-Weiss, Éric Alliez and Jean-Claude Bonne, J. M. Bernstein, and Judith Butler. As I hope to demonstrate, it is not so important whether or not these authors agree with one another or even whether they are explicitly engaged with Bergson's philosophy. More significant is their shared commitment to antirepresentation and anti-intentionality as well as a range of related ideas about trauma, violence, direct action, and perceptual ambiguity.

By "New Bergsonism" I mean the renewed interest in Bergson's perceptual psychology since the 1988 reissue of *Matter and Memory* and the English publication of Gilles Deleuze's *Bergsonism* the same year by the same press, events that went hand in hand with a diminished focus on Bergson's ontology of change. The latter was the central concern of an earlier generation of Matisse commentators interested in Bergson, including John Elderfield, Jack Flam, Lawrence Gowing, and Pierre Schneider, as well as Matisse's contemporary critics, such as Matthew Prichard and Georges Duthuit. This earlier focus on flux and change has been slowly eclipsed by a perceptually and affectively oriented discourse centered on viewer response. It is the latter that my analysis aims to challenge and to offer in its place a new set of terms.

Chapter 3, "The Influence of Others: Matisse and *Personnalité*," considers Matisse's mixed fascination with and aversion to what he called "the hypnotic power of the image."[57] Matisse became a master of visually hypnotic effects but also felt the limitations of any mode of production that depended for its significance on the beholder's reactions. He worried that if artworks contained hypnotic power, then he could not be certain he was not continually under the spell of other artists (as his critics suggested). Matisse expressed his anxieties about mass hypnosis in his frequent warnings against "the influence of others."[58] His answer to the problem was to imagine a kind of selfhood that would block or filter out any harmful influences; he called this his *personnalité*—a concept that anchors his writings and structures his pictorial practice. Ultimately, Matisse devised a simple and powerful formula: to achieve personal autonomy was to achieve pictorial autonomy, what he called the "totality that constitutes a *tableau*."[59] To make a self was like making a picture: to be both social and autonomous, open and organized, constructed and free.

Theories of hypnotic influence emerged at the beginning of the twentieth century as a standing threat to the unitary self because they made the constitution of the self dependent on others. The intensity of Matisse's simultaneous courting and denial of influence spoke to its deep emotional resonance in his art and writings. But my concern is not with a critique of the (unified) self—a problem adequately put to rest, or kept alive for career purposes—but rather with the critique of the *denial* of agency. No matter how the self is described—humanist or posthumanist, singular or multiple, integral or institutional, centered or decentered, whole or fragmented—the problem of agency remains. Even if the idea of the self is a fiction (which I largely assume here), we are still called upon to act and make choices. To say that the self is constructed does not say anything about what that self is supposed to do. So while I characterize Matisse's *personnalité* as fully malleable and socially constituted, my ultimate concern is not with the fixed *or* multiple nature of the self, but with the larger problem of affectively grounded accounts of art and how those accounts seek to avoid or deny the problem of intentionality. The consequences of this denial are political. Without an appeal to intention—trying to understand what someone meant by something (a sign, a mark, a gesture, a sound, a word, an idea)—there are no grounds for disagreement. Another way to put this is to say that reporting what a work makes one think of or feel is not advancing interpretations about what the work means. It is also to say that if the work is seen as requiring the beholder's response to give it meaning, then none of those responses can have any more purchase than another. Hence there can be no grounds to disagree about their significance. Or the question might be: What would it be like to disagree about—rather than calibrate—what happens to a beholder before a work of art?

Chapter 4, "Matisse and Mimesis," builds a new account of Matisse's intentions through close readings of a range of works painted between 1895 and 1917. The focus of this analysis is a sequence of interrelated paintings, several of which have rarely before been seen and which have never been considered as a series. I will argue that from his earliest paintings up to the early Nice period, Matisse's work continuously alternated between "phenomenological" and "realist" modes, between a view of the world as continuous with the painter's body but set at a distance and a view of a scene proximate to the artist but whose forms are often opaque and unreadable.[60] It is this alternation that reveals Matisse's ongoing attempt to negotiate the terms of mimetic identification and specular detachment but that also reveals the limitations of the effort to reconcile them.

In the Conclusion, "From Art to Object: The Case of Paul Valéry," I introduce a figure whose work encapsulates the concerns of the book as a whole. The poet and critic Paul Valéry (1871–1945) was a friend to both Matisse and Bergson, and he was grappling with a set of generational concerns about representation, intention, hypnosis, and audience that gripped them as well. As I noted above, Valéry stands in a privileged place in Barthes's (and Blanchot's and Adorno's and Derrida's) history of anti-intentionalism. But the situation is far more complicated than Barthes suggests. What makes Valéry's work so difficult and so valuable today is that he held two strong and conflicting views of artistic meaning. On one hand, Valéry was an arch-intentionalist, affirming that "one is led to a *form* by a desire to leave the smallest possible share to the reader—and by the same token to leave oneself the least possible scope for arbitrariness and uncertainty."[61] On the other hand, he was increasingly committed to an anti-intentionalist or participatory position, declaring that his "verses have whatever meaning is given them."[62] And in a phrase that entered into the postmodern literary canon, he proclaimed, "Once a work is published its author's interpretation of it has no more validity than anyone else's."[63] What makes Valéry's case so instructive as a version of modernism is that it straddles the line between intentionalism and anti-intentionalism, representation and literalism, and in doing so clarifies the stakes raised by these terms. As I will show, Valéry's ultimate dissatisfaction with representation led him to invent what became the dominant mode of twentieth- and twenty-first-century thought: the death of the author and the birth of the reader. That he resisted his own narrative will also be my subject.

Semiotics against Representation

A final point about the claims sketched above. There is a dominant mode of art historical analysis that appears related to mine. In art history, semiotics is the strongest instance of a representational paradigm available. Signs, on this model, fundamentally mediate one's relation to the world. Semiotics insists we abandon our "transparent" apprehension of the world and replace it with an autonomous linguistic system that produces "an unreflecting totalization . . . which has its [own] reason and of which man knows nothing."[64] The problem this view poses, from my perspective, is that it can knowingly parse the difference between signs and something else. If signs are truly total, then the question of transparency and arbitrariness falls away. Signs exist in a situated context, one in which we are always in the position to interpret them, never in a position to evaluate their existence.

So what is most striking about the semiotic model is that it is fully compatible with its antirepresentational opposite, literalism. To take one canonical example, Rosalind Krauss claims in "The Motivation of the Sign" (1992) that one must "maintain the integrity of representation" by showing how "meaning [is] something always-already mediated by the operations of the sign."[65] For Krauss, our most basic perceptions are shaped by socially, politically, and historically coded representations. This claim is basically right, but it is impossible to imagine its epistemological import. If our access to the world is fundamentally mediated by signs, then *knowing* that fact cannot help us to make better decisions. Whatever position one takes, whatever "critical distance" such knowledge might entail, is just as socially, politically, and historically mediated as any other. What it means, or should mean, to "maintain the integrity of representation" is to maintain that there is no outside, no special knowledge, no critical advantage that one could access through signs. This is what Leah Dickerman says, for instance, in her account of Dada: "Its adherents recognized themselves to be immersed, with no position above or outside that would allow a more reflective view."[66] And yet it is hard to find a claim *less* adhered to by Krauss and her semiotics-inspired colleagues. A still more basic and countering claim made by semioticians (and Lacanians) is that certain artworks interrupt the classical codes of representation, setting in motion a shift from "preconscious perceptual activity . . . to a conscious one."[67] But what could that "conscious" activity get us that is in any way less mediated than the "unconscious" one? If our access to the world is "mediated" by the "operation of the sign," if one is truly "immersed [in representation], with no position above or outside"—and I assume one is—then we should give up on the idea that knowing or thematizing the fact that our access is mediated could matter to what we do.

Of course Krauss and Bois respond directly to this dilemma. It turns out that neither one of them is much interested in the operation of the sign, or the critique of transparency, despite the attention they lavish on it. Or rather, they are interested in mediation only insofar as those smoothly functioning signs are *disrupted* by what Krauss calls their bodily *"preconditions."*[68]

From a certain perspective, everything Krauss writes is driven by the effort, as she calls it, to overcome the "fear of representation" and the "traditional Platonic dislike of representation."[69] And it is certainly true that Krauss rejects the false "dualism of perception and representation," given that the latter "always remains suspect because it is never anything but a copy, a re-creation in another form, a set of signs for experience." In her discussion of the "photographic conditions of surrealism," Krauss shows how surrealist photography helps us to "experience the real itself as sign" or, more decisively, to "experience *reality as representation.*" But if reality really is representation—which I assume it to be, but without the pathos this is presumed to entail—then the "experience" of it being so doesn't actually amount to much. Or it doesn't amount to anything. At the center of *October* aesthetics more generally is the lapsed enlightenment claim to see, to experience, to consciously grasp reality as it really is: representation. Which is another way of saying it wants to deny the reality of representation at the moment it declares representation's ubiquity. So even though Krauss wants to say that surrealist photography "exploits the special connection to reality with which all photography is endowed," that it is indexically a "deposit of the real itself," she also wants to insist—in seemingly the same breath—that this reality requires some kind of artistic (or art historical) intervention ("exploitation") to reveal this fact to the deceived beholder. The surrealist found objects, Krauss writes, "are presentations of . . . reality as configured, or coded, or written."[70] The surrealist photographer presents the fact that reality is representation. But what could that presentation tell us about reality? Or rather, from what position is the photographer (or art historian) working that allows him or her to present reality's reality as representation? It is only from somewhere *outside* representation (however limited or contingent) that the claim could make sense. Or it makes sense only from a perspective that denies the more fundamental claim that, as Nietzsche famously put it, "perspectival seeing is the *only* kind of seeing there is."[71] This is further to deny what Nietzsche called, in an 1871 note, "originary representation," the "internal representation" that precedes every externalization, preceding as well the self-conscious *staging* of representation for beholders. With Krauss we might ask how far we ultimately are from the classical realist claim to transparency (the one she terminally laments) when she asserts that a photograph can help us directly "experience *reality*," even if that reality is itself representation. Matisse, I will argue, provides a counter mode of production to the semiotic one with his pathos-free involvement with a reality mediated by representation. His work silently counters at every step the desire, however fleetingly inhabited or critically oriented, to become "an eye which supposedly looks out in no particular direction."[72]

Krauss's halfhearted commitment to the "always-already mediated" account of reality emerges in her more explicit commitment to the Bataillean task of "liberating our thinking from the semantic."[73] One way to free a sign from the semantic is to see it as an index. The photograph, in Krauss's account, acts as the model for the work of art that is in some crucial sense more like an object and less like a sign. It is the indexicality of the photograph, its causal connection to the things photographed, that automatically sidelines the artist's intentions. "It is the order of the natural world that imprints itself on the photographic emulsion and subsequently on the photographic print," Krauss writes. This causal "imprint" interrupts the "aesthetic intention" associated with "Art."[74]

Another way to free the sign from the semantic is to see the sign *syntactically* (photographs, Krauss insists, can be syntactic, too). Syntax—the sign's specific place in a configuration on or within a flatbed picture surface, for instance—requires the active participation of the beholder in deciding between competing and mutually exclusive significatory possibilities. The problem of semiotic undecidability is at the center of Bois's analyses. Writing about El Lissitzky, Bois explains how the political import of his work has nothing do with any "specific political content." Rather, El Lissitzky's writings and works of the early 1920s revolve around the "eminently ideological goal" of "jar[ring] the spectator out of his or her age-old lethargy."[75] Real politics, once the artist is exempted from the equation, happens between a formal configuration and the beholder's perceptual apparatus. As Bois sees it, illusionistic perspective is fundamentally conservative in its enforcement of a hierarchy of vision. The visual hierarchy at the center of Bois's oeuvre is the putatively preconditional one of figure versus ground. El Lissitzky's mode of axonometric design enforces an "overall foundering of perception." Here's how it works (we will see a variant of it in his account of Matisse): "Not only would lines parallel one another endlessly forwards and backwards, but the perceptual security that the illusionistic system of perspective affords by repressing the basic ambiguity of any visual apprehension of depth would be deconstructed, giving way to an ambiguity that would force the spectator to make constant decisions about how to interpret what he or she sees: is this figure hollow or in relief?"[76] That a work of art can "force the spectator" to make decisions when there are no firm grounds to make a decision (between "plus and minus," for instance) is, Bois contends, a source of trauma. Once perceptual preconditions—those hierarchies of vision—become the ground of politics, then, according to Bois, El Lissitzky's critique of traditional modes of perception emerges as more fully political than any belief about the world could be.[77]

For Bois, what is at stake in looking at an El Lissitzky is the classical ideology that "facing the painting [is] facing the horizon." This "position," he writes, "is clearly anthropomorphic." Why? Because it is "linked to our standing on the ground, to our submission to the law of gravity." Submitting to gravity (do we have a choice?), Bois contends, is the "plastic manifestation of the rationalist philosophy of conscience."[78] But what is the "rationalist philosophy of conscience" if not the belief that one can *reveal* to a beholder how gravity shapes perception itself?

The beholder's active pursuit of meaning on indeterminate grounds (figure/ground ambiguity) is said to expose something crucial about the nature of signification, something that is lost to one's naturalized sense of reality: that perception functions hierarchically. As I have tried to suggest, it is hard to see what consequences could follow from one's knowledge of either the mediated or the hierarchical nature of signification. To say one's encounter with the world is shaped by one's socially, culturally, and politically inherited signs says nothing about whether the signs we use are true or false, good or bad, liberating or limiting. *That* judgment must follow from a set of arguments, the very political ones rejected by Bois; it could never be revealed through a disturbance in one's perceptual faculties or an awareness of the material setting of signification. But what is this bodily disturbance, this indexical desire, if not the emergence of a set of truly natural, transparent, nonideological facts that precede the existence of signs? If we do not accept the foundationalism of the latter claim, then coming to know how reality has been shaped by power-laden signs can never tell us much about what to do with our signs.

In chapter 3 I argue that an awareness of the mediated nature of signs is the *condition for* Matisse's practice and not an enlightened or traumatic discovery. "It is difficult to begin without borrowing," Thoreau wrote in 1854,[79] and Matisse nowhere hides the fact that he is expressing himself on terrain explored by others. Matisse's citational practice acknowledges the borrowed nature of signification without this inducing any hand-wringing or celebration about iterability, regress, and reference. One of Matisse's primary aims was to animate or reanimate the signs he inherited. Signs, for him, were neither arbitrary nor natural, but rather dead or animate, habitual or vital, passively assumed or fully intended.

Critics will contest the validity of my claim that representation is the ground upon which artworks differ from the world. To suggest that artists might embrace or accept representation as a condition for their practice, rather than view it as a necessary evil, will raise in some minds the specter of postmodernism. One standard account of modernism is to see it as a set of historical efforts by subjects in complex relation—half marginal, half central—to the wider capitalist culture and driven by the desire to *test* that culture's regime of representation, even if that aim was recognized by those agents as impossible. (Whether those tests were intentional or not is immaterial from this perspective.) T. J. Clark presents the most powerful account of the modernist war against representation along these lines. According to Clark, "everyone"—he means postmodernists—assumes there is nothing "besides representation." It is Clark's aim, following Debord here, to recover the ways in which modern artists attempted to "represent representation's opposite—'lived experience' . . . or 'imagination.'"[80] While this opposite to representation is "represented"—it is not grounded in some natural referent—it nonetheless orients Clark's accounts around a duality of image and object, representation and materiality. For Clark the materiality of painterly practice, the painter's involvement in the task of squaring image and object, momentarily but decisively interrupts the smooth functioning of painterly discourse and its ideological suppositions. That a work can fail to satisfy an existing representational regime, thereby calling attention to the difference between art and world and, in the process, offering an alternative to the world in its current form, is for Clark its reason for being. Representation, how it encodes the world according to its given categories and hierarchies, is the problem that art tries to solve. A few questions emerge: Why is lived experience opposed to representation rather than a version of it? What would be the problem in calling lived experience a mode of representational immediacy, a flourishing of its potentials rather than its opposite or negative? What, after all, is the testing of a representational regime for, if not for more adequate, more inclusive forms of representation?[81]

That modernism was an epic and failed struggle to overcome representation in the name of something more real is a peculiar lesson to draw from it. The enduring notion that representation is an act of denial of the real (of the body, of materiality, of life) requires its own historical diagnosis. I offer the beginnings of that here. What I will try to show is how representation, far from interposing a wedge between us and the world, can bring us closer to it. I will also show how thinking representation and intimacy, mediation and connection, difference and identity go together is to think one's way into Matisse's art and Bergson's philosophy.

ONE

Painting as Affect Machine

> [With *Harmony in Red*] we are confronted with a wall of painting forcing its color saturation onto us. A certain form of violence is implied by this kind of address.
>
> —Yve-Alain Bois, in *Art since 1900*

> The violence of sensation is opposed to the violence of the represented (the sensational, the cliché). The former is inseparable from its direct action on the nervous system . . . it must have nothing of the nature of a represented object.
>
> —Gilles Deleuze, *Francis Bacon: The Logic of Sensation*

SAVAGE, BARBARIC, CRUDE. The insults once hurled at Henri Matisse—and at modernism in general—have been resurrected by today's critics to describe the impact of paint on the beholder. Matisse's lines and colors make the viewer mad, reversing the traditional association of the artist with madness. Alastair Wright, for instance, catalogs the various invectives directed at Matisse's fauve works and suggests that, although much of it appears "generic," "throw-away," and "hackneyed," nonetheless "it was true."[1] *What* was true? The "lack of verbal fixity" in the discourse about the work "mirrors" and "corresponds" to "something in the paintings." The language of madness used to describe the work is a product of madness itself: to "look at such paintings is, in effect, to look as a schizophrenic." Adding further injury, Wright asserts that Matisse's inconsistent facture "generate[s] blindness" in the viewer.[2] The force of Wright's argument is to show that certain artworks produce affects regardless of who the viewers are (as long as they are upright and bifocal), when they are (it is not ultimately a historical claim), what their attitudes toward the work are (active or passive), or whether the artist intended this response or not (line, color, and handling, independent of the artist, do the work). The unsuspecting viewer of Matisse's fauve work comes to it with the belief that it will deliver something, something expressive of the artist's inner life or a mimetic reflection of the world, and what the viewer discovers instead is a violent encounter with paint itself. Matisse's victims cannot help but discover themselves—their bodies, their senses, the visual hierarchies that shape their worlds—on the way to seeking a transcendence that does not exist.

Wright's vision of a traumatic encounter with "paint itself" comes at the end of a longer history. It is as old as modernism itself. The *post* of postmodern simply means a radicalization of basic modernist claims. That those claims are mistaken is the point of this chapter and of the book as a whole. But while modernism may have invented the idea that art is a matter of direct encounter between paint and bodies, the artists I consider largely saw the limits of that claim as well.

My epigraphs above are drawn from some of the most influential voices in postmodern discourse about paint and bodies. Bois describes the violent aggression of Matisse's walls of paint (Figure 1.1), and Deleuze feels the "violence of sensation" before works by Francis Bacon. What they both assert is a connection between seeing a painting and the experience of trauma. For Bois and Deleuze, certain privileged works bypass representation and come into direct contact with the viewer's nerve endings. (Lest we underestimate the seriousness of the claim, Deleuze repeats the phrase "direct action on the nervous system" no fewer than eight times in the space of fifteen pages.)[3]

The historian's task, Deleuze suggests, is not to interpret a work of art but to determine its efficacy. The historian must set aside the task (or disease) of "interpretosis" in order to evaluate the degree and quality of affective impact.[4] What establishes the picture's "maximum violence" is not, as we might expect, a pictorial thematic or an artistic intention. A work's content and the artist's intention are irrelevant, and if they are too emphatically present, Deleuze states in *Francis Bacon,* "the scream is botched" (34/29). While Deleuze is conventionally anti-intentional in his attitude toward the artist, he grants agency to paint itself: form "asserts its intention to break away from the figurative" (34/29). For Bois the "hypnotic frenzy" induced in the beholder's body by Matisse's *The Dance (II)* (Plate 1) is a function not of representation but of "declaration";[5] the "violence of paint," as Deleuze sees it, has "nothing to do with" what is "represented" (34/29).[6] The performative account of painterly form is not in addition to the work's representational status but is an action against representation.

This is what Judith Butler means when she says of both Matisse and Deleuze, "To the extent that the means of representation—paint and line—are what act upon the nervous system, they do so not only at the expense of representation itself, but explicitly *against* representation."[7] Represented violence can only divert one's attention from what Deleuze calls in the opening sentence of *Francis Bacon* the "very special violence" of form.[8] As I will show, this

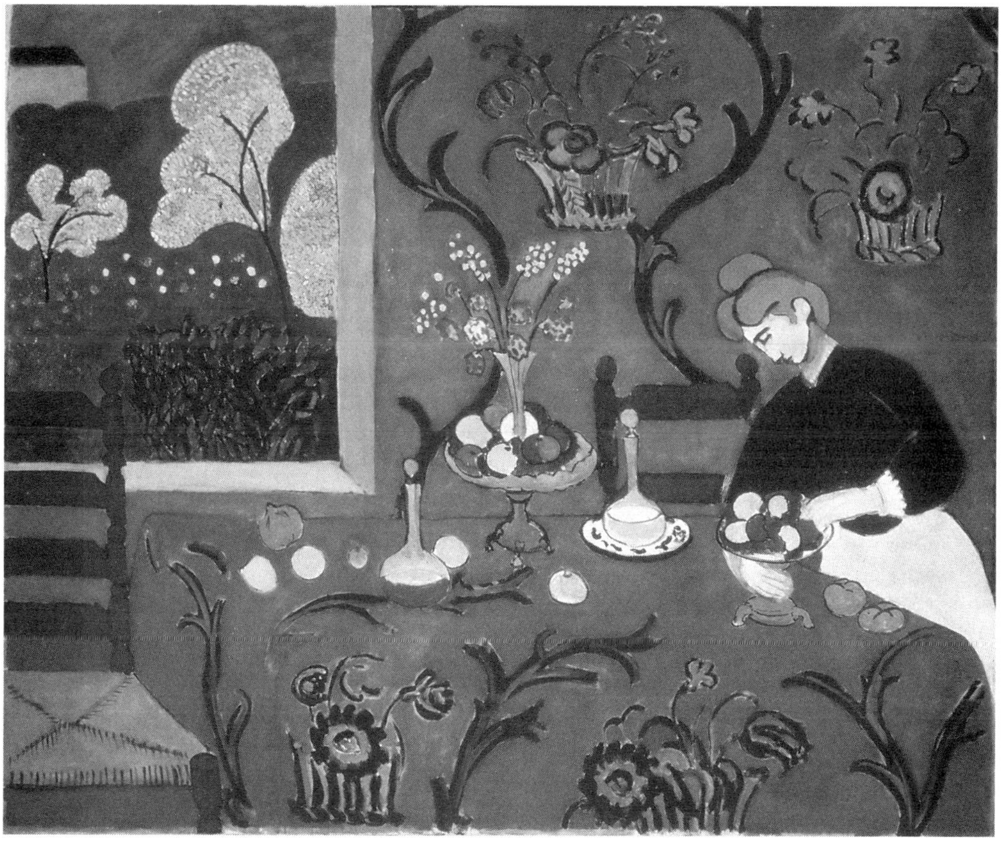

Figure 1.1. Henri Matisse (1869–1954), *Harmony in Red*, 1908. Oil on canvas, 180 × 220 cm. State Hermitage Museum, St. Petersburg, Russia. Copyright 2013 Succession H. Matisse / Artists Rights Society (ARS), NY. Photograph Archives H. Matisse; copyright 2013 Succession H. Matisse.

interest in the violence of color and line is far from special. On the contrary, it constitutes one of the most enduring and failed ideals of modernist theory and practice.

The idea that the formal qualities of a work directly affect the viewer's physical, psychological, or emotional state has a long pedigree. Compare, for instance, Deleuze's view of a picture having a direct action on the nervous system with Wassily Kandinsky's claims that the "principle of art is efficacious contact" and that "color is a means of exerting a direct influence upon the soul."[9] "The purpose of any potential work of art is to produce some kind of effect," he declared. Accordingly, "Color contains within itself a little-studied but enormous power, which can influence the entire human body as a physical organism."[10] Kandinsky was specific about the effects produced by these colors: "Yellow, when directly observed . . . has a disturbing influence; it pricks, upsets people, and reveals its true character, which is insistent and aggressive." Rather than figurative representation, Kandinsky believed that color, texture, and tone were the true means of enacting an emotional transfer between artist and viewer. Then again, it was not the artist or the lack of figuration that really mattered to Kandinsky. "Every object (regardless of whether it was created directly by nature or by human hand) is a being with *its own life* and, inevitably, with *its own effect* flowing from it," he observed.[11] Kandinsky's lines and colors had their own life, as did natural objects, and that is why he could speak of his pictures as bearing agency. The "content of a picture," he wrote, "is not what it represents, but that which the viewer *lives* or *feels* under the effect of the form and the agency of the colors of the picture."[12] So while it is traditional to call Kandinsky an expressionist, what that really means for him is that "objects" express themselves whether the artist intends them to or not.[13] Ultimately, it is the picture, or the combination of lines and colors within the picture, that bears agency, not the artist. The artist "arranges" the independently expressive object-forms. And it is this claim about the affective and anti-intentional nature of line and color that far outweighs the differences between Kandinsky and Deleuze.

So while Deleuze rejected Kandinsky's abstraction—the painter is said to drain pictorial "tension" within an "internal optical space"—and had no interest in the specific emotions contained within specific colors, he fully replicated Kandinsky's more basic claims about the agency of line and color.[14] And while it is largely irrelevant where the affect is going—whether it hits Kandinsky's "soul" or Deleuze's organless body—it is crucially important that both of them imagine a mode of sensorial immediacy that denies the possibility of disagreement or misunderstanding and replaces those possibilities with questions about what actually happens to the beholder. And what actually happens to the beholder is not up for discussion in the way an intention is.

Because, as Deleuze writes, the "work of art is a being of sensation and nothing else" and the "artist creates blocks of affects," it makes little difference whether one is talking about the artist's or the viewer's response.[15] But what does matter is the response. That is why the most common form of the affective approach occurs when Bois asks his readers, "What happens when the eye grapples with a top quality Bonnard?" And again: "What happens to us in front of one or other of [his] works?"[16] This is a question directed not at understanding Bonnard's intentions—an approach Bois rejects—but at what the work does to the beholder regardless of those intentions. Bois is concerned not with understanding how Bonnard sought to express heightened modes of multisensory experience—an interest, he might say, we can never really know—but rather with the actual effects produced by the work on the beholder. The peculiar value of affective analysis is that it cannot be shown to be wrong in the way an interpretive analysis can. While one can misunderstand what an artist meant by a sequence of lines and colors, what happens to one's body when it responds to those lines and colors is immune to this kind of communicative failure. One can presumably discover through sophisticated forms of empirical analysis, such as PET scans and fMRIs, what roughly "happens" to the eye or nervous system when it encounters a work, although Bois and Deleuze insistently, if mysteriously, avoid this consequence of their approach.[17] On the other hand, and unlike the effect of the work, one can never analyze an intention empirically.

The material absence of an intention, or its identification with aspects of the work, is the ground upon which acts of interpretation, rather than assertions about the viewer's experience, make sense. If there is no claim made regarding understanding an intention, then there is also no claim made for interpretation. Which is just to say, talking about how color and line affect you is not the same as talking about what they mean. Those affects may or may not end up being relevant to a question of interpretation, but they are not yet addressed to it. It is the special privilege of affects that they occur regardless of an intention and are not available to traditional modes of evaluation, but matter only insofar as they occur or do not. A related but slightly different point is that Bois's answer to the question of "what happens" to the beholder—whether the work in question is Bonnard's, Matisse's, Picasso's, Mondrian's, or Barnett Newman's—is that "we are hit full in the face."[18] For Bois the value of the work—what makes it "top quality"—lies in the degree of effect it has on the subject who views it. The quality of the effect is a matter of the degree to which the work solicits an awareness of the preconditions of representation, the unconscious hierarchies by which we divide up the world.

The First Affective Turn

My claim is not that Bois and Deleuze are necessarily distorting the past they are describing, but rather to show how their claims are part of a long history of modernist concerns. One way of describing my aim in this chapter is to provide a history of how a dominant mode of postmodern theory derived from a set of failed beliefs of modernist theory and practice: namely, that color and line produce bodily responses that function and mean independent of the artist's agency. It would be a mistake, that is, to characterize *affective formalist* discourse, as I will call it, as either modernist or postmodernist. It flows continuously, with brief interruptions, from the nineteenth century to the present.[19] Against the claims of affective formalism I will argue that the beholder's affective response to a work is irrelevant except insofar as those affects are taken to be intended by the artist.

Affect theorists could find support, for instance, in Matisse's claim made at the opening of the Chapel of the Rosary in Vence (Figure 1.2):

> Colors . . . have in themselves, independently of the objects that they serve to express, an important action on the feelings of those who look at them. Thus simple colors can act on the intimate feelings with much more force, the simpler they are. A blue, for example, accompanied by the brilliance of its complementaries, acts on the feelings like a sharp blow on a gong. It is the same with yellow and red, and the artist must be able to play them according to necessity.[20]

Matisse sought to make his pictures as forceful as possible, likening their impact on the viewer to a "sharp blow on a gong." He conceived the chapel at Vence, "uniting all my researches," as a more powerful vehicle than any canvas in its capacity to control the beholder's total emotional experience. And because color acted independently of its object, it proved the ideal medium for expression (no iconographic knowledge was required on the beholder's part). But then again, the colors acted independent of the artist's own intentions, so it is hard to see that they properly express his will at all. The Vence chapel allowed for the possibility of meaning without misunderstanding, but it was at the expense of the artist's capacity to mean beyond the arrangement of autonomous forms containing their own expressive life. That this kind of statement is especially rare in Matisse's writings and seems intimately associated with his late turn toward architectural ensembles, a turn away from *tableau* form and toward something like an environment, helps puts in relief his more consistent claim that his work embodied his inner expressive aims (the "great thing is to express one's self").[21] As I will show, it is unusual to see Matisse describe color, or any aspect of his work, as embodying meaning "independent" of his expressive will—it is even rarer to see him celebrate that independence as a relief from his intentions.

Traumatic Rhythms

Matisse's view that his colors produced an effect like a mallet on a gong comes at the end of a long tradition of analogizing the visual arts with music. "The art of the colorist is obviously related to mathematics and music," Eugène Delacroix famously declared.[22] And when Delacroix coined the expression "the music of the painting," he was thinking of a specific invention, the piano. The piano was a privileged instrument by virtue of two features: its capacity for complex polyphonic harmonies (color chords) and its percussive immediacy. Like a pianist, the painter was said to play the keys of the viewer's soul. "Thus died . . . Delacroix, who . . . for forty years played upon the keyboard of human passions," his obituary read.[23] Or in Kandinsky's famous analogy from *On the Spiritual in Art* (1912): "Color is the keyboard. The eye is the hammer. The soul is the piano with its many strings. . . . The artist is the hand which, by playing on this or that key (i.e., form), affects the human soul in this or that

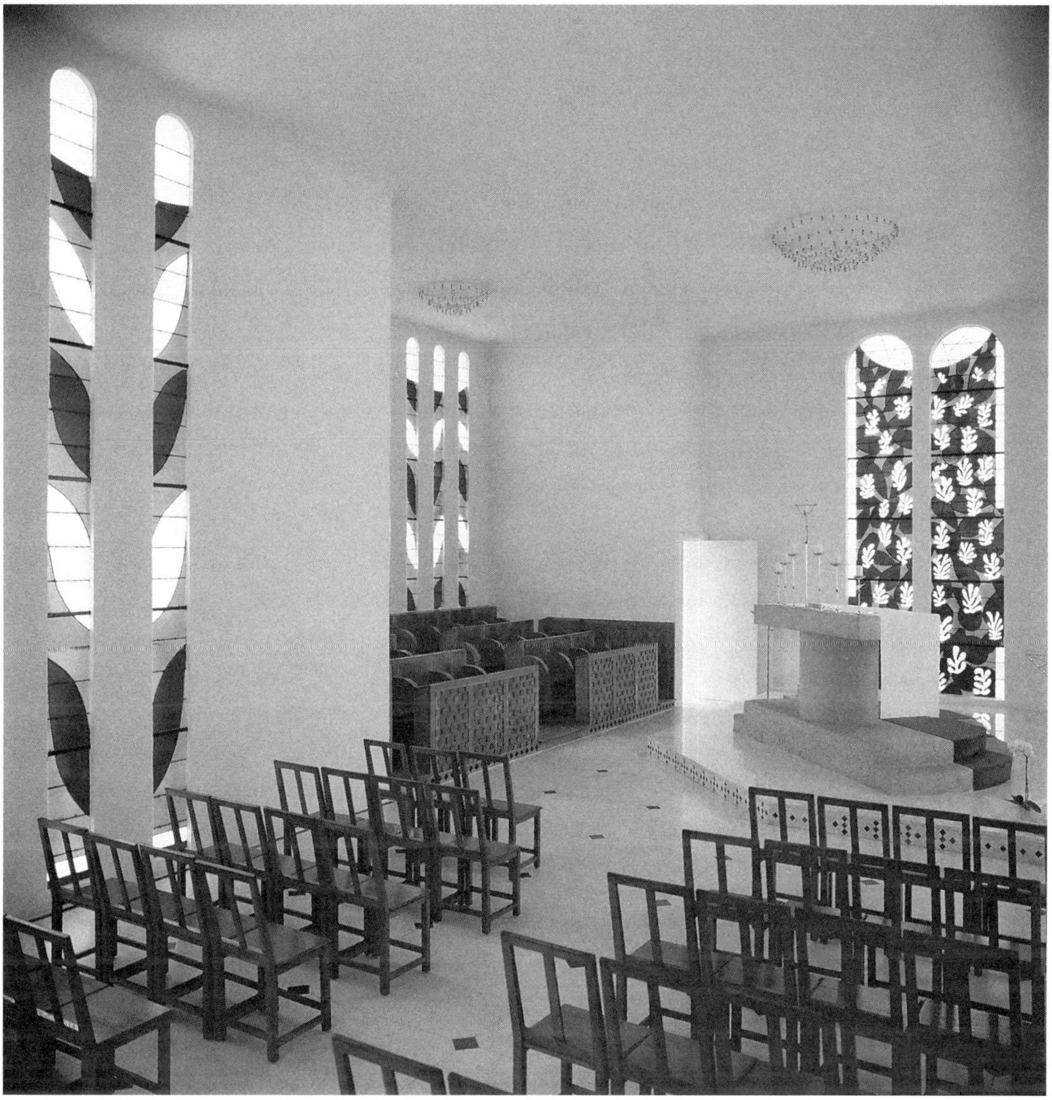

Figure 1.2. Henri Matisse (1869–1954), general view of the interior of the Chapel of the Rosary, Vence, France, 1948–51. Copyright 2013 Succession H. Matisse / Artists Rights Society (ARS), NY. Photograph copyright The Bridgeman Art Library BAL309545.

way."[24] For Kandinsky, as for Delacroix, there were both violent and harmonious color chords, and with sufficient training, artists could manipulate them to produce the desired emotional results.[25]

It was painting's percussive effects, the capacity of line and color to create powerful visual *rhythms,* that inspired Delacroix. This rhythmic commitment first emerged in a stirring diary entry on the making of *The Massacre at Chios* (1824) (Figure 1.3):

> My picture is beginning to develop a rhythm, a powerful spiral momentum. I absolutely must complete it. . . . I must get fullness. Even though it loses in naturalness, it will gain in richness and beauty. If only it hangs together! . . . That silent power that speaks at first only to the eyes and then seizes and captivates every faculty of the soul! Here is your real spirit; here is your own true beauty, beautiful painting, so much insulted, so grievously misunderstood and delivered up to fools who exploit you.[26]

When Delacroix exploited painting he was no fool. As though inducing a mesmeric trance, the spiraling form was intended to take control of "every faculty of the [viewer's] soul." It was Delacroix's view that a powerful rhythmic pattern affected the beholder more directly and more securely than an appeal to the beholder's understanding or memory, either of which could fail. But unlike the artists who followed his example, Delacroix never conceived of his forms as acting independent of his intentions. His pictures would seize the viewer's soul because he intended that effect to come off, not because his colors did so of their own accord.

Consider Delacroix's famous analogizing of nature to a dictionary. As the poet uses words to make poems, so the painter uses natural forms (trees, rocks, rivers) as the elements of composition. Of course, a painter does not put nature into paintings in the way a poet puts words into poems. Moreover, nature does not bear meaning in the way words do. Not until the Symbolists did Delacroix's analogy begin to make sense or, rather, did it begin to be taken *literally.* In the 1890s Delacroix's ambiguous analogy took on the sense in which both nature and words (or lines and colors) were thought to bear significance in themselves and beyond the artist's intended use of them. That this later view actually has little to do with Delacroix's meaning should be clear from the following passage:

> Nature is just a dictionary, you hunt in it for words . . . you find in it the elements which make a phrase or a story; but nobody would regard a dictionary as a composition in the poetic sense of the term. Besides, nature is far from being always interesting from the point of view of the effect of the whole. . . . If each detail is perfect in some way the union of these details seldom gives an effect equivalent to that which arises, in the work of a great artist, from the total composition.[27]

While in Delacroix's time "nobody" would take natural elements as a composition—"nobody would . . . confound . . . the dictionary with eloquence," Delacroix's friend Charles Blanc observed[28]—the history I am tracing shows how it was that many people came to take nature (or objects) as a composition. For Delacroix it was the "total composition" of the "great artist" who made nature more than a sequence of "interesting" details. Nonetheless, it was

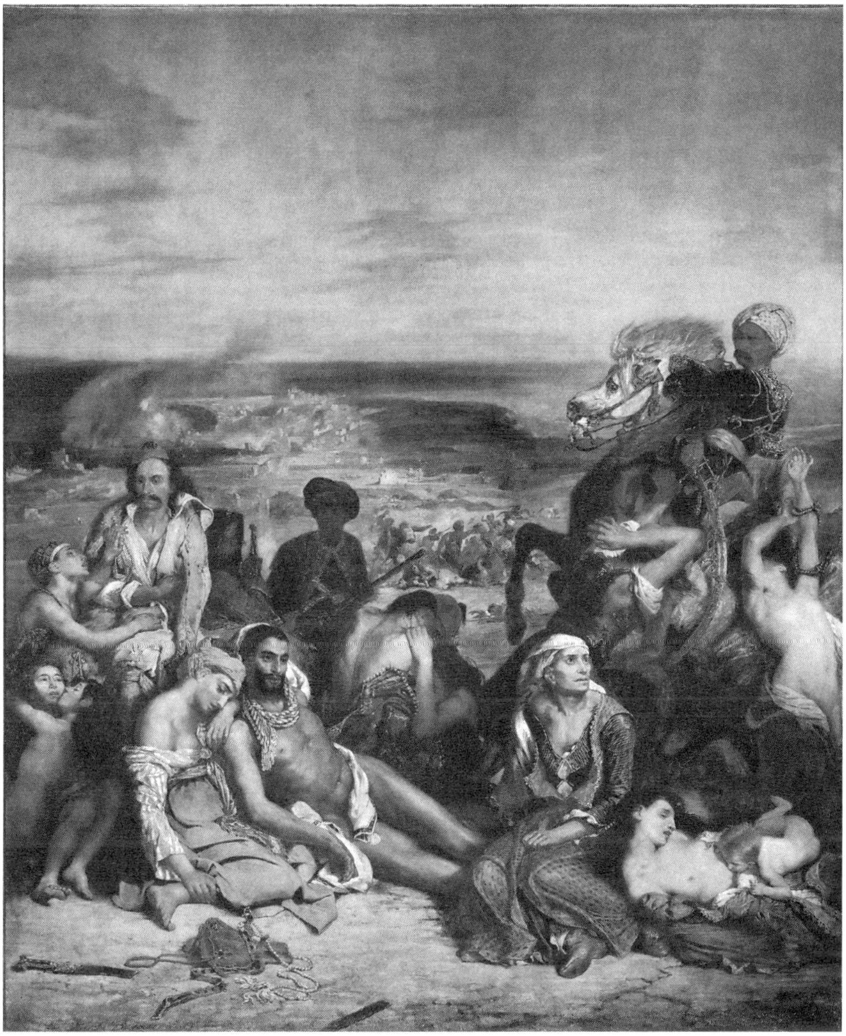

Figure 1.3. Eugène Delacroix (1798–1863), *The Massacre at Chios*, 1824. Oil on canvas, 419 × 354 cm. Louvre, Paris, France. Photograph by Erich Lessing / Art Resource, NY.

Delacroix's deep fascination with beholder response that set in motion a tendency that found its conclusion in the contemporary theory of affect.

By the time we arrive at the writings of Bois and Deleuze, the artist's intention to produce effects (violent or otherwise) is irrelevant. Above all, these writers are committed to the rhythmic and percussive nature of line and color (the hammer action) hitting the nervous system (vibrating steel strings), as though colors and lines are forces that carry charges beyond any specific human motivation. While Bois describes the "pulsating repetition" and "syncopated rhythm" of an ornamental fabric in Matisse's work,[29] Deleuze conceives of a systolic–diastolic rhythm, describing the "almost unlivable Power" of the "rhythmic unity of the senses" made visible by painters such as Cézanne (39/33). This rhythm, according to Deleuze, does not reinforce representation—by metaphorizing the sounds and movements of rustling leaves, or water lapping against rocks, depicted in numerous works by Cézanne—but testifies to a chaotic experience "beyond representation," "neither rational nor cerebral" (41/34, 45/37).[30] Similarly, Bois conceives of Matisse's "pullulating arabesques and color flashes" as literally inducing "blindness" in the beholder.[31] Bois contends that after Matisse eliminated rhythmic themes from his work (as in *The Dance*) a deeper "internalized" rhythm was generated. "It is the rhythm of a pendulum at the core of our vision," he explains.[32] Once Matisse's painting sets in motion an "irresolvable oscillation of our perception" a set of psychological effects inevitably follow. Matisse's *Music* (1910) (Figure 1.4) "affects us so much," Bois writes, because it triggers an action along the "principal nodes of psychic life," those "constitutive of human beings as a species."[33] As these last phrases make clear, Bois is not interested in making claims about how paintings functioned in the past or in a specific context or according to an artist's intention, but in making claims about psychobiological response. What would it be like to dispute a claim based on the actions occurring at the "pendulum at the core of our vision" or along the "principal nodes of psychic life"?

The essential move, for both Bois and Deleuze, is from the *representation* of rhythm to the *production* of rhythms that seize the beholder's body as though automatically or by "surefire" means.[34] For both writers, the relay of optical rhythms to the beholder is a violent encounter. Deleuze imagines the embodiment of a pictorial "catastrophe," while Bois conceives of rhythmic effects as a disturbing event identified with psychic trauma.[35]

In her 1990 essay "The Im/pulse to See," Rosalind Krauss further establishes the influential claim that paintings can be traumatic.[36] She identifies the trauma of the gaze in Picasso's late work with a doubly violent force that inheres in special types of formal patterning. The optical beat, she explains in her opening phrase, "has the power to decompose and dissolve the very coherence of form on which visuality may be thought to depend." It is this "pulse or beat that the modernist artist senses all too well as the enemy of his craft."[37] This rhythmic beat, Krauss explains, has nothing to do with the representational, even if its emergence is bound to a representational setting.[38] In exploiting this beat a range of artists sought an "active aggression against the very prerogatives of vision."[39] The visual beat, by interrupting pictorial form, also disrupts the viewer's normative sense of self that was authorized by classical hierarchies of vision. For the viewer standing before Duchamp's *Rotoreliefs*, the visual beat of the oscillating cone is said to produce an unstoppable relay of affects, by turns painful and pleasurable, that corrode and ultimately dissolve

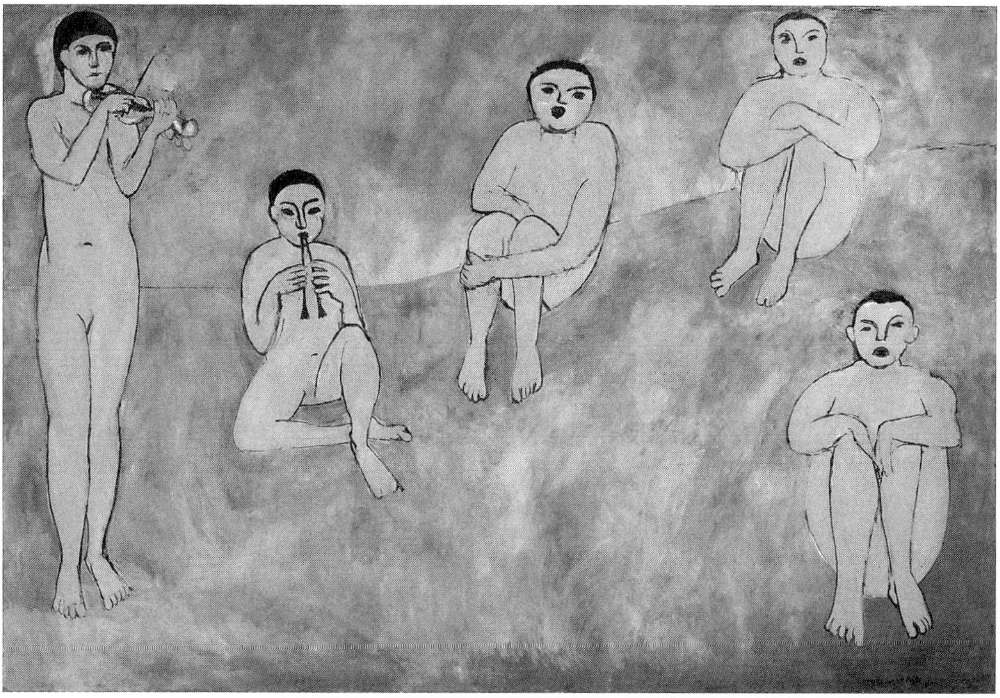

Figure 1.4. Henri Matisse (1869–1954), *Music*, 1910. Oil on canvas, 260 × 389 cm. State Hermitage Museum, St. Petersburg, Russia. Copyright 2013 Succession H. Matisse / Artists Rights Society (ARS), NY. Photograph courtesy The Art Archive at Art Resource, NY.

the chain of coherencies securing both work and subject. At stake for Krauss, Bois, and Deleuze is an interruption in the normal function of the beholder's nervous and perceptual systems.[40] And coming to feel the bodily preconditions of sight is also to feel the way one unconsciously divides the world into hierarchies. Unable to unify figure and ground, the beholder is forced to become aware of the temporality, and materiality, of vision. When the beholder is unable to achieve an instantaneous comprehension of the visual field, he or she discovers that the assumptions on which that vision is grounded—the coherence of the self—are undermined; the beholder is de-formed, blinded, by the visual assault of the syncopated image.

Of course, it would be a mistake to imagine that Krauss or Bois have much interest in the meditated nature of meaning except insofar as it leads to the "rupture" that occurs when the artist's or viewer's illusions about transparency come to nothing. So despite every warning about mediation, about being "immersed [in the world], with no position above or outside that would allow a more reflective view,"[41] everything comes down to a moment of rupture, a violent *standing apart* from one's immersive engagement with the world. The pulsating and temporal "attack on the idea of *immediacy*," Krauss writes, "give[s] rise" to "visual disruption."[42] Disruption here reiterates the modernist fantasy Krauss is critiquing—that a work of art can "play on the viewer's sensations"—only now the tune is traumatic rather than expressive.

Krauss is certainly correct to say that many modernist painters adhered to the ideal of the logically self-sufficient surface as described by scientific treatises on aesthetics throughout the nineteenth century.[43] Modernist painters, Krauss explains—citing Duchamp—"refuse to 'go beyond' the retina to the gray matter." But the question is not whether artists "arrest at the retina" (Duchamp again) or go beyond it, but whether the work's actual effect on the beholder (on the eyes, soul, heart, brain, or nervous system) is significant to the meaning of a work at all. Whether the aesthetic encounter is conceived in terms of temporal dilation, carnalized seeing, or a disembodied instantaneity is irrelevant from my perspective. What is at stake is a view that turns the meaning of the artwork into the actual experience of the viewer's body. Whatever those actual bodily effects are, they are different for each body. And those differences need not be reconciled. If the artwork is construed as an affect machine—"nothing but affects," as Deleuze puts it (35/30), or a "chaos of unrepressed affect," as Krauss does[44]—then any view of art as available to conflicting interpretations of a work's meaning is rendered invalid. What would it be like to disagree about affect? *Can* there be disagreement, or just registration and calibration of the difference between irreducible sensations?

Actual versus Intended Effects

I have relied up to this point on a distinction that I now hope to clarify and elaborate further. There are two types of artistic effect: actual and intended. An *intended* effect is one the artist sought to produce in the beholder. This effect could have existed prior to the work's creation or could have arisen in the process of its making. As I suggested in the introduction, some artists, such as Le Corbusier and Edward Weston (many twentieth-century photographers followed him here), insisted on artistic "preconception" or "previsualization," while other artists, such as Matisse and Picasso, typically described their intentions as something that emerged in the process of production or in hindsight after a work was completed. An *actual* effect, on the other hand, is an effect that occurs in the viewer's mind or body regardless of the artist's intention to make that effect come off.

Bertolt Brecht clarifies this point in a notebook entry titled "On Non-objective Painting" (ca. 1939), in which he introduces the distinction between a "perceptual object" and a work that bears "specific perceptions [bestimmten Empfindungen]." Perceptual objects, like any objects in the world, "generate nameless sensations [unnennbare Empfindungen erzeugt]"; objects of specific perception, on the other hand, are objects to which some responses are relevant and some are not. Likely thinking of Matisse's *Red Studio* or similar works, Brecht states:

> You paint, for instance, something red and indeterminate, and some cry at the sight of this red and indeterminate [Unbestimmtes] thing because it reminds them of a rose, while other people cry because it reminds them of a child covered in blood who has been torn to bits by flying bombs. Your task is then completed: you have composed a perceptual object of lines and colors.[45]

Against the production of perceptual objects, objects that produced open-ended experiences, Brecht offers that "things should not be seen just 'differently,' but that they should be seen in a quite specific way [bestimmter Weise]." The reason a perceptual object is the art form of the ruling classes, Brecht contends, is that there is no ground on which to dispute its claims. Comparing one's sensations before an object with those of another viewer is not the same as disagreeing about what the work means. Something that bears specific meaning, on the other hand, renders certain perceptions irrelevant and others relevant. And like Brecht, I am not concerned, at least in this chapter, with making a case for any specific set of intentions; I am concerned with saying that intention is crucial to the possibility of meaning at all. If readers, for instance, come to disagree with my account of Matisse, that is unrelated to the question of whether art history (or the humanities more generally) aims to understand various forms of intentionality or whether our practices are committed to understanding what happens to the viewer (historically or currently), regardless of what any artist intended.

The difference between actual and intended effects can be further clarified by the following two examples: one drawn from Adolf Loos, the other from André Derain. Loos, like Le Corbusier, conceived of intentions as largely preceding the act of construction. According to Loos, "The artist . . . first senses the effect that he intends to realize. . . . He senses the effect that he wishes to exert upon the spectator—be it fear or horror in a prison, reverence in a church, respect for the power of the state in a government bureau, piety in a tomb, a sense of homeyness in a dwelling, gaiety in a tavern—this effect he evokes by the material and the form."[46] And again: "The architect uses materials to arouse feelings in us which are not inherent in those materials themselves."[47] The idea is simple enough. According to Loos, the artist's task is to express an idea or a sensation to the spectator through the artist's structures. Moreover, Loos makes clear that the intended effect is not one "inherent" in the materials themselves. If the effect were internal to the materials, then the artist's intentions would be at best of marginal significance and at worst nullified by the "agency" of the materials.

Contrast Loos's notion of material noninherency with Derain's claim that "stone, color, etc., no matter the material . . . has its own life, independent of what we make it represent."[48] (Kandinsky followed Derain a few years later in saying "every object . . . is a being with its own life.") For Derain, stones were like colors and both had a life independent of what the artist intended. While Derain did not say anything about the beholder's experience before those stone-colors, following the logic of his claim requires an account of the beholder's attitude toward a "perceptual object." In Derain's view, the encounter with his work was like the encounter with a stone. And while Derain saw stones as having a "life" of their own, it would be impossible to say whether one correctly or incorrectly understood that life. Once the work of art functioned "outside painting," as Derain further insisted, once it had been turned into a stone (i.e., something for which the maker's intentions were irrelevant), the only experience that could possibly matter would be the beholder's own. Kandinsky clarified Derain's point when he said, "Every being will produce a different effect upon different people."[49] Whatever one felt before Derain's stone-painting, any divergence from another's experience could amount only to that—to difference—and not to disagreement. One could not plausibly disagree about what a stone meant in the way one could about an intention, but one could certainly register what it meant to oneself.

Or consider these two statements by Matisse. On one hand, he claimed that his "sole intention" was to "express [himself] *totally* . . . in form and color" and that the "work is the emanation, the projection of self."[50] On the other hand, he suggested that it was not simply his intention to express himself through color but that "colors . . . have in themselves, independently of the objects that they serve to express, an important action on the feelings of those who look at them."[51] The former claim is intentional and expressionist in impulse; the latter is anti-intentional and oriented toward the beholder's response (in the way Derain's statement above is). To parse and differentiate these all-too-familiar types of claims within modernist discourse is one of the aims of this book, to show how they typically fail to be properly distinguished is another, and to show that they are and should be kept ontologically and logically distinct is yet another (this the interpreter's task, I should say, not the artist's).[52]

The question at stake is not whether the beholder's experience before the work counts, but rather *how* it counts. On one account, the beholder's experience is taken as the source of meaning irrespective of the artist's intention. On the other account, an experience is relevant only insofar as it is directed at, and by, the effort to understand or to feel what the artist wanted the beholder to feel (even if the artist had no way to articulate or know that intention in advance of creating the work or even after). As I have been arguing, if one chooses the latter option, one can disagree about the meaning of a work; if one chooses the former, difference is logically dissociated from disagreement.

Of course most writing in the humanities tends to skirt the distinction or to opt for something in between actual and intended effects. Why can't one have one's own experience, something independent of any shared meaning, *and* try to understand what the artist meant? Or what about those artists who intended that the beholder's experiences be the work of art itself? The latter position was articulated, perhaps for the first time, by Duchamp when he said, "I attach even more importance to the spectator than to the artist."[53] But the artist does not decide whether the beholder has an experience before a work of art. The artist may try to frame or focus the beholder's experience of the work and thereby to distinguish that experience from the experiences the beholder had before he or she engaged with the work—which is to say, to distinguish the beholder's experience of the work from the beholder's *experience in general.* And that difference between the work of art and the world will be meaningful only if the beholder's experience of the work of art can *fail* to come off. (No one will tell you that you failed to experience yourself correctly. To say that you may have missed what was going on in *The Dance* makes paintings different kinds of things from other objects of experience.) An unfailing effect—an effect produced by the artist's materials or their form or their color; say, for instance, if the field of red in Matisse's *Harmony in Red* (Figure 1.1) unquestionably produced the sensation of anxiety—would render the artist's intention beside the point. Indeed, even if the beholder's experience were guaranteed to correspond to the artist's—if the artist's intention always came off—then there would be no grounds for disagreeing about what the artist meant. To do so would be like two people disagreeing about whether one is sad. Affects are not meanings. Research, such as Derain's and Kandinsky's, into producing various affects in the beholder avoids (one may suspect that it is meant to avoid) the task of expressing anything. Then again, an artist—Matisse, for instance—may use the affect-producing potential of colors, materials, and other formal properties of art objects expressively.

Let me take up one last time Brecht's distinction between the indeterminately red painting, a "perceptual object," and another red painting—*Harmony in Red*—that makes one feel "in a certain way." But rather than Brecht's scented rose or lacerated child, let me offer the example of hunger. If one feels hungry before Matisse's *Harmony in Red* one might assume that hunger is not an effect intended by the artist and therefore not factor it into one's interpretation. One is often hungry. Perhaps I will say I feel hungry in front of the canvas, and Bois will say he feels a disturbing oscillation "at the core of [his] vision." We do not disagree, nor can we, as long as we continue to understand ourselves as describing our experiences. We can begin to disagree only if we claim that our responses fulfill Matisse's intentions—that is to say, if we found an interpretation of the work on hunger or optical oscillation. But to describe the difference between our responses as a disagreement would be to disagree about what Matisse intended, not about whether I was hungry.

Consider, finally, the issue of color in Matisse. What if we disagree about whether the dominant color in *Harmony in Red* is scarlet or vermilion? Or about whether it is bright red (or bright enough to be scarlet, rather than vermilion)? Then we would be appealing to our sensations, but in order to fix our description of the thing. So, our experiences would be pertinent to our interpretation of the picture—insofar as it matters to us what color Matisse chose, which it must. But then, we might say, having been relined, it is not bright any longer (but still vermilion), but we know that Matisse meant it to be a scarlet. So our interpretation will be an interpretation of a scarlet field, not of the vermilion one we are looking at. The point is simply to say there are ways our bodily experience (of brightness, for instance) would be pertinent to interpretation, but there are even more significant ways in which the artist's intentions *still* trump those experiences when we interpret the work. Tracing the history of how bodily experience came to *be* the work's meaning—and how the artist's intentions came to be seen as secondary or irrelevant—is the aim of the rest of this chapter.[54]

The Origins of Affective Formalism? The Case of Nicolas Poussin

Since the mid-nineteenth century, art historians have argued that the nature of form and affect took a special turn with the art and writings of Nicolas Poussin (1594–1665). Several critics have argued that Poussin founded affective formalist discourse in his famous letter to his patron and friend Paul Fréart de Chantelou on the theory of the Modes. Inspired by Giuseppe Zarlino's sixteenth-century treatise on music, Poussin explained to his discontented patron that different pictures required different modes of execution.[55] "Those fine old Greeks," he told Chantelou, "inventors of everything that is beautiful, found several Modes by means of which they produced marvelous effects." These Modes, when properly deployed in a picture, have "the capacity and power to arouse the soul of the spectator to diverse emotions . . . and to produce particular effects."[56] Traditional readings of this text have assumed that Poussin's references to these "effects" were his way of talking about creating a unity of subject matter and form to provoke specific kinds of response in the beholder. So while most commentators have taken Poussin's theory of the Modes to imply a special attitude toward iconography and form, a small set of readers have argued that the letter is a cleverly coded anti-iconographic manifesto.

Paillot de Montabert reintroduced Poussin's modal theory into France in the 1820s, and through him it was given wide currency by Swiss aesthetician David Sutter (1811–80) in his *Esthétique générale et appliquée* of 1856. According to Sutter, "Lines have a meaning and even their own language to express the different modes, and the order according to which they are combined determines the character and harmony of the subject represented."[57] There is noticeable tension already in Sutter's wording. On one hand, he says that lines bear their own meaning and language; on the other, he asserts that it is the artist's job to order and combine them in order to best express the artist's intent. By suggesting that lines have "meaning" at all, and that they are not the means by which to express meaning, Sutter set in motion an idea that would have significant consequences for art writing from that point forward.

Similar tensions emerged with Charles Blanc's (1813–82) influential *Grammaire des arts du dessin* (1867). According to Blanc, it was not iconography that Poussin was speaking of in his letter on the Modes but the sensations released by the arrangement of lines. Here is Blanc:

> The horizontals, which express, in nature, the calmness of the sea, the majesty of far-off horizons, the vegetal tranquility of the strong, resisting trees, the quietude of the globe, after the catastrophes that have upheaved it, motionless, eternal duration—the horizontals in painting express analogous sentiments, the same character of eternal repose, of peace, of duration. If such are the sentiments the painter wishes to evoke in us, if such is the character he wishes to stamp upon his work, the horizontal lines should dominate in it, and the contrast of other lines, instead of attenuating the accent of horizontality will render it still more striking. Witness *The Testament of Eudamidas* [Figure 1.5]; in it Poussin has repeated the horizontal lines. Lying upon his death-bed, the citizen of Corinth forms the dominant line of the arrangement. The lance of the hero repeats this line and, prostrate like him, seems condemned to the repose of its master and to affirm a second time his death.[58]

Poussin's painting expresses tranquility after long struggle not in terms of imagery—the wizened, sickened, and furrowed body of Eudamidas, the doleful resignation of his wife's gesture, and the stoic repose of his friend accepting his obligation are of secondary significance—but by virtue of the emotions excited in the beholder by the picture's linear organization. The lance hanging high above Eudamidas's prostrate body did not find its source in Lucian's narrative but in the painter's psychological and physiological need to reinforce the physical sensation of repose.

For Blanc, the painter communicated emotion less by iconography than by "harmonies morales."[59] If Sutter observed a fixed relationship between lines and subject matter, then Blanc saw a fixed relationship between the lines in the work and the beholder's response. There was, he said in the *Grammar,* a natural "affinity between sentiment and color" (145).

But for all his emphasis on the putatively natural significance of the artist's means, Blanc's writings are still oriented toward what the "painter wishes to evoke in us." Or rather, there is a tension throughout the *Grammar* between

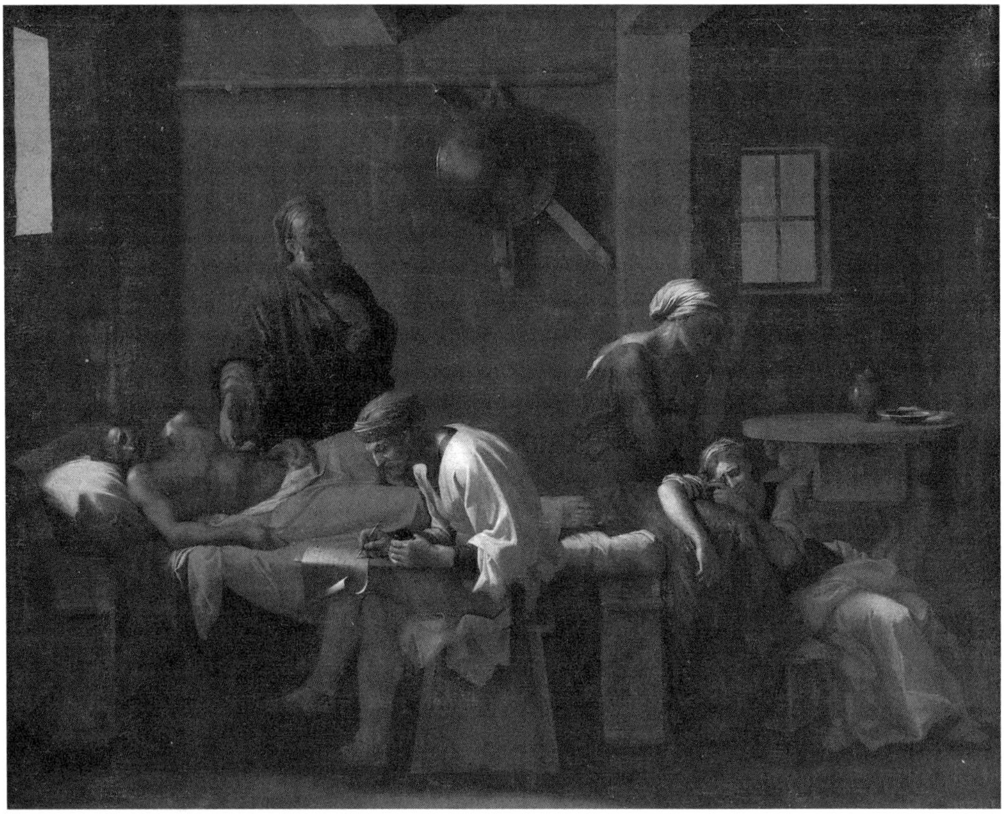

Figure 1.5. Nicolas Poussin (1594–1665), *The Testament of Eudamidas,* 1644–48. Oil on canvas, 110.5 × 158.5 cm. Statens Museum for Kunst/National Gallery of Denmark, Copenhagen, www.smk.dk.

the effort to naturalize forms (what line and color mean "in themselves") and the effort to stress the artist's capacity to *make* forms meaningful regardless of what they "naturally" suggest. (This tension would virtually define Symbolist aesthetics.) In a key passage, Blanc writes of how the artist must

> try his *doses,* distribute to his tints their places and roles, calculate the extent he will give them, and make, as it were, a secret rehearsal of the drama his coloring will form. He must employ the resources of white and black, foresee the optical mixture, know the vibration of colors, and finally take care of the effect the diversely colored light is to produce. (158)

Each sentence pulls in opposing directions, split between the viewer's response and the artist's aims. Blanc is concerned with the independent "drama" of colors (how they optically mix, vibrate, and produce light) and equally with the artist's mastery of these effects through proper distribution, calculation, and prediction. But the most telling analogy is the one he draws between colors and drugs. Colors need to be administered in doses—too little and they will not take effect, too much and they will overwhelm the beholder.

What makes Blanc a less-than-perfect model for affective analysis is the attention he lavishes on intentionality—so much so that at key moments he seems to deny the significance of the beholder's response *tout court.* In the opening pages of the *Grammar* Blanc defines painting's "primitive purpose" against that of sculpture. It is the difference, in his view, between pictorial autonomy and the open-endedness associated with "real things." Blanc clarifies:

> Appearance suffices and must suffice. Why? Because if painting were palpable it would become sculpture. The cubic reality would take from the image its essentially spiritual character and shackle the flight of the soul. Framed in real things, its expression would lack unity, would be contradicted by the changing spectacle of nature, by the ceaselessly varying light of the sun, and its factitious colors would grow pale, would fade out before those of the colorist, *par excellence.* (3–4)[60]

Painting was not exactly a "real thing," according to Blanc, because one's experience of it was more unified than the experiences elicited by the "ceaselessly varying" world of nature. Of course the beholder's experience, like nature itself, was "ceaselessly varying" from moment to moment, body to body. So to withdraw the work from the "changing spectacle" of nature was to deliver it up to its "spiritual" purpose outside of time.

For many of Blanc's admirers his skeptical attitude toward "natural life" could be discarded while his "science" remained intact. And it is this version of Blanc—one who studied the beholder's innate responsiveness to line and color—that became the model for future writers. Mécislas Goldberg, for instance, took up Blanc's "harmonies morales" at length in a book that shaped Matisse's aesthetics. Goldberg's *La Morale des lignes* of 1907 served as a loose model for Matisse's "Notes of a Painter" of one year later.[61] Goldberg considers the "mysterious moral laws of angles, lines and lights," citing Blanc on the "notation of emotional reality."[62] Following Blanc, Goldberg addresses the symbolic power of lines, declaring "vertical, spirit: horizontal, material," and of curves, "the spiritual will tend toward the right angle; the brutal, material will tend toward circular form."[63] Goldberg's book is a commentary on the drawings of Matisse's friend André Rouveyre, whom Goldberg quotes as saying, "Every line that descends towards the center of the earth makes a tragic expression while those that rise are comic."[64] The idea is further supported by a citation from Gabriel Séailles describing how the "horizontal line awakens the idea of repose, the vertical line the idea of action."[65] But like Blanc's, Goldberg's appeal to aesthetic laws was an effort to escape the limitations of an affective theory of art. The whole point of the book was to differentiate "autonomous" works, works whose meaning was "independent of fleeting sentimentality and momentary emotion."[66] Matisse followed Goldberg in his rejection of the "succession of moments which constitutes the superficial existence of beings and things, and which is constantly modifying and transforming them."[67] While "the appearance" of things "is continually changing," Matisse claimed that "the [artist's] intentions . . . remain constant."[68] Goldberg's and Matisse's rejection of momentary and changing reality—one that necessarily included the changing nature of the beholder's reactions—and their emphasis on the artist's capacity to control pictorial effects, is at odds with the wider drift of aesthetics in the twentieth century.

Even though E. H. Gombrich (1909–2001) was impatient with most variants of psychovisual aesthetics, he reserved special praise for Blanc's "interest in the perceptual and emotional effect of elementary forms" and his "bold attempt to reduce instinctual law to first principles, anticipating to some extent the methods of twentieth-century psychology."[69] Blanc's putative commitment to the primacy of response was what made him a model for Gombrich's aesthetics. For Gombrich, beholder response was a way to get over an even more central problem, the primacy of the artist. Whatever an artist *thought* he or she was expressing was often at variance with what the artist was *actually* expressing through lines and colors. Gombrich assured his readers that "artists have been aware of the expressive potentialities of shapes and colors long before expressionist theory seized upon that aspect of painting." That is because these expressive potentials had nothing to do with what traditionally goes by the name of expression. According to Gombrich, all viewers could gain "access to the workings of traditional symbolisms," even of the most recondite variety, if they properly tuned in to the "structural relationships within a scale or matrix" of meaning. Gombrich provided an example of the matrix: "When we say [à la Kandinsky] that *u* is dark blue and *i* bright green, we are talking playful nonsense, or serious nonsense if we are in earnest. But when we say that *i* is brighter than *u,* we find a surprising degree of general consent."[70] It was on the basis of this general consent—based in turn on biology and not on artist "nonsense"—that Gombrich developed his prolific analyses of pictures. Although Gombrich rejected expressionist theory—the idea that "a given shape or color were inherently 'charged' with an expressive meaning that would explode in the mind of the beholder"—he nonetheless believed that conflicting aesthetic responses could be "reduced to unanimity" when a work was situated within its proper context.[71] "There *is* such a thing as a gay melody and a cheerful color," he declared in "Expression and Communication." He continued, "There is some inborn disposition in all of us to equate certain sensations with certain feeling tones."[72] While there is little to dispute about the very broad validity of Gombrich's claim about inborn dispositions, there is little to recommend concerning the relevance of these facts for interpreting works of art.

It is on the basis of these facts (or generalities) that the whole discourse of "neuroarthistory" has evolved in recent years in the effort to apply cognitive and neuronal research to artistic interpretation and aesthetic experience. Neuroarthistory seeks to overcome the problem of interpretation by replacing it with the results of sensory stimulation (an approach Bois and Deleuze roundly reject, but one that is the logical outcome of their interest in "what happens" to the beholder before a work of art).

On the face of it, the ambitious group study *The Artful Mind: Cognitive Science and the Riddle of Human Creativity* (2006) has nothing to do with the mode of affective analysis elaborated by Derain and Kandinsky, Bois and Deleuze.[73] As I will show, contemporary attempts at neuroarthistory are not only compatible with that position but also provide crucial support for its claims. In one of the more well-known studies presented in *The Artful Mind,* David Freedberg claims that Poussin was the first to solve the riddle of human creativity. According to Freedberg, art historians have been blinded to Poussin's discoveries by an undue focus on iconography and contextual matters and by too much focus on the notion of meaning itself. "Context," Freedberg writes, "conditions and contaminates response." To remove contextual contaminates—what would that look like?—would be to begin to respond properly to form. Above all, Freedberg is "concerned with such responses as might arise from vision unmitigated by prior circumstantial knowledge and as uncontaminated as possible by contextual factors, whether individual, social, or historical." Poussin discovered not simply that different subjects required different treatments but that different treatments can trigger different reactions in the beholder (77). Freedberg explicitly rejects the "conventional claim that the expression of the emotions within the paintings should somehow be appropriate to the kind of subject to be depicted" (79) and instead insists that Poussin's "real project is much more radical." Poussin's forms, in and of themselves, "arouse the soul of the beholders to particular emotions" (80). Freedberg concludes his account with his most forceful claim: "Expression of emotion is not the real subject of Poussin's letter [on the Modes]"; rather, "the excitation of the emotions is" (79). To observe the difference between *expressing* and *exciting* emotions is to capture the force of the neuroarthistorical project, and it is this interest in establishing that difference that makes Freedberg's account indistinguishable from the commitments of Bois and Deleuze to separate representation from sensation and expression from affect.

What all of these neomodal accounts share—sub-Blancian formalism and neuroarthistory, Bois's semiotics and Deleuze's affect theory—is an attempt to solve the puzzle of representation by doing away with it. By turning artworks into affective machines stripped of knowledge and context, one dissolves the problem of interpretation into the problem of verifying the (hidden) sensory code embedded in the work. But on this account it is hard to see what the incentive is to discover the code, as it is always already exciting emotions in us whether we care to discover them or not. It is also hard to see what the special appeal of an artwork would be in this system, as affects are generated in us all the time and by everything.

Brain, Color, Line: Symbolism as Affect Theory

In a late collection of conversations titled simply *L'Art,* Auguste Rodin sought to clarify the crucial difference, as he saw it, between nature and art:

> A beautiful landscape affects us not only through the more or less agreeable sensations it induces, but through the ideas it awakens. The lines and the colors one observes in it move us, not by themselves, but through the profound meaning we attach to them. . . . Look at the masterpieces of art. All of their beauty comes from the thought, from the intention which their authors believed to divine in the universe.[74]

Rodin's effort to differentiate ideas and sensations, form and meaning, and to see both in terms of intention became an increasingly minority approach by the beginning of the twentieth century. Under the influence of psychovisual aesthetics, artists and theorists began to separate and reify form and meaning and shift their attention away from the artist's intent (much less a divinized universe) to the beholder's response. Rodin's (Kantian) dissatisfaction with a view of art reduced to "agreeable sensations"—although their agreeableness is not at issue—a view that functions at the expense of the artist's intentions, was wildly out of fashion by the time his conversations were published in 1911. How it was that sensations came to replace intentions as the site of artistic meaning is the history I aim to sketch here.

The remainder of this chapter will be taken up with a discursive history of the affective turn in France in the years prior to and following the major works of Matisse and Bergson, roughly between the years 1885 and 1930. Because what I offer is a limited discursive history, it requires vast supplementation by a set of analyses of the visual production of the artists I consider (this is part of the job of chapters 3 and 4, for instance). I would assume that this other history would look different from the one I present here. That is to say, a history of the visual production of the artists discussed here would likely conflict with the discursive history I present. Nonetheless, it is the case that the artists' writings I consider here were intended to be construed as part of their larger practice and were intended to support their visual productions, and for that reason they bear analysis.

My history is framed by two core figures in the modern theorization of affect: Paul Gauguin—beginning with a series of extraordinary letters to Émile Schuffenecker—and Antonin Artaud, whose theater of cruelty inspired a later generation of writers, artists, and theorists to imagine forms of art and experience free of representation. Unlike the authors of several recent accounts of this period, I will not privilege scientific writings over artist writings; rather, I see the scientific and artist writings in tandem and as coming to a similar set of conclusions about the relationship between form and experience and about the ambiguity of the artist's role in the viewer's increasingly independent encounter with painted surfaces.[75]

To capture some sense of the paradigm shift from artist to audience that occurred between Delacroix's generation and Blanc's, we can briefly consider the criticism of Charles Baudelaire (1821–67). While Baudelaire was one of the most consistently intentionalist writers of the mid-nineteenth century, for a later generation his writings laid the foundations for a theory of beholding that fundamentally undermined the artist's capacity to make forms meaningful.

In "The Salon of 1846" Baudelaire followed Delacroix's claim that a work of art should be judged not only according to its composition and subject matter but also according to its effect on the beholder.[76] Like Denis Diderot before him, Baudelaire compared the picture to a self-governing machine: "A picture is a machine all the systems of which are grasped by the expert eye."[77] Aesthetics was concerned with the proper functioning of the machine and with providing rules for its operator. Baudelaire provided a formula: "The impact produced on the soul of the viewer is in direct relation to the means the artist uses." Delacroix, by "ruthlessly sacrificing detail to whole," was able to "leave a deep impression [on the spectator], the intensity of which is increased by distance" (119/67). With sufficient distance from a painting—at the moment when line and color became pattern—the pictorial effects would take hold of the beholder, "leaving an unforgettable memory in the mind." (Note that it is "memory" that is a key value for Baudelaire here, not sensation.) It was at this proper viewing distance that the emotional capacities of color emerged from behind the veil of subject matter. "The power of line and color," he declared, are "absolutely independent of the subject of the picture." The artist's hold on the beholder was like a "whirlpool"; the beholder feels "as though he is in the grip of vertigo, constrained to follow the author in his entrancing deductions" (616/185). It is as though the artist's freedom were measured by the artist's constraint of the beholder.[78]

And yet the further Baudelaire pressed Delacroix's suggestions, the more the threat to artistic agency emerged into view. Writing about colors, for instance, he was tempted to grant *them* the kinds of agency he tended to give to the artist. "Colors in themselves may be gay and playful, or playful and sad, or rich and gay, or rich and sad, commonplace, melancholy or original," he wrote (108/57).[79] He went on to muse about a hypothetical "analogist who has drawn up a solidly established complete scale of colors and their associated feelings" (109/58). (Baudelaire could not have imagined how powerful such ideas would be for artists and aestheticians later in the century.) In his discussion of Delacroix in "The Universal Exhibition of 1855" the faint outline of an anti-intentionalist approach comes into view:

> First, it must be noticed, and this is most important, that, even seen from too far for the viewer to analyze or even understand the subject matter, a picture by Delacroix will already have produced on the soul an impression, either happy or melancholy. It is as though Delacroix's style of painting, like sorcerers and hypnotists, can project its thought at a distance. This strange phenomenon is accounted for by the power of the colorist, the perfect tone key and by the harmony (pre-established in the painter's brain) between color and subject. It seems that this color thinks by itself, independently of the objects it clothes. (237–38/136–37)

With each sentence Baudelaire introduces a slightly different thought. First is the (now familiar) idea that the work of art is said to make an impression on the beholder beyond the subject that is represented. Second, Baudelaire suggests that the painter's style, not the painter, is hypnotic in its capacity to grip the beholder at a distance. Third, he claims that artistic effects are the combined result of the artist's skill and the "pre-established harmony" between form and subject matter. Fourth is the idea that color is an "independent" force that acts on its own beyond any subject matter but also *beyond the artist's will.* All of these characteristics would recur either in whole or in part throughout the history of affective formalism, and as this history unfolded certain aspects would be privileged while others were left behind. As we saw in the writings of Blanc, the "independence" of color stands in *conflict* with the artist's independence. As I will show, with the Symbolist turn, colors came to *dominate* the artist's intentions and began to produce effects on their own.

Although they have never been considered in these terms, the art and writings of Gauguin (1848–1903) constitute one of the most forceful and influential expressions of affective theory and practice in the modernist period. Looking back to Delacroix's, Baudelaire's, and Blanc's writings, Gauguin found inspiration for his own theory of color but also found something lacking in the earlier accounts. Gauguin cited Delacroix throughout his journals, including the famous passage on the music of painting: "A given arrangement of colors, lights, shadows produces an impression. This is what we might call the music of the painting. Often you are seized by that magical harmony before you even know what the subject of the painting is, as when you enter a cathedral and are too far away from the painting to make it out clearly."[80] Whereas Delacroix hoped to fuse subject matter and form, playing one against the other, for Gauguin painting's music consisted fundamentally in its formal elements. Subject matter was a "pretext" for a more pressing concern, what he called the "direct and mysterious affinities" of line and color with the beholder's "brain."

The artist could exploit those affinities through the careful control of his medium. Gauguin explained:

> They are intended, absolutely! Everything in my work is calculated, meditated over at great length. It's music, if you like! I borrow some subject or other from life or from nature, and, using it as a pretext, I arrange lines and colors so as to obtain symphonies, harmonies that do not represent a thing that is real . . . and do not directly express any idea, but are supposed to make you think the way music is supposed to make you think . . . simply through the direct and mysterious affinities that exist between our brain and such arrangements of colors and lines. (109/138)

Gauguin's emphatic pursuit of intended effects—his stress on how every element was "calculated" to produce experiential results—was at odds with his emphasis on human biological wiring, on the "brain." Like Delacroix, Blanc, and Baudelaire before him, Gauguin suggested that his intended effects took special hold on the viewer only if the effects were free from any "direct idea" conveyed by the artist. Both reference and subject matter were unreliable in their dependence on memory and knowledge. It is as though his desire for expressive communication was so overriding that Gauguin was willing to risk the loss of his own agency in order to secure his effects. Why? Because Gauguin's interest in the "mysterious affinity" between the viewer's brain and form had no bearing on whether he intended that connection or not. The very intensity of Gauguin's intentionalist aims—to have the work be wholly expressive to a beholder, as though transparently so—led him to imagine a kind of effect that worked independent of his intentions.

Gauguin's ambiguous commitment to intentional effects emerged most clearly in an inner dialogue about the expressive effects of natural elements. "Why are willow trees with their hanging branches called weeping willows," Gauguin wondered. "Is the sycamore melancholy because it is planted in cemeteries?" His answer was decisive: "No, it is the color that is sad."[81] Sycamores found their way into cemeteries not because of any associations related to their forms, but because their color was sad. Following Gauguin's logic, feeling (melancholy) did not derive from a context or association (cemeteries), but rather inhered in form itself (color). Like later neuroaestheticians, he viewed context and associations, much less intentionality, as irrelevant factors in the affective transfer of sensation from artist to beholder. Associations, as Gauguin saw it, were suspect products of debased European socialization and had to be trained out of future artists if they were to experience and produce expressive effects properly.[82] Moreover, as I will show, Gauguin's analogizing of nature to art—his assertion that they are both expressive on a formal level—would have sweeping consequences for later Symbolist thought.

In an even more crucial turn of phrase, Gauguin declared that expressive effects were tied directly to the spectator's *nervous system,* bypassing the unreliable means of memory and knowledge as well as representation itself: "All of our five senses reach *the brain directly,* impressed by an infinity of things and no amount of education can suppress them," he wrote to Schuffenecker.[83] "I conclude from this that there are lines that are noble, deceitful, etc. . . . The straight line gives a notion of the infinite; the curve limits creation. . . . Colors are even more revealing . . . than lines, due to their power over the eye."[84]

And if lines and colors could be deceitful, could they also be jealous? If we take Gauguin's theory seriously, then a picture such as *Aha oe feii? (Are You Jealous?)* (1892) (Figure 1.6) has little to do with what we see and everything to do with what we feel before it. Gauguin fully endorsed a critic who suggested, "If this picture represents jealousy, it is with a fire of pinks and violets and not by virtue of its subject-matter."[85] On this account, whatever linguistic difficulties a European viewer encounters with Gauguin's titles are beside the point, as is the confusion most critics and viewers experience when they attempt to interpret the picture as a representation (an "idea") of the emotional state of jealousy. What, after all, suggests the emotion of jealousy here? Very little. That is because the interrogative of the title does not relate to what one sees, but rather to what one feels before it. So when Gauguin said he "put a little fear into the head" of Tehura, the nude in *Manao tupapau (The Spirit of the Dead Watching)* (1892) (Figure 1.7), he meant it quite literally, not as a matter of iconography. Once the sensation of fear was inscribed in the lines and colors of the picture, the viewer could not help but feel fearful standing before it, even if what initially drew the viewer to it was the suggestive subject. For an affective formalist it was not enough to be anti-iconographic, one also had to reject the idea that one could *express* oneself to another through line and color. Why? Because to express oneself was to leave oneself open to miscommunication. In order to circumvent the possibility of misinterpretation, of being misunderstood or even ignored, one had to go beyond iconography and expression to create forms that worked independent of the agent. So when Gauguin put fear into the head of Tehura he was not expressing his feelings about Tehura but applying the "laws" of form that functioned independent of his effort to mean something by them. If an expression could fail to come off—if it produced an emotional blank—then he could discover something more reliable in the action of colors and lines. When line or color interacted with a "brain," it could not help but produce an effect. Which is to say, form by itself did the job no human could do; it could mean (or rather stimulate) without stepping onto the risky terrain of representing one's feelings to another.

Gauguin's preferred term for this kind of reliable emotional transfer was *contagion.* "Contagion emanated from Tehura's terror," he wrote of *Manao tupapau* in *Noa Noa* (1901).[86] "Purple, dark blue, and orangey yellow," the picture "rings in the eye like a funeral bell," he reflected (64/89). While the viewer was

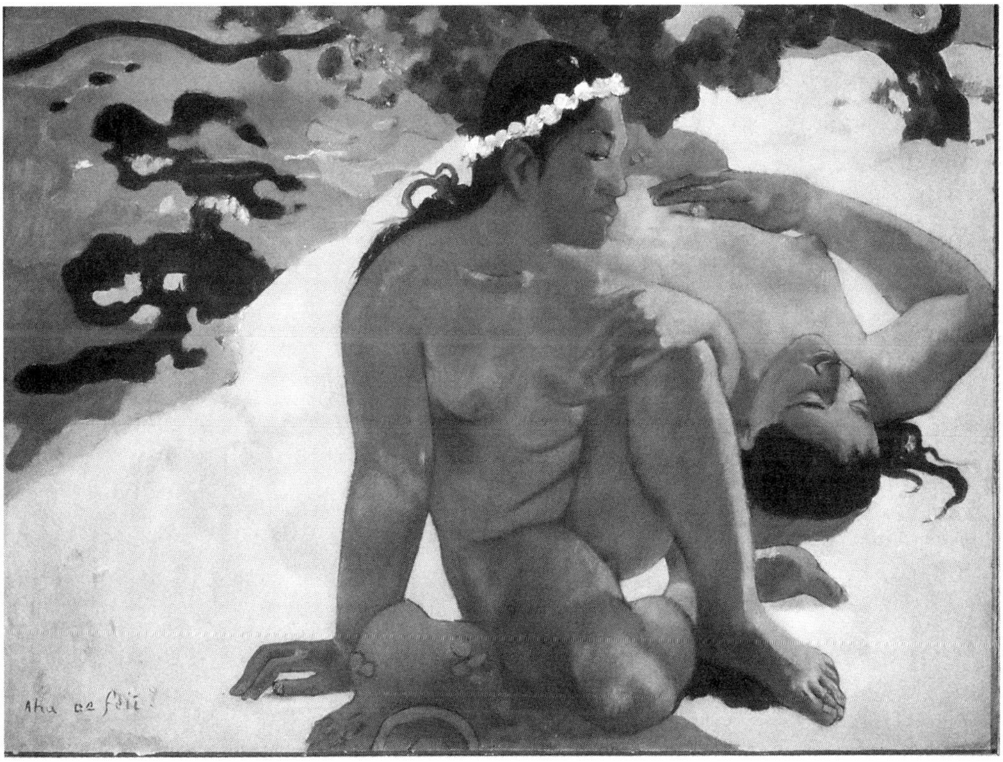

Figure 1.6. Paul Gauguin (1848–1903), *Aha oe feii? (Are You Jealous?)*, 1892. Oil on canvas, 66 × 89 cm. Pushkin Museum of Fine Arts, Moscow, Russia. Photograph courtesy of Scala / Art Resource, NY, ART15856.

inevitably drawn to Gauguin's works by virtue of their supercharged atmosphere, what the viewer received was something entirely different. Expressive content was a "pretext" for the generation of actual effects.[87]

Because subject matter appealed to the beholder's knowledge, it was necessarily limited to a small range of viewers who could decipher it or who would identify with the ideas depicted. Form, on the other hand, was a more universal and more secure mode of connecting with a beholder. "Most well-meaning souls today verbally acknowledge that beauty is very variable, relative, etc.," Gauguin wrote. "I am an artist who does not feel that way at all" (147/181). Instead of variability of reaction, Gauguin appealed to aesthetic laws both to create his work and to explain how they functioned. There are "laws making it possible to create by means of quite different aspects of matter . . . all human feelings," he explained. With a firm grasp of these laws, artists could create works that "no reasoning can withstand."[88] But by exchanging the unreliability of expression for the infallibility of form Gauguin also succeeded in

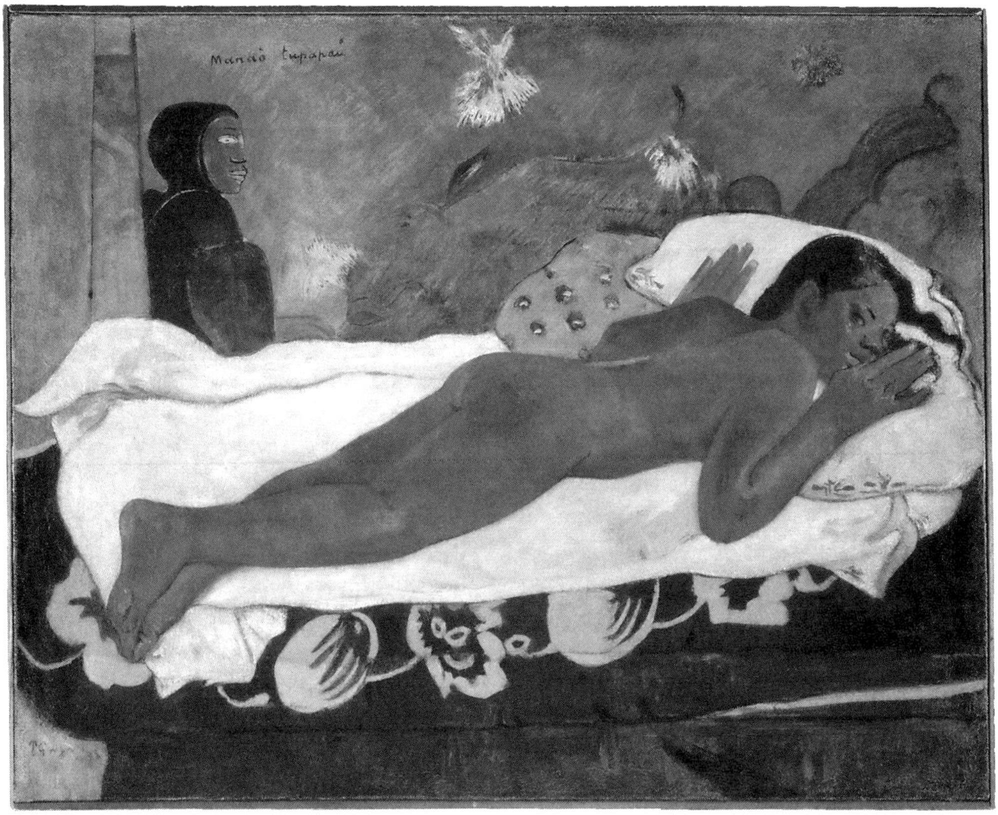

Figure 1.7. Paul Gauguin (1848–1903), *Manao tupapau (The Spirit of the Dead Watching)*, 1892. Oil on burlap mounted on canvas, 116.05 × 134.62 × 13.34 cm. Albright–Knox Art Gallery, Buffalo, New York. Photograph courtesy of Kharbine-Tapabor / The Art Archive at Art Resource, NY, ART392586.

undermining his own purposes. A form that resisted all reasoning was also a form that resisted meaning itself.

Gauguin's disciples, the Nabis, largely reproduced the ambivalent logics of their master. Maurice Denis (1870–1943) famously proposed a new doctrine based on Gauguin's work and words in his "Definition of Neo-Traditionism" of 1890: "It is through the canvas itself, a flat surface bathed in color, that our emotions whether bitter or soothing, are provoked."[89] Édouard Vuillard immediately caught the drift of Denis's aim: "Conceive of a picture really as a series of harmonies, moving away from the naturalistic idea." Vuillard then added a crucial proviso: "The word harmony means nothing but science, knowledge of relationships and colors."[90] A few years later, in his "Notes on Religious Painting" (1896), Denis attempted to unify the thoughts of leading avant-garde painters—including Gauguin, van Gogh, Cézanne, and Seurat—under the banner of Idealism. What all these artists shared was such an "intense passion for the truth" that they were forced to "deform" vision to conform to the laws of nature. According to Denis:

> These artists wanted to submit to the laws of harmony that govern the relations of colors, the agencies of lines (researches of Seurat, Bernard, C. Pissarro); but it is also to bring more sincerity in the rendering of their sensations. Given the structure of the eye and its physiology, the mechanism of associations and the laws of sensibility . . . they drew from it the laws of the work of art and by conforming to it, obtained straight away the most intense expressions. . . . There was, they discovered, close correspondence between forms and emotions![91]

It is a confusing and complicated set of claims. On one side, Denis observed the "laws," "agencies," "mechanism," the physiological "structure of the eye," and on the other, he affirmed the expressive rendering of the artist's sensations. Denis's loose usage of "agency" pointed both to the artist and to the "life" of the artist's lines and colors. It is as though Denis wanted both the scientific rigor of Neo-Impressionism and the individual expressiveness of the romantic symbol. It was the very imprecision of the formula that allowed him to identify artists who shared little ideological ground (Pissarro, for instance, loathed Bernard). Of course, one advantage of the appeal to laws was to make style and ideology irrelevant. But as I have also been showing, the appeal to laws threatened to make the artist irrelevant as well.

Denis's discovery of the "correspondence" of form and emotion came at the end of a line of thought that began with Baudelaire. Recall how Baudelaire described a "harmony (pre-established in the painter's brain) between color and subject," Blanc observed a "secret relationship" between line and sentiment, and Gauguin wrote of the "mysterious affinity" between form and the brain. All of these statements, by *naturalizing meaning,* render the painter's expressive purposes ambiguous. Only with Gauguin did this ambiguity become clarified. He was the first to shift meaning away from the conflicted terrain of interpretation and toward the interaction of form and the nervous system. And that interaction, I have argued, was not really *meaningful* at all; it was just a fact of the matter (scientists such as Charles Féré were trying to measure those reactions at the time, even if Gauguin avoided that route). Because it was the interaction of form and physiology that did the real work here, the artist became something like an arranger of independently expressive lines and colors. So what role do the artist's "feelings" play? Or rather, *how* do they matter? Summing up this moment we might say that Gauguin and the Nabis wanted it both ways: they wanted to preserve their intentionality but also make their intentions safe from the contingencies of interpretation.

It should be clear that the effort to neutralize artistic intentionality was not simply a matter of Symbolist depersonalization. Stéphane Mallarmé

(1842–98), for instance, when he affirmed his "elocutionary disappearance" into his words, never imagined that they thereby would not be expressive of his intent. As he described his "very new poetic" in 1864 (speaking of *Herodias*): "I'm inventing a language . . . which I could define in these few words: *paint, not the object, but the effect it produces.* Therefore the lines in such a poem mustn't be composed of words; but of intentions, and all the words must fade before the sensation."[92] Rather than appealing to any putative laws of expression, Mallarmé conceived of an intensified form of intentionality, as though his words could wholly dissolve into their significance once the artist's *self-conscious* manipulation of their meaning—"the old lyric breath, the enthusiastic personal direction"—was set aside.[93]

Despite some later disagreements, in his early writings Roger Fry (1866–1934) closely adhered to and largely replicated Denis's difficult example.[94] Writing of the *Avignon Pietà* (ca. 1455), Fry discerned the painting's emotional core in terms of the "orderly connection" of its forms: "It is the four parallel diagonal lines to the right cut at right angles by the willfully rigid line of the dead torso and balanced on the left by the prominent mass of the donor that convey to us, quite apart from their meaning as representation, so deep a sense of pity and awe."[95] In this early writing Fry still conceded there was meaning apart from form (a difference he would soon dispense with). By the time Fry wrote his influential "Essay in Aesthetics" of 1909, form and meaning had collapsed into one:

> When the artist passes from pure sensations to emotions aroused by means of sensations, he uses natural forms which, in themselves, are calculated to move our emotions, and he presents these in such a manner that the forms themselves generate in us emotional states, based upon the fundamental necessities of our physical and physiological nature. The artist's attitude to natural form is, therefore, infinitely various according to the emotions he wishes to arouse.[96]

Fry's phrasing is fraught with ambivalence. One can see him trying to sustain intentionality ("emotions he wishes to arouse") and deny it at the same time (natural forms "in themselves" "move our emotions," and the "forms themselves generate in us emotional states"). It is the artist's task to create forms so as to arouse emotional responses in the beholder, and yet those emotions appear to be the "physical and physiological" product of the "forms themselves," for which the artist can have only limited responsibility.[97] Clearly the problem of intentionality haunted the generation of artists and writers from Baudelaire and Blanc to Denis and Fry. While none of them could conceive of the work of art without the controlling mechanism of the artist's will, they also increasingly saw that agent as something more akin to an affective trigger than to an expressive subject.

The Expressive Language of Objects: Neo-Impressionism as Affect Theory

Given the heated debates between Symbolists and Neo-Impressionists, it is easy to lose sight of the concerns shared by the warring factions.[98] At the center of fin de siècle debates on the science of form were the contested aesthetics of Charles Henry (1859–1926). Henry, best known as director of the Laboratory for the Physiology of Sensations at the Sorbonne, presented his "Introduction to Scientific Aesthetics" in the August 1885 edition of *La Revue contemporaine.*[99] Henry began his study with a brief but commanding history of the science of aesthetics from Leonardo and Lomazzo in the Renaissance to Humbert de Superville, Blanc, and Edgar Allan Poe in the nineteenth century. Colors, he argued, following Blanc, "have precise expressive values . . . they have even been linked to the most complicated ideas: hope to green, faith to blue, and so forth." And lines, he asserted, depending on their orientation and location, were experienced as pleasurable or painful.[100] Henry further described how artists could produce a "directed stimulation of energy" through "the methodical excitation of nervous and psychic activity" in the beholder.[101] Artists took their lesson from Henry and came to see aesthetics as a tool that would allow them to control the beholder's "nervous and psychic activity."

Artists and writers with widely divergent approaches took their cues from Henry. Whether it was a "maximum of satisfaction" they sought ("hopeful" or "faithful" colors) or, as was the case with Henry's friend Paul Signac (1863–1935), the maximum *shock* to the senses ("painful" lines), Henry provided the formula.[102] One of Henry's most influential claims concerned the "forces" contained in pictures: "Variations in the release of available force in the picture are represented exactly by changes in the direction of this force." Gustave Kahn provided an important gloss on the idea: "Colors, like any form of stimulation, trigger a varying force of response in a subject."[103] It should be clear that for Henry (and Kahn) what was at stake was viewer response; the artist was responsible for "variations" of response or pulling the sensational trigger. Henry set a new task for painting: maximize sensory response.

It was this pursuit that prevailed over any disagreement between the Neo-Impressionists and Symbolists. Albert Aurier (1865–92), for instance, in a revealing statement in his posthumously published study of "Les Peintres symbolistes" (1892), observed the basic agreement between Henry's science and Symbolist modes of intuition:

> Objects, considered abstractly—the diverse combinations of lines, planes, shadows, colors—constitute the vocabulary of a mysterious but miraculously expressive language that one must know in order to be an artist. . . . There would, of course, be many things to write on the question of the abstract symbolic elements of drawing, on the possibility of their deformation in the expressive mode. The notes and sketches of Leonardo da

> Vinci are proof that he understood the capital importance of this science. Humbert de Superville seems to have suspected it when, in his *Essay on Unconditional Signs in Art,* he established his expressive schemas of the human face. In our time, Charles Henry, who would not be suspected of having Symbolist ties, preoccupies himself with this problem and has written several interesting notes, although too superficial, on the signification of linear directions and chromatic combinations.[104]

This was Aurier's special take on the Swedenborgian theory of "correspondences." What made it special was not only that Aurier imagined "objects" constituting an "expressive language" but also that he saw lines and colors themselves as "objects" abstracted from natural elements. Colors and lines like natural objects bear meaning in themselves. "Forms, lines, colors," Aurier wrote, are "directly signifying elements," they each contain a "magic irradiation."[105]

When Baudelaire (citing Delacroix) described "Nature" as a "dictionary," he immediately added that "no one ever considered the dictionary as a *composition.*"[106] For Baudelaire, the natural dictionary was anything but "miraculously expressive." It was the painter, and not the painter's means, that made color and line significant. Aurier dramatically altered the claim when he said that "the artist sees objects only as *signs,* letters of an immense alphabet that only the man of genius knows how to spell."[107] For Baudelaire it was less a matter of the artist's spelling out nature's meaning than of the artist's creative response to it. In his poem "Correspondences," Baudelaire described nature as "a temple . . . where often words emerge, confused and dim." When those "perfumes, sounds and colors" begin to "respond to one another" it is by virtue of the artist's willing them into a connection.[108] For Aurier, on the other hand, the artwork expressed nature's words through form. To "deform" the likeness of an object in a picture was to release the object's (and not the artist's) expressive magic.

Aurier was also among the first to cite the significance of Humbert de Superville's *Essay on Unconditional Signs* (1827–39), a book that loosely shaped the views of Blanc, Henry, and Seurat, while Superville's illustrations served as sources for several of Gauguin's works.[109] Christine Poggi usefully summarizes Superville's claims:

> According to Superville, the naturally expressive features of the human face pointed to the existence of three "unconditional signs" of human emotion: lines moving upward were generally agreeable and signified agitation, explosion, and joy; horizontal lines signified equilibrium, calm, and order; and lines moving downward, which were generally disagreeable, signified concentration, solemnity, depth, and sadness. Three colors could be associated with these affective qualities: red, white, and black, respectively.[110]

Poggi glosses her summary this way: "Thus for Superville and for Henry . . . both color and the directional movement of line expressed universal human emotions independently of their descriptive or anecdotal function."[111] I would submit that what Superville passed on to later generations was not centrally about how color and line functioned independent of their descriptive purpose (a point about the origins of abstraction), but how color and line were not "conditioned" by intentionality at all.[112] An "unconditional" sign was a sign that functioned outside of an intentional framework. Whether the artist wanted his signs to bear an affective quality was irrelevant to their actually having them. To displace the artist's intention in this way was alternately an attractive and a threatening prospect—it suggested that one could generate emotions without being (fully) responsible for them.

Among the artists most inspired by Superville's writings was Georges Seurat (1859–91). As Martha Ward has shown, after 1889 Seurat increasingly came to follow Superville's example by placing his focus on beholder response. Seurat spoke of making his work "efficacious" and of producing a "well-ordered synthesis" that could "impose itself [on the spectator] as the resultant."[113] In an 1890 letter to Félix Fénéon, Seurat described his effort to introduce "a formula for optical painting."[114] A few months before Seurat wrote to Fénéon, novelist Georges Lecomte publicly identified Seurat's *Chahut* (1889–90) with the work of Henry. "A cheerful sensation will not be expressed only by bright reds, oranges, greens, and so forth," Lecomte observed, "but by lines directed from low to high and by angles whose summits are turned towards the base. Everything will be calculated with this concern in mind."[115] Lecomte's terms express the tension between intended and actual effects that was basic to Seurat's procedures. Nonetheless, Seurat bristled at the affiliation to Fénéon: "Already M. Lecomte had sacrificed me to Charles Henry."[116] But it is hard to say exactly what irritated Seurat about the association with Henry. Whatever Seurat's aversion to fashionable Henryism, Lecomte's terms became the shared language of Neo-Impressionism for several years to come.[117]

Arsène Alexandre, for instance, in his 1891 review of the Salon des Indépendants, described the work of both Seurat and Signac in terms derived from Henry: "Any given scene is an ensemble of lines from which one tries to find a result with a view to producing a determined effect [un effet déterminé]."[118] Similarly, Signac observed how it was "by the harmony of lines and colors which he manipulates in accordance with his needs and will, and not by his subject that the painter should move the spectator."[119] If Impressionism was an effort to record, and to represent, the artist's sensations before nature, then Signac's Neo-Impressionism turned its energies in the direction of the viewer. Signac attempted to strip his work of everything that would detract from the immediacy of emotional response. According to Signac, "Anecdotes, evocations that suggest subjects and titles, stifle the sensation."[120] Signac determined that the best forms were the ones that required the least amount of translation from mind to body. "Rarely a drawing, a statue, excites the anger of an uncomprehending public—an audacity of color, always. Any pure and frank color shocks," he declared in the aptly titled "The Disgrace of Color."[121] Drawings and statues failed to move their viewers not only because of their lack of color, but also because of their subject matter. It was a capital error "into which the best informed revolutionaries . . . have too often fallen to require a precise socialist tendency in works of art," he explained. By "socialist tendency," Signac meant the depiction of workers, class strife, or the sentimental lives of the downtrodden. Rather than revolutionary subject matter, the real revolution "will be found much stronger and more eloquent in pure aesthetes—revolutionaries by temperament." Only "artists haunted by pure art" had the "power to move" their audiences. These aesthetes unconsciously "give a solid pick blow to the old social edifice."[122] Signac's sense of the fallibility of depicted forms—that the representation of workers fighting capitalists did not produce, at least not securely, the kind of political result he desired—led him to reject the possibility of intending to produce an effect at all. His appeal to Henry's science of color was ultimately an effort to avoid the problem of representation and substitute for it a belief in the capacity of works to produce political effects regardless of the artist's political aims. Surefire politics: pull the (color) switch, generate the belief.

The Life of Stones: The Ambiguity of Affect in Fauvism

Emerging out of the Symbolist and Neo-Impressionist debates on color, Matisse and the fauves viewed the violent shock of color as a primary weapon in their artistic arsenal. Although it has not been properly construed, a wide-ranging debate within fauvism concerned the role of color in composition. The debate centered on whether color was an independent "force" (a term in wide circulation at the time) or an instrument of the artist's expressive will.

André Derain (1880–1954) offered the most decisive formulation of a new materialism of color. Combining the political commitments of Signac with the formal principles of Gauguin, Derain conceived of colors as agents with their own will and desires. In a series of fascinating letters from London to Matisse, Derain formulated the principles of his materialism. "I think what we're missing is an idea, an idea to express outside painting," he told Matisse in March 1906. By "idea" he did not mean a literary or conceptual content. As he emphatically explained, what he sought was something "outside" art altogether. We should "push to its conclusion what we were discussing, that is to say no longer to do anything that represents anything." By making a work that did not "represent anything" he meant something more than a kind of visual abstraction. A work that did not "represent anything" was itself a work that functioned "outside painting" altogether.

Derain pursued the idea in his next letter to Matisse. He began with a traditional lament over conventional modes of representation—his "emotions are too general in their nature to convey with a sentence, a word, by language, which binds and traps them in far too tight a circle. They are not part of the usual conventions of practical civilization"—and concluded with a rejection of representation itself. That representation was something unsatisfying because too open to misunderstanding was a view driven by Derain's deeper skeptical commitments. His skepticism emerged clearly in a 1902 letter: "Doubt is everywhere and in everything. Some people . . . declare themselves openly for form. But behind it all, doubt subsists."[123] To overcome this primary doubt about communication Derain sought a mode of absolute reliability. Expressive emotions, in his view, resided *in* things. Derain explained to Matisse: "We might be the only generation to have realized that stone, color, etc., no matter the material in which the human spirit finds pleasure, has its own life, independent of what we make it represent."[124] Like Gauguin, who asserted that trees and colors contained their own expressive energies, or Aurier, who wrote of the expressive qualities of objects, Derain believed that stones and colors signified independent of any representational framework and, more important, independent of any human will (rocks, like colors, contained their "own life"). So while it was obvious to say that stones did not "represent anything" and that they existed "outside painting," Derain's revolutionary gesture was to say that the painter's colors were more like things and less like means to depict or express things.

Like Signac, Derain inserted his materialism into a broadly political context. Colors were a special kind of thing: they were weapons. "No matter how far we moved away from things . . . it was never far enough," he said, looking back on fauvism. "Colors became charges of dynamite. . . . They were to blow out the lights. Everything would be raised above reality."[125] Colors, when held within frames, acted less like stones and more like representations. The solution was to make colors like bombs; he would set the charge and blow up the representational setting. Doing damage to representation was doing damage to the social conventions that authorized it.

While Derain's "political" attitude was largely shared by the fauves, his metaphysical materialism was not. Maurice de Vlaminck (1876–1958), for instance, expressed what seemed like a similar set of concerns in a statement published in an anarchist journal: "I want to burn down the École des Beaux-Arts with my cobalts and vermilions and translate what I feel without troubling about what painting was like before me."[126] Derain rejected "translation" as a mode of expressive communication because it was openly prey to mistranslation by the viewer. Moreover, Vlaminck does not make any appeal to the independent "life" of his colors here. His colors were intended to express his (violent) feelings about the world. Whatever view he might have held about the agency of his colors was overridden by his more basic commitment to self-expression.

While Matisse shared the politicized language of color as shock, his theory of color was more complex than that of the other fauves. Everything, he said, was directed toward "one goal," to "exteriorize [extérioriser] the shock produced by external events and things outside me [l'exéterieur]."[127] Matisse was explicit about the violence suggested by his theory of shock. "I have the need to kill someone before I begin to paint," he told Pierre Courthion in a 1941 interview; "I have energy to use up." The "energy" that was pent up in the artist would be "discharged" in the process of making the work. "When you are [ready to kill]," he said, "you will arrive all at once before the object that provokes the discharge: it is necessary to render the shock."[128] Matisse's phrasing is ambiguous. It is unclear for whom he intends the shock: himself or the viewer. At other times, Matisse was more explicit about the violence directed at the beholder. He spoke of his works as machines to re-create the shock of sensation: "For me, a color is a force. My pictures, made up of four or five colors that have clashes between them, produce the sensation of energy. . . . It is color that generates a certain expression in the mind of the spectator, expression planned by the combination."[129] The phrasing ambiguously shifts between artistic control ("planning") and the independent action of the colors (how they "generate" effects).

Looking back, Matisse came to reject the much-lauded immediacy of fauve color. Fauvism could no longer "command any power over the mind,"[130] because "an avalanche of color has no force." "Color attains its full expression only when it is organized."[131] The wording is again complicated. While color attains to "its" expression, it is the artist who is responsible for the expressive impact. The duality is replayed over and over again: "Painting requires organization by very conscious, very concerted means, as in the other arts. Organization of forces—colors are forces."[132] The stress falls in equal parts on the artist's intentionality and on the colors as independent "forces."

But perhaps Matisse's clearest statement on color comes from his "Notes of a Painter." There he rejected what he called "theoretical knowledge" of color and stressed instead color's expressive purpose. "The chief function of color should be to serve expression as well as possible," he wrote. "My choice of colors does not rest on any scientific theory; it is based on observation, on feeling, on the experience of my sensibility. . . . I simply try to put down colors which render my sensation."[133] There is no suggestion here of forces or the independence of his means, only the centrality of the artist's sensibility. In chapters 3 and 4 I will show that it is this intentional account of color—one that grants little credence to the "agency" of color and line, but a great deal to the artist's sensibility—that best captures the attitude of Matisse's broader artistic aims.

Robert Delaunay (1885–1941) was the first great interpreter of fauve color, and he wrote at length about color theory in the wake of fauvism. Above all, Delaunay admired the "truculence and brutality" of Matisse's *Woman with a Hat* (1905) but ultimately found that the "violent colorings" of fauvism did not amount to anything more than an "*irritating* impressionism."[134] And while Delaunay shared the fauve fascination with color's capacity to "act directly on the viewer," he attempted to activate his pictures in a less aggressive manner.[135] Through a precise manipulation of colored surfaces based on an understanding of a range of color theories, including those of Blanc, Féré, Henry, and scientist Michel Chevreul, Delaunay described how he could stimulate "extra-rapid vibrations" that would be "physically perceptible by the naked eye." Working through color theory, Delaunay came to believe in the production of "undeniable" effects that would strike the viewer like a "punch" (coup de poing), a notion that became one of the more influential formulations of affective formalist discourse.[136]

As Pascal Rousseau has observed, Delaunay's image of the punch was given explicit theorization in Gabriel Mourney's 1913 *Gil Blas* article on "Art and Muscle." Mourney analogized the experience of a boxer who had been punched in the eye (probably Arthur Craven) with the experience of a painter with his colors. The punch planted on the boxer's retina revealed something deep and absolute about the nature of human vision (thus the difference between the boxer's vision and everyone else's). And it was this difference that revealed something crucial about how colors functioned in a picture and how colors functioned "in themselves." Mourney, like Bergson, believed that form distorted reality, forcing it into a straitjacket of instrumental reason. Being punched in the eye nakedly exposed what had been distorted by form: "sonorous reds . . . acid greens . . . pure oranges . . . vigorous and bold blues . . . intense blacks and immaculate whites" emerge as unadulterated realities. Beyond form, beyond any representational setting, colors were free to be themselves. Mourney summed up the results of the boxer's revelation: "Because form doesn't exist, form is nothing. There is only the *tache*. . . . We are therefore resolutely for the *tache*, and against form."[137] To be for the *tache* and against *form* is to turn a representational signifier into a material mark. It is not as if the colors that appeared to the boxer's blasted eye were *representations* of the world; the example was meant to register the opposite: they were the biological manifestation of color *without representation*. If we follow Mourney's (and Delaunay's) example we can imagine a life for colors in the same way that Derain imagined a life for colors and stones beyond "what we make them represent" and that Kandinsky imagined color and everything else as a "being with its own life."

The Theater of Affect

Antonin Artaud's "Van Gogh, the Man Suicided by Society" (1947) is a study of artistic genius. The genius was misunderstood because there was nothing to understand. Encountering a work by van Gogh was encountering a frozen flow of sensations. Artaud's nemesis, his stand-in for the failed effort at understanding genius, is Gauguin. "A candlestick on a chair, on a green straw-bottomed armchair, a book on the armchair, and there the drama is revealed. Who will enter? Will it be Gauguin or some other ghost?" That it was Gauguin who entered the scene and acted out the role of van Gogh—who played his interpreter—was for Artaud a catastrophe. "There was a basic human schism between the personalities of van Gogh and Gauguin," he explained. While Gauguin "thought that an artist should seek the symbol, the myth, enlarge the things of life," van Gogh believed myth should be drawn directly from the "most earthy things in life."[138] This is the difference, as Artaud saw it, between conscious and unconscious mythmaking. Then again, whether the myths were conscious or unconscious was largely irrelevant to Artaud's more basic concerns. While Gauguin's myths emerged from tradition (or from his head), van Gogh's were not really myths at all but more like *events*: they "restored directly to sight, hearing, touch, smell . . . launched afresh into current reality, reintroduced into circulation."[139] The difference between Gauguin and van Gogh was a version of the difference between intentionality and nonintentionality. Van Gogh's works, as objects that emerged from the earth, automatically stimulated affective response (as would any object), while Gauguin's works, as representations of emotional states, were expressively dependent on the unreliable transfer of memory, knowledge, and feeling between artist and beholder.

Artaud's dream of a "theater of cruelty"—perhaps the most influential vision of affective formalism for the second half of the twentieth century—was continuous with the nineteenth-century formalist tradition and at the same time unflinchingly fulfilled the logic of its claims.[140] Artaud, that is, overcame the basic ambiguity of Symbolist discourse as I have considered it so far. Although theater was Artaud's subject, painting was his model for the kinds of effects he sought. His book *The Theater and Its Double* opened with a long ekphrasis on an anonymous Renaissance painting in the Louvre, *Lot and His Daughters* (ca. 1500) (Figure 1.8). Artaud's description offered a hint of what the new theater might look like or, rather, feel like:

> Its emotion is visible even from a distance; it affects the mind with an almost thunderous visual harmony, intensely active throughout the painting, yet to be gathered from a single glance. Even before you can discern what is going on, you sense something tremendous happening in the painting, and the ear, one would say, is as moved by it as the eye. . . .
>
> It seems as if the painter possessed certain secrets of linear harmony,

> certain means of making that harmony affect the brain directly, like a physical agent. (33–35/49–52)

While Gauguin and Kandinsky imagined the affective transfer of complex ideas and emotions to the beholder, Artaud's painter induced something entirely different: trauma. Once the pictorial "agent" (réactif) took hold, the effects were "immediate and painful" (42/63); they produced a "violent action" upon the viewer's nervous system. The sounds and scenes of the new theater would "shake the organism to its foundations and leave an ineffaceable scar" (77/119). According to Artaud, this violent action would resuscitate a dying viewer, reviving the blasé audience's blunted "nerves and heart" (84/131). It was the aim of the new theater to work on the viewer "like the plague," to "drain abscesses collectively" through piercing spatial, aural, and visual effects. The administration of intense and sudden shocks would ultimately revive understanding and relieve humankind of its "endlessly renewed fatigue" (86/135).

Of course Artaud dreamed of going beyond painting to produce an environment that would thrust the viewer into van Gogh's universe of sense. Artaud's theater would leave behind the limited effects of the painted canvas for a "total spectacle addressed to the spectator's entire organism." Through the intensive mobilization of objects, gestures, and signs, forms can "break through language in order to touch life" (13/19). Artaud offered a stark dualism of life and representation. Only an all-encompassing spectacle—a world composed entirely of shapes, sounds, images devoid of meaning—could penetrate the blunted sensibilities of the modern subject:

> The theater is the only place in the world, the last general means we still possess of directly affecting the organism and in periods of neurosis and petty sensuality like the one in which we are immersed, of attacking this sensuality by physical means it cannot withstand. . . .
>
> It is in order to attack the spectator's sensibility on all sides that we advocate a revolving spectacle. . . .
>
> . . . Words say little to the mind; extent and objects speak; new images speak. . . . But space thundering with images and crammed with sounds speaks too. . . .
>
> On this principle we envisage producing a spectacle where these means of direct action are used in their totality; a spectacle unafraid of going as far as necessary in the exploration of our nervous sensibility, of which the rhythms, sounds, words, resonances, and twitterings, and their united quality and surprising mixtures belong to a technique which must not be divulged. (81–87/125–35)

There was a "difference in kind" between understanding and emotion, language and life, representation and reality (13/19). Immersed in the thundering

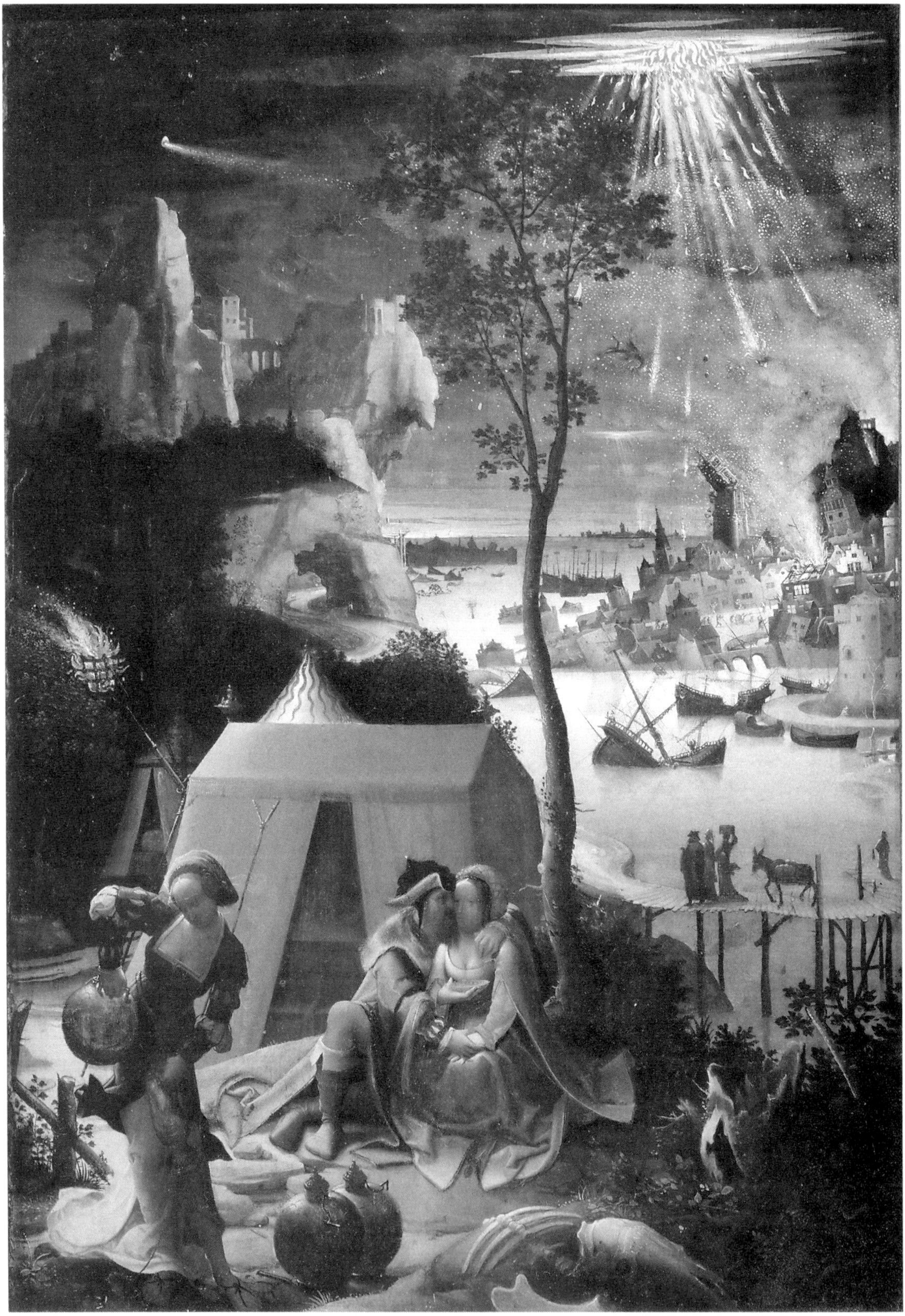

Figure 1.8. Anonymous Flemish painter, *Lot and His Daughters*, ca. 1500. Wood, 48 × 34 cm. RF 1185. Louvre, Paris, France. Photograph by Erich Lessing / Art Resource, NY, ART212964.

images and sounds of the new theater, the mind was physically unable to process them in terms of meaning. Understanding paled before the "violent physical images [that] crush and hypnotize the sensibility of the spectator seized by the theater as by a whirlwind of higher forces" (83/128).

Artaud's theater was clearly inspired by Futurist models. Filippo Marinetti, Emilio Settimelli, and Bruno Corra earlier spoke of "sweeping the audience through *a labyrinth of sensations*" and of *"symphonizing the audience's sensibility by exploring it, stirring up its laziest layers by every means possible . . . [and] throwing nets of sensation between stage and audience; the stage action will invade the orchestra seats, the audience."*[141] Far outstripping Futurist explorations of onomatopoesis, gesture, and noise, Artaud invented wholly new modes of affective artillery.

At the center of Artaud's arsenal was the actor. Artaud introduced a new figure, the "affective athlete." The actor-athlete was especially skilled in the manipulation of forms to create precise nervous response. The artist became an athlete the moment his words lost their meaning and became sensations. "Words will be construed in an incantational, truly magical sense—for their shape and their sensual emanations, not only for their meaning," he insisted in *The Theater and Its Double* (86/125). The halfhearted suggestion that words will be valued not only for their meaning but also for their sensational qualities was soon eclipsed by the view that meaning prohibited words from becoming shapes.

Turning words into sounds, and shapes into sensations, was also to turn language out from meaning. Deleuze follows Artaud's "schizophrenic thought as it plunges into universal depths where the word loses its meaning but not its affect." It was Deleuze's aim to theorize the moment when language turned into an "unlanguage of howls and syncopated rhythms."[142] Deleuze notoriously took Artaud's image of the body without organs, composed only of sensate flesh and nerves, as his aesthetic and political ideal.[143] To become all flesh and nerve was to become a purely affective being, and to become an affective being was to no longer conceive of communication as a matter of representation and interpretation, but as the transmission of sensation from body to body.[144]

Viewers are affected by art not because they understand what they feel but because, as Artaud argued, works of art function like "a blood transfusion"—"a bloodstream of images, a bleeding spurt of images in the poet's head and in the spectator's as well" (82/127). Artaud's brief and enigmatic play "The Jet of Blood" (1925) offers a powerful vision of aesthetico-biological transmission.[145] Although even the barest summary of the action is difficult to manage, the play begins with a scene of romantic love. The scene quickly dissolves into mayhem as a nurse rushes onto the stage to denounce the encounter as incestuous. The nurse's fear of incest between the two lovers is also an image of a bind that runs deeper than language.[146] Incest raises the theoretical possibility of a transfer of sense beyond the logic of representation. Ultimately, for Artaud, the viewer was physically touched by the image, and image comprehension became a matter of biological contagion. And because affect was not interpretation, the viewer did not need to understand the work in order to be altered by it. It was far better if the viewer did *not* understand the work so that its affects would become its meaning. But then again, the question about what an image meant was replaced by the sensation the image produced. As I have been arguing, when a work's meaning becomes a matter of what the work does, then the question of disagreement becomes impossible, for no experience, no affect, can ever be right or wrong. To imagine a world where what matters is "what happens" to us is also to imagine a world where bodies differ but never disagree, because there is nothing to disagree about.

TWO

Freedom and Memory

Bergson's Theory of Hypnotic Agency

> There have been men . . . whose function has been to see and to make us see what we do not naturally perceive. They are the artists. . . . As these artists speak, shades of emotion and thought appear to us which might long since have been brought out in us but which remained invisible; just like the photographic image which has not yet been plunged into the bath where it will be revealed. The poet is this revealing agent. But nowhere is the function of the artist shown as clearly as in that art which gives the most important place to imitation, I mean painting.
>
> —Henri Bergson, "The Perception of Change"

Bergson Today

In his survey of modern art in France, Christopher Green offhandedly remarks that Bergson was "the most influential philosopher in France between the 1890s and the 1920s."[1] Indeed, Bergson's philosophy, unlike any other at the time, swept through Europe and the United States in the opening years of the twentieth century. His work appealed not only to university students and professors but to popular audiences as well.[2] Bergson's precipitous climb to the heights of the intellectual world in the early decades of the twentieth century was followed by an equally precipitous decline. According to Zeev Sternhell, "Though Bergson had undoubtedly been the main figure in philosophy in the 1920s, [by that same time] there were practically no more Bergsonians left in France."[3] And by the 1950s H. Stuart Hughes could glibly note that "although Bergson's present-day influence is almost nil," he nonetheless felt "obliged . . . to try to explain why it was that he was so highly regarded in his own time."[4] Bergson's fortunes have turned once again. One is now obliged to confront Bergson's preeminence both within and beyond the humanities.

Bergson has received massive approbation not only from humanists and social scientists but also from scholars in fields as diverse as physics, law, psychiatry, environmental ethics, and business management. Without a doubt, this broad revival of interest is due to the writings of French philosopher Gilles Deleuze (1925–95). One can almost pinpoint the date of Bergson's resurgence: 1988 saw the simultaneous publication of the English translation of Deleuze's *Bergsonism* and a reprinting of the English translation of Bergson's most important volume, *Matter and Memory* (1896), both by Zone Books.[5] Since that time, a wide range of books, essays, conferences, symposia, special journal issues, and courses on Bergson have appeared, and his presence can be felt throughout intellectual life today.[6]

A brief sampling of the range and depth of the New Bergsonism may clarify his present hold on the humanities and beyond. Bergsonism has emerged as a force in new media studies;[7] photography;[8] architectural theory;[9] electronic music;[10] the history of Russian, French, British, and American avant-garde poetry and literature;[11] the history of art from Leonardo da Vinci to Robert Rauschenberg;[12] Native American and African aesthetics;[13] Hollywood and avant-garde film;[14] feminist theory;[15] trauma theory;[16] political and legal theory;[17] environmental and ecological politics;[18] cancer and autism therapy;[19] educational theory and reform;[20] and business management strategy.[21] While all of these studies pay homage to Bergson, their understanding of his philosophical enterprise tends to be highly selective. Certain keywords are in high circulation in these texts—*difference, multiplicity, memory, duration, expression, delay, attention, distraction, affect,* and *virtuality,* to name the most significant—while others, including *becoming, change, élan, intuition,* and *spirit,* have fallen into relative disuse. The new emphasis in Bergson studies has largely fallen on his perceptual psychology and ontology of memory at the expense of his pragmatism and theory of freedom; and as I will also show, Bergson's commitment to intentionality has been all but erased from the record.

"Appropriating Freedom": Bergson's Allegory of Anti-Intentionality

In the December 1908 issue of the *Revue Philosophique* Bergson published a study of the phenomenon of déjà vu. The essay, "Memory of the Present and False Recognition," reviews the clinical literature on déjà vu, or "false recognition," and shows how a certain phrase, "I was a spectator of my own actions; they were inevitable," appears over and over again.[22] Déjà vu describes an uncanny sensation where the subject feels "a stranger to himself," a "simple spectator at what he is saying and doing."[23] Reports on déjà vu are marked by this double sensation: at once detached observation and intense, but somnambular, action.

Metaphors of acting, theater, staging, and spectatorship saturate the clinical record. The split subject "compares himself to an actor playing his part automatically, listening to himself and beholding himself play."[24] Inside the patient live two personalities, "one of which moves about the stage while the other sits and looks." These "two different selves" constitute "an independent spectator of a scene" and another who "seems to be playing in a mechanical way" as though he were moving about a "stage-world."[25]

Bergson leaves the reader in suspense as to the broader import of the phenomenon. That something crucial is at stake emerges only slowly as he glosses the clinical record. The split subject is at once free and bound. One of these personalities "appropriates freedom," the other acts out of "necessity." The "free spectator" in his seat watches the actor "automatically playing his part."[26] (The actor, in Bergson's philosophy, is never in full possession of his freedom while reciting his lines.) The momentary split induced by déjà vu between free and automatic action, intended and nonintended behavior, offers a glimpse of the *difference* between "appropriated" action and "habitual" action.

Several years before, in *Matter and Memory,* Bergson reflected on the distinction between free and automatic behavior. He described the act of appropriation as one of *self-representation.* The "conscious automaton" is someone who "continually acts his life" and who is unable to "truly represent it to himself."[27] Memories that are not given subjective validity "no longer *represent* our past to us, they *act* it."[28] The special nature of déjà vu is that it *experientially captures the difference* between representation and action, intended behavior and mindless doing. In the trancelike moment of déjà vu there is a "*feeling* of automatism, and of a state comparable to that of an actor playing a part. What is said and what is done, what the person himself says and does, appear 'inevitable.'"[29] That they are not in fact inevitable, or not wholly so, is at the root of Bergson's philosophical claims about agency.

Bergson hoped that this minimal difference or delay within the present moment would serve as instruction for his readers. As Bergson saw it, automatic behavior so fully pervaded normal human conduct that it threatened to erase from awareness any alternative. In our "normal condition," he explained, "there is no consciousness of it [memory]," just as we would be "unconscious of our shadow were our eyes to throw light on it each time they turn in that direction."[30] Déjà vu momentarily interrupts the light projected on the world, paradoxically allowing us to see what is in front us. The minor break in the stream of life is enough for representation to wedge itself into the breach. The delay or replay of a recent action grants the subject a passing glimpse into what it was he or she was doing and at least suggests what it would have been like to do it *differently.* As a philosophical idea, then, déjà vu concretizes or allegorizes the difference between actions that are appropriated by us, taken as being ours, and those that are left unattended, as though they are owned by someone else (as I will show, Bergson used metaphors of paternity as well as ownership to describe the difference).

Bergson's philosophy is oriented around these remarkable missed encounters between automatic and intentional behaviors. Déjà vu is a minor episode, one of those "rare" moments when there is a "temporary enfeebling of general attention to life," but one that bears philosophical weight for Bergson. To be *in*attentive to life is to be momentarily free from life's grip. It is in those half-reflective, half-immersive moments that the eye and mind can allow "itself to look at what it has no interest in perceiving."[31] It is the act of looking without perceiving that defines the intuitive agency of the artist. Most forms of *conscious* intention, on the other hand, are nothing but rule-based behaviors drained of subjective authority.

Bergson's most extensive treatment of intentionality appears in *Creative Evolution* (1907). Here Bergson considers the way philosophers and psychologists typically picture the workings of inner life, and he shows how limited the available accounts of intentionality really are. When philosophers and psychologists train their perceptual eye on man's fluctuating inner life they are able to discover only what is already known. For every act "we shall easily find antecedents of which it may in some sort be said to be the mechanical resultant." Bergson calls this mechanical diagnosis of action "the realization of an intention," but it provides a false picture of reality. Only an act that "involves the whole of our person and is truly ours" is free; a free act must include something that "could not have been foreseen." For an act to be truly ours, the realized intention must also introduce a "*new* reality" into its fold.[32]

Bergson's model for this fuller mode of intentionality is the artist. He describes two types of intention: conscious or "realized intention" and unconscious intention or the "intention of life." An intention that is realized is one that is automatic, driven by habit or routine. The intention of life, on the other hand, is a mode of action that involves the subject's whole being, one that is saturated with the subject's expressive need to make him- or herself known. That this expressive need will never find an adequate form is the source of the artist's continuing and evolving efforts. Traditional modes of intentional analysis picture the mind "merely as assembled," as a sequence of associated ideas, but "not as mutually organized." "The intention of life," Bergson says, "escapes" the grasp of the perceiving eye. It is "just this intention of life" that the "artist tries to regain" by an act of sympathetic intuition.[33]

A few years earlier, in his study "The Life and Work of Ravaisson" (1904), Bergson provided his fullest description of artistic agency. In a discussion of the portraiture of Leonardo da Vinci, Bergson distinguished between the outward character of the portrait and the sitter's inner life, which was the artist's true object:

> Let us look for a moment at the portrait of *Mona Lisa* or even at the picture of *Lucrezia Crivelli*: does it not seem to us that the visible lines of the figure rise

> toward a virtual center, located behind the canvas, where would be revealed at once, gathered into a single word, the secret we shall never have finished reading, phrase by phrase, in the enigmatic physiognomy? That is where the painter has placed himself. . . . True art aims at portraying the individuality of the model and to that end it will seek behind the lines one sees the movement the eye does not see, behind the movement itself something even more secret, the original intention, the fundamental aspiration of the person: a simple thought equivalent to all the indefinite richness of form and color.[34]

Although the perceiving eye cannot see it, the "original intention" of the sitter stirs deep beneath the representational facade. It was the artist's task to grasp the sitter's intention and convey it to the beholder through form and color. That this "single word" of the sitter's personality could not be fully uttered—that it was both revealed and concealed by the artist, requiring close and repeated attention by the beholder—helped explain the continuing hold of Leonardo's achievement. Leonardo, on Bergson's account, was like a depth psychologist. He sought to picture his sitter's deepest thoughts, beliefs, and desires. Situated at the virtual center of his subject, the painter marks his surface "phrase by phrase," seeking the elusive goal of expressing himself and the other through his medium.

As I will now argue, there are two major limitations to Bergson's theory of intentionality. First, Bergson was unable or unwilling to describe freedom outside the framework of *vision.* His philosophy is chiefly ocular in orientation. Freedom is to see unhindered, to observe from a distance; body is blind mechanism, literally a creature of habit. Second, and far more damaging, was Bergson's dissatisfaction with what typically goes by the name of freedom. Bergson was rightly skeptical of theories of "*absolute* [freedom], as a radically libertarian philosophy would have it; it admits of degrees."[35] But Bergson's denial of abstract freedom resulted in an even more unremitting skepticism of other minds. In the effort to limit absolute freedom he steered close to a disabling epistemological skepticism. "Our souls are impenetrable to one another," he reflected in *Laughter* (1900). Unlike the artist seeking behind the lines to the sitter's "original intention," normal social interaction is unfathomably mediated by signs. "Certain signs of passion are all that we ever apperceive externally," he reflected. "These we interpret—though always, defectively—only by analogy with what we ourselves experienced. So what we experience is the main point, and we cannot become thoroughly acquainted with anything but our own heart—supposing we ever get so far."[36] Bergson did not linger long on the permanent defect of expressive interpretation, but it nonetheless authorized his skeptical account of social communication. It justified a dualistic picture of intuition and intellect, memory and matter, and made bridging the gap between the two more like a leap over an abyss.

In other words, Bergson, along with Marx, Nietzsche, and Freud, was one of those "Masters of Suspicion" (as Ricoeur put it) who conceived the whole realm of conscious intention, decision, and judgment as a malign illusion, one that hid from view the true causes of agency.[37] Intentionality was a kind of pretension to run the show of our own lives, one that risked suppressing the truly determining role that forces outside the self were playing in our most intimate decisions. The figure for this extrahuman agency, at least after 1896, was *memory.* On this account, the subject did not in fact *appropriate him- or herself* but rather appealed to something *outside the self, outside the social* altogether, for the source of freedom. The "true self" in Bergson stands in absolute tension with another form of agency: "true memory."[38]

In one of his more vivid images, Bergson granted memory a charged form of animation otherwise lacking in humans: "Memories rise and spread abroad and perform in the night of the unconscious a wild phantasmagoric dance."[39] Memory's "wild dance" makes human action seem rather pale in comparison. Bergson, like so many others of his generation and after, could not see how one could be both determined by and dependent on impersonal forces and also be a freely acting subject. And yet, against the grain of his philosophical commitment to memory Bergson sketched a picture of human intentionality that was more than merely a shadow of spiritual forces running the show.

The discussion in the remainder of this chapter will proceed as follows. I will begin with a consideration of Bergson's master concept, memory, and with the problem it raises for his account of freedom. The issue at stake here concerns the traditional philosophical appeal to nonhistorical, nonhuman, nonsocial modes of "agency" to *ground* and *limit* the concept of human agency. As I have suggested up to this point, Bergson did offer a way to describe agency as *self-grounded,* as appropriating an act for oneself. But as I will now show, this self-grounding is undermined by Bergson's ontological theory of memory, which granted it priority over, and was said to be the source of, agency and action. I will go on to explore Bergson's long-standing commitment to hypnosis and "psychical research," both of which are intimately related to but crucially distinct from his account of memory. At first glance, hypnosis would seem to suggest the very *opposite* of agency, as though one were wholly prey to the suggestions of another. But in Bergson's paradoxical formulation of the phenomenon, hypnosis could signify a fully embodied and self-determined mode of action.

The discussion of hypnosis and subjectivity will continue as I turn to Bergson's theory of art and artistic intentionality and reintroduce the problem of affective formalism considered in chapter 1. At the conclusion to the chapter, I will show how Matisse's major interpreters—including Yve-Alain Bois, Alastair Wright, Mark Antliff, Éric Alliez and Jean-Claude Bonne, J. M. Bernstein, and Judith Butler—following certain claims made by Bergson and elaborated by Deleuze, introduce a theory of traumatic subjectivity centered on the encounter between paint and the beholder's perceptual faculties. The question is not whether these authors agree with one another, or whether they explicitly take Bergson as their model, but how they reproduce an identical set of claims about the affective nature of Matisse's work that originates in aspects of Bergson's philosophy. Continuing some themes from chapter 1, I will show the depth of Bergson's relation to affective formalism and, with his investment in intentionality, how he diverges from the art historical accounts inspired by his work.

Ontological Memory

Bergson described normal human action as being "possessed" by habit. Alternately, to assume those habits for oneself, to validate and intend them, was to be "self-possessed."[40] "To act freely is to recover possession of oneself," he explained.[41] But for Bergson, human agency on its own was insufficient to secure freedom. Something in the nature of déjà vu, and *not* in the subject to whom it was happening, *granted* the subject the capacity to be free. When perception momentarily failed, it was not, or not strictly, human intentionality that intervened but *memory itself*. As I will argue, the central paradox of Bergson's theory of freedom was that freedom was bound to something beyond the human. Something about human agency was deficient or contingent, too historical and limited for Bergson's tastes. Memory, in Bergson's terms, was not a psychological or physical entity; it was not tied to a self at all—it was ontological, spiritual, and immaterial.

Memory bears an intentionality all its own: it "crowds upon" and "imprints its *élan*" upon everyday awareness.[42] And again: "The past in its entirety follows us at every instant; all that we have felt, thought and willed from our earliest infancy is there, leaning over the present which is about to join it, pressing against the portals of consciousness that would fain leave it outside."[43] Memory "dances," "crowds," "imprints," "follows," "leans," "presses" against the wall of consciousness, waiting to pounce on the subject at the moment perception lags and the mind wanders. When Bergson spoke of the past "in its entirety" he meant something far more than the return of childhood memories. Memory did not consist of *our* past, the past of any subject; it was the "past *in general*."[44] Deleuze offered various names for this form of memory: "immemorial," "ontological," "world," "cosmic," and "virtual Memory."[45]

If déjà vu is characterized as the temporary doubling of action and observation, then it is founded upon a much more basic doubling of matter and memory that orients Bergson's philosophy as whole from *Matter and Memory* onward. The *"formation of memory . . . is contemporaneous with the formation of perception,"* he writes in the essay on déjà vu.[46] There is a perpetual doubling of the present into perceptual and memory images. Because modern humans are creatures of perception, memory typically appears as an aberrant and threatening fringe of consciousness. Déjà vu is one of those "rare moments" when memory slips into perception, undermines its claims, and creates the conditions for freedom.

But déjà vu is a rather special image of freedom for Bergson. More often than not, Bergson substituted for the modest claims of déjà vu a much more sublime picture of freedom. If the freedom that was glimpsed in the moment of déjà vu was fleeting, then there were unlimited and eternal modes of it as well. The moment of déjà vu was a much more limited version of what happens at the "moment of death."[47] For Bergson, it was under conditions of extreme bodily distress that memory forced its way into consciousness in its totality. Although the past of the world is "all there" in memory, the mind would have to cease its perceptual hunger in order to taste it. If one could take the "leap" into memory, one would be thrust into unimagined pastures of freedom; one could "combine and reshape [the past] in a new way."[48] Bergson dreamed that humankind could even push beyond the human condition, forging "a new species" that could "deliver man from the necessity of being a species."[49] "At the limit," Deleuze writes, the free subject can "play with the whole of creation"; "man is capable of burning the plans, of going beyond both his own plan and his own condition, in order to finally express naturing Nature."[50] But in order to become a "new species" humanity would have to give up its current mode of being human.

Le Moi des mourants: The Pathos of Memory

The phenomenon of déjà vu is part of a wide array of abnormal psychic states that form the empirical backbone of Bergson's philosophy. Bergson was concerned, above all, with accounting for the origins, effects, and lingering threat of disease on normal human personality. Chapters 2 and 3 of *Matter and Memory* as well as several essays in *Mind-Energy* are taken up with surveying clinical and medical studies on brain pathology and "diseases of the personality."[51] Cases of dementia, hysteria, aphasia (sensory and motor), apraxia, dyslexia, amnesia, catalepsy, blindness, schizophrenia, false recognition, and paramnesia (psychic blindness and deafness) are the clinical foundations of Bergson's theory of memory. According to Bergson, all of these pathologies pointed to one result. They showed how "extraordinary cases reveal" what was "ordinarily concealed." "Pathology confirms . . . a truth about memory of which we are all instinctively aware" but are too timid to confront.[52] What was concealed was the fact that memory persisted beyond matter and that "nothing is ever truly forgotten."[53]

The eternal conservation of memory was an idea with wide currency in

Bergson's milieu. Charles Richet, in his 1884 study *Man and Intelligence,* was among the first to raise the claim: "As one has said for a long time, no fact disappears from memory: everything is fixed in it. Everything acts on us and leaves an indelible trace. Our intellectual existence at a moment is the result of all the impressions received in our past existence. How few, in this immense number, are perceived by consciousness."[54] Bergson also cited an 1885 study of amnesia that proved that "memory is a faculty which loses nothing and records everything."[55] While memory persistently "acts on us," we were typically unaware of that fact. The challenge was to make memory part of conscious awareness without it becoming another object of that consciousness.

Bergson took these claims about memory one giant leap further. Memory was not part of *any* existence; it was not the deep memory of the self that was at stake. Memory transcended humanity entirely. The self was an ever-expanding bundle of *"unconscious memory,"* an endless chronicle "of the whole of our past . . . containing the full detail of our previous life."[56]

Chapter 2 of *Matter and Memory* presents the case against the materialist theory of memory. According to the materialists, "memory is but a function of the brain."[57] Although materialist psychology conceives of "pure memory as only a weakened perception, an assembly of nascent sensations," perception is in fact *different in kind* from the actions of memory.[58] Bergson sought to undermine the materialist plot linking psychology and medicine:

> Thus psychological observations and clinical facts seem to conspire. Together they seem to point to the existence, within the cortex, of auditory memories slumbering, whether as a physico-chemical modification of certain cells or under some other form. A sensory stimulation is then supposed to awaken them; and, finally, by an intra-cerebral process, perhaps by trans-cortical movements that go to find the complementary representations, they are supposed to evoke ideas.[59]

Pointing to a range of the clinical studies on brain pathology, Bergson ridiculed this "amazing hypothesis."[60] Despite the materialist consensus, memories were *not* localized in the cellular tissues of the brain.[61] Although memory was inhibited by perception and a damaged brain could erase superficial layers of memory, neither of these facts could alter its metaphysical reality.[62]

Bergson presented a startlingly new picture of the relations among trauma, memory, and the self. Despite the accepted view of trauma as destructive to both memory and the self, Bergson showed how there was no relation between "real memory" and trauma. "Injuries to the brain," he insisted, "cannot destroy memories" because memories were entirely independent of the brain.[63] Memory was not a physical substance that could be destroyed; it was beyond the reach of time, history, decay, or subjective inflection (in this it differed entirely from Freud's *Nachträglichkeit*). Despite the effects of violent shock to the brain, there was no real loss of memory. All of the "memories which are apparently destroyed are really present, and not only present but *acting*."[64] Which is to say, conventional modes of agency have been inverted: human action is habitual, while nonhuman memory is active.

It was Bergson's vitalist theory of memory that was at the center of Jean-Paul Sartre's critique in *Imagination* (1936). It was Sartre's view that Bergson simply cured his dissatisfaction with the limits of human agency, finitude itself, with memory's complete freedom. According to Bergson, memories were introduced into consciousness "by some sort of force belonging to memory itself."[65] As Sartre concisely noted, "Images live."[66] And when "images live," humans do not. Sartre continued:

> According to Bergson, images try "to struggle into the light," and an effort is required "to inhibit their appearance." As soon as the pressure is relaxed, "the motionless memories, sensing that I have removed the obstacles to raising the trapdoor which kept them in the cellar of consciousness, begin to move. . . ." Such metaphors are, at the very least, unfortunately chosen. . . . What now becomes of the role of screening and reflecting assigned as fundamental to the body [described in chapter 1 of *Matter and Memory*]? What of the notable definition, "The unconscious is the inactive," which Bergson seemed to have quite forgotten while describing at length the "dance" engaged in by memories? . . . to attribute an activity of a mental sort . . . to contents of consciousness first carefully severed from the whole of consciousness, is to leave oneself open to the intervention of material forces of a magical sort that prove to be completely inconceivable.[67]

The "magic" of memory pointed to a central problem in Bergson's theory of freedom. If memory was self-propelling agency—it required no external cause or correlate—then the status of human action began to look rather secondary or epiphenomenal. Sartre took up the problem again in *Being and Nothingness* (1943): "If [the past] is unconscious, as Bergson claims and if the unconscious is inactive, how can it weave itself into the woof of our present consciousness? Would it have a force of its own? . . . How does memory emanate from the past as such?"[68]

Despite his vigorous assertions to the contrary, Bergson was a materialist. Memory-images were *things.* On this account, Bergson's doubling of perception and memory was a replay of Hume. Here is Sartre: "For Hume, the image appeared as a weakening of the perception, an echo subsequent to it in time; for Bergson, it was a shadow paired with the perception. In both cases, the image was an exact decalcomania of the thing: opaque, impenetrable like the thing, rigid, frozen, in fine, itself a thing."[69] This thingly double of the human, this ghostly presence haunting perception, was the truly generative force of human action. Against conventional notions of materialism, Bergson presented something like a metamaterialism, a mode of recording every aspect of existence that was immune to the effects of time or loss.

At the conclusion to chapter 3 of *Matter and Memory* Bergson summed up his claim about the ontological nonrelation between matter and memory: "All the facts and all the analogies are in favor of a theory which . . . considers memory itself as absolutely independent of matter."[70] Nonetheless, this claim did not go far enough. In his introduction to the 1910 edition of *Matter and Memory,* Bergson looked back on his earlier claim and found it too timid. He came up with a bolder conclusion: life after death. Here is Bergson in 1910:

> That which is commonly held to be a disturbance of the psychic life itself, an inward disorder, a disease of the personality, appears to us, from our point of view, to be an unloosing or a breaking of the tie which binds this psychic life to its motor accompaniment, a weakening or an impairing of our attention to outward life. This opinion, as also that which denies the localization of the memory-images of words and explains aphasia quite otherwise than by such localization, was considered paradoxical at the date of the first publication of the present work.[71]

Over the fourteen years since the first edition of *Matter and Memory* Bergson saw how there was new evidence, including Freudian psychoanalysis, to prove the veracity of his earlier claims.[72] While materialists obstinately adhered to memory localization, Bergson showed how partial lobotomies proved that memory had no physical location. The real breakthrough came with his discovery that one could remove the brain and memories would be *intensified.*

Following the recent reports of psychical research, Bergson showed that the self was not only independent of the body but also there was an "intensification of personality . . . after the disintegration of the body."[73] Since memories survived the destruction of parts of the brain, he now determined that the soul survived the destruction of the body. "There is an exaltation of spontaneous memory in most cases where the sensori-motor equilibrium of the nervous system is disturbed," he explained. In order to "bring into the foreground the spontaneous memory which was hidden . . . every attempt at motor memory is, to begin with, suppressed."[74] Disturbances of the nervous system, disintegration of the body, *death itself* resulted in an expansion of the self. (Sartre wryly remarked on the idea: "Dreams and hypermnemonic phenomena show what a wealth of imagery may accompany . . . physiological annihilation.")[75] In the new introduction Bergson observed that if one were to "unscrew the vice in which personality has allowed itself to be squeezed by action," then there would follow a "greater dilation of the whole personality."[76] To fully unscrew one's attention to life would of course result in death. Bergson did not hesitate to pursue that conclusion.[77]

Mental pathologies, bodily disintegration, and personality disorders were far from secondary concerns for Bergson. Going where philosophers feared to tread, Bergson established memory as the primordial outside to Western thought. Philosophers "do not readily descend from the heights whereon they love to dwell," he averred. "It goes against them to come into touch with . . . such facts as mental maladies . . . : they would be afraid of making their hands dirty."[78] Bergson had no fear of making his hands dirty.

Matter and Memory begins with a detailed review of brain pathologies and diseases of the personality and goes on to explore a range of bodily privations, including suffocation, asphyxiation, drowning, inanition, extreme insomnia, vertigo, falling from great heights, shootings, hanging, and near-death experience. It was in the analysis of pathologies and physical injuries that Bergson discovered a basic phenomenon of his philosophical enterprise. At the moment of death, and only then, was memory truly revealed.[79] (According to Rouveyre, Matisse got caught up with the idea. "It is well known that the approach of death gives the spirit a sort of condensation and fundamental vision of the whole life," Rouveyre explained, referring to Matisse's 1941 cancer operation.)[80] This moment was "instructive," Bergson said, because it was the only one *within life,* no matter how fleeting, that revealed the active presence of memory. The moment of death was the last stop on a continuum that ran from commonplace déjà vu through sleep and dreams, to insanity, to the hangman's noose. He summarized the idea in a key passage in *Matter and Memory*:

> But, if almost the whole of our past is hidden from us because it is inhibited by the necessities of present action, it will find strength to cross the threshold of consciousness in all cases where we renounce the interests of effective action to replace ourselves, so to speak, in the life of dreams. . . . It is a fact commonly observed that memory is "exalted" in certain dreams and in certain somnambular states. Memories which we believed abolished then reappear with striking completeness; we live over again, in all their detail, forgotten scenes of childhood; we speak languages which we no longer even remember to have learnt. But there is nothing more instructive in this regard than what happens in cases of sudden suffocation, in men drowned or hanged. The man, when brought to life again, states that he saw, in a very short time, all the forgotten events of his life passing before him with great rapidity, with their smallest circumstances and in the very order in which they occurred.[81]

The renunciation of action was the liberation of memory. When the mind was no longer narrowed by perceptual hunger it could expand to encompass the whole of one's past. Memories of childhood returned unaltered, and we could speak languages we never thought we knew. The nature of these forgotten languages remains unclear. Bergson made the point again in *Laughter,* describing an "appeal [that] had been made within us" to "ancestral memories belonging to a far-away past [ataviques souvenirs infiniment anciens]—memories so deep-seated [profonds] and so foreign to our present life that this latter . . . seems something unreal and conventional."[82] Indeed, it was one of Bergson's most sustained claims, and he reiterated the idea at the conclusion to his last book, *The Two Sources of Morality and Religion*: "The innate beliefs of our ancestors subsist in the depths of our inner selves; they reappear as soon as they are no longer inhibited by opposing forces."[83] As these passages suggest, the languages that return to us and that we never thought we knew are part of our *racial* background, which substantially complicates (to say the least) Bergson's concept of the retrieval of the "past *in general*."

Returning to the passage in *Matter and Memory*, Bergson's description moves from sleep and dreams to forgotten languages and childhood, to a concluding image of suffocation and hanging. Déjà vu, sleep, madness, and death were points on a continuum edging toward total perceptual nullity and complete memory recall. "Sleep and insanity"—they belonged together—"detach memory and attention from the sensori-motor functions by which they enter into present reality," he explained.[84] Once again, *detachment* from sensori-motor functions was simultaneously *attachment* to memory. One literally relived childhood when adult life was annihilated. At the clarifying moment of death all that was thought abolished, buried under layers of habit, was discovered unaltered in its pure state of being.

Loosen the pull of perception, and memory springs into view. For all his dissatisfaction with the materialist picture of mind, Bergson could nonetheless describe action in straightforwardly mechanical terms. Matter and memory were a series of contractions and expansions, tensions and releases. Bergson's ocularism reemerges within his account of memory. The moment of death is also a moment of *pure seeing*:

> Should the attention to life grow weak for a moment . . . then our mind, which has of force been kept till then looking forward, loses the tension which strains it and by the recoil is made backward-looking; it surveys its whole history. The panoramic vision of the past is due, then, to a sudden *disinterestedness in life* born of the sudden conviction that the moment is the moment of death [mourir à l'instant].[85]

It is important to see that even here Bergson does not fully dispense with an account of intentionality. The panoramic vision of the dying man is still the result of a "conviction" about his condition. Nonetheless, it is hard to see what kind of action would follow from this conviction.[86]

Bergson expanded his view of the "moment" by considering evidence derived from the study of animal memory. Like suffocation, drowning, and hanging, starvation in animals revealed the unimaginable scope of unconscious memory:

> Consider again what happens in a prolonged fast. It is a remarkable fact that in animals that have died of hunger the brain is found to be almost unimpaired, while the other organs have lost more or less of their weight and their cells have undergone profound changes. It seems as though the rest of the body had sustained the nervous system to the last extremity, treating itself simply as the means of which the nervous system is the end.[87]

The veracity of this claim does not, of course, hold up under scrutiny. What matters is that Bergson believed that when an animal's individual cells decomposed through lack of sustenance, the brain still flourished. Among animals, at least, the brain was the locus of memory. A starving body will use its resources to keep memories intact rather than to prolong its survival.

Bergson cited a series of articles on near-death experience to support his claims for the eternal conservation of memory. The most important of these studies appeared in his notes to *Matter and Memory,* including Forbes Winslow's *Obscure Diseases of the Brain* (1863), L. F. Maury's *Le Sommeil et les rêves* (1865), Théodule Ribot's *Maladies de la mémoire* (1881), A. M. P. Rouillard's dissertation *Les Amnésies* (1885), and Victor Egger's extraordinary 1896 study of drowning and hanging, "Le Moi des mourants."[88] This last work proved the most relevant to Bergson's argument, and he returned to it several times throughout his writings.[89] He referred to Egger's work again in his 1911 study "The Perception of Change," as well as in his 1913 presidential address before the Society for Psychical Research. The formula was the same in both: the moment of death proved the existence of something beyond death. Both passages deserve citation here:

> An attention to life . . . separated from all practical interest, would thus include in an undivided present the entire past history of the conscious person. . . . That is not a hypothesis . . . immediately, as though by magic, the past once more becomes present. In people who see the threat of sudden death unexpectedly before them, in the mountain climber falling down a precipice, in drowning men, in men being hanged, it seems that a sharp conversion of the attention can take place—something like a change of orientation of the consciousness which, up until then turned toward the future and absorbed by the necessities of action, suddenly loses all interest in them. That is enough to call to mind a thousand different "forgotten" details and to unroll the whole history of the person before him in a moving panorama.[90]

Bergson replays here several of the themes discussed so far, but the imagery is more subdued. He does not suggest, for instance, that it is the past "in general" that surges into the "undivided present." But when he considered the matter two years later, he amended the 1911 account and expanded the horizon of memory to include the existential past:

> Many facts seem to indicate that the past is preserved even down to its slightest details, and that there is no real forgetting. You have heard of persons resuscitated from drowning or hanging, who have said that during a moment they had the panoramic vision of the totality of their past. . . . It has occurred to Alpine climbers slipping on a precipice, to soldiers seeing the guns fired at them and feeling themselves lost. The truth is that our whole past is always present behind us, and to perceive it we have but to look back.[91]

The panoramic vision spread out before the Alpine climber pales in comparison to the one that flashes before him as he slips and falls. While both ideas privilege vision, the first is acquisitive, the second, utterly noninstrumental. The (specular) freedom Bergson offers here is purchased at such a high price that it is hard to see how it is not the same as its denial.

For Bergson, commonplace failures of attention such as déjà vu were ultimately unsatisfying in their exemplification of freedom. While they showed us what it would be like to loosen the hold of perception, exposing to view a more layered view of the present, they were a momentary lapse in the acquisitive pursuit of reality. It was the fact of being human, being a practically oriented creature, that dissatisfied Bergson. The solution to the human was death or a Nietzschean overcoming of it. Bergson's fascination with starved animals, asphyxiation, shooting, drowning, and hanging needs to be considered alongside his commitment to "overcoming [dépasser] the human condition."[92] Human nature "turning back on itself and twisting on itself . . . doing violence to its nature" was a truly paradoxical path to freedom.[93] To intuit life required the death of the active mind. It was an either-or:

> Our mind can be installed in the mobile reality, adopt its ceaselessly changing direction, in short, grasp it intuitively. But to do that, it must do itself violence, reverse the direction of the operation by which it ordinarily thinks, continually upsetting its categories, or rather, recasting them. In so doing it will arrive at fluid concepts, capable of following reality in all its windings and of adopting the very movement of the inner life of things.[94]

Bergson presented a paradoxical "vitalism." To go beyond the human required an act of violence against being human.[95] While Bergson believed the moment of death to be "instructive"—it offered a more expansive picture of possible freedoms—he nonetheless could not offer any clear path from the unlimited potential of memory to the (necessarily) limited potentials of human action.

Hypnotic Agency

Before Bergson developed his notion of ontological memory, he appealed to a more traditional model of agency based on philosophical claims concerning "self-determination," "judgment," and "free decision."[96] Unlike the account put forward in *Matter and Memory,* in *Time and Free Will* Bergson described those who make "appeals to memory rather than to judgment" as those who "live . . . and die without having known true freedom."[97] Indeed, throughout his early writings Bergson vilified memory as an inert and superficial capacity. What crucially distinguishes his later concept of memory from "duration" (the core concept of his early writings) is that duration lacks the significance and agency granted to ontological memory. Duration requires the "interference" of the self to make it significant.[98] And in contrast to the moment of death described in *Matter and Memory,* in *Time and Free Will* Bergson described the "great and solemn crisis" as one that is "decisive of our reputation . . . with ourselves." Reputations are not at stake in the moment of death. Rather, when one is forced to decide in a moment of crisis one's true intentions emerge, stripped of any habitual routine. To act in a crisis is to act with intention. In the crisis moment, one is forced to "choose in defiance of what is conventionally called a motive."[99] It is in those moments without clear precedent, without predetermined rules, that one fully grasps one's actions as free.

Bergson's most detailed early treatment of intentionality appears in the section titled "The Free Act" in *Time and Free Will.* Bergson's concern here is to differentiate "reflex acts"—the actions of a "conscious automaton"—from those acts that "belong to us, [and] that we have appropriated."[100] A free act is one that "springs from the self . . . , for our self alone will lay claim to its paternity."[101] Like a father to a child or the "artist and his work," the free act is one that "bears the mark of our [whole] personality."[102]

Bergson provides an extraordinary, and extraordinarily counterintuitive, example of the free act: hypnotic suggestion. The "most authoritative education" pales before the persuasive force of a suggestion received under hypnosis.[103] Ideas received through education adhere only to the surface of one's personality. It is easy to see how learned behavior is not fully self-determined, but how could it be that hypnotic suggestion is more free than a lesson learned? As I will show, Bergson never conceived of hypnotic suggestion as something that actually came from another. Every suggestion that worked or took hold of the subject was simply eliciting something already at work deep within that individual. Consider, for instance, how Bergson compared the effects of suggestion to the "violent anger roused by some accidental circumstance" or "a hereditary vice suddenly emerging from the obscure depths of the organism."[104] These thoughts and feelings were a deep part of one's personality—they were truly intended—but they could emerge only at a moment of crisis. Because they were more like a "personal idea" and less like an external event, "a suggestion received in the hypnotic state is not incorporated in the mass of conscious states."[105] Because it is already part of you, the suggestion feels as though it bears "a life of its own" and at the right moment "will usurp the whole personality."[106] Only if the "entire self assimilated the suggestion," Bergson explained, would it become genuinely "persuasive."[107] If a suggestion truly took hold of you, it would not be felt to be a suggestion at all, but something you suggested to yourself, an autosuggestion. The hypnotic operator was simply the trigger of the action, not the agent.

A few years prior to *Time and Free Will,* Bergson elaborated his theory of hypnotic suggestion in an essay that established the primary concerns of his philosophical enterprise while offering an account of agency different from the one described in *Matter and Memory.* Despite its unfamiliarity even among his admirers, Bergson's first major essay, "Unconscious Simulation in the State of Hypnosis" of 1886, bears close consideration for its proximity to and difference from the claims of his later philosophy.[108]

"Unconscious Simulation in the State of Hypnosis"

Bergson's aim in the essay was to evaluate the findings of a certain doctor, "M. V.," who used hypnotic techniques on a group of teenage boys to prove the existence of thought transference.[109] M. V.'s experiments involved standing before a group of boys, his back to the window, with an open book before him raised to eye level. From the boys' perspective, they could see only the cover of the book and the partially exposed face of the hypnotist. According to M. V.'s report, while the boys were in a hypnotic trance they could read the number as well as the words and lines on the open page before him, although the text was unobservable from their point of view. For M. V., this was a clear case of thought reading, and he assumed that the boys saw the words pass through his mind while he was reading and simply read the words along with him.

Bergson and his colleague Robinet were intrigued by the doctor's account, but they were suspicious of the conclusion. They resolved to repeat the experiments themselves, and they gathered four of the boys from M. V.'s study in order to review his results. According to Bergson's report, by simply waving his hands before their eyes he put the boys into a deep hypnotic trance.[110] As the effects began to take hold, the boys entered into a state of general insensibility akin to catalepsy, wherein "the eyes remained disproportionately open and fixed, the physiognomy completely lacking the expression of intelligence" (525). Once reduced to this cataleptic state, the boys became blank slates upon which Bergson and Robinet could perform their experiments without any conscious interference from the boys. After the boys fell into a trance, Bergson recorded the series of remarkable events that ensued:

> M. Robinet puts himself before a window, standing, his back turned to the light; he puts L . . . e to sleep . . . then he opens a book at random and holds

> it nearly vertically about 10 centimeters before his eyes . . . always keeping his eyes on the sleeping subject; he then orders the boy to indicate the number on the right-hand page. If L . . . e makes a mistake the first time, he quickly corrects his error if we carefully move the book a few centimeters in one direction or the other until he declares he can read it distinctly. . . . We have repeated the experiment several times on three other subjects; but . . . they were far from giving as satisfying results. (526)

Except for some quickly corrected mistakes, L . . . e's reading was nearly flawless. Bergson's account raises several questions. Why was L . . . e so much more adept at reading than the others? What made him "the most interesting" among the boys? Did it have something to do with the fact that, as Bergson noted in passing, L . . . e suffered as a child from severe headaches? Did the childhood ailment bear on his current mental capacities? And then again, what was the significance of the few centimeters' shift in the placement of the book that allowed L . . . e to read more clearly? Bergson, for the moment, leaves these questions unanswered, turning instead to a series of mental feats performed by the group as whole.

When queried under hypnosis as to how they read the concealed words, the boys offered a startling reply:

> If I ask any one of these four subjects, once asleep, how he goes about guessing the page number or the word, he invariably answers: "I see it."—"Where do you see it?"—"There." And, passing his finger under the book, in such a way that he could touch the page I am looking at, he places it with surprising precision on the page number or title that he was required to reveal. I'm astonished that he should be able to read through the book and its cover, I add: "Show me then the cover of the book."—"Here it is." And while pronouncing these words he passes his hand under the book, places it before the page and indicates, not the actual position of the cover, but its symmetrical position in relation to the open page. In sum, the book would seem to be open before his eyes rather than mine; he imagines that he is reading the book, and naturally situates its cover behind the open page. (526–27)

From the boys' perspective they were simply reading a book before their eyes. There was no mention of thought transference or any occult explanation for their actions, nor did they accept any occult explanation when it was offered to them.

A few problems continued to puzzle Bergson, however. Why did the boys, even the talented L . . . e, make mistakes when reading? If it were a true instance of thought transference, then what possible difference could the shift of the book's placement make? Could the manner of their mistakes provide a clue to the problem? P . . . r, for instance, sometimes said "213" when the actual page number was 312, and "75" for page 57, as though he were reading figures inverted in a mirror or seeing through the book and reading the numbers left to right. Was this a previously unrecorded side effect of thought transference, or was something else at fault, something far less mysterious? Bergson did not hesitate to offer a solution to these problems: "In light of these observations it appeared to us natural to suppose that the reader read off the cornea of the magnetizer, it playing the role of a convex mirror" (527). When the possibility of thought transference was ruled out, Bergson posed the only credible alternative: the boys were reading inverted reflections in the reader's cornea from across the room! Bergson noted the obvious difficulties involved, but remained unruffled:

> Without a doubt, the image reflected may be an extremely small one, given that the figures or letters guessed at were scarcely larger than 3mm in height. And supposing that at the cornea a radius of curvature of 7.8mm a very simple calculation shows that this cornea, acting as a convex mirror, presents an image of figures and letters the height of which was a little less than 0.1mm. (527)

Despite the improbability of the claims, Bergson pressed forward with his thesis: "Nonetheless, a parallel hypothesis has nothing unbelievable about it, given the curious hyperesthesia that we have noticed in the state of hypnotism, and that we have provoked by suggestion in many cases. We therefore recommence our experiments" (527).

Bergson's reference to multiple cases of hyperesthesia remained a provocation; he supplied no further details as to their results. Ruling out the "unbelievable" hypotheses of magnetism, clairvoyance, psychometry, telepathy, and thought transference—that is, any *occult* explanation for the phenomenon—he swiftly concluded that the boys were endowed with the more common talent of hyperesthesia. Hypnosis created the condition where something like déjà vu could be elaborated, investigated, and extended far beyond the limits of a temporary lag in perception.

What is hyperesthesia? In the medical literature of the time, hyperesthesia indicated a pathological condition involving excessive sensitivity in the nerves or nerve centers. (It should be noted that all of Bergson's tests hinged on the hyperesthesia of the *optical* nerves, not the senses at large.) Hypnotic suggestion, by decisively relaxing the body, induced a profound change in the shape of the subject's cornea (what Bergson described as a "ciliary spasm") that made the eye for a brief period of time hyperacute, as though it were a microscope. The use of suggestion simply brought this hidden capacity into actuality. Above all, hypnotism showed that the range and possibility of human sensation and human *action* were far more extensive than everyday awareness or conventional science was prepared to accept.

Although Bergson did not detail the available evidence of hyperesthesia, he assumed the sympathetic reader of psychically oriented journals was aware of recent achievements in the field. Reports of hyperesthenic events were in fact widely circulated at the time in journals and newspapers, and seemed to suggest the existence of a vast, unexplored realm of human sensation. In the inaugural issue of the *American Journal of Psychology* (1887), for instance, an anonymous reviewer summed up the current state of research concerning hyperesthesia. The reviewer's tone was confident, animated with the conviction of a breakthrough:

> Hyperesthesia . . . whether normal or morbid, opens up a new world as truly as the microscope or telephone. One tells the form, substance and even color of objects near him by radiant heat, or reads as in a mirror, shadows from walls that seem to others unreflecting; or, in one lately reported case, sees the shadows of heat vibrations over a hot substance cast on a wall by moonlight; the sense of a personal presence is felt by the blow or noise of breathing or heat. The case of Dr. Taguet's patient, who, it was said, was able to read script held behind her head by reflection on a plain card in front of her; the case reported by Dr. Sauvaire, who recognized the suit and number of a card in a different pack, as, it would *seem,* by seeing through it;[111] the case of Roclia's clerk, who seemed to use a piece of card-board as a mirror in which he could see all that took place behind his back; and the well-known case of Bergson's reader of images reflected in the cornea. . . . If these degrees of hyperaesthesia, normal or even hypnotic, are possible . . . the entire experimental basis of telepathy vanishes.[112]

The reader is liable to be stopped short, after being regaled by the achievements of paranormal science, by the author's cautious conclusion. One might expect the account to conclude with a critical gesture toward the limitations of conventional science, but the reviewer seems more concerned with discriminating between paranormal phenomena, focusing on the difference between hyperesthesia and *telepathy.* It is as though the primary question raised by newly discovered psychic phenomena was not whether the dominant scientific trends were misguided but how one occult phenomenon (hyperesthesia) undermined the claims of another (telepathy). And like the anonymous reviewer, Bergson, in "Unconscious Simulation," was similarly concerned with discriminating between types of occult phenomena.[113] Did hyperesthesia indicate an immaterial realm of spirits and forces unavailable to analysis—phenomena typically construed under the general heading of clairvoyance—or was it a radically heightened form of ordinary sensation and therefore available, at least potentially, to analysis, testing, and elaboration?

Bergson was well versed in mapping the uncharted terrain of unconscious phenomena. In a review of Émile Boirac's *Unknown Psychology* (1908) he expressed his admiration for the author's careful discrimination of psychic phenomena:

> 1. *Hypnotic* phenomena, or facts of hypnotism and suggestion; 2. *Magnetic* phenomena, which seem to imply the intervention of forces "unknown, not yet defined, but of a physical nature, and more or less analogous to the physics of radiation, light, heat, electricity, and magnetism. At this stage occur all the phenomena of animal magnetism and telepathy." 3. *Spiritual* phenomena, "which also seem to imply the hypothesis of unknown agents, but this time of a psychological nature."[114]

Like Boirac, Bergson stressed the *material* nature of psychic transmission in his classification of unknown psychology. Boirac's fundamental concern, Bergson noted, was with category 2, "forms emanating from the human organism 'and capable of exercising at a distance on other organisms, maybe even on material objects, an influence more or less analogous to that of forces of physical radiation.'"[115] At the time of "Unconscious Simulation" Bergson considered magnetism a spiritual phenomenon, but by 1908 he had revised his categories and come to believe that "science has taken almost complete possession" of the spiritual world. Psychic research had been codified as a branch of science.[116] This was to fulfill Bergson's earliest ambition to "re-erect the bridge, broken down since Kant's day, between metaphysics and science."[117]

The Problem of Suggestion

As Bergson was fully aware, the scientific establishment resisted every effort to establish links between the empirical world and the immaterial beyond. In "Unconscious Simulation" he painstakingly tried to convince the scientific community of the validity of his methods and his results. But most important, he sought to distinguish his scientific interpretation of the boys' abilities from any spiritual explanation of the phenomena. This latter aim reveals Bergson's acute anxiety concerning the prospect of simulation. At the time he was writing, the widely shared view within the scientific and medical communities was that the doctor, the patient, or the two in collusion were guilty of suggesting (on the doctor's part) or simulating (on the part of the patient) the other's actions. Throughout "Unconscious Simulation" Bergson struggled to defeat this picture of suggestion and to secure what seemed to be paranormal results within the available terms of empirical science. He wanted to demystify hypnosis and to turn the problem of suggestion on its head: every suggestion functioned like an autosuggestion. Far from implanting foreign ideas in the boys' heads, the hypnotic operator freed the boys to become themselves.

Bergson's desire to achieve scientific validity is evident in his determined rebuttal of the telepathic explanations of his colleagues. In order to exclude explanations based on a theory of suggestion for the phenomena they discovered, Bergson and Robinet closely considered the role that unconscious thought transferences may have played in their experiments. To this end, they closed their eyes and "concentrated all of their attentive energies on the figures they were thinking of" and asked the boys if they could read the figures in their minds. According to their reports, these experiments produced no correct responses; there was "no trace of mental suggestion." What Bergson meant by this was that the boys were in no way gaining access to the hypnotist's mind and seeing the words floating about; rather, they were reading—in a purely visual manner—the reflections off the page in the hypnotist's eyes. And these reflections, as opposed to any occult forces, were virtually, if not actually, available to all subjects and replicable in potentially unlimited contexts.

Having ruled out telepathic explanations, Bergson and Robinet continued their investigations, returning to the case of L . . . e, "the most adept of our subjects" (528). Given L . . . e's proven ability to read off the hypnotist's cornea, Bergson and Robinet decided to challenge their subject with a series of more difficult tasks:

> First we showed him a microscopic photograph representing the members of a learned society in England. This photograph in the form of a rectangle of which the largest corner measures around 2mm; a dozen people appear there, sitting or standing around a table. L . . . e was able to describe them to us one after another and mime their appearances. (528)

L . . . e's ability to mimic the actions of the learned society was intended to prove his mastery of the task. A simple description of the scene presumably would have been open to subjective inflection, while mimicry proved the depth, fluency, and immediacy of his vision.

In the name of empirical rigor, Bergson undertook one last experiment to plumb the outermost limits of L . . . e's optical acuity. He placed in the boy's hands a microscopic slide of the "epidermic tissue of an orchid, of which the cells have been colored such that their nucleus was aniline red." The diameter of the cells, he noted, was no larger than 0.06mm (considerably smaller, that is, than the 0.1mm figures on the page). The boy was asked to look at the image and reproduce exactly what he saw on a sheet of paper. "After a minute examination," Bergson observed, "L . . . e drew the cells as hexagons, such as one sees them in a microscope" (528). "These experiments," he concluded, "lavishly prove that the reading of a figure at the height of around 0.1mm is an operation which presents no difficulties for him in a hypnotic state." Under hypnosis, that is, the normal range of human sensibility and the potentials for action were vastly exceeded. The consequence of these experiments was the revision of the picture of possible human freedoms.

Like the work of M. V. before him, Bergson's experiments came under intense scrutiny by other practitioners of hypnosis at the time. Frederic W. H. Myers, fellow at Trinity College, Cambridge, and one of the founders of the Society for Psychical Research, strenuously objected to Bergson's procedures.[118] Above all, Myers protested the conclusions Bergson drew from the last two experiments. As "thought-transference was not formally excluded, since M. Bergson himself knew the photograph and the look of the cells," Myers concluded that Bergson's experiments were crucially flawed.[119] According to Myers, "If we wish to prove that a subject does not receive an image from our minds we should present to him an object with which we are ourselves unacquainted."[120] Bergson, in other words, because his experimental method introduced an element of indeterminacy (his own thoughts, potentially read by L . . . e) into the tests, was unjustified in his rejection of telepathic explanations.

Bergson was troubled by the accusation and asked L . . . e to return so as to duplicate the experiments under stricter protocols. This time he would employ images wholly unfamiliar to himself and to the boy so as to preclude any possibility of mental suggestion. To Bergson's dismay the boy refused the request, and he was unable to reconfirm the results of the first trial. He was unable, that is, to rule out fully the role thought transference might have played in his final examinations. Despite the controversy, Bergson vigorously maintained the specificity of the hyperesthenic thesis against Myers's and every other occult account of the events. As Bergson made clear, occult phenomena were tainted with the lure of suggestion and were to be aggressively rooted out of any empirical investigations. He devoted the second part of the essay to resolving any lingering doubts about the role suggestion played in the proceedings.

Although Bergson repeatedly tried to explain to the boys what occurred in the experiments, they passionately denied his account of the situation. The boys insisted they were simply reading a book that lay open before their eyes. After several attempts to extract a confession from them, Bergson concluded they were acting in "complete good faith." And this was a scandal from his perspective. Could it be that he was suggesting (or inducing), albeit unconsciously, the words to them as he read? Were the boys honest in their explanations precisely because *he*, the analyst, was playing an active, persuasive role in the encounter, steering the boys with nearly imperceptible body movements, such as subtle articulations of the lips, an almost imperceptible sound under his breath, a knowing glance of the eye, toward his desired results?

One year prior to "Unconscious Simulation," Eduard von Hartmann published *Der Spiritismus* (1885), a scathing critique of spiritual phenomena. All paranormal phenomena, von Hartmann argued, could be explained as hallucinations implanted in the minds of the participants by the medium. While the hypnotized were in a trance, hypnotists and mediums produced "mental pictures" of apparitions and conveyed them to their subjects through the power of suggestion. Hypnotized individuals, with the power of suggestion, believed they were in the direct presence of a material body, but in reality they were prey to hallucinations suggested by the hypnotist. Nearly all paranormal phenomena, von Hartmann stated, could be explained by "the wishes, expectations, and beliefs of the people present, of which the [hypnotist] was aware."[121] Following on von Hartmann's claim, two French psychotherapists, Paul-Charles Dubois and Alfred Binet, initiated a protracted campaign against hypnotic forms of therapeutic treatment. For Dubois and Binet, all neurotics were "simulators" and they should be treated as such. Dubois compared neurotics to "army stragglers" and wondered "whether to believe in their hurts and put them in the infirmary, or to handle them roughly and send them back to the ranks." Ultimately, he opted for the latter solution. It should be clear that what was at stake for Dubois with the question of hypnosis was nothing less than "the problem of liberty and of responsibility" itself.[122]

It was at this same moment that Freud began his psychological investigations with a close study of hypnotic phenomena. Specifically, he examined the role of suggestion in the medical treatment of hysterics. Writing against the grain of Bergson, as well as von Hartmann and Jean-Martin Charcot, Freud followed Hippolyte Bernheim in affirming the ubiquity and relative triviality of suggestion within *all* forms of human interaction. In "Psychical Treatment" (1890), Freud sought to reveal the truth behind the "magical" powers of mediums. Heightened, but commonplace, forms of bodily awareness, he observed, could easily explain occult phenomena such as thought transference:

> The affects in the strict sense are characterized by a quite special connection to somatic processes, but, strictly speaking, all mental states, even those we usually consider as "processes of thought," are to some degree "affective," and none of them are without the capacity to modify the somatic processes. Even when a person is engaged in quietly thinking in "representations," there is a constant series of excitations, corresponding to the content of these representations, which are discharged into the smooth and striated muscles, and which can be distinguished by an appropriate reinforcement and can thus explain many surprising, supposedly "supernatural" phenomena. Thus, for example, so-called "thought-reading" can be explained by small, involuntary movements of the muscles that are carried out by the "medium" when he makes someone try, without guiding him, to find a hidden object. The whole phenomenon might more suitably be called "thought betraying."[123]

Our bodies, like an open book, necessarily betray us. Even the most recondite acts of introspective reflection produce external, visually observable reactions or cues that can be read, at least potentially, by any sensitive reader. It was Freud's larger claim, implicit in these remarks, that humans, like animals, read each other all the time: individuals are in continual suggestive dialogue with each other, even if they are unaware of the exchange taking place. One did not need to be a specially endowed adept (as Bergson suggested of L . . . e), or mad (as Charcot claimed), to read the thoughts of others. Strictly speaking, it was not thoughts that were being read, only their expression through bodily comportments and minute motor-muscular discharges and adjustments. It was not even necessary to be hypnotized—human beings' connections with others were so intimate and continuous that one could not help but broadcast one's thoughts and feelings to others in the environment (the limits of what constituted an environment were left out of account). And in sharp contrast to Bergson, Freud, in this early statement, affirmed the role of suggestion in the psychical treatment of patients. Far from wishing to expel suggestion from scientific research, Freud wished to make it more explicit and further its availability as a tool for a scientific-medical account of subjectivity.[124]

A few years later, however, he fundamentally reconceived his early account of the material expression of affect. As Freud saw it, his early view suffered from an overly optimistic assessment of the scientific availability of mental processes. It was as though one could know everything one needed to know about inner life with the right amount of empirical investigation. Freud came to see that life was layered with metaphorical, figurative, and *symbolic* modes of mediation (the unconscious itself, he later explained, was a mode of representation). When he came to write *Dora* in 1905 he fundamentally revised his materialist picture of psychology to one that granted a far greater share to representation. "There is a great deal of symbolism . . . in life," he explained, "but as a rule we pass it by without heeding it." Freud's commitment to symbolism seemed to require a purging of hypnosis:

> When I set myself the task of bringing to light what human beings keep hidden within them, not by the compelling power of hypnosis, but by observing what they say and what they show, I thought the task was a harder one than it really is. Anyone with eyes to see and ears to hear will be convinced that mortals cannot hide a secret. If one's lips are silent, then the fingertips tattle; betrayal oozes out of every pore. And so the task of making conscious the most hidden recesses of the mind is one which is quite possible to accomplish.[125]

If hypnosis revealed the truth of the subject's mental life by compulsion, then psychoanalysis proved to be a far more reliable means of accessing the soul because it avoided the possibility of suggestion. Freud came to believe that humans were, rather than affect machines, "expression machines, and virtually never turned off." Simply to be human was to be the "victim of expression—readable" in every sound and gesture, Stanley Cavell writes of Freud; it is as though "every word and gesture [is] ready to betray [one's] meaning."[126] That our words and gestures could betray *meaning* and not some biological event is the key to the difference between Freud's early affect theory and his theory in 1905, when he turned to more symbolic and representational modes of interpretation. Bergson replayed this turn *in reverse.*

Like Freud, Bergson came to reject hypnosis and took aggressive steps to purge his analysis of the least trace of suggestion. In "Unconscious Simulation" his peculiar strategy was to contain external suggestion by foregrounding, even flaunting, its presence. After all, he tacitly acknowledged that the boys' testimony *was* simulated—he featured this fact in the title of his article—but they simulated it *unconsciously.* The boys were lying unintentionally. Rather than construe the boys' errors either as unintentional mistakes or as conscious deceptions—as did the majority of his critics—Bergson took those errors as a sign of sincerity. In other words, despite the boys' false testimony, no lie was perpetrated. Even though what they said was objectively false and they were in fact reading words reflected off the hypnotist's cornea, regardless of what they said or thought, their deeper, *unconscious intentions* spoke louder than words. Even though "everything happens *as though* we were dealing with the most able of simulators," what Bergson witnessed was "a kind of 'unconscious simulation'" (529). While skeptics may have taken the boys' protestations as simple evidence of simulation or, worse still, of suggestions the analyst fed them, Bergson took their lies as the clearest proof of their honesty.

Bergson showed that every instance of conscious simulation masked an unconscious one. He precluded the intrusion of conscious intentionality or fantastic elaboration. Despite their objectively false testimony, no influence, no suggestion, no transference, no conscious simulation—no collusion of any kind—was performed by the analyst or the patient. Evidence that we might take as *confirming* the inductive nature of hypnotic suggestion—that the operator, consciously or unconsciously, directed his subjects through a set of paces—Bergson took as confirming the opposite: hypnotism was a strictly instrumental means of lowering a subject's inhibitions; it allowed the boys to connect with and act according to their true intentions.

From where, then, did the urge to simulate arise? Simulation was a natural impulse generated by individuals to suppress the responsibilities that go along with "free" action. We tell ourselves lies in order to avoid the responsibility of making decisions and accepting their consequences. Bergson was convinced that with the introduction of psychic research into the techniques of scientific observation, a whole range of previously unobservable virtual phenomena would come into view. Although there are "certain conditions, which we cannot perceive with our means of observation," he explained in his 1887 course "The Metaphysics of Life," it was the means themselves that were flawed; they should not prevent us from knowing the "existence of other worlds" within our own.[127] To attempt to live within those other worlds within one's everyday life was to act freely under conditions of unfreedom.

In the conclusion to "Unconscious Simulation," Bergson drew together all his claims up to that point. Discussing two accounts of mental suggestion, Bergson pointed to recent cases of occult phenomena considered by his colleagues Charles Richet and Pierre Janet. Although he disagreed with their conclusions, he nonetheless found key support for his hyperesthenic hypothesis in their experiments. A whole range of past cases that had been dismissed as performances, the results of suggestion, or simply mysteries could now be reclassified under the rubric of hyperesthesia.[128] Bergson argued:

> While the operator holds a pack of cards and concentrates all his attention on the card at which he is looking, a subject in a state of hypnotism is required to guess the card. The experiment first succeeded 9 times in 14, then 8 in 27. Were all the necessary precautions taken to ensure that the subject could not see the image of the card on the operator's cornea? The same question applies for the picture experiments cited by M. Pierre Janet in his new and interesting paper of February. . . . It is by no means necessary to look directly at a picture held in one's hand for the cornea, in certain positions, to reflect the image. (531)

At first glance, Bergson's effort appeared to be aimed at deflating the pretenses of Richet's and Janet's reports. Where Richet and Janet found "unconscious deception [supercheries]" in the recent experiments made by the Society for Psychical Research, Bergson found a simpler, and now familiar, explanation: the subjects were reading the words reflected off the cornea of the operator. Despite what looked like a skeptical analysis, Bergson's real intent was to deflate the "touch of skepticism" he found in their work. Bergson answered every charge of malicious suggestion, as well as blind faith in the occult, with the truth of hyperesthesia. Although some subjects might *say* they had occult powers to see into other minds, in truth they had a fairly normal capacity to read what was actually *there,* right before their eyes, but typically beyond the range of practical perception.

What Bergson ultimately discovered was not that the hypnotized subjects had a propensity to dissimulate, but that social pressures tended to suppress naturally occurring hyperesthesia, forcing everyone to deny their real intentions. So deep was the pressure of social conformity that rather than admit these powers into consciousness, even hypnotized subjects instinctively turned them into lies. For Bergson, the whole history of conventional science was akin to an act of denial: experimental results were accountable only within a narrowly prescribed range of possibilities. Science expended its energy searching for ways to deny the truth it knew too well but could not come to terms with. Perception made skilled charlatans of us all. Bergson now concluded his account:

> Until he receives the order to perform a tour de force like mind reading, a hypnotized subject will conduct himself in complete good faith as would the least scrupulous and most adept of charlatans, he will unconsciously exercise means whose existence we barely suspect, a hyperesthesia of sight, for example, or other senses, and, unconsciously as well, we will ourselves suggest this recourse to illicit means by giving him a command that he is incapable of executing in another manner. (531)

Mind reading was simply a tour de force, a phenomenon at the extreme limit of hyperacuity, but by no means a supernatural achievement. In order to free those "means whose existence we barely suspect," society would have to lift the crushing weight of social pressure.

In our everyday lives man was forced to be a charlatan against his will. Man deceived others and himself in order to evade the responsibilities that come with acting in line with what one intends. Humankind set up rules, laws, habits, and conventions to avoid the problem of having to express what one means. Even the hypnotic operator remained a charlatan, resorting to "suggestion by illicit means," giving subjects impossible commands rather than confront the intimate truth of freedom and responsibility. It was precisely at the moment man approximated the "super-man" that he recoiled in fear, turning truth into lie, so as to avoid the terrible weight of his freedom.[129] But there was a "super-man" among us. For Bergson, the artist provided an invaluable model of freedom.

Hypnotic Agency: Bergson's Aesthetics

The opening pages of *Time and Free Will* are devoted to a detailed analysis of the nature of feelings. Bergson's aim is to distinguish between the inner and outer, or deep and superficial, emotions. After surveying a range of emotions—including desire, hope, joy, and sorrow—he turns his attention to "aesthetic feelings." Art provides the most compelling philosophical example of the difference between "intensity of feeling" and its extensive or measurable reality.[130]

Bergson begins his analysis of art with a consideration of a dancer's grace. Grace, he writes, does not communicate through the outward line and shape of the dancer's body but rather through that body's submission to "rhythm and measure." Once the rhythmic pattern has been established, the viewer feels as though he can "control" the dancer's movements, as though the dancer were an "imaginary puppet."[131] Bergson immediately complicates this idea when it becomes clear that the moment the beholder takes control of the dancer's body is the one where the beholder finds *himself possessed.* The rhythmic effect is so "irresistible" that it can take "complete possession of our thought and will."[132] So who is possessed, the dancer or the beholder? Or are both possessed by something greater than themselves, rhythmic duration itself?

Before this question gets off the ground, he offers an answer by way of a definition: the "object of art is to put to sleep the active or rather resistant powers of our personality, and thus to bring us into a state of perfect responsiveness, in which we realize the idea that is suggested to us and sympathize with the feeling that is expressed."[133] It is the *beholder* who is possessed by the artist's work. As Bergson goes on to say, the value of a work of art is a matter of the "feelings and thoughts which the artist suggests to us."[134] The artist aims to give us "a share in [his] emotion, so rich, so personal, so novel."[135] Every word of Bergson's account is driven by a vision of artistic intentionality. The artist is like a hypnotic operator lulling the beholder/patient into a trancelike state of receptiveness. Bergson continues his definition of art: "In the processes of art we shall find, in a weakened form, a refined and in some measure spiritualized version of the processes commonly used to induce the state of hypnosis."[136] Art is a "spiritualized" descendant of hypnotic suggestion. But note that it is the processes of hypnosis, rhythm and measure, that art shares and not hypnotic technique itself.

Bergson goes on to survey the arts according to their rhythmic capacities. With music, "rhythm and measure" are said to "suspend the normal flow of our sensations and ideas."[137] If the "normal flow" of our lives is dominated by automatic and nonintended behaviors—those that do not emerge from our "deep-seated self"[138]—then art is able to break up and break through those resistant layers of habit and bring us into "self-possession." That is, we must be *possessed* by the other in order to be *self-possessed.*

Bergson goes on to introduce a formula that will carry broad consequences for subsequent interpretations of Matisse. Like the rhythmic motion of the hypnotist's dangling watch, musical effects cause our "attention to swing to and fro between fixed points, and they take hold of us with such force that even the faintest imitation of a groan will suffice to fill us with the utmost sadness."[139] (How it is that music imitates a "groan" is left unclear.) Like his account in "Unconscious Simulation," Bergson's claim is not that the artist produces sensations in the beholder's mind and body, as in traditional accounts of "suggestion," but rather that those emotions are *already there* in the beholder's self but buried beneath the "normal flow" of conscious intent. As I will show, it is this sense of the *latency* of emotions within the beholder, as well as the artist's intention to evoke those effects, that is refused or neglected by Bergson commentators and entirely absent in the Bergson-inspired interpretations of Matisse. The sense that a work of art can hypnotically "cause our attention to swing to and fro" is affirmed by the Bergsonian interpreters, but that idea is stripped of its intentionalist setting, which requires both the artist's and the beholder's agency.

Bergson's survey of the arts becomes a hierarchy of media. From dance and music to poetry, sculpture, and architecture, the arts become progressively more powerful in transfixing the beholder. This transfixing power is in inverse proportion to *movement*: the more static the work of art, the more hypnotically fixed the spectator. It is a mirror relation. Beneath the static form of the work lies a vital realm of experience; beneath the beholder's conscious actions lie unconscious ones. Bergson's emphasis on the static nature of art requires that every work become an *image*. Bergson's theory of poetry, for instance, is deeply counterintuitive and speaks directly to this ocularism. Reading poetry is an act of "seeing [the poet's] images pass before our eyes." Those images are themselves the product of music, and it is by their "rhythm . . . that our soul is lulled into self-forgetfulness."[140] If we can forget our "moi superficiel," then we can remember our "moi plus profound."[141] Bergson returned to the idea in *Laughter*, with even more explicit reference to the hypnotist's watch: "By a certain arrangement of rhythm, rhyme, and assonance, it is possible to lull the imagination, to rock it to and fro between like and like with a regular see-saw motion, and thus prepare it submissively to accept the vision suggested."[142] No matter how "submissive" this reader is, the vision that is suggested must be one the reader already knows (but has suppressed). If the idea is not the reader's already, the reader's soul will remain unmoved.

Bergson reserves a special place for architecture and sculpture: the least animate media suggest the most powerful hypnotic effects. By virtue of the "fixity" that sculpture "imposes on life" it can induce the same fixity, by way of "physical contagion," on the "attention of spectator."[143] Bergson offers his most paradoxical formulation yet: the "pale immobility of the [sculpted] stone" is in direct proportion to its capacity to "absorb our thought and our will."[144] The more fixed and static the work becomes, the less likely we are to imagine we control it like an "imaginary puppet." Worse still, we seem to become the work's puppet. Of course for Bergson, when the work is truly able to pull our strings, then we are finally in a position to make ourselves free.

For this reason the "startling immobility" of architecture is granted the highest place in Bergson's hierarchy of effects. Bergson takes up the old theme of "architecture is frozen music" and makes it literal: the effects of architecture are "analogous to those of rhythm." The unity of multiplicity and sameness in the arrangement of columns (his model is the classic Greek temple) is matched by the beholder's capacity to perceptually unify repetition and difference:

> The symmetry of form, the indefinite repetition of the same motive, causes our faculty of perception to oscillate between the same and the same again, and gets rid of those customary incessant changes which in ordinary life bring us back without ceasing to the consciousness of our personality: even the faint suggestion of an idea will then be enough to make the idea fill the whole of our mind.[145]

No idea of Bergson's was more broadly influential for interpretations of Matisse than this description of how a formal rhythm "causes our faculty of perception to oscillate." These accounts suppress Bergson's fundamental commitment to freedom and intentionality. As Bergson describes it, trying to grasp the unity and difference within an architectural order sets our faculties in motion and in the process displaces those "incessant changes" of "ordinary life." Two rhythms are in competition here: ordered change and incessant change. It is the *endless temporality* of daily life—automatic behaviors and mechanical habits—that art is able to still and replace with the ordered duration of inner life.

At this point Bergson introduces a key distinction between art and nature. Art, he writes, "aims at impressing feelings on us rather than expressing them."[146] And again: "Nature confines itself to *expressing* feelings, whereas [art] *suggests* them to us."[147] What is the difference between impression and expression, art and nature? Aesthetic effects are *"suggested,"* he says, while natural effects are *"caused."*[148] What he means by "suggestion" here is relatively simple. Like the deepening layers of the "state of hypnosis," aesthetic feelings constitute a series of "distinct phases." At its limit, a work of art can affect us so deeply that it "absorbs us and completely monopolizes our soul."[149] As Bergson makes clear, one does not *evaluate* a work according to its hypnotic strength. The "merit of a work of art is not measured so much by the power with which the suggested feeling takes hold of us as by the richness of this feeling itself."[150] In other words, the meaning of the work of art is not a function of its *natural causality.* It is not the strength of the impact that matters, but the quality of the feeling it communicates. The great artist is someone who can help us "experience what he cannot make us understand."[151] And what the artist helps us to experience is the depth of *ourselves.*

To understand a work, on the other hand, is to consider it like a natural object. Meaning, on this account, is something publicly available for the viewer to read. To compose a work from borrowed elements is the very opposite of the "self-possessed" work. Imitative art, on this account, is almost criminal: "We are strangely mistaken on the role of poetic imagination if we think it pieces together its heroes out of fragments filched [morceaux empruntés] from right and left, as though it were stitching up [coudre] a harlequin's motley."[152] The artist has to look elsewhere for meaning: inside the self. Bergson explains the idea by virtue of a paradox. It was Shakespeare's "homely sort of life" that was the key to his strength. By staying at home, literally and figuratively, Shakespeare could create his characters directly, without the use of "borrowed" models. Macbeth, Hamlet, Othello, Lear *were* him, at the depths of his self. All of the characters created by the poet *"are* the poet himself, plumbing the depths of his own nature."[153] Shakespeare's immobility, like that of the cataleptic boys described in "Unconscious Simulation," and like the "pale immobility of stone" and "startling immobility" of architecture, paradoxically allowed him, by stilling his conscious intent, to broaden his sense of self to incorporate all the feelings of his characters: they were in him and they were in anyone who could connect with his or her "fundamental self."[154]

As I will argue in chapter 3, Matisse entirely shared Bergson's notion of the self, or *personnalité,* as the locus of intentionality. And like Bergson, Matisse continually thematized, pictorially and discursively, the dangers of the "influence of others" on that self. But unlike Bergson, Matisse could never dissociate sociality and independence, openness and self-sufficiency, mimesis and autonomy. And as I will now show, Matisse's Bergson-inspired interpreters dispense entirely with artistic intentionality and replace it with the encounter between paint and beholder. If for Bergson certain works of art can "cause our faculty of perception to oscillate," then that effect is valuable only insofar as it breaks down the walls of the beholder's habituated reactions and reconnects the beholder with the artist's intentions—and with his or her own. That artists and beholders have intentions, or at least ones that bear centrally on the meaning of the work of art, is something that the New Bergsonists deny.

Hypnotic Painting: Matisse and Bergson

Few claims have had a wider impact on the interpretation of Matisse's practice than Bergson's notion of rhythmic duration. Listening to music, watching a dance, or viewing a painting can induce such a state of identification that it can take "complete possession of our thought and will."[155] These rhythmic effects capture the viewer by their formal qualities alone. In what follows I will briefly establish the claims of Matisse's early Bergson-inspired interpreter, Matthew Prichard, and go on to review the dominant accounts of the relation between Matisse and Bergson since the advent of Deleuze's affect-driven philosophy. All of the Bergsonian interpretations of Matisse share a threefold commitment to anti-intentionalism, a replacement of the artist's intention with the agency of his materials, and the belief that those materials produce violent sensory effects. These texts center on the beholder's supposed traumatized affective state. The rhythmic effects of Matisse's works are said to possess, occupy, hypnotize, intoxicate, seize, touch, imprint, stun, stupefy, generate laughter, paralyze, petrify, shock, strike, disturb, blind, breach, penetrate, and induce schizophrenia and madness in the viewer. Because all of these accounts focus on the putatively physical effects of Matisse's work on the beholder outside any intentionalist framework, they deny the reader any terms for disagreement. Because "what happens to you" is not an interpretation,[156] the reader is forced to accept the terms of the argument in the way that Matisse's works are said to affect the beholder: as facts of the matter.

As early as 1910 Matisse's work was interpreted in light of Bergson's philosophy. Curator Matthew Stewart Prichard (1865–1936) arrived in Paris late in 1908 and quickly became acquainted with the Stein circle as well as with art historians Bernard Berenson and Roger Fry. Prichard first met Matisse in 1909 and became a devotee and eloquent defender of his art. In 1910 Prichard also began assiduously attending Bergson's Collège de France lectures and brought the philosopher's ideas to bear on his interpretation of Matisse's work. By all accounts, Prichard's relations with Matisse were strained. It seems Matisse resisted Prichard's efforts to read his work along Bergsonian lines. As Prichard put it early on in their meetings, "To me he quite certainly does not see the real bearing of his own work."[157] Prichard nonetheless proceeded, in a series of extraordinary letters to his friend Isabella Stewart Gardner, to formulate his Bergsonian interpretation of Matisse's art.

Prichard's claims revolve around the beholder's experience. As he puts it in a June 1912 letter to Gardner, "The subject of a picture is our action under the circumstances."[158] Prichard expresses his basic insight in another letter to Gardner:

> A Matisse painting is a *hint* to creative *action,* its seed, germ, and the determination, at the same time, of your state of mind. In Hamlet (à la Craig) the action is guided and carried through: in the Matisse painting it is started only. You are put into a boat and pushed off: the boat may stick in the mud or reeds or may reach the stream. The artist pulls the trigger, you go off or you miss fire. The result is your affair and not his. If you respond the distance you carry depends on the nature of your gun, its aim and its charge. Think of the evocative power of a Byzantine Christ on a double loaded conscience![159]

Prichard's interpretation is largely based on Bergson's claim in *Matter and Memory* that all perception is *"activity"* and "ideo-motor" by nature.[160] Matisse's works trigger the beholder's perceptual activity, but crucially one is not "carried through" by it. On one hand, Prichard seems to suggest that the meaning of the work is largely "your affair"—it depends on the "nature of your gun" and not on the artist's. On the other hand, Prichard seems to recognize that there are better or worse forms of "action" before a picture, ones more closely or distantly attuned to the artist's intent. Prichard says, for instance, that the picture loosely determines our action before the picture, that we can "reach the stream" or get stuck in the mud, and that the beholder can "go off" or "miss fire." Nonetheless, Prichard leaves it ambiguous whether reaching the stream or hitting the target is equivalent to understanding (or feeling) the artist's intention or if it is simply the affective resonance of the beholder's inner life. Above all, what makes Prichard's claims unique among Bergson interpretations is the clear distinction he draws between the work "carried through" by the artist—one automatically productive of an affective response—and the one that requires the beholder's active engagement in the task of understanding. As I will show, the dominant approach to Matisse's work, inspired by Bergson's example, is to see the works as resistant to the possibility to "miss fire."

Over the past thirty years the author most committed to a Bergsonian interpretation of Matisse's practice has been Jack Flam. In an unpublished lecture delivered at the Baltimore Museum of Art in 1976, Flam states that Bergson's *Creative Evolution* was "a book that Matisse read throughout all his life." He goes on to say, "He was reading it in 1908–09 . . . [and] he was reading it again in 1914, even at the end of his life when he was bedridden during the war he wrote a letter to Raymond Escholier . . . saying that he was reading Bergson as if for the first time."[161] Here is the actual phrase from Matisse's 1944 letter: "I spent the day reading Bergson, which I had only skimmed before at home."[162] Evidence of Matisse's broader interest in or knowledge of Bergson is scant at best. The earliest available evidence we have comes from his first trip to Tangier in 1912.[163] There is little proof that Matisse had much awareness of Bergson before this date, and there is little to suggest he read Bergson again (at least with any seriousness) before the summer of 1944. Rather than pursuing a historical link, Flam follows what I take to be a more productive route when he suggests that the "broad concepts of Bergsonism were especially in the air at the time [of the 'Notes of a Painter'], and his ideas were current not only among artists and writers but also found their way, condensed, into the popular press."[164] It is at this level of generality that the most meaningful connections can be made.[165]

In "A Vitalist Critique: Decoration and Spirituality," Catherine Bock-Weiss offers a critical survey of the long tradition of Matisse's Bergson-inspired critics.[166] She considers whether the "religious paradigm" offered by the "Byzantine/Islamic" critics—including Prichard, Duthuit, Schneider, and Labrusse—is an appropriate model for understanding Matisse's work. She approaches the problem from three sides: intention, reception, and aesthetics (167). Even though Bock-Weiss considers reception—what happens to the viewer "regardless of [Matisse's] intention"—as part of her equation, her claims ultimately turn on the artist's intent. The matter is complicated by the fact that Bock-Weiss characterizes the Bergsonian position *itself* as driven by affective response. Matisse's work, she writes, was "not perceived, but received" (162); it was understood in terms of "primary psycho-sensory reaction" rather than what the artist intended (167). In many works, Bock-Weiss suggests, mirroring the Bergsonists, "color acts directly upon the senses." And while Bock-Weiss urges that these effects are "not proper to many . . . Matisse works," she nonetheless observes how "for many viewers" his works are "simple (or complex) purveyors of visual pleasure and mood enhancement" (167). While the latter is undoubtedly true, it is hard to see how it is relevant. It does not constitute a criticism of the Bergsonists (or anyone) if one viewer claims Matisse's work enhances her mood and another says it is sublime, because neither one is making a claim about what the work means. Differing "psycho-sensory" reactions are not disagreements. But it is also clear that Bock-Weiss is not much interested in these differing reactions because her ultimate claim is about what Matisse meant by his works, regardless of how they were received. Matisse "intended his audience to enjoy the same kind of experience" he had when he painted, she explains. Bock-Weiss concludes her case against the Bergsonists by saying that without any "pressure to relate his art to religious experience, his concerns were habitually more materialist, secular, pragmatic" (168). And while I will offer a different set of conclusions in my interpretation of Matisse's practice, Bock-Weiss's claims allow for disagreement in ways many current commentators seek to avoid. It is to those anti-intentionalist critics that I turn now.

Mark Antliff has done more than any other writer to flesh out Bergson's impact on art practice in the first half of the twentieth century in Europe.[167] In "The Rhythms of Duration: Bergson and the Art of Matisse," Antliff boldly claims that "it is the thought of Henri Bergson—with its metaphysics of rhythmic duration—that is the foremost philosophical influence [on] the art of the early twentieth century, [and on] the art and art criticism of the Cubists, Futurists and Fauvists."[168] Focusing on Matisse's series of wartime portraits, Antliff describes how Matisse put himself in a state of "psychic tension" so intense he was able "to perceive the rhythmic duration" of his sitters. Citing Prichard, Antliff relates that one of Matisse's models was so open that her "being agreed to lend itself" to him. She emitted a "constant vibration . . . like a rippling lake." Once she had opened herself to the artist, Matisse proceeded to explore the recesses of her inner self: "She is a flowing stream. She is just a flame, she hangs by a thread, no point is indicated where you can grasp her" (199).[169] Antliff focuses on Matisse's portrait *Mademoiselle Yvonne Landsberg* (1914) (Figure 2.1), the "radiating lines" of which act like "rhythmic overtones." This picture, and an associated drawing, "translated [Bergson's] metaphor [of personality as a flower] into a pictorial form, drawing a generative association between Yvonne Landsberg's burgeoning sexuality, fecundity in nature, symbolized by the budding magnolia, and vibratory rhythm" (200).[170]

So far Antliff's account is compatible with any number of Bergson-type interpretations of Matisse's work that see it as expressing the densely layered nature of the self. What follows next is far different fare. While *Mademoiselle*

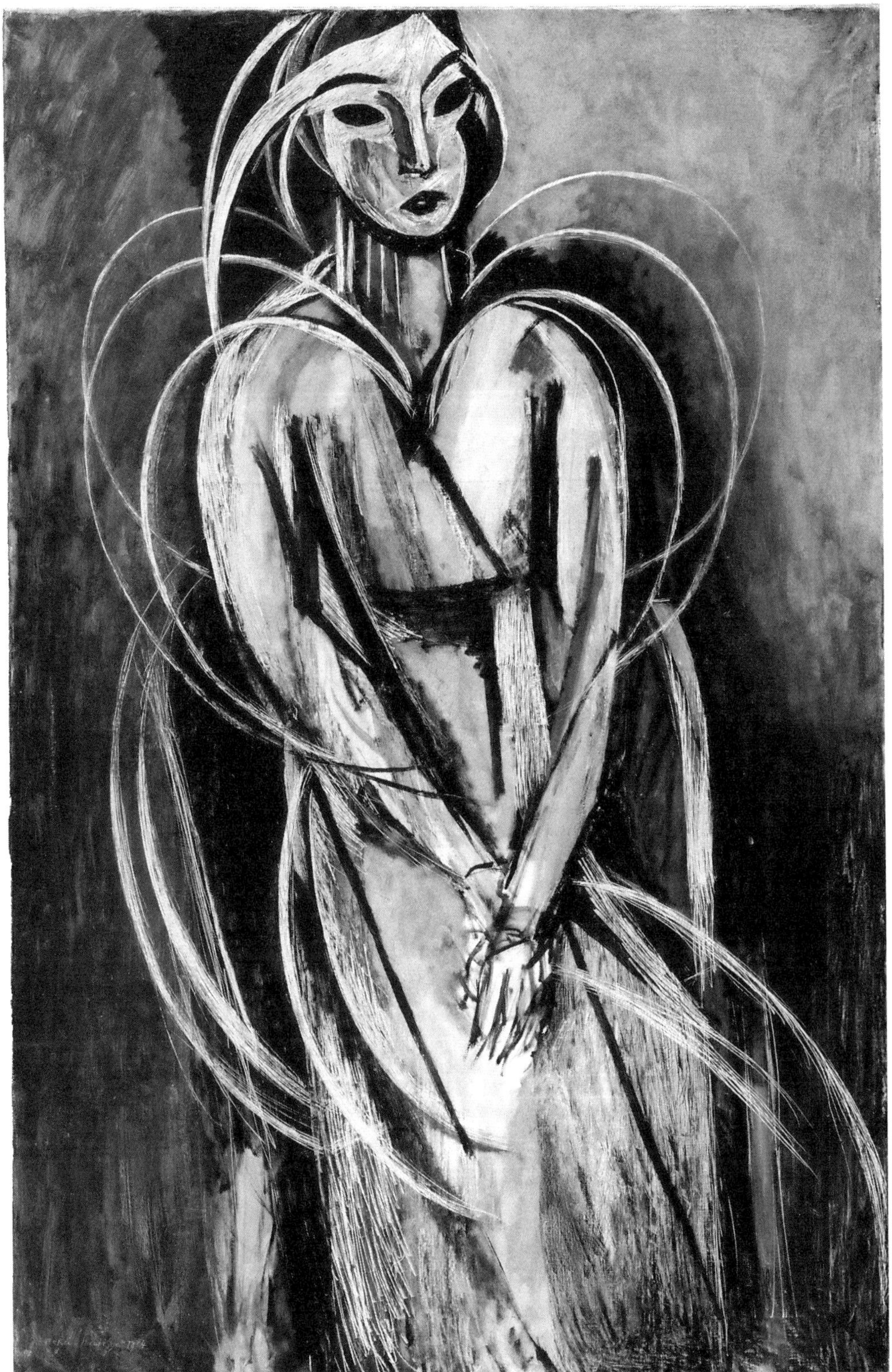

Figure 2.1. Henri Matisse (1869–1954), *Mademoiselle Yvonne Landsberg*, 1914. Oil on canvas, 58 × 38⅜ inches (147.3 × 97.5 cm). The Louise and Walter Arensberg Collection, 1950. Philadelphia Museum of Art, Philadelphia, Pennsylvania. Copyright 2013 Succession H. Matisse / Artists Rights Society (ARS), NY. Photograph courtesy of the Philadelphia Museum of Art / Art Resource, NY, ART184357.

Yvonne Landsberg embodies the "rhythmic pulsation" at the core of Landsberg's personality, it also transmits this erotic effect to the beholder. Antliff cites Prichard's observation that Matisse's drawing acts as "a conduit by means of which a certain tide of sentiment could be caused to flow in others" (201). As we have seen, for Prichard, the flow of sentiment to the beholder matters insofar as it is directed at the artist's intention (the boat, so to speak, enters into the stream). For Antliff, on the other hand, these sentiments, now construed as destabilizing, are incapable of "misfiring." According to Antliff, "*Harmony in Red* causes our attention to oscillate between volumetric depth and an unmodulated decorative surface, as if the fluctuating field of red introduced a rhythmic 'pulse' to our reading of the painting" (191). The work *causes* the beholder's attention to shift between depth and surface, inducing a violent physical sensation. If for Prichard the work is a "*hint* for creative *action*"—one that could fail to come off—for Antliff it is a machine for bodily affects that are perceptually induced.

Antliff's argument closely follows Bois's now canonical account of Matisse. The title of Bois's most comprehensive and influential study of the artist, "On Matisse: The Blinding" (1994), prepares the reader for his central claim: certain Matisse works blind their viewers.[171] This is not a metaphor. A blinding effect is produced when the "Matisse system," as Bois calls it, is "conclusively put in place." Beginning with *Harmony in Red* (Figure 1.1), Matisse's works, according to Bois, produce a "respiratory expansion" that is facilitated by the staccato rhythmic arrangement of Matisse's broad and largely uninflected surface patterns (105). The expansionary sensation is further layered with a "stroboscopic pulsation" in Matisse's most decisive formulation of his system, *Music* of 1910 (Figure 1.4). In the stark opposition between the vermilion bodies of the musicians and the blue/green ground, the work, not the artist, "exploits a contradiction in the spectator between the desire to stare (at the figures) and the desire to perceive the whole painting" (112). The spectator desires to see figure and ground together as a total instantaneous vision. *Music* frustrates that effort as it refuses to resolve into a unity in the viewer's eye.

According to Bois, the perceptual failure to resolve into a unified whole has traumatic consequences. Here is Bois (it is his most basic claim): "One can't stare at the musicians one by one or, in other words, isolate them from the visual field—the surrounding respiration of the color beckons to us—but, with the clarion call of the vermilion bodies on a green-and-blue background competing for its attention, neither can the eye come to rest in a global contemplation" (112). *Music*'s "internalized rhythm" produces an "irresolvable oscillation of our perception," what Bois calls a "hypnosis-effect" between contrary desires to stare and to look. The "spectators are hypnotized" by the swinging movements of their optical nerves (112). "This hypnosis [of the spectator]," Bois explains, "is based on a pendulum in our perception that makes us switch from our incapacity to focus on the figures to that of seizing the whole visual field at once, an oscillation that defines the very invention of Matisse's concept of the 'decorative.'"[172] It is at this point in Bois's argument that historical specificity falls away. Moreover, it is at this point that any effort to evaluate the argument, beyond recourse to ophthalmology to investigate what the eye is actually doing in front of *Music,* becomes impossible. After all, it is not an *interpretation* to say that the pendulum in one's eye is oscillating, but a (presumed) fact of the matter about human physiology. Bois seems to accept this consequence when he describes Matisse's decorative system as "a surefire means to keep the beholder's gaze moving." If the picture bears a "surefire means" of producing "*specific* effects" on its beholder, then Bois forecloses the possibility of disagreement.

In addition to the traumatic *perceptual* effects produced by key Matisse works, Bois suggests an equally traumatic *psychological* result. Matisse's paintings "affect us so much," he writes, because the "principal nodes of psychic life that psychoanalysis presents as constitutive of human beings as a species are operative" in them (100). So while the "principal nodes" of our perceptual faculties are affected by the figure/ground relation, Bois concedes that an iconographic analysis will reveal a similar effect on the level of the psyche. Writing of the black-mouthed figures in *Music,* Bois cites Freud's 1897 letter to Fliess in which he describes "hysterical cataleptic fits" that come with too close an "identification with someone who is dead" (110). While the viewer desires to see *Music* in terms of narrative continuity and secured gender identification, the picture subtly frustrates those desires. Citing Freud's study of the Medusa myth, Bois describes how the "taboo concerning the maternal genitals led to a multiplying of the snakes on Medusa's head." Bois analogizes Medusa's head, via this psychological insight, to the picture's structural organization. The oscillating eye that cannot focus on either figure or ground becomes the castrated subject who quivers in the fated effort to replace by multiplication the missing member. In Bois's words, "The interdiction on focalization . . . leads to a tension in the whole canvas in an endless quivering" (112). Because the flattened and degendered bodies in *Music* offer so little information, the viewer vainly seeks clues elsewhere by which to reconstruct the violated body.[173] But the castrated eye can never find the missing member; there is no sublimation for something that never existed.

Matisse's pictures are agents, and their (bourgeois) viewers are victims. From this perspective, the putatively hypnotic effect of Matisse's paintings does not connote a fluid interchange between subject and object, but rather an assault *from the outside* on an already constituted subject. Bois's reliance on Freud's Oedipal staging of the Medusa myth—involving the triangular relation of child-mother-father—to understand Matisse and Picasso overly sanitizes the complex story. Freud's account is based on Sándor Ferenczi's earlier study "On the Symbolism of the Head of Medusa" (1923) as well as notes from his *Clinical Diary* (1932–33). Ferenczi's model offers a radically non-Oedipal account of the Medusa myth.[174] For Freud, the Medusa myth is a story about a boy who sees the decapitated head of Medusa and must compensate for the fear this induces by becoming erect in terror, thereby consoling himself that he still possesses the penis whose lack the beheaded Medusa embodies.[175] While the boy tries to sublimate the anxiety of castration by multiplying the absent member—the multitude of quivering snakes on Medusa's head—his desire cannot be fulfilled. In contrast, Ferenczi offers a determinately *nonlibidinal, nonspecular* reading of the myth, one that, as Ruth Leys observes, "prevents us from unproblematically assimilating the mimetic scenario to a scene of conscious observation and visualization."[176] Freud's account assumes a fully constituted subject who stands *outside* the scene and looks in on it from a detached position.

Freud's short text and Bois's reading of it are saturated with visual metaphorics. Freud writes of "the sight of something," "catching sight of the female genitals," the "sight of Medusa's head makes the spectator stiff with terror," a sight that "offers consolation to the spectator" by the substitution of stiffness for the absent phallus.[177] In Ferenczi's interpretation, Perseus and Medusa never reach the specular distance necessary to achieve consolation or even a clear victim/aggressor scenario. Boy and monster are wrapped up in a co-determining mimetic encounter that provides no space of detachment, either physical or cognitive, from the scene.

Ferenczi's interpretation of the Medusa myth offers a different conception of trauma from the one described by Freud. For Ferenczi, trauma is never conceived as an event that befalls a passive victim; rather, it implies a more complex history that involves identification with the aggressor, exchange of roles, distortion, memory, and forgetting. Ferenczi's mimetic conception of trauma further suggests treatments at variance with post-Freudian models of narrative recollection. Eschewing Freud's narrative therapeutics, Ferenczi pursued techniques of hypnotic catharsis or "acting-out" with his patients, wherein the "subject" replayed the traumatic event without the requirement of cognitive mastery over it, because there was no pure traumatic material to be mastered. It is unfortunate that Ferenczi's account of traumatic experience has been almost entirely displaced by Freud's specularly driven account. It should suffice to say that traumatic accounts in the visual arts have focused almost exclusively on the externalist vision of a beholder struck, as it were physically, from the outside by the work of art.

Finally, consider Bois's related discussion of Barnett Newman's series of four paintings titled *Who's Afraid of Red, Yellow, and Blue* dating from 1966 to 1968. As mentioned earlier, Bois's account of Newman shares identical features with his account of Matisse. The two largest works of the series were vandalized in the 1980s—*III* (1966–67) "most savagely." This "disaster," Bois writes, "should perhaps not be dismissed as random lunacy (all the more since Newman's paintings have endured an unusual rate of vandalism)." That high rate of vandalism is not simply an accident. Bois asks without apparent irony whether "such a visceral, iconoclastic response was not in part encouraged by the art itself." The engulfing red of the painting, like the red in Matisse's *Harmony in Red* and *The Red Studio,* is "overwhelming: one cannot dodge its blow." "The man who knifed the painting, furiously slashing it three times across," he concludes, "could not bear the heat."[178] Newman's extraordinary pictures strike the viewer and produce their own heat. These claims are *literal*—and the only viable response to the physical blow is either to return it in kind (here by the act of cutting) or to suffer it (and presumably become a different person).[179]

A range of writers have followed Bois's claims regarding the traumatic nature of modernist paintings. In the conclusion to his aptly titled chapter "*Trouble Rétinien*: Fauvism, Madness, and the Schizophrenic Eye," Alastair Wright in his study *Matisse and the Subject of Modernism* (2004) offers a series of sweeping claims on Matisse's behalf:

> Shards of meaning cling to Matisse's pigments, and it is this that makes the work disturbing. Offering to the eye a fragmentary series of signifiers, Fauvism ruptures the sensory and hermeneutic continuity of the eye's operation, pushing into view the disarticulating operation of perception itself. The look dismantles its bearer; the eye becomes a site not of mastery, of a sovereign subject surveying its surroundings, nor of a disinterested modernist contemplation, but rather of disintegration without end. This is the eye as breach, as conduit through which the viewer is opened out onto the world and thus dismantled, unable to synthesize the sensations that cross back and forth across the troubled retina. This, which may be the condition of all vision, is what Fauvism pushes into view, pushes, in the most literal sense, into the eye of the beholder.[180]

"Pushes . . . in the most literal sense" into the eye of the beholder? Wright obviously takes "literal sense," like Bois's notion of the work "literally lodged" in the spectator's body, in a special way. And like Bois, Wright suggests that the eye is a hermeneutic instrument. How, we might ask, would one disagree with the eye's "interpretations"? Or how would one begin to evaluate Wright's sweeping claim about fauvism pushing into view the "condition of all vision"?[181]

Two recent studies have attempted to align Matisse with Bergson's great interpreter, Gilles Deleuze. In 2005 Deleuze's student Éric Alliez, along with art historian Jean-Claude Bonne, published an impressive 384-page study of the artist, *La Pensée-Matisse: Portrait de l'artiste en hyperfauve.* Alliez and Bonne reject every "territorializing" effort to understand Matisse under the terms of representation, interpretation, or meaning. "Representation in general," they write, "implies the subordination of difference to identity, of cognition to recognition." They propose an account that will "tear us away from representation."[182] Against any representational purpose, Matisse proposed a "Physiological Aesthetics" (Nietzsche) or "bio-aesthetics" (Deleuze and Guattari) where "perception becomes the deterritorialized agent of color-forces."[183] Alliez and Bonne cite Bergson's claim that for life *"there is no form,* since form is something immobile and reality is change" (57) in support of their claim about fauvism, which "calls into question the whole concept of Art construed as Form." Matisse's work, they explain, "does not close up on itself in search of an autonomy that would imply a contemplative absorption" but rather produces an *"all-around* radiation of the work beyond the frame," "eliminating every form of opposition between art and life, between the exterior and interior of the work."[184]

La Pensée-Matisse concludes with a detailed analysis of Matisse's *Jazz* of 1947. Plate 16, *Destiny,* takes on programmatic significance for the authors as it announces the arrival of the Deleuzian "body without organs." The right half of the plate is an abstract sign for an embracing couple who face their destiny at left. The destiny of the human itself is at stake. Matisse and his readers face "the *rising swell* of the biomorphic signs-colors, welling up no longer from the 'deliberate' and from 'meaning,' but from the 'instinctive' and the vital sense of 'rhythm'" (318). The rhizomatic body appears with the final three images of *Lagoons,* which are said to exclude the least remnant of representation, meaning, symbolism, or significance. And the absence of meaning seems to necessarily involve us with the presence of violence. With plate 19, the third and final *Lagoon* (Figure 2.2), "fauve color shows its claws: the signs in primary colors, red and blue, bristle, lashing out with their lobes as though administering so many punches, opening them like threatening jaws, or fingering the luminous space to take possession of it and be taken by it" (320). By a mysterious alchemy, the attacked spectator is also a productive one. Like Barthes, Alliez and Bonne insist that once the figure/author is dead, the audience/author is born. They describe the power of the "spectator-actor" to generate meaning precisely at the moment when the artist offers none. *"No image is suggested here,"* they insist, so "each viewer naturally invests these signs with whatever metaphorical movements and emotions he pleases" (320). This emotional investment is legitimate only insofar as it is founded exclusively upon *"the tactile action* of biodynamic signs-colors." Once the spectator gives up on the effort to "interpret" the picture, then can "the picture's spectator-actor *freely build up its expression*" (320). The virtue of Alliez and Bonne's account is that they pursue the logic of affective formalism to its limit. While Bois, Wright, and Antliff certainly secure their accounts on the beholder's affective-traumatic response, they nonetheless resist saying that the beholder actually generates the work's meaning. The object, that is, still plays a key role in their analyses even if the artist does not; the agency of the object stands as a substitute for the absent artist. But as Alliez and Bonne rightly insist, that is a failure of nerve. If it is not the artist's intention that is the object of the beholder's interpretation (all agree on that), then it can only be the beholder itself who defines the work's significance. Every "spectator-actor" makes his or her own work—and those works, like different bodies, embody difference without disagreement.

In his study "In Praise of Pure Violence (Matisse's War)" (2008), philosopher J. M. Bernstein further pursues a Deleuzian account of Matisse's war against representation.[185] According to Bernstein, "Matisse fully announces and institutes the program of painting that Deleuze elaborates in . . . *The Logic of Sensation.*" Bernstein begins by citing Deleuze's claim, discussed in chapter 1, that "what directly interests [the artist] is a violence that is involved only with color and line: the violence of a sensation" (42).[186] Bernstein views the encounter with Matisse's paintings as a "sensory encounter" with paint matter, a

Figure 2.2. Henri Matisse (1869–1954), *Lagoon,* from *Jazz,* 1947. Portfolio of twenty *pochoirs.* Composition of various dimensions; sheet: 16¾ × 25¹¹⁄₁₆ inches. Museum of Modern Art, New York. Published by Tériade Éditeur, Paris. Printer: Edmond Vairel and Draeger Frères, Paris. Edition: 250. Copyright 2013 Succession H. Matisse / Artists Rights Society (ARS), NY. Digital image copyright Museum of Modern Art; licensed by Scala / Art Resource, NY, ART317694.

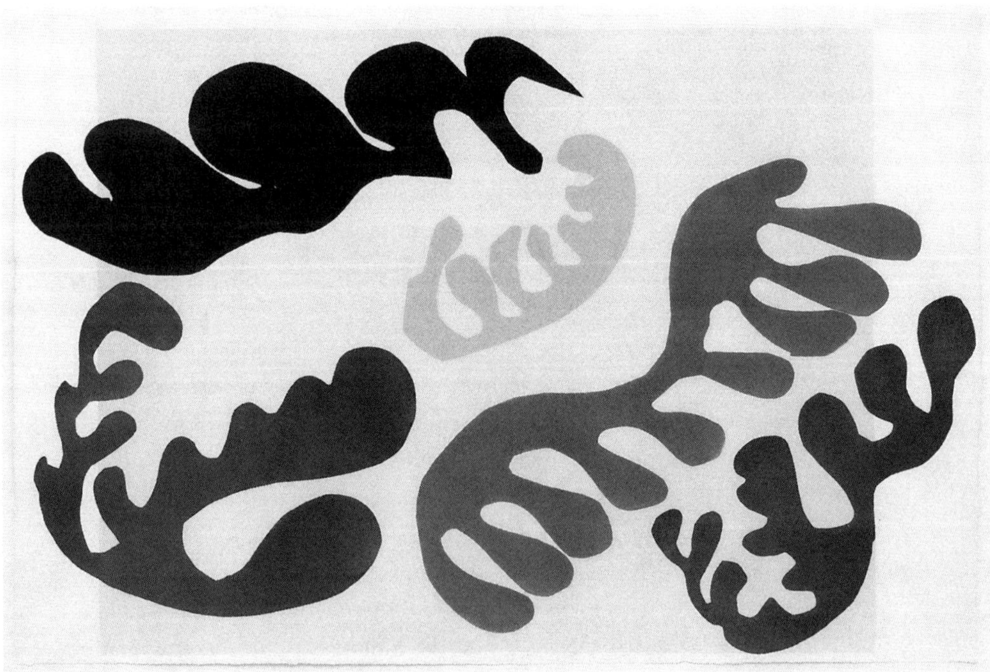

sensation "inseparable from [the work's] direct action on the nervous system" (42, 45, 49).[187] According to Bernstein, it is "representational form itself" (54) that blocks access to "a stratum or aspect of experience submerged in and repressed by ordinary cognitive engagements" (43). To represent is to do violence to the thing represented. (Bernstein does not construe the possible difference between representation and scientific disclosure.) Rather than representing violence, Matisse expresses "pre-representational structures of experience" that modernity is slowly eradicating (42). Matisse's violence against representation is done in the name of what representation has destroyed. The decorative abstraction of *The Red Studio* "liberate[s] lines and colors from their representative function" (45). Once they have been liberated, lines and colors surge into life, producing a "corporealization of the picture surface" (49). Matisse, he writes, "invents and reinvents the body without organs, a body that could be identical with the flow of lines inscribing it" (51). This pictorial body confronts the actual body standing before it. To properly recognize the pictorial totality that modernity refuses us in our lives, one must "blind" one's "understanding eye" and undergo the "dis-orienting barrage of sensation that can be suffered but not claimed" (53). Unlike Bois, Wright, and Alliez and Bonne, Bernstein understands Matisse's categorical violence against the figure as bearing a cognitive result. Matisse's pursuit of "overallness," Bernstein explains, "is the restitution of the claim of embodiment out of its social—and art-historical—destitution, the war upon its normative authority in urban, industrial society" (54). The threatened and dismembered body of modern experience is given affective embodiment in Matisse's supercharged surfaces. The violence of the picture is a mimetic reflection of the violence of the world that produced it. Matisse's violence is a paradoxical last-ditch effort at restoring the violated body. It is only by "blinding vision," Bernstein concludes (citing Bois), that "the claims of color and line can be restituted, and with them, finally, the authority of the fragile and harassed human body."

In her response to Bernstein, Judith Butler concisely sums up his and Deleuze's claims: "To the extent that the means of representation—paint and line . . . —are what act upon the nervous system . . . they do so not at the expense of representation itself, but explicitly *against* representation."[188] But as she also shows, there is a tension in Bernstein's account between his claim about affect and his claim about meaning. There is a tension, that is, between two "bodies without organs": the picture's body versus the viewer's. If the "canvas is fully corporealized," if the picture is given the kind of fullness modernity tends to eradicate, then what is the status of the "body before and outside the canvas?" (60). Butler rightly sees the problem in identifying Matisse's claims about autonomy with Deleuze's claim about the "body without organs." Matisse, she says, confronts Deleuze: "If we were to accept Matisse's claim that the surface is completely self-referential, then we seem no longer to be able to refer to the body outside and before the surface that is reacting and responding to what it sees there" (61). If we are to have that body back, she insists, "we must reject Matisse to return to Deleuze" (61). Pictorial autonomy can only be at the expense of the beholder's autonomy, and Matisse's lively surfaces "cannot save us from the moment when we have to look away to another landscape" (62). Butler asks us to look away from art and look again toward the world. Art's fragile autonomy is exchanged for the limitlessness of experience. And nothing can save us from that.

Looking back over the one hundred–year history of Bergson-inspired interpretations of Matisse, one sees the major shift that occurred from accounts centered on what the artist may have intended to the so-called agency of the picture. And if Bergson could not conceive of the artistic encounter as anything but the beholder's responsiveness to an artist's intentions, then the New Bergsonists retain the interpretive setup but make the object (lines, colors, and marks), rather than the artist, the site of the work's meaning. But then again, it is hard to see how what one does with an object is to either understand it or interpret it. It is the virtue of writers such as Alliez and Bonne to have seen the flaw, the incoherence, of any anti-intentionalist account that retained a notion of agency beyond the viewer's own. So while Alliez and Bonne still speak of Matisse's works as "forces," their real concern is with how those forces stimulate the viewer into becoming a creator. If Prichard worried that Matisse's "ideo-motor" fields of color might misfire—might produce a free field for the viewer's affective response—then Alliez and Bonne's worry is that Matisse's viewers might mistakenly imagine there was something he was aiming at in the first place.

THREE

The Influence of Others
Matisse and Personnalité

> I said to her, "Follow my example; force yourself, above all, to develop personality."
>
> —Paul Cézanne to Ambroise Vollard

> Every artist has been influenced by others and shows traces of that influence in his works; but his significance for us is nothing but *his* personality.
>
> —Ludwig Wittgenstein, *Culture and Value*

"GENIUS IS THE POWER OF RESISTANCE AGAINST THE ENEMY," Matisse told Louis Aragon.[1] This idea may strike a disagreeable note for many readers. Despite our unease with it, this attitude is deeply characteristic of Matisse's approach. Matisse, like Bergson, defined the artist as someone with "sufficient self-mastery to follow his own discipline," a view his official biographer called the "best summation" of his art and life.[2] While the idea of genius as a personal power seems unsustainable, it is more complex than it might first appear. First, Matisse introduced the idea as something "an artist once told me." That is, the expression of self-mastery was articulated through the words of another. Second, the definition of genius was "incomplete" if it imagined a self as complete in itself.[3] As Matisse well knew, a pure self-legislating noumenal subject is "incomplete" without a moment of alienation or self-exposure to the other. The problem is to say how much or how little, how centrally or how minimally, how ratified or how passively assumed? So while Matisse continually insisted that his "certitudes are internal," he just as insistently framed independence *relationally,* in terms of what he called "the influence of other personalities."[4] It is this conflictual attitude—at once independent and imitative, singular and social—that defines the basic modality of his discursive and artistic practice. Moreover, if we are accustomed to seeing the modern artist as someone who forces a separation between his art and his life, separating aesthetics from ethics, then Matisse will not satisfy that desire. To make a picture, for Matisse, was to make and to give expression to a self. But to make a work or create a self—to achieve *autonomy*—was also an effort to establish a connection with the other, one that did not deny the other's difference. Matisse could describe his pursuit of connection—"what is most important is the relationship [les rapports] between things" (89/103)—just as intensely as his effort to preserve difference: "I paint only the differences [les différences] between things" (285). To capture relation with difference, identity with separateness, was to understand picture making as well as what it took to make a self.

Matisse's commitment to self-expression—"What I am after, above all, is expression," he declared in his "Notes of a Painter" (37/42), and the "great thing is to express one's self" (68)—makes his commitment to others much harder to construe. Matisse's continual stress on personal and pictorial autonomy—along with a related set of ideas about independence, individuality, freedom, and self-expression—seemed to leave little room for the existence of others. "He was like a doctor," Lydia Delectorskaya said, he was "completely bound up in himself and his concerns."[5] Georges Duthuit observed that Matisse's "perspective was that of *ego maximus*" in which "'others'" have no share. Duthuit's quotes around "others" suggest how limited and indirect the existence of others was for the artist.[6] "I only take interest in myself," Matisse told Jane Bussy. Bussy repeated the phrase in French—"Je ne m'intéresse qu'à moi!"—to stress the point.[7] And despite the long history of Bergson-inspired efforts to affirm Matisse's commitment to change and becoming, some of Matisse's closest friends and supporters found the opposite at work: "Matisse's fundamental belief is that there is no such thing as essential change. Appearances change, men learn certain things . . . but the man is the same, and it is the man that counts."[8] As unsustainable as this conclusion may be, it speaks directly to Matisse's emphatic pursuit of personal and pictorial autonomy.

What emerges from an examination of Matisse's art and writings is a distinctly philosophical attitude: skepticism. Personal expression seemed to require a denial of "other minds."[9] Less an account of artistic psychology, this denial signifies Matisse's relation with artists, models, objects (including his own body or self), and, most centrally, his medium. The effort here is to imagine the work of art's *meaning* as autonomous, that is, to see it as immune to any responses not the artist's own. Simply put, autonomy will be defined as the spectator's irrelevance to the meaning of the work of art, what Michel Puy described as Matisse's lifelong "disdain of accommodating himself to the spectator's imagination."[10] Matisse's skeptical modernism posited the work of art as something that bears meaning irrespective of any particular viewer's correct or incorrect interpretation of that meaning.[11]

Matisse's skepticism befitted a painter who felt claustrophobic in a culture crowded with Manet, Monet, Seurat, Gauguin, van Gogh, and, above all,

Cézanne. Between the years 1895 and 1905 Matisse tried in picture after picture to inhabit these separate voices and ultimately to make them his own. Escholier described the problem clearly: "Various influences have contributed to the formation of this so 'independent' master! From El Greco to Cézanne, from Turner to Gustave Moreau, from Renoir and Claude Monet to Odilon Redon, to Seurat, and to Signac, it is impossible to count the number of artists who have made an impression on the young Henri Matisse."[12] It is hard to see exactly what role Escholier's scare quotes around "independent" play here. Escholier went on to cite Matisse's friend Marcel Sembat in his defense (Matisse apparently still needed defending in 1937): "Good Lord! He did not create all alone!" Sembat declared. "Of course he looked at Cézanne, Signac and Monet, he looked at Odilon Redon." Accusations of copying haunted Matisse throughout his career, and Sembat raised the issue in order to defeat it: "Copyist? Never! Impossible! If he was stirred by the great discoverers, it was only to gain clarity through their light."[13] Sembat's defense was classically tautological: Matisse saw through the light of others more deeply into himself.[14] But Sembat's commentary raises the crucial problem of citation in Matisse's work, that somehow the basic terms of Matisse's works were derived from others, as though a work was not his unless its elements had been already expressed by another.

Matisse's early critics frequently remarked on his capacity to switch styles from picture to picture, as though he had no personality, no style, of his own. One characteristic criticism lamented Matisse's "inconsistency and a *lack of personality,* the chameleonlike versatility with which he imitated the masters."[15] Louis Vauxcelles described Matisse's work as an "ensemble of supple diversity": "Today he is quite close to Cézanne. To Moreau and Cézanne, with a stop at Signac."[16] "Matisse is by no means the innovator he is taken for," wrote a Russian critic. "His work is a synthesis of Cézanne, Signac, the early Italians, Etruscan vases, and the ancient Greek archaics, rearranged in a popular fashion to suit the modern public. . . . He is almost an academic."[17] Picasso noted how "critics are always talking about this and that influence on Matisse's work" to the extent that were blind to his originality.[18] In the eyes of some critics, Matisse was pathological in his susceptibility to influence. But for Matisse inconsistency and versatility, diversity and mimicry, were paradoxical routes to autonomy.

In his writings Matisse described the problem of other minds as the problem of the "influence of others" (29/56), a topic I consider at length below. But it was pictorially that Matisse expressed his deepest skeptical impulses. Skepticism emerged as an aesthetic concern through figurative modes of facingness, formal and thematic patterns of frontality (early on exemplified by portrait-like vertical formats), as though to wall the beholder off from the space of the picture. Moreover, his insistent attention to the conventions and artifice of the studio setting, as though the studio constituted the artist's primordial or "natural" setting, suggested a world at one remove from the social.

Nonetheless, as I have been suggesting, Matisse's skepticism was far from unified and was often coded as undesirable, even if necessary. Pictorially, the limits of skepticism were registered by breaks, gaps, and openings in the visual continuum that offered a provisional place of contact for the beholder (or for the artist as the work's first beholder). This contact sometimes emerged through the use of internal framing mechanisms such as mirrored self-portraits (I will consider a range of these) or through the inclusion or citation of his own work within his work.

It is a surprising fact of the literature on Matisse that the sense of the work's intense continuity with the beholder, as though one is directly connected with the work or the artist's mental space, prevails over what I take to be the artist's stronger, but far from absolute, impulse toward imagery and expressions of separation, detachment, observation, and control.[19] My brief review of the contemporary literature on Matisse and Bergson in chapter 2 bears out the view that antirepresentational or literalist ideals of *merger* or *affectivity* between paint and beholder have all but effaced crucial issues of severance, separateness, and detachment (what I am calling more generally skepticism) that Matisse insisted on preserving and making salient to the beholder. Although I aim to provide terms for this initial sense of Matisse's work as an independent "world" standing over and against the viewer, I do not intend to deny the equally strong, but perhaps less insistent, sense of continuity felt by the viewer standing before the work, a nonliteralist sense of connection that preserves a sense of difference.[20]

As I have already suggested, philosophical skepticism is a theme closely linked with the modernist problem of autonomy. As Matisse made clear, his ambition was to establish his works as autonomous, to achieve a "totality that constitute[s] a *tableau*" (42/51). While his works attempted to express complex and changing emotional states, the results would be anything but changing. No matter how layered the works' surfaces, he continually described his works as the achievement of "definitive conclusions and precise signs." He spoke of following a "personal logic . . . from one state to another toward conclusive and definitive results."[21] This autonomous state was conceived in two contrasting modes. On one hand, autonomy was understood as a fully expressive representation, as the artist's "condensation of sensations" about the world (38/43). On the other hand, autonomy captured his sense of the work of art as a "sign" existing outside the self, possessing an authority or agency the artist felt was not entirely of his making.[22] Although both sides of autonomy are consistently figured in Matisse's work, my discussion in this chapter bears on three problems or moments in his practice that bring the issue of autonomy into focus.

First, I consider the skeptical tenor of Matisse's discursive claims as an effort to *force* the terms of artistic and personal autonomy. Skepticism emerges here in terms of his simultaneous resistance and attraction to the contemporary discourse of hypnosis. In the most basic terms, hypnosis seemed to threaten constitutive assumptions about the nature of the self. Hypnosis pointed to a silent bond with the other that suggested that the self was porous to the world around it. This connection was something Matisse refused but also sought to reestablish on less passive grounds.

Second, I examine an early figure type of the frontally disposed standing or seated nude in the studio that Matisse made in response to Cézanne's late work as well as a related set of studio-based works that situate the artist in the space of the picture. Both the standing figure type and the "self-portrait" works set up a basic pictorial structure that Matisse articulated throughout his career.

Third, I examine Matisse's complex account of subjectivity, what he repeatedly called his *personnalité,* in terms of the problem of citation, exemplified by a remarkable and little-discussed 1903 sequence of costume pictures inspired by Manet's citational practice.

These three interlocked elements—hypnosis, self-portraiture, and citation—help to define Matisse's notion of personal and pictorial autonomy. The balance of discussion in this chapter falls on the work produced in the years 1900 to 1905 in order to establish what I take to be the basic aesthetic and philosophical parameters of his artistic enterprise as a whole. Chapter 4 continues this discussion but broadens the time frame substantially to include works spanning the period 1895 to 1917.

The Hypnotic Encounter

"He is one of the best mimics I know," Jane Bussy says of Matisse in her ironically titled memoir of his life "A Great Man" of 1947. He could imitate people "with an extreme economy of means; a look, an intonation is enough to conjure up a person." "He missed his vocation," Bussy quotes her mother, Dorothy, as saying, "he should have been an actor." All teasing aside, Matisse seems to have taken Bussy's remarks "with complete seriousness."[23] From the beginning Matisse signaled the dramatic, even staged quality of his practice—scenes of actors, self-conscious models, and artworks frequently situated within studio or domestic spaces appeared over and over again—as though to underline the social, cultural, and historical setting, if not the limits, of his project.

Bussy identifies Matisse's mimetic skills with his artistic economy, his ability to conjure up figures, even complex states of mind and emotion, with little more than a few strokes or bands of color. Matisse propounded this economic ideal in his "Notes of a Painter": "Everything that is not of utility to the *tableau* is harmful." He went on: "A work of art must be harmonious in its entirety: every superfluous detail takes the place of another essential detail in the mind of the spectator" (38/43).[24] In Matisse's view, a poor actor is one who distracts the audience's attention with extraneous, inessential details: if a look is held too long, if an intonation wavers, the effect invariably collapses. The consummate actor is one who imposes on himself a strict regime of exclusion, sacrificing everything to the immediacy of his response in order to seize and hold the spectator's attention.

This dramatic impulse is strongly Diderotian in tenor.[25] According to the great French critic, a composition cannot afford "any idle figure, any superfluous accessory. The object must be one." The artist must have the audacity to eliminate inessentials in the name of producing a unified effect. "When one has the courage to sacrifice those compelling episodes, one is truly a great master, a man of profound judgment," he wrote.[26] Matisse, of course, tested Diderot's claims. How much of the familiar world could one sacrifice and still hold the viewer's attention? How few "compelling episodes" could a work contain and still possess unity? How far could line and color depart from the model and still retain expressive force? (Like Diderot, Matisse knew there *was* a limit, and he never dispensed with "episodes" *tout court.*) For Matisse, the expressive hold of the picture stood in some fragile proportion with its elimination of familiar subject and detail. It was the crucial difference, as he described it, between "premature synthesis"—a work "without density," "ephemeral and momentary"—and complete "synthesis."[27] Matisse characterized the fully realized *tableau* as *hypnotic* in its grip on the beholder: "I want to characterize, eliminating what is not essential and what is therefore detrimental to the hypnotic power of the image."[28]

Matisse's identification of the work with hypnotic effects was paradigmatic for the artist, and according to Bussy it had a strong autobiographical dimension. After lauding Matisse's imitative skills, Bussy steers her reader in a different direction. She tells a story told to her by the artist about his encounter as a child with a traveling hypnotist:

> The hypnotizer mesmerized all the school children, suggesting to them that they were out of doors by the side of a stream with flowers growing all round; they would stoop to pick the flowers, they would try to drink the water, so powerful was the hypnotic suggestion. When it came to him, however, just as he was beginning to fall under the spell, something seemed to snap and through the grass and the stream he saw the carpet on the floor. "No," he cried, "I can see the carpet!" And after that the hypnotizer could do nothing more to him. That incident became a symbol to him in after life. However far fantasy might lead him, he never lost sight of the floor.[29]

Tempting as the hypnotist's suggestions must have been, "something" snapped him out of it at the last moment. The floor beneath the hypnotist's feet pierced through the alluring scene of grass and stream, breaking the mesmerizing spell. Or almost. It was the carpet under the operator's feet that broke the spell. That is, *art*, not nature, supported the operator's illusions.

According to Schneider, Matisse frequently told this story to guests. But why did it bear repeating? What was at stake that made it a "symbol" for his life, as Bussy indicates? Then again, what was the "something" that saved him at the last moment from going under the spell? Why was he the only one among all the schoolchildren to resist the operator's suggestions? And what about this childhood game provoked in Matisse such a strong need to debunk it?

The peculiar idiom of hypnotism and mimicry, openness and mastery, recurs again and again in Matisse's writings, posing an insistent and unresolved problem. In the text that accompanies *Jazz* (1947), for instance, Matisse reimagines the hypnotic encounter and arrives at a similar conclusion. An unnamed interlocutor asks the artist whether he believes in God. "Yes," he replies, "when I work." He continues:

> When I am submissive and modest I sense myself helped immensely by someone who makes me do things that surpass myself. However, I feel no gratitude toward *him* because it is as if I found before me a prestidigitator whose tricks I cannot pierce through. I then find myself frustrated of the profit of the experience that should be the reward for my effort. I am ungrateful without remorse. (173/238)

God, in this impious story, is the great hypnotist. But in this version of the hypnotic episode the artist is unable to "pierce through" the operator's "tricks." Despite his efforts to break the spell, he is left feeling a dupe. Matisse was not satisfied to play the role of an actor following the commands of an unseen director.[30]

Matisse's resistance to the claims of hypnotic suggestion placed him in good company. Freud, at nearly the same moment, described hypnosis as a sophisticated game, something every subject could (and should) resist. And because it was ultimately a game, it could not pose any real threat to the self. Freud considered the matter in his study of group psychology:

> As we know from other reactions, individuals have preserved a variable degree of personal aptitude for reviving old situations of the kind discovered under hypnosis. Some knowledge that in spite of everything hypnosis is only a game, a deceptive renewal of these old impressions, may however remain behind and take care that there is a resistance against any too serious consequences of the suspension of the will in hypnosis.[31]

Without this innate resistance to the suspension of the will, the self was in danger of being shaped and formed by suggestions from the other. For Freud this threat was serious, and, as recent commentators have argued, it effectively defined the difference between psychoanalytic practice and the "magic" of suggestion. Nonetheless, Freud found it impossible to purge psychoanalysis completely of a guilty association with hypnosis.[32] Similarly for Matisse, the lure of influence—of artists, models, objects, his own body—both threatened and animated his deepest commitments to autonomy.

What is striking about Matisse's discursive practice is the way in which the hypnotic episode is repeatedly replayed under the sign of influence. In his first public statement, an interview with Guillaume Apollinaire in 1907, the discussion turned repeatedly on the problem of personality and influence. "I have never avoided the influence of others," he explained. The artist's "personality develops and asserts itself through the struggles . . . against other personalities" (29/56). The first remark suggests one has a clear choice to avoid or accept influences. How does one *decide* when and where influence begins and ends? From where does the decision come? And what is the relation between development and assertion, ideas that seem to move in contrary directions? Development describes, at least minimally, a social relation, while assertion marks selfhood as something resistant to change from without. In *Jazz* Matisse made a more decisive claim: "I have accepted influences but I think I have always known how to dominate them." The "servant," he concluded, "must not become the mistress" (172/237).[33] To be sure, influence was coded, and in this instance it connoted passivity, femininity, and class position. But the influence here was *not* the other, but himself—he was describing a relation to his body.[34] He needed to control his hand so that it would not control him by performing inexpressive gestures (a problem explored at length by Bergson). Controlling himself, like controlling others, was an effort to ensure the *significance* of his marks, to certify they were fully meant, not just casually assumed. In *Degas, danse, dessin* (a book well-known to Matisse), Paul Valéry considered a similar idea: "To ensure the freedom of drawing, so that the draftsman can carry out his will, he must suppress those local autonomies [of his muscles]. The question is one of control."[35] Matisse's effort to "carry out his will" required the active suppression of any influence not fully felt as his own, including that of his muscles. To control bodily "autonomies"—his own or those of others—was an effort to secure a pictorial autonomy.

Variants on the hypnotic episode appear in the early criticisms of Matisse's practice. Duthuit, for instance, reflected on those "moments of panic" in Matisse's work after which Matisse had to "stop . . . to strike the ground and assure himself of its presence."[36] For Duthuit, Matisse's panic was induced primarily by his own formal innovations. Matisse felt compelled to fall back into the arms of realism as though the threat of abstraction loomed too large to take (Duthuit, like others, saw Matisse's Nice-period work as a protracted panic formation). Panic moments, Duthuit declared, produce "bastard pictures." Like Odysseus resisting the Sirens' song—"the rock, the divan, the car-

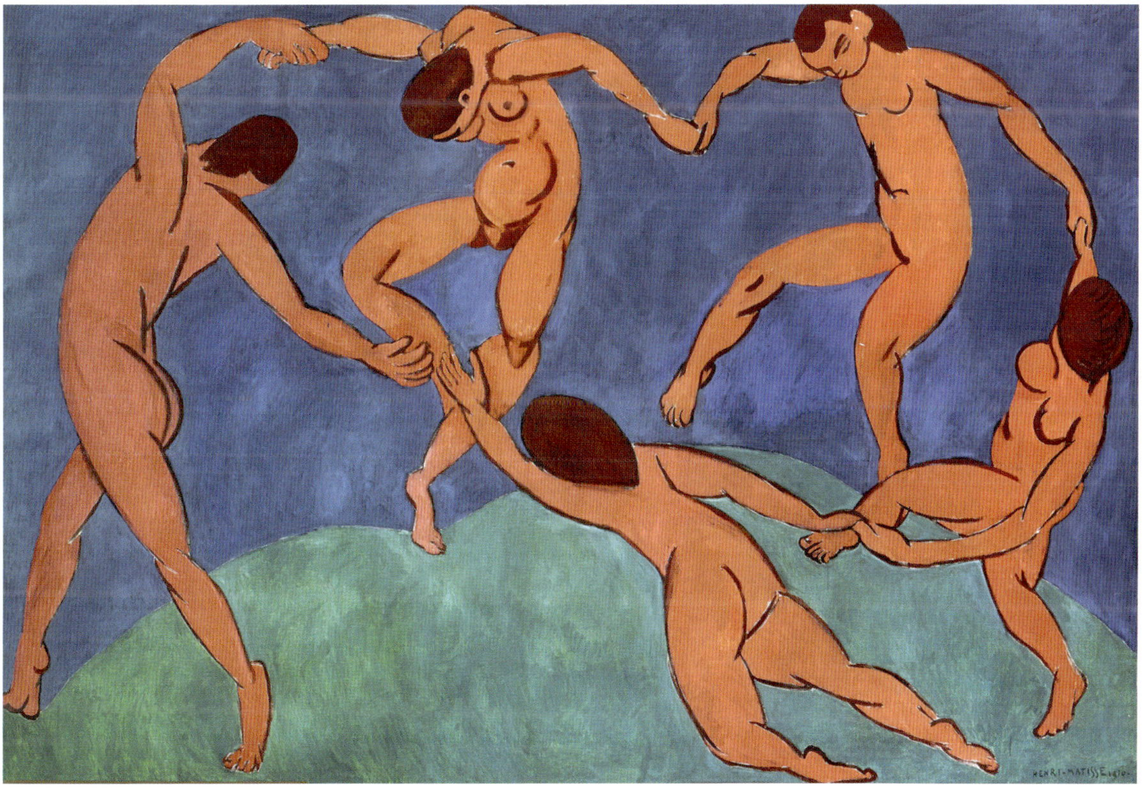

Plate 1. Henri Matisse (1869–1954), *The Dance (II),* 1910. Oil on canvas, 260 × 391 cm. State Hermitage Museum, St. Petersburg, Russia. Copyright 2013 Succession H. Matisse / Artists Rights Society (ARS), NY.

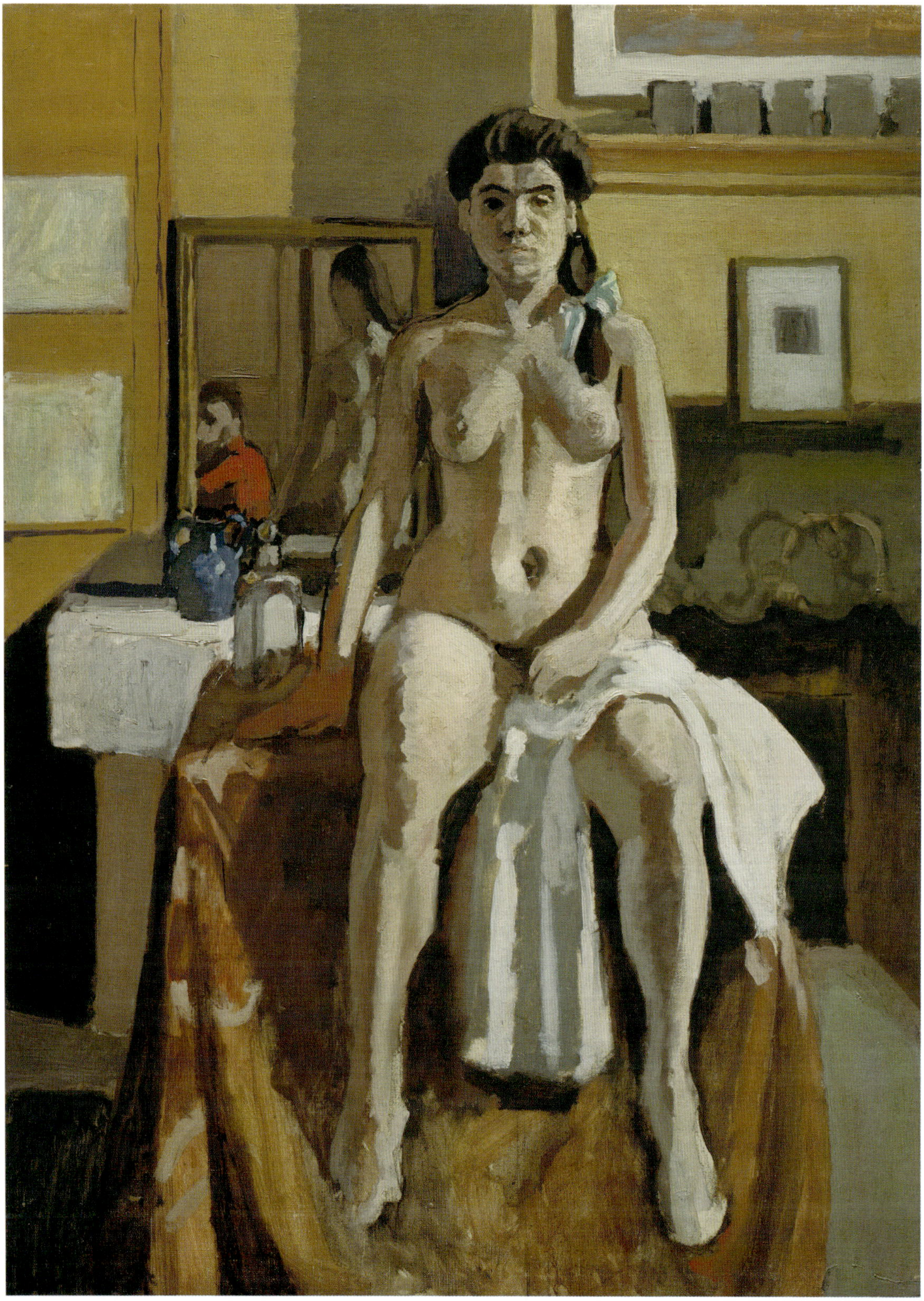

Plate 2. Henri Matisse (1869–1954), *Carmelina,* ca. 1903. Oil on canvas, 32 × 23¼ inches (81.3 × 59 cm). Tompkins Collection—Arthur Gordon Tompkins Fund, Museum of Fine Arts, Boston. Copyright 2013 Succession H. Matisse / Artists Rights Society (ARS), NY.

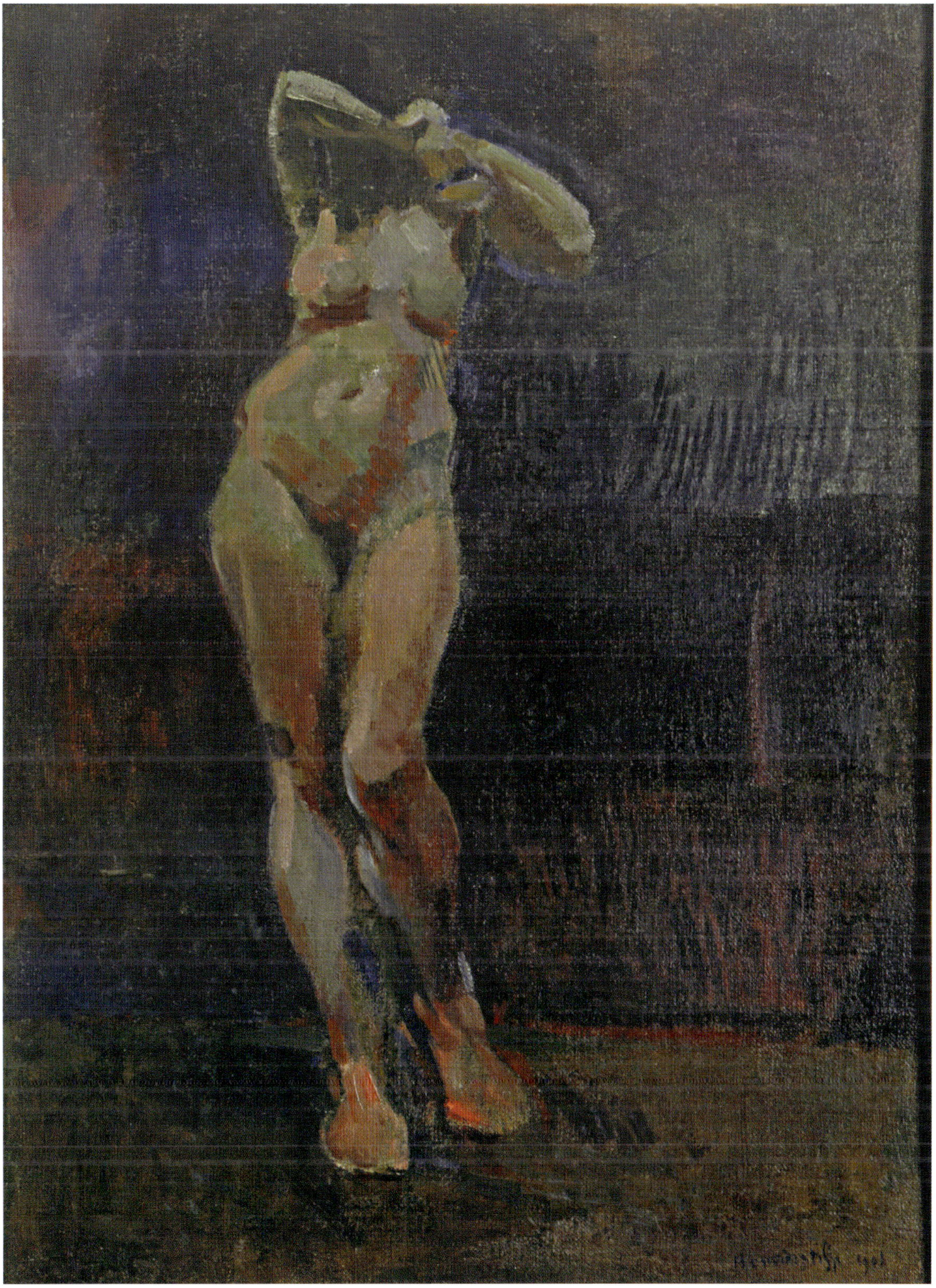

Plate 3. Henri Matisse (1869–1954), *Standing Nude (Study in Blue)*, ca. 1901. Oil on canvas, 80 × 59 cm. Private collection. Copyright 2013 Succession H. Matisse / Artists Rights Society (ARS), NY. Photograph courtesy of Archives Henri Matisse.

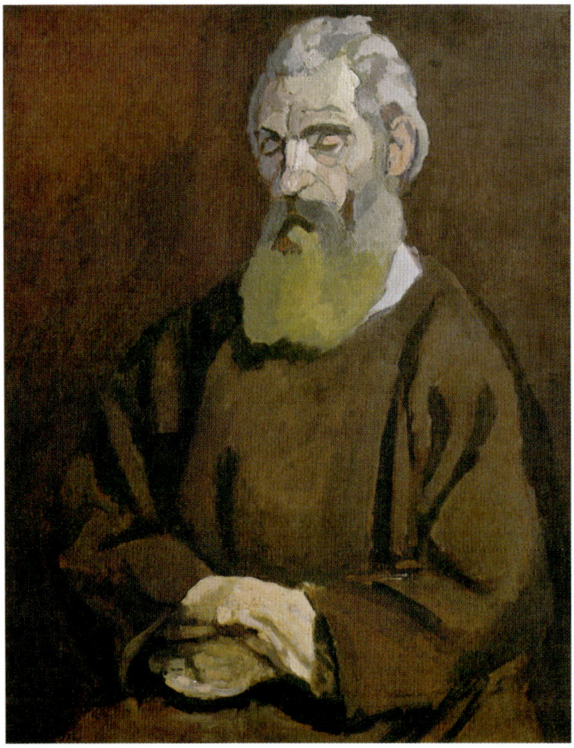

Plate 4. Henri Matisse (1869–1954), *The Monk,* 1903. Oil on canvas, 81 × 65 cm. Private collection. Copyright 2013 Succession H. Matisse / Artists Rights Society (ARS), NY.

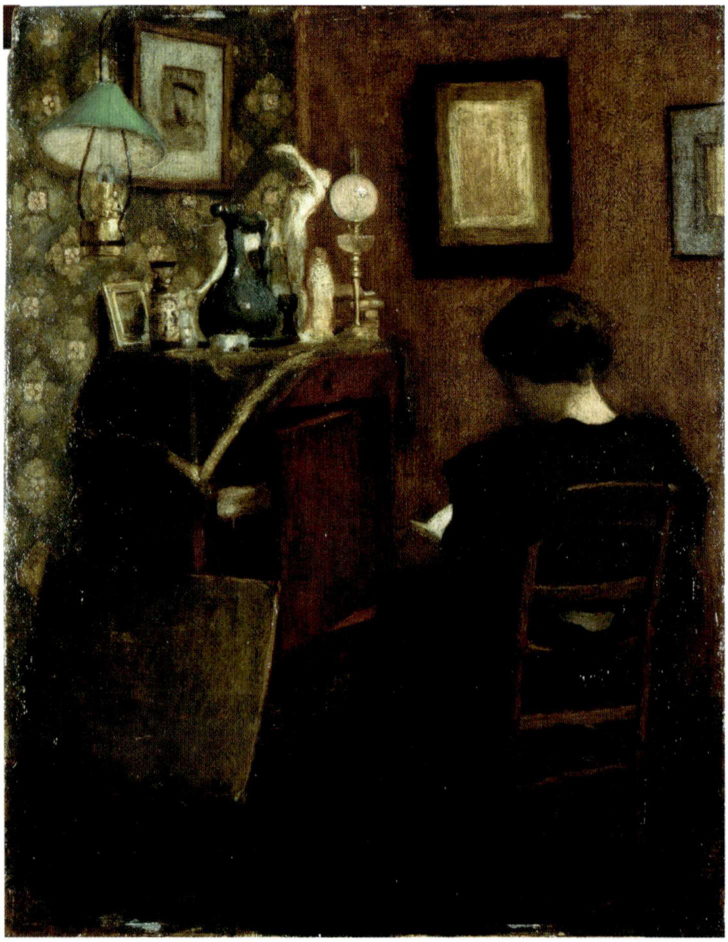

Plate 5. Henri Matisse (1869–1954), *Woman Reading,* winter 1895. Oil on wooden panel, 61.5 × 48 cm. Musée National d'Art Moderne, Centre Georges Pompidou, Paris, France. Copyright 2013 Succession H. Matisse / Artists Rights Society (ARS), NY. Photograph by Jacqueline Hyde. Photograph courtesy of CNAC/MNAM/Dist. Réunion des Musées Nationaux / Art Resource, NY.

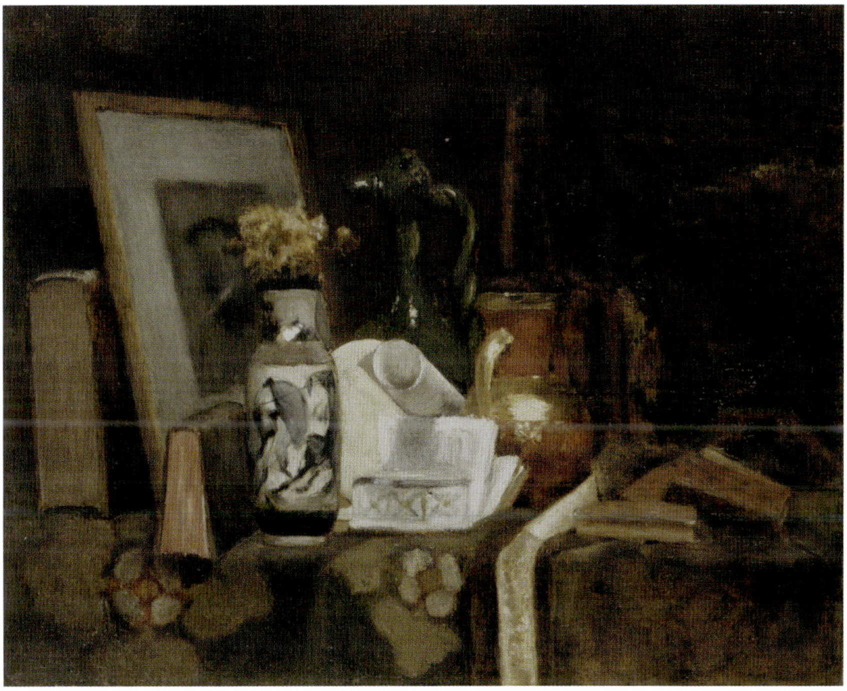

Plate 6. Henri Matisse (1869–1954), *Still Life with Self-Portrait*, 1895. Oil on canvas, 64.8 × 81.3 cm. Columbus Museum of Art, Ohio, gift of Howard D. and Babette L. Sirak, the Donors to the Campaign for Enduring Excellence, and the Derby Fund. Copyright 2013 Succession H. Matisse / Artists Rights Society (ARS), NY.

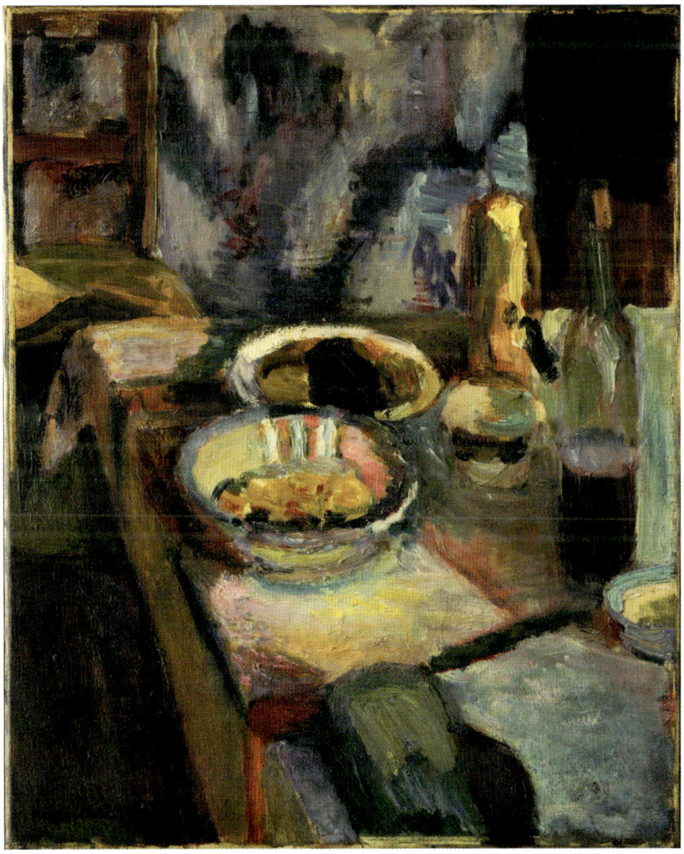

Plate 7. Henri Matisse (1869–1954), *Still Life*, early 1899. Oil on canvas, 18⅛ × 15 inches (46 × 38.1 cm). Gift of A. Conger Goodyear, Museum of Modern Art, New York. Copyright 2013 Succession H. Matisse / Artists Rights Society (ARS), NY. Digital image copyright Museum of Modern Art; licensed by Scala / Art Resource, NY, ART413325.

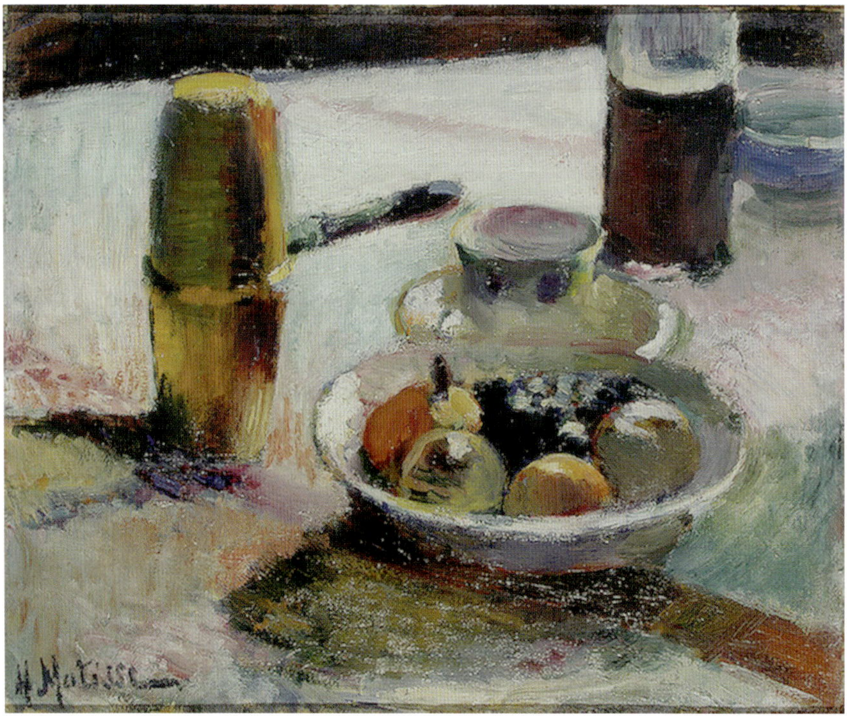

Plate 8. Henri Matisse (1869–1954), *Fruit and Coffee Pot,* 1899. Oil on canvas, 38.5 × 46.5 cm. State Hermitage Museum, St. Petersburg, Russia. Copyright 2013 Succession H. Matisse / Artists Rights Society (ARS), NY.

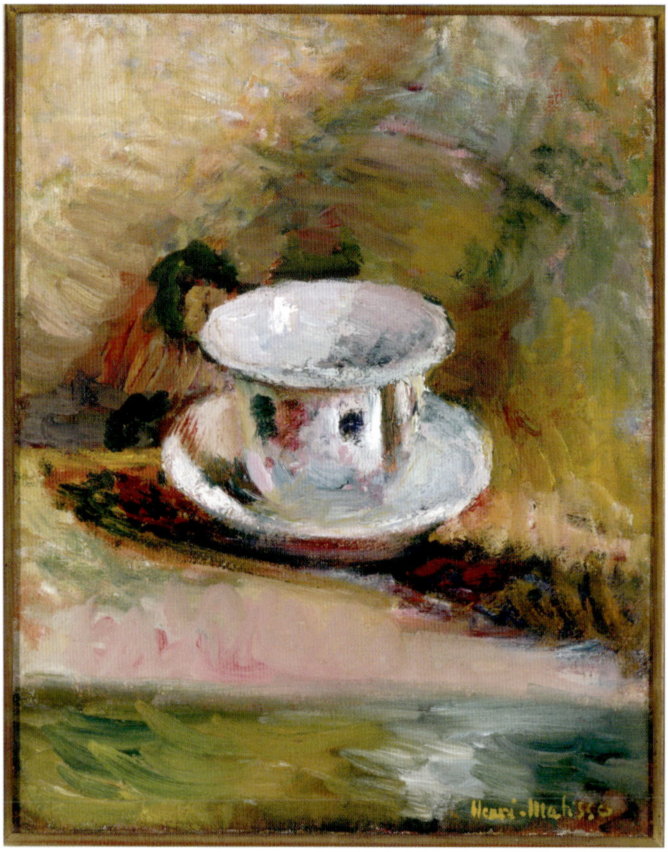

Plate 9. Henri Matisse (1869–1954), *Café Table,* 1899. Oil on canvas, 16 × 12⅞ inches (40.64 × 32.7 cm). San Francisco Museum of Modern Art, bequest of Harriet Lane Levy. Copyright 2013 Succession H. Matisse / Artists Rights Society (ARS), NY.

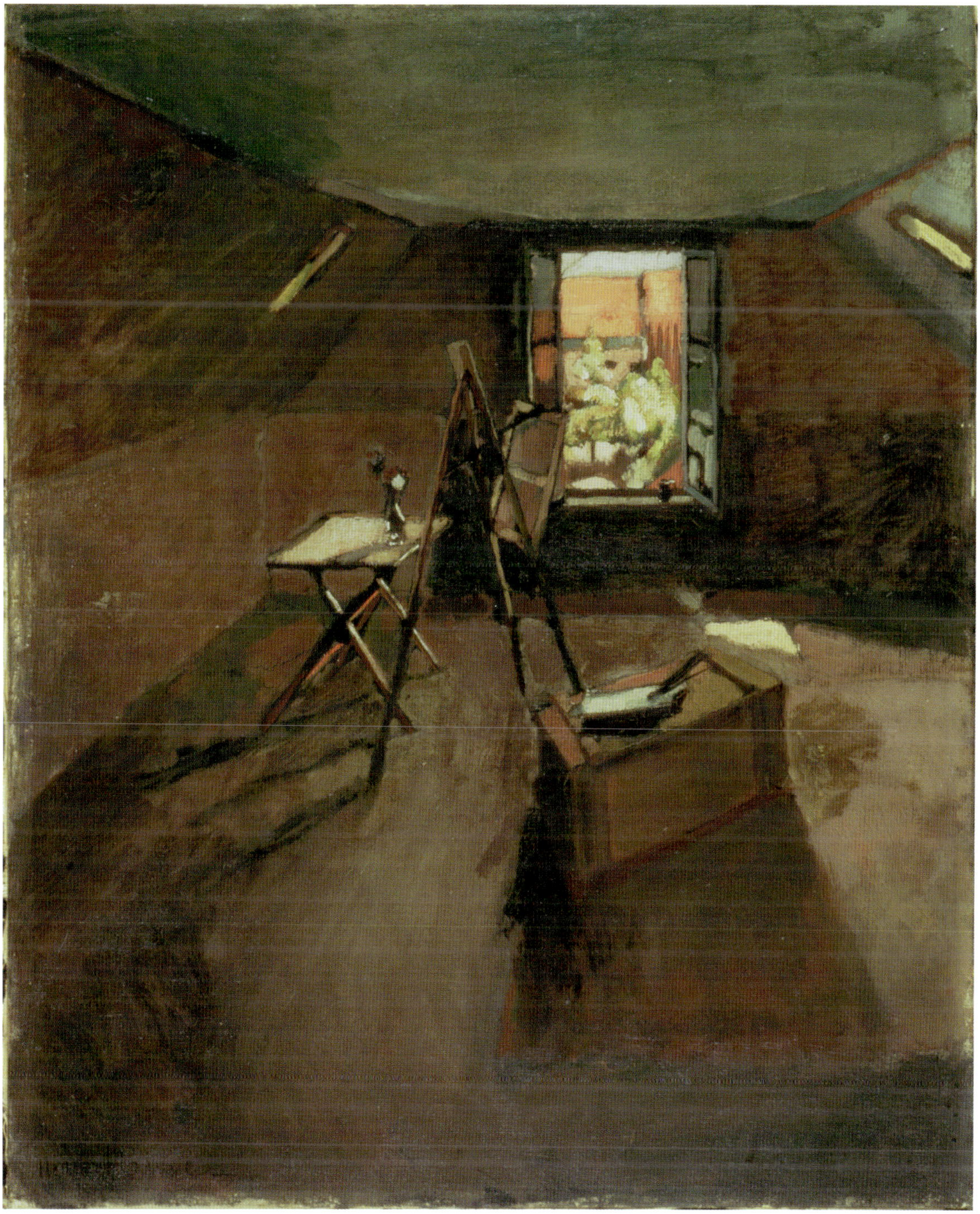

Plate 10. Henri Matisse (1869–1954), *Studio under the Eaves*, ca. 1903. Oil on canvas, 55 × 44.5 cm. Fitzwilliam Museum, University of Cambridge, England. The Bridgeman Art Library. Photograph courtesy of Art Resource, NY, FIT69699.

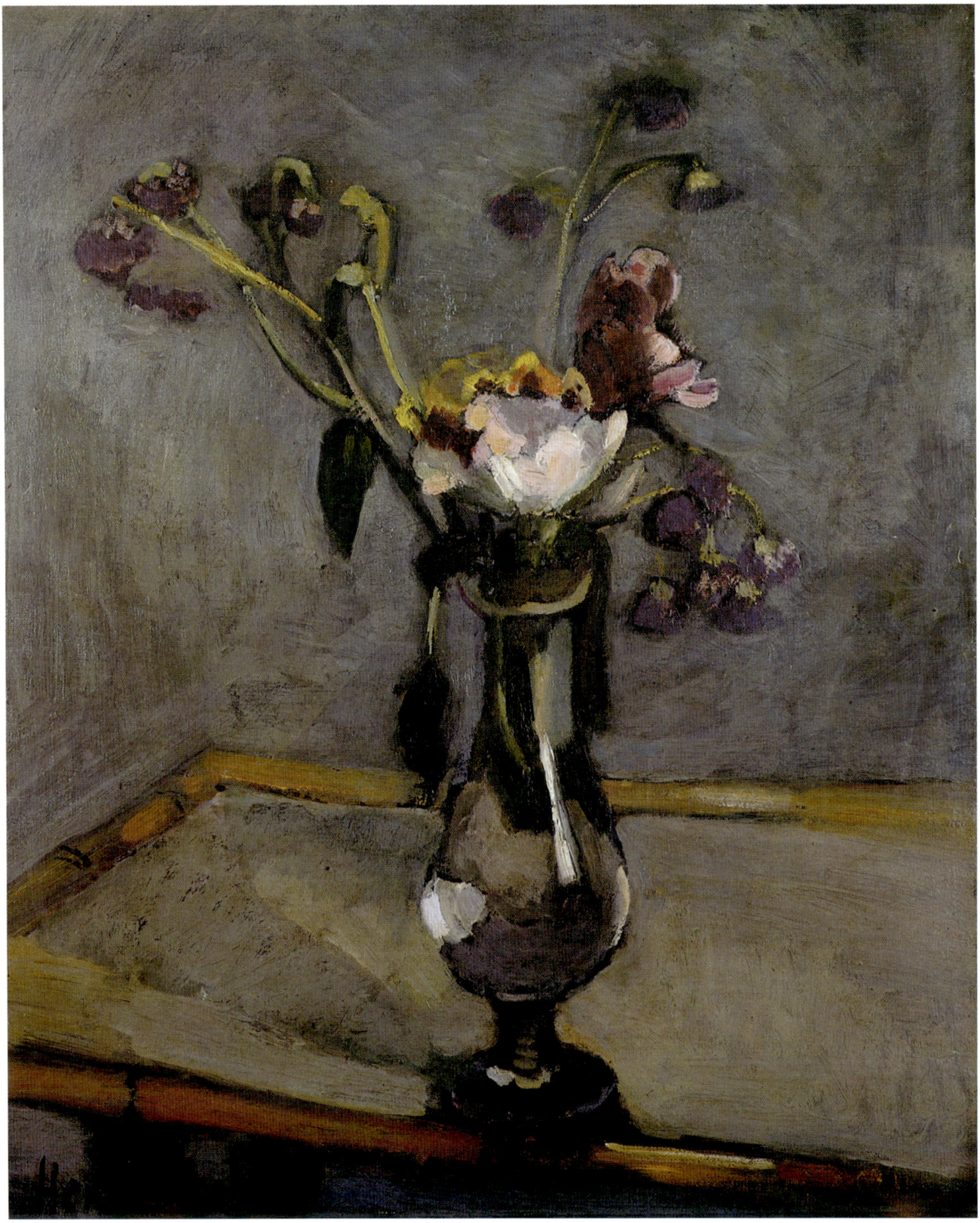

Plate 11. Henri Matisse (1869–1954), *Bouquet on a Bamboo Table,* ca. 1903. Oil on canvas, 55 × 44.5 cm. Private collection.

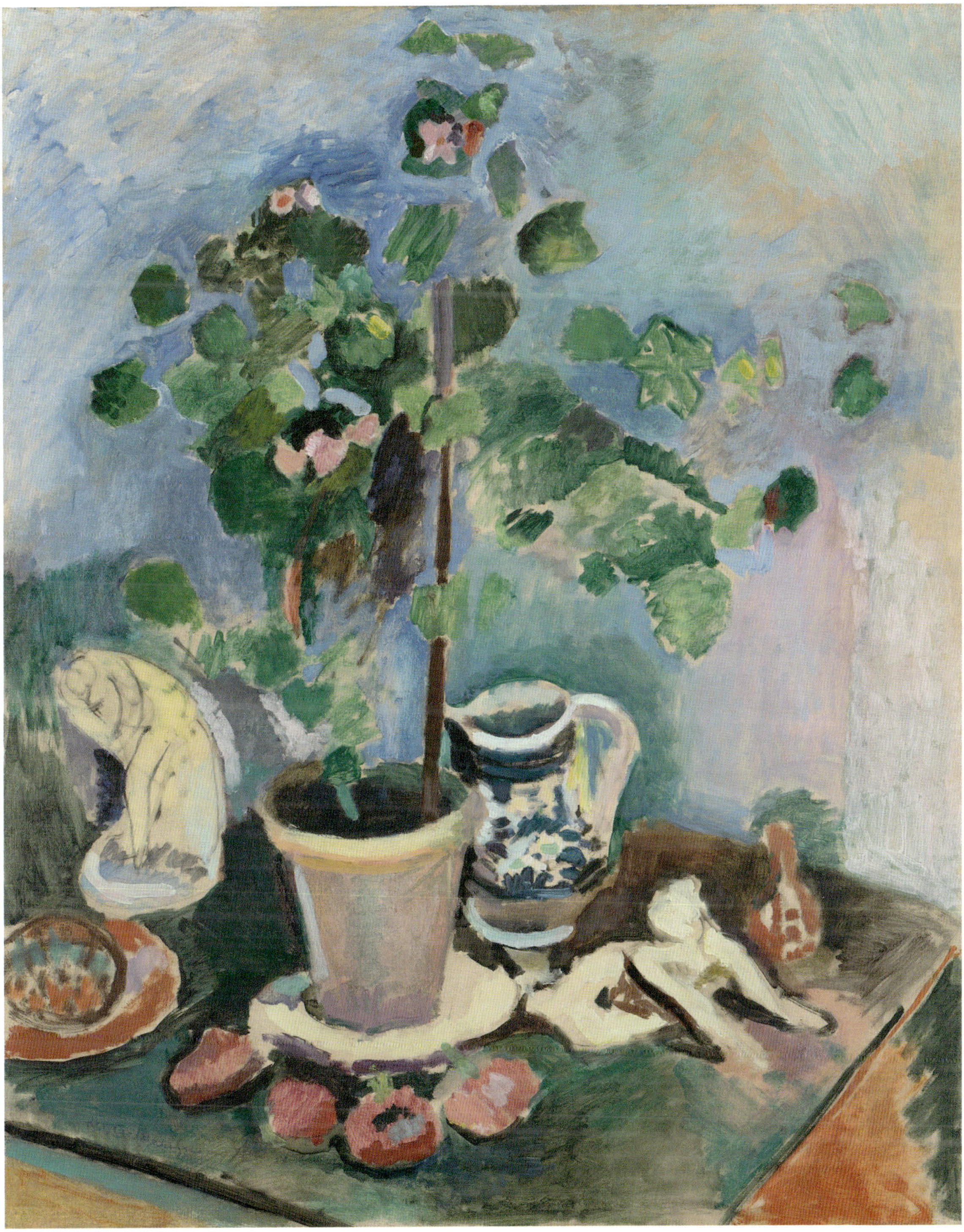

Plate 12. Henri Matisse (1869–1954), *The Geranium,* autumn 1906. Oil on canvas, 100.3 × 81.5 cm. Joseph Winterbotham Collection, 1932.1342, Art Institute of Chicago.

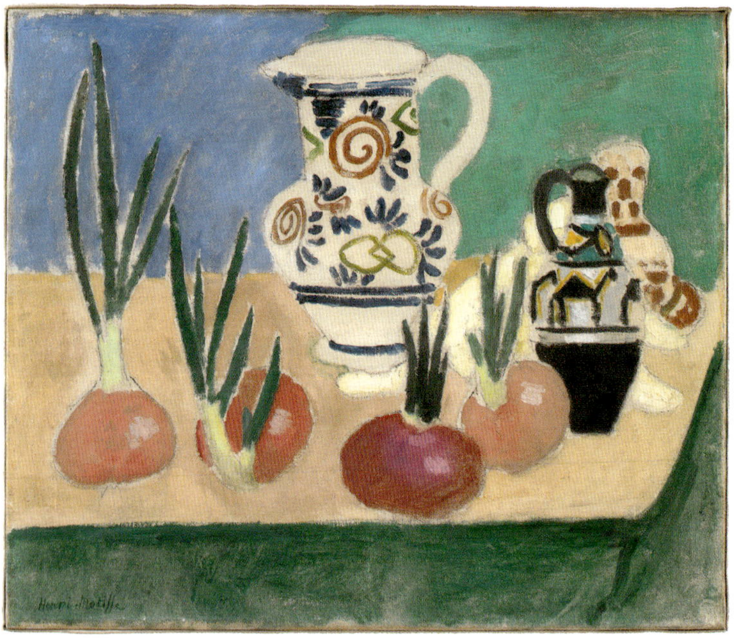

Plate 13. Henri Matisse (1869–1954), *Pink Onions,* ca. 1906. Colored paper and tempera cutout glued on paper, 40.5 × 86 cm. Statens Museum for Kunst/National Gallery of Denmark, Copenhagen. Copyright 2013 Succession H. Matisse / Artists Rights Society (ARS), NY. Photograph courtesy of Scala / Art Resource, NY.

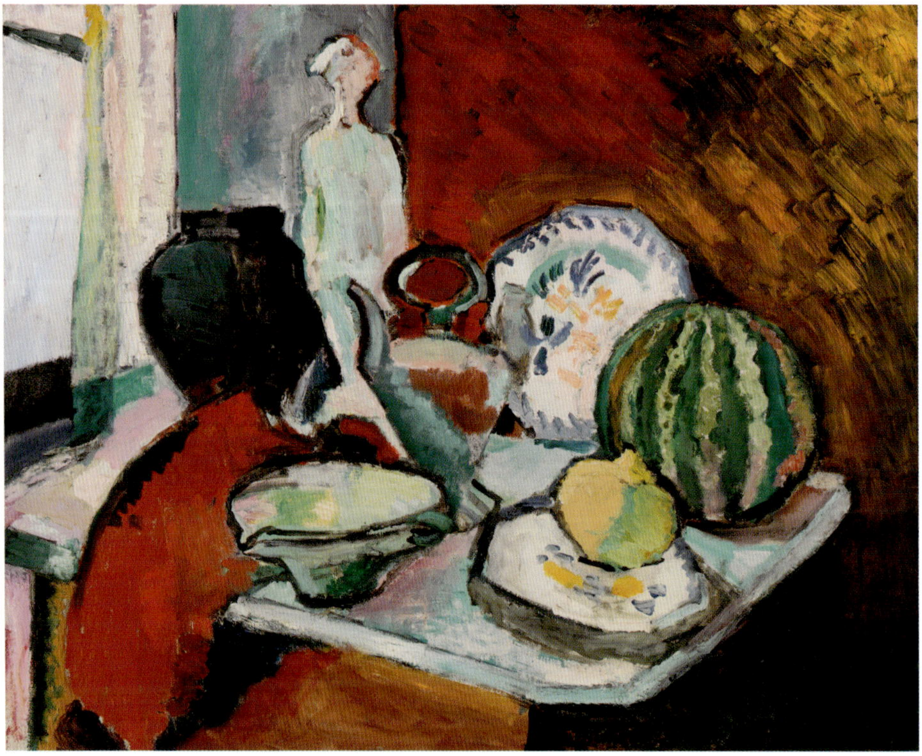

Plate 14. Henri Matisse (1869–1954), *Dishes and Melon,* spring 1906. Oil on canvas, 65 × 81 cm. The Barnes Foundation, Merion, Pennsylvania. Copyright 2013 Succession H. Matisse / Artists Rights Society (ARS), NY. Photograph: The Bridgeman Art Library International BRN 160639.

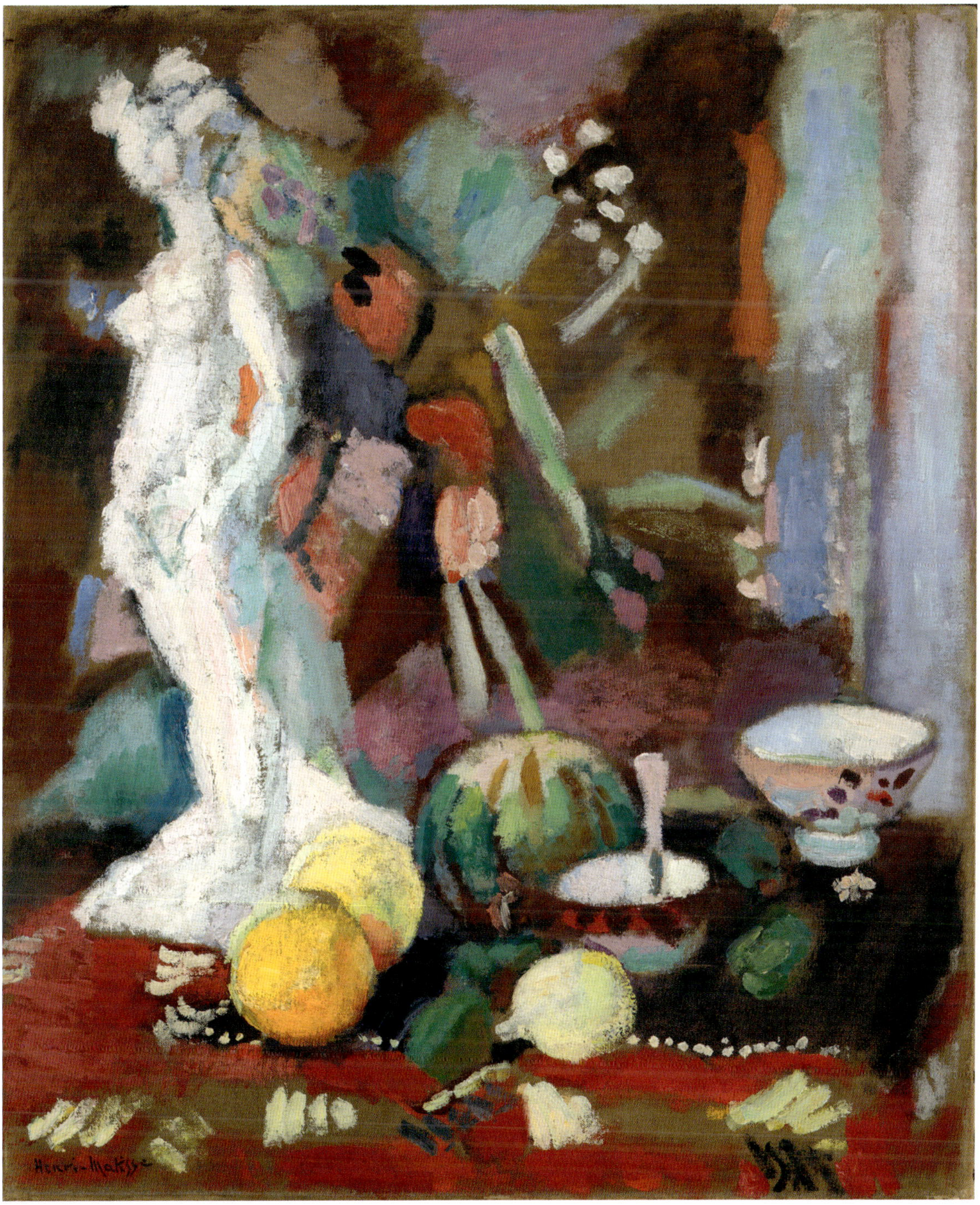

Plate 15. Henri Matisse (1869–1954), *Still Life with Plaster Figure*, 1906. Oil on canvas, 54 × 45.1 cm (21¼ × 17¾ inches). Bequest of Mrs. Kate L. Brewster, 1948.121, Yale University Art Gallery, New Haven, Connecticut. Copyright 2013 Succession H. Matisse / Artists Rights Society (ARS), NY. Photograph courtesy of Yale University Art Gallery / Art Resource, NY.

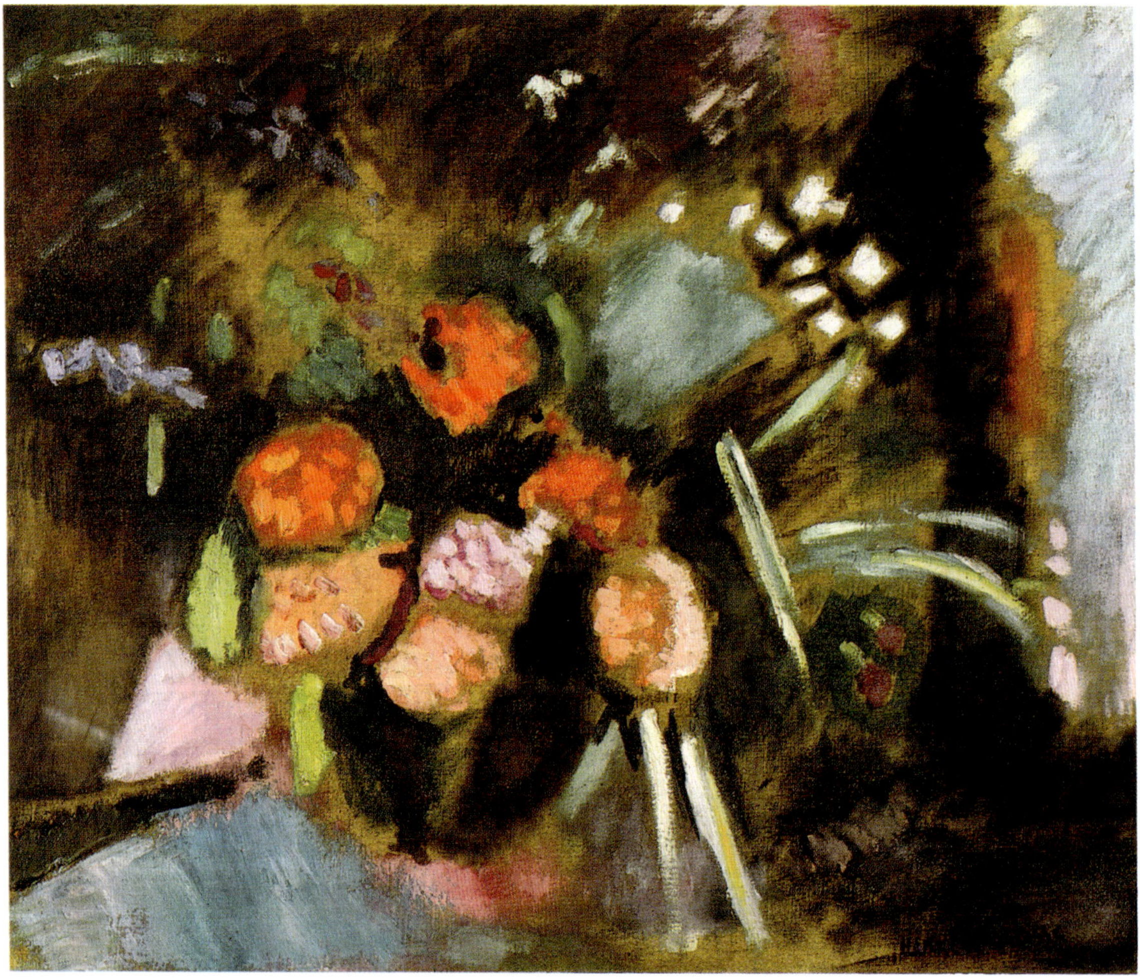

Plate 16. Henri Matisse (1869–1954), *Flowers,* 1906. Oil on canvas, 58 × 71.5 cm. Collection The Duke of Roxburghe, England. Copyright 2013 Succession H. Matisse / Artists Rights Society (ARS), NY.

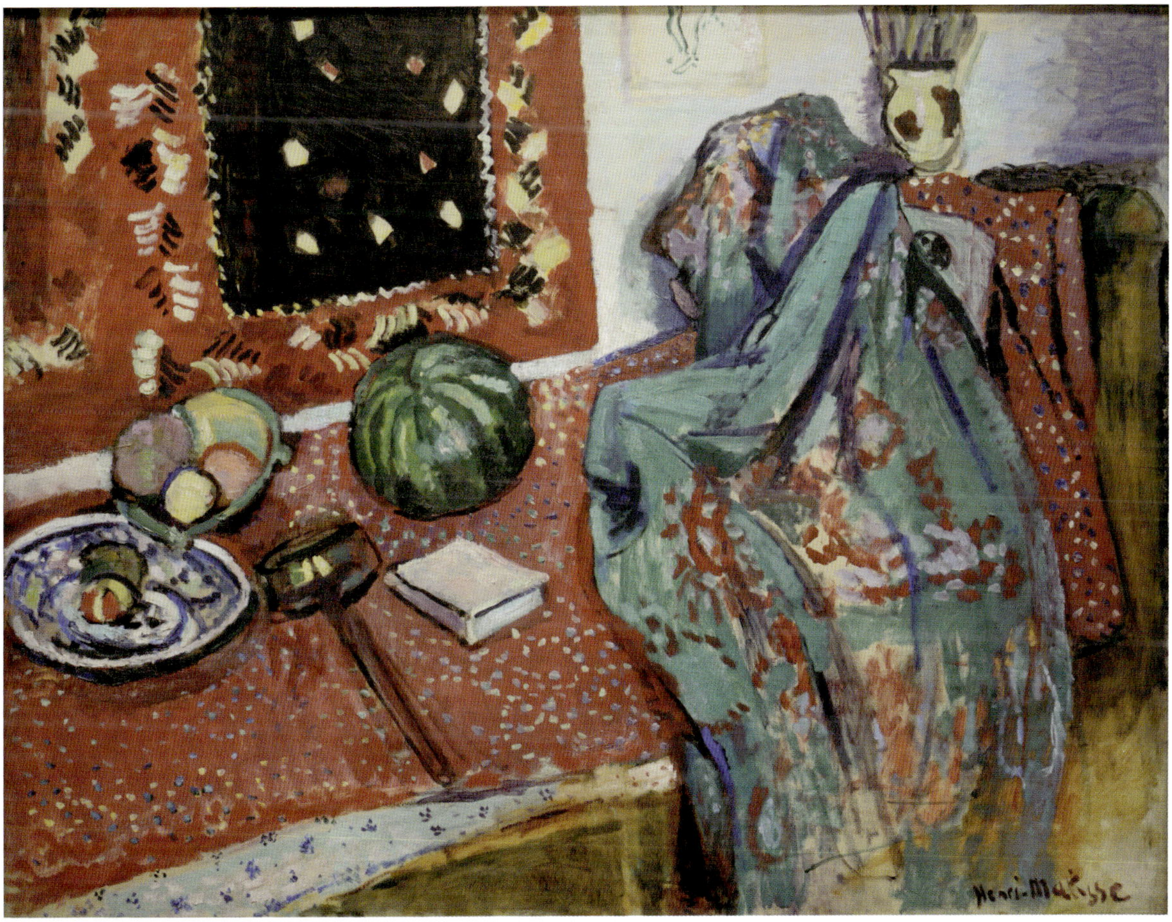

Plate 17. Henri Matisse (1869–1954), *The Red Rugs,* 1906. Oil on canvas, 89 × 116.5 cm. Musée des Beaux Arts Grenoble, France. Copyright 2013 Succession H. Matisse / Artists Rights Society (ARS), NY. Photograph courtesy of Gianni Dagli Orti, The Art Archive at Art Resource, NY, AA384622.

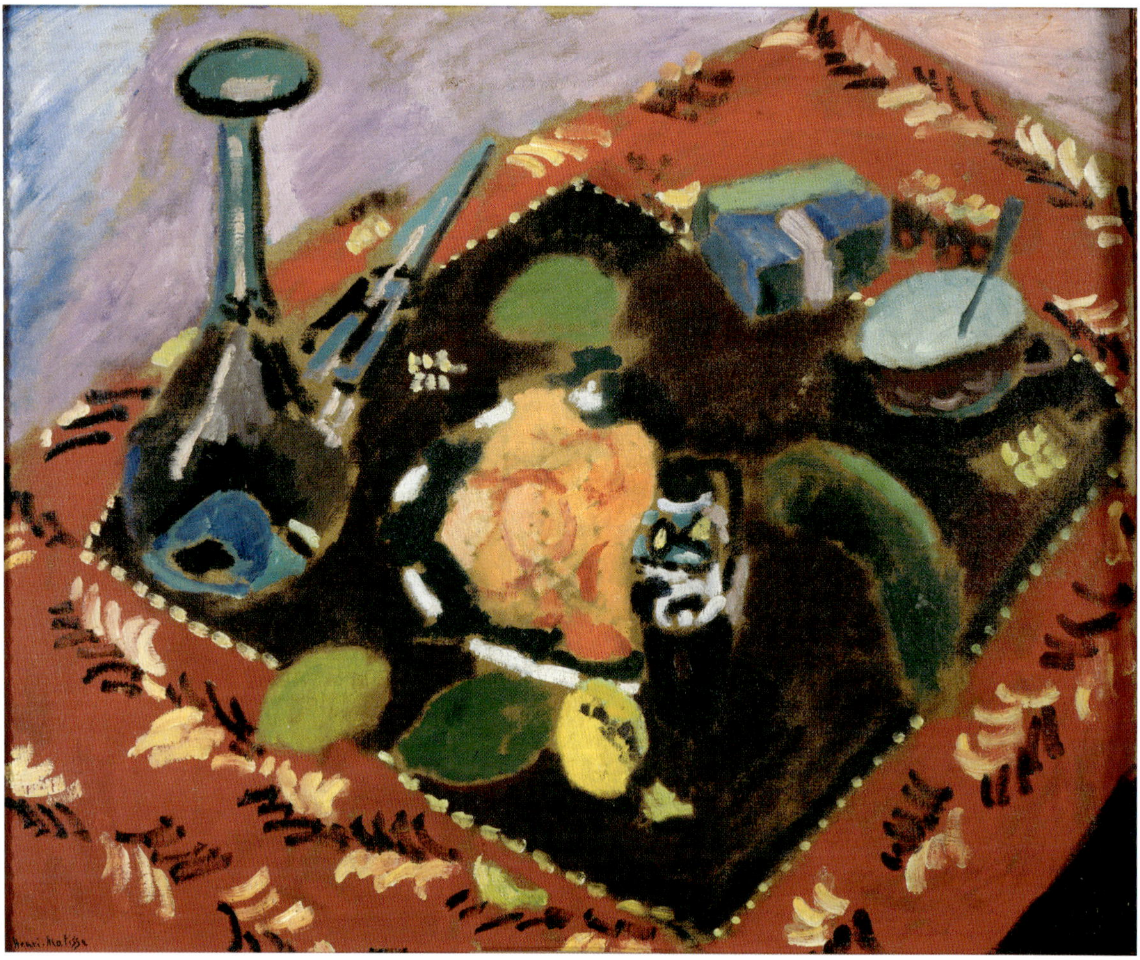

Plate 18. Henri Matisse (1869–1954), *Dishes and Fruit on a Red and Black Carpet,* 1906. Oil on canvas, 100 × 80.6 cm. State Hermitage Museum, St. Petersburg, Russia. Copyright 2013 Succession H. Matisse / Artists Rights Society (ARS), NY. Photograph: Courtesy of Scala / Art Resource, NY, ART395467.

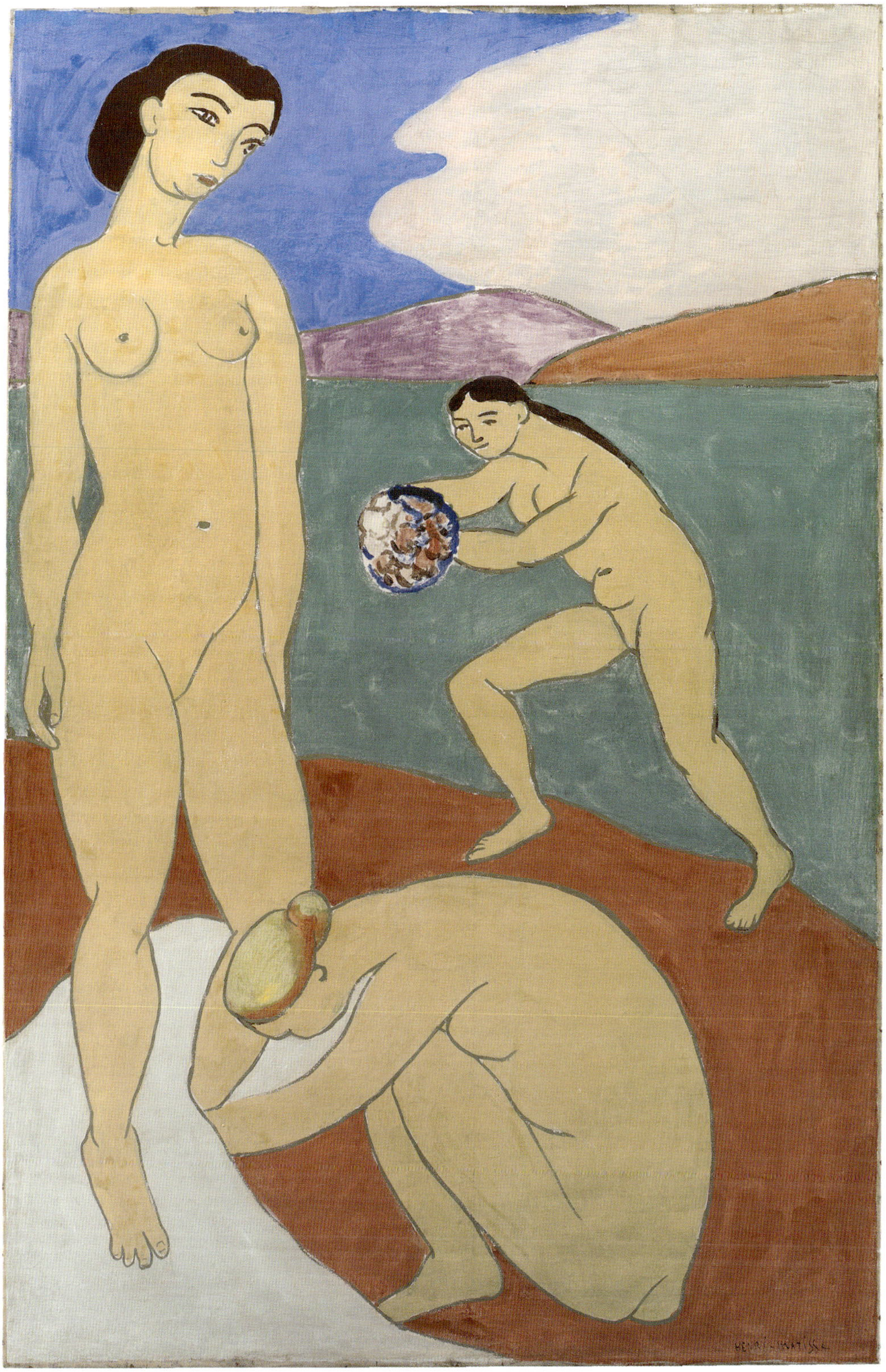

Plate 19. Henri Matisse (1869–1954), *Le Luxe II,* 1907–8. Casein on canvas, 209.5 × 138 cm. Statens Museum for Kunst/National Gallery of Denmark, Copenhagen.

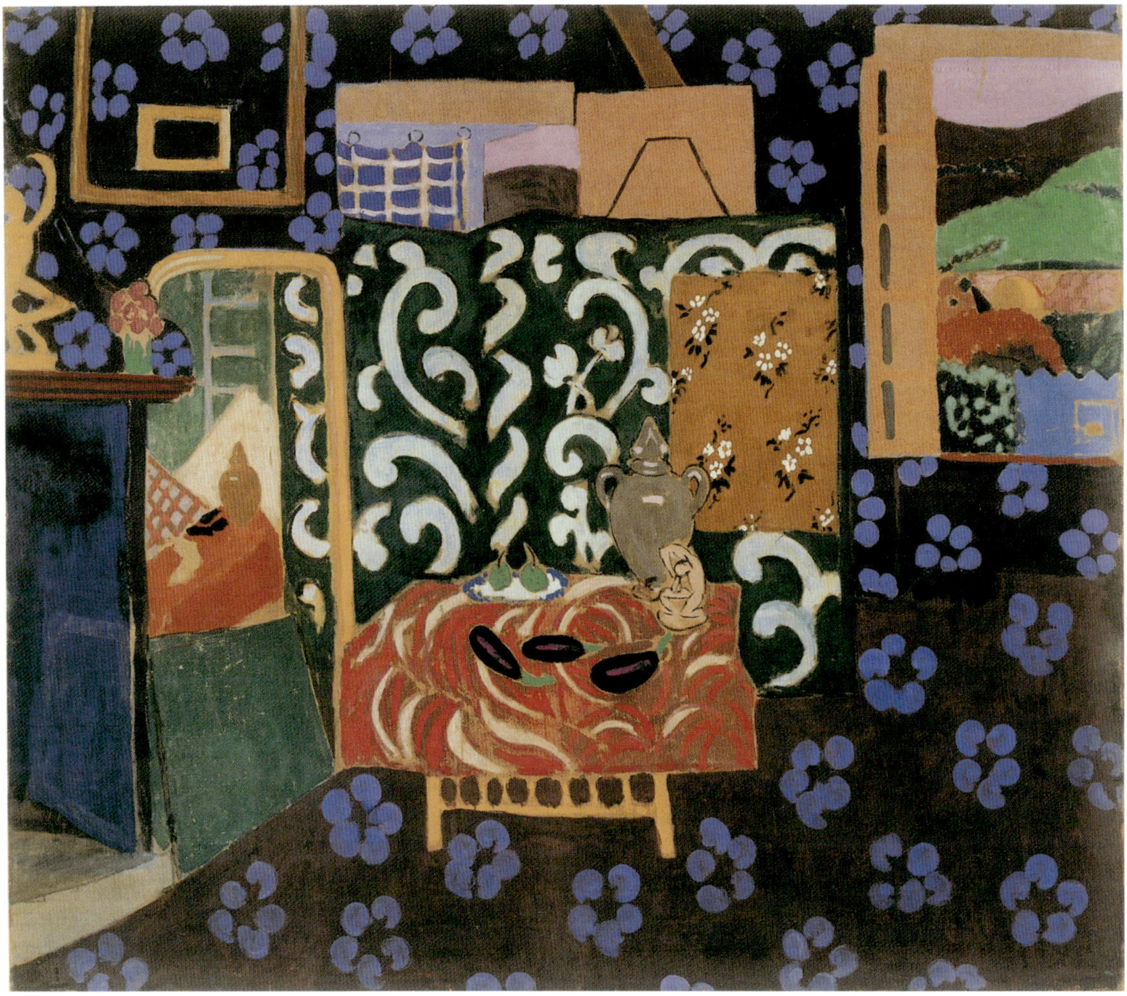

Plate 20. Henri Matisse (1869–1954), *Interior with Aubergines,* 1911. Musée des Beaux Arts Grenoble, France. Copyright 2013 Succession H. Matisse / Artists Rights Society (ARS), NY. Photograph courtesy of Gianni Dagli Orti, The Art Archive at Art Resource, NY, AA384624.

pet, bound to their vertical post and weighing on the ground with all their bulk"—Matisse resisted panic as he made his fated attempt to master his own legacy.[37] Unlike Matisse, Duthuit made no distinction between the "rock" and the "divan," between life and art. For Matisse, the panic of the hypnotic episode was stopped by the ground of *art* (the "divan" underneath the hypnotist's feet). Unlike his Impressionist and Post-Impressionist predecessors, Matisse avoided reference to nature as his foundation (thus his seeming aversion to landscape). Put more strongly, the influences Matisse attempted to overcome were precisely those artists who laid claim to nature. Even his artistic hero, Cézanne, who consistently appealed to the "truth" of the external world, required a heavy extraction from his stated intentions.

The Influential Master: Cézanne

With whom, and with what, was Matisse competing? Matisse was consistently asked about his influences throughout his career. "What was the greatest single influence on your art?" His answer was always ready to hand: "above all, Cézanne" (255); he is "the master of us all."[38] Among all the turn-of-the-century painters who staked out a truly Post-Impressionist art, a potential model for Matisse's own overcoming of Impressionism, Cézanne was closest of all. Coming to understand Cézanne's aims was the task of a lifetime. Matisse's attitude toward him was characteristically conflicted. Consider, for instance, his idiosyncratic, or willful, reading of Cézanne from the "Notes of a Painter":

> Look at one of Cézanne's pictures: all is so well arranged that no matter at what distance you stand or how many figures are represented you will always be able to distinguish each figure clearly and to know which limb belongs to which body. If there is order and clarity in the picture, it means that from the outset this same order and clarity existed in the mind of the painter. . . . Limbs may cross and intertwine, but in the eyes of the spectator they will nevertheless remain attached to and help to articulate the right body: all confusion has disappeared. (40/47–48)

Matisse's Cézanne was like no other. To even the most acute eye, distinguishing limb from limb in Cézanne's final *Bathers* (Figure 3.1) is a challenge. Matisse's repeated emphases on clear arrangement, integrated and connected bodies, order and clarity, and a total lack of confusion are eccentric terms to describe Cézanne's work, even if they capture something crucial about Matisse's own.

Who, for instance, is the imagined spectator who finds Cézanne's crossing and intertwining of limbs to be a means of articulating difference? Compare this, for instance, with T. J. Clark's discussion of Cézanne's *Large Bathers,* and in particular the "'double figure'"—overlaying buttocks and shoulders—at the right of the picture: it is "a figure of one body necessarily being in another,

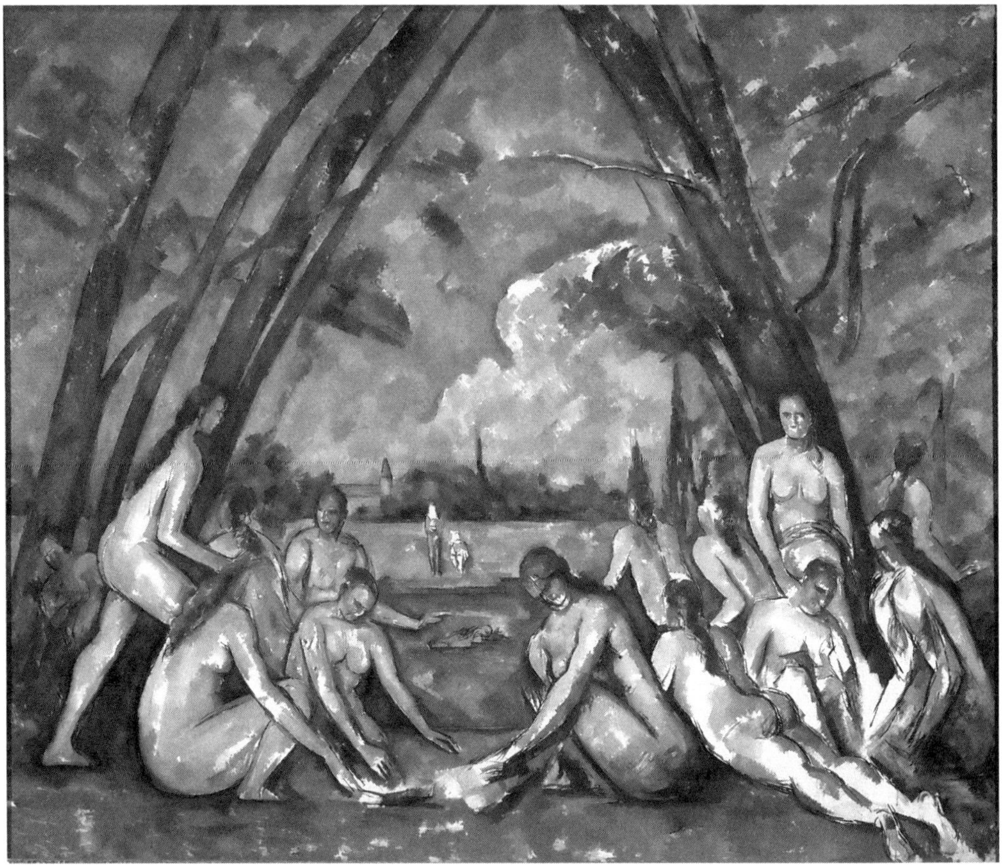

Figure 3.1. Paul Cézanne (1839–1906), *The Large Bathers,* 1906. Oil on canvas, 82⅞ × 98¾ inches (210.5 × 250.8 cm). Purchased with the W. P. Wilstach Fund, 1937. Philadelphia Museum of Art, Philadelphia, Pennsylvania. Photograph from Philadelphia Museum of Art / Art Resource, NY.

entering every body it encounters, always and interminably reading the configurations someone else's body takes by trying them on for size."[39] If Clark still insists on Cézanne's difference from his depicted bodies, other commentators have gone further. Susan Sidlauskas describes a world where "boundaries between self and other dissolve, and the artist imagined himself somehow one with the colors that composed them, a fusion that he articulated in almost primal terms."[40] For Matisse, such a fantastic ideal of bodily merger could only be construed as failure, a melodrama of oneness. The Cézannian ideal of merger denied the fact of separateness: of the work, of the world, of the other. But it also denied the possibility of *overcoming* that difference, as it posited an identity that was there from the start, as though in the act of perception itself.

Matisse's emphasis on the wholeness and independence of Cézanne's bodies perhaps signaled their opposite: these mingling and ambiguous bodies evoked the specter of influence, of a fusion of bodies and limbs that denied *les différences* he aimed to preserve. While Matisse affirmed (or exaggerated) the autonomy of Cézanne's bodies, it was not ultimately to cancel their sense of interconnection—Cézanne's bodies, he noted, "cross and intertwine"—but rather to deny the ease with which that effect of unity might be generated.

Matisse's effort to assimilate Cézanne's example often took an extreme and tautological form. "Cézanne you see is a sort of god of painting," he told an interviewer in 1925. Matisse was acutely aware of the burden Cézanne's example posed for artists coming after him. Rather than downplay his influence, Matisse challenged his authority. "Dangerous, his influence? So what? Too bad for those without the strength to survive it" (80/84). That he referred to "surviving" influence speaks to the emotional register Cézanne's example provoked.

"You must deny the influential master," Matisse told his students (158, 189/198). Characteristically, the phrase is a quote, this time from Cézanne himself. It is taken from a letter Cézanne wrote to painter Charles Camoin, who was a friend of Matisse:

> The understanding of the model and its realization is sometimes very slow in coming for the artist. Whoever the master is whom you prefer, this must only be a directive for you. Otherwise you will never be anything but an imitator. With any feeling for nature and some fortunate talents . . . you should be able to dissociate yourself; advice, someone else's methods must not make you change your own way of feeling. Should you momentarily be under the influence of someone older than you, believe me, as soon as you begin to feel vividly, your own emotion will always emerge and win its place in the sun—gain the upper hand, confidence—what you must strive to achieve is a good method of construction.[41]

Cézanne's warning about becoming an imitator may have gone down hard with Matisse. When he first read the letter sometime in 1905, he had just emerged from the most overtly Cézannian moment of his career. But he could also take comfort in Cézanne's words. The master's emphasis on craft, on finding the right "method of construction," seems to win out against the "feeling for nature." Matisse could perhaps sense with relief that influence was, as Cézanne suggested, "momentary," and that his fauve work would have sufficiently loosened him from the master's grip. Once he triumphed over, or validated, the master's method as his own, he could resist every other influence that challenged him on the path to autonomy.

It is worth pausing to reflect on a remarkable analysis of Cézanne that bears directly on Matisse's vision of autonomy. Roger Fry's 1917 review of

Vollard's biography of Cézanne reveals the impact of Matisse's own ideas on the critic's writings. Fry controversially implied that biography was a particularly apt genre to understand Cézanne's practice. Vollard's book revealed the nature of the true artist as a "strange species" who lived "irresponsibly and irredeemably [for] himself." Cézanne was the "perfect realization" and "unmitigated form" of the artist. Cézanne's "outrageous egoism" made him "ineducable" in a "world where every one else is being perpetually educated"; moreover, in a "world where the individual is squeezed and molded and polished by the pressure of his fellow-men the artist remains irreclaimably individual."[42] So while the artist is shaped and influenced at every moment by his surroundings, it is his special gift to resist the world and to exert pressure back onto it. Fry described Cézanne's personality in terms that bear directly on Matisse's view of the self: "Every word and every gesture he records sticks out with the rugged relief of a character in which everything is due to the compulsion of inner forces, in which nothing has been planed down or smoothed away by external pressure—not that external pressure was absent but that the inner compulsion—the inevitable bent of Cézanne's temperament, was irresistible." He was driven by the "dread of any possible invasion of his personality," Fry concluded.[43] Cézanne's resistance to invasion by "external pressure" by virtue of the strength of his "inner compulsion" mirrored Matisse's claim that "the influence of other personalities can do no harm" because the artist's "certitudes are internal" (29/56). As Fry wrote of the form and the self that resisted being "smoothed away," Matisse described the perfect sculpture as one that "could be rolled down a hill till most of the surface elements were knocked off" and the "form would still remain."[44] Like Matisse, Fry drew no distinction between personal autonomy and artistic autonomy—both required resistance to pressures forced upon the artist by "worldly ideals and ways of life."

Of course it would be absurd to imagine a solipsistic denial of the world. My concern is to understand the significance and intensity of Matisse's and, more generally, modernism's commitment to personal and pictorial autonomy. No concept could be more out of favor in view of the triumph over the past forty years of the "death of the author." In general, "critical" or historicist interpretations of autonomy have been far too quick to see it as impossible or unfulfilled, to expose the limits of selfhood in iterability and repetition. To reveal the constructed, social, ideological nature of the self is thought to be an achievement, but it fails to show what an agent is supposed to do with that knowledge (the genesis of an act tells us nothing about what it is to take an action). Matisse's commitment to autonomy was itself driven by a dissatisfaction with every historical account of the self, as though identifying an artist's relation to the past amounts to undermining the self's future. What would it be like to preserve agency in the face of, or in the name of, a kind of utopian or perfected heteronomy? That is Matisse's question and achievement.

Self-Hypnosis

While the concept of influence played a defining role in Matisse's relation with Cézanne and with the past more generally, it was by no means restricted to the realm of aesthetics. Fears about influence took on broader consequences in fin de siècle culture. Above all, influence was associated with the cultural phenomenon that gripped Matisse's generation: hypnosis. Hypnotic experiments were covered by nearly all the major French newspapers and journals in the second half of the nineteenth century. While frequently characterized as a game, for some psychologists and sociologists hypnosis suggested something far more serious about the nature of the self. What Matisse and others of his generation found disturbing about influence was the idea that one's thoughts may not come from one's own mind but through the imitation of another. Hypnosis described a model of identification that involved a "blind" subjection to the other; it was "blind" in the sense that the hypnotized subject was unconscious of the hypnotist's commands (the hypnotist could also be blind to his effects). Influence was ubiquitous, and it was impossible resist.

Although Matisse's encounter with hypnosis occurred when he was at a young age and it was identified with a kind of imaginary theater, hypnosis took on more serious consequences for a new breed of crowd psychologist. In their groundbreaking studies of crowd behavior, Gabriel Tarde and Gustave Le Bon pointed to the hypnotic encounter as a view into the anarchic potential of social interaction. "We know today," Le Bon wrote in *The Crowd* (1895), "that by various processes an individual may be brought into such a condition that, having entirely lost his conscious personality, he obeys all the suggestions of the operator who has deprived him of it, and commits acts in utter contradiction with his character and habits." In the hypnotic state the subject "has become an automaton who has ceased to be guided by his will" and becomes the passive vehicle of another's will.[45] For the crowd psychologists, hypnotism implied a potential annulment of the boundary between self and other, leaving one dangerously susceptible to the influence of others. Reflecting on this history, Mikkel Borch-Jacobsen has described hypnotic suggestion as "a 'bond' that inextricably mingles the 'self' with the 'other'—a bond that transcends all (op)position of identity . . . and that must therefore be characterized as a non-bond."[46] Ruth Leys has similarly shown how "hypnosis threatened to dissolve the distinction between self and other to such a degree that the hypnotized subject came to occupy the place of the 'other' in an unconscious identification so profound that the other was not apprehended *as other*."[47] What Borch-Jacobsen's and Leys's scare quotes around "self," "other," and "bond" indicate is how the hypnotic state points to a fluid moment prior to the distinction between self and other. According to Borch-Jacobsen and Leys, hypnotic identification designates a process that is formative *of* the ego and for that reason is anterior to subject/object differentiation. But as Borch-Jacobsen and Leys also explain, no matter how deep the hypnotic bond runs, it should not be confused with the affective *merger* with the other. At no point in the hypnotic encounter does the self/other distinction actually fall away, leading to some elusive sensation of oceanic oneness. And while the hypnotic bond suggests a closer and more basic relation between self and other than any traditional account of subject and object, it nonetheless preserves a sense of difference. Or rather, the experience of hypnotic attachment is accessible only through a mode of representation, even if that form of representation is not one of conscious awareness.[48] What is important to observe is that the ideal of affective merger could present as fatal a denial of the self as the counter-ideal of solipsistic individuation.

For Matisse, hypnosis signified both the ubiquity of influence and the artist's necessity to actively and continuously *appropriate* those influences for himself. The fact of being named by the other was never in question—this is what makes Matisse's claims to autonomy sustainable—only being named without an appeal to one's own agency, to one's ontological capacity to ratify or validate an influence as one's own.

Matisse explored two broad strategies to neutralize or overcome what he felt to be the stultifying effects of generalized hypnosis. First was to conceive a mode of *self-hypnosis,* to imagine a form of production the source and consumption of which was his own self or *personnalité.* Second was to reconceive hypnosis as an artistic *technique,* to harness what he called the "hypnotic power of the image" and turn suggestive effects onto the beholder and thereby draw influences away from himself.

Michel Puy, in his groundbreaking study of fauvism (perhaps dictated in part by Matisse), spelled out the basic terms of Matisse's claim to self-hypnosis. "The artist obeys reasoning less than the suggestions of his own nature," Puy wrote. "He is directed by an interior force that he knows poorly but it . . . always leads him back on his way."[49] Matisse was not hypnotized by the other but by a voice within himself. Puy, that is, relocated the source of suggestion from the operator to an autosuggestive impulse.[50] Matisse projected a vision of sacrifice and struggle against the anarchic forces within him, as though every battle with the other was the shadow of a more basic struggle. "From beginning to end" Matisse's life and art constituted "one long resistance," an "unceasing fight against himself," Escholier wrote.[51] Prichard observed how Matisse "feels in himself something greater than himself, a Socratic demon, the enemy."[52] Matisse described his unconscious drives as "alien" to his worldly life: "I was urged on by I know not what—some force that I see today is quite alien to me in my everyday life."[53] Matisse put the matter most directly and eloquently in a 1938 letter to Georges Besson, describing the relation to his self as an encounter with an "other mind": "There are so many things I would like to understand,

and most of all *myself*—after a half a century of hard work and reflection the wall is still there. *Nature—or rather my nature—remains mysterious.*"[54] The "wall" is a surrogate for the work itself, and if there was a wall within the self, then the relation of the self to others could only be more attenuated.

What makes Matisse's fantasies of autohypnotic production something more than aesthetic ideology is that they were part of a larger effort to defeat what he called "theatrical effects."[55] The significance of his inner "demon" was that it could *not* perform for the other, because the artist was not consciously aware of its workings. Gilot observed how the "artist obeyed his daemon, his forceful inner drive, which irresistibly propelled him forward" and explicitly identified it with the practice of self-hypnosis:

> Matisse could talk, consider what he saw, and at the same time sustain intense concentration that bordered on self-hypnosis. He was present and yet self-absorbed, pursuing some thought of his own, perhaps unconsciously reabsorbing or reintegrating some work in progress before projecting it anew as soon as [Picasso and I] had left.[56]

Matisse's self-absorption was the condition for his projecting the world "anew." He reestablished hypnotic other-directedness in an internal space in order to fictively escape the possibility of self-consciously performing for the other.

Alongside and in tension with autohypnosis, Matisse conceived of the artist as a hypnotic operator who could place his viewers, rather than himself, in a kind of trance. By establishing the "hypnotic power of the image" he could reverse the flow of influence from others to himself. As the hypnotic operator, he could control expressive effects and induce feelings in the mind and body of the beholder. In this way every hypnotic imitation *of* the other could be turned into a form of hypnotic power *over* the other. "The ideal is for the spectator to be captured without them being aware, by the mechanism of the picture," he explained.[57] Capturing the spectator was his way of not being captured in return.[58] But unlike self-hypnosis, which fantasized a closed circuitry of production and consumption, the painter as hypnotist actually threatened to undermine his agency. On first view, this seems implausible. If the artist was a kind of hypnotist, then his work would simply embody the effects he intended to produce in his spectators. But then again, that agency was limited by the hypnotic process itself. In order to secure the production of pictorial effects, it was not enough for the artist to *intend* to express himself to the spectator (something that could surely fail to come off). The "mechanism of the picture" was something *not* dictated by his intentions. The picture became a quasi-impersonal force, a more reliable means of producing an effect than any human agency. Following the logic of affective formalism discussed in chapter 1, the very extremity of Matisse's desire to produce a response threatened to make his expressive aims negligible. When Matisse played the role of the hypnotist, thereby *forcing* viewers to feel what he wanted them to feel, he was simultaneously expressing his ultimate skepticism about the capacity of his works to carry meaning for another.

The Theater of Skepticism

Matisse not only described the relation between his inner and outer self, artist and beholder, in terms of hypnotic suggestion but could also conceive of the picture space as a confrontation between two selves: one masterful and observant, the other passive and blank. In an important late text titled "Exactitude Is Not Truth," Matisse underscored the role detachment, spectatorship, and inner resolve played in his practice, above all in his self-portraits. "My self-portraits," he wrote, reveal "the same man, who always remains an attentive spectator of life and of himself" (180/174). It is "the same man . . . in terms of his character, his personality, his way of considering things, his reaction to life, and in terms of the reserve he displays in relation to life which stops him from uncontrolled surrender to it." This skeptical *reserve* is perhaps most explicitly rendered in his quizzical self-portrait in a striped shirt of 1906 (Figure 3.2), in which he displays the look Apollinaire described as the "bespectacled gaze" of the "Cartesian master" peering out (or down) at the world.[59] While his left shoulder tilts out toward the beholder, its form pressed against the picture plane, his upper body inclines into space, his bare neck opening a poignant gap between head and body. The stately head, as well as his right upper arm and shoulder, are enclosed in thick black contours, detaching them from the ambient space of the setting as well as symbolically withdrawing them from the space of the beholder. Even the moment of closest proximity, the painter's left shoulder that seems to slide outward and across the frame, is simultaneously withdrawn into the picture space by virtue of the black modeling on the far side of the shoulder, which, unlike any other moment in the picture, firmly situates the body inside the illusory space. Pictorial modes of openness and closure are mirrored by Matisse's qualified account of his own "inner reserve." As he went on to explain in "Exactitude Is Not Truth," he rejected an "uncontrolled surrender" to life, not life itself. Skeptical reserve stood side by side with the effort to "identify completely with one's subject" (181/175).

Matisse's skepticism is continuous with a larger cultural tradition, one that stretches back to Diderot and the French philosophes. In his study *The Paradox of Acting* (1773–78), Diderot described the great actor as someone who "excels in simulating" but who "feels nothing" for the characters he plays on stage. The actor is never fully mesmerized by his role and stands mentally detached from the spectacle he performs. No matter how far the actor "loses himself," he always carries within him "an unmoved and disinterested onlooker." Diderot wanted to dislodge the traditional (or sentimental) notion of

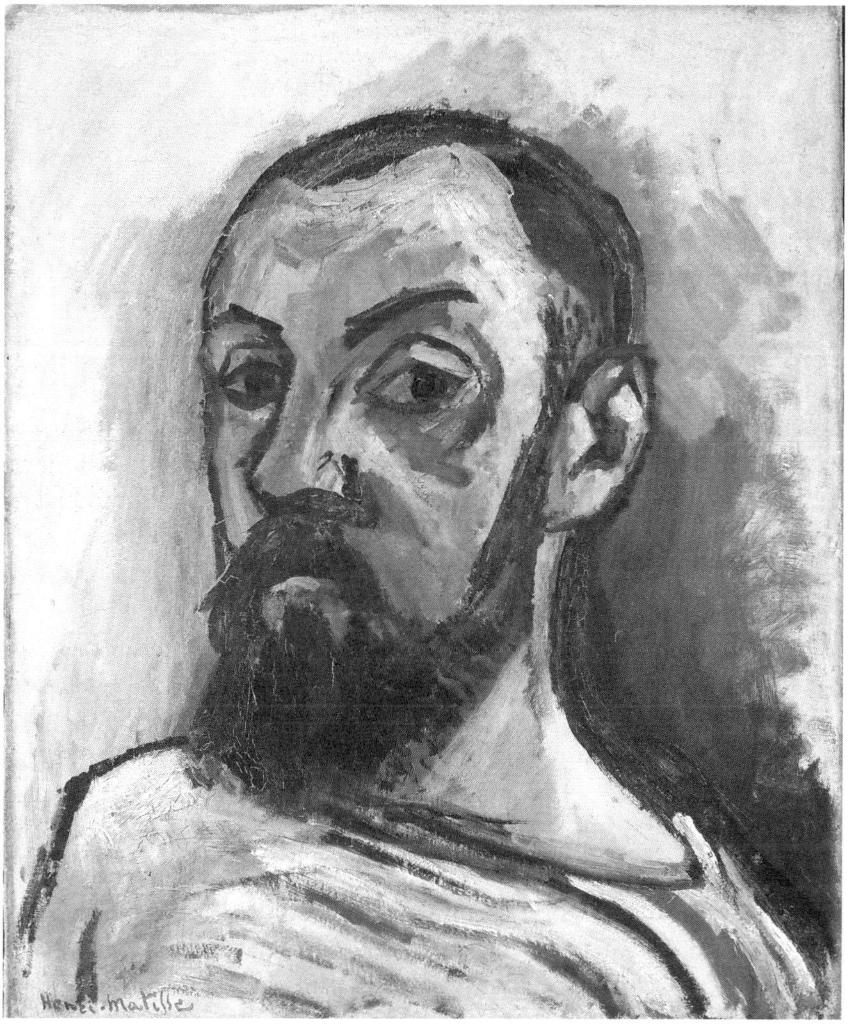

Figure 3.2. Henri Matisse (1869–1954), *Self-Portrait,* 1906. Oil on canvas, 46 × 55 cm. Statens Museum for Kunst/National Gallery of Denmark, Copenhagen, KMSr78. Copyright 2013 Succession H. Matisse / Artists Rights Society (ARS), NY.

the actor as someone who merges completely with his role, who believes his own tears and who takes no distance from the emotions he projects on stage. Diderot's supreme actor was self-possessed, full of "sureness," "cool reflection," and "self-command" no matter how far he sank into his role.[60] (Being absorbed in one's role was not the same as the mystical loss of self.) Diderot's actor offered a complex vision of artistic autonomy: the actor's lines and gestures were of course learned—they were not his—but that fact had no bearing on the individuality of the actor's performance, which could certainly rise to the level of original achievement or "genius."

Matisse followed Diderot's cues in a late piece of writing. "The objects in my paintings are like actors," he explained, and a "good actor can have a part in ten different plays; an object can play in ten different pictures, ten different roles" (208/247). Matisse's prized piece of glazed cotton, printed with a stylized pattern of arabesques and baskets of flowers, plays dramatically different roles in the *Blue Still Life* of 1907, *Harmony in Red* of 1908, *Blue Tablecloth* of 1909, and the *Still Life with Geranium* of 1910. Following the toile de Jouy's migrations throughout his oeuvre, one can see it change identity with each role. Whether pinned against the wall, lying on a table or on the floor, or bunched up in a corner—changing color according to its role within the picture—it is transformed by its setting and is frequently more visually animated than the figures and objects it surrounds or supports. Indeed, Matisse's oeuvre encompasses a relatively small cast of recurring characters: chocolate and coffeepots, flower vases, books, goldfish bowls, his own painting and sculpture, and a small number of foreign models as well as members of his family appear again and again from his earliest works to his last. He would later describe the form of method acting performed by his subjects "theme and variations."

But no matter how many roles his actors played, the artist remained the director. "The artist must make the object worthy of interest," he explained. "It says only what he makes it say." "The object," like the actor, "is not so interesting in itself. It's the milieu that creates the object" (207/246–47).[61] While the milieu *creates* the object-actors—they are lost in their roles—Matisse creates the milieu where the objects play their part. Without the artist's projection of "love" onto his objects, they would remain stiffly independent, lacking any animate "relations."

At other times Matisse saw himself as the cameraman, observing the scene from a distance: "I create the cinematography of my model's private feelings. In my work I am as unobtrusive as a cameraman who is standing at the front of a train and who films the various aspects of an unknown countryside."[62] From model to countryside, the artist simultaneously creates the feelings he depicts and watches them as they unfold. He is both the observer behind the camera and director of the actor's feelings.

Matisse's fascination with the mechanisms of theater, cinema, and spectacles is well documented. Spurling relates how Matisse stayed up late into the night watching a film crew outside the casino in Nice. He was captivated by the director's total control over the scene (he particularly admired the megaphone as a means to project one's voice across a vast space).[63] He was so taken with the spectacle that he made a rough sketch of the scene, taking special note of the director's surveying role (Figure 3.3). Like the actor who remained a spectator of the feelings he represented on the stage, the artist performed his role with awareness that the feelings embodied in his pictures were his own, even if—only if—they were borrowed from another.

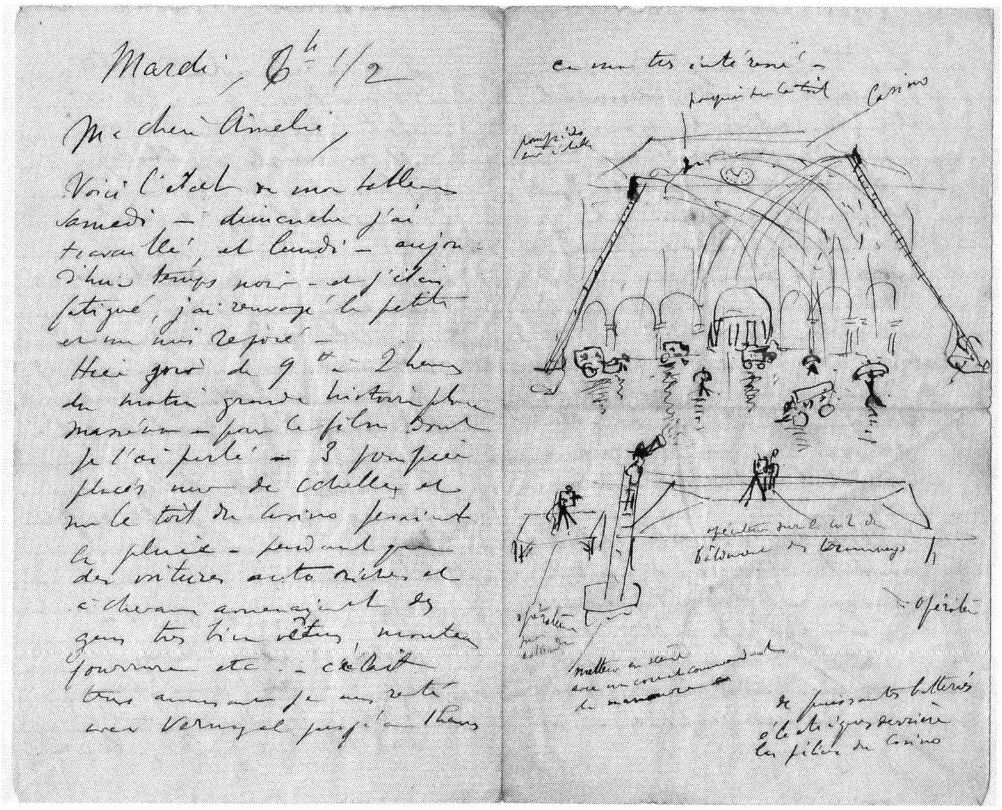

Figure 3.3. Henri Matisse (1869–1954), sketch of a film set in an undated letter to Mme Matisse, ca. 1921–23. Copyright 2013 Succession H. Matisse / Artists Rights Society (ARS), NY. Photograph Archives H. Matisse; copyright 2013 Succession H. Matisse.

The Painter in the Picture

Matisse discovered that one solution to the problem of other minds was to see the other as a form of the self, perhaps the most intimate and mysterious part. While this view did not require the explicit projection of his likeness into the space of the picture, it could nonetheless suggest that as well. It was Gilot's view that no matter what subject Matisse depicted, he began by psychologically projecting himself into the picture: "He puts a model in front of him almost as a decoy, to pacify his rational mind, while at the same time the person, object, or landscape is only there as a mirror reflecting his own project, his imaginative self in the process of becoming. He looks through the model rather than at the model" (84–85). Gilot captured the skeptical tenor of Matisse's works, as though there was a space of aloofness or reserve at the center of them, as though models simply did not exist for the artist except as mirrors of his self. For Gilot, it was the artist's model, and not any explicit mirror imagery, that figured the process of "rationalization." What I want to explore here is not simply the metaphorical claim of mirroring self-reflection, but the figurative or thematic role that mirrors, and more generally framing and the inclusion of his own work within his work, play in his practice.[64]

Consider, for instance, the complex representational setup of *Carmelina* (ca. 1903) (Plate 2). This work marks an early instance in an unfolding sequence of works in which Matisse takes the circuitry of representation as his subject. Beyond its seemingly realist commitment to optical accuracy, *Carmelina* projects an almost pedagogic atmosphere (a tone aided by its muted color), as though it were an exercise or demonstration of the materials, procedures, powers, and limits of representation.

In *Carmelina* the mirror-reflected artist appears diminutive—we see his right shoulder and back, his right arm (mirror reversed) extended toward the canvas just beyond the frame, his face, a sequence of bare indicators of flesh, beard, and hair—as though withdrawing from any direct encounter with the sitter's exposed body. The sitter's back, right arm, and hair—pulled into a tight ponytail, tied with a bow, and draped over her left shoulder—are reflected in the mirror while the painter appears to be at work on the picture we are now looking at. While frames, and frame-like surrogates, are projected throughout the scene, they stand in different and sometimes opposing relations to one another. One of the most curious moments in the picture is the framed image that lies suspended over the fireplace mantel, its top edge parallel to the mirror at left drawing a clear comparison between the two shapes. The framed image on the right is flat and unreadable, which seems to echo the frontality and blankness of the sitter's stare. The shape of the mirror resting on the table at left is more articulated than the other framed elements, and while the forms reflected in it are sketch-like, they are nonetheless legible and seem to open the studio space into a fictive distance, but one that projects outward, pointing to *this side* of the picture surface.

The large mirror draws a comparison with a range of framed and frame-like elements throughout the scene. Above the suspended image on the right appear a sequence of five vertically oriented rectangular boxes on a shelf; behind and above them appears another, larger, framed picture (we see only the lower edge of the frame, mat, and a glimpse of the image). To the left of the mirror hover two white rectangular forms, evoking a patterned decor of the door or wall (these forms reemerge in the mirror-space, now appearing behind the artist).

The picture is organized around a grid of horizontals and verticals. Along the right side a vertical line articulates the right side of the fireplace and continues through the suspended or leaning frame above. This vertical is balanced along the left side with the strong vertical of the left edge of the mirror. One of the most unsettling moments in the picture is the assertive vertical drawn across the sitter's chest. This line continues on the other side of the body along the turning edge of the far wall, drawing together the most salient and recessive elements in the picture.

The drama of the picture hangs on the balance and tension between the blank frontality of the framed elements, analogous to the wall-like expression of the sitter's gaze, and the sense of physical and emotional depth around the figure of the painter in the mirror. The mirror, that is, functions in an entirely different way from the other framed elements in the picture, as though its peculiar dual status as flat and deep were wholly to the point. Moreover, it is the moment where the two "bodies"—model and painter, surface and depth—touch, even if it occurs in the doubly fictive mirror-space that is the key to the picture's expressive charge.

Writing of *Carmelina* and related works, Jean Guichard-Meili reflects on "the frequent presence of the painter himself in his work." For Guichard-Meili the presence of mirrored reflection in Matisse's work was an effort to sustain personal autonomy while simultaneously denying the autonomy of the subjects depicted:

> Often it is his face that appears, reflected in a mirror at the back of the scene: an alert face, watching the model and watching himself. In this way, the importance of the creator in his creation is asserted. . . . it is thus a reminder of the fact that the subject does not exist in its own right, and that it has no autonomy. It becomes what the painter wishes it to be.[65]

In Guichard-Meili's formulation, the loss of autonomy within the picture is equivalent to the artist's achievement of selfhood outside the picture.[66] It is of course too pat a formula, but it nonetheless manages to frame the problem of self-reflection in clear terms. Revising Guichard-Meili's description, I would say that *Carmelina* figures two distinct and interrelated modalities. On one hand, it is a figure of skepticism or "rationalization" figured above all in the "materiality" of the picture surface and in the blankness of the sitter's stare, one that is further exemplified by the artist's detached presence overlooking the scene from within the picture space. Moreover, I would suggest that this figurative opacity and detachment captures the artist's felt sense of *discontinuity* with his work, as though it were the product of something beyond or outside his control. On the other hand, *Carmelina* is an assertion of the artist's sense of proximity or continuity between himself and his work, a moment captured in the poignant "touch" of artist and model, one that occurs within the mediated space of the mirror. I interpret this mirror-space connection—a characteristic moment, I will suggest—as Matisse's way of mitigating the directness and proximity of the gridded and exposed body while also figuring his sense of the contingency and fragility of expressive connection more generally. I would further note how the lower reaches of the picture surface—the cloth that hangs across the sitter's lap, the spread of the tablecloth beneath her feet, legs that seem almost to dissolve as they approach the lower or most proximate edge of the picture plane—intimate another potential moment of connection between artist and beholder, one that stands in contrast to the stark frontality of the picture's main themes.

Matisse's near obsessive use of mirrors, windows, and his own body or surrogates for his body, as with the numerous inclusions of his own work within his paintings, constitutes a project centered on picturing himself and thereby making himself present to his work. Of course there was no moment, as it were, when the self was made present to itself, and Matisse began to feel and search for a way to express its opposite, the sense of discontinuity or skeptical reserve that was his more "natural" mode of being in the world. Evidence seems to suggest that as his career went on, the process of identification became more and more fraught with psychological and pictorial difficulty for him. Gilot observed how his "representation of himself appeared more and more frequently in his own creations" (172).[67] It is the frequency and intensification of modes of self-portraiture that spoke to its significance as well as its limitations.

Three further works replicate and intensify the structural features of mirror reflection that emerged with my analysis of *Carmelina*. The little-discussed *Still Life with a Checked Tablecloth* of 1903 (Figure 3.4) features a still life arrangement of fruit, vases, and a basket spread across a red-and-white checked cloth that drapes down the edge of a mantelpiece (perhaps the same one that appears in *Carmelina*). As it spills down the front, its left edge creates a sharply contoured vertical while its right side folds back on itself, creating a hollow that is echoed in the shape of the handles of the containers.

The composition is ordered around a sequence of horizontals and verticals formed by the cloth, fireplace, and mirror above. The foreground elements are positioned flat up against the picture plane, while the hanging cloth evokes the texture of the canvas support beneath. At top left, nestled behind the objects, rests a broad mirror that reflects back partial features of the artist's face, signaling his location in the space outside the picture and analogous to the space where we stand. The picture expresses a sense of continuity between the still life objects in the foreground and the mirrored space behind. The broad handle of the tipped basket, for instance, reaches over the mirror frame and into the space of reflection, thereby fictively projecting into our space before the picture. The reflection is treated as though the handle at once stands out from the mirror and is continuous with the space behind it.

More than thirty years later Matisse returned to the original setup of *Carmelina* with *The Red Blouse* of 1936 (Figure 3.5). Concentrated on the distended upper body of the sitter, her red blouse is dramatically set against the deep blue-green of the chair. The sitter's form is awkwardly surmounted by a mirror reflection of the artist's head, with hat and glasses, in the upper right

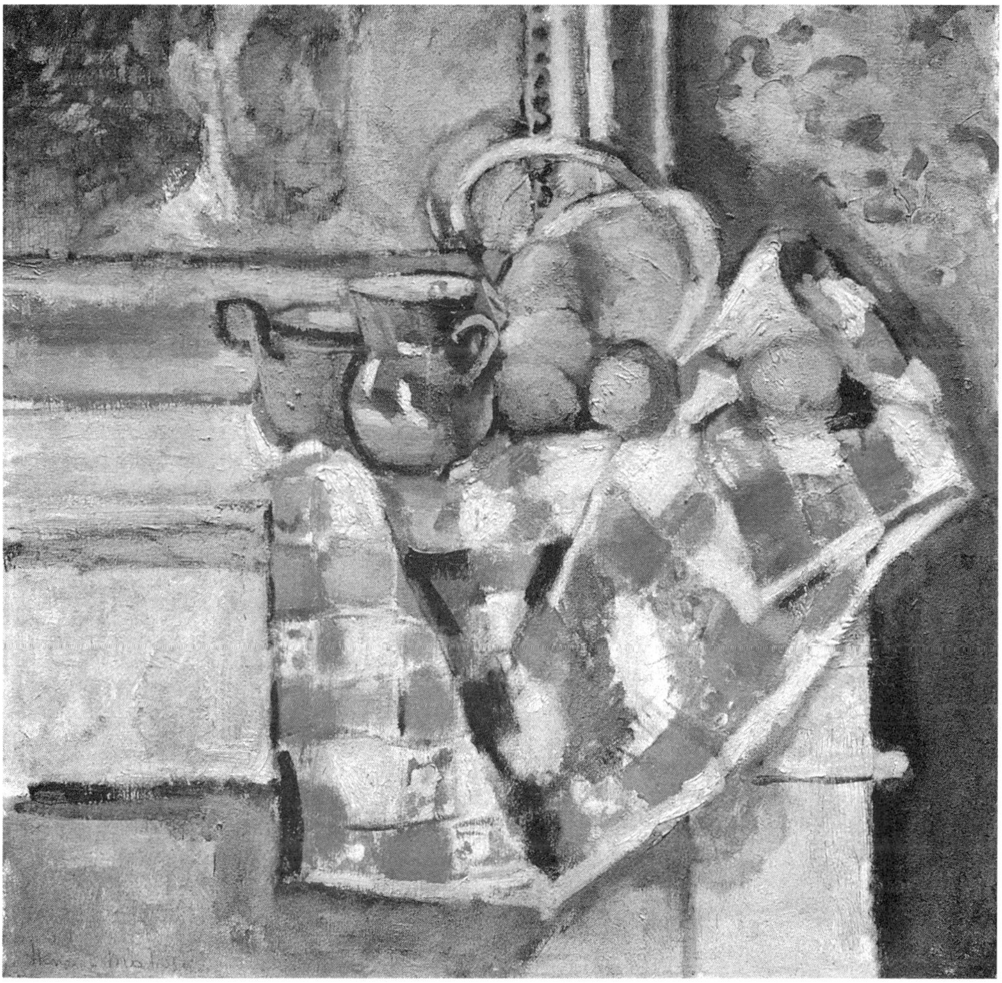

Figure 3.4. Henri Matisse (1869–1954), *Still Life with a Checked Tablecloth*, ca. 1903. Oil on canvas, 52.3 × 54.6 cm. Private collection. Courtesy of Peter Willi. Copyright 2013 Succession H. Matisse / Artists Rights Society (ARS), NY. Photograph courtesy of The Bridgeman Art Library / Peter Willi / PWI198896.

corner. The artist's bearded face seems almost to rest on the upper edge of the chair back. The brim of his hat echoes the sitter's collar, while his eyes, concealed behind lenses, parallel those of the model. The sitter's frontally disposed body fills up the picture surface, while the massive chair nearly blocks visual access into the space, producing a feeling of closure reinforced by the artist's guarded insertion into the scene.

Finally, consider *The Swimmer in the Aquarium* of 1946, plate 12 of *Jazz* (Figure 3.6).[68] The dramatically simplified scene shows the fully extended and horizontally disposed body of a swimmer, its form loosely contained within

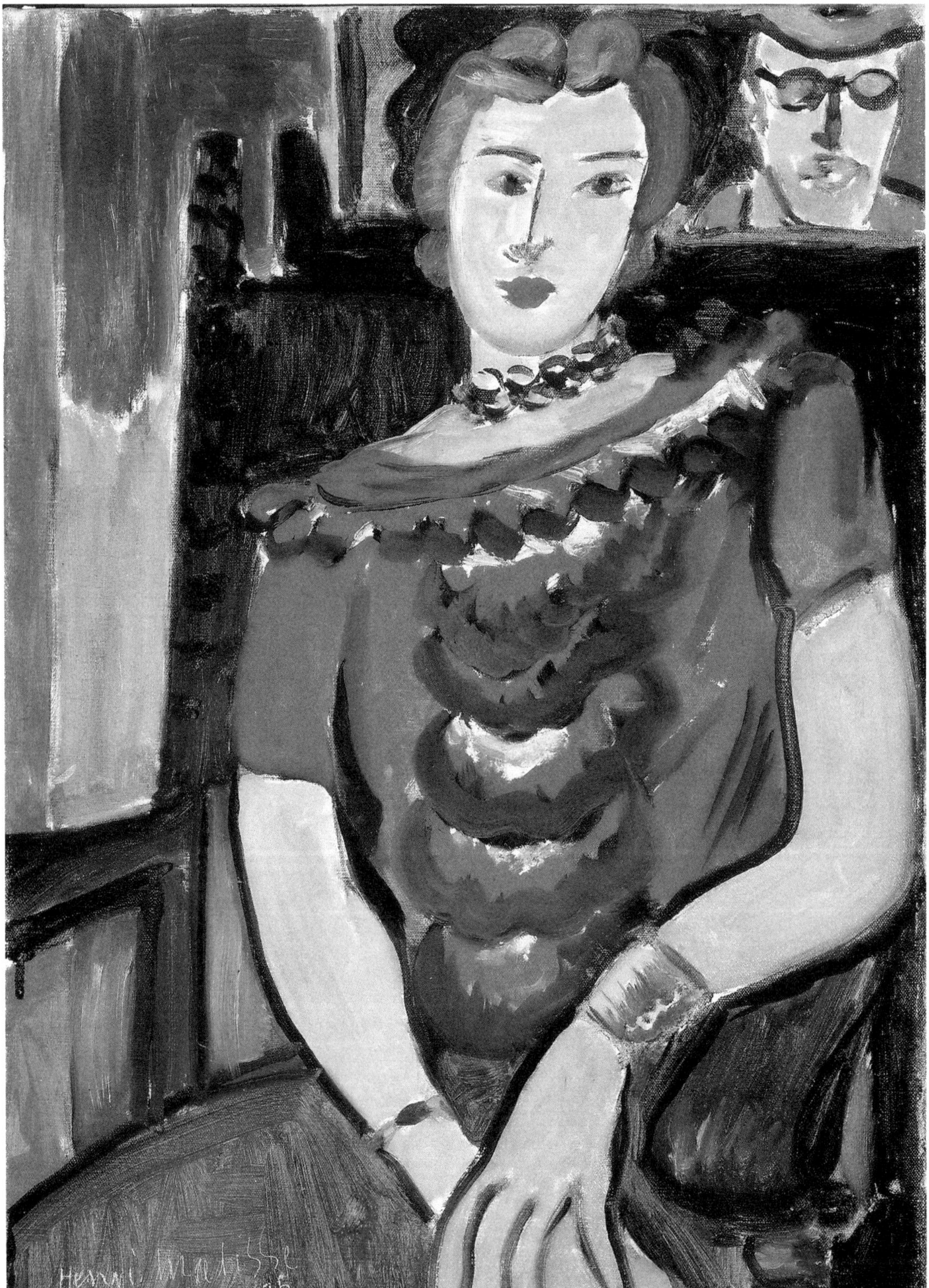

Figure 3.5. Henri Matisse (1869–1954), *The Red Blouse,* 1936. Oil on canvas, 18⅜ × 13⅛ inches (46.7 × 33.3 cm). Bequest of Marion Koogler McNay, McNay Art Museum, San Antonio, Texas. Copyright 2013 Succession H. Matisse / Artists Rights Society (ARS), NY. Photograph copyright McNay Art Museum / Art Resource, NY.

four floating rectangles (five if we include the white ground). The pictorial drama is driven by the complex play of the colored rectangles that seem to alternately hover near the surface and recede into space. The swimmer's white body is further framed by the bright-red form of an onlooker (the artist?) peering in or down from the bottom right. The two forms seem situated in radically different bodily and spatial registers. While the flattened and distended form of the swimmer spans the whole of the picture space, the two or three vertically oriented rectangles behind it seem to reiterate and intensify the figure's blank frontality. And yet the sense of pressure against the surface is mitigated by the suggestion of water flowing around the forms, as though the red face below floats in the same substance as the swimmer despite its seemingly detached location beyond the glass box. (Or perhaps it is not a face at all, but a rock toward which the swimmer lunges for security?)

What sets these four pictures (spanning forty years) apart from Matisse's wider oeuvre is their explicit thematization, through the use of a mirrored

Figure 3.6. Henri Matisse (1869–1954), *The Swimmer in the Aquarium*, from *Jazz*, 1947. Portfolio of twenty *pochoirs*. Composition of various dimensions; sheet: 16¾ × 25¹¹⁄₁₆ inches. Museum of Modern Art, New York. Published by Tériade Éditeur, Paris. Printer: Edmond Vairel and Draeger Frères, Paris. Edition: 250. Copyright 2013 Succession H. Matisse / Artists Rights Society (ARS), NY. Digital image copyright Museum of Modern Art; licensed by Scala / Art Resource, NY, ART317687.

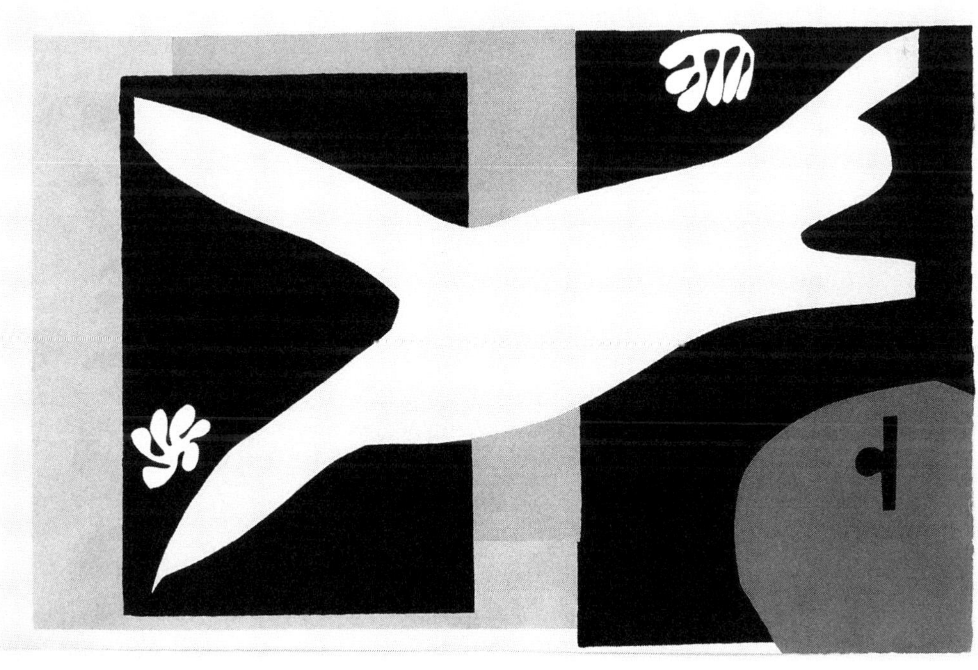

self-portraiture or fictive projection of the artist (or his surrogate) into the picture space, of issues of skepticism and embodiment. In the next section I explore a closely related pictorial arrangement but one that does not include an explicit representation of the artist within the picture. Nonetheless, the structural features of these works replicate the dual and conflicted nature of the "self-portrait" works while marking out a shared set of features for Matisse's work as a whole.

The 1901 Standing Figure Sequence

In the summer of 1901 Matisse visited his parents, who were vacationing in the Swiss Alps. The trip lasted two weeks and he returned home with about a dozen small oils on cardboard, including works such as *The Alps in Savoy* (Figure 3.7) and *Pine Trees* (Figure 3.8), both of which were subsequently owned by Picasso. Little information is available about this trip, but later in his life Matisse reflected back on his Alpine experience and made a revealing statement: "I don't believe mountain landscapes can be of much profit for painters. The difference in scale prevents any intimate contact. A few weeks in the mountains are excellent, but as a complete rest from work."[69] These small landscapes can be seen as reflections on the problem of difference in scale between human and natural worlds. The placement of a foreground cabin in *The Alps in Savoy,* with its vertical pole connecting human and natural, subtly but significantly organizes and orients the natural world in terms of human scale. Alternately, I would suggest that *Pine Trees* is one of the few pure landscapes Matisse produced. The view taken here shifts the horizon to the space above the cabin, offering the viewer a survey of the mountain range beyond with little effort to establish a sense of human measure. Although I will not pursue the claim here, I would suggest that it was his unhappy aesthetic encounter with mountain landscapes that first established Matisse's commitment to an art of human scale, or to what he called spaces of "intimate contact."

When Clement Greenberg declared in 1953 that while "Matisse himself feels no predilection for landscape," he was nonetheless "the greatest" landscape painter of the century, he knew he was offering a deeply unorthodox opinion and one that Matisse would likely not have recognized.[70] Matisse was forthright about his *figurative* ambitions; as he put it in his "Notes of a Painter" of 1908, "What interests me most is neither still life nor landscape, but the human figure. It is the human figure which best permits me to express my so-to-speak religious feeling towards life" (41/49). This figurative orientation is actually difficult to construe, given his mainly still life and landscape production of his first ten years of work, but it comes fully into view with a series of standing nudes in the studio produced in the weeks and months prior to his trip to the Alps.

Looking at the work Matisse produced between 1900 and 1905, it is clear that the structural arrangement balancing frontality and continuity featured

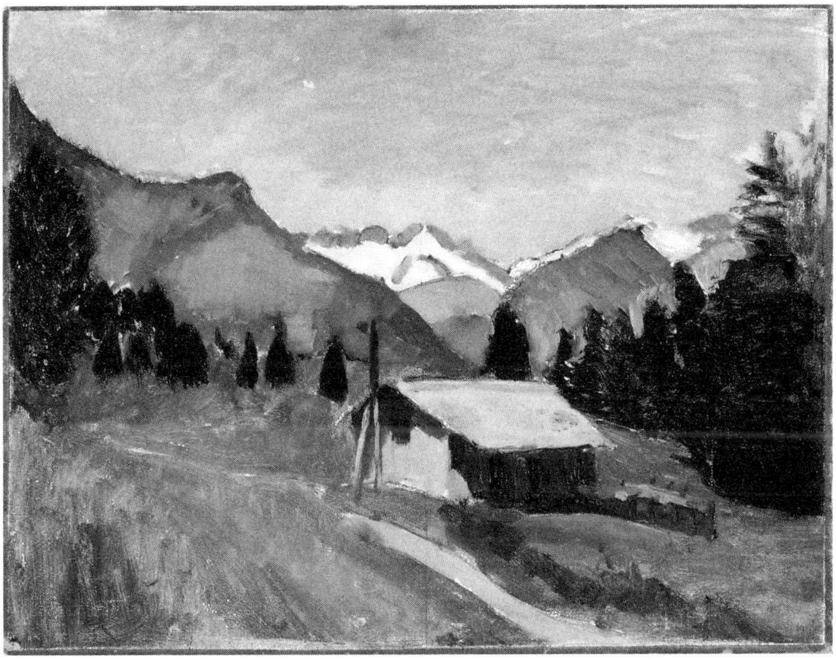

Figure 3.7. Henri Matisse (1869–1954), *The Alps in Savoy,* ca. 1901. Oil on canvas, 36 × 48 cm. Musée Picasso, Paris, France. Copyright 2013 Succession H. Matisse / Artists Rights Society (ARS), NY. Photograph by G. Blot and C. Jean. Courtesy of Réunion des Musées Nationaux / Art Resource, NY, ART145901.

Figure 3.8. Henri Matisse (1869–1954), *Pine Trees,* ca. 1901. Oil on cardboard, 36 × 48 cm. Musée Picasso, Paris, France. Copyright 2013 Succession H. Matisse / Artists Rights Society (ARS), NY. Photograph by R. G. Ojeda. Courtesy of Réunion des Musées Nationaux / Art Resource, NY, ART145900.

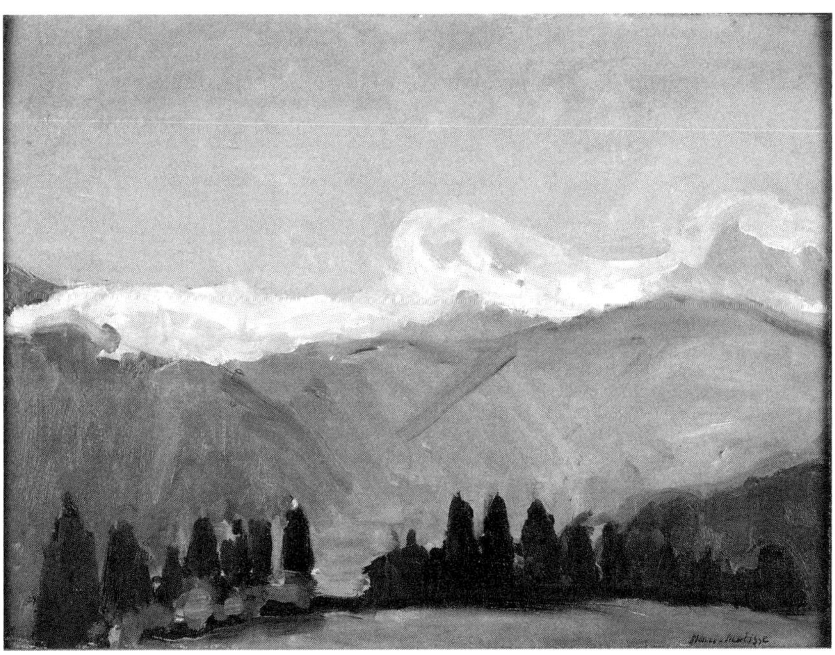

in *Carmelina* is a particular variant on a more long-standing figure type. The standing nude figure type first emerged in his work in response to Cézanne's great *Standing Nude* of 1898–99 (Figure 3.9), which he saw at Vollard's gallery around 1900.[71] The upward reach of the arms, spread stance, and arched back stretch open the body, which is dramatically silhouetted against the blank background wall. Matisse copied the form in several drawings (Figure 3.11) that largely maintain the basic setup of Cézanne's figure but extract it from the interior setting. In *Standing Nude (Study in Blue)* (Plate 3), Matisse preserves the basic arrangement of the Cézanne but crucially complicates the area around the face. Here, the figure's arms are raised and the hands are clasped over the face, hiding it completely from view, while the lower part of her exposed body presses forward toward the picture plane. The figure's thickly treated flesh draws her out from the receding atmosphere of the studio space, while her covered face reverses the forward lean of her body and draws the head—almost entirely lost to sight—deep into the space. The scene as a whole is driven by a tension between the assertive handling, heightened colorism, and inflated sexuality of the body and the model's gesture of emphatic, even strenuous, withdrawal from the space of the beholder into the blue of the wider setting.

Standing Nude (Study in Blue) is part of an extraordinary and little-discussed series of small-scale works—etchings, drawings, and paintings—that exemplify Matisse's conflicted attitude toward representation, a conflict figured by twin modes of embodiment and facingness. Throughout the standing nude sequence the model's face is occluded by various modes of blotting, blanking, deleting, erasing, or painting over. In *The Model* (Figure 3.12) the figure's right arm is awkwardly and mysteriously raised up around the side of her lowered head, her face purposefully distorted and illegible; in *Standing Nude* (Figure 3.10) the figure's pose is equally static, the body fully exposed, while the face is blanked out as though in preview of the two rightmost bathers in the great *Bathers by a River* of 1909–16.

Two related works—an etching with drypoint and a drawing—further explore the psychological and pictorial problems raised by the Cézannian form. In these works the figure's naked body is fully exposed to view while the face is withdrawn, either through arms and hands raised in the act of weeping (Figure 3.14) or by an arm dramatically pulled across the face (Figure 3.15), as though the figure is withdrawing in shame. I am tempted to read the shape of the body in *Standing Nude, Arm Raised* (Figure 3.15) as a surrogate face, staring outward at the beholder, as though facingness were an irresistible fact of both the body and the picture surface.

One way to understand the sequence as a whole is to see these works as a complex response to Cézanne's monumental figure types. They attempt to merge or reconcile two aspects of Cézanne's nudes. On one hand, Matisse

Figure 3.9. Paul Cézanne (1839–1906), *Standing Nude*, 1898–99. Oil on canvas, 92.7 × 71.1 cm. Private collection. Photograph by Erich Lessing / Art Resource, NY.

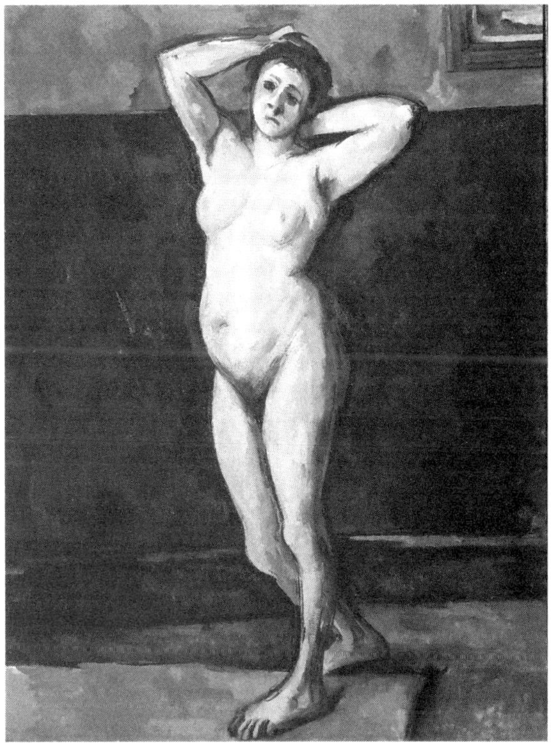

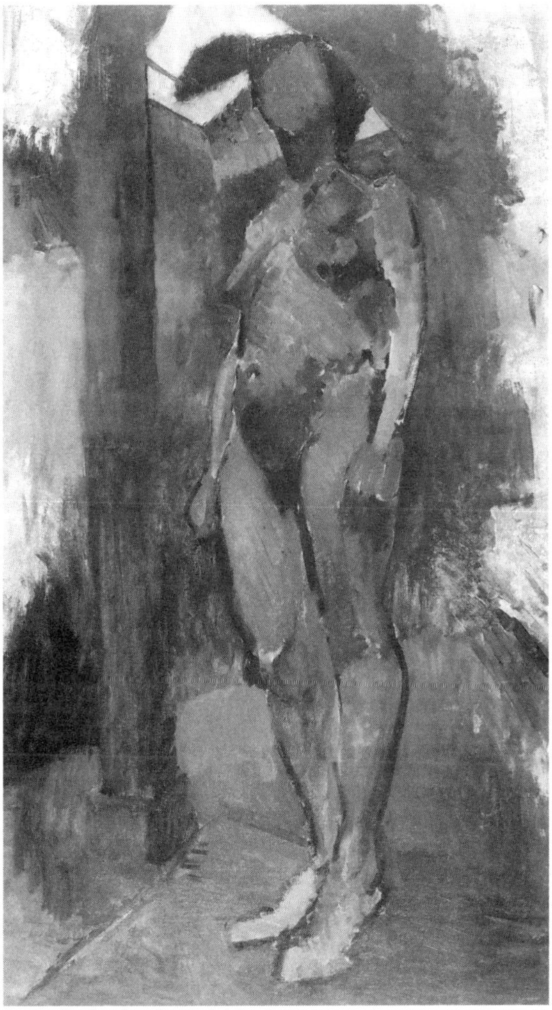

Figure 3.10. Henri Matisse (1869–1954), *Standing Nude*, ca. 1901. Oil on canvas, 44.5 × 78.7 cm. Fine Arts Museums of San Francisco, Bequest of Aurelie Henwood to the de Young Museum in memory of Lucille and Gardner Dailey. Copyright 2013 Succession H. Matisse / Artists Rights Society (ARS), NY.

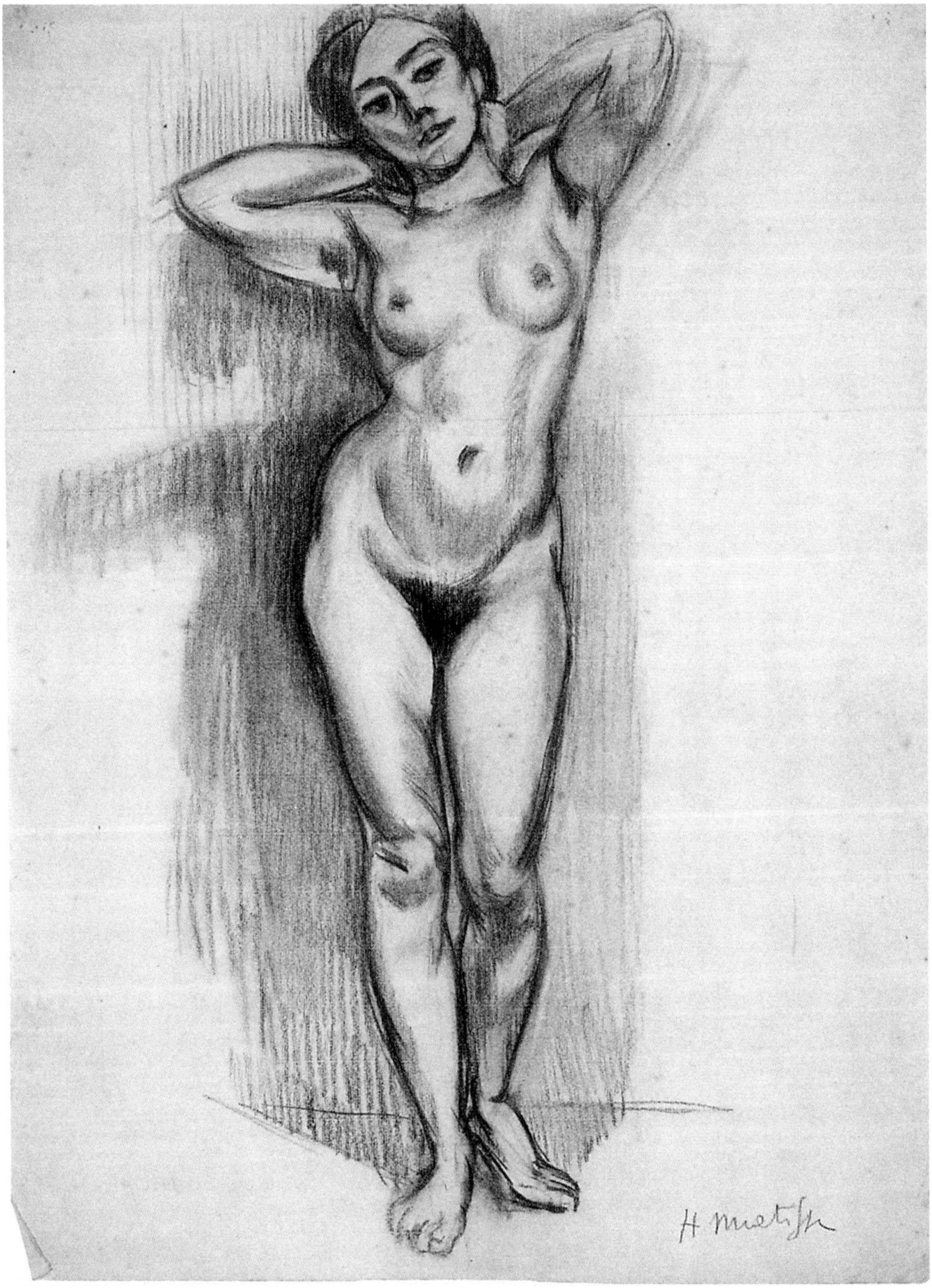

Figure 3.11. Henri Matisse (1869–1954), *Standing Nude,* ca. 1905. Charcoal with erasing, 63 × 47 cm. Pierre and Maria-Gaetana Matisse Foundation Collection. Copyright 2013 Succession H. Matisse / Artists Rights Society (ARS), NY.

Figure 3.12. Henri Matisse (1869–1954), *The Model,* ca. 1900. Oil on canvas. Musée d'Art Moderne de la ville de Paris. Copyright 2013 Succession H. Matisse / Artists Rights Society (ARS), NY.

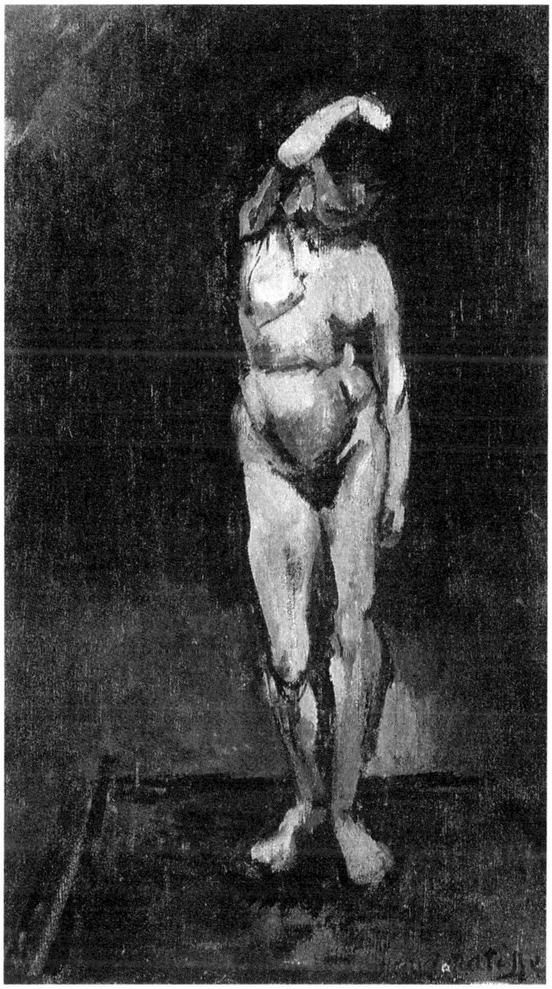

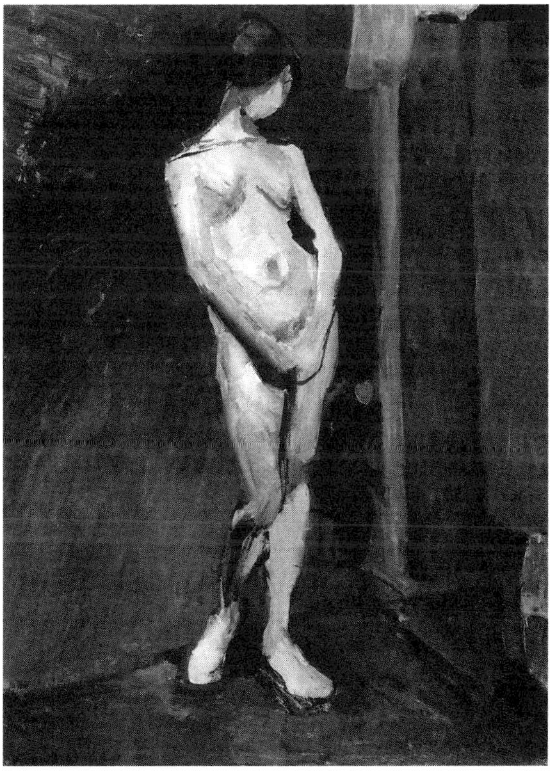

Figure 3.13. Henri Matisse (1869–1954), *Nude Study in Blue,* ca. 1899–1900. Oil on canvas, 73 × 54.3 cm. Tate Collection, bequeathed by C. Frank Stoop, 1933. Copyright 2013 Succession H. Matisse / Artists Rights Society (ARS), NY.

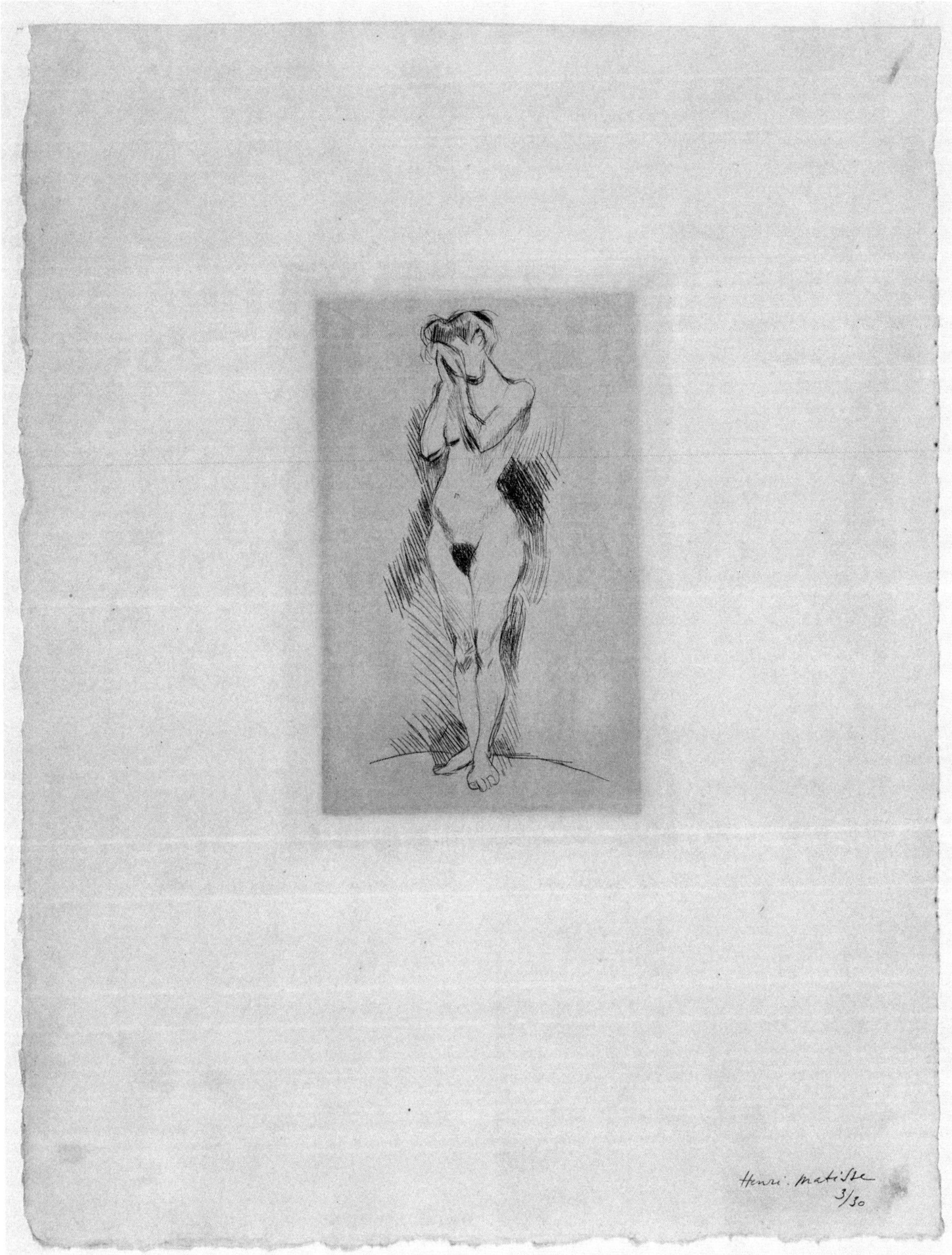

Figure 3.14. Henri Matisse (1869–1954), *The Weeper,* 1900–1903. Etching and drypoint; plate: 5 7/8 × 3 13/16 inches (14.9 × 9.7 cm), sheet: 12 5/8 × 10 1/16 inches (32 × 25.5 cm). Abby Aldrich Rockefeller Fund, Museum of Modern Art, New York. Copyright 2013 Succession H. Matisse / Artists Rights Society (ARS), NY. Digital image copyright Museum of Modern Art; licensed by Scala / Art Resource, NY, ART413278.

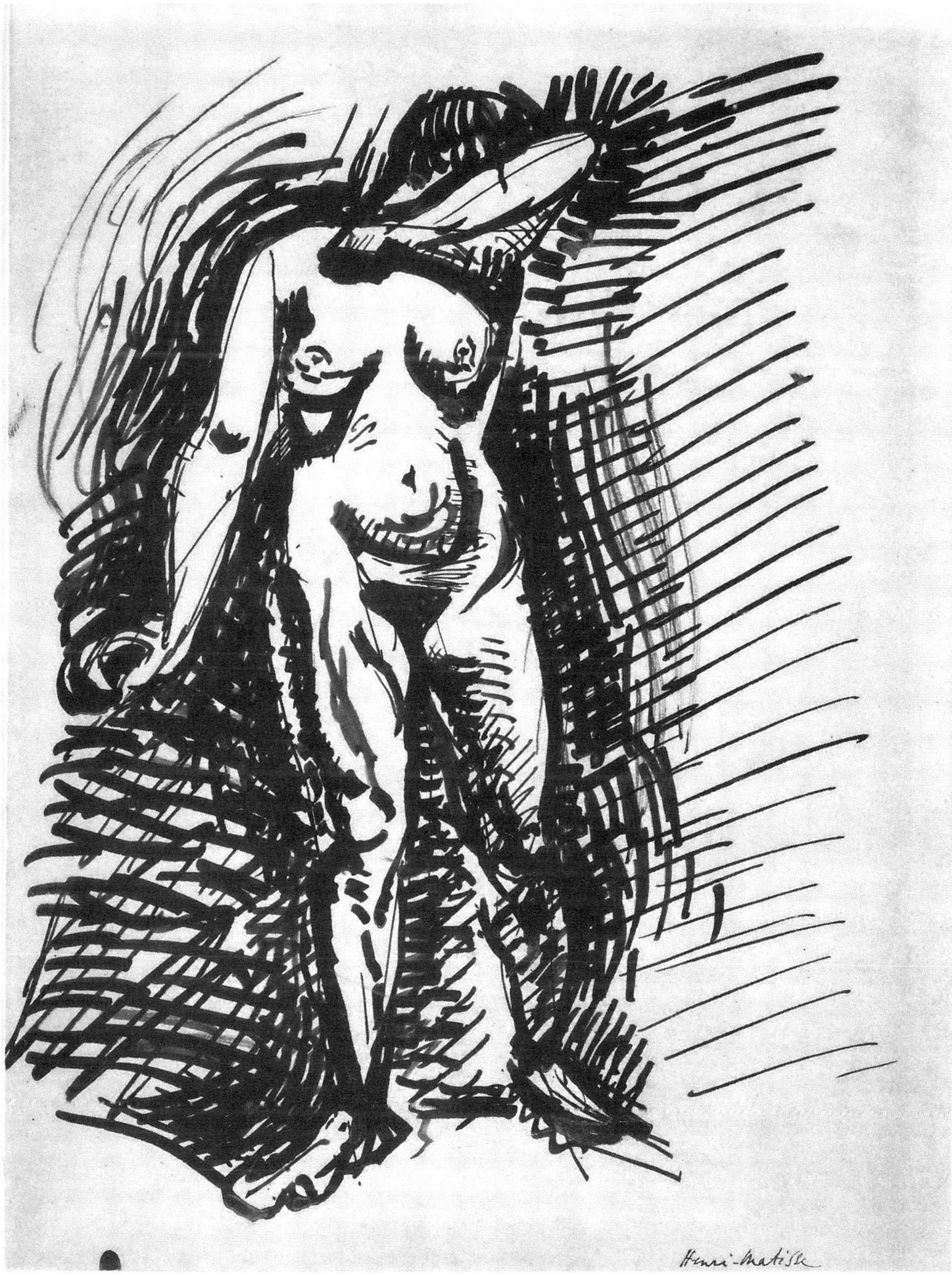

Figure 3.15. Henri Matisse (1869–1954), *Standing Nude, Arm Raised,* 1901–3. Brush and ink on paper, 10⅜ × 8 inches. Gift of Edward Steichen, Museum of Modern Art, New York. Copyright 2013 Succession H. Matisse / Artists Rights Society (ARS), NY. Digital image copyright Museum of Modern Art; licensed by Scala / Art Resource, NY.

exaggerates the tense and exposed naked body seen in Cézanne's *Standing Nude,* an exposure that is analogous, I would suggest, to the artist's own experience standing before the work and reflecting its brute, material qualities. On the other hand, Matisse's standing nude sequence is an attempt to overcome or annul or neutralize that felt sense of bodily and material exposure by occluding the face and pressing the body back into the setting or withdrawing the figure deeper into itself (just how much or how little psychology we can sense in these figures is a question I will not pursue here).

For that reason, we might say *Standing Nude (Study in Blue)* is closer to Cézanne's upright and frontally disposed *Bather* of around 1885, who fills up the space proximate to the picture plane, and whose bared form is laid out for the viewer's lingering gaze (Figure 3.16).[72] Despite the sense of exposure, the figure seems to *resist* the pressure of the beholder's look; his head is tilted down, his eyes averted and withdrawn deep into himself—he is withholding as much as he gives. His complex posture suggests he is at once moving out toward the beholder and yet massively rooted to the terrain at his feet. Although Matisse's standing nudes are more extreme in their standoff between exposed frontality and emphatic withdrawal, they are nonetheless keyed to the problems raised by Cézanne's monumental nudes.

Then again, Matisse's response is more complicated still as he declaratively situates the action within the normative space of the studio, as though landscape, and its automatic displacement of the beholder, was not an option available to him. That Matisse's works are largely produced in interiors and studios, a fact made thematic in numerous works, is essential to their meaning in the way Cézanne's figure inhabiting a landscape is significant for his. Once again Matisse was concerned to thematize the explicitly human constraints on his practice, an idea that was not typically emphasized in Cézanne's great landscape paintings or in Impressionism more generally. As though to foreclose any easy suggestion of merger of artist, figure, and ground, Matisse modeled his practice on Cézanne's studio-based works.

While the pedagogic tone of the standing figure sequence recedes with the emergence of Matisse's fauve work, he nonetheless continued to grapple with the structural problems raised by the picture group. *Interior with a Young Girl (Girl Reading)* of 1905–6 (Figure 3.17), for instance, reiterates key characteristics of that sequence but deploys them within a more ambitious setting. A young woman is seated at a table reading a book. Her head is arched down, her left arm is bent at the elbow, and her left hand is pressed into her hair as though curling it in absorbed distraction. The sitter's right hand is pulled in close to her chest against which the book rests. Beneath the book is a wooden book rest that effectively draws the volume and her upper body into a close connection, further enforcing the charged atmosphere of concentration. On the table before her lies a still life grouping of a chocolate pot, fruit dish, and

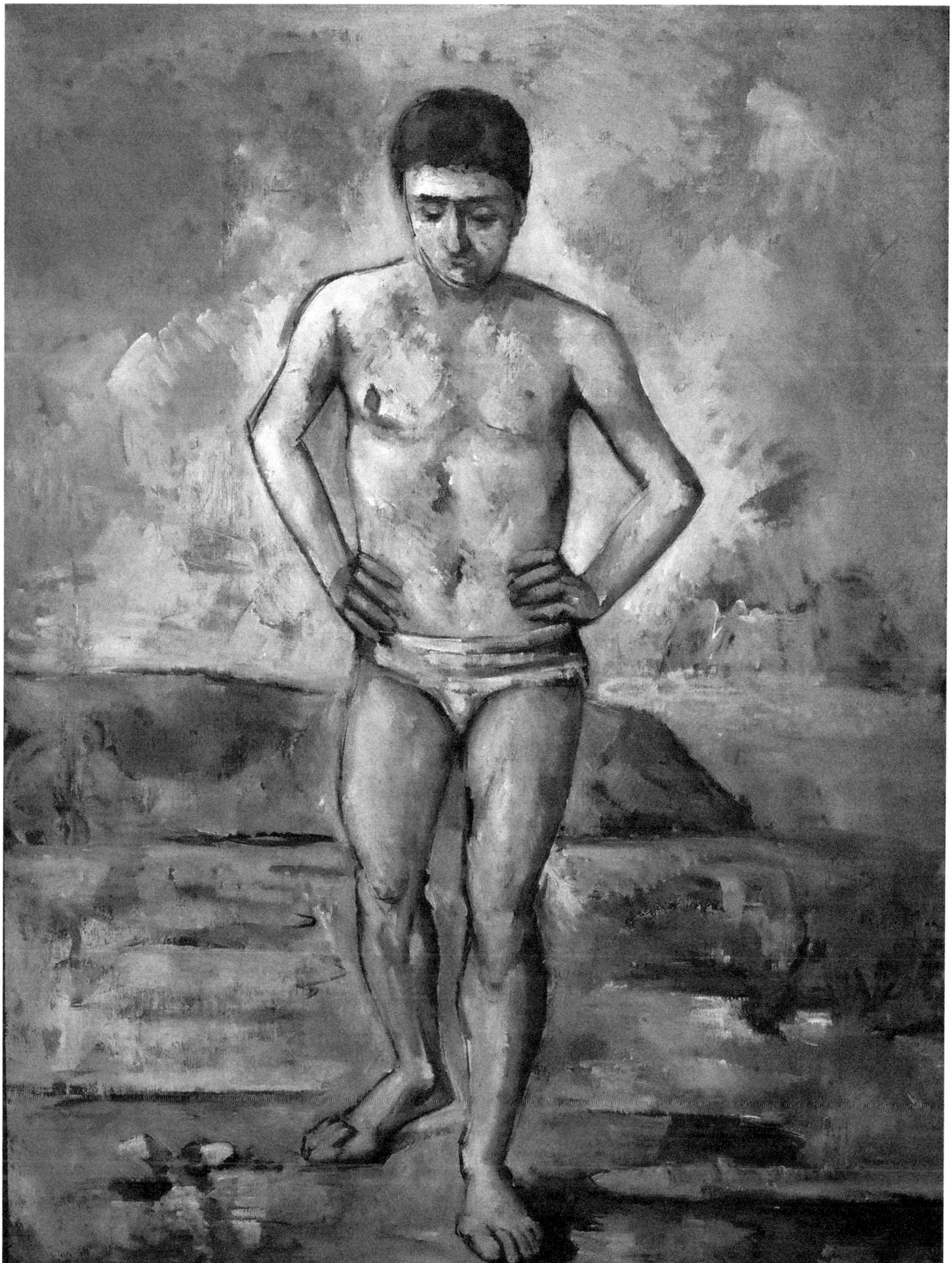

Figure 3.16. Paul Cézanne (1839–1906), *The Bather*, ca. 1885. Oil on canvas, 50 × 38⅛ inches. Lillie P. Bliss Collection, Museum of Modern Art, New York. Digital image copyright Museum of Modern Art; licensed by Scala / Art Resource, NY.

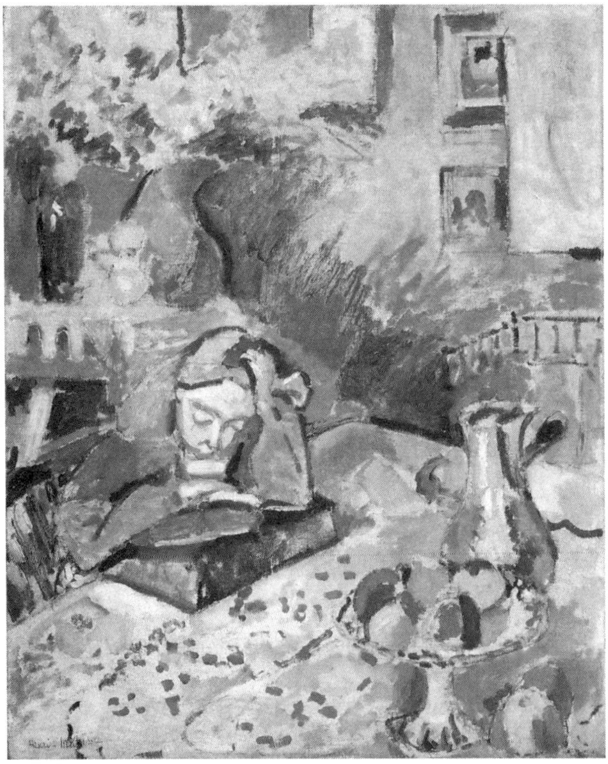

Figure 3.17. Henri Matisse (1869–1954), *Interior with a Young Girl (Girl Reading)*, 1905–6. Oil on canvas, 28⅝ × 23½ inches (72.7 × 59.7 cm). Fractional gift of a private collector to the Museum of Modern Art, New York. Copyright 2013 Succession H. Matisse / Artists Rights Society (ARS), NY. Digital image copyright Museum of Modern Art; licensed by Scala / Art Resource, NY.

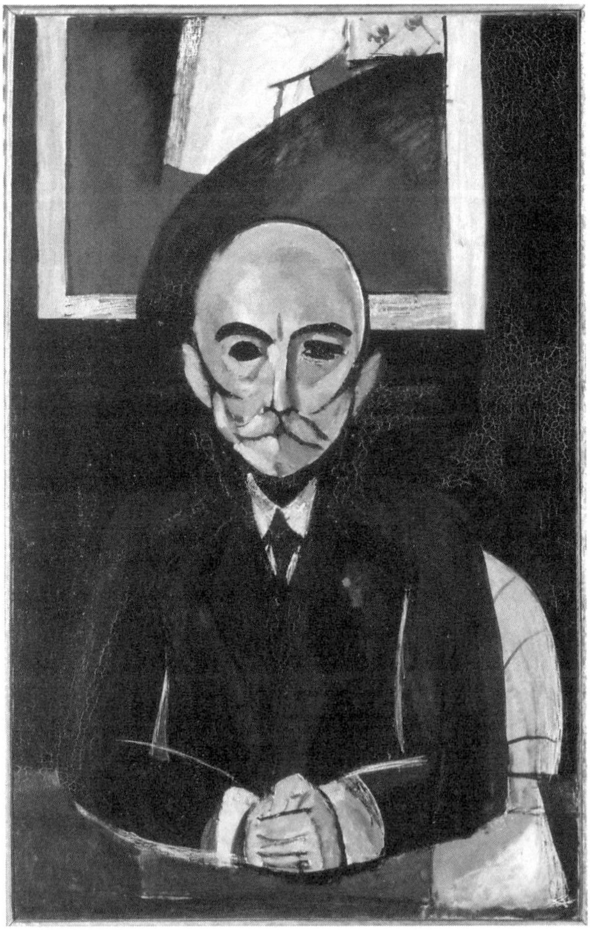

Figure 3.18. Henri Matisse (1869–1954), *Auguste Pellerin II*, 1917. Oil on canvas, 150.2 × 96.2 cm. AM1982-97. Musée National d'Art Moderne, Centre Georges Pompidou, Paris, France. Copyright 2013 Succession H. Matisse / Artists Rights Society (ARS), NY. Photograph by Christian Bahier/Philippe Migeat. Photograph courtesy of CNAC/MNAM/Dist. Réunion des Musées Nationaux / Art Resource, NY.

two loose pieces of fruit resting on the table. Despite the fact that the foreground fruits provide blasts of vermilion, orange, purple, and green, the forms do not spread into the larger setting, as they are effectively contained by the raised fruit dish. The color flashes within the dish seem to further secure her rapt state of attention by pointing up her unawareness of, her indifference to, the fruit and warming chocolate just beyond her reach. The latter seem to be offered as much to the viewer as to the sitter.

The foreground scene does not prepare us for the dramatic space above and behind the figure. The sitter appears oblivious to the blaze of color and jagged lines seeming to press in on her from above. Matisse has set up an exemplary contrast between the still life grouping against the far wall and the one that appears on the table. Hues of red, green, and yellow in the foreground arrangement seem to do opposite work in the background, dissolving firm contours into flat color patches, rendering the wider decor illegible.[73] The picture turns on the contrast and tension between the concentrated and attentive state of the sitter and the directed outwardness of the picture's wider setting.

The persistence of the structural dynamic described above is evident in a work that might seem to share little with the standing figure group or *Girl Reading.* The portrait *Auguste Pellerin II* (Figure 3.18), completed in the months prior to Matisse's relocation to Nice late in 1917, reiterates the structural pattern of the earlier works. The portrait depicts Pellerin, the great entrepreneur and art collector, seated at home, his stately arms resting foursquare on a broad desk, his eyes directed outward, his gaze seeming to meet our own. And yet, despite the figure's intense outward stare, his eyes do not in fact meet ours; they are blackened hollows that seem to merge with his jacket and the general atmosphere of the room. The active cancellation of the sitter's look even while he assertively engages the beholder produces an absorptive effect in the face of its outward negation.

Bois has observed that "only a handful of his paintings . . . show the sitter in a frontal pose, sternly regarding the beholder. In general, Matisse's sitters . . . appear absent-minded—'absorbed' . . . —their gaze a directionless blur."[74] This, I think, grasps one half of the pictorial equation. More to the point, Gilot reflected on the dual character of Matisse's portraits, describing figures whose "eyes look so lost in total absorption of an inner vision that they stare blindly in front of them, utterly unaware of a viewer out there" (258). While the figures stare directly out at the viewer with all the candor of a Manet, they are nonetheless lost to us, withdrawn into a world of inward contemplation.

Original Quotation: The 1903 Costume Sequence

It should not surprise us that Matisse's next major encounter with the past was with Manet. At the conclusion of the standing nude sequence Matisse began another ambitious campaign, this time of costumed figures in interiors. *Lucien Guitry (as Cyrano), Bevilacqua as Toreador,*[75] *The Monk* (Plate 4), *Female Guitarist, Standing Guitarist,* and *Guitarist* (Figure 3.19) constitute a small and closely interrelated costume group. Four of these works were featured in his first one-man exhibition at the Galerie Vollard in June 1904 and again at the Salon d'Automne of that year. This series from the winter of 1902–3 constitutes his most direct confrontation with Manet's example in his career.[76] Like Manet, Matisse makes no effort to disguise the circumstances

Figure 3.19. Henri Matisse (1869–1954), *Guitarist,* 1903. Oil on canvas, 55 × 46 cm. Private collection. Copyright 2013 Succession H. Matisse / Artists Rights Society (ARS), NY. Photograph courtesy of Archives Henri Matisse.

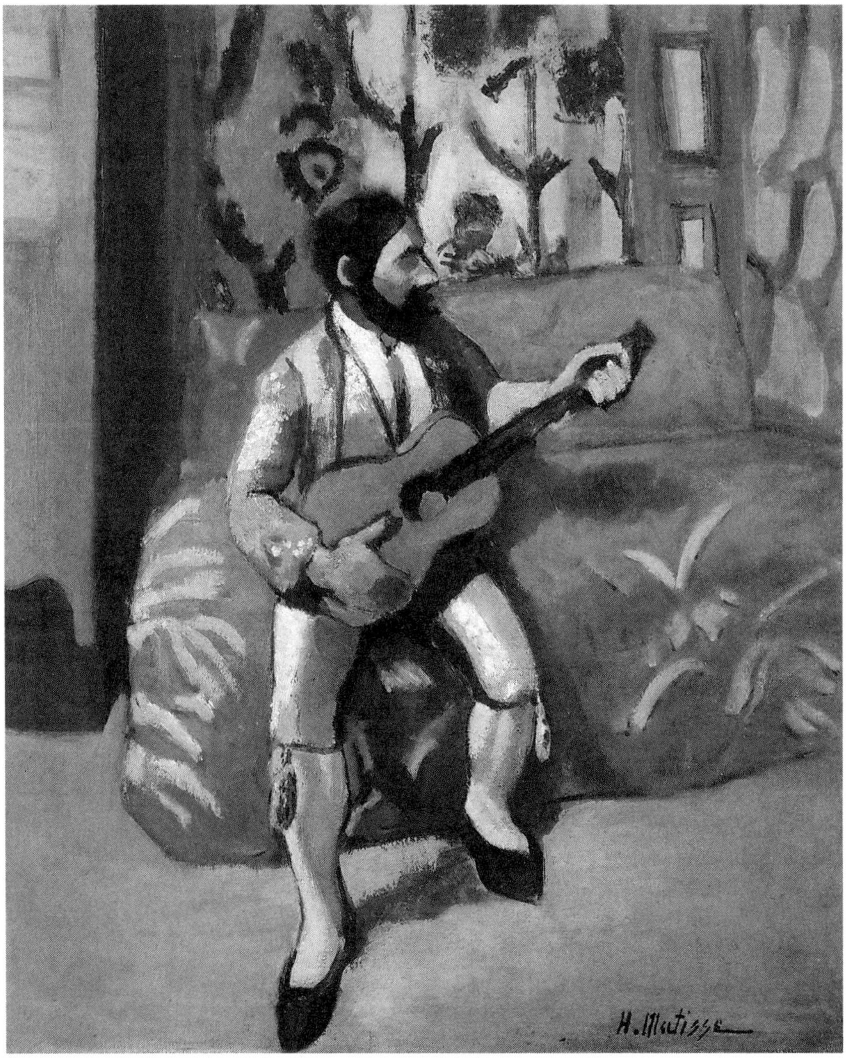

in which the works are made, but rather emphasizes the artifice of the studio ambience.[77]

Citing Manet's own citational costumed figures of the early 1860s, Matisse's *Guitarist* foregrounds the staged quality of the scene but crucially *resists* the assertively outward look of Manet's central figure types. While Matisse's work emphatically declares the artifice of the depicted action—the studio props, the awkward handling of the guitar, the heightened and dissonant color contrasts, and aggressive mark making—despite all of this the sitter feels lost to us, his gaze abstracted and turned from view, his body pulled in two directions at once, both toward the viewer—the guitar face drawn parallel to the picture plane—and away, head turned, his eye a great blank.

Matisse's resistance to the outwardly directed gaze of Manet's figures was, I would suggest, overdetermined. We know, for instance, that the confrontational look of *Olympia* (Figure 3.20) had little purchase on his pictorial concerns.[78] Matisse went so far as to say that *Olympia* "remains very close to the traditional painting of the old school" and that "it is not, for this very reason, one of his best." While Matisse found little to admire in *Olympia,* he thought *The Dead Toreador* of around 1864 (Figure 3.21), which he saw at the

Figure 3.20. Édouard Manet (1832–83), *Olympia,* 1863–65. Oil on canvas, 130.5 × 190 cm. Musée d'Orsay, Paris, France. Photograph courtesy of Scala / Art Resource, NY, ART150433.

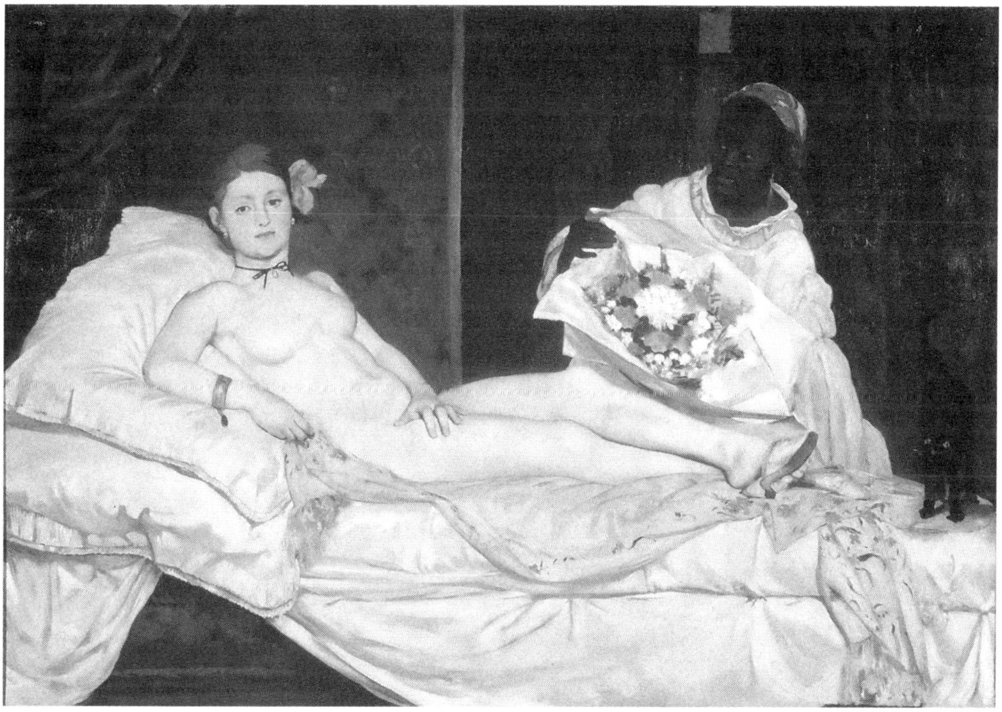

National Gallery in Washington, D.C., in 1930, was the very "finest" of Manet's works (295).[79] This is a deeply idiosyncratic judgment. *The Dead Toreador* is among the most atypical Manet paintings the artist ever conceived (it was, we know, cut from another picture). What clearly differentiates *Olympia* from *The Dead Toreador* is that the latter is one of the few works by Manet that expresses a quasi-absorptive state of mind or action; I say "quasi-" because there remains the unmistakable sense that this absorption itself is something of a pose.[80] Indeed, what Matisse found so appealing about *The Dead Toreador* was that the figure's condition—dead—made it humanly unavailable to the forms of facingness made explicit by Manet. I would add that Matisse's fascination with *The Dead Toreador* adds a layer of significance to Matisse's choice, in 1895, to copy Philippe de Champaigne's *Dead Christ* (Figure 3.22). It is as if Champaigne's subject were a premodern equivalent to Manet's *Dead Toreador,* but without the least suggestion of Manet's outward-facing gaze and with a maximum resistance to conventional modes of empathetic identification.[81] Nonetheless, two aspects of *The Dead Christ* should be noted, as they further complicate its meaning. First, the upturned crown of thorns at the bottom left implicitly acknowledges the flatness of the picture surface, and second, the dead Christ is not dead in the way the toreador is—he is at least *potentially* animate, in the way only Christ can be.

Matisse's encounter with Manet is further charged in his stunning *Monk* (Plate 4), which is part of the costume sequence. While the sitter's posture suggests a deep state of contemplation—eyes closed, hands drawn in close to his lap, the deep shadows along the creases of his robe granting his form a

Figure 3.21. Édouard Manet (1832–83), *The Dead Toreador,* ca. 1864. Oil on canvas, 29⅞ × 60⅜ cm. Widener Collection, National Gallery of Art, Washington, D.C.

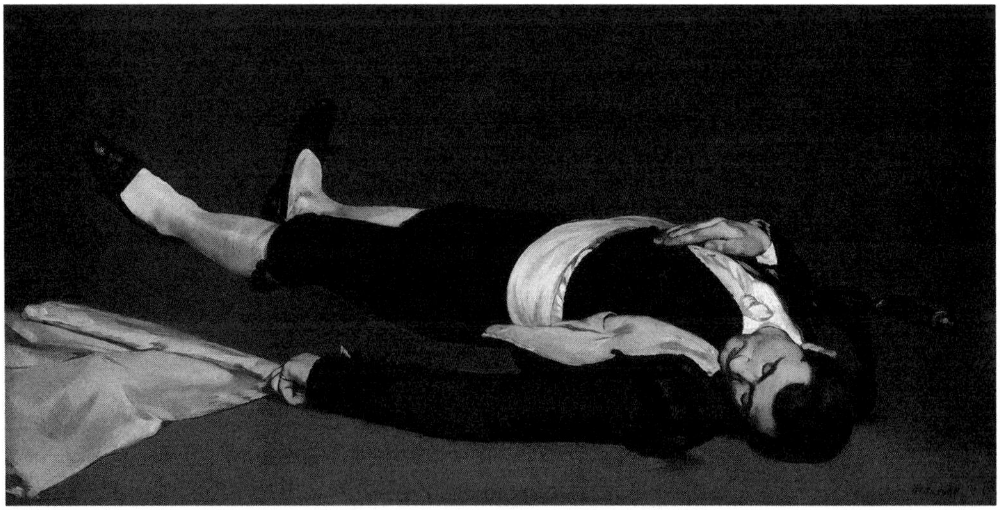

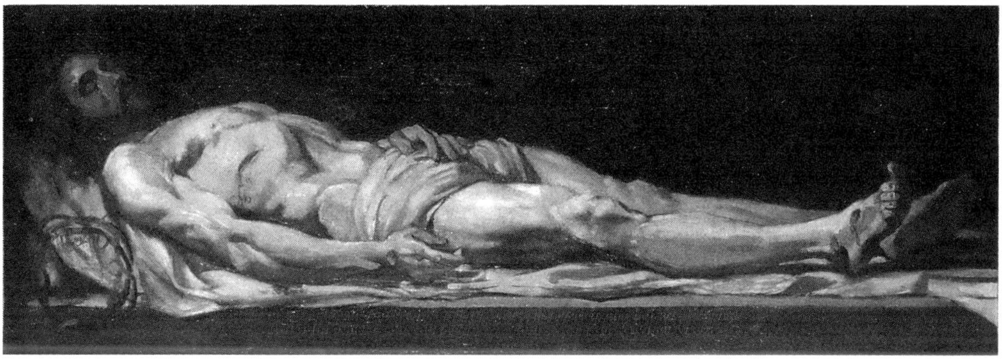

Figure 3.22. Henri Matisse (1869–1954), *The Dead Christ, after Philippe de Champaigne*, 1895. Oil on canvas, 67 × 194 cm. Musée Matisse, Nice, France. Bequest of Madame Henri Matisse, 1960. Inventory 63.2.16. Copyright 2013 Succession H. Matisse / Artists Rights Society (ARS), NY. Photograph from City of Nice Photographic Service.

weighty repose—the handling, especially around the face and hands, is obdurate and abrasive, consisting of thick, loosely applied dabs of earth tones with intense highlights.[82] The sitter's bodily orientation at once leans out toward the beholder, as though taking note of our presence, and away from us; the model's state of mind could be described as definitively inward, concentrated, closed. The broad, brown, indeterminate background, highly reminiscent of Manet's Velázquez-inspired single-figure paintings of the 1860s, at once draws the figure into the larger atmosphere of the scene and detaches him by virtue of his massive physical presence.[83] In *The Monk* the evident formal qualities of surfaceness and facingness, as well as the artifice of the mise-en-scène, refuse to be reconciled with the intensely inward-directed scene of devotion. At no point does the viewer imagine the scene depicted here as "natural" or given; it is, rather, fully contrived by the artist and may even be read as a disguised self-portrait.[84] The citational or nonnatural character of the work is further signaled in terms of its allusive qualities. Manet's *Monk in Prayer* of 1865 (Figure 3.23) as well as Manet's absorptive source, Corot's *Seated Monk, Reading* of 1857 (Figure 3.24), are clearly marked sources for Matisse's costumed monk.

The beautiful drawing *Italian Man (Bevilacqua)* (Figure 3.25) from the same sequence further exemplifies Matisse's basic structural concerns. Although this figure's inwardness is not overtly religious in its appeal, the attitude of inward contemplation is just as intense as in *The Monk*. And like the monk's spatial orientation, the Italian man's posture powerfully counters his inward state of mind as his body is directed out toward the beholder with his lower body pressed close against the picture plane. This bodily dynamic finds a haunting equivalent in Matisse's treatment of the sitter's eyes. I am at a loss to say whether what I see here are eyes that are open or closed or

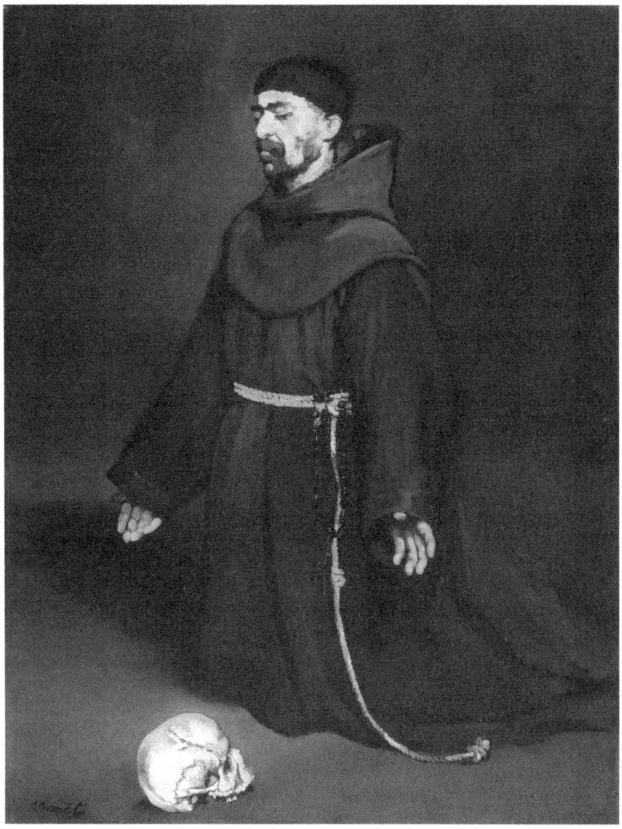

Figure 3.23. Édouard Manet (1832–83), *Monk in Prayer,* 1865. Oil on canvas, 146.4 × 115 cm. Anna Mitchell Richards Fund, Museum of Fine Arts, Boston.

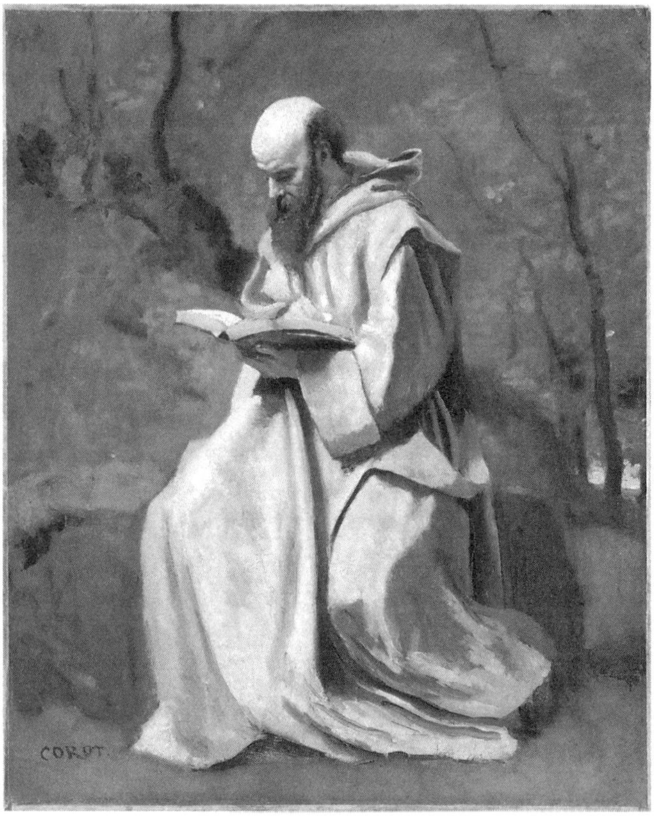

Figure 3.24. Jean-Baptiste-Camille Corot (1796–1875), *Seated Monk, Reading,* 1857. Oil on canvas, 55 × 45 cm. RF2604. Louvre, Paris, France. Photograph by Hervé Lewandowski. Photograph courtesy of Réunion des Musées Nationaux / Art Resource, NY.

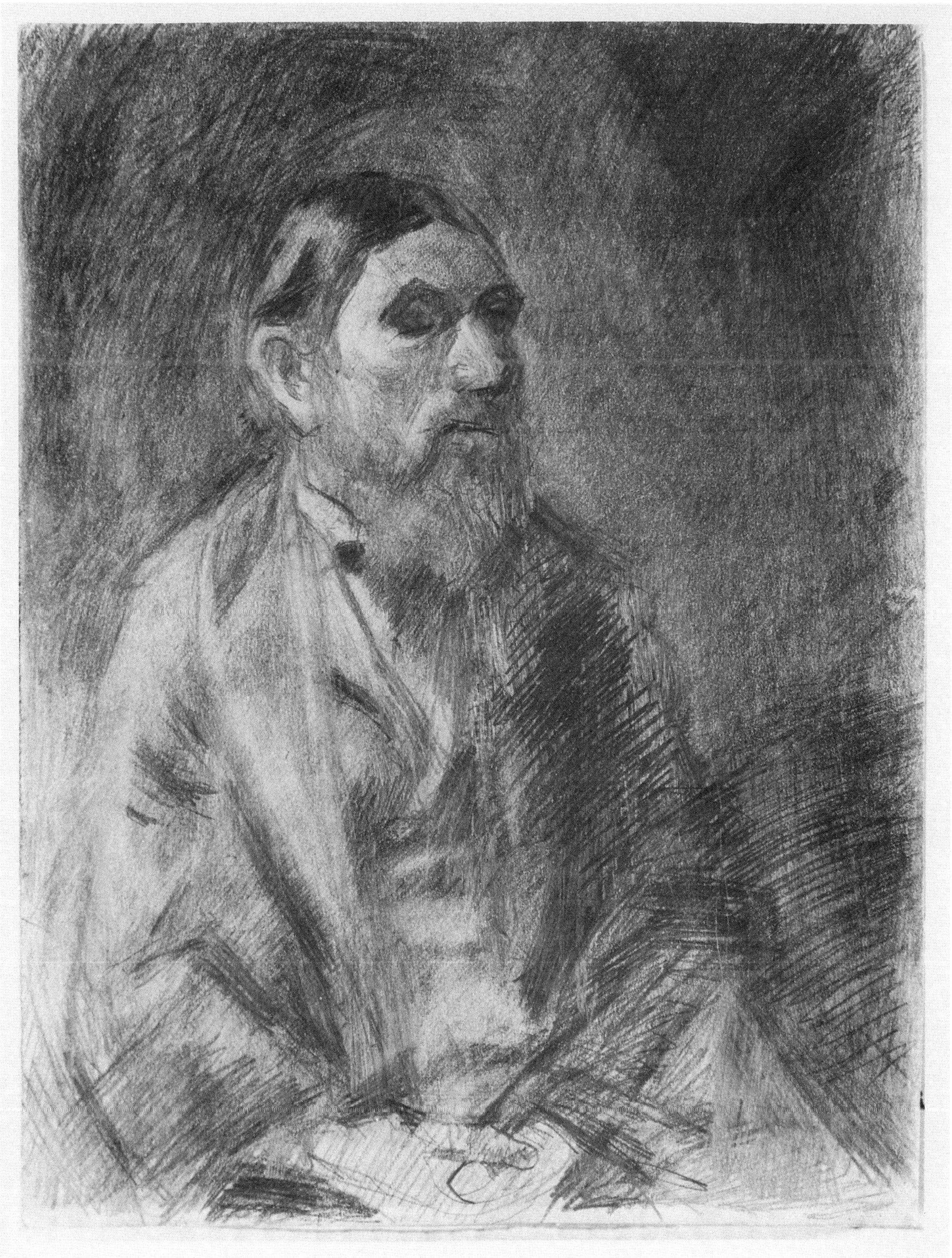

Figure 3.25. Henri Matisse (1869–1954), *Italian Man (Bevilacqua)*, ca. 1902. Graphite pencil on orange paper, 31.4 × 24.8 cm. Musée Matisse, Nice, France. Bequest of Madame Henri Matisse, 1960. Inventory 63.2.84. Copyright 2013 Succession H. Matisse / Artists Rights Society (ARS), NY. Photograph from City of Nice Photographic Service.

some combination of the two. Further still, observe the passage of aggressive horizontal and diagonal marks along the right side. This mode of handling bears little of the concision or subtlety one expects from traditional absorptive techniques (in this instance, the artistic model is surely Fantin-Latour's tremendous self-portrait drawings of the early 1860s).

Viewed as a whole, the standing nude and costume sequences force the problem of beholding in a new way. They present a tense standoff between suggestions of inwardness, withdrawal, even denial of the beholder's presence and exposure, outwardness, artifice, and acknowledgment of the beholder's physical location before the work.[85]

As mentioned previously, the most obvious points of reference for the group are Manet's deeply reflexive Spanish-costume pieces of the 1860s. And while Matisse's works refer back to Manet's work directly, they can also be seen as citing indirectly Manet's own sources: Velázquez, Rembrandt, Hals, Watteau, Chardin, Goya, Delacroix, and Corot are further displaced referents to these pictures.[86] Matisse's roll call of artistic heroes closely mirrors Manet's own: "Goya, Dürer, Rembrandt, Corot, Manet are my favorite masters," he said, adding Chardin to the top of the list (68).[87]

Matisse's costume pictures embody a complex layering of sources. *Lucien Guitry,* for instance, cites Manet's *The Tragic Actor* as well as Velázquez's *Pablo de Valladolid*; *Bevilacqua as Toreador* cites Manet's *Young Man in the Costume of a Majo* (1863) and *A Matador* (1865–67) as well as a plate from Goya's *Tauromaquia* (ca. 1815). His two toreador guitarists reference Manet's series of guitarists (several in Spanish dress), including *The Spanish Singer* (1860), *The Street Singer* (1862), *The Guitar Player* (1866 or 1867), and *The Music Lesson* (1870), as well as, more indirectly, Manet's sources, such as Delacroix's *Young Guitarist in a Costume of the Italian Renaissance* and Watteau's *La Finette* (ca. 1717) and *Mezzetin* (ca. 1718–20).[88]

A similar set of concerns emerges with a range of related works in dialogue with Manet and his sources. *Carmelina* recalls Velázquez's *Las Meninas* as well as Manet's Velázquez-inspired *Self-Portrait with Palette* (1879); *Luxe, calme et volupté* of 1904–5, looks back to Manet's *Déjeuner sur l'herbe; Woman with a Hat* of 1905 takes Hals's *Willem Coymans* of 1645 as its point of departure; and as Schneider has aptly observed, Matisse's *Music* of 1910 looks back to Manet's *Old Musician.*[89] Matisse's early works, as many commentators have noted, raise the question of citationality in a central way. What kind of account of originality do they offer?

Like Manet's, Matisse's costume series contains a complex layering of art historical sources crossing a wide range of nationalities—Spanish, French, Dutch, Italian—and epochs, as well as reflecting on the art of the recent past. It is tempting to follow Carol Armstrong's account of Manet's costume works and see Matisse's similar practice as an instance of "sheer excess," embodying a "multiplication and refusal to add up . . . quotations" as well as a "resistance to assimilating and naturalizing them."[90] Alastair Wright has followed Armstrong's lead in his study of Matisse. Wright argues that "the play of insistently visible sources"—he notes the presence of Raphael, Poussin, Manet, Seurat, Signac, Cézanne, Puvis de Chavannes, and Gauguin behind *Luxe, calme et volupté*—"points not behind the surface—to the implied presence of the artist—but across it: a relay, an array of connections, leads from one style to the next, from one motif to the next, across the surface and out to Matisse's predecessors."[91] Historically overloaded, artistic subjectivity is dispersed into an infinitely regressive palimpsest of sources. According to Wright, citation in Matisse signals something far more disturbing than the iterability of one artist's expressive intentions; it shows "the impossibility of painting escaping from its own system." According to Wright, Matisse's example reveals "art as always a repetition."[92]

Wright's is a revelation story about the nature of artistic expression. If Matisse began with a naive belief in the transparency of his expressive marks, he came to discover a disturbing truth about the arbitrary and iterative nature of signification. Wright's sweeping theory of arbitrariness and iterability removes any possibility of differentiating among or evaluating various forms of citation. Artists have the option of denying the truth of arbitrariness or staging it for others, but they cannot escape it. The "truth" about arbitrary signs is available, however, only if there is some initial proposition about natural or transparent ones. Matisse made no such proposition, nor do I take it to be a central feature of modernist practice. The only general assumption we might make about Matisse's approach to the problem of expression is that there were no transparent signs available to him. Matisse was closer to the Emersonian or Nietzschean tradition that assumed that all art "is a quotation." "All minds quote," Ralph Waldo Emerson wrote in "Quotation and Originality." "By necessity, by proclivity, and by delight, we all quote." The "inventor only knows how to borrow." "All our literature is a quotation," Emerson affirmed (without pathos).[93] For Emerson, and for Matisse, quotation is the condition for expression, not its negation.

Another way to put this is to say that reviewing the cause or history of a mark reveals nothing about the significance of that mark. For Matisse, repetition (figured, for instance, by the space of the studio and the depiction of his own works within his works) was a fact about the nature of art, and expression was impossible without the threat of one's signs being taken for another's. Signs, on this account, are not arbitrary (or they are arbitrary only from a naively naturalist point of view) but normative. Matisse viewed signs as the condition for the possibility of expression, despite their being, or rather because they were, not natural or given in their significance. Matisse's assumption was that most available forms of signification had lost their expressive capacity, that they were not his or anyone's any longer, and that extraordinary efforts were required to reanimate them. So what Wright and others stigmatize or celebrate as arbitrary or iterative because not transcendentally or absolutely grounded sublimes signification, placing the bar so high that nothing could fulfill the demand for transparency. These commentators are then in the (safe) position of exposing the failed nature of the attempt at pure signification. On this account, the terms of semiotic analysis are insufficient for understanding Matisse's approach to expression—he assumed a normative, improvised, and dependent context of meaning—which reestablishes the problem of expression on the other side of quotation. To say a sign is borrowed is not for that reason to say it is arbitrary or merely conventional.[94]

Personnalité and the Logic of Imitation

The end of my argument is in view, but before reaching it I want to consider the significance of a motif in Matisse's writings touched on earlier, one that bears directly on the problems of skepticism and autonomy I have been examining: the motif of *personnalité.* Matisse's fascination with *personnalité* comes to the fore in his first published statement, an essay in the form of an interview with Apollinaire that appeared in the literary journal *La Phalange* in 1907. I quote it here at length, as it encompasses virtually the whole of his theory of the self:

> "I have worked in order to enrich my brain by satisfying the diverse curiosities of my spirit, and by striving to know the different thoughts of ancient and modern masters of plastic art. And this study was also material, because I tried at the same time to understand their technique." Then, having poured me some *rancio* liqueur . . . you wanted to recount for me the incidents of this perilous voyage to the discovery of personality. It goes from science to consciousness, that is to say to the complete forgetting of everything that was not in your own self. How difficult! . . . Instinct offers no guide. It got lost, one is trying to find it.
>
> "Then," you said, "I invented myself by considering my first works. They rarely deceive. I found there a thing that was always the same and which at first glance I thought to be a monotonous repetition in my pictures. It was the manifestation of my personality, which appeared the same no matter what different states of mind I passed through. . . . I strove to develop this personality by counting above all on my instinct, and by frequently returning to principles." (28/54–55)[95]

The word *personnalité* appears no fewer than nine times in the short interview, and it raises more than a few questions. How does one discover one's personality? What is the nature of the "thing" that was always the same in his pictures?

What balance is struck between notions of development and stasis in his account? The matters are left unresolved for the moment.

After a brief discussion of Matisse's masterful technique, his reputed economy of means—with only "four or five spots of color, or by drawing four or five lines," he is able to produce a powerful "plastic expression"—Apollinaire turns to the decisive question of influence. The interview continues:

> To one who works in this way the influence of other personalities can do no harm. His certitudes are internal. They come from his sincerity and the doubts that bother him become the source of his curiosity.
>
> "I have never avoided the influence of others," Matisse told me. "I would have considered this cowardice and a lack of sincerity toward myself. I believe that the personality of the artist develops and asserts itself against other personalities. If the fight is fatal and the personality succumbs, it means that this was bound to be its fate." (28–29/56)[96]

To be sincere with oneself means to be open to influence.[97] The moral of the story is to say that if one's personality is fundamentally shaped by others, then one never really has a personality to begin with. Matisse made the point several times over. "It's a lack of sincerity to shrink from influences that naturally affect you," he said. What, then, of those unnatural influences? Matisse suggested there is natural filter that roots out any malign influences in advance.[98] As in his aesthetic reflections, Matisse never assumed a direct connection with the natural world; any connection was always shaped in advance by its setting within a normative context. Matisse later addressed the matter of influence in a more declarative way, insisting, "It is necessary to accept influences, but in order to react to them, to triumph over them."[99]

Matisse fed on the influence of others, as though to discover what he meant by his marks and his signs. What appeared from the outside to be the loss of self was simply a self in the process of defining itself in terms of how much it could imitate and still sustain a moment of "inner reserve." "All formal languages help him to develop his personality," Apollinaire suggested. Apollinaire's phrasing significantly reduces the tension between self-assertion and development by simply collapsing the terms into a single phrase: development of personality. He continued:

> It is by incessantly having his art confront other artistic conceptions, and by not closing his mind to the arts related to the plastic arts, that Henri Matisse—whose personality is so rich that it might have developed in isolation—has attained the greatness and the confident conviction that distinguish him. (29/57)

At this point Matisse's (and Apollinaire's) theory of the self threatens to derail. On one hand, Apollinaire stressed Matisse's profound openness to the other, his "incessant" confrontation with other artists and ideas. On the other hand, Apollinaire suggested how negligible the impact of the other really was on his personality. Matisse's inner life was so rich, it could develop in isolation. What purpose, then, did the exhaustive cataloging of influences—"the hieratic Egyptians, the refined Greeks, the voluptuous Cambodians, the productions of the ancient Peruvians, the statuettes of African negroes," "Giotto, Piero della Francesca, the Sienese primitives, and Duccio" and "Rembrandt" (29/57–58)—serve if they were ultimately insignificant to his development?

Published in the wake of the fury over the fauve exhibitions of 1905 and 1906, the Apollinaire interview was in part a form of damage control. Bois has described the piece as "the brief of a bad lawyer camouflaging a retreat."[100] (For Bois, the retreat was from Picasso; as I am arguing, that is to construe the problem too narrowly.) The main issue Apollinaire's catalog of influences was intended to resolve was the sense that Matisse was inordinately susceptible to influences. Apollinaire offered a succinct formula. "The influence of other personalities can do no harm," because "his certitudes are internal" (29/56). But Apollinaire's defense also suggested the limitations of this skeptical ideal. If one's certitudes were in fact internal, one would have no need to court influences. Apollinaire flaunted the excess of influence on Matisse and then withdrew the claim at the last moment as though it were irrelevant to begin with.

Matisse took up Apollinaire's terms (if they were ever his) to describe the character of his artistic models. Those who influenced Matisse were also characterized as immune to influence—that is what made them so influential. "Manet," he said, "was open to all influences at once." But then again, "he had to discard all that he had acquired through education and keep only what came from himself" (295).[101] This was the same idea put forward by Matisse's teachers. It was Gustave Moreau who said, "Don't be afraid to lean on the masters! You'll always rediscover yourself there. You don't have the same soul: it's impossible that you won't rediscover your originality."[102] Eugène Carrière was less sanguine about the prospect of imitation: "Accept nothing that comes from outside of oneself or without the consent of one's own nature."[103] Matisse offered similar advice to his own students, saying that an artist's "personality could draw freely upon sources" with the proviso that they only draw upon those "in which they would be able to feel secure" (188–189/316).[104] Matisse further sharpened his rhetoric on this point. "Never think of other artists," he told his students; for a true artist, "others will not exist" (108). And when asked what role other artists played in his work, he insisted, "No one ever teaches us anything."[105]

Matisse occasionally characterized influences as foreign agents that literally entered into his bloodstream. It was important to take such bodies in, to build up one's immune system, and purge them from one's system. In a 1903 letter to his friend Simon Bussy, he suggested the need for "a good purge," one that "could rid me of the good or bad browsings, foreign to my nature that I've picked up along the way these past six years."[106] Once he rid himself of the foreign influences, his true nature could emerge unaltered and immunized by the encounter.[107]

Marcel Sembat perhaps best captured the terms of Matisse's conflicted logic of the self:

> Notice that Matisse is original without trying. I know no one more insistent about the necessity of influences. . . . He feels strong enough to assimilate, digest, and incorporate everything from outside. . . . He has examined everything, and with passion. . . . He has learned all the lessons and has used whatever techniques served his character and suited his genius.[108]

Matisse was at once "insistent" in his engagement with others (Apollinaire also spoke of "incessant influence") and powerful enough to "digest and incorporate" them all. Sembat offered a syllogism: the more he could assimilate, the stronger his personality; the stronger his personality, the more he could assimilate. As tautological as this claim is, its strategic import is great. It largely replays the terms of Matisse's self-hypnotic or autosuggestive practice described above.

I have yet to consider the most bewildering moment in the Apollinaire interview. Matisse recounted a story about seeing again his first still life, painted seventeen years earlier. Looking at it now he "found something that was always the same." It suggested to him a kind of "monotonous repetition" in his work. He made the same claim near the end of his life: "From the *Joie de vivre*—I was thirty-five then—to this cut-out—I am now eighty-two—I have remained the same" (207/246).[109] "Every quality I have ever obtained is in [my first] canvas, at least in embryo," Matisse reflected.[110] And to Sembat he observed how his work was "like an egg! In this egg lay the complete germ of new works."[111]

Matisse's assertion of personal stasis strikes one as perverse given the dramatic stylistic shifts throughout his career. Even though he traversed an astonishing range of styles, he nonetheless claimed his works carried the same "essential substance" from his first pictures to his last (100).[112] While looking at a photograph of one of his 1890s landscapes he observed, "Everything is there." "Basically, after that, I only developed this idea further." This is an intentionally puzzling claim, and one that seems hard to sustain. Matisse's skepticism verges here on narcissistic withdrawal (as skepticism always might). Consider, finally, Matisse's most assertive claim to inner certainty: "You know, you have only one idea, you are born with it and all your life you develop your fixed idea, you make it breathe" (175).[113] As I have tried to show, Matisse's "fixed idea" developed according to the terms of pictorial and personal autonomy: at once unified, complete, and open to limited or novel modes of connection.

Matisse offered his most elaborate definition of the self in a 1941 interview with Pierre Courthion:

> You are in everything you do, in your first paintings as well as your last. But it is the development of the personality that exists already in the first painting that brings that personality into the world, because it has developed itself. It already existed, but it was in the state of a cell [Ça existait déjà, mais c'était à l'état de cellule].[114]

Apollinaire's phrase from the first interview—"development of the personality"—returns here unaltered. But the logic of the claim is further strained. Matisse's phrasing moves back and forth between development and preexistence, evolution and embryo. As in all of the instances cited above, it is the cellular state that assumes priority.

"The mode of the *cell,*" Philippe Lacoue-Labarthe and Jean-Luc Nancy write in their study of political panic, "twice implies the subject: once as a constituted individual in which each cell consists; then as the organized whole which reproduces on a larger scale the individuality of the members with all the characteristics of self-sufficiency of this individuality."[115] Matisse's aesthetics hinges on this double-cellular subject. No matter how far the influence of others penetrates into the cells of the self, there is another cell, another subject, that protects the health of the person from contagion. Matisse's emphasis on his sources, on the "incessant influence" of his artistic masters, is countered by an internal mechanism that shapes and molds those influences according to the needs of his *personnalité.* And while this picture of personal and aesthetic autonomy is strained to the limit, it is not as willful as it might appear. First, as I have stressed throughout, Matisse positively thematized the role of influence in every aspect of his personal and artistic life. He never conceived of his practice without the definitive pressure of other minds on it. Second, Matisse's preformationist theory of the self was driven by a defense against what he perceived to be the pervasive affirmation of unity and oneness, melodramas of unity and merger offered by a range of Post-Impressionists, which, as I have also suggested, find their counterpart in current modes of affect theory.[116]

A concluding glance at three documents that span the whole of Matisse's career will help bring these matters to a point. In an extraordinary 1896 letter to his painter friend Victor Roux-Champion, Matisse first articulated his commitment to ideals of personal and pictorial autonomy. That this letter constitutes something of an early artistic credo is clear from his general tone and use of enumeration to make his points. "I believe I'm speaking like a pedagogue!" he told Roux-Champion. "You know, it's not for nothing that I have a degree." He went on to offer his friend a "formula" for sincere art:

> Work with white, work with blue, work with red, if it's necessary paint with your feet if the heart tells you to, and tell those who are not satisfied to take

> a hike. That's the true way to become personal and as it is today as at all times only personalities count, it's sincerity above all that one should aim at. You're interested in nature? Right? Why? Because of this or that. Put all of it into what you do and you will already be an original artist. That's the formula. But *be personal above all,* and for that *be sincere.*
>
> If you were as strong as Holbein you would not exist yourself, you would be just a double. It would be better to paint a bit of water, a willow and a fine sky (like Corot) with emotion than to make yet another variation on the most beautiful Leonardo.
>
> One more point, that's all.
>
> You can come here [but . . .] you will not see my studies so they won't be able to influence you, you will be alone with nature and you can have your *impressions* at leisure. That's the best advice you can get. What's good? What's bad? I have no idea; it will all depend on two things: 1. emotion, 2. sincerity.[117]

Virtually all of the motifs of the Apollinaire interview appear in this letter of more than ten years earlier. While imploring Roux-Champion to avoid copying Holbein and simply paint "a bit of water, a willow and a fine sky" with emotion, Matisse paused to insert a telling reminder: be sincere *"like Corot."* Being personal means being as personal as the models one is copying.

This citational view of the self was reinforced at the conclusion to the "Notes of a Painter." The final page of Matisse's discussion was devoted to a response to Sâr Joséphin Péladan's critique of Matisse's mimicry of other artists:

> Whether we want to or not, we belong to our time and we share in its opinions, its feelings, even its errors. All artists bear the imprint of their time, but the great artists are those in whom this is most profoundly marked. . . . Whether we like it or not, however insistently we call ourselves exiles from it, between our period and ourselves solidarity is established, and M. Péladan cannot escape this. (43/53)

Matisse's solidarity with his period was not something he typically celebrated. To be "imprinted" by the world was precisely what he resisted. Or rather, he resisted the idea that one was devoid of the capacity to *print oneself* on the world in exchange. As though to suggest a deeper sense of solidarity with his time, Matisse fought against fictive Symbolist communities as well as Sâr Péladan's ontology of difference.

Many years later, Matisse rejected the surrealists along the same lines he refused Péladan. "We are not the masters of our production," he explained. "It is imposed on us" (123/128). Imposed on us by what? At first, Matisse's answer is familiar: "My latest paintings" express "my essential core [fond]."[118] And yet there is another line of thinking here, one that imagines a broader conception of self. There is, Matisse said, "a development that comes not only from the individual." The artist's essential core is itself a product of "the civilization that precedes us."[119] "We are born with the sensibility of a given period of civilization," and for that reason "one can't do just anything."[120]

As I have argued, Matisse's claim to inner certainty was also a claim to self-alienation. Personality, self-certainty, expressive significance were functions of self-sacrifice. Robert Pippin offers a powerful exploration of these issues in his discussion of Hegel's vision of social agency:

> Actually to have an intention *is* to struggle to express that intention in a public and publicly contestable deed, subject to . . . interpretations by others that can greatly alter one's own sense of what one is about. It is . . . to "sacrifice" the purity and certainty (and so security) of one's self-understanding and to subject oneself to the reactions, counter-claims and challenges of others. Were one to remain in the Inner Citadel of Subjective Certainty [Matisse's so-called internal certitudes] . . . one's self-understanding would have to remain suspended in doubt—the question of whether I am actually committed to what I take myself to be . . . would be left suspended, and because of that could be counted as much a fantasy of resolve or intention or commitment as genuine. Action must be understood as a self-negation in this sense, a negation of the subject's pretension to complete ownership of the nature and import of the deed, and therewith the sharing of such authority with others.[121]

Matisse, of course, was loath to admit the shared authority of his utterances. Or rather, he insisted on his final responsibility for those utterances, even if all the words were formerly owned by others or had lost their ownership in a deadening round of clichés.

Winter Landscape

Matisse took various stands on the issue of the other: hate, defiance, reserve, acceptance, embrace, affirmation. Whatever his stance, the other was the pivot around which his practice revolved. Not surprisingly, the issue of self-expression was given its most basic and perplexing formulation in terms of Matisse's encounter with Picasso.

Françoise Gilot, in an intriguing account of Picasso's *Winter Landscape* (1950) (Figure 3.26), articulated many of the issues that frame Matisse's vision of self-constitution. It was a picture that thematized the question of influence with the artist who most deeply intertwined with Matisse's own sense of self. *Winter Landscape,* Gilot argued, was an allegory of the relationship between Matisse and Picasso. Not surprisingly, it was a relationship constrained and driven by the anxiety of influence. *Winter Landscape* was also at the center of a minor conflict between the artists. Matisse so admired the work that he

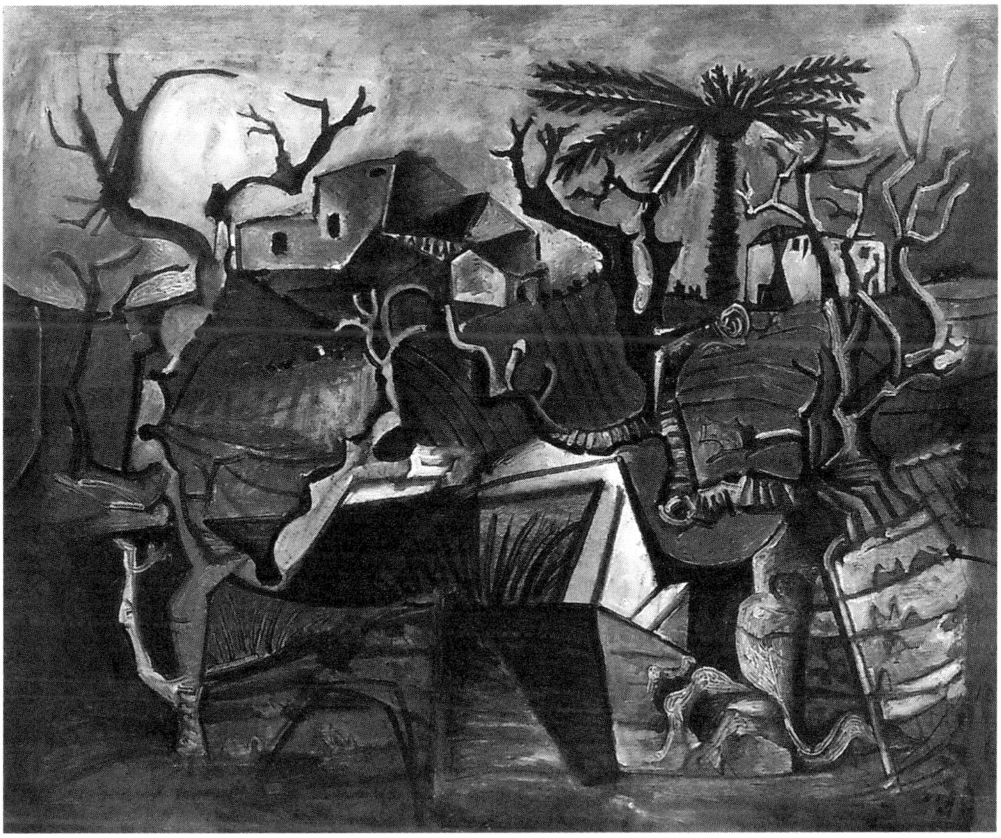

Figure 3.26. Pablo Picasso (1881–1973), *Winter Landscape*, December 22, 1950. Oil on wood on panel, 102.9 × 125.7 cm. Collection of Kate Ganz. Copyright 2012 Estate of Pablo Picasso / Artists Rights Society (ARS), NY.

asked to borrow it from Picasso. Picasso agreed, and Matisse gave it pride of place on his mantel at the Hotel Régina (Figure 3.27). When Picasso requested its return, Matisse stalled. Picasso had to resort to a ruse to get it back.

According to Gilot, Matisse is evoked at two moments in the work. The two trees in the foreground were figures for the fraught relation between Gilot and Picasso: "The tree trunks were as distant as possible and the tortuous branches shied away from each other in agony except for two fingerlike twigs that almost touched but did not join, like the image of God and Adam in Michelangelo's Sistine Chapel ceiling or the two hands in Matisse's *The Dance*." Gilot was being deliberately provocative with her literalism. In this instance, Gilot's iconographic decoding rose above psychologism and opened a new interpretive layer. Gilot's sense that Matisse's *Dance* might be behind Picasso's picture seems improbable but actually captures an important quality of the work. According to Gilot, Picasso's enclosed surfaces are pierced at key

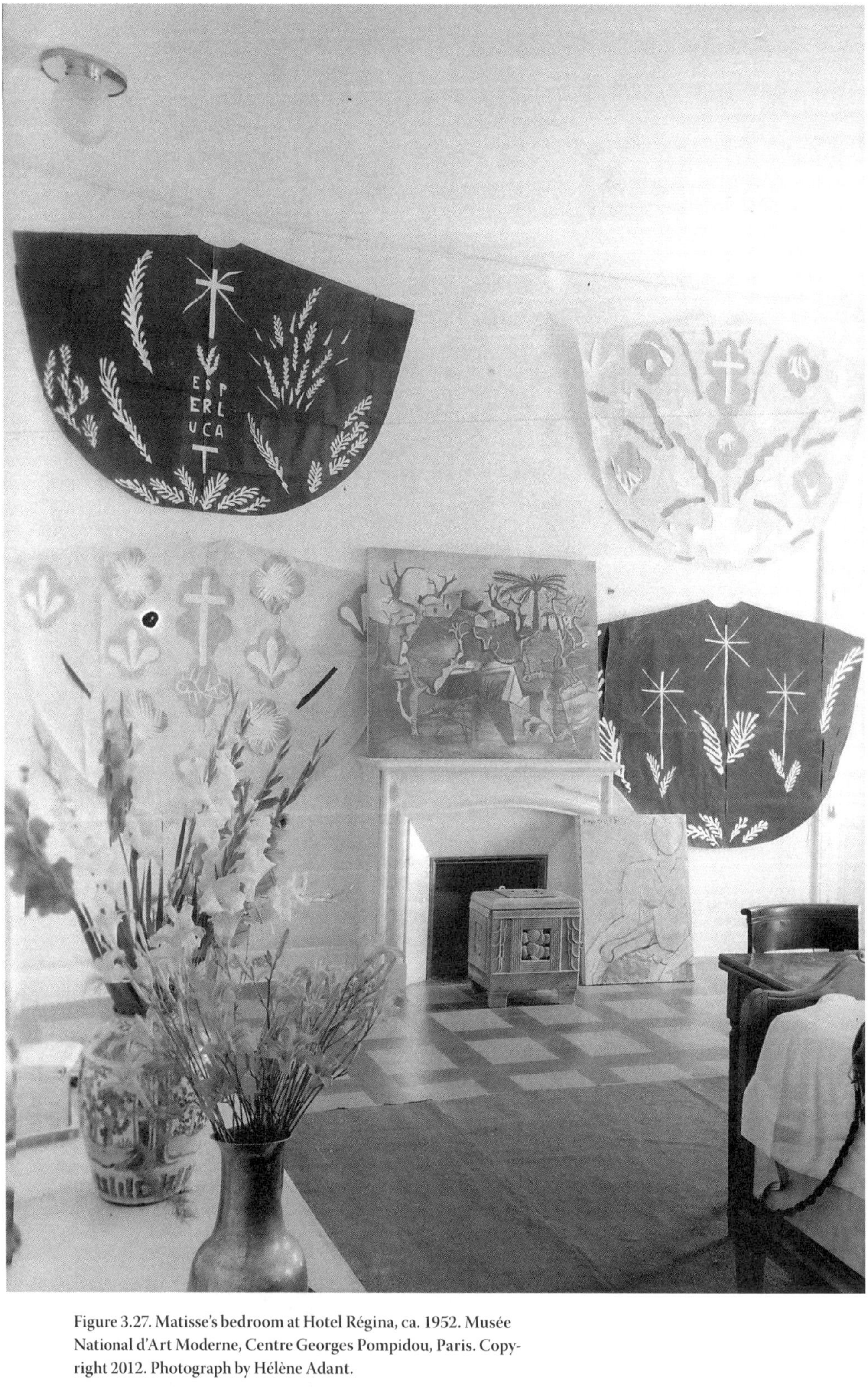

Figure 3.27. Matisse's bedroom at Hotel Régina, ca. 1952. Musée National d'Art Moderne, Centre Georges Pompidou, Paris. Copyright 2012. Photograph by Hélène Adant.

moments to include contact inside the picture as well as to offer a fictive moment of connection between painter and beholder. "To the right," Gilot said, "one could recognize a simple cubic house that evoked Matisse's villa, 'The Dream,' all the more so because the silhouette of a huge palm tree loomed close to it" (220). Gilot was figured as the "lithe and feminine" tree at the left; Picasso was the "prowling" tree at right. At the top left looms the "ghost hamlet" of "society." Gilot suggested that Matisse was figured by the villa and palm at top right.

The work is about influences: the influence of women on men, of the "feminine" Matisse on masculine Picasso, of life on art. Gilot's description offers a range of suggestive themes along these lines:

> The palm tree and the two leafless tress formed a triangle of interest. The palm tree's penetration of the soil just above the most vulnerable breach between two main branches of the male tree was counteracted only by a dead stump, which did not fend off its action, suggesting Picasso's terror of being put in tutelage, or influenced, or dominated. Irrepressible, however, some palm-fronds extended laterally and insinuated themselves in each nook and cranny, and one frond was prolonged by a ray of light that struck a leafless branch of the male tree, while another lightbeam flashed its way to the feminine tree on the left. (220–21)

The mimetic triangle concerns Gilot, Picasso, and Matisse, who were closer than they had ever been at this moment.[122] Gilot pointed to the fragile opening in the upraised branches of the dying tree (Picasso) where the palm (Matisse) penetrated the soil below. Picasso was invaded, penetrated by the reach of his friend despite his efforts to guard himself against the influence. It is a picture, ultimately, about the "irrepressible" power of influence. In Gilot's reading, the picture captures the sense in which Matisse's art, and his person, insinuated themselves into Picasso's own. It is tempting to read *Winter Landscape* as an inverted image of the problem I have been considering throughout: Matisse's skeptical denial of other minds. It is an inverted image because, unlike Picasso, Matisse refused the role of the dying tree, one penetrated, despite his efforts, by the other. Perhaps Matisse's fascination with the painting says more than Matisse could verbalize. Although it is an image of resistance, even terror of influence, it nonetheless keys us to its inevitability.

Gilot of course knew she was in danger of (over)reading the painting. "I was supposed to praise . . . composition, tone coordination, and contrasts between negative and positive space," she worried (221). Gilot noted that Picasso "disliked references to feelings," and she clearly touched a nerve. She concluded in a way that also touched on Matisse's concerns: "He recoiled from discussing matters of sensitivity and sensibility with anyone, since that would have allowed another human being to come too close to his innermost core" (222).

Lawrence Gowing once described Matisse's art as one of "deliberate self-engrossment," verging "close to narcissism." Matisse was, Gowing reflected, "the painter of the self absorbed in self-hood." And as this self-regard "grew on him, it held obvious limitations from which he did not always escape."[123] These are the limitations of skepticism. The self, as Freud observed, is available to the self only "when it has been put to the use of cathecting . . . objects, that is, when it has become object-libido." It is the object world that directs the subject's activity. When the self becomes its object, it paradoxically becomes accessible as a self.[124] At its limit, the skeptical self threatens to fade into its objects. Borch-Jacobsen powerfully describes the conflictual dynamics of skeptical self-constitution:

> What is it all about, this desire . . . called "egoist" or "narcissistic"? It is about being an "I," a "self"—that is, a subject: closed-in upon itself, free of all bonds, absolute in this sense. But if I desire to be an I, if I desire myself, then according to the most elementary logic, it must be because that is not what I am. Thus this singular desire is not the desire of any subject.[125]

Matisse's work reveals the limits as well as the possibilities of skepticism. His claim to the inviolability of the self stood alongside an equally decisive insistence that his self was not his, or not his alone. His desire to overcome the influence of others was also, unmistakably, a desire for others. But that relation could not be assumed; it had to be earned. Matisse's quest for closure was rooted in a critique of immanence, in a view of the self as something passively constituted. One might say that for Matisse a history of the self was not an account of the self. Personal and pictorial autonomy was the effort to make one's name within a world of empty ones. Matisse's effort to attain autonomy expressed his ultimate need for a connection to fulfill it. But any connection worth having could not spare him the difficulty of acknowledging separateness.

FOUR

Matisse and Mimesis

> Enigma of the noble expanse
> oh magnificent visage
> serenely woven
> from a pure flight
> into a stroke
> certain of path
> by a sudden rift.
> He saw
> the distant as near.
> He freed.
> (to free: to protect an arrival into hesitant nearing)
>
> —Martin Heidegger, "On a Drawing by Henri Matisse"

> Renoir told me: "When I have arranged a bouquet in order to paint it, I go round to the side I had not seen."
>
> —Henri Matisse, *Jazz,* 1947

In "Portraits" of 1954, Matisse's last published statement, he reflected how "portraiture demanded . . . a complete identification" with the model. Or rather, portraiture required the "possibility of almost complete identification" with the model.[1] This kind of verbal complication tells us something important about his artistic aims. While Matisse's art was driven by his desire for identification with the other—the artist seeks to "identify himself perfectly with his subject" (181/175)—the consummation of this aim was thwarted by his equally strong sense of the *difference* between himself, his work, and the world. In this chapter I explore how Matisse's practice thrived on a dual fantasy: one of total affective merger with his medium and with the viewer and an equally strong desire for separation or detachment, as though art were a way to seal himself off from others and the world. Fantasies of expressive immediacy, what Matisse called "direct action on the viewer," exist side by side with fantasies of *in*expression, that "nothing can be transmitted," as though we remain ontologically outside one another.[2] Matisse's notion of identification remains internally divided, drifting toward merger with the other and an equally emphatic denial of the other.

At times Matisse followed Leo Tolstoy's utopian view of artistic communication as the capacity to *"evoke . . . by means of movements, lines, colors, sounds, or forms expressed in words, so to transmit that feeling that others experience the same feeling."*[3] In Matisse's words, "It is through design that the feelings and the soul of the painter travels without difficulty into the spirit of he who looks on" (185).[4] This attitude characterizes Matisse's "expressionism." He described his practice along these lines in his "Notes of a Painter": "What I am after, above all, is expression" (37/42). And again, the "artist expresses his interior visions" (54/61); the "great thing is to express one's self" (68). And while this expressionist Matisse is the most familiar one, he equally stressed his inexpressiveness, his inability or disinclination to make himself known. Although his worked surfaces and vibrant colors seemed to make available his "interior visions," Matisse's critics saw those same surfaces as withholding meaning.

In the early critical reviews of Matisse's work he was excoriated for his reserve, as though his pictures were *about* expression, but not expressive themselves. There is no word in wider circulation among his early critics than *theory.* Maurice Denis lamented the "excess of theory" in Matisse's fauve works, describing them as "artificial and willed," the product of "pure reason," Neoplatonic "noumenal paintings [noumènes de tableaux]."[5] André Gide described Matisse's works as the "exposition of theorems." They were the "products of theory," he wrote, "everything in them can be deduced, explained; intuition plays no part."[6] Louis Vauxcelles described them as "schematized," nothing but "theories, system and the abstract"; Matisse's work "resolutely distances itself from the object [s'écarter résolument de l'objet]."[7] Charles Morice lamented how "science and calculation are more perceptible than instinct in Matisse's work."[8] Like Vauxcelles, Jacques Rivière saw Matisse as someone who "stands *apart* from things when he paints," detaching himself "to the point of actual separation" from the world. All that was left in the works was "intellectual splendor," a "sparkling and inert extract."[9]

What made Matisse's skeptical reserve particularly intolerable for his critics was the sense in which his "fauve" color and handling were identical with his muteness and withdrawal. His surfaces seemed excessive in their exemplification of the artist's inner life, as though he was a van Gogh in extremis. In his recent interpretation of Matisse's *Woman with a Hat* (1905), T. J. Clark persuasively argues that Matisse's detachment from his surfaces was itself an expressive gesture. Matisse's skepticism was not an effort to deny the world, but a paradoxical attempt to attach himself to it.[10] According to Clark, *Woman with a Hat* is an expression of Matisse's incapacity to express himself fully in a world that he felt was increasingly unavailable to emotional understanding. Matisse's desire to express "qualities of intensity, depth, directness, vividness," qualities that were in the process of being "outlawed . . . vulgarized and commodified," could be expressed only through "flatness," "cold technique," and "rigorous masking and formality."[11] Matisse's critics were right to see his works as *performances* of expression, rather than the real thing. Matisse's performance of spontaneity was intended to signal the unavailability of expression as a viable mode of representing modern experience. My account shares with Clark's a sense that Matisse's skepticism was less than fully intended, or motivated by a deeper desire for attachment. But I also see, and see Matisse as striving to maintain, the sense that skepticism registers something true about the nature of communication and that it is not simply the result of the alienating conditions of modernity. It was Matisse's implacable sense of isolation, and his desire to bridge it, that provoked his expressive efforts in the first place. Put another way, if there were no ontological separation between the artist and his world, there would be no need and no occasion for expression.

The effort to bridge difference without subsuming it, to deny neither his difference from the world nor his connection to it, brought Matisse to a mode of aesthetic understanding that precluded fantasies of immediacy or detachment. Borrowing the term from Philippe Lacoue-Labarthe, I describe this alternate approach as mimetic.[12] *Mimesis* does not refer to traditional notions of imitative representation but rather to the artist's conflicted psychic relationship with the other. In psychoanalytic terms, mimesis is a mode of identification between self and other so intense that it evokes the loss of difference between self and other. By virtue of the intensity of this unconscious identification it can suggest a sense of blissful annihilation as well as the painful loss of boundaries. It is immersive and binding but also detached and rivalrous. Mimetic identification is psychically fraught, inherently conflictual and ambivalent, suggestive at once of possessive mastery and traumatic openness. And however evocative mimesis is of either ecstatic or traumatic communion with the other, it remains constitutively unavailable to the subject as a direct experiential encounter.

Matisse's contemporary Freud theorized "identification" in ways that speak directly to the artist's aims. In his middle-period writings Freud observed the deep-rooted ambivalence that haunts every form of identification. "Identification is ambivalent from the very first; it can turn into an expression of tenderness as easily as into a wish for someone's removal."[13] Tenderness and removal—identification is a paradoxical form of *"devouring affection"* for the other (Freud associated the idea with the dual nature of cannibalism—to destroy and to ingest, to remove and to adore—a theme that will be important for my interpretation of Matisse's work).[14] Moreover, Freud suggested that this ambivalent identification with the other is the original condition of the self. "Primary identification" is the state of being prior to the discrimination of subject and object, self and world. It is the simultaneous and contradictory need to master, possess, and consume the other, and to merge with or *become* the other.[15] It is this mimetic framework of mastery and merger, (self-)possession and openness, difference and continuity that offers the most useful terms for understanding the pictorial dynamics of Matisse's enterprise.

Freud's notion of "devouring affection" or "tender removal" is closely echoed in Matisse's descriptions of his practice. At times Matisse framed his practice in violently conflicted and sexualized terms:

> I reckon I've made progress when I recognize more and more clearly in my work a detachment from the support offered by the model (the presence of the model, who counts not so much to provide possible information about her constitution as to keep me in a state of emotion, in a sort of flirtation which ends by turning into a rape [viol]. Whose rape? A rape of myself, of a certain tender feeling [attendrissement] before the sympathetic object).[16]

Artistic progress requires a disinterested attitude toward the live model in order to achieve a more "synthetic" expression of the passing moment. Then again, the "model" itself is fabricated. Progress is a detachment from an already mediated source, the "support offered by" the model and not the model itself. What role, then, does the model play? Before we can answer that question Matisse's language takes a turn. The artistic process is redescribed in sexualized terms. Absorbed in an erotically charged state, the artist allows himself to be "raped" by the "model." Matisse travels a wide distance between the initial image of "detachment" and the final scene of masochism, the "rape of myself." The imagery is fraught with ambivalence: it is suggestive at once of violent mastery and of exposure, *attendrissement.*

In the next section I follow the threads of Matisse's conflictual mimesis, considering four discursive variants—traumatic repetition, possession and merger, ecstasy and absorption, imbibing and impregnation—and one visual instance that provides a basic pattern for his artistic practice. This larger discursive framework will set the stage for the sections that follow, where I trace a sequence of works from the first half of his career.

"I've been shattered"

In October 1944, Matisse's daughter Marguerite was released from a makeshift prison camp at Belfort, situated at the northeast border between France and Germany. Imprisoned for her collaboration with the French Resistance during World War II, Marguerite was held for nearly six months, first at Rennes and then at Belfort on her way to the concentration camp at Ravensbruck, north of

Berlin. Severely beaten and tortured by the Gestapo (her eardrum was burst with a bludgeon), she attempted suicide and was saved by her fellow prisoners. Upon her escape, she traveled to Nice to visit her father and arrived there in January 1945. There are conflicting reports as to the nature of their reunion. According to Gilot, Matisse was anxious to move on from the event and to pick up where father and daughter had left off before the war. "Let's not talk about any of these events," he told Marguerite, "let's just resume our relationship." Looking back on the meeting, Gilot saw how Matisse "always appeared cool and collected . . . he did not allow himself to succumb to his own emotions." Gilot noted his typical emotional reserve: "It was as if he made himself unavailable for personal feelings."[17] But a second thought crossed the first, and Gilot saw something beyond his "autocratic attitude." Despite appearances, Matisse's manner "did not prove a lack of sensitivity" but "perhaps the opposite."[18] For two weeks Matisse and daughter spent their days together as she recounted the details of her ordeal. Matisse recalled the moment to his son Pierre. "I was literally hypnotized" by her stories, he said. He continued:

> I saw in reality, materially, the atrocious scenes she described and acted out for me. I couldn't have said if I still belonged to myself. . . . I was aware several times in her presence of taking part in the greatest of all human dramas—in a side of the existence of others which it is rare to be able to live through with such intensity, to the point where you no longer feel yourself existing separately.[19]

Marguerite's stories haunted him for weeks. "I'm in the anguished swirl of memories of the captivity of my daughter, I've been shattered by it [j'en suis anéanti]," he told André Rouveyre.[20]

Matisse's language evokes the heightened emotional nature of their reunion. Indeed, the sensation of no longer feeling any separation from the other, of "literally" or "materially" living the other's life, describes a traumatic scenario. What is unusual about the scenario is that it is suggestive of *Matisse's* traumatic condition, not Marguerite's. Matisse's shattered senses seem to express *his* sense of witnessing. Matisse was hypnotized by his daughter's words, as though he suffered with and through his daughter's suffering. What is striking about this role reversal is that Matisse concedes his usual position as observer and becomes an actor in the "greatest of human dramas" (that it is still a mode of staging, and not a *literal* encounter, is basic to the mimetic scenario). He is acting *with,* not outside, his subject. Matisse's hypnotic identification is brought about under the extreme conditions of shared traumatic experience between father and daughter. As Ruth Leys describes it, trauma has been defined as

> a situation of dissociation or "absence" from the self in which the victim unconsciously imitated, or identified with . . . the traumatic scene in a condition that was likened to a state of heightened suggestibility or

> hypnotic trance. Trauma was therefore understood as an experience of hypnotic imitation or identification— . . . *mimesis*. . . . Trauma was understood as an experience that immersed the victim in the traumatic scene so profoundly that it precluded the kind of specular distance necessary for cognitive knowledge of what had happened. . . . [Thus] the effort to cure patients by getting them, through the use of hypnotic catharsis or by other means, to recollect and narrate the dissociated traumatic origin was destined to fail.[21]

The traumatized subject who is forced into a situation without physical or emotional reserve can fall into a state of hypnotic receptivity so intense that it can lead the subject to an unconscious identification with the other, even if that other is the aggressor.[22] The hypnotic state induced by trauma was seen to be so all-consuming that there was no space for the kinds of emotional detachment necessary for self-narration or diegesis. Lacanian psychoanalysis, on this account, becomes incompatible with its Freudian models. Lacan privileged narration—dissociated from any "real"—as a therapeutic device to set the sufferer on the path to healing. Unlike Lacan, Freud did not typically grant narration a formative role in the healing process. Freud observed that the traumatized subject was so physically and psychologically bound up with the past that he or she tended to repeat or hypnotically "act out" the past, rather than mentally organize it, which rendered any narrative therapeutics compromised from the start.[23]

At first glance this view of trauma seems at odds with Matisse's account of his daughter's mental state. Matisse's language is saturated with a set of dramatic images. Far from traumatized, Marguerite *performs* her experience for her father, as though she had gained cognitive mastery over the events. As Matisse tells it, she performed the atrocious scenes of her captivity as part of a "great human drama." While Marguerite may have gained some mastery over the events, Matisse encountered her words as "reality, materially." In this scenario Marguerite is the detached artist-director, while Matisse plays the hypnotized actor. This is not to suggest that Marguerite was not traumatized by her torture and imprisonment or to suggest that the traumatic events were contagiously transferred from victim to witness. The scenario is too complicated by mimetic bonds to allow the disentanglement of fact and fantasy. What is remarkable about the descriptive evidence is how a kind of role reversal occurred, as though Matisse stood on the side of the hypnotized at the same time as he engaged in a form of heightened emotional attachment to his daughter. Moreover, each actor played multiple roles. Marguerite acted out her trauma, as though temporarily standing apart from it, taking her father through its paces. Matisse hypnotically identified with his daughter's trauma but also signaled the fictive-dramatic nature of the encounter.

Matisse's ambivalent mode of identification was replayed three years later in a far more public way with the appearance of his epistolary introduction to the 1948 retrospective of his work at the Philadelphia Museum of Art. The letter offered some unusual counsel for young artists:

> It is necessary for the artist to possess Nature. He must identify himself with her rhythm, by efforts that prepare for the mastery, for the power, by which he will later be able to express himself in his own [propre] language.
>
> The future painter must be able to foresee what is useful to his proper [propre] development—drawing and even sculpture—everything that will let him merge with [se confondre], to identify himself with Nature, by incorporating the things [s'insinuant à travers les choses] . . . that arouse his sensations. (182–83/313)

His language carries connotations of sexual aggression and physical ownership. The artist must penetrate, master, and possess the object that arouses his sensations. By the end of the passage, sexual mastery mixes with ideals of merger and physical incorporation.

At nearly the same moment, Matisse transcribed some reflections on his travels to the South Seas of sixteen years earlier, which similarly expressed his psychically conflicted state of mind. The "enchantments of the sky, the sea, the fish, and the coral in the lagoons plunged me into the inaction of total ecstasy [ravissement complet]" (169).[24] The rapturous moment of ecstasy brought with it the threat of passive inaction. Why, he asks, is it "only now that these wonders have returned to me with tenderness and clarity" (169)?[25] Tenderness was never an unequivocal value for Matisse, as it carried shades of passivity and weakness. (The addition of "clarity" to tenderness further suggests his unease.) The loss of self implied by ecstasy was rendered ambiguous by virtue of its recollection; it had been filtered through time and memory.

Matisse summed up his ecstatic recollection of the South Seas in a concluding analogy: "With my eyes wide open I absorbed everything as a sponge absorbs liquid [j'absorbais tout, comme une éponge absorbe le liquide]" (169).[26] While the desire to absorb everything *into* the self points to the intensity of Matisse's desire to consume the world, it also suggests a more unsettling loss of boundaries, as though the self is entirely composed of what it takes in. In Tahiti he was "absorbed by the ambience, shattered [anéanti] and without thought in the face of the novelty of everything I saw there, unconsciously storing up so many things."[27] (As he explained to Brassaï around the same time, "It's more important to absorb things than to try to capture them from life.")[28] Although the experience of being overwhelmed, without thought, connotes a kind of sublime passivity, these experiences were said to be "stored up" in the self and given their ultimate expression many years later.

As Matisse repeatedly explained, it was essential for him to enter into, to become his subjects in order to render them properly in paint. He continually stressed his need to "steep" himself, sponge-like, in the world, to digest his subjects inwardly in order to express them on canvas. "My work consists in steeping myself in things [m'imbiber des choses]. And after that, it all comes out."[29] And again, in more eroticized terms: "I have no imagination, I have to impregnate myself in things [je me'imprègne des choses], I have to receive before I can give."[30] Active and passive, mastery and exposure seem to collapse into one. He is both impregnating things and being impregnated by them. Giving and taking, possession and exposure, Matisse's mimetic imagery offers a bewildering confusion of normative distinctions between subject and object, conscious and unconscious, artist and world.

Louis Aragon offered a similarly charged image but positioned Matisse more securely in the role of master: "Matisse drew this chair endlessly, patiently, in a secret flirtation with the room, until he should have absorbed enough to discover its mystery. . . . Matisse would say of . . . that flirtation, it is like the conversation of a pick-pocket with his victim: 'during that time, he lifts his watch.'"[31] Here, the artist's victim is a chair and the flirtation is a ruse. The encounter has also lost its mimetic complexity; the self is comfortably organized around its objects (which one might concur reflect Aragon's attitudes more than Matisse's).

Consider a final variant of Matisse's discursive claims, one that encapsulates their mimetic character. "It is by going back into the object [rentrant dans l'objet] that one enters into one's own skin [rentre dans sa propre peau]."[32] Subject and object, inner and outer mingle within a shifting set of boundaries. It is impossible to establish the idea as either auto-affective mastery (loss of self as a means to self-definition) or affective merger (loss of self into the other). Similarly, when speaking about his ambitious *Parakeet and Mermaid* (1952–53) Matisse collapsed the terms of artistic control and empathetic loss, as though they were two sides of the same experience. "I had to do this parakeet with colored paper. Very well! I became a parakeet. And I rediscovered myself in the work."[33] The rediscovery of self is one and the same with the encounter with the other.

A visual totem of Matisse's mimetic approach will set the stage for the rest of this chapter. In 1900, speaking of his *Jaguar Devouring a Hare (after Antoine-Louis Barye)* (Figure 4.1), Matisse observed how over time he began "identifying himself with the passion of the wild beast [fauve], expressed in the rhythm of the masses."[34] Whatever passionate connection with the beast he was referring to, it was experienced at several removes. He was working from Barye's idealized image of the jaguar eating its prey. He described the act of identification as a movement from passion to rhythm, feeling to form. The idea is related to his remarks in the "Notes of a Painter" that "if I have an Italian model, whose first aspect only suggests the idea of purely animal exis-

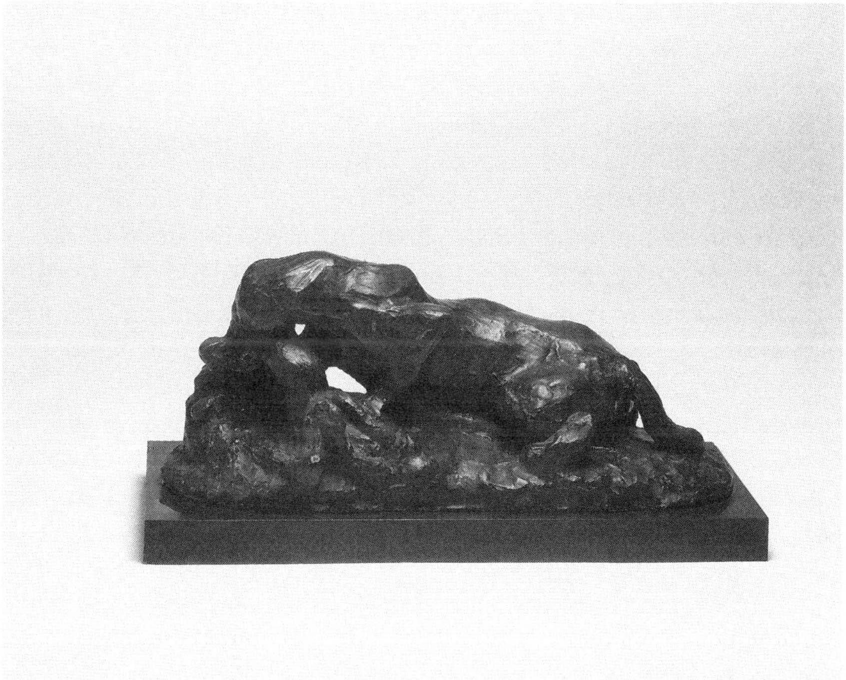

Figure 4.1. Henri Matisse (1869–1954), *Jaguar Devouring a Hare (after Antoine-Louis Barye),* 1899–1901. Bronze, 22.5 × 56.0 × 22.4 cm. AM1991-283. Musée National d'Art Moderne, Centre Georges Pompidou, Paris, France. Copyright 2013 Succession H. Matisse / Artists Rights Society (ARS), NY. Courtesy of CNAC/MNAM/Dist. Réunion des Musées Nationaux / Art Resource, NY, ART168632. Photograph by Philippe Migeat.

tence, I discover among the essential traits, I penetrate among the lines of his face, those which translate the character of deep gravity that persists in every human being" (41/49). Even here it is important to see that Matisse's access to the "human being" is through the *idea* and *model* of it. Matisse's carefully tuned language significantly complicates any effort to either celebrate or criticize his practice as either perceptually based or sublimatory. There is no clear path that runs from external violence to aesthetic measure, from animality to essence, from passive to active, as both terms are so powerfully imbricated with one another.[35]

The subject of *Jaguar Devouring* allegorizes the very process of aesthetic and erotic seizure. According to Matisse, by taking successive *"constats"* of his subject, by multiplying views of the model, he could progressively enter into it until it became part of himself. "To work on my subject until I have it sufficiently inside me to be able to improvise" is how he described his working process.[36]

Barye's original depicts a jaguar in the act of snapping the spine of a subdued hare. The beast's legs are propped, his stomach compacted, back gathered and tensed with strained muscles. The overpowered hare, his long, limp ears and flaccid forepaws dangling lifelessly to the ground, sounds a tragic note of resignation. Matisse was seemingly less interested in the tragic contrasts of Barye's piece than in its embodied expression of identification. Matisse's version is a more compact mass, as though beast and prey, in the heat of action, are fused into one indissoluble whole. When it is struck by light reflecting off its densely worked surface, the mass appears animate and fleshy. As the jaguar fingers his prey in a gesture of "devouring affection," so it appears Matisse manipulated the clay. While Barye focuses the action on the struggling beasts, Matisse stresses his encounter with the pliable and resistant material. Matisse saturates the surface of the clay with marks of his presence. These marks reveal the artist's desire to remain present to his work, to almost merge with its features, and yet the accumulative nature of the marks signals the intensity and impossibility of continuing that presence once the work has been completed. Matisse seemed reluctant to come to that conclusion, as the work carried on for nearly three years.

The Side Not Seen

In the "Notes of a Painter" Matisse outlined two broad artistic approaches, one realist, the other imaginative:

> [There are] painters who work directly from nature and those who work purely from imagination. For me, I think neither of these methods must be preferred to the exclusion of the other. Both may be used in turn by the same individual, either because he needs the presence of objects in order to receive sensations and thereby excite his creative faculty, or because his sensations are already classified, in either case he will be able to arrive at the totality that constitutes the *tableau.* (42/51)[37]

As Matisse made clear, realism and imagination can be "used in turn by the same individual." Matisse called this the "eternal conflict" of "design and color in the same individual."[38]

Not surprisingly, Matisse's definition of the nature-based approach is anything but straightforward. He differentiates here the "presence of objects" from the sensations that excite the creative faculty. Without attempting further explication of this layered idea, I will nonetheless continue to call this tripartite approach to nature "realism." I will also assume, as I have argued up to this point, that Matisse's realism is conceived as anything but a direct contact with the natural world or bodies within it.

His account of the imaginative approach presents fewer difficulties. It describes someone whose sensations are "already classified" before engagement with the world. But it also suggests that the world is more immediately present to hand for such a person than for the realist, who requires constant stimulus. Matisse's imaginative approach was given explicit formulation in terms of his window imagery, where "space is one unity from the horizon right to the interior of my work room, and . . . the boat that is going past exists in the same space as the familiar objects around me; and the wall with the window does not create two different worlds" (146).

If the works discussed in chapter 3, including the standing nude and costume sequence, constitute Matisse's *conflictual* mode of aesthetic presentation, then in what follows I describe a related and more generalized practice that splits the terms of disconnection and connection, skepticism and merger into dialectically organized sets of paired or tripled works. Between 1895 and 1917 Matisse explored the tension between two modes of representation: first, a declarative form of *realism,* where objects are situated close to the beholder, filling up the picture surface, and yet maintain their separate, distinct identities. The term *realism* here is not intended to indicate a mode of reference to the world outside the work; rather, it is a descriptive term to articulate Matisse's indebtedness to the French realist tradition. With the second approach, the one I call *phenomenological* or embodied, Matisse figures space as something that involves the beholder, as the picture surface suggestively runs up to and under the viewer's feet but, for all its sense of fluidity, nonetheless situates objects at a distance. These two modes are two relations to the world. Together and individually, they challenge the reduction of one's relation to the world to the terms of subject and object, cause and effect upon which affective formalism and its skeptical opposite are founded. In pictorial terms, realism and phenomenology chart the two sides of Matisse's ambivalent mimesis. Realism designates Matisse's skepticism, his detached or observational attitude toward his medium and the world. Phenomenology captures Matisse's immersive relation to his medium and through it to the beholder and the world. Further still, these two modes project an image of the artist's practice that is distinctly at odds with the claims of a range of recent commentators following in the wake of Bois's writings who contend that Matisse founded a formal "system" for creating psychically affective responses and that he elaborated this system throughout his career. Rather than a system, Matisse's practice is better seen as a set of problems around expression underwritten by a set of largely unconscious, but no less intentional, structural concerns about the nature of representation.

Matisse's phenomenological approach is captured in an early work, *Woman Reading* of 1895 (Plate 5). We look in, as if from a distance, on a scene of absorption. Caroline Joblaud, the artist's lover at the time, is seated in a chair reading a book. Her head is tilted down, her neck exposed; her posture indicates a deep involvement in her activity. The flesh tone of her neck and the white edge of the book stand out in sharp relief against the stuffy green and brown scheme of the interior. At the far corner of the room, perched on top of a broad cabinet, lies a miscellaneous array of precious and semiprecious objects (they will be seen again presently). The clutter of objects contrasts with the bareness of the partially exposed cabinet interior beneath; on its single visible shelf lies a large volume laid flat, presumably the location where the sitter found her book. To the left of the cabinet, and appearing to lean against it, lies a canvas resting on a portable easel, the image fully obscured. Although the room is adorned with five images, only one of them is legible. Hanging above the still life is an early self-portrait; the artist's partially faded physiognomy enhances his spectral presence throughout the scene.

The room's complex spatial organization—how far, for instance, is the woman from the far shelf or from the pictures on the back wall?—further complicates the picture's emotional tone. It is at once a space of intimacy and protection and one of disorientation and detachment, as though we are not part of this world, but looking in on it from outside. The muted brown and green color scheme, broken only by flesh-colored highlights and the bright pages of the book, further adds to the expansive yet closed atmosphere. Overall, the image is charged with a latent sense of drama or psychological unease. Could the still life grouping on the far shelf be seen as actors performing a play whose script is unavailable? Could these objects be staging a fantasy in the mind of the reader, phantasmatic equivalents of the fictive characters in her book?

Abruptly telescoping the perspective of the distant scene atop the cabinet, *Still Life with Self-Portrait* (Plate 6) reiterates the far object group with subtle rearrangements and additions. The patterned vase barely visible at the left of the group in *Woman Reading* now plays a leading role, and a curious transformation has occurred: a flower pattern, which in the first picture functions as wallpaper, appears now as a cloth laid across the chest that supports the group. At the center of the scene lies a brightly lit roll of paper (presumably a drawing); it leans precariously on a book turned on its spine, the open pages of which partially cover Matisse's portrait medallion of Joblaud (Figure 4.2). There is a slight, but unmistakable, expressive charge in the proximity of the portrait to the image just to the left of it: it is the self-portrait that hangs on the wall in *Woman Reading.* Now wedged between two scruffy leather-bound books turned on their edges, the self-portrait no longer surveys the scene from above but is fully set into the cluster of objects that are Matisse's subject. In *Still Life with Self-Portrait* objects are drawn in close; Matisse emphasizes their presence as tactile, material entities. A strong light falls from the left, sharply illuminating the vase, plate, drawing, and cabinet and throwing their contours into relief. But for all this vividness, the objects keep their distant, separate identities, bound to one another, yet independent.

I want to point briefly in passing to a set of four works from this period that establish what I take to be the central problematic of Matisse's early ca-

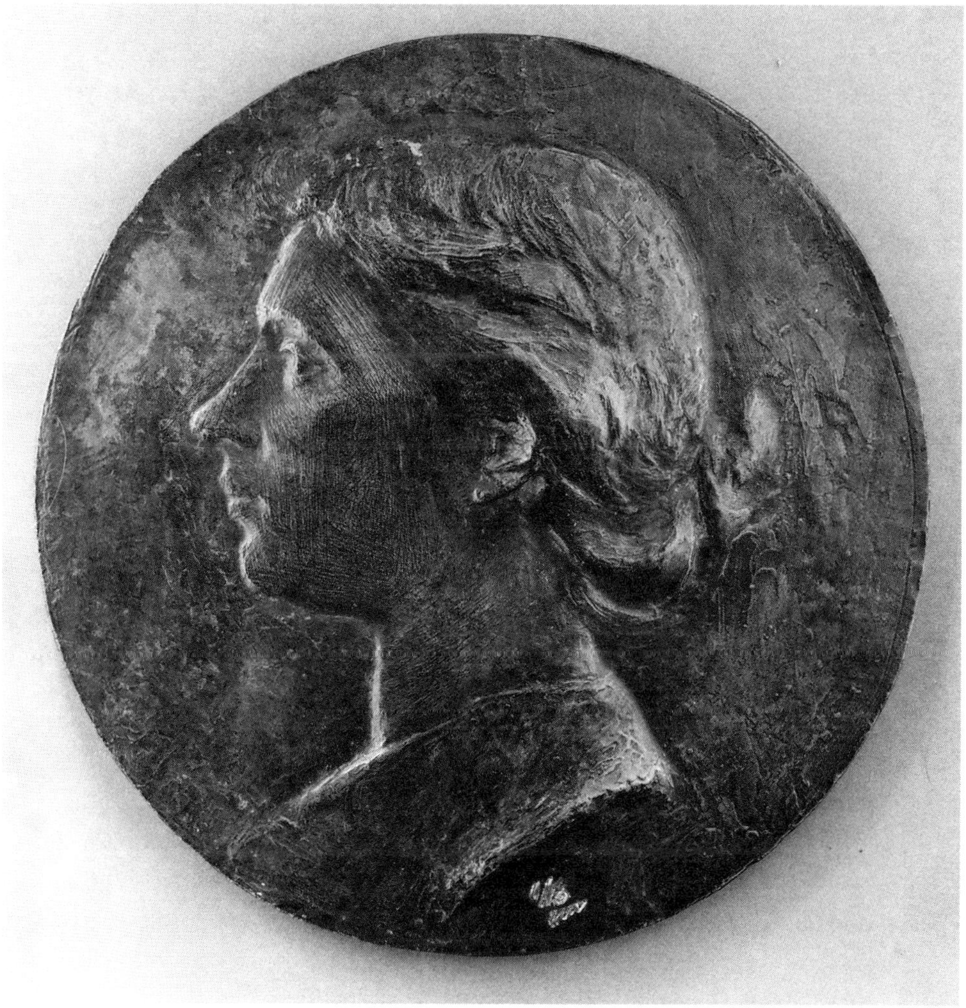

Figure 4.2. Henri Matisse (1869–1954), *Portrait Medallion (II)*, 1894. Bronze, 25.4 cm diameter. Musée Matisse, Nice, France. Copyright 2013 Succession H. Matisse / Artists Rights Society (ARS), NY. Photograph courtesy of Archives Henri Matisse.

reer. These pairs turn on the questions I have raised so far, shifting as they do between a detached, high-angle view over the scene to a more proximate, tactile presentation of the same or slightly altered material, as though objects were turning themselves, or opening, to the artist and the viewer's less scrupulous, but perhaps more attentive, gaze.

Although a seemingly undistinguished Dutch-inspired still life, Matisse's *Still Life with Fruits and Bottles* of 1896 (Figure 4.3) elaborates on the complex representational issues that emerged with *Woman Reading* and *Still Life with Self-Portrait* of the year before. *Fruits and Bottles* is a modest scene comprising a black-handled knife, four loose fruits (three apples and a lemon, which appears peeled in the foreground), a plate of grapes and pears, two wine bottles (one opaque, the other transparent), a decanter, a decorated pitcher, a silver coffeepot (it rests on another table behind the one in the foreground, only its surface visible), a small white bowl mostly obscured by the half-empty bottle in the foreground, and a baguette along the back edge of the table. All the forms, except for the coffeepot, rest atop a white tablecloth that visibly hangs over the closer edge of the table below the fruit dish and baguette along the left side. Although the tabletop is crowded with forms, they are positioned in such a way as to stress their individual identities. Tension is generated between the separate forms and their seeming to touch, even inflect one another at their edges. Consider, for instance, how the apple at the center of the composition seems to create a dark shadow along the lower portion of the decanter. Then again, this "shadow" may be a view into the decanter (its punt barely visible) resting on the table. The differentiation of forms along the table surface is set in contrast to the shapes in the fruit dish, which seem to lose their individuated forms and to fuse into a singular mass. Once again, the painter's viewpoint ranges above and over the elements, looking down on the scene from a detached perspective.

Compare this with the *Still Life with Clay Pitcher and Black Knife* (Figure 4.4) of the same year. The viewpoint has dramatically shifted, and we are drawn in close to the forms on the table. That this is the same table is evident by the recurrence of the knife, three apples (the peeled lemon has been conspicuously removed), the decorated pitcher with blue patches, the red wine bottle, the baguette (now positioned parallel to the left edge of the frame but dramatically foreshortened), and a closer view of the coffeepot, which now visibly rests on a lower table behind this one. Where the former image evoked a sense of detachment, the closer viewpoint brings the objects more proximately into the viewer's space. While the knife and the shadow create a sense of visual recession, other markers secure the presence of the picture plane. Indeed the baguette lines up along the left edge, so the pitcher and wine bottle seem to share a vertical limit along their left sides, one that is echoed in the shadow of the center-left apple and marked by the handle of the knife in the foreground. A vertical is also evoked by the brightly lit reflection on the slope of the pitcher. This vertical orientation is subtly countered by the horizontal mouth of the pitcher and the top of the coffeepot (the latter is further echoed by the shoulder of the wine bottle).

Several elements from the *Fruits and Bottles* and *Clay Pitcher and Black Knife* pairing recur in a closely related still life set of 1897. In *Still Life with Two Bottles* (Figure 4.5) the dark setting of the previous works has given way to a brighter, more silver-toned atmosphere. The play of reflections across the still life elements marks Matisse's growing awareness of Impressionism, and the

Figure 4.3. Henri Matisse (1869–1954), *Still Life with Fruits and Bottles,* 1896. Oil on canvas. Copyright 2013 Succession H. Matisse / Artists Rights Society (ARS), NY. Photograph courtesy of Archives Henri Matisse.

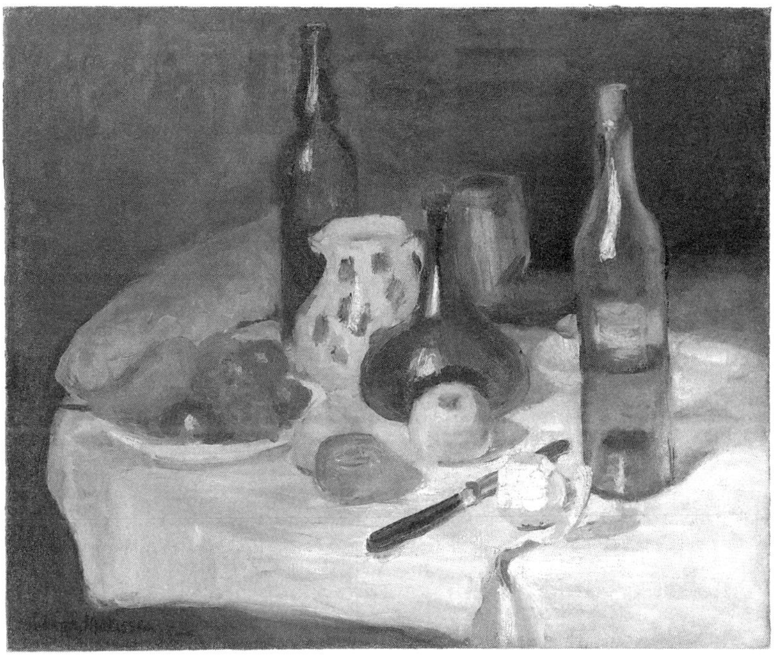

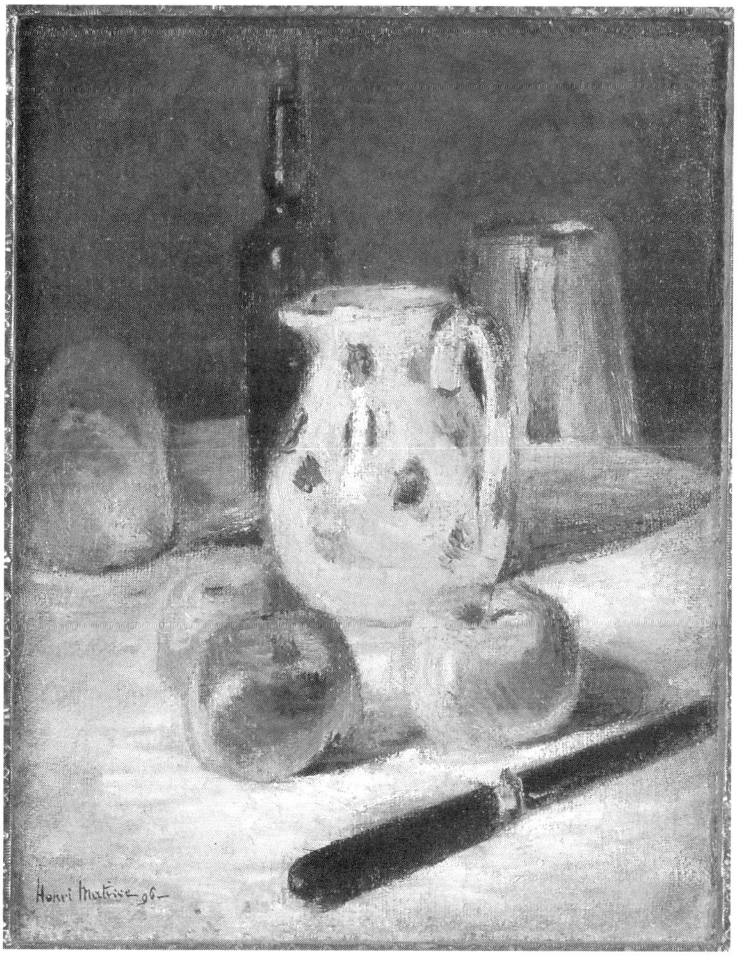

Figure 4.4. Henri Matisse (1869–1954), *Still Life with Clay Pitcher and Black Knife,* 1896. Oil on canvas, 42 × 33.5 cm. Musée Matisse, Nice, France. Bequest of Madame Henri Matisse, 1960. Inventory 63.2.11. Copyright 2013 Succession H. Matisse / Artists Rights Society (ARS), NY. Photograph from City of Nice Photographic Service.

contrasts of materials and surfaces are richer than anything he has attempted up to this point. The viewpoint is raised slightly above the scene, granting the eye visual access across the forms and into depth. The foreground space is oriented around a fruit dish with four apples arranged in a loose cruciform shape. A white-handled knife, its blade resting along the edge of the dish—the whole form is visible—repeats the decorative line of the tablecloth as well as the line produced by the edge of the tablecloth in the foreground. Behind the dish lies a decorated white teacup, a bottle of white wine (the glass is transparent) and a

Figure 4.5. Henri Matisse (1869–1954), *Still Life with Two Bottles,* 1897. Oil on canvas, 73 × 60 cm. Private collection. Copyright 2013 Succession H. Matisse / Artists Rights Society (ARS), NY. Photograph courtesy of Archives Henri Matisse.

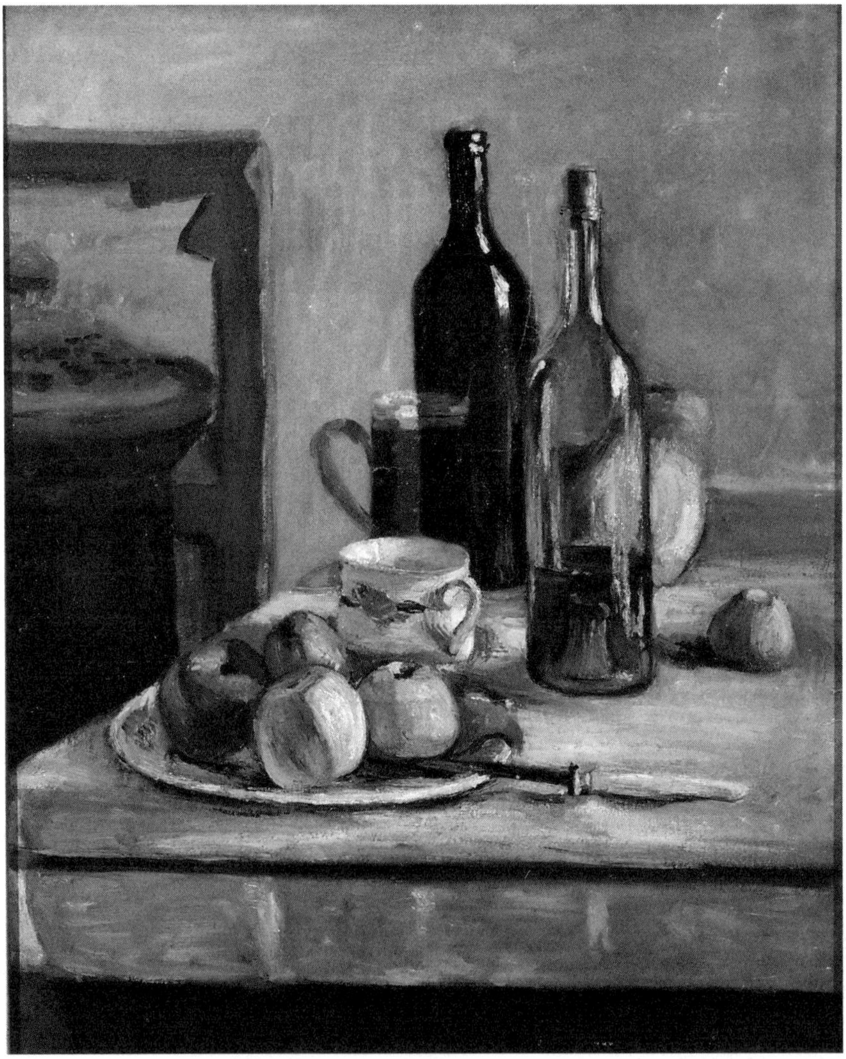

taller, more opaque bottle of red wine situated farther along the table surface. Matisse has positioned a stray apple along the right side of the tabletop near the transparent bottle. Located in a position similar to the one in *Clay Pitcher and Black Knife,* and directly behind the bottle of white wine, a foreshortened baguette is set parallel to the picture edge. Near the back edge of the table lies a large-handled blue mug, its form just visible through the dark bottle before it. To the left of the table and farther back in the space appears an oven or furnace behind which a canvas leans against the wall with its surface turned away from the viewer (the proximity of heating source and canvas is striking).

Still Life with Apples (Figure 4.6) develops a motif out of *Two Bottles,* and once again the viewer is drawn in closer to the scene depicted in its complement, but the elements are now arranged and treated in a different manner. The tablecloth that hangs down along the foreground plane is decorated with a red horizontal line that carries across the surface, although it mysteriously seems to tilt onto the tabletop along the right side. The knife that appears in *Two Bottles* has been turned ninety degrees to create a strong vertical. This line directs our vision in a similar way to the vertical pull of the baguette that appeared in *Two Bottles* but whose form is no longer visible. A fruit dish with

Figure 4.6. Henri Matisse (1869–1954), *Still Life with Apples,* 1897. Private collection. Copyright 2013 Succession H. Matisse / Artists Rights Society (ARS), NY. Photograph courtesy of Art Resource, NY.

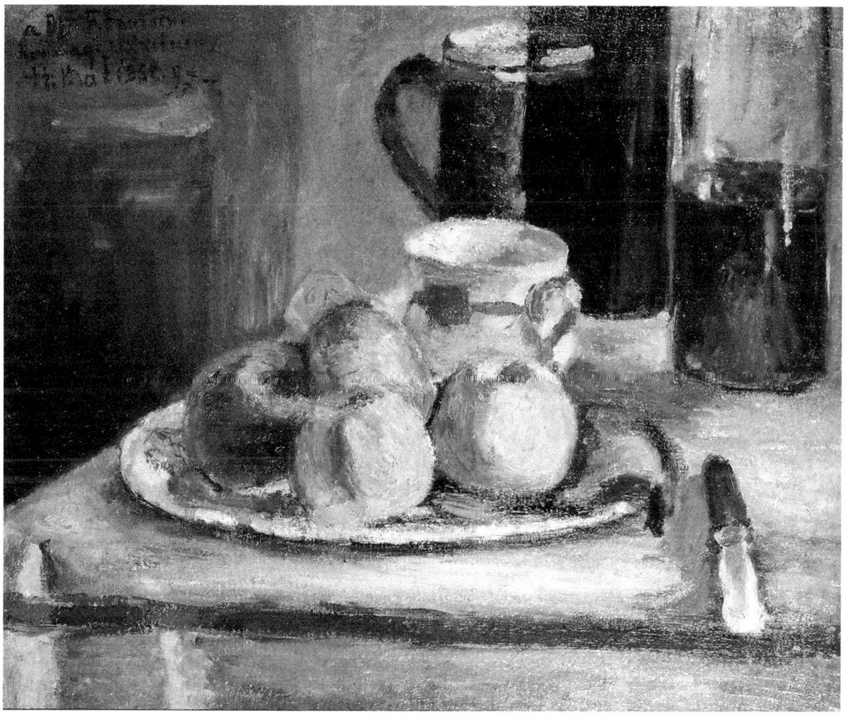

four apples, a cup, wine bottles, and mug are situated in roughly the same locations as in *Two Bottles,* but the forms seem more compacted within the compressed table space.

Matisse's treatment of the surface in *Still Life with Apples* contrasts decisively with that of the companion work. Here the forms emerge out of thickly applied dabs of viscous paint, their contours so loosely defined that the elements tend to merge with their neighbors. Most surprising is the treatment of the space near the back left, where the furnace and canvas back merge into one indistinct mass that would be impossible to recognize if not for the information provided by the companion picture. The formal constraints on this close-up image contrast widely with *Two Bottles.* While the individual elements are more loosely defined, Matisse gives up none of the formal rigor apparent in *Two Bottles.* An underlying grid is suggested by the decorative foreground stripe and vertically situated knife. And while the canvas back has become less distinct as an individual form, its contours imply the existence of a tautened grid in the upper-left section of the canvas. The underlying structure is further articulated by the horizontal pattern of the cup, by the half-empty bottle, and by the far edge of the mug, which are balanced and countered by the vertical lift of the wine bottles.

Matisse elaborated many of the structural features of *Two Bottles* and *Apples* in several sets of paired works at the time. While *Two Bottles* projects a sense of cool objectivity, *Apples,* a more intimate image, combines a tight formal logic with a loosely applied surface texture. Here, Matisse slackens the contours of the individual forms while retaining the specific weights and textures of the objects. A further level of intimacy is suggested in *Apples* with the boldly inscribed dedication at upper left. Matisse called the picture his "little Chardin" and dedicated it to his childhood friend Fernand Fontaine on his wedding day. (It was at the wedding feast that Matisse and Amélie Parayre met; they were married in January of the next year.)

Matisse and his wife arrived at Ajaccio, Corsica, in February 1898 as part of their extended honeymoon (they had spent the previous weeks in London). It was a highly productive period for Matisse, and in just over two months on the island he painted fifty-five paintings, most of them of small scale. Although the majority of these works are painted in an assertively new style of boldly applied dabs of thick paint and nonnaturalistic color, *Room at Ajaccio* (1898) (Figure 4.7) stands out as a rather sober and unassuming study of his spartanly furnished surroundings at the Villa de la Rocca. *Room at Ajaccio* balances between an attention to particular features (including bed, night table, lamp, hat, jacket, and carpet) and the overall surface design. The space is clearly makeshift and seems to function as both bedroom and studio for the artist (the reverse of a canvas is visible once again against the back wall). A jacket is casually slung over the bedpost, the vertical lines of its folds transferring their upward lift across the surface, echoing the line of the bedspread, table legs, and the fireplace along the right side. Spread across the foreground, a patterned carpet is situated in such a way as to draw the eye into the space, producing a sense of recession in what is likely a diminutive space, as well as blocking that recession by drawing the form flat against the picture plane. This oscillating effect occurs through a subtle manipulation of the shape of the carpet, the edges of which project the form into space (its lines are picked up by the floor mat beside the bed) while the decorative border, which is echoed by the lamp shade, seems to lift the form off the floor, bringing it in line with the picture plane. Similarly, the hatched lines of the central design sharply cut into the space while at same time lifting free of the framing border, generating a flickering surface effect.

Although it has never been noted in the literature, Matisse developed another pictorial motif from within this space. Traditionally dated to around

Figure 4.7. Henri Matisse (1869–1954), *Room at Ajaccio*, 1898. Oil on canvas, 80 × 95 cm. Private collection. Copyright 2013 Succession H. Matisse / Artists Rights Society (ARS), NY.

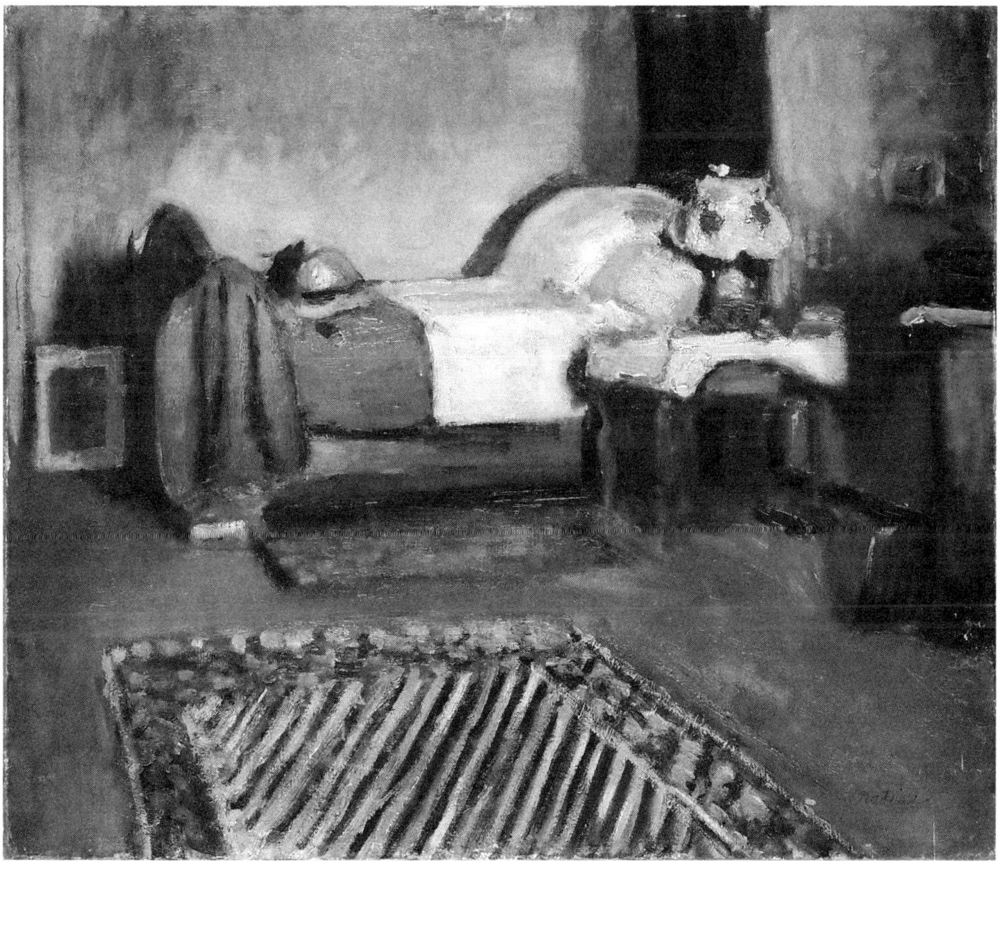

1896, the *Still Life with Black Knives* (Figure 4.8) is in fact a motif drawn out of the same room at the Villa de la Rocca, and it should be dated to the spring of 1898. The wide-angle view of *Room* has been altered as we are drawn in close to a still life arrangement situated along the left side of the space. The same bed as in *Room* appears in the far corner, as well as the straw hat and the jacket, which is now draped over the far end of the bedpost. To the left of the bed rest a number of canvases, two tall and narrow ones and a smaller rectangular one that may be the same canvas seen along the left side in *Room*. It now appears that the space serves a triple function: bedroom, studio, and kitchen.

The foreground is dominated by a seemingly casual arrangement of elements. Two pears on a plate, a baguette, two wine bottles, a cup, a silver dish with a spoon lying within a broader ceramic bowl, a blue-patterned pitcher

Figure 4.8. Henri Matisse (1869–1954), *Still Life with Black Knives*, 1898. Oil on canvas, 60 × 85 cm. Fonds National d'Art Contemporain. Copyright 2013 Succession H. Matisse / Artists Rights Society (ARS), NY. Photograph courtesy of Archives Henri Matisse.

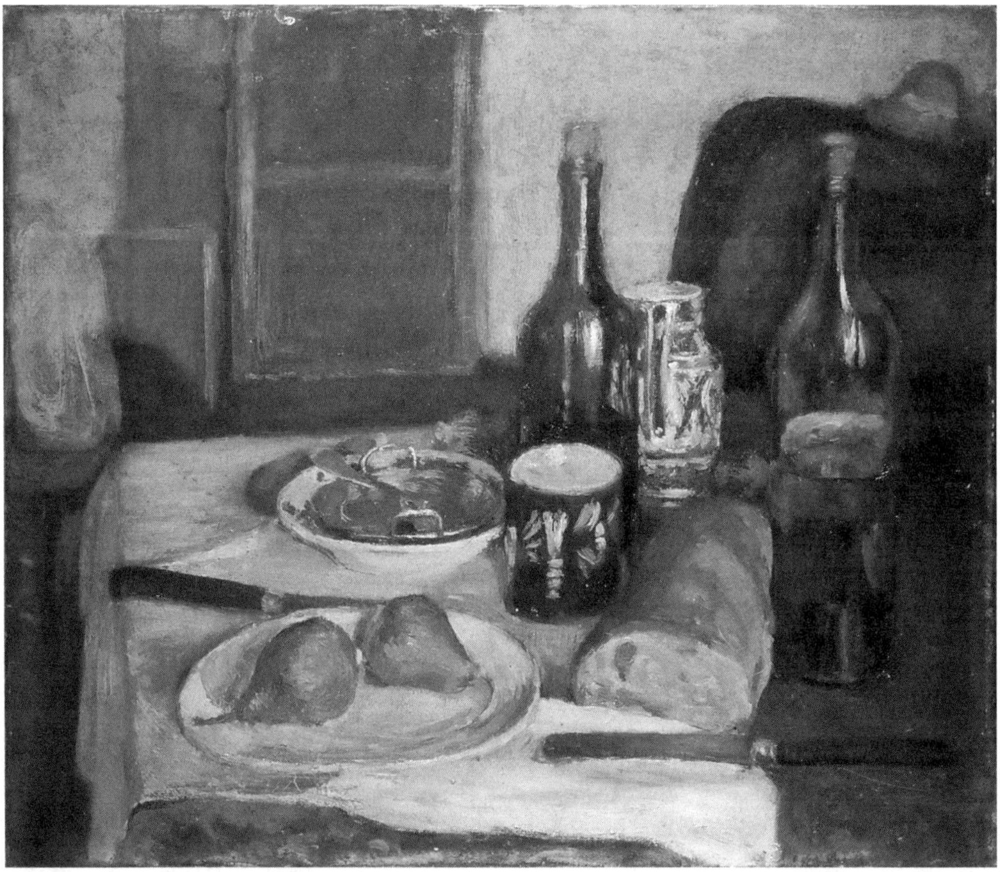

(which has appeared in several earlier still lifes), and two knives, which give the picture its name. The hovering perspective of *Room* has given way to an encounter with more weighty forms. The tilted table surface seems to present the elements in such a way as to lift them up and project them out toward the beholder. Despite the air of informality, *Black Knives* is as carefully organized as *Room.* The distant lines of the reversed canvas once again subtly project across the foreground space. While the canvases, bed, and back wall are almost completely drained of their mass, the foreground forms are weighted and clearly defined against their neighbors. The lines of the distant stretcher bars further echo across the foreground space, mirroring the lines of the knives, tablecloth, and bottles (the closer label turned away from the viewer) and the pattern on the vase. Matisse has generated a high degree of tension between the loose gridding of the picture surface and the specifically evoked textures of the elements, but in the end it is the clearly defined forms that seem to have won out against their formalization.

Another pair from the same Ajaccio moment turns on an even more dramatic contrast between phenomenological and realist modalities. The unassuming *Still Life with an Oil Jug* (Figure 4.9) presents a flat table surface atop which rest a pair of salt and pepper shakers, a short silver cup wedged within a group of six or seven apples or oranges, a reflective glass surface with what is likely a baguette behind it, a piece of fruit in the distance, and an oil jug at the far edge of the table. Matisse has chosen an unusual viewpoint, one taken from a lowered position, the table surface spread out at eye level. The picture is organized around a sequence of horizontals and verticals that echo and rhyme across the surface, binding the various elements together, while sharp notes of color and fleshy textures establish the separate identities of the various forms.

The most gripping and peculiar moment in the picture is the carefully managed reflection in the partially full glass (or mirrored surface) at the right. I cannot help but see in it a blurred reflection of the artist—a vertical form against a blue ground along the left side—and another figure, shown against a white ground (this is impossible to establish for certain). A vertical line down the center of the glass seems to both divide and bind the forms to what might be shimmering liquid beneath.

At first glance the little-known *Still Life with Pitcher* (Figure 4.10) seems worlds apart from the studied simplicity of *Still Life with an Oil Jug.* A closer look reveals that *Pitcher* is indeed a view of the same still life arrangement seen from a different perspective. We are situated close to the oil jug that loomed in the distance in the paired work. Just to its right and above stands the salt and pepper shakers, which now lie at the far edge of the table. While the densely painted forms along the right side are illegible, the silver cup and oranges reappear along the left side. The angle of vision has been slightly shifted as well. We now look down and across the space at about a sixty-degree angle, which

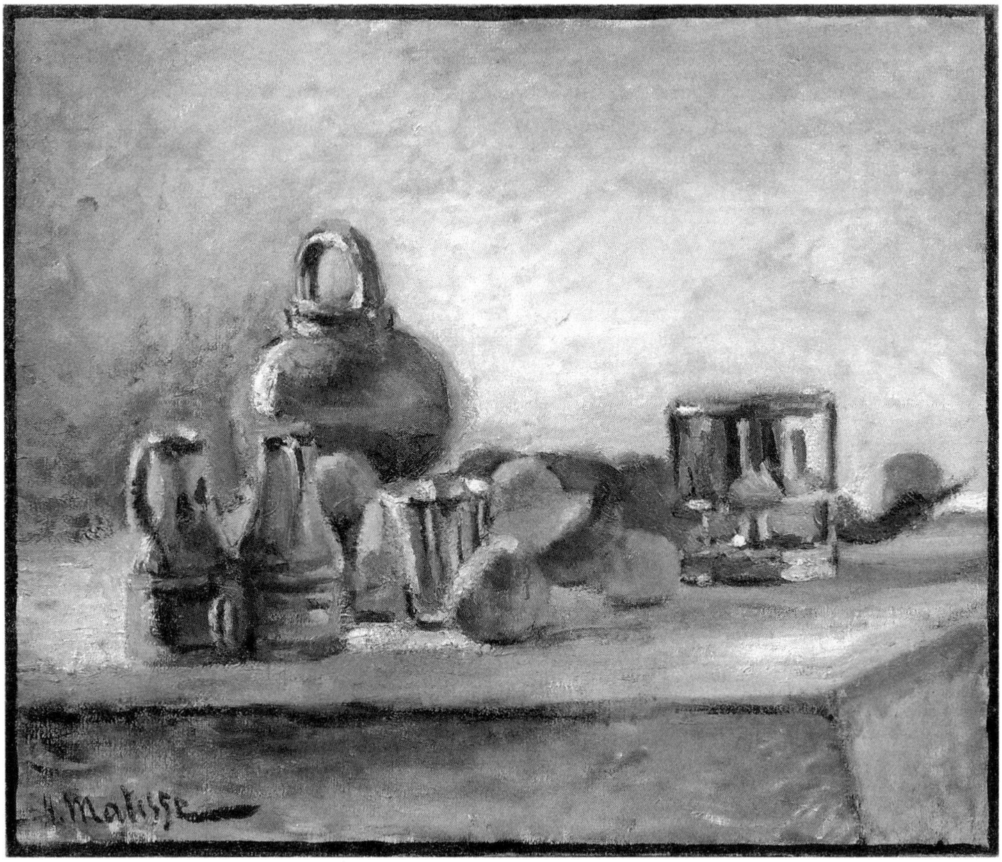

Figure 4.9. Henri Matisse (1869–1954), *Still Life with an Oil Jug,* 1898. Oil on canvas, 38 × 46 cm. Private collection. Copyright 2013 Succession H. Matisse / Artists Rights Society (ARS), NY.

Figure 4.10. Henri Matisse (1869–1954), *Still Life with Pitcher,* ca. 1898. Oil on canvas, 12 × 21 cm. Copyright 2013 Succession H. Matisse / Artists Rights Society (ARS), NY.

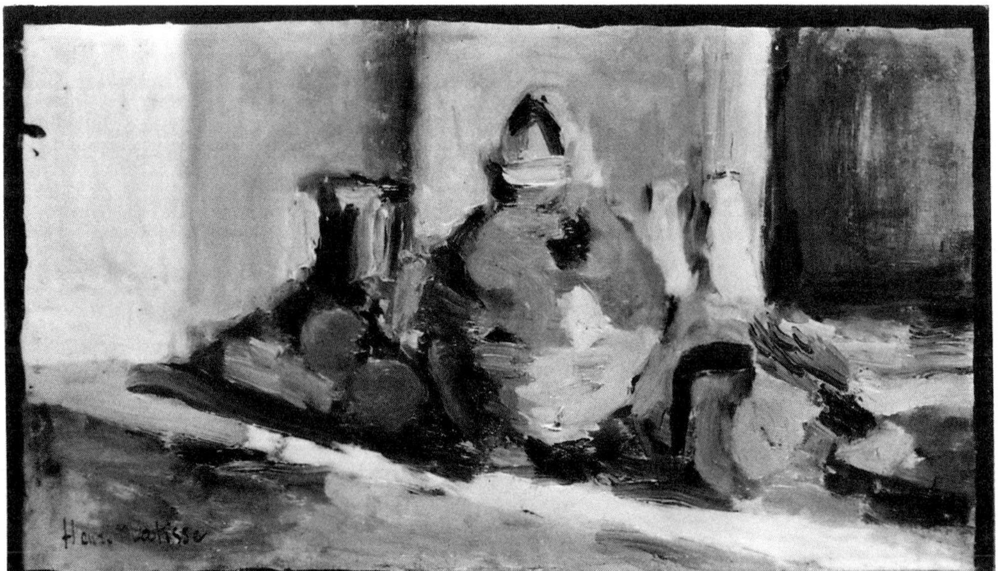

should reduce the apparent height of those objects in relation to the pitcher, but they are curiously expanded and inflated here. The most striking contrast with the companion work is its heavily worked surface. Thick dabs of viscous paint are applied with seeming abandon, evoking a set of tactile sensations associated with the character of the depicted elements. Suppressing light/dark modeling, suggestions of contrasting weights and textures emerge through the rough application of paint and heavy contours.

The most haunting element of the scene is the starkly rendered reflection in the mirrored surface at the right. The upper right section is dominated by the distended and disembodied visage of the painter (or another figure) looking out upon the scene and imaginatively at the viewer. Given the lowered vantage point, it is difficult to see this as a mirror reflection, as the figure's chin is roughly flush with the far edge of the table surface. The angle of vision more convincingly depicts the almost ninety-degree viewpoint shown in *Oil Jug.* In fact, it would not be going too far to say that *Oil Jug* presents us with a view from the mirror image, while *Pitcher* renders the scene from the painter's perspective. Like the suspended self-portraits in *Woman Reading* and *Interior with a Top Hat* (1896), as well as the mirror-reflection works discussed in chapter 3—notably *Carmelina* and *Still Life with a Checked Tablecloth*—there is a specular undercurrent here. It is as though Matisse resists the drift of merger that his newly conceived formal principles, ones largely drawn from the example of van Gogh, seem to imply.

Painted early in 1899 after his return to Paris from his honeymoon, *Still Life* (Plate 7) is notable for the first appearance of Matisse's beloved toile de Jouy. Here the fabric screens off the background, and the V shape at its center mirrors and pulls up flat the dense receding shadow across the tabletop. The viewpoint is high, and the space sweeps precipitously from back to front until it reaches the lower edge of the picture surface, which seems to almost spill out into the beholder's space. Sloping in a sharp diagonal across the surface, the side edge falls off at a sharp angle, revealing the dark flooring to the left. The most striking element of the picture is the impastoed treatment of the surface. The dense layers of marks both physically divide elements from one another and provide a sense of continuity across the individual zones of paint. Degrees of finish and unfinish, precision and ambiguity, draw the eye across the surface, inviting it to wander without clear direction from moment to moment, zone to zone. The separate forms of coffeepot and cup, wine bottle, and bowls of fruit seem to struggle to emerge from the thickly crusted surface. Although each object is defined against its neighbor by heavily applied contours and sweeps of intense color, the overall tone is muted, and the forms tend to merge with their surroundings. The baguette at the most proximate edge exemplifies a tension between the dense, individuating work-up of paint and an equivalent loss of definition. From the baguette in the foreground to the space near the back wall, it seems the painter's focus shifted between amorphous patterns and the stiff verticality of the chair back. As the eye moves across the hanging fabric along the far wall it is stopped short again by the fluid black-and-red zone at the right, where the focus becomes hazy, and the space, which defines both the edge of the wall and the coffeepot on the table, confounds clear spatial organization.

Compare this now with *Fruit and Coffee Pot* of 1899 (Plate 8). The arrangement of the five forms—a plate of fruit, a gold coffeepot, a cup on a saucer, a half-empty bottle of wine, and a blue dish at the far edge of the picture surface, although the middle of the table—seem to invert the pictorial conventions of *Still Life.* One's focus no longer ranges high over and above the objects, but is drawn in close, each form clearly articulated against its neighbors spread out along the tablecloth that fills up almost the whole of the surface. Although the objects are spaced at clearly defined intervals, they are nonetheless held together through the sharp angle of the coffeepot handle. The handle seems to touch and inflect the cup at its furthest reach, while the lip of the cup touches the lower edge of the bottle, which in turn touches and inflects the blue bowl at the far edge. The four separate elements are gathered and echoed by the round pieces of fruit in the foreground bowl, while the deep blue of the grapes is picked up by notes of color across the surface, from the handle of the coffeepot to the upper edge of the surrounding space. The common theme, we might say, is states of liquidity.

Compare this again with *Still Life.* Although the treatment is sharply different from its companion, *Fruit and Coffee Pot* is in fact a view taken from *within Still Life.* It is the view, as it were, from the distant chair in *Still Life,* looking out and across the table before us. *Fruit and Coffee Pot* shows us, literally and, I want to say, figuratively, the other side of things. Matisse has exchanged the hovering viewpoint for one of clarity and directness. And although we are brought closer to these objects the clarity does not obscure differences, or a sense of distance; rather, distinctions are further articulated the closer they seem to cross over into our space.

Matisse draws us to a further point of proximity and difference in his little-known *Café Table* of 1899 (Plate 9). Extracted from the still life ensemble, the coffee cup has also been drawn nearer along the table surface. I see the intense line drawn across the middle ground, the cup seeming to rest on its surface, as the shadow that falls from the grip of the coffeepot just outside the picture's right edge. Matisse has given up none of the thick, loose handling of *Still Life,* but he has deployed it here to a different end. Applied to a singular, proximate, familiar object, the loose handling and heightened color lose their burden of skepticism and grant the object, and the world, a kind of flesh, or even a face.

A similar set of concerns emerges in another pair from the months following the costume sequence discussed in chapter 3. One's first impression of

Studio under the Eaves (Plate 10) is of spatial dislocation and expressive opacity. The scene is a makeshift studio the artist created in the attic of a temporary home in northern France. The room, which appears vast and feels as though it sweeps under one's feet, is sparsely decorated and contains only the barest of spatial indicators. About halfway between the floor at the canvas edge and the distant casement window lies a broad packing crate, on top of which lies a palette with three brushes lodged in the thumbhole. Closer to the window, and angled away from the viewer, stands an easel with a canvas suspended from it. To the left of it stands a small bamboo folding table, two of its legs intersected by those of the easel. Although the artist is absent from the scene, his tools project his presence throughout the room. The picture's drama lies in the stark contrast between the open window and the dull brown of the attic space. While the thin, vertical skylights on the sloping side walls seem to exacerbate the room's claustrophobic feel, the enclosure is punctuated by the dazzling light that bursts in through the distant window.

As disorienting as *Studio* is, its pendant, the remarkable *Bouquet on a Bamboo Table* (Plate 11) casts a vision of familiarity and solidity despite the fragile and makeshift support on which the depicted vase rests. This view, I take it, is what we would see if the picture suspended on the studio easel were to be made visible. *Bouquet* draws the viewer in close to a handful of purple dahlias; the upward tilt of the table, the bouquet resting on the outermost edge, draws the object into the utmost proximity. Although the vase rests insecurely on the table, it nonetheless gives the impression of security, the base creating a well-defined shadow that cuts through the thick gray of the surface. Speaking of the paired works near the end of his life, Matisse reflected that "this painting of the attic is one my best pictures as is the one of the flowers." He valued *Bouquet* above all for its sense of "atmosphere and intimacy."[39] Intimacy is a precise term for what we see. It implies a desire for closeness and communication but also suggests a remainder of difference, of an independent existence that makes the desire for intimacy possible. It is the experience of intimacy that Heidegger expressed in his poem on Matisse. Matisse opened the world to the beholder in order "to protect its arrival into hesitant nearing." Hesitant nearing might come close to describing Matisse's basic aesthetic attitude.

During the fauve period Matisse's perspectival approach grew more complicated and layered, and in the summer of 1906 he produced some of the most exploratory works of his career. In terms of technique and genre, *The Geranium* of 1906 (Plate 12) eludes established categories. Situated above the scene, the viewer peers down on a stagelike proscenium consisting of two sculptures, a plate, a painted vase, four onions, and the geranium featured in the title. Although it is difficult to make out, the figurines are Matisse's own *Woman Leaning on Her Hands* of 1905 and his remake of the classical figure of the thorn extractor. The atmosphere seems charged with animation, as though we are peering into a glade with figures moving about in a landscape. The leaves of the geranium seem suspended in the air by layers of paint, their forms floating free of their roots, creating a canopy or a frame for the ambiguous drama below.

If *The Geranium* seems charged with dramatic tension, then its companion, *Pink Onions* (Plate 13), projects an atmosphere of faux naïveté (Matisse told his incredulous friends it was painted by the local postman).[40] Pressed forward against the picture plane, the four onions from *The Geranium* reemerge in a wholly new expressive and pictorial configuration. Distance gives way to proximity, and narrative drama shifts to a kind of absurd intimacy. Without a doubt the boldest moments of the picture are the broad planes of largely unmixed color constituting wall, tabletop, and space below. And yet, despite the determined simplicity of the presentation, key elements remain illegible. Consider, for instance, the ill-defined white-and-red-checkered form near the back right. A glance at the elements along the right side of the *The Geranium* might help us make sense of the related passage in *Pink Onions.* The white-and-red form is more clearly articulated, but its purpose is still unidentifiable. Behind it stands a rendering of Matisse's sculpted portrait of his wife, *Woman Leaning on Her Hands.* And this moment seems as emotionally laden as the earlier one in *Still Life with Self-Portrait* where the relief portrait of Joblaud pressed against the artist's self-portrait among the books and curios. In both works a private encounter is made available to the beholder while key features (as well as their personal sense) remain obscure. Simplicity here does not provide for clarity, but perhaps for something more intimate than knowledge.

One further picture should be included in this pictorial dialogue between *The Geranium* and *Pink Onions.* Matisse painted a small "portrait" of the camel-design vase in *The Rose* (Figure 4.11). The neck of the vase is decorated with a diamond shape in heavy black outline, its form loosely mirrored in the open shape of the rose above. The distinct frontality of the form exerts a kind of pressure against the surface, as though the whole image is turned out toward the beholder, the leaves acting as surrogate limbs, the vase supplying a body. The emphatic silhouette of the *The Rose* is similar in character and setting to *Bouquet on a Bamboo Table,* as it too extracts the vase and flowers from a larger grouping in order to fix our attention on the individuated form. For all its colorful display, the vase is set back in the shallow space, reserving a discrete distance from the beholder's approach.

At the same moment that Matisse was at work on the *Geranium* group, he was pursuing the most complex set of interlocked works he had attempted up to that point. As a whole, the summer of 1906 marks a turning point in Matisse's career as he begins analyzing and organizing the basic themes, mo-

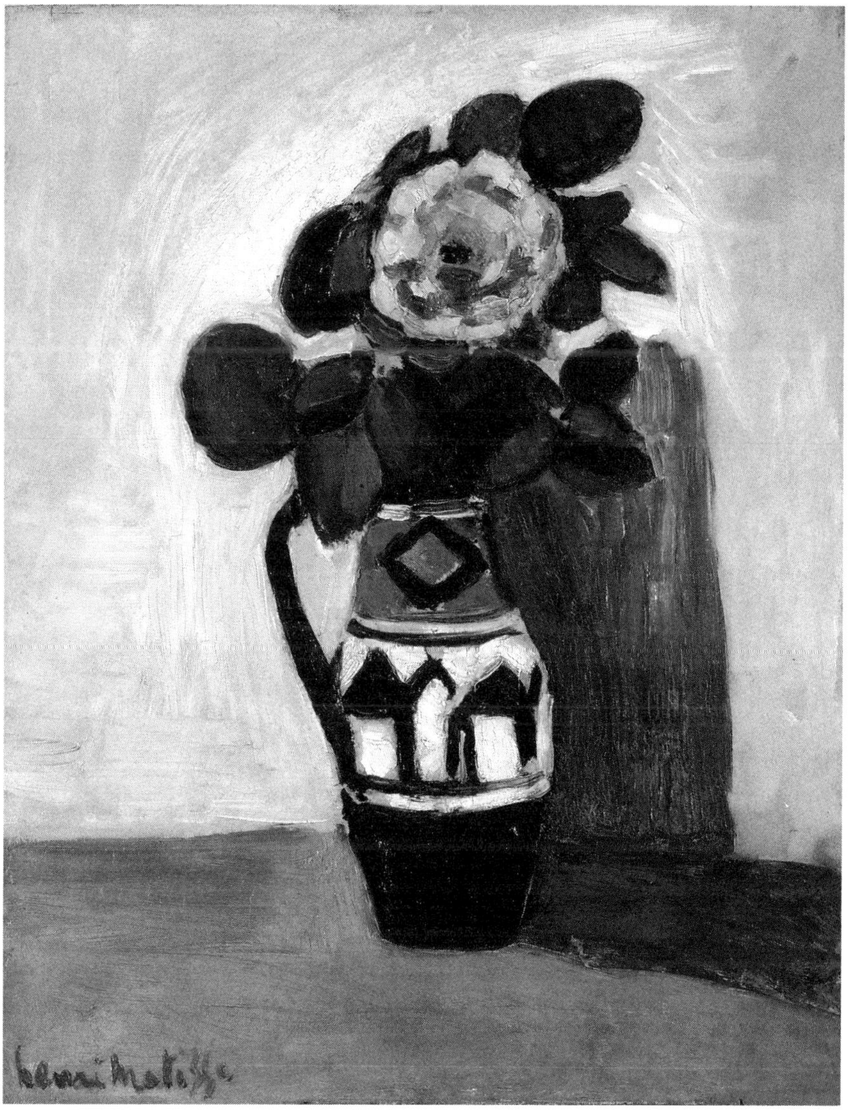

Figure 4.11. Henri Matisse (1869–1954), *The Rose*, ca. 1906. Oil on canvas, 40.6 × 31.8 cm. Norton Gallery of Art, West Palm Beach, Florida. Copyright 2013 Succession H. Matisse / Artists Rights Society (ARS), NY. Photograph Archives H. Matisse; copyright 2013 Succession H. Matisse.

tifs, and techniques explored in *Le Bonheur de vivre* (Figure 4.12) and to which he will return throughout his career. Looking back years later on *Le Bonheur*, he observed, "It was painted through the juxtaposition of things conceived independently but arranged together. Whereas afterwards, I tried to get more unity in my compositions."[41] In order to achieve that unity, he began by radically *disassembling* the independent elements. The analytical process of dividing up his practice through the exploration of contrary stylistic approaches,

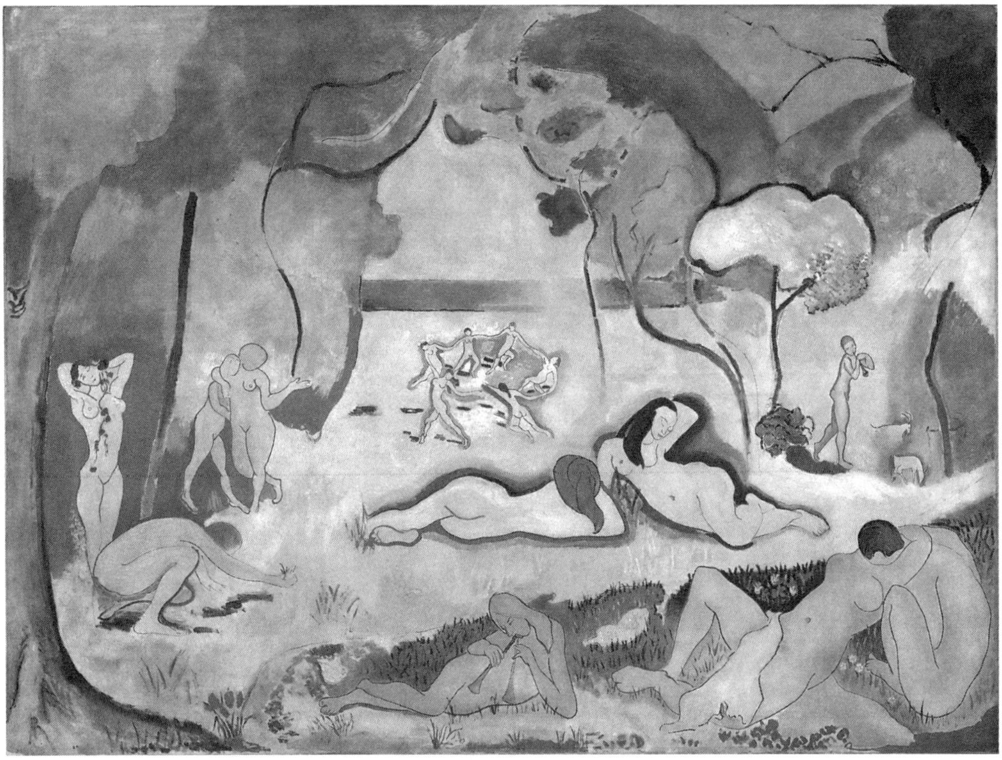

Figure 4.12. Henri Matisse (1869–1954), *Le Bonheur de vivre*, 1905–6. Oil on canvas, 175 × 241 cm. The Barnes Foundation, Merion, Pennsylvania. Copyright 2013 Succession H. Matisse / Artists Rights Society (ARS), NY. Photograph: The Bridgeman Art Library International.

while retaining the same thematic elements, was itself an attempt to unify his efforts on the level of structure.

After returning from Algeria in late May, Matisse spent the summer of 1906 in Collioure, remaining there until the opening of the Salon d'Automne in October. That Matisse consciously developed an interlocking or multilayered approach to pictorial problems at this time is exemplified by his submissions to the Salon, which included *Still Life with Plaster Figure* (Plate 15), *Flowers* (Plate 16), and the ambitious *Red Rugs* (Plate 17).[42] Two further paintings are connected with the group at its start—*Dishes and Melon* (Plate 14), likely from the spring of 1906—and at its conclusion—*Dishes and Fruit on a Red and Black Carpet* (Plate 18), which was likely completed in the fall, after his return to Paris. One further work closely associated with the sequence is the plaster cast form of *Standing Nude* (Figure 4.13), a portrait of his daughter Marguerite, which appears in two of the still lifes.

The six works are associated with one another through a shared set of still life elements as well as through an underlying structural design. Four of

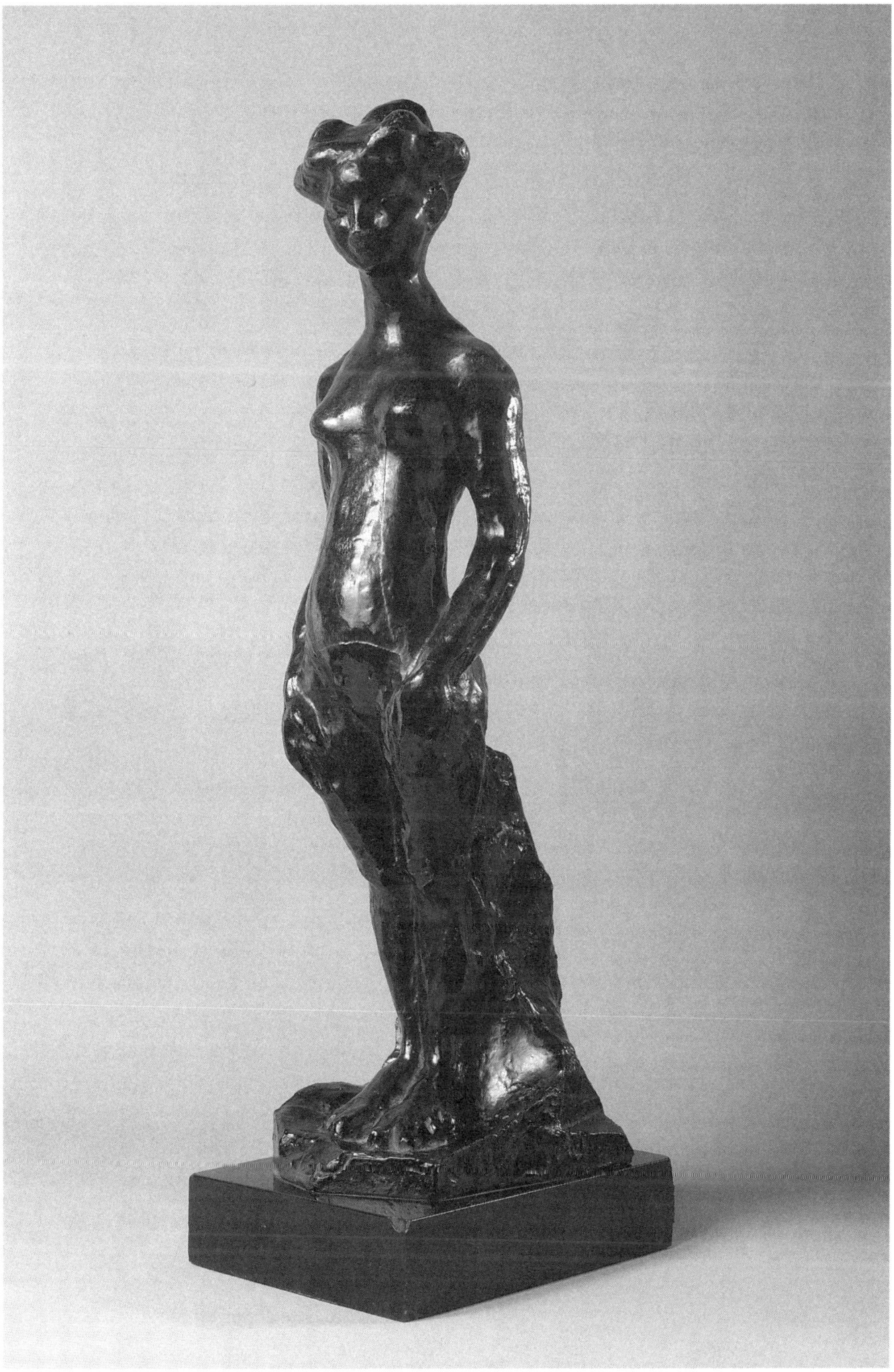

Figure 4.13. Henri Matisse (1869–1954), *Standing Nude,* 1906. Bronze, 83 × 12.7 × 16.5 cm. Private collection. Copyright 2013 Succession H. Matisse / Artists Rights Society (ARS), NY. Photograph copyright The Bridgeman Art Library International / Lefevre Fine Art Ltd., London.

the five pictures are of modest dimensions: the Barnes Foundation's *Dishes and Melon* is twenty-six by thirty-two inches, Yale's *Still Life with Plaster Figure* is twenty-two by eighteen inches, the Duke of Roxburghe's *Flowers* is twenty-three by twenty-eight inches, and the Hermitage's *Red and Black Carpet* is twenty-four by twenty-nine inches. *The Red Rugs* at Grenoble, at thirty-five by forty-six inches, is significantly larger than the works associated with it. The size and scale of *The Red Rugs* indicates its role as the summa of the series as a whole.

Although Matisse had included sculptures in his earlier still lifes, the first work in the sequence, *Dishes and Melon,* is among the first to feature one of his own sculptures since his *Still Life with Self-Portrait* of 1895. The plaster figure is symmetrical, the neck elongated, the head disproportionately large, hands drawn in close to the body. While Flam suggests that *Standing Nude*'s presence within the still life serves as the first of Matisse's "symbolic . . . personifications of femininity among the flowers and fruits,"[43] in the Barnes picture the artist seems to have redirected all of its bodily energy to the inanimate elements that surround it. The fruit, especially the lemon and melon, contain a heightened sense of inner life while the body seems to recede, its physiognomy a blank. And although the plaster figure does not appear in all of the works in the sequence, her ghostly presence sets the tone for the group as a whole. The red rug in the Grenoble picture, for instance, carries an indescribable charge of corporeal animation although it conspicuously lacks the sculpted form.

Still Life with Plaster Figure shares many elements with the Barnes picture, although the formal qualities are poignantly inverted. The two oranges, lemon, melon, decorated bowls, and plaster statuette blend with their surroundings, and no element is given special emphasis. Whereas the space is deep and tactile in the Barnes picture, it is shallow and watery in the Yale work. Colors in *Plaster Figure* are subtle and vaporous, and the forms seem to blend with their neighbors and with the setting at large. Consider, for instance, the Cézannian moment where the green lines above the melon appear to merge with the ground, as though the flowery forms along the far wall have sprouted from the melon's rind.

Flowers closely relates to *Plaster Figure,* a connection Matisse made when the pictures were exhibited together. The image of *Flowers* appears along the far edge of the table surface in the Yale picture, filling up the space of the distant wall.[44] Although the bouquet has been extracted from the still life setting in way that evokes the example of *Still Life with Self-Portrait, Café Table, Bouquet,* and *The Rose,* its form is more diffuse than the clearly defined forms in those works. The formal features of *Flowers* are reminiscent of the work of Édouard Vuillard and seem to slow down one's perceptual apprehension of the scene, the picture's forms tending to expand like a watery burst or an abruptly raking light against a translucent surface. The expansiveness of *Flowers* serves even more effective purpose in *Plaster Figure,* where it enlivens what would otherwise be a static ground, acting as a binding agent for the still life elements in the foreground and visually identifying the foreground space with the ground and with the surface as a whole.

Matisse brought back from Algeria a striking black-and-red carpet, a prayer mat, that seems to migrate throughout the sequence. Folded and creased, the carpet simultaneously unifies and divides the elements on the table surface in *Dishes and Melon.* It is an unobtrusive presence in *Plaster Figure*; the statuette, fruit, and bowls rest securely atop its surface. In *The Red Rugs* it is tacked against the back wall like an abstract picture, its central black square framed by the red ground. Finally, in *Red and Black Carpet* the mat is given its full due; here, it spreads out to fill up the picture surface, although it distinguishes itself from the literal support by taking the shape of a loose rhomboid most visible around the edges. The still life elements seem to float on its aqueous ground; the table support beneath is all but invisible. The loosely arranged still life group comprises four fruits, a cucumber, a bowl with a spoon resting on the rim, the camel-frieze vase (the same that appears in *Pink Onions* and *The Rose*), a large semitransparent glass decanter, and an unidentifiable orange element positioned at the center of the composition.

In *Red and Black Carpet* relations of local color, especially between the red decorative border and the green forms within the black field, establish the illusion of depth, rather than darks and lights. The olive greens, whites, velvety black, blues, and orange float and ripple on the ground of the darker tones as though viewed through a transparent fluid. And yet every form appears fixed in its place. Unlike the exaggerated handling and abrupt contrasts of the fauve works of the preceding summer, here the delicate color contrasts and light pressure from the brush produce an undulating surface evoking the liquid nature of the still life elements contained within it.

The Red Rugs, likely painted just prior to *Red and Black Carpet,* is the most ambitious of the sequence. The picture is organized around a complex interplay of three-dimensional and two-dimensional forms, as though it is an effort to fuse together the various strands of the problems worked out in the previous works. The Algerian carpet hangs on the wall, and to the right of it appears the lower half of a small drawing. Even the most basic question as to whether the supporting ground for the still life group is a table or a low couch is unclear. At left the support appears hard and flat, and near the center, beneath the red rug, appears to be a leg support for a table. But to the right, as the rug seems to curve upward, its raised edge seemingly held down by a slim vase with flowers, there appears the left arm of a couch.

Spread across the flat surface appear several familiar elements from the previous works, including a decorated plate with fruit, the melon, and the Algerian carpet. Additional elements are included, such as a closed book, a second plate with fruit, which inexplicably seems to rest on or lean over onto the decorated plate at left, and perhaps another book that peers out from underneath the blue-green rug at the right, just below the flower vase. The blue-green rug dominates the right half of the composition and carries a charge of animation as the broad vertical shadow down the center of the rug unequivocally falls into an armlike configuration. At the lower-right edge of the picture the rug pulls up flat, seeming to almost fuse with the picture surface near the signature at bottom right. It appears as though the picture is bathed with diffuse figurative energies despite the lack of figurative content.

Consider, finally, the relation between *Dishes and Melon* and *Red and Black Carpet,* the first and last pictures of the sequence. In the Barnes work the items are sharply defined, inscribed within heavy contour lines, with the paint laid on thick on and around the elements, whereas in *Red and Black Carpet* they seem to float in an abstract space, the thinly applied paint producing a kind of watercolor effect. Although there are considerable stylistic differences between the works, their formats are roughly the same, and their sizes are nearly identical. Then again, the works seem opposed in their treatment of the central forms. The bulging and volumetric watermelon at the center of the Barnes picture contrasts with absence and dispersion at the center of the Hermitage picture, as though suggestive of the watermelon's fleshy interior.

Like Matisse's standing nude sequence discussed in chapter 3, the group produced over the spring to fall of 1906 can be seen as Matisse's further effort to come to terms with Cézanne's example. I would suggest that the 1906 group stands in close dialogue with Cézannes's *Plaster Putto* of around 1895 (Figure 4.14)—a picture Matisse knew well as it was owned by his dealers Bernheim-Jeune—and related works. The most obvious points of comparison emerge with Matisse's *Dishes and Melon* and *Plaster Figure* viewed alongside Cézanne's *Plaster Putto.* Like Matisse's sequence, Cézanne's picture is a meditation on the process of translation between reality and representation, the latter emphatically signaled by its studio setting. While the cupid itself (both like and unlike Matisse's *Standing Nude* plaster), looming up in the foreground, is a proud display of artistic mastery, this prideful stance is immediately undone when it is conceived as part of the larger play of representations that encompass it.

Plaster Putto raises a series of questions that bear closely on Matisse's own spatial complexities, especially that of *The Red Rugs.* What, for instance, is the surface on which the plaster cast is standing? Is it a table? If so, how far off the floor is it? And if that is the floor several feet down below the table, what sense can we make of the oversized green apple at the top of the picture? Or the blue material in the foreground that seems to start from the tabletop, but whose destination is unclear? What type of space does it fall back into along the left? And what is the strange figure near the top and to the right? It seems to be a plaster cast, but if it is, why does the floor recede so dramati-

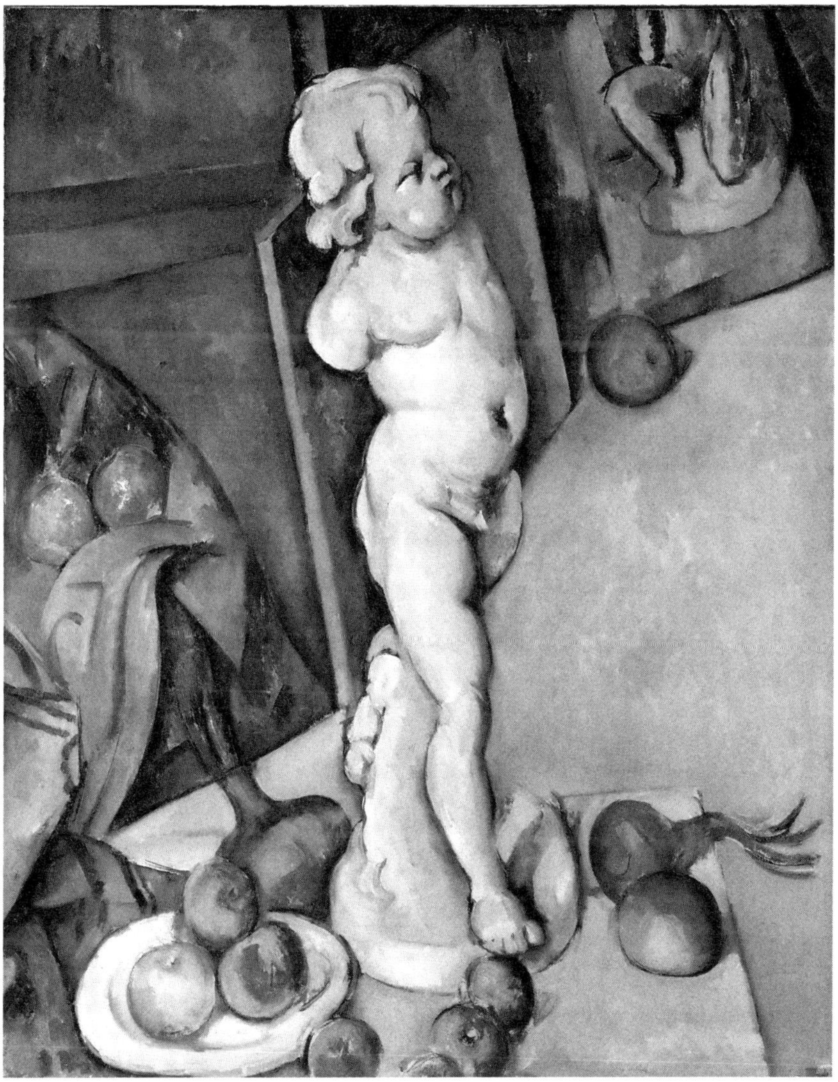

Figure 4.14. Paul Cézanne (1839–1906), *Plaster Putto,* ca. 1895. Oil on paper, mounted on wood, 70 × 57 cm. Courtauld Institute Galleries, London, England. Photograph by Erich Lessing / Art Resource, NY.

cally beneath it? Then again, is the figure a plaster cast or is it framed image of a plaster cast within the picture? Representation seems multiplied or layered throughout the scene, leaving the beholder several removes from any conceivable referent.

Of course some of these questions have answers. *The Peppermint Bottle* (Figure 4.15) in the National Gallery in Washington, D.C., is clearly the "picture" that rests along the left side of *Plaster Putto. Peppermint Bottle* shows us the same fruit and blue material that appears propped up against the left-side wall in *Plaster Putto.* In *Plaster Putto* Cézanne engineered the transition between the cloth in the foreground space and the "picture" at the left in such a way that one cannot be sure where the cloth begins and ends or which element is real and which is depicted. Or consider how the onion along the left side of the foreground still life group (the "real" one) in *Plaster Putto* imperceptibly blends into the "depicted" still life group at left. The canvas propped against the far wall raises similar quandaries. It is the painted image of another sculpture—the so-called *écorché de Michelange*—and one is surely meant to take the measure of the difference between the several modes of representation on display. Cézanne painted several instances of the *écorché,* or *The Flayed Man,* throughout his career, which suggests that he is painting after his own painting within this picture. If that is the case *Plaster Putto* leaves us at least four removes from reality—from a painting of real fruit to the

Figure 4.15. Paul Cézanne (1839–1906), *The Peppermint Bottle,* 1893–95. Oil on canvas, 26 × 32⅜ cm. Chester Dale Collection, National Gallery of Art, Washington, D.C.

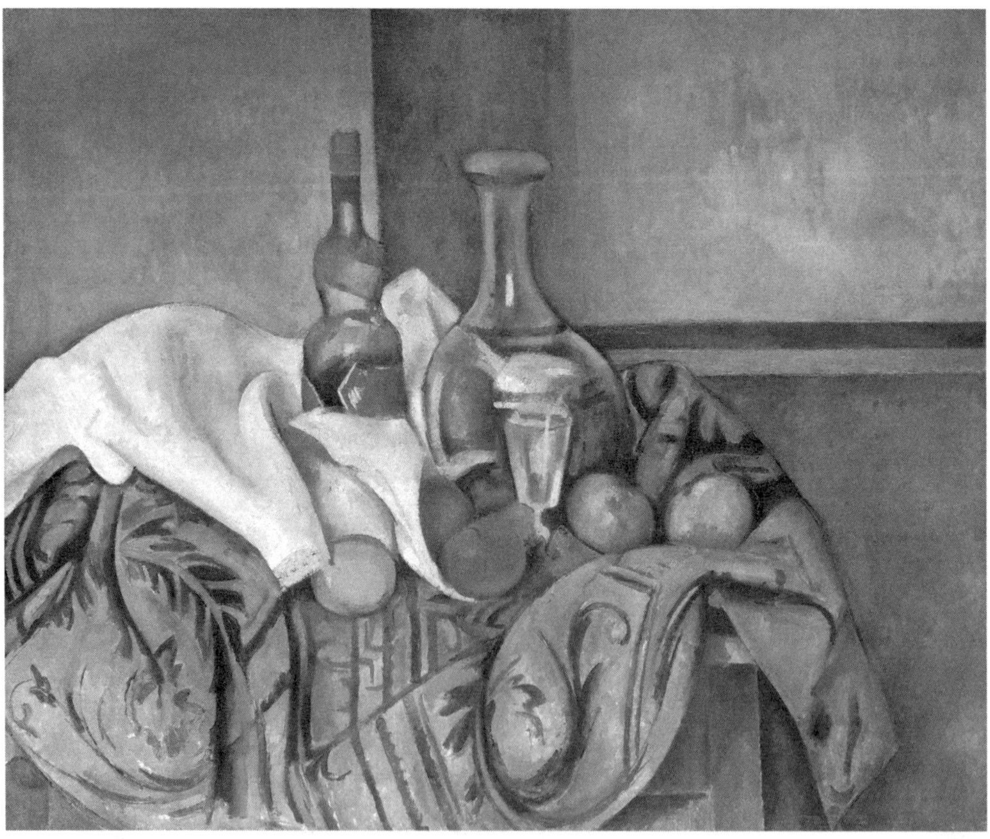

painting of a "real" plaster cast of boy, to the painting of painted fruit and the painting of a painting of a plaster cast of a man.

Further complicating these representational quandaries, Cézanne painted several more works out of and around *Plaster Putto. Still Life with Statuette* (Figure 4.16), from the same moment, with nearly all of the same elements, programmatically shifts the scene into a horizontal format, compressing the elements, expressing a sense of the figure's bulk or weight where *Plaster Putto*'s verticality suggests a sense of upward lift or release. Or consider another scene extrapolated from the *Plaster Putto* mix. The space in *Stoneware Pitcher* (Figure 4.17) is dramatically contracted; the beholder seems to be thrust into the foreground space of *Plaster Putto.* The triumphant putto has been removed, and in its place is a broad clay pitcher that spans the crucially complicated space between table, ground, and still life section at the left. Although the onions have disappeared, the apple count remains the same; that is, if we accept that the two on the left in *The Peppermint Bottle* may have fallen

Figure 4.16. Paul Cézanne (1839–1906), *Still Life with Statuette*, 1894–95. Oil on canvas, 63 × 81 cm. National Museum, Stockholm, Sweden. Scala / White Images / Art Resource, NY, ART402289.

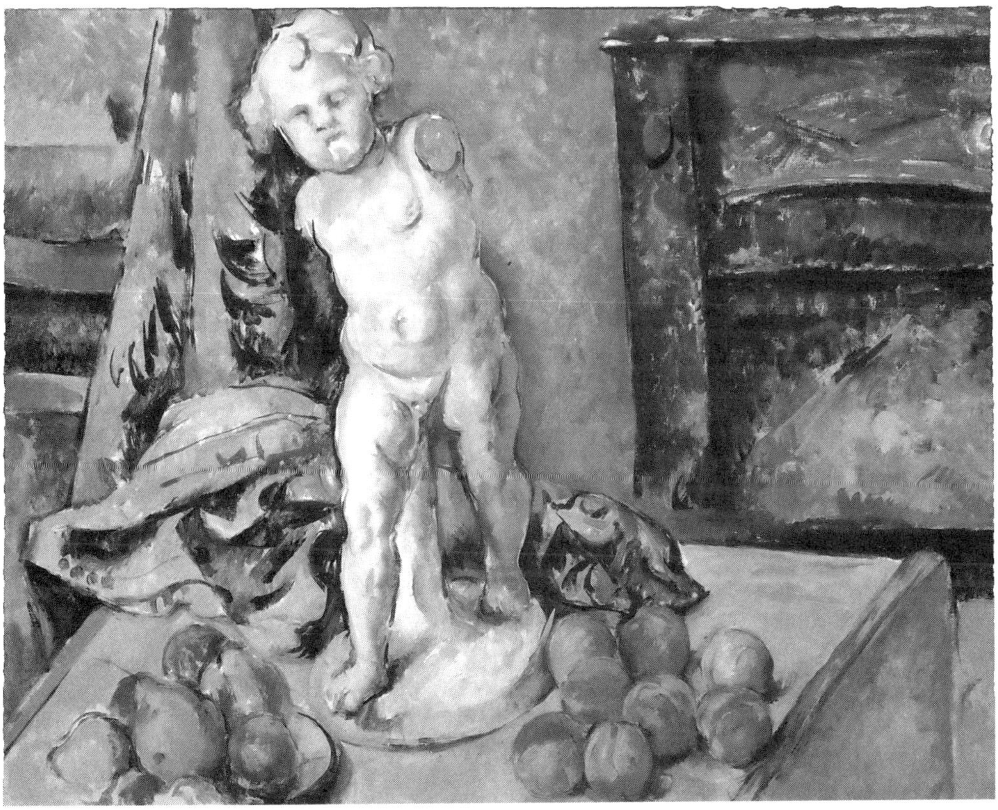

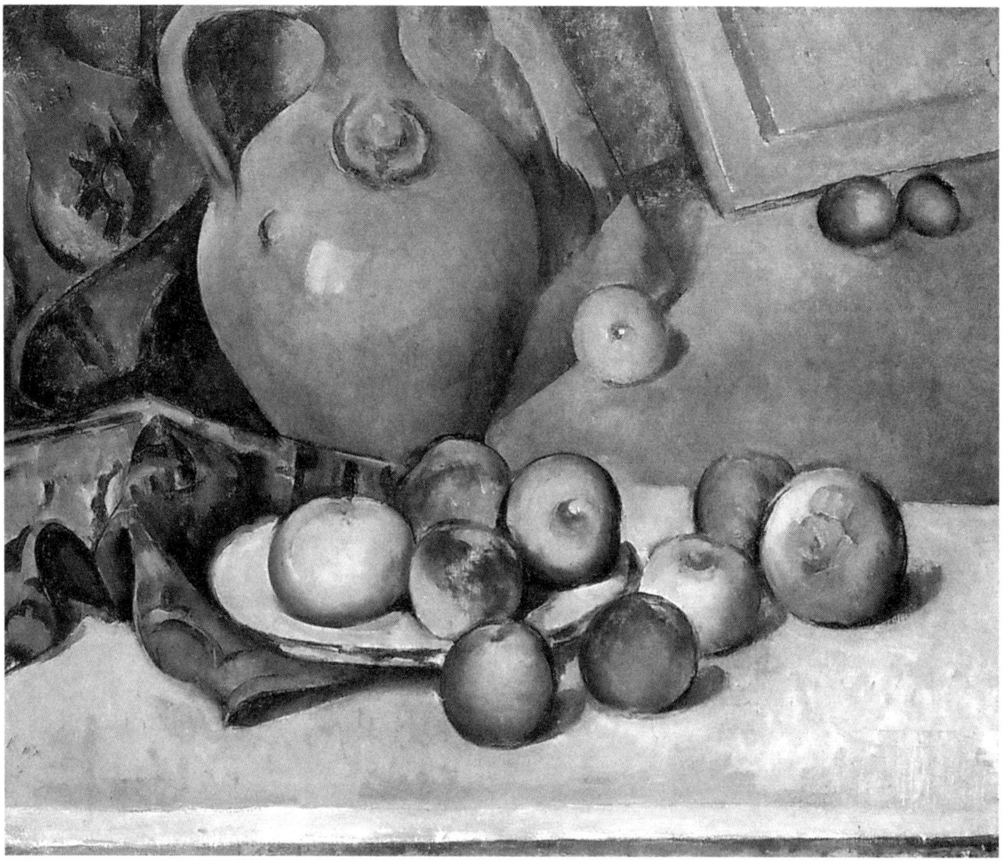

Figure 4.17. Paul Cézanne (1839–1906), *Stoneware Pitcher,* 1893–94. Oil on canvas, 38.2 × 46.0 cm. Fondation Beyeler, Riehen/Basel, Switzerland.

off their fictive table and entered into the (fictive) background. The rightmost edge of *The Peppermint Bottle* is barely visible while the left side is swarmed by the more real than illusory blue cloth.

That Matisse could find inspiration in Cézanne's own efforts at creating layered representations and interlocking sequences of work would present a rather controversial interpretation of the master's work. Above all, it would suggest how the *Plaster Putto* group stands at the furthest remove from any realist account of Cézanne's concerns. If this is the "truth in painting" that Cézanne spoke about, it was *painting's* truth on offer, rather than any worldly one. Even if Matisse had little awareness of the extent of Cézanne's commitment to a kind of perspectival analysis, he would have been fully responsive to the manner in which Cézanne could extrapolate works from within works as a means to explore fluid and tactile, phenomenological and realist strands of representation.

Matisse's still life sequence of 1906 marks the culmination of his intensive investigation of conflicting representational modalities. In the works that followed, Matisse attempted to draw together the separate strands of his realist and phenomenological approaches. But it was also in the summer of 1906 that Matisse initiated one of his most radical and perplexing procedures: the explicit creation of paired and doubled works.[45] *Young Sailor I* and *II* (1906), *Le Luxe I* (Figure 4.18) and *Le Luxe II* (1907–8) (Plate 19), *Nasturtiums with "Dance" I* and *II* (1912), *Interior with Goldfish* and *Goldfish and Sculpture* (1912), *Interior with a Goldfish* and *Goldfish and Palette* (1914), *Piano Lesson* and *Music Lesson* (1916 and 1917), *Auguste Pellerin I* and *II* (1916 and 1917), and *Laurette Reclining* and *The Studio, quai St.-Michel* (1916–17) offer dual approaches to a single theme, sharing nearly all the same features but depicted in differing, often opposing styles. In the first versions of these works, the rendering is relatively naturalistic and descriptive while the picture surface is treated as though a fragile membrane, with mild pressure exerted on the brush. The second version, by contrast, tends to be more hard-edged and abstract; the surface is often densely worked or layered and the aesthetic character more symbolically charged. The paired works give explicit evidence of the expressive ambivalence that shapes Matisse's career, the "eternal conflict" of "design and color in the same individual" he spoke about.[46] It is as though these works literalize conflict for the viewer, projecting an image of the artist divided against himself. And while these pairs are among the artist's most well-known and most admired works, and constitute further evidence of his ambivalent mimesis, my focus lies less with Matisse's stylistic ambivalence than with his overall structural and spatial complexities within a set of static or semistatic figurative and thematic groupings.

A closer look at one set of paired works, *Le Luxe I* and *II*, will exemplify some of the problems raised by the paired format as a whole. As though extracting a detail from the left-hand section of *Le Bonheur*, Matisse treats *Le Luxe I* (Figure 4.18) in a loose, quasi-Impressionist manner. If the handling is evidence, the scene is taking place in the present, while the bathing thematic—including an anointed goddess with her flower bearer and a servant to dry her naked form—evokes a mythic pastoral past. The conflict between the spontaneous feel of the surface treatment and the archaic quality of the imagery is reconciled in its companion piece. *Le Luxe II*, painted over the winter of 1907–8 (Plate 19) is among Matisse's most extreme ventures into the mural-design aesthetic that gripped him in the wake of his encounter with Giotto's frescoes in the summer of 1907. The most dramatic feature of the work is the flat, wall-like implacability of the casein bands of red, green, blue, and white, a flatness made all the more extreme as it is reinforced by the blank-faced, distended shape of the figure on the left. Removed from the wider pastoral setting of *Le Bonheur*, the standing figure, as though unrolled from clay, accentuates

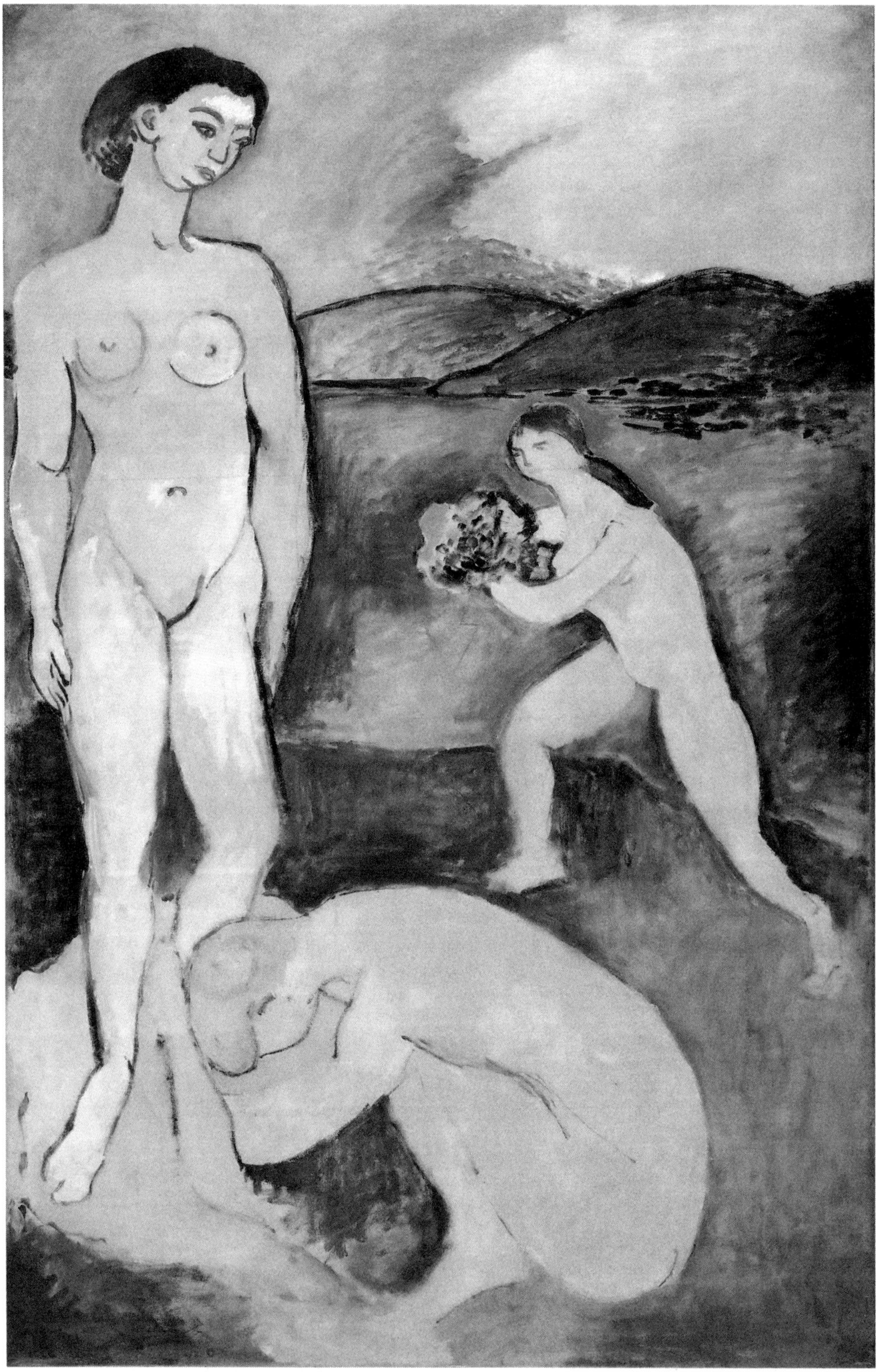

Figure 4.18. Henri Matisse (1869–1954), *Le Luxe I,* 1907. Oil on canvas, 210 × 138 cm. AM2586P. Musée National d'Art Moderne, Centre Georges Pompidou, Paris, France. Copyright 2013 Succession H. Matisse / Artists Rights Society (ARS), NY. Photograph by Philippe Migeat. Photograph courtesy of Réunion des Musées Nationaux / Art Resource, NY, ART421166.

the strong verticality of the format while her uninflected body blocks the beholder's fictive access into the pictorial space. The blankness of the swollen form is reiterated in the circle of flowers, a parodic and inexpressive display of mythic iconography, near the center of the composition. Then again, the decorative unity of the surface is broken at the bottom left, where the white drapery seems to spill over into the beholder's space, sweeping us up into the composition. Nonetheless, there is a countermovement in the reenclosure of the squatting figure at bottom. Matisse creates a perceptual puzzle in the space of the standing figure's left leg. On closer inspection it becomes unclear whether we are looking at the standing figure's leg or the squatting figure's right arm. The intensity, if that is the right word to describe the action here, of the squatting figure's engagement with her task of drying the standing figure's legs draws the beholder *into* the space, as though it were a surrogate for our involvement in the scene. Nonetheless, despite the seeming concentration of the action, the figures are all so devoid of a sense of inner life, all of the forms so resolutely outward in their display (perhaps this is the true theme of the work), that it is difficult to identify with the squatting figure's absorbed engagement with her task.

By virtue of its frontality and lack of psychological depth, the upright figure in *Le Luxe II* effectively walls out the viewer only to be pierced by the unbounded flow of color along the lower edges of the picture. With the *Bathers with a Turtle* from the spring of 1908 (Figure 4.19), Matisse manifestly reintroduces psychology along with intensely modeled forms. And while Matisse reengages with absorptive thematics—one might say the bending figure in *Le Luxe* is tripled and monumentalized—the narrative action is so minimal as to read as a parody of absorbed action (gazing at or feeding a turtle does not sustain much embodied senses of empathy). Absorption here works *against* empathetic identification. The inward-turned gesture of the central standing figure makes it appear that she is in the process of devouring herself. Each figure suggests a painful sense of withdrawal from her neighbors and her surroundings. Like the dwarfed turtle they collectively contemplate, the figures are enclosed within their private atmospheres. But unlike the turtle, these bodies have adopted their isolated condition. Combining traits of infantilism and cannibalism, the standing figure, hand plunged partway into her mouth, is a stark image of impotent auto-affection.

In an unfinished picture, *Still Life with African Sculpture* (1908–9) (Figure 4.20), which features a small Congolese Vili figure Matisse purchased late in 1906, Matisse depicts a gesture similar to that of the standing figure in *Bathers with a Turtle.*[47] According to most commentators, Matisse's interest in African art fell stillborn after this early encounter. Nonetheless, the small figure, performing its slow act of literalizing inwardness, expresses a basic quality of his artistic enterprise, the one described by Freud as "devouring

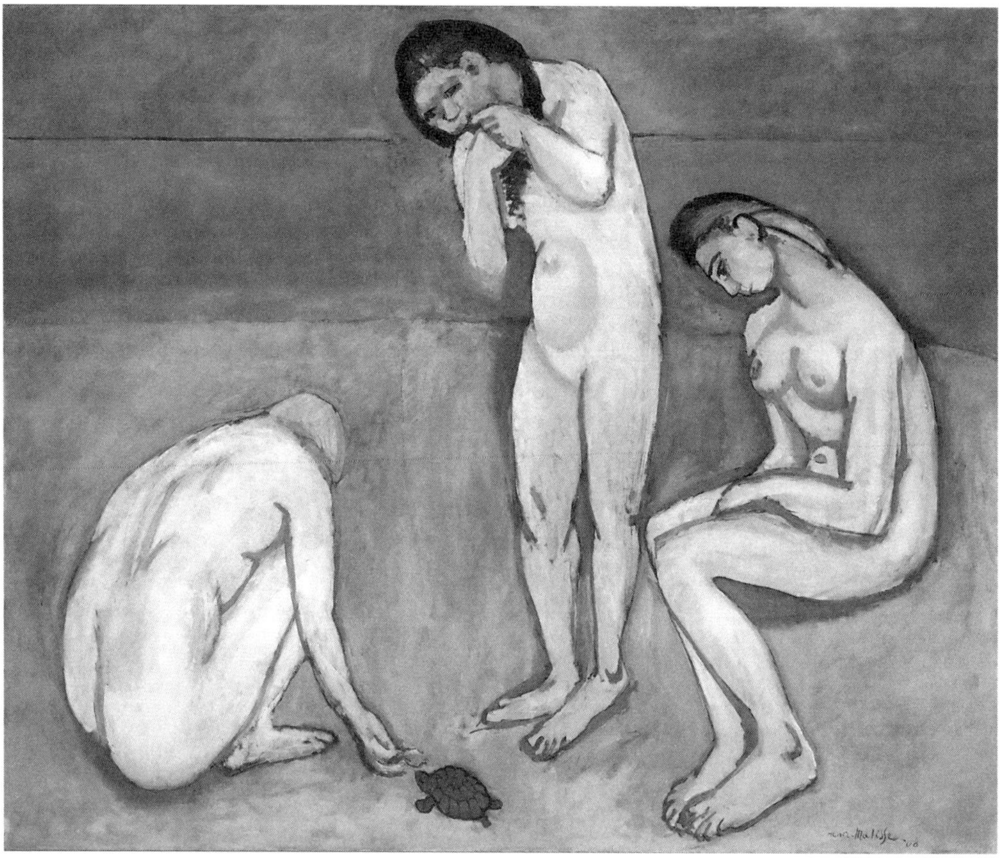

Figure 4.19. Henri Matisse (1869–1954), *Bathers with a Turtle*, 1908. Oil on canvas, 179.1 × 220.3 cm. St. Louis Art Museum. Gift of Mr. and Mrs. Joseph Pulitzer Jr. Copyright 2013 Succession H. Matisse / Artists Rights Society (ARS), NY.

affection" for the other (or for oneself as the primary other) and which was exemplified for him by the phenomenon of cannibalism. Here too the sense of enclosure or inwardness is not complete. I read the blank section along the lower edges of the canvas, stopping at the feet of the figurine, as well as the outline of an empty form at the left, as though touching the foot of the glass, as suggestive of the artist's embodied involvement in the space. Either through psychological blankness (as in *Le Luxe II*) or through total "inwardness" as in *Bathers with a Turtle* and *African Sculpture*, these figures forestall or at least decelerate the viewer's need to psychologically enter into the space of the composition. As I have also suggested, Matisse never achieved in practice this act of narcissistic or self-devouring enclosure (a limit case of skepticism), as these pictures provide space for empathetic engagement, if of a more limited, and perhaps more powerful, kind.

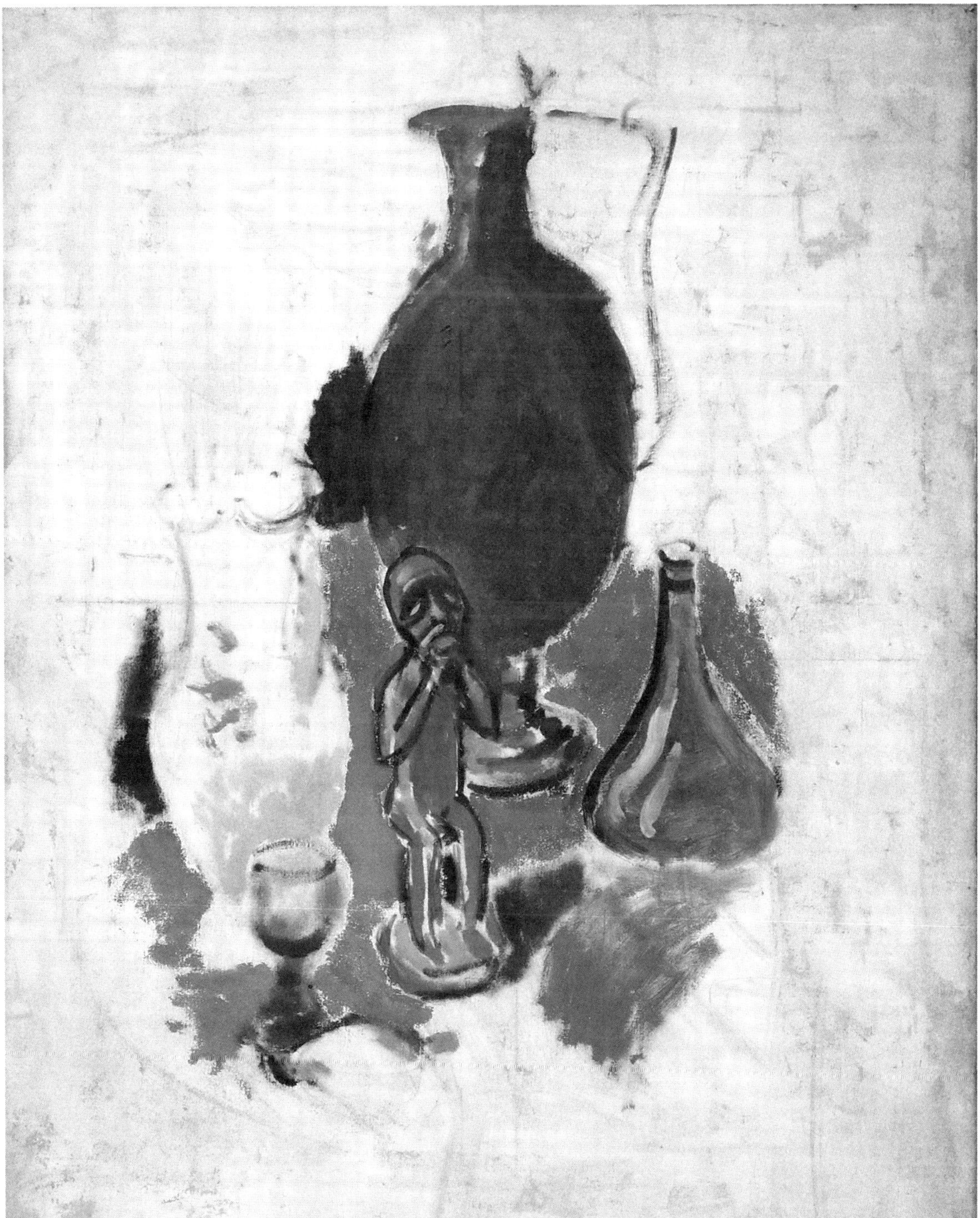

Figure 4.20. Henri Matisse (1869–1954), *Still Life with African Sculpture,* 1908–9. Oil on canvas, 105 × 70 cm. Private collection. Copyright 2013 Succession H. Matisse / Artists Rights Society (ARS), NY. Photograph courtesy of Archives Henri Matisse.

In his analysis of *Bathers with a Turtle* Yve-Alain Bois effectively grasps the wider skeptical tenor of Matisse's work (other minds extended to nonhuman creatures). "Matisse tells us that we can no more converse with a tortoise than we can among ourselves," Bois writes. "The painting is about an irremediable absence of communication, about the impossibility of telling stories; that's why each nude is in her own bubble, why they don't touch or overlap, why their gazes don't converge on the inoffensive reptile."[48] Bois's sense of the picture's "absorptive thematic" centered on figures "remote in [their] own thoughts," "oblivious" to the other, and expressive of "separateness, dearth of language, and asociality" well captures the general atmosphere of the work.[49] Indeed, the standing figure's gesture, whatever it denotes, suggests the preclusion of speech. The picture projects the classical image of other mind skepticism gone awry.

But even this claim—the claim to muteness and difference—in *Bathers with a Turtle* cannot ultimately be sustained. Although each figure is driven in upon itself and cut away from its surroundings (look, for instance, at the sharp vertical cut along the right bather's calf), the figures are nonetheless, as Wilhelm Niemeyer noted at the time, "linked by the breath of a common elementary line."[50] The thick, bold contour lines that surround each figure, most assertively around the right arm of the standing nude, serve at once to enclose the bodies, dividing them from one another as though they have developed a second protective skin, like the tortoise shell below, and to bind them together across the surface. Bois describes the "dialectic opposition between the formal coalescence of the group, cemented with all the energy of the dynamic structure and the 'common elementary line,' and the incurable isolation of each of its members."[51] "Coalescence" and "isolation," rhythmic unity and linear enclosure, well describe the conflicted dynamic of the picture. Further still, the underlying identification between and across the figures pierces their enclosure and opens the bodies up, suggesting their (limited) connection to the world around them and to the space before the canvas. It is the very force and evidence of division and separation, the density of contour lines that enforces their psychological remoteness, that expresses the inescapability of inhabiting the same world as the beholder.[52]

But Bois's dialectical analysis of *Bathers with a Turtle* becomes less persuasive when he pursues a more familiar line of thought. Competing with Picasso, the "master bedazzler," *Bathers* shows us the "next step" in the Medusa-like "blinding" process perfected by Picasso in *Les Demoiselles d'Avignon.* The stiffened figures in *Bathers* literalize the results of blinding visual castration; "petrification" constitutes a reaction formation generated by the loss of the phallus. Bois's analysis drifts into a more static framework concerning "primary psychic nodes" of "human development" (mostly occurring through the eye), which also turns his interpretation into an account of the psychic and biological causes and consequences of the picture.[53]

And although Matisse's *Bathers* is clearly in dialogue with Picasso's *Demoiselles,* another approach would consider the structural consistency of Matisse's fantasies of skeptical isolation and unbounded connection. From *Still Life with Crab and Clay Pitcher* (Figure 4.21), a little-known early work of 1896, to his final image *The Snail* (Figure 4.22), Matisse was gripped by imagery and themes of isolation as well as by expressions of vulnerable and fleshy interiors (consider the dialectical interplay of enclosure and exposure evident in his copy after Chardin's *The Ray,* 1897–1903). Even the modest *Crab and Clay Pitcher* sustains a degree of dialectical tension in the relation between the forward tilt of the pitcher and the crab's broad pincer that reaches over and across the threshold of the picture plane, fictively reaching out toward the beholder, at once threatening and solicitous, despite its literal and fictive enclosure in another world.[54]

Matisse's skeptical temper was given its most insistent expression in a sequence of works depicting a crouching and enclosed figure extrapolated from *Le Luxe* and *Bathers with a Turtle.* Continuing the squatting figure type at the left of *Le Bonheur* and more centrally figured in *Le Luxe* and *Bathers*

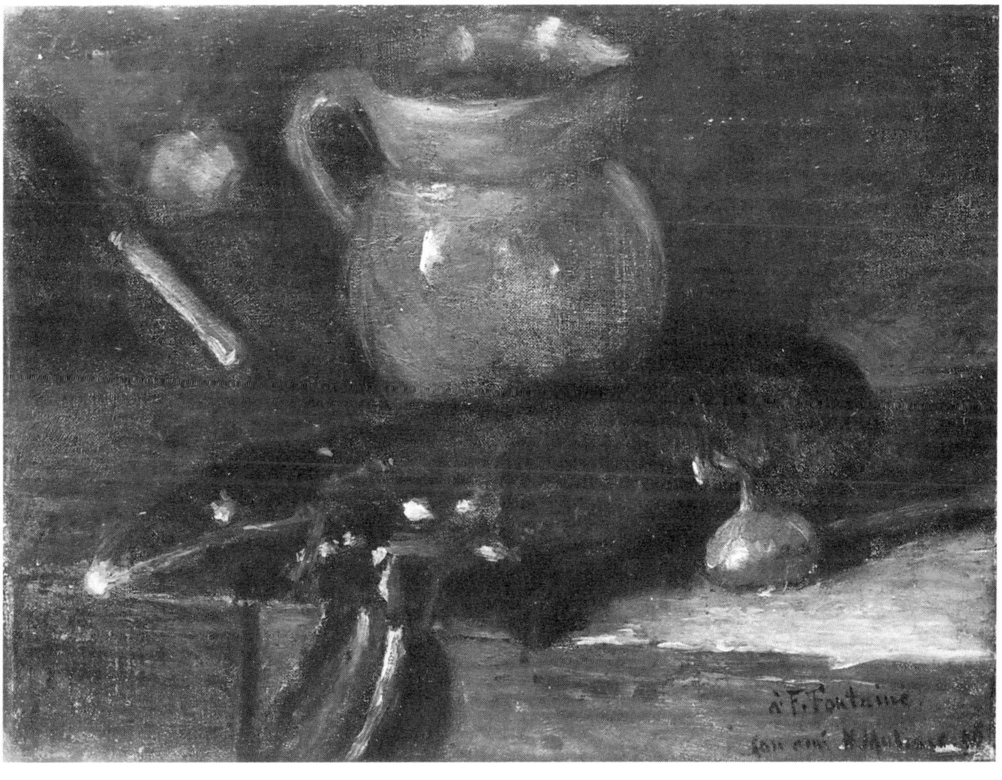

Figure 4.21. Henri Matisse (1869–1954), *Still Life with Crab and Clay Pitcher,* 1896. Oil on canvas, 25.5 × 35 cm. Private collection. Copyright 2013 Succession H. Matisse / Artists Rights Society (ARS), NY. Photograph courtesy of Archives Henri Matisse.

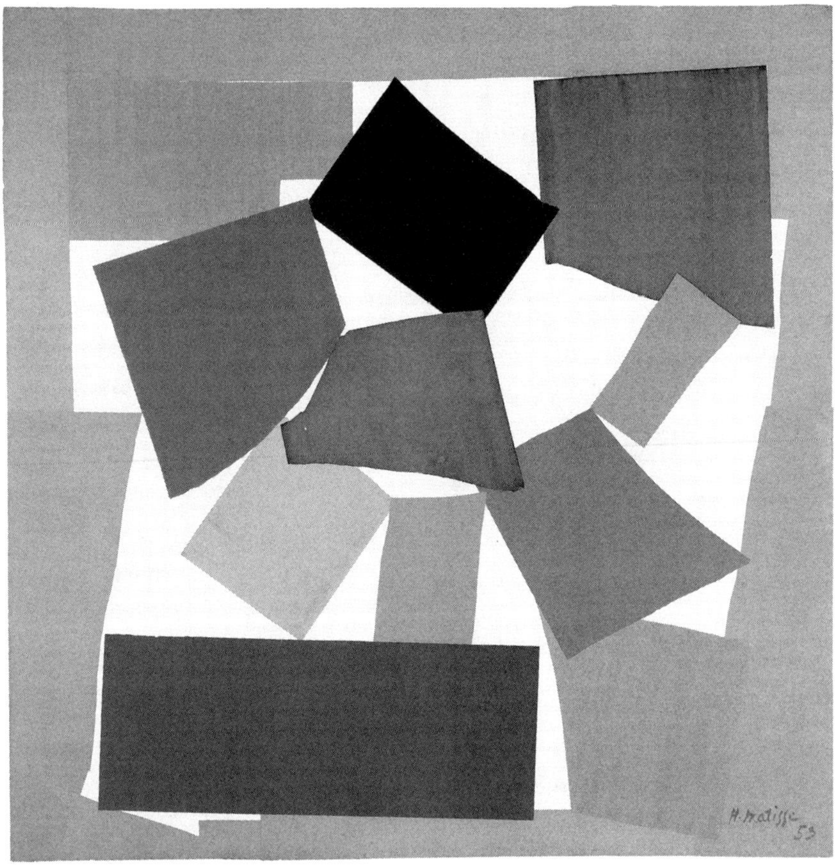

Figure 4.22. Henri Matisse (1869–1954), *The Snail*, 1953. Gouache on cut-and-pasted paper, 112¾ × 113 inches (287 × 288 cm). Tate Gallery, London, England. Copyright 2013 Succession H. Matisse / Artists Rights Society (ARS), NY. Photograph courtesy of Tate, London / Art Resource, NY.

with a Turtle, Matisse further detaches the form from its figurative and narrative context. In the years following *Le Bonheur* the crouching figure type recurs in a wide range of styles, formats, and media. *Woman by a Stream* (1906), *Thorn Extractor* (1906), *Plate with Nude* (1907) (Figure 4.23), *Small Crouching Nude with Arms* (1908), *Seated Figure, Right Hand on Ground* (1908), *Small Crouching Nude without an Arm* (1908), and *Small Crouching Torso* (1908) (Figure 4.24) constitute a sequence of determinately inward figures whose bodies are thrust in upon themselves as their backs and legs press against the limits of their media. The sequence as a whole unfolds toward greater degrees of involution and internalization, ending in the final, extraordinary *Small Crouching Torso,* whose bodily features are all but consumed within the circular egg-like form.

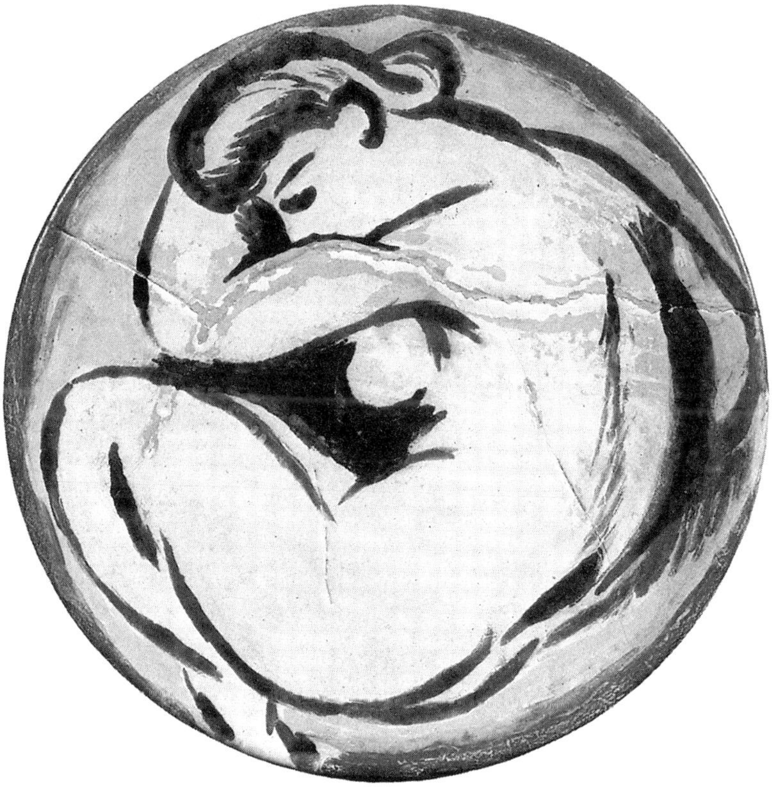

Figure 4.23. Henri Matisse (1869–1954), *Plate with Nude,* 1907. Ceramics, 35 cm diameter. Private collection. Copyright 2013 Succession H. Matisse / Artists Rights Society (ARS), NY.

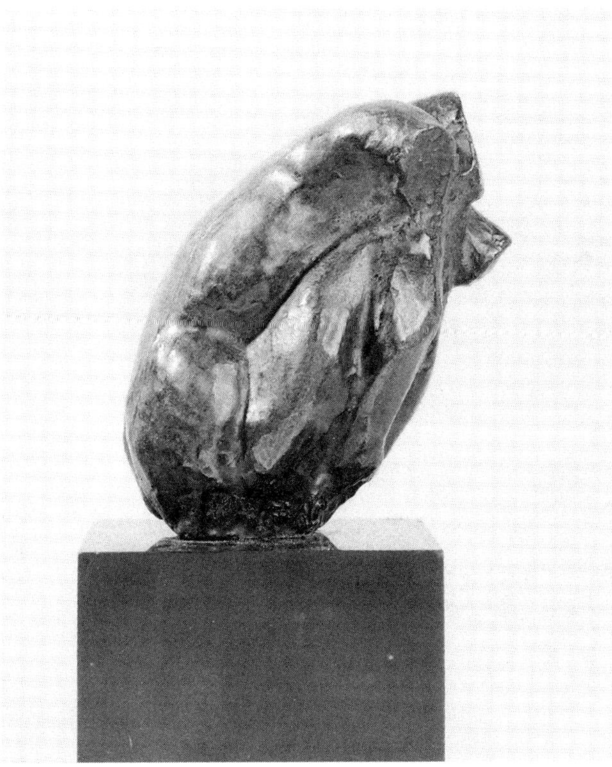

Figure 4.24. Henri Matisse (1869–1954), *Small Crouching Torso,* 1908. Bronze, 0.140 m × 0.700 m × 0.850 m. RF3398. Musée Matisse, Nice, France. Copyright 2013 Succession H. Matisse / Artists Rights Society (ARS), NY. Photograph courtesy of Réunion des Musées Nationaux / Art Resource, NY, ART403882.

Although *Small Crouching Torso* is only three inches in height and would hardly seem to bear much expressive or philosophical significance, it was highly prized by the artist, and he kept a version of it with him until the end of his life. The legs of the figure are tightly compressed against the torso, while the arms, the bearers of touch and contact, have been dramatically cut off above the elbow, leaving stumps not much larger or longer than the neck against which they press. Although the body bears as little internal differentiation as seems possible while still evoking a measure of animate or bodily presence, its surface is rich with tactile cues. We know that this tactile quality was a key feature of the work, as we have a photograph in which the artist affectionately grips the figure with both hands (Figure 4.25). Matisse's unusual decision to sculpt it without a base especially licenses this kind of handling. While the figure is determinately withdrawn and nearly illegible, it nonetheless projects a sense of energy across its surface. Even the mutilated arms carry an ambivalent expressive charge, as though they have been refashioned into

Figure 4.25. Unknown photographer, Henri Matisse with *Small Crouching Torso*, ca. 1950.

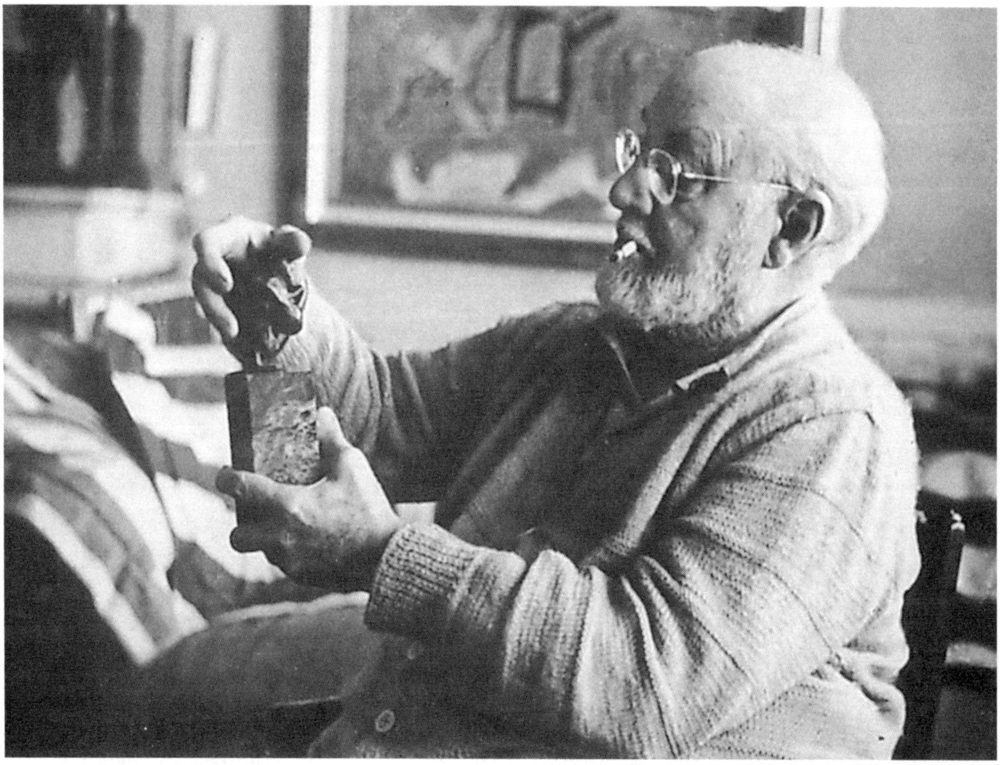

tiny feelers, irrepressibly reaching beyond the sculpted mass, awaiting the beholder's absent touch.

I will not dwell on the potential sources for this figure, but several points of reference deserve brief mention. The leftmost crouching nude in Cézanne's *Large Bathers* of 1906 (Figure 3.1), a painting Matisse saw at the 1907 Cézanne memorial exhibition at the Salon d'Automne (or at Vollard's even earlier) seems a likely source.[55] Matisse would also have been familiar with a range of sculptural precedents for Cézanne's figure. Auguste Rodin's *Crouching Woman* of 1880–82 (Figure 4.26), based on a figure from the tympanum of *The Gates of Hell,* similarly depicts an inwardly drawn figure whose distended right arm and hand grasp her left ankle, while her left hand presses against her bare chest. The figure writhes at once in agony and in pleasure, as though the two conditions are inflections of a singular and contradictory experience of the body. Aristide Maillol's *Woman with Crab* of 1903 (Figure 4.27) draws on Rodin's example with the peculiar addition of the crab at the figure's feet. The inclusion of the crab, a clear antecedent for *Bathers with a Turtle,* distinctly lightens the emotional tenor of Rodin's image. The figure is no longer simply drawn in on itself but now interacts with another involuted creature. But interaction is perhaps not the right word to describe the action in the Maillol work. As with Matisse's *Bathers,* the inclusion of the shelled creature only frustrates the viewer's sense of connection. Any deep interaction between the two awkwardly counterpoised species is foreclosed in advance.[56]

Matisse's iterations of the crouching figure project an ideal of physical and mental isolation, and, like related images of turtles, crabs, and snails, they seek a condition undisturbed by conflict with the world or by divisions within itself. Although this bodily ideal suggests narcissistic plenitude, in *Bathers with a Turtle* it further registers the effort required to extricate oneself from the indifferent other. As Alex Potts observes of the antique figure of the *Thorn Extractor,* an image Matisse copied in 1906 and included in *The Geranium* (Plate 12): "The state of total self-absorption is achieved at a huge cost, and in the end comes closer to self-annihilation than self-affirmation. . . . The utopian fantasy of a totally unconstrained and undisturbed enjoyment of self, which renders redundant any potentially troubling or frustrating interaction with the outside world, is presented equally as the nightmare of a solipsistic isolation, a kind of death."[57] The *Crouching Torso* group and related works evoke an ideal of "total self-absorption," but one that is poignantly incomplete, every enclosure pierced by animated, if fragile and disjointed, limbs that (blindly) reach out toward the world, half awaiting connection, half averse to it.

The dialectic of skepticism and connection is organized in a widely different manner with the works Matisse made after the crouching figure sequence. He seems to signal a completely alternative conception with the shift from

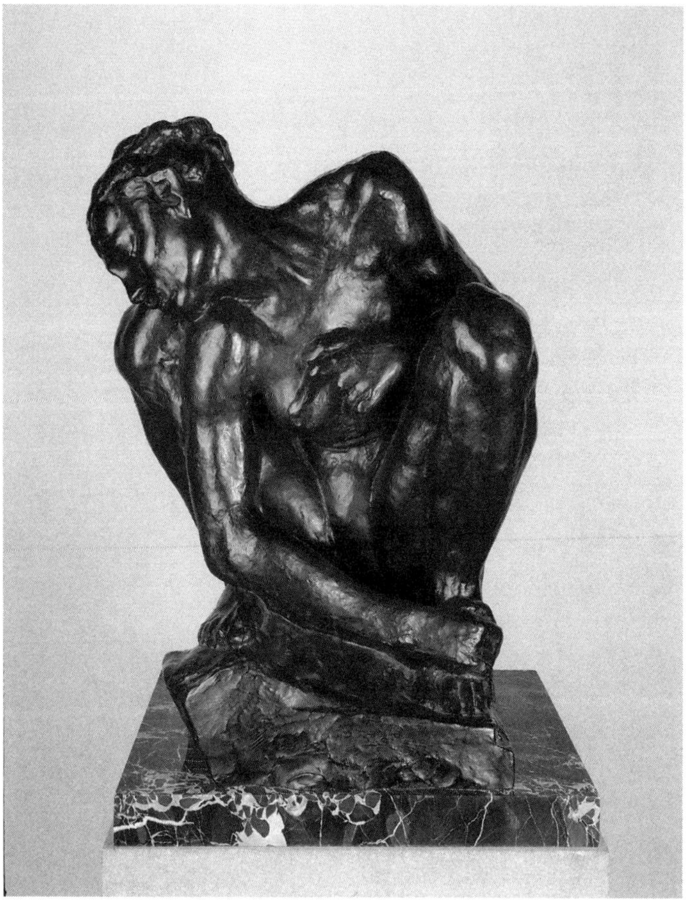

Figure 4.26. Auguste Rodin (1840–1917), *The Crouching Woman,* conceived 1880–82; cast 1925. Bronze, 33 × 21 × 18 inches (83.8 × 53.3 × 45.7 cm). Cast by the founder Alexis Rudier, Paris. Rodin Museum, Philadelphia, Pennsylvania. Bequest of Jules E. Mastbaum, 1929. The Bridgeman Art Library. Photograph courtesy of Philadelphia Museum of Art / Art Resource, NY.

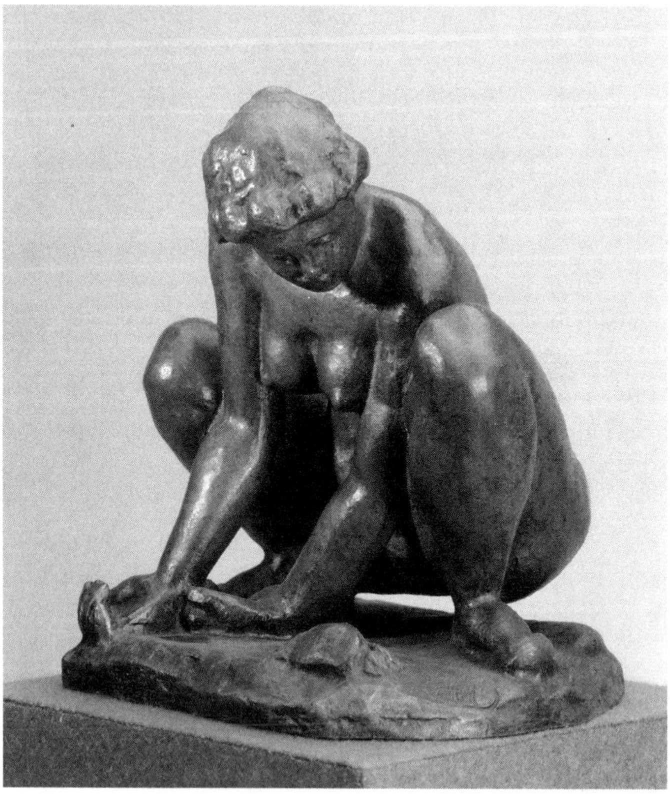

Figure 4.27. Aristide Joseph-Bonaventure Maillol (1861–1944), *Woman with Crab,* 1903. Bronze, 18.7 × 15.2 × 12.7 cm. Gift of Thomas B. Walton, 1971.779, The Art Institute of Chicago. Copyright 2012 Artists Rights Society (ARS), New York / ADAGP, Paris.

the slow-moving turtle and self-absorbed type of *Bathers with a Turtle* to an ecstatic image of release with *The Dance (II)* from 1909–10 (Plate 1). The group of dancers mined from *Le Bonheur* has been reduced by one, and the colors keyed up to bands of minimally inflected green and blue; the bodies, enclosed with black contours, are a searing vermilion. Despite the suggestion of aggressive and frenzied movement, the bodies seem attracted or perhaps dictated—pulled, twisted—by the shape of the horizontal format. The figures seem to be thrown "against the perimeter of the canvas," as Elderfield observes. "Think of the hard lines of the stretcher or the frame, they affect the lines of your subject," Matisse told his students, and *The Dance* seems to illustrate that claim.[58] The sheer vertical stretch of the figure on the left, whose bounding form almost challenges the horizontal enclosure, finds its response in the figure balancing on one leg to "his" left (I will call "him" the "bending figure"). The bending figure's arms, back, and distended neck all serve to articulate and reiterate the horizontal limits of the canvas. It is hard to tell whether these bodies are vainly struggling against their container, as suggested by the bending figure, or celebrating their disembodied freedom from the earth, as with the "bounding figure" at left. Feet, hands, heads touch or graze the material limits of the picture surface as though they are simultaneously drawn to it by a magnetic attraction and then repulsed by it when they abrade against it. The turning bodies seem closed in upon themselves and closed off from the viewer, as though what provides them with a collective identity is their unified *indifference* to us, as though we represent the opposite of their elated sense of anonymity (an effect, it bears noting, that is roughly the opposite of Picasso's *Demoiselles d'Avignon*).

Nonetheless, there are aspects of the picture that mitigate the sense of "totality" suggested by the enclosed form of the dancers' bodies. Consider, for instance, the poignant break in the clasp of hands between the foreground and leftmost figures. This highly charged moment where three bodies seem to collide but do not touch offers a chance opening for the beholder to complete the circle. The break in the chain is mirrored or doubled below the hands and legs by an expansive stretch of green, the broadest unoccupied space in the picture, which projects an inescapable sense of *unboundedness* that surges outward toward the beholder. For a moment, perhaps decisive and fleeting, the beholder is solicited to enter into the dance. The contingency of this pictorial call, something like a hairline fracture in the total image, is as though immediately mitigated by the reenclosure of the unclasped hands around the lower legs of the bending figure above. Notice how the unclasped hands meet along the right leg of the bending figure, and the contour line that defines the foreground figure's index finger continues uninterrupted into that of the bending figure's legs above, one line improbably defining a hand and two legs. Even the open palm of the bounding figure to the left seems to clasp the leg of the bending figure beside "him," who in turn might be instinctively drawing away from that figure's clutching hand. Which is to say, the open call to the beholder upon further reflection appears compromised, the figures even more deeply enclosed upon themselves, stopping or slowing down our empathetic drift into the scene. It is precisely in the fixing of this tense movement and countermovement of closure and opening, totality and breach, that Matisse labored over the color and compositional details of *The Dance (I)* and *The Dance (II).* It is the space where the unclasped hands meet over the bending figure's legs that has undergone the most decisive transformation, as though the work was only complete when the movement between closed unity and immersive solicitation was at its most intense.

Jacob Tügenhold, in his review of the 1910 Salon d'Automne, observed how Matisse's work was the product of a "dual personality." Matisse, he said, was split between the "half-dreams of a naïve primordial structure" and "frenzied American-style life of today."[59] Modern and primordial, frenzy and control, capture something of the polarities of Matisse's psychic and aesthetic attitude. Tügenhold's reference to "primordial structure" suggests the ways in which Matisse's work is driven by a mural-like tendency to create allover designs that stand resolutely apart from the viewer, complete in their formal and temporal detachment. And yet this sense of mythic remove is seemingly eclipsed by the "frenzy" of movement, the sense in which not only the figures but the colors spill out into the beholder's space, which threatens to immerse or enfold them into its world. Charles Caffin, upon seeing *The Dance* at the same Salon, described it as the "expression of purely physical abandonment of lusty forms to sense intoxication."[60] But when Matisse was prompted about the picture, he characteristically emphasized a strictly *pictorial* sense of intoxication. "You can conceive a dance in a static way," he explained. "The static is not an obstacle to the feeling of movement. It is a movement set at a level which does not carry along the bodies of the spectators, but simply their minds" (190). In his effort toward the "*representation* of movement" (39/45), he made an overt appeal to the imagination. In one of his more explicit formulations Matisse described an ambivalent state of mind: he was "such a romantic, but with a good half of the scientist, the rationalist."[61]

Matisse reengaged Cézanne's *Plaster Putto* several years after the 1906 sequence with his ambitious and challenging *Interior with Aubergines* of 1911 (Plate 20). *Interior with Aubergines* constitutes Matisse's most profound investigation of the nature of the frame. Even the most superficial effort to count the number of frames or frame surrogates in this work is difficult to manage. From left to right, there is a fireplace, a rectangular book of drawings or a painting at the fireplace's lower edge; the book of drawings leans against a mirror; above the mirror appears a vertically oriented frame, which is open at the top and within which lies a smaller rectangle (an image within the frame?);

to the right of the mirror stands a broad, decorated folding screen to which is attached a vertically oriented decorated textile; to the right of the folding screen is what appears to be an open window looking out on a landscape; finally, peering out above the folding screen is another opening, perhaps a door onto a room, perhaps a bathroom, with a curtain hanging from three visible rings. The enclosures can be multiplied tenfold if we consider the array of self-contained rectangles and squares within the space. Consider the eight squarish forms that appear below the red tablecloth at center, or the shutters along the left side of the open window, or the rectangles on the shower curtain (if that is what it is), or the ladderlike form (reflecting the window shutter?) in the mirror at left, or the checkered triangular form angled out of the mirror-space (is it reflecting the tablecloth that hangs down the back of the table, so that the squares visible at the lower edge of the red tablecloth might be another one underneath?).

Despite or by virtue of the relentless production of framing devices, there is a sense in which nothing is securely closed upon itself. At every moment, the closures double, mirror, echo, or spread onto their neighbors (consider, for instance, what happens to the folding screen when it touches the thick yellow contour of the mirror). At the center of the composition appears the sculpted form of the *écorché,* resting on the table surface.[62] In 1903 Matisse made a sculpted version of the figure (Figure 4.28) and began to include it in several works. The figure's anatomy is clearly defined, especially that of his left leg and right arm, while the head leans down toward the stumped form of the right arm. Unlike Cézanne, Matisse seems more engaged with the expressive nature of the "academic" figure, or at least with the contrast between the elegant lines of the form and the expression of writhing pain. Lawrence Gowing glosses the potential philosophical and pictorial significance of this figure: "Matisse's early figurines often sprouted wing-like forms, raised arms or little faun-like horns, like emanations of natural energy. The hands that are clasped to the head of the flayed and twisted *Écorché* speak of a Michelangelesque realization of that which is agonizing in the bodily condition. The little figure is like a personification of an anxiety that haunted Matisse."[63] The anxiety he refers to is Matisse's "nearly obsessive" and "narcissistic" desire for the wholeness and physical integrity of the body, an attitude I have characterized throughout as conflicted or ambivalent.[64]

I take the *écorché*'s double status—as an image of intense suffering that renders it unavailable to familiar modes of empathetic identification and yet fully exposed to the world and therefore engaging our response, whatever that might be—to be at the root of its interest for Matisse. Then again, the *écorché* is paired in *Interior with Aubergines* with a "bounding" figure along the left edge on the mantel above the fireplace, as though reversing the profile and challenging the emotional tenor of the *écorché.* More generally, it is as though

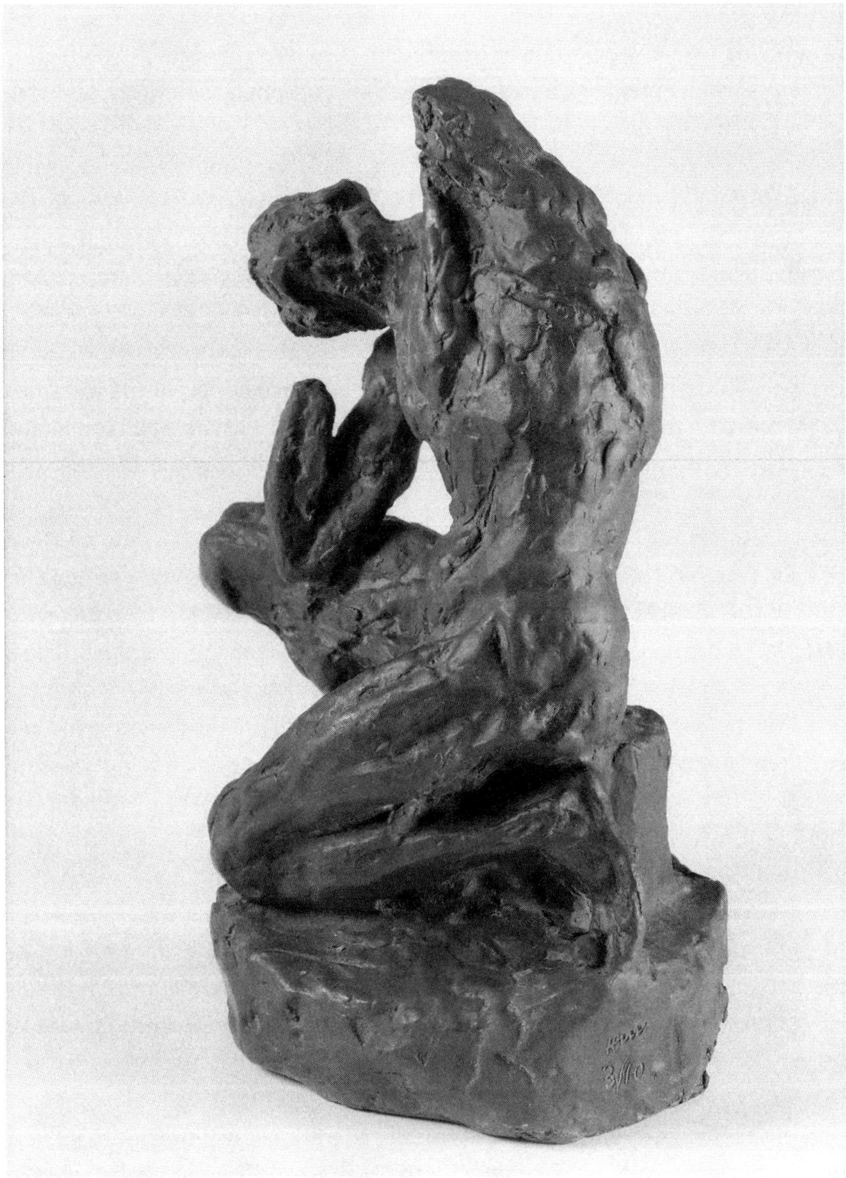

Figure 4.28. Henri Matisse (1869–1954), *Copy after Puget's Écorché,* 1903. Bronze, 22.5 cm. Cast by Valsuani, 1958. Musée d'Orsay, Paris, gift of Mrs. Jean Matisse, 1978; on deposit at Musée Matisse, Nice, France. Inventory D.78.1.42. Copyright 2013 Succession H. Matisse / Artists Rights Society (ARS), NY.

by the proliferation of picturing or mirroring representation Matisse expresses the limits of skepticism as a form of knowing. As its counter, Matisse amplifies the picture surface, and the blue-and-black patterned "ground" seems to sweep up under and immerse the beholder in the swirl of the imaginative and seemingly limitless space (paradoxically but crucially, Matisse projected this sensation of limitlessness within an *interior*).

It is characteristic of Cézanne to situate the *écorché* at the upper or outer limits of the picture space. Matisse, on the other hand, places the figure at the center of the composition. Moreover, Matisse made the *écorché* the central actor in a work paired with *Interior. Still Life with Aubergines* (Figure 4.29) brings the disorienting fantasy of *Interior* to a halt, slowing the beholder's distracted gaze and telescoping it into the still life grouping at the center of the ensemble. As in the *Bouquet on a Bamboo Table* and *Pink Onions,* the elements here are rendered in a technically ingenuous manner. The handling is broad and loose, sketched like a child's crayon drawing. The colors—orange, yellow, blue, green, black, and cream—are unmixed, laid on in flat and broad strokes. The "lightness of touch and thinness of paint application," Elderfield observes, "serve to join all parts of the picture together and to the surface with which color is identified."[65] The red wall hanging in *Interior* is now yellow, and the dark-blue screen with light-blue patterning has also been transposed. The eggplants are starkly rendered along with the two pears, the double-handled vase, and the *écorché* from the larger ensemble. While the flayed man's form is abstract and muted, the outline of his raised arms unequivocally registers the gesture of misery. "Suggestive of suffering and death," the flayed man, Elderfield notes, "is dwarfed by the rounded voluptuous pot and isolated in a halo of flame-red brushstrokes from the exotically colored fruit, [and] seems to connote the frailty of human presence, if nothing more, in the paradisal garden presented by the still life."[66] Although the figure is dwarfed and drained of the vitality of the still life elements around it, it nonetheless registers the frailty of human presence more decisively than if it were in competition with its surroundings.

Consider, finally, a grouping Matisse completed in the months just prior to his relocation to Nice in late 1917. *The Painter in His Studio* (Figure 4.30) is a complex meditation on the problems of representation, while *Laurette in a Green Robe (Black Background)* (Figure 4.31) is a portrait that captures the natural ease of the sitter. Laurette, in a capacious green robe, lounges in a chair, her slippers loosened from her feet. With only the barest of spatial indicators, she appears suspended on a pink swirl formed by the curvilinear shape of her lush Second Empire armchair. When she reappears on the easel in *The Painter in His Studio* she has been reduced to a schematic play of color forms. How far, Matisse seems to ponder, can a sequence of marks depart from their referent and declare themselves as "expressive" yet still carry, in their rhythm and consistency, effective connotation? The balance between image and affect is different in *Green Robe* and *Painter in His Studio.* In *Green Robe* space has been evacuated, while the body is intact; in *Painter in His Studio* space has been retrieved, indeed it is exemplified by the sweeping orthogonals of

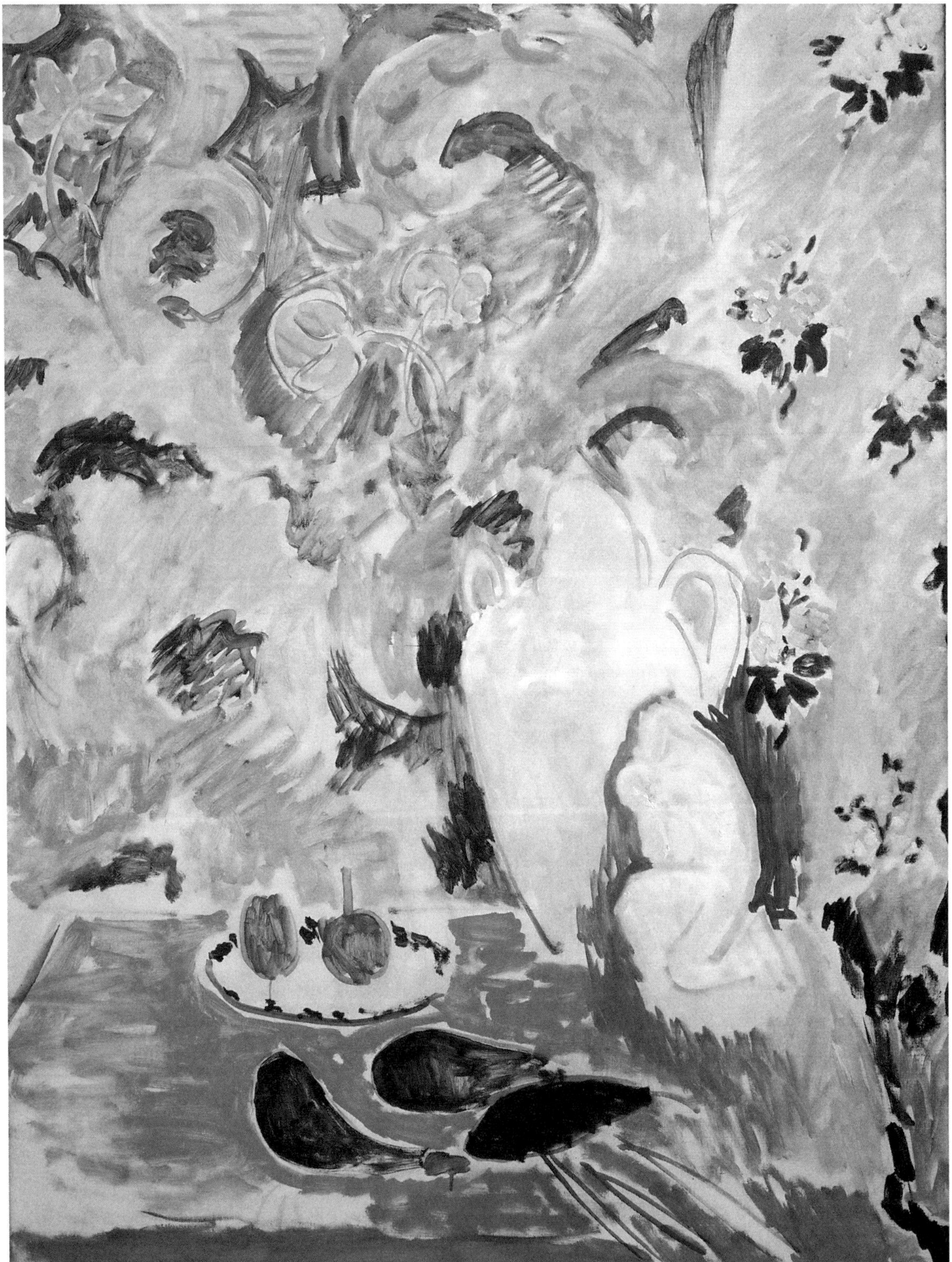

Figure 4.29. Henri Matisse (1869–1954), *Still Life with Aubergines,* summer 1911. Oil on canvas, 45¾ × 35⅛ inches. Louise Reinhardt Smith Bequest, Museum of Modern Art, New York. Copyright 2013 Succession H. Matisse / Artists Rights Society (ARS), NY. Digital image copyright Museum of Modern Art; licensed by Scala / Art Resource, NY.

Figure 4.30. Henri Matisse (1869–1954), *The Painter in His Studio,* 1916. Oil on canvas, 146.5 × 97 cm. AM 2585P. Musée National d'Art Moderne, Centre Georges Pompidou, Paris, France. Copyright 2013 Succession H. Matisse / Artists Rights Society (ARS), NY. Photograph courtesy of CNAC/MNAM/Dist. Réunion des Musées Nationaux / Art Resource, NY.

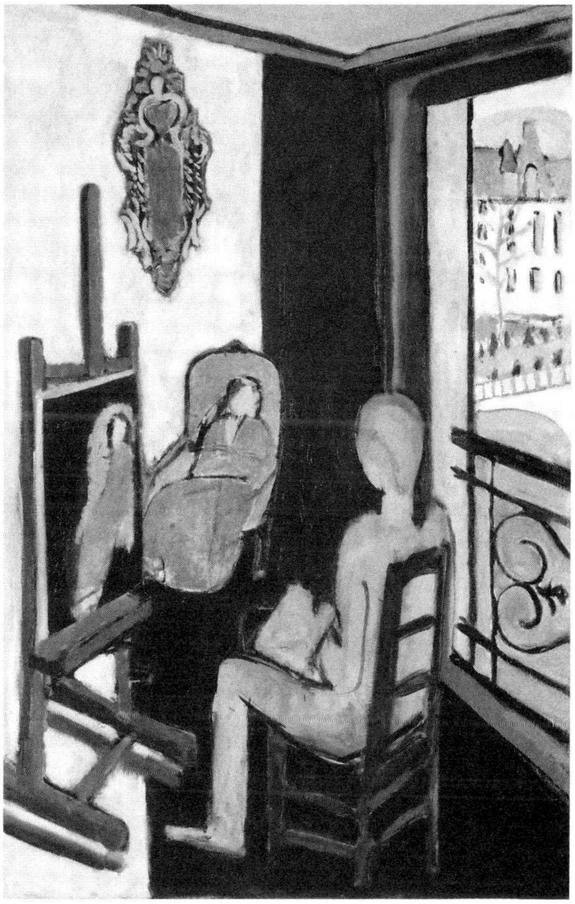

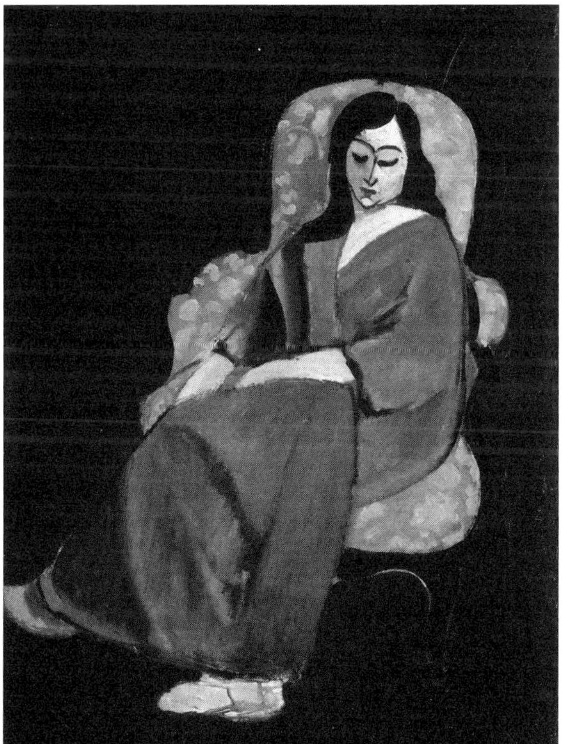

Figure 4.31. Henri Matisse (1869–1954), *Laurette in a Green Robe (Black Background),* 1916. Oil on canvas, 28¾ × 21⅜ inches (73 × 54.3 cm). Jacques and Natasha Gelman Collection, 1998 (1999.363.43), Metropolitan Museum of Art, New York. Copyright 2013 Succession H. Matisse / Artists Rights Society (ARS), NY. Photograph copyright Metropolitan Museum of Art / Art Resource, NY.

window frame, chair, and easel, but the body has been drained of its sensuous appeal—Laurette's curves have been ironically displaced into the rococo mirror on the wall, another, perhaps ironic, figure for art. In the charged space between artist and model, representation literally intervenes, suggesting at once connection and the gulf between the painter and his world—a gulf ratified by the black-and-white division of the surface—and a connection that is sealed at the electric moment where Laurette and her chair seem to fuse with the image on the easel, as though the loss of sensuous appeal has been regained in what Matisse called the "condensation of sensations that makes a picture" (38/43).

The power of this pair of paintings derives from their ability to keep the question of representation open, to strike a balance between closed unity and empathetic openness without collapsing these terms into a surefire effect or a visual pattern. Neither picture moves, in its reductions, toward a predetermined triumph of "less is more," but rather keeps line, color, markers of space in suspension between constraint and incisiveness, construction and weightlessness.

As all of Matisse's paired, layered, and sequential pictures suggest, to express oneself to another does not involve a theory or a system of representation, but rather a series of preliminary, investigative, and contingent approaches. How could it be otherwise? If expressing oneself to another were terminally mediated, then we would be locked in our affected bodies. Then again, if it were direct, if bodies or selves could communicate without need of representational mediation, would there be anything to say? At its best, Matisse's expressionism foreclosed either a skeptical withdrawal from other minds or possessive mastery over them. Although Matisse was tempted to seek alternatives to representation, his work is better seen as a profound reflection on the limits and powers of expression as a mode of understanding. What his work reveals is something about the nature of expression more generally: that to express oneself to another requires an acknowledgment of the other's difference; this difference both threatens isolation and makes every connection like an unrepeatable gift. To refuse the gift, to retreat into a solipsistic space of pure representation, or to take it for granted, to circumvent representation and seek to transmit affects directly through paint and surface, would involve a denial of the other and of oneself.

CONCLUSION

From Art to Object
The Case of Paul Valéry

> Any beautiful work is a *closed* thing.
>
> —Paul Valéry, *Notebooks*

> The "meaning" of a poem, like that of an object, is the reader's business. *Quantum potes, tantum aude.* [Dare to do all you can.] The poet's job is to construct a sort of verbal entity that will have the solidity, but also the ambiguity, of an object.
>
> —Paul Valéry, *Notebooks*

CORMAC MCCARTHY'S *Blood Meridian, or The Evening Redness in the West* (1985) bears an epigraph from a surprising source, Paul Valéry.[1] Surprising because McCarthy's story is a nightmarish vision of brutal violence against Native Americans by American settlers during the westward expansion—hardly a typical Valéryean theme—and surprising given McCarthy's stated aversion to a certain strain of literary artifice. "Proust and Henry James," McCarthy has famously observed, were "not literature" because they did not "deal with issues of life and death."[2] But Valéry, apparently, was not part of that tradition. Despite what we may know of Valéry (that he was a member of the Académie Française and an author of carefully constructed Symbolist poetry and prose in the tradition of Mallarmé), he was in fact an author of life and death.

The passage McCarthy cites is from a little-known 1895 essay by Valéry titled "The Yalu," a sprawling meditation on the difference between Eastern and Western cultures.[3] "The Yalu" presents a dialogue between a European (we are meant to infer the poet himself) and a Chinese scholar "from the land of Tsin." The scholar announces his fear that Japanese forces are gearing up for war with China once again. "They are imitating us," the European reflects. The scholar is unimpressed by the comparison because the European is not worthy of imitation. Why? Because the Europeans "are afraid of death." While the Chinese excel in patience, orderliness, and a "feeling for the irregular," Europeans know only unbounded intelligence.[4] Intelligence is a tool of fear; it is a means to evade awareness of mortality. The scholar offers a dark meditation on the failure of the European mind (the passage appears as McCarthy's epigraph):

> You are in love with intelligence, until it frightens you. For your ideas are terrifying and your hearts are faint. Your acts of pity and cruelty are absurd, committed with no calm, as if they were irresistible. Finally, you fear blood more and more. Blood and time.[5]

While the European uses his intelligence to mask his mortality, the scholar, who is "learned in writing" as well as "war command," knows something more powerful than intelligence. "We do not wish to know too much," he reflects, echoing Euripides's sense that "it is not always wisdom to be wise." Although the Chinese can be "cruel, subtle, or barbarous," what makes *their* acts of pity and cruelty "reasonable" is that they are built on a foundation of blood.[6]

The men from the land of Tsin "feed . . . in the most favorable valleys of the earth." To the outside world China appears a meaningless "sea of individuals," but in reality the men of Tsin form a living "family." There is an "unbroken line [of descent] from the earliest days" to the present, the scholar affirms. While the European is cut off from his roots by his haphazard intelligence, the Chinese empire forms a bloodline "woven of the living, the dead, and Nature." "Think of the web of our race," the scholar says, think how "we are joined by memory to our fathers" while the exhausted Europeans "endlessly re-begin the work of the first day."[7] The scholar analogizes his "family" to a massive wall, built up brick by brick through the ages, that holds them together—and holds "the others" out. "Every man here feels that he is both son and father, among thousands and tens of thousands, and is aware of being held fast by the people around him and the dead below him and the people to come, like a brick in a brick wall." Outside this "miraculous structure of his ancestors" man is reduced to "nothing."[8]

Many years later, in his essay "On Nations" (1927), Valéry drew again on the analogies between nations, families, and walls, now without the allegorical veil. "Nations are strangers to one another," he wrote, and however "sincere they desire to converse, to understand each other," the conversation necessarily "comes to an end," because there is an "impassable barrier against depth and duration" between various nations.[9] While there is an "inner bond that rivets together" a nation over time (the technology here has been updated), this bond effectively blocks others from passing through. But unlike in his early claim, wherein the racial family forms the only secure bond, he now suggested that race is only one of various possibilities. There are shared historical phenomena that can bind a nation together, including "language, or territory, or memories, or interests."[10] But these historical bonds, on closer inspection, are natural phenomena in disguise: they were "discovered, just as the nebulae were." "Just as it was discovered that the Earth is part of a certain system," he affirmed, "so it was discovered that a person is *this* by birth and *that* by his livelihood."[11] Valéry discovered that class, like race, is something you are born with.

The same year, in his "Notes on the Greatness and Decline of Europe," Valéry showed how the "actions of a few men" derive directly from "natural causes." "As natural causes produce hail, typhoons, and epidemics, so intelligent causes affect millions of men, the great majority of whom submit to them as to the vagaries of the sky, the sea, the earth's crust."[12] In order to restore Europe's greatness, Valéry concluded, a dictator must emerge to "act upon the masses in the manner of blind, physical causes"; only then would Europe have a real politics.[13] To be sure, the dictator does not persuade either by his policies or by coercion, but, like the poet, with the direct power of his words.

And yet, at this same moment, Valéry was exploring a wholly different account of causality. For "even the coolest calculator," he wrote in "The Struggle for Peace" (1933), "one cannot figure with sufficient probability a definite end."[14] This led to a thought that he would repeat in virtually every scrap of writing from this point forward (especially, as I will show, in his aesthetics): "It has become impossible to foresee not only the final outcome but even the immediate effects" of one's efforts.[15] "No one will ever be able to predict or circumscribe the almost immediate consequences of any undertaking whatever," he reflected in "On History."[16] This is the *"transcendent"* fact of modernity. Humankind's means of "representation and understanding" the world have been fundamentally "outstripped" by the facts. The future "is endowed with *essential unpredictability,* and this is the only prediction we can make."[17] So while in his early writings he was committed to finding the "exact conjunction between the sensuous *cause,* which constitutes the form, and the intelligible *effect,* which constitutes the content,"[18] after 1927 he became increasingly skeptical of relating causes with effects, leaving effects open to the "unpredictable" play of the reader's desires.

The consequences of Valéry's revision of causality are fundamental to a shift in the burden of artistic meaning from the *author*—the central figure of his early writings—to the *reader,* who dominates his later aesthetics. Nonetheless, as I will also argue, behind both terms lies an even deeper commitment to a form of literary materialism that turns *representation* itself into a self-generated *agency.*

Literary Sadism

"Imagine, I am seeing blood," Valéry wrote to Gide in May 1891. Valéry was responding to the violence at Fourmies in northern France, where gendarmes shot and killed ten workers at a mass strike at a textile mill. Here is Valéry rather unhinged:

> Those soldiers who fired on the crowd, I envied them and oh to fire on all the World! I detest the masses, and even more, the Others! . . . I am exhausting an art form in a quick spasm, and am so panic-stricken that I am haunted by a panorama of slaughter, and blinded by ravaged lights. I almost wish for a monstrous war in which to flee amid the shock of a crazed and red Europe. . . . I don't know what blood is speaking in me, or what wolf of olden times yawns in my boredom, but I feel it there. . . . Does this barbarian surprise you? . . . Ah! how much night there is! To grasp it! To brood it . . . and to laugh at holding it captive—a Star! It is difficult. Well then! Blood![19]

Gide was worried. "Can this warrior be you?" Like the soldiers firing on the crowd, "You dream of the impact of shuddering weapons as well."[20] But Gide assured his panicked friend that no matter how "drunk" one gets on words, they "are no more than literature."[21] Nonetheless, Gide shared his friend's sense that "we have literature 'in our blood,' like the germ of a disease." It is literature itself that provokes such immense "desires for battle." Gide coined a term to describe this literary impulse: "like those who, tired of loving, want to bruise some bit of white flesh—it is sadism, my friend—literary sadism."[22] It is the white flesh of the page that Valéry really wants to damage, despite his call to literal violence. But Valéry did not make much of this distinction; it was the identity of the two that generated his literary ambitions. To damage a page was to damage its reader in turn.

Gide's dream was starkly different from his friend's. Rather than literary sadism, Gide presented a picture of masochism, of Mallarméan self-annihilation. "To forget one's self, to adore . . . it was for that, was it not, that we have loved all that literature," he reflected. Gide admitted that his dream was as "brutal and frantic" as Valéry's, and it too passed beyond literature; it was nothing less than mass suicide along with the workers at Fourmies. Here is Gide: "To end up like an animal, without thinking . . . completely numbed through intoxication, since otherwise we would be afraid of dying; to end up with *the others,* in a pile, without speaking, since we would not know one another. But what vinegar and gall it would take, O Lord!, at that supreme moment, to put our soul to sleep!"[23]

Valéry resisted Gide's aesthetic of intoxicated self-annihilation, always placing the active mind against the passive contemplation of religious thought. Gide, on the other hand, was averse to Valéry's belief, stated over and over again, that art was a matter of calculation, of abstraction and "chemical study." "You speak ill of 'artificial flowers' and Wagner," he scolded Gide, "but note, and this is the essence of my system, that although they may not be as beautiful as the real ones, they come out ahead from the point of view of the doing."[24] Fake flowers require active control, while "two beings who make love are reduced to jelly."[25]

Valéry conceived of language as humankind's greatest means of controlling unstable matter, the most unstable matter of all being the *crowd*. "Of all possible feelings, the strongest in me is that of *security*," he told Gide. "I have no confidence in what comes and goes. I don't trust it."[26] Valéry's security system, his barrier against the crowd, at least early on, was writing. To write was to order, shape, and mold the formless crowd. "The crowd rules," he told Gide in 1891, a few months after Fourmies. The crowd "invades one's brain . . . [it] submerges the inner temple and makes the individual a thing of the world." But "you don't understand," he chastised Gide, "you think of your public too much."[27] While Gide embraced the formless liberties of the crowd, and the loss of self it invited, Valéry sought to escape its clutches. "This Paris which I . . . detest more and more flows round me like a river, and it is a Lethe seething with resonant oblivion."[28]

Human Material

A year prior to the publication of McCarthy's novel, Gilles Deleuze published a study of Irish painter Francis Bacon that shared with the American author's work a similar set of concerns.[29] At the center of Deleuze's book lies a commitment to an aesthetic of blood, and once again Valéry is the inspiration. Deleuze cites Bacon's paraphrase of Valéry: "I don't want to avoid telling a story, but I want very, very much to do the thing that Valéry said—to give the sensation without the boredom of its conveyance."[30] Throughout the book Deleuze discriminates between two forms of pictorial violence. "When talking about the violence of paint, it's nothing to do with the violence of war," he quotes Bacon as saying. Glossing Valéry and Bacon, Deleuze explains the difference between the violence of form and the violence of representation: "The violence of sensation is opposed to the violence of the represented (the sensational, the cliché). The former is inseparable from its direct action on the nervous system, the levels through which it passes, the domains it traverses: being itself a Figure, it must have nothing of the nature of a represented object."[31] Deleuze's claim is to be taken literally. "Great" works of art are able to produce unmediated affective experiences that directly attack the viewer's sensorium. Like McCarthy, Deleuze extracts an image of Valéry that is violent and brimming with bodily excess. While McCarthy cites "The Yalu" as his source, Deleuze cites an even earlier text, Valéry's first essay, "On Literary Technique" (1889).

"On Literary Technique" was Valéry's manifesto, and he rarely deviated from its principals throughout his career. His opening remarks announced his primary ambition: "Literature is the art of playing on the soul of others. It is with this scientific brutality that the problem of the aesthetics of the Word . . . has been set for our age."[32] Valéry's concerns could hardly be more explicit. Above all, he was anxious about problems of communication with his reader.

After all, metaphors work only if the reader can grasp the sense of at least two disparate terms and drawn them together. For Valéry this process invited failure. He was no longer certain whether audiences would grasp his metaphors, and even if they did the experience would take place over time and would thus be prey to potentially uncontrollable associations. The science of effect would overcome these problems and put art back on a secure foundation.

Valéry found support for his brutal science in Edgar Allan Poe's "Philosophy of Composition" of 1846. As Valéry explained, Poe offered the reader "knowledge of the different notes that must be sounded in another's soul . . . [so as to] predict with certainty the overwhelming effect of a bleak refrain" on a reader.[33] Valéry's fascination with tightly controlling the outcome of formal effects led him to analogize the work of art to an expressive machine: "The work of art takes on the character of a machine to impress a public; to arouse emotions and their corresponding images."[34] To stamp the audience like a machine, like a typewriter against white paper, was no innocent metaphor. Metaphors of the artist as machine dominate his writings: the composer is an emotional mechanic, the medium is the machine, and the reader is the raw material shaped by the poetic mechanism.

A few years earlier, in his influential "Notes on Wagnerian Painting" (1886), Teodor de Wyzewa declared, "Art, as Wagner tells us, must create life . . . utilizing colors and lines only as emotional signs, marrying them to one another with the sole purpose of producing within us, through their free play, an impression like that of a symphony."[35] Valéry shared the Wagnerian view that the artist's role was to "create life" through colors and lines, but he believed that artists had more reliable means of creating their audience than broad waves of sound; they could precisely shape, mold, and form the viewer with a science of pictorial form. Valéry mused of a future where pictures would be made in "a picture-making laboratory, with its specialist officially clad in white, rubber-gloved, keeping to a precise schedule, armed with strictly appropriate apparatus and instruments, each with its appointed place and exact function."[36] The furthest thing from an Impressionist, Degas was imperious, cruel, and rigorous in his manipulation of form to shape the viewer's emotional state.[37]

But it was Valéry's great protagonist, "Monsieur Teste"—a character influenced by Degas[38]—who, although immune to aesthetic effects himself, achieved perfection in transmitting them to others. M. Teste "had known quite early the importance of what might be called human *plasticity.* He had investigated its mechanics and its limits." According to his anxious escort, if Teste had "turned upon the world the controlled power of his mind, nothing could have resisted him."[39] What kind of ideal is it that makes the artist and his work literally irresistible? And if there is no resistance, how do we judge a work's success? If success is defined in terms of the artist's ability to suggest complex, perhaps unrecognized or unfamiliar, states of mind or feeling to the viewer, then what is it to judge success in terms of the degree of physiological impact?

In addition to Poe, Valéry found support for his machinic ideal in a more unlikely source. It was Leonardo da Vinci's writings, paintings, and technical drawings (often of machines) that authorized Valéry's vision of a violent and masterful formalism. In his ambitious "Introduction to the Method of Leonardo da Vinci" (1894), Valéry focused on the *method* announced in the title. To maximize his effect on the public, the artist, like a mechanic, must render his materials properly:

> What is called in art a *realization,* is in fact a problem of rendering—one in which the private meaning . . . plays no part, and in which the principal factors are the nature of those materials and the mentality of the public. . . . on the basis of psychology and probable effects . . . every combination of elements made to be perceived and judged depends on a few general laws and on a particular adaptation, defined in advance for a foreseen category of minds to which the whole is specially addressed; and the work of art becomes a machine designed to arouse and assemble the individual formations of those minds.[40]

Metaphors pile up. The artist is at once scientist, mathematician, composer, and mechanic (he will also assume the role of zookeeper). With adequate knowledge of psychology, physiology, and probability, Valéry argued, the artist can impress, assemble, and shape his listeners' minds with utter precision.

Just after the publication of the "Method of Leonardo," Valéry, like his fictive counterpart in "The Yalu," who is trained in both art and warfare, entered the War Department in Paris and commenced his first retirement from poetry. Before his retreat, he wrote a sequence of four essays for *Mercure de France* dedicated to the problem of methods: "The Conquest by Method," "Instruction and Training of Troops," "Semantics," and "Time." Valéry was explicit about the aim of these texts: "The most important phenomena of life can serve as the basis and the subject of sustained mathematical operations—that life is not above human calculation." As he concluded, "Life can be dealt with." And when the artist went to work, he went to work on the senses: "In art we should see the artist working directly on each of the senses, on each of the psychological needs of his public and aim directly at his man. Wagner did it."[41] To be the Wagner of poetry was indeed Valéry's early aesthetic ambition. Nonetheless, as though recognizing the sheer *effectiveness* of his aims—the ease with which he achieved aesthetic response from his readers, and therefore the nonartistic nature of the result—he (temporarily) withdrew from pursuing them.

From his first article in 1889 to his death in 1945, Valéry expanded and explored his singular theory of poetic affect. At the conclusion to *Monsieur Teste* he succinctly described the central claim of his earliest writings: "The effect on others, never forgetting their mechanics— . . . and not only treating them as *selves* but as machines, animals—whence an *art*."[42] This is a twofold process: first, to break through the resistant layers of the reader's self, and second, to tame the inner workings of one's animal-machines. Above all, Valéry maintained that literature is "a question of fact—and, in short, of force"; only now he suggested that "if the reader—any reader—feels the effect of it, the poet *ipso facto* is *justified*."[43] On this point the only difference between his early and later writings is the chastened admission that if only *one* reader is physically altered by the poem, the poet's practice is justified.

Valéry came to acknowledge the limitations of his desire to produce an effect on others, and later in his career he turned his attention away from the reader and literature more generally to better know and acknowledge himself.[44] At the conclusion to "Monsieur Teste's Logbook" (1925), for instance, Valéry offered a hint of disillusionment with the poetics of pure intentionality, as though it threatened to become its opposite: theater. "Disgusted with . . . doing what succeeds, with the *effectiveness of methods*, try something else."[45] It was as though the complete transmission of one's intentions at once limited what it was that one intended and, worse still, inevitably felt forced upon the reader. The potential collapse of intentionality into a kind of posturing emerged in a key text on Mallarmé:

> It was necessary to renounce the surest means of pleasing, the tender or touching effects which are directly obtained by a sort of provocation of the reader's memories of passions. The highest art can certainly not consist of arousing emotion by way of emotive objects. What is simpler than to make people shudder or wax tender by the artistic representation of death, grief, or tenderness? That is hardly *creation*. It is easy to captivate a public by a spectacle or a speech that goes straight to our weaknesses, that tortures or swells our hearts, making us live a fictional life by playing on our naïve energies. . . . As for me, nothing so cools my emotions as to recognize the desire to maneuver me, and to see the simple mechanism of it.[46]

And while Mallarmé refused these types of surefire means, theatrical effects were commonplace within modernism. In his book on Degas, Valéry described the limitations of the art of effects:

> If the habit of facility . . . becomes the dominating factor [in creating art, then] . . . it reduces to nothing the slightest necessity for concentration on the reader's part, in order to *secure* with *instantaneous effects, rhetorical shock tactics*. . . . Modern art tends almost exclusively to exploit sensory

> sensibility. . . . It has a marvelous flair for arousing our attention, and for exploiting every means to that end—intensification, contrast, the startling, or the enigmatic. It can capture, by the subtlety of its means or the audacity of its execution, certain very valuable effects: states of extreme transience or complexity, irrational values, inarticulate sensations, resonances, correspondences, intuitions of shifting depths. . . . But these things are bought at a price.[47]

As though acknowledging the very *ease* of producing results—that the poet achieves his aims with little effort and a range of literary tricks—Valéry sought more difficult material to render. This he found in his own mind, still conceived as a plastic material to be molded, although of a fundamentally more resistant kind.

To express one's intentions transparently, without resistance—to achieve an artistic effect with certainty—was equal to artistic failure. If the work succeeded in communicating its meaning directly, Valéry reasoned, then the work itself was flawed. Expressive transparency set the aesthetic bar both too high and too low. Too high because Valéry assumed there would be those—any but the "happy few"—who did not respond to his work (or simply did not care), at least not according to his intentions; too low because the effect produced, if it were certain, would be of such generality as to make it uncompelling as a stand-in for meaning.

A Throw of the Dice Might Abolish Chance

In the March 1929 edition of the *Revue des Vivants,* Valéry published a two-part essay on the problem of conventions. The world seemed held together by an increasingly intricate web of conventions, the vast majority of which one accepted without consent. Although these conventions were the products of human intention, they seemed to function independent of any agent. As Valéry saw it, the sheer complexity of conventions had grown exponentially with the rise of technologies of instantaneous transmission—radio, the phonograph, photography, and cinema. The second part of the essay, called "Hypothesis," reflected on these technologies as mechanisms that had hypnotically imposed a network of conventions on producers and consumers.

Valéry foresaw a time when it would be possible to "act from a distance, not only on man's sense but also on the most hidden elements of the human psyche."[48] The prediction was grounded, once again, in a theory of hypnotic suggestion: "By stimulating the system and very sources of man's mental and affective life, some remote and unseen operator will impose illusions, impulses, desires, and artificial disorders" on our minds.[49] And like Matisse and Bergson, Valéry saw the stakes of this pervasive influence as nothing less than the reliability of "our *identity*." All of our beliefs in the "*indivisible*, autonomous" self were being eroded by invisible waves of sight and sound. Our "secret substance" was unprotected "against external influences"; we were continually shaped by "*everything* or *anything*" in our surroundings.[50]

Valéry ruminated on "the physics of wave transmission" and new "kinds of action at a distance," comparing their power to the "great orators, founders of religions, leaders of nations" of the past. Only now the stakes were raised. What if these leaders were to marshal the new technologies for their causes? He imagined a terrifying world where "the power to make men live more rapidly or more slowly, to imbue them with tendencies, to make them tremble or smile, to abase or exalt their courage, or if need be, to stop the hearts of an entire people, might be known, defined and applied!"[51] In all these reflections, Valéry circled around his main concern: the integrity of the self. "What then of the pretensions of the self?" He went on: "At every moment of their lives, men would wonder whether they were the source of their own actions or whether, in their own deepest sense of their existence, they were marionettes."[52]

Valéry's most panicked (and influential) reflection on this generalized state of hypnosis emerged in his 1935 study "The Outlook for Intelligence." We should be wary to "believe *our own words*," he warned. "I mean that a word that comes into our head is generally not ours."[53] Guy Debord would have been hard-pressed to imagine a starker vision of spectacular society:

> You know . . . how *talkative* the modern age is. Our cities are plastered with gigantic letters. The night itself is peopled with words of fire. In the morning, numberless printed sheets are in the hands of passers-by, of travelers in trains, and lazy people in their beds. We have only to turn a knob in our room to hear the voices of the world and sometimes our masters' voice. As for books, never have so many been published. Never has so much been read, or rather, skimmed over! . . . our verbal sensibility . . . is being brutalized, dulled, degraded. Our inner language is wearing out. . . . Furthermore, the daily output of vast quantities of published matter, the flood of printing and broadcasting, wash over our judgments and impressions from morning to night, mangling and mixing them, making of our brains truly a gray matter in which nothing stands out, nothing can last, and we have an odd sense of the monotony of novelty; we are bored with wonders and extremes.[54]

The eternal sameness of the new made it impossible for the self to render judgment on the difference between quantity and quality, what was a cause and what was an effect.

The collapsing "pretensions of the self" Valéry described were part of a broader "pretension of foresight."[55] Selfhood depended on foresight, on the ability to discriminate between causes and effects and, above all, match them up. Accommodating new experiences within a range of habits was crucial to self-maintenance. The "whole man . . . hangs on the possibility of being modified in face of an event, so that the man and his complexity may preserve what is required to keep on living, for the self to maintain its continuity, recognize itself and go on being itself."[56] The self required "a capacity for adapting to a certain amount of the unexpected." But what happens when the "unexpected itself" has been transformed?[57] Because spectacle indiscriminately turned causes into effects and effects into causes, chance seemed to reign supreme and agency became a kind of accident. Mallarmé's dream of the abolition of chance—to "conquer chance, word by word"—was beyond belief.[58] If self-maintenance was a game played against the odds, then spectacle rendered even that game obsolete. We are all playing a new game, one whose rules are obscure to the player: "Instead of playing a straightforward card game with destiny, as we used to do, knowing the rules, knowing the number of cards and face cards, we are now in the position of a player who discovers with amazement that his partner's hand contains face cards he has never seen before, and that the rules of the game change with every deal." Not even the most veteran gambler could play the odds when the rules changed as one played. If the gambler was the supreme modernist fiction—someone who could turn seemingly limitless chance into meanings—then in the new (postmodern) situation, "no calculation of probability is possible anymore."[59]

Valéry described postmodernity as the site of "incalculable risk,"[60] defined by the *"impossibility of localizing anything."*[61] If the self depended on its capacity to temporarily defeat or suspend risk, then the confrontation with the sheerly incalculable threatened to defeat the self in return. According to Valéry, the new science and technology stripped the world of its legibility by stripping it of its predictability. Consequently, our ability to read effects back to their causes even hypothetically was radically undermined. "Effects," he observed, "are so rapidly becoming incalculable from their causes, and even contradictory to their causes, that henceforth it will perhaps be thought puerile, dangerous, and senseless to look for the causal event, to try to produce it or prevent it."[62]

For Valéry, the work of art was the last and most essential "causal event" produced by human beings. "In poetry you have to make an accidental relation—that of sound and sense—appear natural; . . . appear to be a law," he wrote in the *Notebooks.*[63] Artworks were the only human thing remaining in which cause and effect were proximate enough that it was possible to discern their necessary connection. Valéry saw Mallarmé as the great master of chance from a now invalidated past. If Mallarmé's art flirted with the senseless, it was in the effort to recover sense from the dice throw, but now science and spectacle made that aim pointless. Mallarmé's effort to transform every verbal cliché into something animate and particular was no longer viable: "In effect he was defending himself, even in matters of detail and in the elementary functions of the mental life, *against automatism*."[64] To convert automatisms into meanings—as I have argued, this was Bergson's project as well—was the poet's lifework.[65] But what happened to the idea of art when automatisms of a particularly incalculable sort defined life itself? Valéry explored two possibilities for artistic response to the new aleatoric regime: either withdraw into skeptical isolation or try (and fail) to transcend chance through chance procedures. While the former was Valéry's central position—and the one I consider in the remaining sections of this chapter—it was his engagement with chance, as a paradoxical mode of intentional agency, that stands in tension with his ontological skepticism and offers a vision of artistic practice closely in tune with Matisse's procedures (even if neither saw it).

Valéry described a hierarchy of the arts based on the proportion, as he saw it, of *intentionality* and *chance* within each medium. The "nobility of an art depends on the purity of the *desire* that gives rise to it, and the artist's uncertainty as to the happy outcome of his *activity*," he explained.[66] For Valéry, artistic value was largely a function of the relation between the depth of the artist's mastery of his medium and the degree to which that medium resisted the artist in turn. Therefore, "the more uncertain he is of the results of his efforts, on account of the nature of the *material* he wrestles with and the means he employs for subjugating it, the purer is his desire and the more evident his worth."[67] In other words, the artist requires the utmost "positive resistance" to his intentions in order for his intentions to be construed as properly *his* and not merely a matter of habit or routine.

In Valéry's hierarchy, Matisse—at least as a painter or draftsman—might not fare well. For the "true artist," Valéry explained, "pen or brush seem too light." True artists "worry about the lastingness of what costs them so little and develops so easily." The greatness of art consists in the artist's courting of chance; it is a matter of creating "imaginary difficulties" for oneself, "inventing quite arbitrary conventions or rules, putting checks on the freedom they have learned to distrust, a veto on the safe and immediate realization of *all* that they desire."[68] To invent a convention for oneself was to replace or at least contest the unreflective conventions one lived by in one's everyday life.

Within Valéry's hierarchy of the arts, ceramics came out on top. The ceramicist played with the most unpredictable medium of all: fire. For Valéry, the quality of a medium was defined by its capacity to "veto" the artist's most immediate intentions by interposing a seemingly unbridgeable separation between cause and effect. It was this gap that "explains why working in marble seems worthier than working in clay." If clay absorbs the artist's least touch, marble resists it to the same degree. He went on:

> And that explains why engraving is more honorable than etching; and fresco (to be carried out within a time limit, and involving a reciprocal

> and intimate relationship between *action, material,* and *duration*) nobler and worthier than any kind of painting which allows for *repeated* effort, retouching, alteration.
>
> But among all the arts, I know of none more hazardous, none less certain of the outcome and consequently more noble, than those which call for the use of *Fire.*[69]

Working with fire tested the most exacting of technical and imaginative procedures. No human agent could possibly foresee the total outcome of his efforts when the vase emerged from the kiln and confronted the cool air. But unlike those who confronted the ubiquitous unpredictability discovered by the new sciences, the artist who played with fire projected an image of almost superhuman agency, someone who could, at least *potentially,* overcome the most extreme contingencies of matter. "By their nature the arts of fire exclude or punish any negligence," Valéry explained. They "allow no relaxation or respite, no fluctuations of thought, courage, or temper. They emphasize, in its most dramatic aspect, the close combat between man and form. *Fire,* their essential agent, is also their greatest enemy." For the ceramicist, chance was both medium and adversary. Fire, Valéry explained, is a "formidable precision instrument," but one whose "physical or chemical *constants* are difficult to observe." Unlike the painter, for whom frequent corrections are part of the creative process, the ceramicist works in a medium in which "any slip is fatal, and the work ruined."[70] What marble, engraving, fresco, and ceramics held in common, and what clay, etching, and painting seemed to lack, was the artist's direct involvement with material contingencies, as though working with these media challenged chance on its own terrain such that the artist's inevitable failure to master these contingencies was also the source of any possible success.

For Valéry it was the artist, and not the medium, that really defined the work's significance. It was the *presentness* of the artist to his work that privileged the "arts of fire" over every other medium. "While the fire is in action, the man himself is aflame," Valéry wrote. As the artist watches the fire burn, "he is like both gambler whose fate is to be sealed by a fall of the dice [la chute d'un dé], and a soul in anxious prayer."[71] It was the intensity of the artist's physical and intellectual concentration on his task—one that by necessity exceeded any human capacity for control—that defined the superiority of his task. "The hand that lit, fed, stoked, and tempered the fire, is all alert for the one and only moment for withdrawing the incandescent shape which the fire has created, and will destroy in a moment longer, just as life, in its blind and monotonous power, does with its creatures."[72] While life was "blind and monotonous," the artist, distinguished by his seemingly absolute alertness, wrested order from randomness, rhythm from monotony. It was this tenuous mastery of the incalculable that led Valéry to describe ceramics as "a crowning of man's capital achievement."[73]

Valéry went on to define "Great Art" as something that "requires the artist *to bring to bear all the powers of his mind.*" Moreover, great art equally "require[d] the consumer to deploy all his faculties."[74] It was the latter assessment that led Valéry to a very different ontology of art in the 1930s. Although the work required the viewer's or reader's sustained attention, that attention was not directed, as one might expect, to understanding what the artist meant. Rather, the reader was to "find something quite different from what the author intended: conceivably, what the author wanted was less than what the attention of the reader or auditor gives him."[75]

In the end, it was the impossibility of the artist's complete control of his medium that spelled both his success and failure. No matter how skilled the artist was in his calculations of the dynamics of fire, mastery of that medium was ontologically unavailable. While every work of art is "wrenched from the domain of chance," every great work is equally a hymn to failure. "All reality," Valéry wrote, reflecting again on Mallarmé, "has no other excuse for existence except to offer the poet the chance to play a sublime match against it—a match that is lost in advance."[76] However present the artist was to his medium, it would transcend his desire for the communication of his intentions. Or rather, it was the capacity for the medium to exceed the artist's intentions—the sense in which loss was written into the effort from the beginning—that defined an artistic intention in the first place. As Valéry wrote:

> But all the fire worker's admirable vigilance and all the foresight learned from experience, from his knowledge of the properties of heat, of its critical stages, of the temperatures of fusion and reactions, still leave immense scope for the noble element of uncertainty. *They can never abolish Chance [Elles n'abolissent point le Hasard].* Risk remains the dominating and, as it were, the sanctifying element of his great art.[77]

For Valéry the problem of ceramics and its involvement with the unpredictable dynamics of fire was an allegory for the larger problem of the artist making an object that he intended to make. Chance, in ceramics, intervenes in a central way with the artistic process, as it does for different reasons in Valéry's discussion of photography (which I address below). How far can the artist loosen his established intentions, how much of chance can he incorporate, and still call the work *his*? From the artist's perspective, playing a match against the world and losing could be the same as winning, as high degrees of chance had been confronted if not defeated; for the reader, on the other hand, the artist's profound sense of concentration in the production of his work necessarily makes for an open-ended object with unlimited possibilities of *self-creation.*

For Valéry the sciences of radical indeterminacy and the spectacular society that emerged from it presented the author with two contrary conclusions about the nature of contemporary art. On one hand, it lodged radical unpredictability at the heart of the work of art. Valéry's reflections on the reader all point toward this new condition of artistic *production*, wherein the reader became the author. When effects were permanently separated from their causes the work entered into a wholly new situation defined by skepticism. At times, Valéry was unmitigated in his skeptical attitude: "No one agrees on anything except by mistake, and all harmony among human beings is the happy fruit of an error."[78] When it comes to aesthetic experience, "there will never be any accurate way of comparing what has happened in the two minds" of author and audience.[79] And because "everyone does not react in the same way to a work of art," the work's meaning "varies with the individual and the circumstances."[80] For Valéry, this condition of objecthood adheres to every work of art, no matter what the artist intends.[81] On the other hand, as I have argued in this section, Valéry conceived of an entirely alternative possibility, that the embrace of chance granted the artist an unprecedented capacity to express his intentions, as though it made his deepest intentions available for the first time.

Valéry's imaginative effort to turn every contingency into inevitability, unpredictability into certainty, emerges in a sequence of reflections on technology and media written between 1927 and 1935. Valéry's "The Conquest of Ubiquity" of 1928, for instance, an essay made famous by Walter Benjamin when he quoted it in the epigraph to "The Work of Art in the Age of Its Technological Reproducibility" (1936–39), offers a complex vision of new forms of technological indeterminacy. Valéry began the essay with a now-familiar lament on new technologies of reproduction that were "changing the very notion of art."[82] "Just as water, gas, and electricity are brought into our houses from far off to satisfy our needs in response to minimal effort, so we shall be supplied with visual or auditory images, which will appear and disappear at a simple movement of the hand, hardly more than a sign."[83] He called this new art the "home delivery of Sensory Reality" (another delivery system to be "enslaved" by, he groused). And yet a few paragraphs later his tone began to change. What seemed a terrifying vision of effects without causes (a world of nonintentionality) transformed into one of absolute intentionality. "To be able to choose the moment of enjoyment, to savor the pleasure when not only our mind desires it, but our soul and whole being craves and as it were anticipates it, is to give fullest scope to the composer's intention, for it permits his works to live again in a vibrant milieu not very different from that in which they were created. In recorded music the work of composer or performer finds the condition essential to the most perfect aesthetic returns."[84] To loosen the artist's grip from the work and send it out into the world had the uncanny result of binding it more tightly to the artist's truest intentions. One can now listen to music, score in hand, when one is at home and in the right mood for it and in a space that is closer to the composer's own when he wrote it. The composer's intentions are given their "fullest scope" and "most perfect" realization at the moment they circulate freely in the world.[85]

Valéry considered sculpture, as he did engraving and fresco (if not oil painting), as a medium that bore a degree of risk analogous to the "arts of fire." In a brilliant reflection on Renée Vautier's creation of his own portrait bust, Valéry pondered how the sculptor courts chance at every opportunity (Figure C.1). "He [or rather, she] invents hidden conditions and restrictions, invisible obstacles which . . . impede his acquired facility, delay his satisfaction, so as to draw from him . . . what he did not know he possessed."[86] While the ceramicist worked directly with chance, the sculptor must seemingly invent it for himself. And yet, like the ceramicist, the sculptor confronted almost untold contingencies in both the production and, more centrally, the reception of his work. Once again the comparison was with painting: "Whereas painting repudiates the wall it hangs on, opening on to a fictive world which simulates not merely the objects placed in it but also its own space and light, sculpture is established in the same dimensions as the spectator; it accepts the same light, and its radiance, like its shadows, are *real*."[87] Sculpture offered resistance to mastery and an exposure to contingency that Valéry considered lacking in painting. This is, of course, another version of the praise he accorded the "arts of fire." But unlike the problem raised in the ceramics essay of making the object one intended to make, a related but different problem is raised in the sculpture essay, that of the work's effect on the beholder. Valéry worried not just about producing the work he intended to make but also about how the finished work would be understood by its viewers. He was not satisfied, that is, simply to make the work he intended, leaving the response out of the equation as an imperfect gauge of an artist's intent; he wanted also to see that the work he intended *produced exactly the kinds of responses* he desired. In fact, it was the limitations of the latter pursuit—that the work could never ultimately produce the response the artist intended to produce—that set off the whole issue of anti-intentionality for him. While sculpture raised the specter of open-ended reactions, it nonetheless signaled the continuing possibility of artistic control of beholder response. As I will show, only *writing* could establish the possibility of a truly anti-intentional situation. For Valéry intentionality adhered to every aspect of the visual arts, as though it were inscribed in the least visible mark.

Because sculpture was apprehended in "real" space, the sculptor was playing with contingencies that seemingly exceeded those faced by the ceramicist; fire, for the sculptor, becomes a matter of the changing light of reception. Valéry describes the new situation: "But the spectator, immobile with regard to the *tableau,* can move in relation to a statue, so that the work can thus be viewed from an infinity of angles. Yet again, the local light can also change its

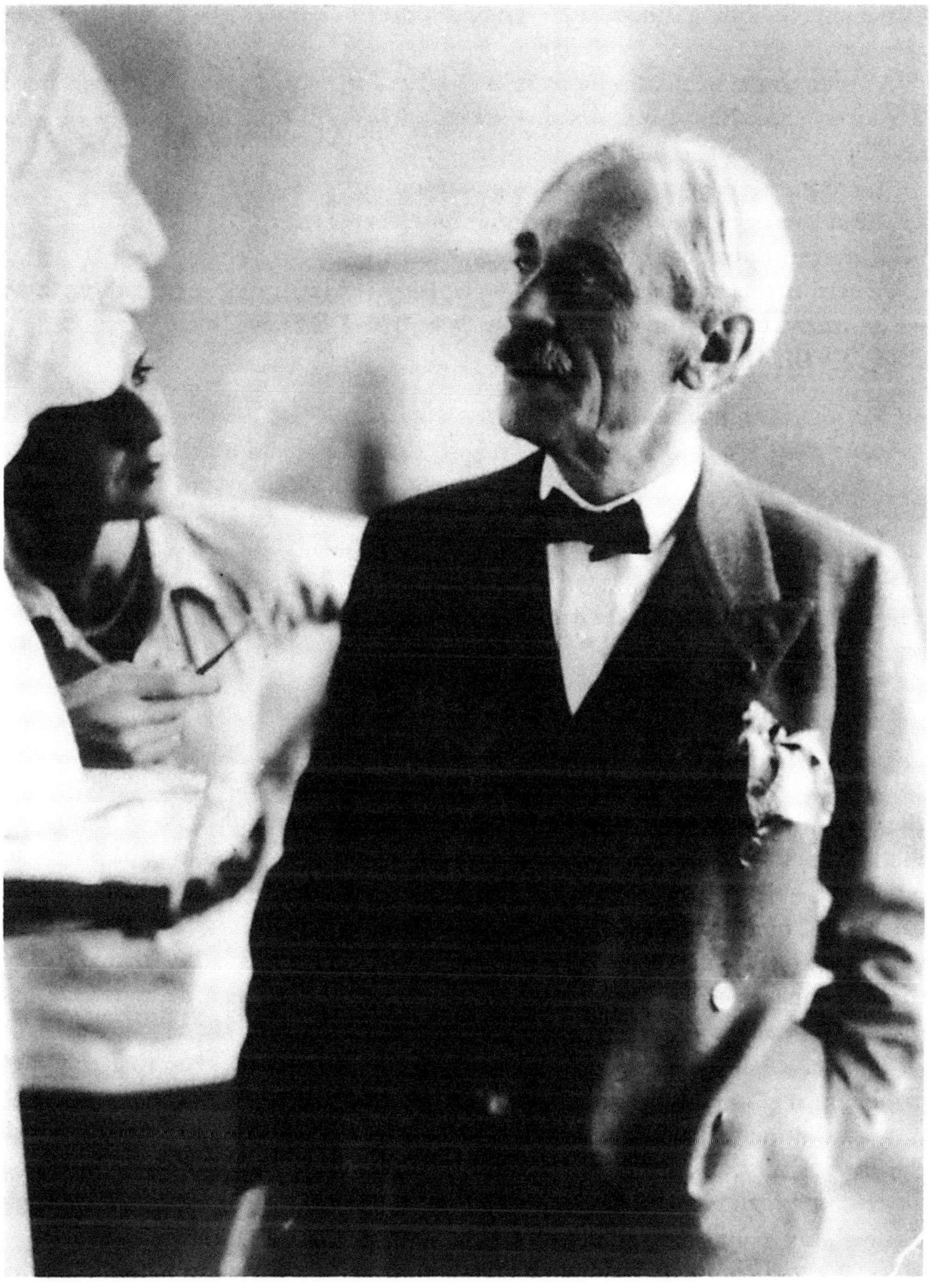

Figure C.1. Unknown photographer, Paul Valéry with the sculptor Renée Vautier, 1934.

angle of incidence, which involves incalculable changes in refraction."[88] Given these circumstances, one might assume the artist was once again placed in an impossible situation. The work seemed to be swamped in the experiential contingencies of viewing. But unlike poetry, whose words left the artist's control in the act of publication, with sculpture the artist could at least *potentially* control the situation of the work's reception. Thus Valéry turned his attention to the artist: "The work must therefore be conceived in a way that will satisfy the eye from an infinite number of possible positions, each of which may be related to an infinite number of possible angles of the light. Every step the observer takes, every hour of the day, every lamp that is lit, can endow the sculpture with a certain aspect which is quite different *from all the others*."[89] Once again the open-endedness of the beholder's reception of the work seemed to swamp any possible expression of intent. The work threatened to become an imponderable object of experience with every change in the angle of vision, every alteration in lighting. And yet, Valéry's ideal artist seemed to be defined by his capacity, or attempt, to master conditions beyond his control. Failure haunted the sculptor's slightest gesture: "So the artist has to make only the slightest move, and what he has just done to his work may at once appear regrettable. An improvement in relation to a given point of view is transformed, thanks to a slight movement, into a grave blunder. And the same applies to the slightest change of position in the source of light."[90] Valéry summed up the potentially disastrous situation: "Every moment of the sculptor's work is menaced by an *infinity of infinite* contingencies. He [or she] risks with each instant losing from one point of view what he has gained from another."[91] It was the artist's task to stare down the menace of infinite experiential regress that adheres to objecthood. The artist was someone who, *"while at work, has the ability to keep in mind all the necessary questions"* and "strives, through an incessant modulation, to link all the successive moments of execution with such a subtle feeling for form that it defies analysis."[92]

A few years earlier, Ezra Pound considered a similar set of problems with regard to the work of Constantin Brancusi. Brancusi, Pound wrote, pursued a "maddeningly more difficult exploration [than other sculptors] toward getting all the forms into one form."[93] The difficulty lay, he said, in making "every one of the thousand angles of approach to a statue . . . interesting." A successful sculpture, he insisted, was "one which gives satisfaction from no matter what angle of vision."[94] Pound, like Valéry, imagined a mode of intentionality that transcended any possible technical achievement. But that was not the point. The point, rather, was to saturate the work with as much technical and imaginative intentionality as the artist could manage. To act like God and to fail was to be an artist; to be a human and to fail was pitiable.

The situation that Valéry described in "My Bust" was one in which the artist was the work's primordial beholder. What happened when this intimate producer/consumer relation was broken? This was the central problem of poetic or musical *performance.* It was the *ontological* break, both spatial and temporal, between writer and reader that made Valéry skeptical of literature at large (that is, when he was not celebrating this break, as I will discuss in the next sections). "I have always regarded literature with great doubts as to its true value," Valéry observed in his extraordinary "Letter about Mallarmé" of 1927.[95] Why? Because literature lent itself to modes of reception that were ontologically impossible to master, and, what is worse, this unpredictability was often courted by writers. Valéry presented a case against linguistic expression by virtue of its promiscuity:

> The magic spell literature can exert on others implies—by the very nature of language—a quantity of errors in comprehension, and since those misunderstandings are so necessary that *the direct and perfect transmission of an author's thought,* if such a thing were possible, *would entail the suppression and almost the obliteration of the finest artistic effects,* it follows that anyone who reflects on this situation is likely to feel a certain distaste for spending his time in speculating about the inexact, or in trying to provoke others into having astonishing thoughts and emotions as little foreseen by ourselves as the consequences of a spontaneous act might be.[96]

Literature was both limited and liberated by its suggestive capacities. And it was this very suggestiveness—the openness of its signs to unforeseeably various readings—that rendered it insufficient as an intentional medium. Its insufficiency lay in its seemingly foundational failure to achieve the *"direct and perfect transmission of an author's thought."* Of course it was not as if Valéry thought the latter possible, but one had to take aim at the impossible and to expose oneself to failure. The stakes were different with literature, as contingency was not something the writer could even potentially control. This was the difference between Valéry and his master, Mallarmé. "Where I saw only conventions," Valéry explained, "he tended to suppose a hidden necessity." It was Mallarmé's "idealism," the way he "burdened himself with verbal ideas taken from the Philosophers (Hegel)," that marked the divide between Valéry and the Symbolist generation.[97] It was Hegel's *Logic* that inspired Mallarmé's theory of chance: "Science's job . . . consists in grasping the necessity hidden under the appearance of contingent being."[98] Even more ambitiously, Hegel insisted in *Reason in History* that "philosophical reflection has no other object than to get rid of what is accidental."[99] Mallarmé's (and Hegel's) unified science was unavailable to Valéry; literary science was defeated by the actual sciences of the day. Whereas Mallarmé's idealism permitted him to imagine the "perfect transmission" of his ideas to his readers (even if they did not recognize it), for Valéry this was a game of chance, sheer *accident,* at least for the writer. Valéry continued:

> Even when those incalculable reactions of the reader are favorable to our work, as sometimes happens, and infinitely sweet to our happily surprised vanity, still a deeper pride complains of being offended in its rigor. It wants nothing to do with a fame that is only an accidental and external attribute of the person, and it does not hesitate to make us feel all the wide distance that it places between *being* and *seeming*.[100]

A chance meeting of author and reader was no meeting at all. And for Valéry the only kind of meeting literature *could* offer was a chance one. When it came to literature, any "proposition involving . . . an author, a work, a spectator . . . is meaningless."[101]

Then again, and from a seemingly different angle, Valéry saw the sign's musicality, its suggestiveness, as the mark of its intrinsic theatricality. Which is to say it was not exactly the work's open-endedness that made literature so flawed, but rather the author's anxiety about that openness that undermined the work's authority over the reader. The author's necessary awareness of the endless suggestiveness of his signs led inexorably to a kind of morbid self-consciousness that seemed to adhere to every word. Valéry "could not think of Mallarmé without *egotism,*" because he could not detach the writer's words from the writer's efforts to make his words mean.[102] "*Homo Scriptor,* the man with a pen, cannot help thinking about the effect on his reader of what he puts down on paper," Valéry reflected in an essay on Gérard de Nerval.[103] Words, like the throw of the dice, cannot abolish chance, but the author could not help but imagine that he could. The author "gambles, unconsciously or otherwise, on the power of words." And it is this *sense* behind the words of a desire for authorial control that infects the written word like a poison. It is as though the moment the author tries to enforce his meaning, the question of his sincerity is put in doubt. "But the certainty that such a calculation must have taken place inevitably awakens in the critical reader a certain presumption of *qualified sincerity* . . . he knows that the intention or the vocation to influence others makes us other than ourselves."[104] Ultimately, Valéry could not decide whether theatricality was a matter of the author's attempt to control his words or the corrupting influence of the words themselves. Valéry often seemed to slide between the two. Consider this: "Literature corrupts everything it deals with, since it is in its essence an unnatural development of the powers of language, and that there is no form of sincerity . . . that it can express which may not leave us with the thought, that they are the most deliberate, the most cunning of artifices."[105] When language assumes full agency, it also assumes total deception (no human agency can compete with its illicit demands). Nonetheless, it might be more correct to say that Valéry's putative aversion to the open-endedness of words was ultimately an aversion to the (putative or projected) insincerity of the author. It was as though the author, simply by using words to describe things, made his words unnatural, diverting them from their natural course. On this view, even the most sincere renunciation of authorial control—Mallarmé's desired "elocutionary disappearance into his words"—not only could not abolish authorship but also came to feel like insincerity itself.

If the writer dealt in incalculables when he considered the reader, then the photographer seemed to present something closer to Valéry's favored dialectic of intentionality and chance. "The writer who depicts a landscape or a face, no matter how skillful he may be at his craft, will suggest as many different visions as he has readers," Valéry explained in a 1939 essay on photography.[106] As a counter to literature's affective promiscuity, photography enforced a kind of "eviction of the word by the image." "Bromide proves stronger than ink," he observed, "whenever the thing speaks for itself . . . without having recourse to the wholly arbitrary transmissions of language."[107] Against language's arbitrariness of association, photography offered especially "natural" signs. But Valéry immediately turned photography's strength into its weakness. Photography was really useful for its negative definition of literature: it "discourages us from describing."[108] The "true nature" of literature was revealed by comparison with photography's grasp of the "mere presence of things."[109] Moreover, photography, as a strictly nonart medium, helped define the ontological status of art. After photography had done its job of "apprehending sensible things," then it became clear: *"All the rest is literature."*[110]

Valéry went on to offer a "Philosophy of Photography," the results of which are unexpected.[111] Given his commitments to chance and the nonintentional, photography came up surprisingly short. He so thoroughly excluded photography from the space of art that he collapsed it into complete transparency with the world it records. "The snapshot," he declared, "has rectified our errors . . . it shows us what we would see if we were uniformly sensitive to everything."[112] It solves the "ancient and difficult problem of *objectivity.*" But the thought of objectivity was soon eclipsed by a more profound reflection on the philosophical implications of the medium. "Is there any emotion more deeply philosophical," Valéry wondered, "than the one we experience as we anxiously wait—beneath that rather diabolical red light which turns a glowing cigarette into a green diamond—for the emergence to visibility of that mysterious *latent image*"?[113] Rather than a simple capture of "sensible things," the photograph became an allegory for consciousness itself. No longer focused on the photograph's contents, Valéry turned his attention to the other aspect of the medium, the way the image develops in the darkroom, a space whose function is not unlike that of the kiln for the ceramicist. It is here that chance reemerges at the center of the artistic act. "Little by little, here and there, a few spots emerge like the first stuttering of awakening consciousness," he observed.[114] And as the image slowly emerges from the blank paper, the mind gathers its thoughts: "Watching this configuration as its disparate elements, each one trivial in itself, proceed by leaps to form a recognizable picture, we cannot but think of certain precipitations as they occur in our minds, of memories that come into focus, of certitudes that suddenly crystallize, of the creation of certain rare lines of verse that fall into place, abruptly wresting themselves from the chaos of our inner speech."[115] It is as though the world captured by the photographic lens is the artist's own creation, his own thoughts projected outward. Watching the image emerge from the sensitized paper is like watching marks turn into meaning. And yet Valéry quickly closed the analogy, returning to the idea of objectivity as defining the photographer's "noble" task. It is the "self-denial and perseverance of the inventors" that "redounds upon the nation," he concluded, and not their special kind of verse.

Writing a few months later on the relation between performer and composer, Valéry again raised the skeptical situation. Speaking of the performer's freedom in relation to the composer's text, he observed that "there is no work, however fine, that is not susceptible of a wide variety of interpretations, all equally plausible."[116] And yet, despite this putatively fundamental open-endedness, Valéry still held that what the performer performs is an *interpretation* of the composer's intent. He closed the discussion by reflecting on the singular nature of the work by virtue of its openness to interpretation: "The richness of a work of art consists in the number of meanings or values it can assume, while still remaining itself."[117]

The Reader as Producer

Although it has gone unremarked in the literature, Valéry made one of the most decisive and influential turns in the history of modern literary thought. His emphasis throughout the writings discussed so far was on the author's imperative to closely control his words so as to calculate the desired effects on the reader, and then again on the impossibility, but potential desirability, of this mode of intentional communication. One of his most dramatic statements concerning the artist's prerogative to control the reader appears in an unlikely place, an essay on the art of Camille Corot:

> Delacroix, Wagner, Baudelaire—all great theorists, bent on dominating other souls by sensorial means. Their one dream was to create the irresistible effect—to intoxicate, or overwhelm. They looked to analysis to provide them with the keyboard on which to play, with certainty, on man's emotions, and they sought in abstract meditation the key to absolutely certain *action* upon their subject—man's nervous and psychic being. . . . [It was] the ambition of such violent and tormented minds, anxious to reach and as it were *possess* (in the diabolical sense of the term) that tender and hidden region of the soul by which it can be held and controlled entire, through

> the indirect path of the entrails and organic depths of being. They wish to enslave; . . . to bring us into bondage.[118]

Delacroix, Baudelaire, and Wagner formed an exclusive trinity of artists collectively "bent on dominating other minds by sensuous means." The beholder had no hope of resisting the effects of the artist playing him or her like an instrument. Valéry spoke of music more generally as the medium with "almost total powers of possession," because it "plays with life's depths, . . . rousing, soothing, exploring the whole nervous system—and all this by an almost instantaneous and irresistible agency": the musical capacity for control was the exact *opposite* of Corot's aims.[119] "Nothing could be remoter from Corot than the ambition of such violent and tormented minds." Although Corot started out with a strict pictorial method, he left it behind in the pursuit of "vagueness" and the "indefinable" emotion obtained by "improvisation," "chance," and "fortunate accidents."[120] This more "poetic" approach lends itself to a new form of *reception.* The viewer is now free to discover whatever meanings he or she finds in the work. "We have reasons for liking what we like," and what we like is outside the artist's control. What we like are works that "act upon us as an object would."[121] When "works of art are . . . objects in the material sense of the term," they of course bear no intended meaning.[122] Objects are significant from the perspective of the viewer; they apply only in *"each particular case."*[123] And the artwork as object, like any object in the world, is open to an "infinite number of interpretations."[124]

Valéry's most sustained reflection on the relation between artist and audience, art and objects, emerge within his "Reflections on Art," delivered before the Société Française de Philosophie in 1935. Here Valéry insisted on an absolute "nonidentification" between "producer and consumer."[125] It is a fundamental mistake, he averred, to imagine any "direct communication" between artist and audience. So "whenever you hear an artist say despairingly that he has not been able to express himself as he wished, he is under a misapprehension." And while this "absurdity" "may make the artist do his best to translate his thought into his work," the effort to express oneself to another is doomed to failure. "All the artist can do is to fashion *some thing,*" Valéry said, "that will produce a certain effect on someone else's mind."[126] And again, more succinctly still: "What we call a work of art is the result of an action whose *finite aim it is to provoke infinite developments in someone.*"[127] The relation of cause and effect in the work of art simply mirrors that of cause and effect in the world. Poems, according to Valéry, produce a kind of physiological reflex action in the reader, one whose effects are incalculably related to their cause.[128]

But Valéry offered his most peculiar assessment when he suggested that artistic intentionality, although of a rather literal kind, spelled the end of art. If the writer could "communicate directly" with the reader, then "all art would collapse."[129] It is important to see that the failure here is *not* that the work of art would become something like a telepathic device between writer and reader and therefore representation would be rendered meaningless. Rather, the ultimate aim of art is to generate unlimited effects in the reader; those effects would disappear without an independently productive reader. "The whole effect of art," Valéry explained, "would be impossible without the interposition, between the author and his audience, of a new and impenetrable element capable of acting upon other men's being." It is this "impenetrable element"—the artwork as object—that provokes the reader to become a writer. The function of the artist is not to create works of art, or even to express something through a medium, but to *"make others create."*[130] It is the strict "*independence* between the act and the result of the act" that opens up the space for the reader to become the writer.[131]

It is not as if Valéry was uninterested in the kinds of intentionality artworks embody; rather, he believed that the unreliability of communicating those intentions created an impossibly skeptical situation. Valéry clearly saw the difference in response required by works of art, as intended objects, versus objects more generally, but he found the distinction too capricious. "Colors and sounds," he stated, outside an intentional framework, "are indifferent to me: I perceive them but disregard them."[132] Although he was "vaguely affected" by everything in the world, "should the need or occasion arise, my attention would isolate the relation [between two forms] and, from a comparison of tones, I should derive some pictorial intention."[133] He called this transformative moment when his affects became organized "artistic or aesthetic attention." Nonetheless, he rejected the aesthetic attitude as too "restrictive," because the "art object is not constantly an art object, nor is it an art object for everyone."[134] Because artistic intentionality emerges as an issue only in specially restricted settings—studios or museums, for instance—and it does not follow the work into the world at large, it can be of only limited interest to those for whom these settings matter—artists.

On occasion Valéry played the part of "creative viewer," as though to exemplify the limitations of intentionality. One vivid instance occurs in his description of an unnamed Corot engraving. Although it is a landscape without any identifiable subject matter, it nonetheless suggested to Valéry "a delicious episode from *Parsifal*."[135] While Corot did not—indeed, could not—intend anything of the sort, it is the virtue of landscape that it evokes in the viewer a vision from the past. In Valéry's case, it was a highly specific vision: "At dawn, after the endless night of torment and despair, King Amfortas tortured by an ambiguous wound, mysteriously, voluptuously inflicted as a punishment on soul and body alike, has his litter carried out into the country air—The Impure One, come to breathe the cool of the morning."[136] As though his description were not explicitly subjective enough, he insisted that the landscape evokes "only a bar or two" of Wagner's score.

The dramatic oscillations in Valéry's views about intention are most evident in "Odds and Ends," a collection of thoughts written between 1924 and 1930. There he explained, "One is led to the *Form* adopted by a desire to leave the smallest possible share to the reader."[137] Just a few pages later he offered a very different picture of the reader's share: "Once a work is published its author's interpretation of it has no more validity than anyone else's. If I make Pierre's portrait and someone finds it more like Jacques than like Pierre, there's nothing to be said against this; his opinion is as good as mine. My intention was merely *my* intention and the work is—what it is."[138] Valéry continued the thought in his "Commentaries on *Charmes*" (1928): "If a painter does a portrait of *Socrates* and a passer-by recognizes *Plato,* all the creator's explanations, protests, and excuses will not change this immediate recognition."[139] Of course Valéry was right to say that the artist's intention in making the portrait of Pierre or Socrates does not count as making it look like either Pierre or Socrates. But Valéry seemed to take this (inevitable) consequence of (mistaken) viewer response as signaling something more than simply an unsuccessful work. Rather, Valéry wanted to see that when someone sees the picture as Jacques or Plato, the work actually becomes a portrait of that person. Which is to say, Valéry saw the inevitable limitations of the production of intended effects—that they are not surefire—as the license for an affectively generated aesthetics: the work means whatever the audience thinks it means, regardless of what the author intended.

At the same moment as the "Commentaries" Valéry offered a more limited, or perhaps confused, assessment of this "fundamental condition of literature":

> One must reckon with the element of misunderstanding which is a fundamental condition of literature. It often happens that an attentive reader . . . will discover in a given text intentions and hidden folds the author did not know were there and would never have seen without this reader's intervention. . . . So you see a work is fashioned under such conditions that it completely escapes the author once it leaves his hands. It is virtually impossible for him to make an exact reckoning of the way in which that work will be received, judged, and understood. . . . Paradoxical as it may seem, inspiration is more likely to come from the reader than from the author.[140]

Here Valéry suggests that the reader's "intervention" is to see something that the author intended but did not see when he made the poem. He further suggests that the poet, at some limit case of intentionality, could potentially "make an exact reckoning" of how a work would be received. But these two claims stand in tension with Valéry's more ongoing claim (at least after 1927) that a poem, once it is written, is an object for the reader's productive usage, that it "completely escapes the author" upon publication.

If we are to believe Valéry's account of the turn from a rigorous intentionalism to an equally rigorous anti-intentionalism, it revolves around an encounter with the philosopher Alain. In a story recounted in his "Commentaries on *Charmes*"—his most influential statement of anti-intentionalism—Valéry explains how a friend lent a copy of his last book of poems to the philosopher. Alain returned the volume to Valéry with extensive commentaries filling up the margins. Reading over the philosopher's notes, Valéry was forced to reconsider the nature of authorial intention: "Does he understand you? . . . Has he unfolded your aims?" he wondered to himself.[141] His answer is clear: no. Or rather, there is no problem of meaning. Even to seek a meaning in a poem is misguided. Why? Because "my verses have whatever meaning is given them. The one I give them suits only myself and does not contradict anyone else. It is an error contrary to the nature of poetry, and one which may even be fatal to it, to claim that for each poem there is a corresponding true meaning, unique and conformable to, or identical with, some thought of the author's."[142] It is left to the reader to create whatever meaning the work might have. Like any physical object, "the action of a text modifies minds, each according to his nature and state, provoking combinations latent within a certain head, but whatever reaction is thus produced, the text is . . . capable of indefinitely generating other phenomena in other circumstances or in another person."[143] It is the writer's job to fashion the poem-object, the meaning of which is generated by its various respondents. Alain's interpretation is as good as any reader's, including the author's: "Once a work is finished and presented, whether in verse or prose, its author can propose or affirm nothing about it that would have any more weight or would explain it more exactly than what anyone else might say. . . . An author can, no doubt, inform us of his intentions; but it is not a question of these; it is a question of what subsists, what he has made independent of himself."[144]

Once the author has released the work into the world, its meaning is beyond the control of the author and becomes a purely public property. "How can people manage to cling to their opinion once it has been voiced and has parted company with what created it?" he mused.[145] And again, in an essay looking back on *Le Cimetière marin:* "Whatever the author may have *wanted to say,* he has written what he has written. Once published, a text is like an apparatus that anyone may use as he will and according to his ability: it is not certain that the one who constructed it can use it better than another."[146] It is the notion of the work of art as *apparatus* that is perhaps the most influential claim in Valéry's canon, and it is this idea that Benjamin picks up in "The

Author as Producer" (1934). According to Benjamin, "a writer's production must . . . place an improved apparatus at the reader's disposal." "This apparatus," he continues, "will be the better . . . the more readers or spectators it turns into collaborators."[147] To see the reader as a collaborator, one who refunctions the artist's work for his or her own ends, is to take seriously Valéry's suggestion that the work of art is an object, like other objects in the world, something that subsists beyond every artistic agency.

I have traced Valéry's commitment to anti-intentionalism in such detail because he virtually invented the position that dominated literary theory from this point forward. In William Wimsatt and Monroe Beardsley's version of idea, the poem is "detached from the author at birth and goes about the world beyond his power to intend about it or control it. The poem belongs to the public. It is embodied in language, the peculiar possession of the public."[148] The publicly available poem, what was called in the French context a *text* rather than a work, seemingly detached the artist from the "work" while still maintaining a sense of its nonprivate meaning. The public meaning of the work was intended to sustain the difference between the text and the reader, while still insisting on the ontological gap between writer and text. Thus Wimsatt and Beardsley ask us to consult our "grammars, dictionaries, and all the literature which is the source of dictionaries . . . all that makes a language and culture," to secure the meaning of a text without making any fallacious appeal to the author. But what could that "public" information actually provide us? If a word in the dictionary has more than one meaning, or contrary meanings, then on what grounds could we choose one over another? One can only admit or rule out evidence—choose one "public" meaning over another—by appeal to the author's intention.[149] While Wimsatt and Beardsley follow Valéry in his anti-intentionalism, they cannot abide by his affirmation of readerly affect. Although Wimsatt and Beardsley rejected what they called the "Affective Fallacy"—the notion that the reader's experience creates or produces the work's meaning—more recent commentators have shown that they could not logically sustain that critique if they maintained a strong anti-intentionalist position. Simply put, if the work does not mean what the author intends it to mean, there is no alternative available but that the reader is the one who creates meaning.

At the same moment as Wimsatt and Beardsley, Maurice Blanchot offered a similar critique of intention of "public" meaning in *The Space of Literature* (1955). Citing Valéry, Blanchot explained that "whatever [the writer] does, the work withdraws him from what he does and from what he can do."[150] As the work withdraws from the author, so the reader enters into that gap and recreates the book herself. "The reader becomes an author in reverse," Blanchot reflected. "The true reader . . . is apt to return, drawn by an imperceptible pull, toward the various prefigurations of the reader which have caused him to be present in advance at the hazardous experience of the book."[151]

So by the time Roland Barthes published "The Death of the Author" in 1967, Valéry's double position—anti-intentionalism and readerly affect—was already established as a central option within the literary theoretical canon. Indeed, in his brief history of "writers who have long since attempted to loosen the Author's sway," Barthes places Valéry at the center. Valéry, he says, despite some hesitations, "never stopped calling into question and deriding the Author; he stressed the linguistic and, as it were, 'hazardous' nature of his activity, and throughout his prose works he militated in favor of the essentially verbal condition of literature, in the face of which all recourse to the writer's interiority seemed to him pure superstition."[152] And as Barthes further suggests, Valéry's critique of intention simultaneously led to the effort to "restore the place of the reader."[153]

Despite its current canonicity, Valéry's delineation of a publicly defined work of art did not go unchallenged at the time. Picasso provided a cogent, if off-the-cuff, assessment of Valéry's claims. Picasso knew Valéry from their collaborative production of an edition of Valéry's *La Jeune Parque* in 1921, which included a lithographic frontispiece portrait of the poet. It was an unhappy encounter, at least for Picasso.[154] Valéry's poetics, he later said, were a variant of the "old grab bag" theory of art.[155] Picasso took issue above all with Valéry's view that a *"creator is one who makes others create."*[156] If the viewer was a creator on par with the artist, then it followed that the work was open "for everyone to reach into and pull out what he himself has put in." Valéry proposed exactly that: to each his own. "I want my paintings to be able to defend themselves, to resist the invader," Picasso retorted. He went on:

> Valéry used to say, "I write half the poem. The reader writes the other half." That's all right for him, maybe, but I don't want there to be three or four or a thousand possibilities of interpreting *my* canvas. I want there to be only one and in that one, to some extent, the possibility of recognizing nature.[157]

The point of Picasso's censure was not to suggest that nature carries an independent meaning that the artist could secure, but to say that whatever meaning the work expresses, it has that expression by virtue of the maker's intention alone, and not by virtue of a possible viewer's—necessarily unlimited—intentions. If the work does not carry one meaning, Picasso argued, then it carries an infinite amount of meanings, one for each viewer. Of course what Picasso got wrong about Valéry is that Valéry did not actually think that there were a thousand possibilities of *interpreting* his work, but that the reader is actually making a new work when he or she reads it. Thus the force of Valéry's minidialogue: "I understand this text badly. Never mind! I'm discovering fine things, he's pulling them out of me. . . . It is my *error* that is the author."[158] (And yet, even here, Valéry continues to suggest that there *is* an author, and that he can recognize the author's intentions, he just chooses to ignore them to make his own work.) Then again, if all readers are actually pulling themselves from the work, as Picasso lamented and Valéry seemingly celebrated, then they are not interpreting a work but creating it for themselves.

"Verbal Materialism"

Are we left with two Valérys, one concerned with the author, the other with the work of readers who encounter the text like an object? What could possibly bind the two accounts of meaning—intentionalist and anti-intentionalist, authorial and affective—that seem to bifurcate Valéry's career? Which, if any, is the "real" Valéry? Is he the brutal scientist of form, seeking to produce the most "direct and irresistible effects" on his readers? Or is he the linguistic and scientific skeptic who knows that *"the man who thinks he is having an influence is not* (or is having one contrary to his intentions)."[159] Is there a core around which both ideas circulate?

While an author may not be able to control reference, he may nonetheless produce autonomous configurations of language, what Valéry simply called "form." Strip away the author and the reader, and we are left with material form. According to Valéry: "It is the form alone which commands and survives. It is the sound, the rhythm, the physical proximity of words, their effects of induction or their mutual influences which dominate at the expense of their capacity for being consummated in a defined and particular meaning."[160] But it would be a mistake to think that Valéry's problem with conventional approaches to poetry was with the reduction of poems to a "particular meaning." Rather, he described a mode of poetic production that is devoid of *any* meaning. It is the poem as sound and rhythm and the physical characteristics of the page that generate unpredictable sensations in the reader; poems generate personal poems. "The action of the text's presence modifies minds," Valéry affirmed again and again, "to each according to its nature and state."[161]

From beginning to end, Valéry assumed that poems are an "action." Writing has a direct effect on the reader; only after 1927 did he see those effects as multiplied to infinity. Each body that comes into contact with the work generates a new affect. It follows that every encounter with a work generates a different affect depending on the viewer's state of mind and body and the physical setting of the work.

What binds the early Valéry and the later, then, is a view of the work as a material action and *not as a representation.* For this reason Deleuze and McCarthy are right to see Valéry as committed to an aesthetic of "blood," or to a "direct action on the nervous system." Adorno similarly traced the inner logic of Valéry's poetics when he wrote that for Valéry "form involves no consideration of the receiver or the producer."[162] Rather, the work contains a living "material substratum," the "language of things themselves."[163] That is to say, language and meaning leave the hands of living agents and get established in the things themselves. The literary action that Adorno describes is the "eruptive revelation of negative experience," the expressive emergence of a forgotten and repressed language of suffering that "precedes objectness."[164]

What makes Valéry a writer of "life and death," then, is his view of the work of art as something stripped of its meaning and replaced by its agency. When Valéry was asked what his poems meant, he turned the question around to show that they did not in fact mean anything, but they *did* something: "If I am questioned; if anyone wonders (as happens sometimes quite peremptorily) what I 'wanted to say' in a certain poem, I reply that I did not *want to say* but *wanted to do,* and that it was the intention of *doing* which *wanted* what I *said.*"[165] Valéry's contorted formulation captures the shape of the thought it expresses. The sentence turns on two opposed meanings of *intention.* The first involves an all-too-conventional notion of intention: what an author wants to communicate, his message, as it is delivered in the poem. As Valéry suggests, this is an unsupportable (and uninteresting) notion of a literary intention. But the second meaning strips the poem of human intention altogether and makes *language* an agent; his words make him do what *they* want him to do. This is, as I have argued throughout this book, the canonical move of anti-intentionalism: to set up a false notion of intention—art as the communication of an inner message or preformed idea, for instance—and replace it with an equally false ideal of art as a machine to produce affects. Of course as I have tried to suggest in my discussion of Valéry's engagement with chance, he was also fully aware—and fully practiced—a mode of *mimetic* intentionality.

Fictive Politics

"Law is the *interlude between acts* of force," Valéry observed in a series of notes titled "On Political Parties."[166] Laws, like predictions, are pure fictions. And behind every fiction lies its truth: material force. Many years later, Jacques Derrida followed Valéry's thought when he redescribed conflicts of interpretation as disguised "conflicts of force."[167] Derrida's well-known "substitution of mark for sign" further followed Valéry's course in their shared ambition to establish the authority of readerly affect.[168] Marks, by their nature, mean different things to different readers, while a work, composed of words, has only one meaning, the author's.[169] For Derrida as for Valéry, because there is no possibility of discovering the correct interpretation of a mark, every act of interpretation is necessarily the "imposition of meaning."[170]

For Valéry the result of the redescription of signs as marks and interpretations as impositions was to show that "everything pertaining to *practical politics* is necessarily *superficial*."[171] Valéry suggests a simple reversal of priorities. In place of practical politics (parties, policies, reform) appears a more effective means of control—*fictive* politics (words and ideas). To found a society based on policies, Valéry asserts, glossing Montesquieu, is misguided and destined to failure. "Mere coercion of bodies by bodies," he explains, "can never found an order." To truly persuade the masses, "fictional forces are needed."[172]

Anti-intentionalism is the technology that provides the means of warfare. As a material thing, a word can be deployed by and against the public will. On this account, Valéry's literary and political ontologies are identical. This identity clearly emerged in his 1933 essay "Literature and Politics." "Nothing is more remarkable," he observed, than "to see that ideas, separated from the intellect that conceived them, isolated from the conditions of their birth, . . . can become *political agents* . . . weapons."[173] When words no longer mean what one intends them to mean, then political agency is no longer tied to political belief. In their place are bodies doing battle with a new kind of weapon: "Language is good, it does its job when used . . . like a tool—pliers or a drill—or a kind of currency—or a weapon."[174] "Verbal materialism" was Valéry's weapon. The verbal materialist "can *look down* on . . . all who are enslaved to words by credulity—who *must* believe that their speech . . . signifies some reality. But as for you, you know that the *reality of discourse* is only the words and the forms."[175] Beneath every intention, behind every meaning, beyond every representation lie the blood and viscera of the form-object. And when one experiences the great work of art, its form-matter can plunge into the reader's bloodstream and infect the reader like a disease. By its very nature, the work as object "acts so powerfully, grips the viscera, collapses the diaphragm. Indeed, a certain note in a certain register attacks the substratum of life."[176]

At the beginning of *The Logic of Sense* (1969), Deleuze seizes on Valéry's materialism. "Valéry had a profound idea: what is most deep is the skin," Deleuze reflects. Deleuze does not offer a citation, but the phrase is taken from Valéry's *Idée Fixe,* a book Valéry described as "exclusively for the medical profession"; it was published by a pharmaceutical firm.[177] Those beholden to the philosophy of depth, Deleuze insists, will inevitably be wounded by Valéry's intuition. "The more events traverse the entire, depthless extension," Deleuze writes, "the more they affect bodies which they cut and bruise."[178] Deleuze could quote Valéry's fictive Doctor on this account: "However much we dig beneath the surface, we remain . . . ectodermal." It is "viscera" all the way down.[179]

Acknowledgments

THIS BOOK HAS BEEN MANY YEARS IN THE MAKING. I wrote a dissertation largely on Matisse, but what I wrote then has not found its way in here, except around the edges and maybe in negative. There is no doubt my advisers (Whitney Davis, T. J. Clark, and Martin Jay) shaped my way of seeing, even if they won't find all the evidence of that here. Davis's boundless intelligence, analytic rigor, and unflagging support have been a major source of encouragement for many years. Clark's teachings and writings on modernism have been my most constant source of inspiration during the past twenty years. My debt to him is unlimited.

My short time studying with Michael Fried and Walter Benn Michaels at Johns Hopkins University took effect many years later with the force of a *Nachträglichkeit.* Reading Michaels's *The Shape of the Signifier* just after I completed my dissertation was a disaster for my work; things have improved since then. At nearly the same moment, Fried's *Menzel's Realism* altered, or showed me, a way of seeing. Fried's writings have been a major source of inspiration throughout the writing of this book. Independent of my encounter with Michaels's and Fried's work, but ultimately related to it, was my reading of Ruth Leys's writings on mimesis, hypnosis, and trauma. Any reader of *Against Affective Formalism* will see the impact of *Trauma: A Genealogy* (2000). My dialogues with Ruth during the past few years have been among the most productive in the shaping of this book (although she is blameless for its faults).

Eric Michaud's groundbreaking histories of modernist ideology, especially in *La Fin du salut par l'image* (1992), were centrally important for me early on. For many years now Charles Palermo has been a constant interlocutor and an even more constant friend. Charles has been with this project (and several others) from its inception, and he has helped me say what I want to say in the way I want to say it. His comments have been invariably on the mark; his friendship, invaluable.

Marnin Young has been a sympathetic sparring partner for years. Brian Kane has been a model of generosity and courage for as long as I can remember.

Michael Schreyach has been an unbroken source of support and a cherished friend for a long time.

I owe a debt of thanks to friends and colleagues who read aspects of the book, including Jennifer Ashton (who offered invaluable advice and suggestions), Howard Caygill, Michael Clune, Lisa Florman, Gordon Hughes, Jeremy Melius, Richard Neer, and Robert Pippin. Pippin's work in particular has been crucial for my understanding of Bergson. Early on in the project I received important feedback from my colleagues at the Getty, including Tom Crow, Simon Critchley, David Doris, Lynn Hunt, and Bertram Kaschek. Other friends and colleagues along the way have been Yve-Alain Bois, Jean Campbell, Jérôme Cornette, Stephanie D'Allesandro, Rachael DeLue, Brigid Doherty, John Elderfield, Graham Finlay, Dani Follett, Hal Foster, Michael Golec, Robert Hobbs, John Lysaker, Walter Melion, Eric Michaud, Andrew Mitchell, Alex Potts, Michael Schreffler, Blakey Vermeule, Aron Vinegar, and Anne Wagner.

Georges Matisse has been especially generous and patient with his assistance in tracking down lesser-known works of Henri Matisse—there are surprisingly many.

Parts of this book were written with the support of the Huntington Library, Deutscher Akademischer Austauschdienst, and a postdoctoral fellowship at the Getty Research Institute. I received generous support for illustrations from a Dean's Faculty Research Grant at Virginia Commonwealth University, from Emory College at Emory University, and from the College Art Association Millard Meiss Publication Fund.

This book is dedicated to Bridget and Nicholas. Their love makes everything else small in comparison. The book would not have been started or finished without them.

Notes

Introduction

1. There are numerous studies of the debates generated by Descartes's representational epistemology. The ones I have found most useful are three works by John W. Yolton, *Thinking Matter: Materialism in Eighteenth-Century Britain* (Minneapolis: University of Minnesota Press, 1983); *Perceptual Acquaintance: From Descartes to Reid* (Minneapolis: University of Minnesota Press, 1984); and *Perception and Reality: A History from Descartes to Kant* (Ithaca, N.Y.: Cornell University Press, 1996); and Steven M. Nadler's *Arnauld and the Cartesian Philosophy of Ideas* (Princeton, N.J.: Princeton University Press, 1989). For Yolton and Nadler, the succession of materialist critiques of Descartes throughout the eighteenth century and beyond, especially the one that emerged with the writings of Thomas Reid, were fundamentally misguided. According to Nadler and Yolton, a better way to understand Cartesianism is to see it as a special form of representational thinking that avoided falsely skeptical consequences. "For many of these early modern thinkers," Nadler writes of the Cartesian tradition, "ideas are acts of the mind, not objects of quasi-observation" (9). Nadler and Yolton elucidate and defend the "act theory of ideas." According to this theory, Nadler says, "the mind [is put] in direct cognitive contact with the external world—no intervening proxy, no *tertium quid*, gets in the way" (6). What is important to stress here is that the Cartesian notion of "direct realism" was founded upon "direct *cognitive* contact" between perceiver and world. Direct realism, that is, is not a material act of "touching" or the unmediated presence of objects to the mind or body. To think representation and directness, idea and embodiment, together is the aim of this study and of my interpretation of Matisse.

2. Alexander Rodchenko, "Working with Mayakovsky" (1939), in *Rodchenko and the Arts of Revolutionary Russia*, ed. David Elliott (New York: Pantheon, 1979), 102; Piet Mondrian, "Natural and Abstract Reality: A Trialogue," in *The New Art—The New Life: The Collected Writings of Piet Mondrian*, ed. and trans. Harry Holtzman and Martin S. James (New York: Da Capo, 1993), 114. There are major disagreements even here about the status of art. Mondrian, for instance, never wavered from the view that contemporary conditions were not right for the dissolution of art into life. ("Only as 'work of art' can Neo-Plasticism be realized as 'our environment,'" he explained in 1922. Piet Mondrian, "The Realization of Neo-Plasticism in the Distant Future and in Architecture Today" [1922], in *The New Art*, 170.) Rodchenko, on the other hand, after 1919 condemned outright art and representation: "The Productivist Group stands for ruthless war against art in general," he and Varvara Stepanova wrote in "The Program of the Productivist Group" of 1920, rpt. in *The Tradition of Constructivism*, ed. Stephen Bann (New York: Da Capo, 1974), 20.

3. Jacques Derrida, "The Parergon" (1979), in *The Truth in Painting*, trans. Geoffrey Bennington and Ian McLeod (Chicago: Chicago University Press, 1987), 73. Derrida's most sustained critique of the antirepresentational impulse appears in "Sending: On Representation,"

trans. Peter Caws and Mary Ann Caws, in *Transforming the Hermeneutic Context: From Nietzsche to Nancy,* ed. Gayle L. Ormiston and Alan D. Schrift (Albany: State University of New York Press, 1990), 107–38. Derrida's claims deserve citing here: "We might say . . . that a criticism or a deconstruction of representation would remain feeble, vain, and irrelevant if it were to lead to some rehabilitation of immediacy, of original simplicity, of presence without repetition or delegation, if it were to induce a criticism of calculable objectivity, of criticism, of science, of technique, or of political representation. The worst regressions can put themselves at the service of this antirepresentative prejudice" ("Sending," 119).

4. Henri Bergson, *Time and Free Will: An Essay on the Immediate Data of Consciousness,* trans. F. L. Pogson (New York: Macmillan, 1913), 171; Bergson, *Oeuvres,* ed. André Robinet, centennial ed. (Paris: Universitaires de France, 1963), 112.

5. Matisse, quoted in Georges Duthuit, *The Fauvist Painters* (1949), trans. Ralph Manheim (New York: Wittenborn, Schultz, 1950), 85.

6. Henri Matisse, *Matisse on Art,* ed. Jack Flam, rev. ed. (Berkeley: University of California Press, 1995), 185.

7. Henri Matisse, interview by Pierre Courthion, 1941, transcript, p. 132, Pierre Courthion Collection, J. Paul Getty Research Library, Los Angeles, Calif., my translation. (Throughout, unless otherwise credited, all translations are my own.) The theory of affective energies or "forces" was being defined in Matisse's time by Freud in his materialist writings of the 1890s. In a May 1895 letter to Wilhelm Fliess, Freud described his aim to "investigate what form the theory of mental functioning assumes when one introduces the notion of quantity into it, a sort of economy of nervous forces." *The Complete Letters of Sigmund Freud to Wilhelm Fliess, 1887–1904,* ed. and trans. J. M. Mason (Cambridge, Mass.: Harvard University Press, 1985), 129. Pathologies are understood to be quantitatively linked to displacements, investments, discharges of what Freud later called "quota of affect," which "corresponds to the drive in so far as the latter has become detached from representation and finds expression, proportionate to its quantity, in processes which are sensed as affects." Sigmund Freud, "Repression," in *The Standard Edition of the Complete Psychological Works of Sigmund Freud,* ed. and trans. James Strachey (London: Hogarth Press, 1975), 14:152. These are obviously complicated matters, and they cannot be fully treated here. What matters from my perspective is the relationship between affectivity and representation. The currently dominant account, the one I am considering here—offered by Jean-François Lyotard, Gilles Deleuze, and Michel Henry among others—construes affect "detached from representation" as the pure presentation of the drive, dispensing entirely with the unconscious or redefining the unconscious as the space of affects. But as Mikkel Borch-Jacobsen has shown, it is a mistake to oppose affect and representation. According to Freud, the instinct or drive is represented by a *Vorstellung,* which itself gets repressed. Affects, that is, are *displacements* of the drive and not the drive itself. See Mikkel Borch-Jacobsen, "The Unconscious, Nonetheless," in *The Emotional Tie: Psychoanalysis, Mimesis, and Affect,* trans. Angela Brewer and X. P. Callahan (Stanford, Calif.: Stanford University Press, 1993), 123–54. While my account is indebted to, and in broad agreement with, Borch-Jacobsen's analysis, I use the term *affect* here and throughout in the sense provided by current-day affect theorists who affirm its opposition to representational mediation (for Borch-Jacobsen, affect theory substantially distorts the Freudian sense of the term).

8. Éric Alliez and Jean-Claude Bonne's whole enterprise is founded on the distinction between the qualitative or psychological theory of color (aligned with Delacroix, van Gogh, Gauguin, Cézanne, and Kandinsky) and Matisse's quantitative or affective theory of color. As they put it, "For Matisse there is a clear difference between vital expressivity and psychological expressionism." Éric Alliez and Jean-Claude Bonne, *La Pensée-Matisse: Portrait de l'artiste en*

hyperfauve (Paris: Le Passage, 2005), 77; see also the section titled "Expressivité vitale vs expressionnisme psychologique," 61–64. This difference is anything but clear in Matisse, but as I am arguing, both accounts are mistaken, and for the same reasons: the denial of representation.

More generally, Deleuzian discourse categorically separates affect and emotion. According to Brian Massumi, emotion is defined as "the conventional, consensual point of insertion of intensity into semantically and semiotically formed progressions, into narrativizable action-reaction circuits, into function and meaning." Emotion, therefore, in representing affect, is also its "capture and closure." Brian Massumi, "The Autonomy of Affect," in *Parables for the Virtual: Movement, Affect, Sensation* (Durham, N.C.: Duke University Press, 2002), 28. I consider the larger claims of affect theory in my review of *The Affect Theory Reader.* See Todd Cronan, "'Radically Private and Pretty Uncoded,'" *Radical Philosophy* 172 (March/April 2012): 51–53.

9. Yve-Alain Bois, "Matisse," in Hal Foster, Rosalind Krauss, Yve-Alain Bois, and Benjamin H. D. Buchloh, *Art since 1900: Modernism, Antimodernism, Postmodernism,* vol. 1, *1900 to 1944* (London: Thames & Hudson, 2004), 104.

10. Yve-Alain Bois, "On Matisse: The Blinding," trans. Greg Sims, *October* 68 (1994): 92, 100; hereafter cited in the text.

11. Bergson, *Time and Free Will,* 15; Bergson, *Oeuvres,* 14.

12. Yve-Alain Bois, *Painting as Model* (Cambridge: MIT Press, 1990), 203.

13. Roland Barthes, "The Death of the Author" (1967), in *Image-Music-Text,* trans. Stephen Heath (New York: Macmillan, 1978), 147; hereafter cited in the text.

14. Immanuel Kant, *Critique of Judgment* (1790), trans. Werner S. Pluhar (Indianapolis: Hackett, 1987), 61. More recently, Kant too has been taken up by affect theorists. What has struck them is the idea, as Kant repeatedly puts it in the *Lectures on Metaphysics,* that form is "the manner in which we are affected [affiziert] by objects"; it is the manner as distinct from our knowledge of "content" or from empirical contact with objects. Which is to say on a certain reading Kantian formalism is a matter of the affects, of subjective intuition, while traditional notions of literary critical or art historical formalism, often thought to emerge from Kant's *Third Critique,* is really something entirely different from what Kant introduced. Most post-Kantian formalisms contend that form is something that inheres *in* the object, while for Kant form is projected into an object by the intuitional activities of its maker or beholders.

15. Ibid. Robert Pippin considers these issues in "The Significance of Taste: Kant, Aesthetic and Reflective Judgment," *Journal of the History of Philosophy* 34, no. 4 (October 1996): 549–69.

16. Of course Kant does not want to simply exchange judgment for sensation, thereby rendering the aesthetic judgment something overly conceptual. Rather than affirm concepts over sensations, Kant continually stresses the centrality of "inner sense and sensation" in every aesthetic judgment. I will call this "inner sense" the viewer's response insofar as it is understood as a response the artist could have intended. What is crucial about the latter, as opposed to affects, is that it is open to dispute.

17. Kant, *Critique of Judgment,* 45.

18. G. W. F. Hegel, *Aesthetics: Lectures on Fine Arts,* trans. T. M. Knox (Oxford: Clarendon Press, 1975), 33; Hegel, *Vorlesungen über die Ästhetik I,* ed. Eva Moldenhauer and Karl Markus Michel (Frankfurt: Suhrkamp, 1986), 53–54.

19. Hegel, *Aesthetics,* 32.

20. This is the opposite tendency to the one found in Mondrian. Far from calling for the "end of art," Mondrian pushed in the opposite direction under pressure from van Doesburg and Oud to enter into "life" through architecture. "The architect today," he insisted, functions *"outside art."* Against the architect, Mondrian embraced the autonomous work of art. "In our time each work of art has to stand on its own," he wrote. "The Neo-Plasticist," he continued, "must

abstract the environment, for he recognizes that there can only be harmony through *equivalence;* for him, harmony between nature and the man-made is *fantasy—unreal.*" Mondrian, "The Realization of Neo-Plasticism," 170.

21. Leah Dickerman, "Bauhaus Fundaments," in *Bauhaus, 1919–1933: Workshops for Modernity* (New York: Museum of Modern Art, 2009), 24. Dickerman's dualism of representation and sensation is unqualified. According to Dickerman, Bauhaus artists like Kandinsky desired to "supplant the communicative with the sensory" (ibid.).

22. Rosalind Krauss defines opticality as the "suspension of the work in space as if it were nothing but pure optical glitter . . . a condition that establishes the corresponding illusion that its viewer is similarly bodiless." Rosalind Krauss, "Using Language To Do Business as Usual," in *Visual Theory: Painting and Interpretation,* ed. Norman Bryson, Michael Ann Holly, and Keith Moxey (New York: HarperCollins, 1991), 88. The largely irrelevant nature of the critique of the subject—an obligatory accompaniment of the critique of representation—will emerge in what follows.

23. André Gide, "Promenade au Salon d'Automne," *Gazette des Beaux-Arts* 34 (December 1, 1905): 483.

24. Jacques Rivière, "Une Exposition de Henri Matisse" (1910), in *Études* (Paris: Gallimard, 1912), 47. In chapter 4, I consider the various early criticisms of Matisse's work, most of which center on Matisse's putative skepticism.

25. My interpretation of Matisse's "absorptive" mode is indebted to Michael Fried's writings on modernist painting, including *Courbet's Realism* (Chicago: University of Chicago Press, 1992); *Manet's Modernism, or, The Face of Painting in the 1860s* (Chicago: University of Chicago Press, 1998); "Caillebotte's Impressionism," *Representations* 66 (Spring 1999): 1–51; and *Menzel's Realism: Art and Embodiment in Nineteenth-Century Berlin* (New Haven, Conn.: Yale University Press, 2002). See also my review of *Menzel's Realism* in *Zeitschrift für Kunstgeschichte* 4 (2006): 578–92.

26. This account of subjectivity was most famously criticized by Martin Heidegger in essays such as "The Age of the World Picture" (1938), in *The Question Concerning Technology, and Other Essays,* ed. and trans. William Lovitt (New York: Harper Torchbooks, 1977), 115–54.

27. Mikkel Borch-Jacobsen, *The Freudian Subject* (1982), trans. Catherine Porter (Stanford, Calif.: Stanford University Press, 1988), 40.

28. Matisse, *Matisse on Art,* 42; Matisse, *Écrits et propos sur l'art,* ed. Dominique Fourcade (Paris: Hermann, 1972), 52.

29. Henri Matisse, letter of March 31, 1912, quoted in Hilary Spurling, *Matisse the Master: A Life of Henri Matisse, the Conquest of Colour, 1909–1954* (New York: Knopf, 2005), 115, 149.

30. Matisse, *Matisse on Art,* 162.

31. Henri Bergson, *Creative Evolution,* trans. Arthur Mitchell (New York: Henry Holt, 1911), 159; Bergson, *Oeuvres,* 617. It is important to see that Bergson identifies hypnotism—a central concept of this book—with the complete absence of intention. Bergson often describes perceptually directed activity as being "riveted to . . . material objects," living "in a state of somnambulism, outside itself, hypnotized on its own work" (*Creative Evolution,* 175; *Oeuvres,* 630).

32. Henri Bergson, *Matter and Memory,* trans. N. M. Paul and W. S. Palmer (New York: Zone Books, 1988), 82; Bergson, *Oeuvres,* 228.

33. Bergson, *Matter and Memory,* 155; Bergson, *Oeuvres,* 296.

34. Bergson, *Creative Evolution,* 198; Bergson, *Oeuvres,* 648.

35. Bergson, *Creative Evolution,* 198; Bergson, *Oeuvres,* 648. Bergson saw any thoughtful action as the opposite of "absorptive." One of his guiding aims was to extract human beings from what he saw as their mindless immersion in habit, "confined to the present and absorbed, to the exclusion of all else." The life of an animal is "absorbed at every instant by the actions it performs

and the attitudes it must adopt." An animal "no doubt plays rather than thinks its ideas" (*Creative Evolution*, 205–6; *Oeuvres*, 654). On this account, to think one's ideas is to truly intend them.

36. Bergson, *Time and Free Will*, 231–32; Bergson, *Oeuvres*, 151.

37. Bergson, *Creative Evolution*, 219; Bergson, *Oeuvres*, 665.

38. On this topic I am indebted to the writings of Ruth Leys and Mikkel Borch-Jacobsen. See Ruth Leys, *Trauma: A Genealogy* (Chicago: University of Chicago Press, 2000); and Borch-Jacobsen, *The Freudian Subject.*

39. Robert Pippin has succinctly described the standard case against intentionality: "The critique of human subjectivity is essentially the result of . . . the 'masters of suspicion': Marx, Nietzsche, and Freud. These are the first to suggest that the domain of conscious intention, decision, and judgment is merely an appearance, while the true determinates of what we take ourselves to be consciously determining are actually inaccessible to consciousness. The domain of our conscious attentiveness is a kind of illusion, a pretension to run the show of our own lives, whereas it is actually some manifestation of the relation between the mode of production and the relations of production in a given society, or the will to power, or the unconscious. What poststructuralism did, which is essentially a post-Heideggerian phenomenon, is intensify the skepticism about the possibility of running any show, by destabilizing the attempt to identify these so-called true forces of determination—the unconscious, the will to power, economic relations of class, and so on. Such an intense skepticism that we could ever come to any determination about those latent forces leaves one in a condition of complete indeterminacy." According to Pippin, this view is "unintelligible." What practices could or should follow from one's belief that intention is an illusion? "What would it be to properly acknowledge this fact, in one's life, from the first-person point of view? Are you supposed to wait around indefinitely, to see what your indeterminate forces do?" As he explains, the problem is not an abstract one of coercion versus freedom, but rather one of making decisions within the "constructed realm of possibilities"—what I am calling the "space" of representation—in order to establish "social conditions under which the life you lead seems to be the one you have determined." That it might only "seem" to be one's own, and not purely or absolutely one's own, is a necessary consequence of finitude. "After Hegel: An Interview with Robert B. Pippin," by Omair Hussain, Platypus, June 1, 2011, http://platypus1917.org. This discussion roughly summarizes the terms of Pippin's *Modernism as a Philosophical Problem: On the Dissatisfactions of European High Culture,* 2nd ed. (Oxford: Blackwell, 1999).

40. An excellent place to start is G. E. M. Anscombe's *Intention* (Oxford: Blackwell, 1958). See also Stanley Cavell, "A Matter of Meaning It," in *Must We Mean What We Say?*, updated ed. (Cambridge: Cambridge University Press, 1976), chap. 8.

41. Marcel Duchamp, *Marcel Duchamp: Work and Life,* ed. Pontus Hultén (Cambridge: MIT Press, 1993), entry for April 5, 1957.

42. Marcel Duchamp, "The Creative Act" (1957), in *The Writings of Marcel Duchamp,* ed. Michel Sanouillet and Elmer Peterson (New York: Da Capo, 1973), 139.

43. Matisse, *Matisse on Art,* 40.

44. Ibid., 161. Similarly, Matisse's student Hans Purrmann quoted the artist saying, "A picture is like a game of cards: you must figure from the very beginning on what you will have at the end; everything must be worked out backwards and always finished before its begun." Hans Purrmann, "From the Workshop of Henri Matisse," *The Dial* 73 (July 1922): 36.

45. Matisse, quoted in Jack Flam, *Matisse: The Man and His Art, 1869–1918* (Ithaca, N.Y.: Cornell University Press, 1986), 374. Robert Pippin offers a sustained analysis of this publicized mode of agency in *Hegel's Practical Philosophy: Rational Agency as Ethical Life* (Cambridge: Cambridge University Press, 2008), chap. 6.

46. Pablo Picasso, "A Picture Not Settled Beforehand," in *Picasso on Art: A Selection of*

Views, ed. Dore Ashton (New York: Da Capo, 1972), 30, 28. See also, in the same volume, "Intentions," 32.

47. Jackson Pollock, "My Painting," in *Jackson Pollock: Interviews, Articles, and Reviews,* ed. Pepe Karmel and Kirk Varnedoe (New York: Museum of Modern Art, 1999), 18.

48. Duchamp, "The Creative Act," 139.

49. Discussion following "The Creative Act," in *Marcel Duchamp: Work and Life,* entry for April 5, 1957.

50. Picasso, "A Picture Not Settled," 29, 30, and 28.

51. Freud interpreted "chance events" as "actions and manifestations of persons." His aim was to "trace [unconscious actions] back to a thought." One way of describing the point of psychoanalysis is to not "let chance count as chance but to interpret it." Sigmund Freud, *The Psychopathology of Everyday Life,* ed. James Strachey, trans. Alan Tyson (New York: W. W. Norton, 1960), 258–59. Pollock followed Freud on this account. "I don't use the accident—'cause I deny the accident," Pollock said to William Wright. Wright responded: "I believe it was Freud who said there's no such thing as an accident. Is that what you mean?" "I suppose that's generally what I mean," Pollock replied. Jackson Pollock, "Interview with William Wright," in Karmel and Varnedoe, *Jackson Pollock,* 22. For an excellent discussion of these matters, see Walter Benn Michaels, "Action and Accident: Photography and Writing," in *The Gold Standard and the Logic of Naturalism: American Literature at the Turn of the Century* (Berkeley: University of California Press, 1987), chap. 7; and Michaels, "The Death of a Beautiful Woman: Christopher Nolan's Idea of Form," Electronic Book Review, October 1, 2007, http://www.electronicbookreview.com.

52. Empson used the term "unconscious intention" in an interview with BBC television; quoted in John Haffenden, *William Empson: Against the Christians* (New York: Oxford University Press, 2006), 656. The term was first used extensively by Empson's teacher I. A. Richards. Paul Valéry poked a good deal of fun at the kinds of intentionality Freud and Empson were interested in. Here, for instance, is Valéry in his *Notebooks* mocking the surrealist vision of "unconscious intentionality": "Intentionally seeking to call forth the unintentional, consciously soliciting the 'unconscious,' is a rather curious project—a procedure that artists have always attempted more or less, but that has only recently been acknowledged and made into a doctrine; formerly practiced with the intention of discarding from the trawl all but the 'good' catches; recently, with that of holding on to everything—i.e. of *crediting* everything with value." Paul Valéry, *Cahiers/Notebooks,* vol. 2, ed. Brian Stimpson with Paul Gifford and Robert Pickering, trans. Rachel Killick, Robert Pickering, Norma Rinsler, Stephen Romer, and Brian Stimpson (Frankfurt: Peter Lang, 2000), 315. As should be clear, Valéry does not simply reject unconscious intentionality, as he suggests it is one of the basic modes of artistic agency; rather, he rejects the effort to grant every gesture, even the most lazy, with heightened significance.

53. Jacques Derrida, "Signature Event Context" (1972), in *Limited Inc,* trans. Samuel Weber and Jeffrey Mehlman (Evanston, Ill.: Northwestern University Press, 1988), 18.

54. Barthes, "The Death of the Author," 147.

55. This turn helps make sense of the rise of viewer-oriented aesthetics under postmodernism. Nonetheless, as I argue in chapter 1, the "participatory" turn emerged from a set of Symbolist premises.

56. Bois, "Kahnweiler's Lesson," in *Painting as Model,* 95.

57. Matisse, quoted in Françoise Gilot, *Matisse and Picasso: A Friendship in Art* (New York: Doubleday, 1990), 77.

58. Matisse, *Matisse on Art,* 29; Matisse, *Écrits et propos sur l'art,* 56.

59. Matisse, *Matisse on Art,* 42; Matisse, *Écrits et propos sur l'art,* 51.

60. Maurice Merleau-Ponty's phenomenology provides a model for the immersive pole of

Matisse's practice. Writing about art, Merleau-Ponty affirms the difference between his phenomenology and specular philosophies of experience: "I do not see it [spatial relations and objects in space] according to its exterior envelope; I live it from the inside; I am immersed in it. After all, the world is around me, not in front of me." Maurice Merleau-Ponty, "Eye and Mind" (1961), in *The Merleau-Ponty Aesthetics Reader: Philosophy and Painting,* ed. Galen A. Johnson (Evanston, Ill.: Northwestern University Press, 1993), 138. As I will argue, the loss of difference this immersive relation suggests prompted Matisse's equally salient commitment to "realism," a standing apart from the world not in order to know it better, but in order to acknowledge its difference.

61. Paul Valéry, *Analects,* trans. Stuart Gilbert (Princeton, N.J.: Princeton University Press, 1970), 105.

62. Paul Valéry, *The Art of Poetry,* trans. Denise Folliot (Princeton, N.J.: Princeton University Press, 1989), 155.

63. Valéry, *Analects,* 109.

64. Claude Lévi-Strauss, *The Savage Mind* (1962; Chicago: Phoenix Books, 1966), 252.

65. Rosalind Krauss, "The Motivation of the Sign," in *Picasso and Braque: A Symposium,* ed. Lynn Zelevansky (New York: Museum of Modern Art, 1992), 273.

66. Leah Dickerman, "Introduction," in *Dada* (Washington, D.C.: National Gallery of Art, 2006), 7.

67. Bois, *Painting as Model,* 203.

68. For Krauss the "fact" that vision is "porous" to the "operation of its internal organs" is something that "forever undermines the idea of vision's transparency to itself." This fact shows that the "density and opacity of the viewing subject" is the "very precondition of his access to sight." See Rosalind E. Krauss, *The Optical Unconscious* (Cambridge: MIT Press, 1993), 121–22.

69. Rosalind E. Krauss, "The Photographic Conditions of Surrealism," in *The Originality of the Avant-Garde and Other Modernist Myths* (Cambridge: MIT Press, 1986), 95.

70. Ibid., 113, my emphasis.

71. Friedrich Nietzsche, *On the Genealogy of Morals,* trans. Douglas Smith (New York: Oxford University Press, 1996), 98.

72. Ibid.

73. Rosalind Krauss, "*Informe* without Conclusion," *October* 78 (1996): 105.

74. Krauss, *Originality of the Avant-Garde,* 211.

75. Yve-Alain Bois, "El Lissitzky: Radical Reversibility," *Art in America* 76, no. 4 (April 1988): 167.

76. Ibid., 172.

77. That the critique of the hierarchy of vision is a progressive political idea has recently been interrogated by Walter Benn Michaels in "Neoliberal Aesthetics," in *The Beauty of a Social Problem,* forthcoming from the University of Chicago Press. "The core commitment" of antihierarchical politics, Michaels writes, "is to the recognition of an equality that already exists but that our falsely hierarchical vision has kept us from seeing." As Michaels rightly observes, the central damages that shape modern life are not a product of our "falsely hierarchical vision" but are a "function of capitalism." Michaels aims to show that attending to the former is unrelated to the latter and that truly progressive politics is not a matter of dispelling illusions about privileged realities (about the self, about identities)—it is not about *vision* at all, but about economic inequality and exploitation.

78. Bois, "El Lissitzky," 174.

79. Henry David Thoreau, *Walden* (1854; Oxford: Oxford University Press, 1999), 38. For a discussion of the role of citation in Emerson and Thoreau, see Stanley Cavell, "Emerson, Coleridge, Kant (Terms as Conditions)," in *In Quest of the Ordinary: Lines of Skepticism and*

Romanticism (Chicago: University of Chicago Press, 1988), 29–40; and Cavell, *A Pitch of Philosophy: Autobiographical Exercises* (Cambridge, Mass.: Harvard University Press, 1994), 44–45. I consider Matisse's approach to citation in chapter 3.

80. T. J. Clark, foreword to *Guy Debord,* by Anselm Jappe, trans. Donald Nicholson-Smith (Berkeley: University of California Press, 1999), ix. Clark's frustration with the (postmodern) representational attitude—one shared here—leads at times to overstatements such as the following (made in collaboration with Retort): "It is only twenty-first century intellectuals who believe that everything human is always already representation. If we could take them back to a stockyard or a guildhall or a Glasgow 'steamy'—or indeed to a 'market' before the Right eviscerated the notion—they would soon see that human beings have other ways of making each other meaningful besides branding and signing. And it is the interaction of these different ways—of these different materialities and intentionalities—that make up a human world." "Capital, Spectacle, and Modernity: An Interview with Retort," by Soren Whited, Platypus, November 1, 2008, http://platypus1917.org.

For Clark and Retort, human action at its most expressive seems to exist at the limits of representation. A few questions emerge here: Are the interactions that made up the life of a nineteenth- or early twentieth-century guildhall or marketplace outside exchange? Isn't it the guildhall or marketplace that makes "material" experiences possible? That is to say, isn't representation *prior to* interactions, and isn't it representation that makes experience into an experience and defines a "world" against sameness? And if I take this broadly representational position, I do not see that it entails a view of knowing as branding or conceptualizing.

But these issues are complicated. In one of his most sustained reflections on representation, Clark glosses Debord's "hostility to the very idea of 'representation.'" Clark rightly worries about what these issues might suggest: "Do they not lead us inevitably back to a Rousseau-and-Lukács realm of transparency and face-to-faceness and therefore usher in a politics of purity and purging to match?" But rather than "anathematizing representation in general," Clark sees Debord as "proposing certain tests for truth and falsity in representation and, above all, for truth and falsity in representational *regimes.*" Clark asks, "Why is it so difficult to think . . . 'representation' as plural rather than as singular and centralized: representations as so many fields or terrains of activity, subject to leakage and interference . . . constantly crossed and dispersed . . . subject to retrieval and cancellation. Why should a regime of representation not be built on the principle that images are . . . transformable (as opposed to exchangeable)" (foreword, ix–x). It is this pluralized or transformable notion of representation that stands as the central alternative to representation as a mode of (conceptual) exchange.

A good deal hinges on what Clark means by the "transformable" image. He defines this alternate regime as one where images are "disposable through and through, and yet utterly material and contingent; shareable, imaginable, coming up constantly in their negativity, their nonidentity, and for that reason promoted and dismantled at will" (foreword, x). But is it right to say representation is a matter of promotion or dismantling? One's relation to a representational regime, as I have been arguing here, is more immersive and constitutive of subjectivity, and while certainly open to change by agents in a shared social and historical setting, these changes do not require an attitude toward representation at all.

Perhaps the clearest instance of the transformable image emerges in Clark's discussion of El Lissitzky's work. Clark approvingly cites El Lissitzky's notion of a revolutionary symbol that "acquires its name later" and whose "meaning is revealed later still." Clark describes this process as one where meaning ascription, "if it happens, [occurs in] some future history of use and misuse (some number of convolutions) in social practice." To say that it is social practice that makes meaning, and not the artist, is to construe an artwork as something closer to an object and art history as something closer to anthropology (how meaning is determined by changing uses).

Then again, it is hard to see what "misuse" means in this context if the meaning is something that emerges with the history of the object. See T. J. Clark, *Farewell to an Idea: Episodes from a History of Modernism* (New Haven, Conn.: Yale University Press, 1999), 252.

Moreover, one might ask how far Clark's transformable ideal is from the Deleuzian notion that "social institutions . . . receive a strictly immanent determination, and thus remain always and completely susceptible to restructuring, reform, and destruction (in the spirit, for example, of the Communards, who insisted that all representation be subject to immediate revocation)." Michael Hardt, *Gilles Deleuze* (Minneapolis: University of Minnesota Press, 1993), 120.

81. I don't imagine Clark would disagree with the spirit of this line of inquiry, but he would disagree about the value or viability of representation today. In his most recent work, Clark seems to suggest a détente in the battle between revolutionaries and reformists. Or rather, he sees them both as future-driven modes of thought and practice to be avoided. But Clark's insistence on a "piece-by-piece, assumption-by-assumption dismantling of the politics we have," now in a tragic key, flirts with vanguardist models he seeks to avoid. T. J. Clark, "For a Left with No Future," *New Left Review* 74 (March/April 2012): 73. The effort to make modern modes of representation fulfill their claim to freedom—this is the burden of my history—might be construed as an effort at "revival, resuscitation" of a failed system (ibid., 74).

1. Painting as Affect Machine

1. Alastair Wright, *Matisse and the Subject of Modernism* (Princeton, N.J.: Princeton University Press, 2004), 56. Wright's account is internally divided between historical and ontological claims. On one hand, he describes Matisse's "mobilizing the signifying codes" of the past and "leaving them in disarray"; on the other hand, this critique of codes speaks to the "condition of all vision" (ibid., 65, 86). The paradox is at its sharpest in the following phrases: "Color is always mediated" and yet color is a "brute materiality" (ibid., 85, 88).

2. Ibid., 85. "Crucially," Wright contends, "it was the *viewer's* own perceptual faculties that were . . . afflicted" by Matisse's paintings (ibid., 81).

3. The phrase appears on pages 31, 32 (twice), 34, 40, 43, 44, 45, and 88 in Gilles Deleuze, *Francis Bacon: The Logic of Sensation*, trans. Daniel W. Smith (Minneapolis: University of Minnesota Press, 2003); Deleuze, *Francis Bacon: Logique de la sensation* (Paris: Éditions de la Différence, 1981), 27, 28, 29, 34, 35, 36, 37, 70. Further page references to the English translation of this work, followed by page numbers in the French edition, will appear in the text. Deleuze cites two immediate sources for his view of the affective immediacy of artworks. Writing about Antonin Artaud, Deleuze describes "words that act directly on the body, penetrating and bruising it." Deleuze, *The Logic of Sense*, ed. Constantin Boundas, trans. Mark Lester with Charles Stivale (New York: Columbia University Press, 1990), 87; Gilles Deleuze, *Logique du sens* (Paris: Éditions de Minuit, 1969), 107. I will not dwell on Artaud's example here, as I will consider his work in my conclusion. Deleuze further cites Francis Bacon's distinction between "paint which conveys directly and paint which conveys through illustration." Here is Bacon: "It's a very, very close and difficult thing to know why some paint comes across directly onto the nervous system and other paint tells you the story in a long diatribe through the brain" (quoted in *Francis Bacon*, 26). The latter phrase was featured in the introductory wall text for the 2008–9 exhibition *Francis Bacon: A Centenary Retrospective*, at Tate Britain and the Metropolitan Museum of Art, New York.

4. The philosophy of "schizoanalysis," Deleuze writes, "never consists in interpreting." Gilles Deleuze, *Dialogues*, trans. Hugh Tomlinson and Barbara Habberjam (New York: Columbia University Press, 1987), 143. Rémi Labrusse pursues a similar interpretation of Matisse. "The work of interpretation," he writes, "must not concern the work—which, in itself, signifies

nothing—but the function that it fulfills." That function is viewer-driven, if not exactly affective; it is "an invitation [to the spectator] to creative action," Labrusse quotes Matthew Prichard as saying.

5. Yve-Alain Bois, "1910," in Foster et al., *Art since 1900,* 1:365.

6. The distinction between representation and action is foundational for this line of argumentation, and it loosely follows J. L. Austin's distinction between performatives and constatives: "If a person makes a [performative] utterance . . . we should say that he is *doing* something rather than merely *saying* something." J. L. Austin, "Performative Utterances," in *Philosophical Papers,* 3rd ed., ed. J. O. Urmson and G. J. Warnock (Oxford: Oxford University Press, 1979), 235. According to this popular usage of Austin, performatives are special in their capacity to be neither true nor false but simply "felicitous" or "infelicitous," their only disability being that they "can fail to come off in special ways." To conceive of art as a "performative"—as "*doing* something" rather than "*saying* something"—is to value the *experience* of a work over and against its *meaning.* For Austin, of course, a performative requires a recognized intentional context to "do" anything.

7. Judith Butler, "Response to J. M. Bernstein," in *The Life and Death of Images: Ethics and Aesthetics,* ed. Diarmuid Costello and Dominic Willsdon (Ithaca, N.Y.: Cornell University Press, 2008), 58. I consider Butler's response at the conclusion to chapter 2.

8. According to Deleuze, there is "a violence that is involved only with color and line: the violence of a sensation (and not of a representation)." Deleuze, *Francis Bacon,* xxix.

9. Wassily Kandinsky, *On the Spiritual in Art* (1912), in *Complete Writings on Art,* ed. Kenneth C. Lindsay and Peter Vergo (New York: Da Capo, 1994), 160. Kandinsky's claim is drawn from Émile Jacques-Dalcroze in his study *Eurhythmics:* "Sound acts directly on the soul and finds an echo there because . . . music is innate in man." Kandinsky quotes this phrase in one of the epigraphs to chapter 6 of *On the Spiritual in Art,* "The Language of Form and Color." Kandinsky conceived of words in the same fashion as pictures: the repetition of a word, he wrote, can "bring out unsuspected spiritual properties . . . and deprives the word of its external reference. Similarly, the symbolic reference of a designated object tends to be forgotten and only the sound is retained. We hear this pure sound . . . [which] *exercises a direct impression on the soul.*" Quoted in John Elderfield, introduction to *Flight Out of Time,* by Hugo Ball (Berkeley: University of California Press, 1996), xxvi–xxvii, my emphasis. It is important to note that Kandinsky's view did not change substantially over time. In his brief tenure as director of the Institute of Artistic Culture (INKhUK) he continued his research into the "effect of the artistic means employed on the experiences of the man apprehending it, i.e. on his psyche." Quoted in Cristina Lodder, *Russian Constructivism* (New Haven, Conn.: Yale University Press, 1983), 79.

10. Kandinsky, *Complete Writings on Art,* 457, 159.

11. Ibid., 168, my emphasis.

12. Ibid., 180–81, 402.

13. Deleuze defines his philosophy as expressionist, and it is in the way Kandinsky's is (that is, not about the expression of the self, but in the expressive capacity of matter). See Gilles Deleuze, *Expressionism in Philosophy: Spinoza,* trans. Martin Joughin (New York: Zone Books, 1992).

14. According to Deleuze, Kandinsky drained pictorial tension within a "pure and internal optical space." Deleuze, *Francis Bacon,* 85/68.

15. Gilles Deleuze, *What Is Philosophy?,* trans. Hugh Tomlinson and Graham Burchell (New York: Columbia University Press, 1994), 164.

16. Yve-Alain Bois, "Bonnard's 'Passivity,'" in *Pierre Bonnard: The Work of Art: Suspending Time* (Paris: Musée d'Art Moderne de la Ville de Paris, 2003), 53–54.

17. The answer to the mystery of why Deleuze resists empirical modes of analysis of what

happens to the beholder before a work of art may be found in his critique of the spatial character of neuronal imaging. Simply put, science is unable to capture the full range of affective experience with two-dimensional representations.

18. Bois, "Bonnard's 'Passivity,'" 54.

19. Although her focus is literary modernism, Jennifer Ashton explores the continuity between modernism and postmodernism along the lines I am pursuing here. See Jennifer Ashton, "Modernism's Old Literalism: Pound, Williams, Zukofsky, and the Objectivist Critique of Metaphor," in *From Modernism to Postmodernism: American Poetry and Theory in the Twentieth Century* (Cambridge: Cambridge University Press, 2005), 119–45.

20. Matisse, *Matisse on Art,* 195–96; Matisse, *Écrits et propos sur l'art,* 257.

21. Matisse, *Matisse on Art,* 68.

22. Delacroix, quoted in Paul Signac, *From Eugène Delacroix to Neo-Impressionism,* trans. Willa Silverman (New York: Rockefeller University Press, 1992), 218. Matisse was a great admirer of Signac's text and read it closely when it appeared in 1899. For a thorough discussion of Matisse's involvement with Neo-Impressionist color theory, see Catherine C. Bock, *Henri Matisse and Neo-Impressionism, 1898–1908* (Ann Arbor, Mich.: UMI Research Press, 1981).

23. Quoted in Eugène Delacroix, *The Journal of Eugène Delacroix,* trans. Walter Pach (New York: Viking Press, 1972), 30.

24. Kandinsky, *On the Spiritual in Art,* 160. In a review of a 2006 Kandinsky exhibition at Tate Modern, Ossian Ward supported Kandinsky's synesthetic claims by citing the results of contemporary neuroscience. "Recently . . . a group of neuroscientists has been able to prove that synaesthetes [like Kandinsky] do indeed 'see' sound. A series of brain scans showed that, despite being blindfolded, synaesthetes showed 'visual activity' in the brain when listening to sounds. Now all that is left is to find the gene that may be responsible." Ossian Ward, "The Man Who Heard His Paintbox Hiss," *Telegraph,* June 10, 2006, http://www.telegraph.co.uk. No doubt a good deal of effort is being invested in the discovery of the "synesthetic gene"; my question is what relevance that discovery will have for understanding Kandinsky's, or any artist's, practice.

25. Film director Alfred Hitchcock spoke of "controlling the audience's thoughts" and, in a rather literal interpretation of his job, "directing the viewers. You might say I was playing them, like an organ." In Francois Truffaut with Helen G. Scott, *Hitchcock,* rev. ed. (New York: Touchstone Books, 1985), 269.

26. Delacroix, *Journal,* 85; journal entry, May 7, 1824, in Delacroix, *Journal: 1822–1863,* ed. André Joubin (Paris: Plon, 1996), 78.

27. Delacroix, quoted in John Rewald, *Georges Seurat* (New York: Wittenborn, 1943), 10.

28. Charles Blanc, *The Grammar of Painting and Engraving* (1867), trans. Kate Newell Doggett (London: Hurd and Houghton, 1874), 5.

29. Bois, "Matisse," in Foster et al., *Art since 1900,* 1:105.

30. Deleuze's and Bois's insistence on the nonrepresentational quality of this rhythmic experience is indebted to the writings of Jean-François Lyotard. See, for example, Lyotard's "Beyond Representation," preface to the French translation of Anton Ehrenzweig's *L'Ordre caché de l'art* (Paris: Gallimard, 1974), in *The Lyotard Reader,* ed. Andrew Benjamin, trans. Jonathan Culler (London: Blackwell, 1989), 155–68. For a trenchant and too little known critique of Lyotard's and Deleuze's position, see Philippe Lacoue-Labarthe, "The Scene Is Primal" (1974), trans. Karen McPherson, in *The Subject of Philosophy,* ed. Thomas Trezise (Minneapolis: University of Minnesota Press, 1993), 99–115.

31. Bois, "Matisse," in Foster et al., *Art since 1900,* 1:101.

32. Bois, "On Matisse," 112. Bois repeats the (causal) claim in *Art since 1900:* "This hypnosis [effect of *Music*] is based on a pendulum in our perception that *makes us* switch from our

incapacity to focus on the figures to that of seizing the whole visual field at once, an oscillation that defines the very invention of Matisse's concept of the 'decorative.'" Bois, "Matisse," 1:104, my emphasis.

33. Bois, "On Matisse," 100, 112.

34. Deleuzian art historian Simon O'Sullivan shows how replacing representation with affect fundamentally changes the way art history is done. "A certain kind of art history might disappear," he writes, "that which attends only to art's signifying character, that which . . . positions art *work,* as representation." Rather than representation, "what becomes important is what a particular art object can *do.*" Art history thereby "changes from a hermeneutic to a heuristic activity . . . a kind of *creative* writing." Simon O'Sullivan, "The Aesthetics of Affect: Thinking Art beyond Representation," *Angelaki* 6, no. 3 (December 2001): 130.

35. Deleuze describes the emergence of pictorial "catastrophes" in his discussion titled "The Diagram," chapter 12 of *Francis Bacon* (81–90/65–71). "Painting as Trauma" is the title of Bois's study of Picasso's *Les Demoiselles d'Avignon.* According to Bois, Picasso's painting set off Matisse's pictorial response, *Music* of 1910. I will consider Bois's analysis of *Music* in chapter 2. See Yve-Alain Bois, "Painting as Trauma," *Art in America* 76, no. 6 (1988): 130–40, 172–73.

36. Rosalind E. Krauss, "The Im/pulse to See," in *Vision and Visuality,* ed. Hal Foster (Seattle: Bay Press, 1988), 51–78. Mark Antliff follows Krauss's claims here in his study "The Rhythms of Duration: Bergson and the Art of Matisse," in *The New Bergson,* ed. John Mullarkey (Manchester, England: Manchester University Press, 1999), 184–208. I will consider Antliff's essay in chapter 2.

37. Krauss, *Optical Unconscious,* 205–6. This section expands and includes her argument in "The Im/pulse to See."

38. Ibid., 322.

39. Rosalind Krauss, "1993," in Hal Foster, Rosalind Krauss, Yve-Alain Bois, and Benjamin H. D. Buchloh, *Art since 1900: Modernism, Antimodernism, Postmodernism,* vol. 2, *1945 to the Present* (London: Thames & Hudson, 2004), 631.

40. "Dependent on the connection of the eye to the whole network of the body's tissue, this [rhythmic] force wells up within the density and thickness of carnal being, as, tied to the conditions of nervous life, it is by definition a function of temporality." Krauss, "Im/pulse to See," 51, 62; see also Krauss, *Optical Unconscious,* 216. Bois refers to this passage in his study of Matisse, calling for "a psychoanalytic analysis of rhythm." Krauss, he says, provides this "starting with the notion of the 'matrix' elaborated by Jean-François Lyotard [as well as in her work] . . . devoted to Duchamp and his optical machines." Bois, "On Matisse," 102.

41. Dickerman, "Introduction," 7.

42. Rosalind Krauss, "Reading Photographs as Texts," in *Pollock Painting,* ed. Hans Namuth and Barbara Rose (New York: Agrinde, 1980), n.p. I thank Michael Schreyach for bringing this text to my attention.

43. For a detailed account of this enterprise, see Jonathan Crary, *Techniques of the Observer: On Vision and Modernity in the Nineteenth Century* (Cambridge: MIT Press, 1992).

44. Krauss, *Optical Unconscious,* 304. Krauss's commitment to affective aesthetics goes back to her earliest writings. Her epigram to her "Sense and Sensibility: Reflection on Post '60s Sculpture," *Artforum* 12 (November 1973), is drawn from Jean-Luc Godard: "Every scenario and every mise-en-scène . . . must . . . start from affection" (43).

45. Bertolt Brecht, "On Non-objective Painting," rpt. in *Modern Art and Modernism: A Critical Anthology,* ed. Francis Frascina and Charles Harrison (New York: Harper & Row, 1982), 143–44. For another translation, one I have consulted here, see Brecht, "On Non-representational Painting," in *Brecht on Art and Politics,* ed. Tom Kuhn and Steve Giles, trans. Laura Bradley, Steve Giles, and Tom Kuhn (London: Methuen, 2003), 239–42.

46. Adolf Loos, "The Principle of Cladding" (1898), in *Spoken into the Void,* trans. Jane O. Newman and John H. Smith (Cambridge: MIT Press, 1982), 66. It should be clear that intention for Loos is not a matter of internal mental representation. Loos rejected the priority of the plan over the architect's embodied and changing "sense" of a site.

47. Adolf Loos, "The Old and the New Style in Architecture" (1897), in *On Architecture,* ed. Adolf and Daniel Opel, trans. Michael Mitchell (Riverside, Calif.: Ariadne Press, 2002), 33. In these early writings Loos had not yet firmly established his distinction between architecture and building.

48. "A Selection of André Derain's Letters from London and *Modern Thought and Painting,*" trans. Nancy Ireson with John House, in *André Derain: The London Paintings* (London: Courtauld Institute, 2006), 136.

49. Wassily Kandinsky, "On the Question of Form" (1912), in *Complete Writings on Art,* 246.

50. Matisse, *Matisse on Art,* 212.

51. Ibid., 196–97; Matisse, *Écrits et propos sur l'art,* 258.

52. Recent turns in affect theory have gone so far as to completely reimagine the difference between intended effects and actual affects and to see them in inverted terms. A highly instructive, if not so recent, example of this occurs in Peter Eisenman, "The Affects of Singularity," *Architectural Design* 62, nos. 11/12 (November/December 1992): 43–45. Here Eisenman sets out to clarify the distinction between affect and effect and ends up utterly confusing their meanings. Even though "'affect' and 'effect' sound alike" they mean "quite different things," Eisenman writes. An effect "is something produced by an agent or cause," and it has a "function or meaning" (43). Eisenman's disinterest in distinguishing between agents and causes, functions and meanings, reveals just how foreign the question of intention is to most current accounts. Eisenman's concern is to trace the "loss of affect" over the "last 200 years" and to redress this history by privileging affects over effects. Against the pursuit of effects—they are, he says, "no longer valid"—Eisenman offers a new theory of affect, which he defines as the "conscious subjective aspect of an emotion considered apart from bodily changes" (43). While Eisenman is wary of reducing affects to the body, his next sentence makes this concern rather ambiguous as he defines affects as "simply the sensate response to a physical environment."

Eisenman aims to clarify the distinction between affect and effect—what I am calling actual effects and intended ones—by virtue of example. Here is Eisenman: "When I lecture in a foreign country, everyone listens with headphones to a technical translation of my words. . . . At the same time the translator desperately tries to tell the audience what I mean. And what I mean is precisely what is at issue. The audience feels it must understand what I say—it must have an effective response to my present. But I want them to feel my presence, my affect. Like the audience at my lecture, people all over the world are . . . losing the affect of being in space. The loss of individual response to unmediated stimuli is one consequence of the phenomenon [of mediation]" (43). Eisenman offers two senses of the word *meaning.* There is the "technical translation" of his words, what he calls the effort to "understand what I say." But there is another more important sense of *meaning,* what he calls "presence." His speech "means" in mutually exclusive ways: in terms of understanding or effect and in terms of presence or affect. Rather than "desperately trying" to "understand" his words, audience members should, Eisenman suggests, grasp what is right in front of them, their "individual response" to the stimuli provided by the sounds emitted by the speaker. (How the latter constitutes "meaning" and not just a sensation or assertion is left unexplained.) Once he has established the primacy of presence over understanding, Eisenman shifts his attention to what he calls the "crucial" part of his argument. Media "sets out to destroy the possibility of individual affect" (45). While affects allow for the "possibility of mistake, the misgotten message, error and untruth," the effects produced by mass forms of media cannot. But how can a "personal form of behavior" be mistaken? How can an affect contain a "message" at all (from where and to what)? What could an affect be mistaken about if *not* an effect intended by an agent? One can always be wrong or have a disagreement about what an architect meant to happen to us within a built environment, but what one's "individual affect" is in those spaces is not open to dispute. Nonetheless, as Eisenman's talk about the "possibility of mistake" makes clear, he is confused about his own account of affect. In the end, he treats affects like effects, even at the expense of the logic of his claims about the primacy of presence over understanding. The essay was reprinted in Peter Eisenman, *Written into the Void: Selected Writings, 1990–2004* (New Haven, Conn.: Yale University Press, 2007), 24–35.

53. Duchamp in 1961, quoted in *Marcel Duchamp: Work and Life.* While Duchamp grants the spectator more importance than the artist here, he more often said, "I give the [spectator] as much importance as the one who makes it." Marcel Duchamp and Pierre Cabanne, *Dialogues with Marcel Duchamp,* trans. Ron Padgett (New York: Viking Press, 1971), 70. The incoherence of the latter claim will emerge in my discussion of Valéry in the conclusion.

54. I owe a debt of thanks to Charles Palermo for helping me think through the issues raised here.

55. According to Anthony Blunt, Poussin's theory of the modes was drawn from Zarlino's *Istituzioni armoniche,* first published in 1558 and republished several times throughout the century. See Anthony Blunt, "L'Origine de la lettre de Poussin sur les modes d'après un travail recent," *Bulletin de la Société de l'histoire de l'art français* (1933): 125–43.

56. Poussin's letter is reprinted in Anthony Blunt, *Nicolas Poussin,* vol. 1 (London: Pallas Athene, 1995), 367–70.

57. Sutter, quoted in Barbara Maria Stafford, *Symbol and Myth: Humbert de Superville's Essay on Absolute Signs in Art* (Cranbury, N.J.: University of Delaware, 1979), 181.

58. Blanc, *The Grammar of Painting and Engraving,* 41–43; hereafter cited in the text.

59. Blanc, *Les Artistes de mon temps* (Paris: Firmin-Didot et Cie, 1876), 62.

60. Blanc returns to the comparison between painting and sculpture in his discussion of chiaroscuro in the *Grammar.* While the following passage deserves detailed analysis, it is beyond the parameters of the present discussion. "It is not with the painter as with the architect or the sculptor, whose palpable creations are subject to the mobile and changing power of natural life," Blanc writes. He continues: "A monument that appears simple and grand by moonlight may lose these qualities in the light of day, if it is loaded with details and dwarfed by superfluous ornaments which were lost sight of in the uncertain light of the moon. A piece of sculpture expressive, almost tragic, like the *Pensieroso* of Michael Angelo, might change its character if its place were changed, and if, instead of being lighted from above, it received its light from below, which would disperse the profoundly melancholy shadows that envelop the face of the hero. On the contrary, the painter draws his light from his color-box. . . . It is the sun, it is true, that lights up the canvas of the painter, but it is the painter himself who lights up his picture. In representing in it, according to his pleasure, the appearances of light and shadow he has chosen, he throws upon it a ray of his own spirit.

"Free thus to illuminate his drama in a way that shall be invariable, he need not fear lest the external light should ever come to contradict the sentiment which has inspired him" (126–27).

I quote this passage at length because it indicates the limits of Blanc's interest in the beholder's "natural life." Blanc's main concern is the status of actual or external light versus the painter's depicted light. The former is "mobile and changing," while the latter is "invariable." Similarly, one might say the beholder's "mobile and changing" experience is part of his or her "natural life" and therefore unrelated to the artist's sentiment, which does not change with the climate. For a contrasting view of sculpture, but based on the same aesthetic principles regarding intention, see my discussion of Valéry's "My Bust" in the Conclusion.

61. Indeed, Goldberg's publisher lived in Matisse's building. For a discussion of the relation between Goldberg's text and Matisse's "Notes," see Flam, *Matisse on Art,* 34–35.

62. Mécislas Goldberg, *La Morale des lignes* (Paris: Léon Varier, 1908), 21–22.

63. Ibid., 58, 87.

64. Ibid., 18.

65. Ibid., 73–74.

66. Ibid., 75. For a neurobiologically oriented account of Goldberg's significance, see Semir Zeki, "Art and the Brain," in *The Brain,* ed. Gerald M. Edelman and Jean-Pierre Changeux (New Brunswick, N.J.: Transaction, 2001), 71ff.

67. Matisse, *Matisse on Art,* 39; Matisse, *Écrits et propos sur l'art,* 42.

68. Matisse, *Matisse on Art,* 121; Matisse, *Écrits et propos sur l'art,* 132.

69. E. H. Gombrich, *The Sense of Order: A Study in the Psychology of Decorative Art* (Ithaca, N.Y.: Cornell University Press, 1979), 168.

70. E. H. Gombrich, *Art and Illusion: A Study in the Psychology of Pictorial Representation* (Princeton, N.J.: Princeton University Press, 1956), 370.

71. Ibid., 373, 370.

72. E. H. Gombrich, "Expression and Communication" (1962), in *Meditations on a Hobby Horse, and Other Essays on the Theory of Art* (Chicago: University of Chicago Press, 1963), 58.

73. David Freedberg, "Composition and Emotion," in *The Artful Mind: Cognitive Science and the Riddle of Human Creativity,* ed. Mark Turner (Oxford: Oxford University Press, 2006), 73–89; hereafter cited in the text. For a summary account of the history of and recent tendencies within neurologically informed visual analysis, see John Onians, *Neuroarthistory: From Aristotle and Pliny to Baxandall and Zeki* (New Haven, Conn.: Yale University Press, 2008).

74. Auguste Rodin, *L'Art: Entretiens reunis par Paul Gsell* (Paris: Grasset, 1911), 218–19.

75. Eric Michaud, in a series of brilliant studies of modernist ideology—above all *La Fin du salut par l'image* (Paris: Editions Jacqueline Chambon, 1992)—has laid the groundwork for the genealogy I sketch here. As Michaud argues, modernism turns on a "series of constant points": "the will to master the effect produced on the spectator, the necessity that follows from the discovery of the most effective means to commune souls; and recourse . . . to the direct action of colors and lines. Painters aim to go beyond the mediation of objects, their representation, figures, and iconic images. To discover—or invent—a mode of direct action in which the immediacy was such that it would affect the sensibility of man without delay, by short-circuiting memory and reason." Eric Michaud, "La Fin de l'iconographie: Une Nouvelle Rhétorique du sensible," *Cahiers de Musée National d'Art Moderne,* no. 5 (1980): 448.

Michaud traces the fraught and often dubious role formalism has played in art from romanticism to the Third Reich. According to Michaud, artistic and critical practices of formalism were frequently driven by broadly political ambitions to control and shape a passive and pliable audience. For Michaud, artistic efforts at "direct action" on the beholder are largely identified with notions of mastery and control. My point is to show how the same trajectory Michaud has sketched reveals a more basic tension between intention and affective response. Moreover, I argue that the central modernist belief in the "direct action" of line and color tended to undermine the artist's intentions while at the same time making those intentions unassailable. Affective formalism, on my account, was driven by the desire to negate the artist's responsibility to make forms meaningful to the beholder by appealing to aesthetic laws or rules or conventions outside the artist's control. In my conclusion I will argue that the attention artists paid to the beholder ultimately turned the beholder into an agent when the artist no longer was one. That is, my story ends with a result different from Michaud's: rather than a pliable mass, the audience becomes "creators," replacing the artist's will with their own.

76. For a useful discussion of Baudelaire's writings on Delacroix, see Armand Moss, *Baudelaire et Delacroix* (Paris: A. G. Nizet, 1973); and Elizabeth Abel, "Redefining the Sister Arts: Baudelaire's Response to the Art of Delacroix," *Critical Inquiry* 6, no. 3 (1980): 363–84.

77. Charles Baudelaire, "Salon de 1846," in *Curiosités esthétiques: L'Art romantique, et autres oeuvres critiques*, ed. Henri Lemaître (Paris: Garnier, 1986), 117; Baudelaire, "The Salon of 1846," in *Selected Writings on Art and Literature*, trans. P. E. Charvet (London: Penguin Books, 1992), 65. Further page references to *Curiosités esthétiques*, followed by corresponding page numbers in the *Selected Writings*, will appear in the text.

78. According to Baudelaire, Constantin Guys, the so-called painter of modern life, worked so thoroughly on the imagination of his viewers that he was able to "put them under the influence of [the artist's] imperious code" (470/406–7).

79. Here Baudelaire closely followed Delacroix's idea that "yellow, orange, and red induce and represent ideas of joy and of riches." The latter phrase is cited by Signac in *From Eugène Delacroix to Neo-Impressionism*, 217; and Kandinsky in *On the Spiritual in Art*, 161.

80. Paul Gauguin, *The Writings of a Savage*, ed. Daniel Guérin, trans. Eleanor Levieux (New York: Da Capo, 1996), 129; Gauguin, *Oviri, écrits d'un sauvage*, ed. Daniel Guérin (Paris: Gallimard, 1974), 160–61. Further page references to the English translation of this work, followed by page numbers in the French edition, will appear in the text.

81. Paul Gauguin, *Correspondance de Paul Gauguin: Documents, Témoignages*, ed. Victor Merlhès, vol. 1 (Paris: Fondation Singer-Polignac, 1984), 89. As Brian Massumi puts it, "The primacy of the affective is marked by a gap between *content* and *effect*: it would appear that the strength or duration of an image's effect is not logically connected to the content in any straightforward way." Brian Massumi, "The Autonomy of Affect," *Cultural Critique* 31 (Autumn 1995): 84.

82. In his "Response of the Symbolists" of 1886, Gustave Kahn argued that the Impressionist themes of everyday life were to be replaced by Gauguin's new "center of action," the "viewer's brain." See Gustave Kahn, "Réponse des symbolistes," *L'Evénément* (September 28, 1886); Kahn, "Response of the Symbolists," quoted in John Rewald, *Post-Impressionism from Van Gogh to Gauguin* (New York: Secker and Warburg, 1978), 134. The directness of color effects led Gauguin to muse on recent "attempts by medical science to cure madness by means of color" (179/145). Indeed, Gauguin conceived color as a means to induce madness, and he saw van Gogh's illness as the result of colors acting on an (inordinately susceptible) brain.

83. There is a striking coincidence between Gauguin and Deleuze on this account. Although Deleuze would reject Gauguin's phrasing here, he nonetheless shared a similar view of art's expressive capacity, with one (minor) proviso: for Deleuze, to act on the *brain* (as Gauguin suggests) rather than the nervous system would not go far enough. According to Deleuze, if a work were to "pass through the brain" it could not act directly upon the nervous system. Deleuze, *Francis Bacon*, 32/28.

84. Gauguin to Émile Schuffenecker, *Correspondance de Paul Gauguin*, 88.

85. Achille Delaroche, quoted in Philippe Jullian, *The Symbolists* (London: Phaidon, 1973), 225.

86. Paul Gauguin, *Noa Noa: The Tahiti Journal of Paul Gauguin*, trans. O. F. Theis (New York: Chronicle, 2005), 73.

87. At the same moment Gauguin was formulating his thoughts on the agency of line and color, one of the most influential affect theorists of the later nineteenth century, Charles Féré, was publishing the result of his experiments with a dynamometer that could "prove" the efficacy of Gauguin's claims. The dynamometer was a device that measured and recorded through graphic notation a subject's response to stimuli. In his 1887 book *Sensation and Movement*, Féré used colored lights to show how chromatic sensations produced a variety of sensorimotor responses in his subjects. According to Féré, cool or "moon" colors reduce nervous agitation,

soothing a subject's nerves, while warm or "sun" colors increase somatic activity, producing uncomfortable excitations of the nerves. From his experiments with the dynamometer Féré drew a startling conclusion about the nature of aesthetics. He argued that the metaphorical language used to describe the world was actually a literal account of the world translated into language. While Gauguin intuited that there were "sad" and "happy" colors, for Féré these intuitions were based in fact. Féré summed up his experiments with the dynamometer this way: "It is without metaphor that we say that red is a hot color." Charles Féré, *Sensation et mouvement: Etudes experimentales de psycho-méchanique* (Paris: Germer Baillière, 1887), 106. To translate metaphors into realities was to turn intentions into causes. But Féré's most influential finding was the discovery of "psychomotor induction." Looking at a work of art, Féré observed, was like sensing electrical currents, whereby lines "provoke the execution of specific movements" and colors "determine a dynamic effect." Féré, cited in Eric Michaud, "La Construction de l'image comme matrice de l'histoire," *Vingtième Siècle: Revue d'Histoire*, no. 72 (October–December 2001): 41.

88. Gauguin to Schuffenecker, *Correspondance de Paul Gauguin*, 87–88; Gauguin, "Letters to Emile Schuffenecker," in *Symbolist Art Theories: A Critical Anthology*, ed. and trans. Henri Dorra (Berkeley: University of California Press, 1994), 186–87.

89. Maurice Denis, "Définition du Néo-Traditionnisme" (1890), in *Théories, 1890–1910: Du Symbolisme et de Gauguin vers un nouvel ordre classique*, 4th ed. (Paris: Hermann, 1964), 10; Denis, "Definition of Neo-Traditionism," trans. Peter Collier, in *Art in Theory, 1815–1900: An Anthology of Changing Ideas*, ed. Charles Harrison and Paul Wood with Jason Gaiger (Oxford: Blackwell, 1998), 867. Denis's theory is in turn indebted to the writings of Édouard Dujardin. As Dujardin forcefully explained in the conclusion to his Nabi manifesto "Cloisonnism" (1888): "It is evident that different colorations would yield different sensations." Édouard Dujardin, "Aux XX et aux Indépendents: Le Cloisonisme," *La Révue indépendante* 6, ser. 3 (March 1888): 492; Dujardin, "Cloisonnism," in Dorra, *Symbolist Art Theories*, 181, translation modified.

90. Édouard Vuillard, journal of August and October 1890, quoted in Guy Cogeval, *Vuillard: Post-Impressionist Master* (New York: Abrams, 2002), 25, 20. I owe this reference to Marnin Young.

91. Denis, "Notes sur la peinture religieuse" (1896), in *Théories*, 33–34.

92. Stéphane Mallarmé, *Selected Letters of Stéphane Mallarmé*, ed. and trans. Rosemary Lloyd (Chicago: University of Chicago Press, 1988), 39.

93. Stéphane Mallarmé, *Oeuvres complètes*, ed. Henri Mondor and G. Jean-Aubry (Paris: Gallimard, 1945), 211. For a brilliant assessment of these complicated issues in Mallarmé, one that does far more justice to the changing role intentionality plays in his writings between his work in the 1860s and *Un Coup de dés*, see Danielle Follett, "The Ghost of God: Studies in the Nineteenth-Century Poetics and Aesthetics of Chance: Baudelaire, Mallarmé, Proust" (Ph.D. diss., Johns Hopkins University, 2007).

94. Fry translated Denis's 1907 essay on Cézanne into English. See *Burlington Magazine* 16 (January/February 1910): 207–19, 275–80.

95. Roger Fry, "The Exhibition of French Primitives—Part II," *Burlington Magazine* 5 (July 1904): 379, quoted in Richard Shiff, *Cézanne and the End of Impressionism: A Study of the Theory, Technique, and Critical Evaluation of Modern Art* (Chicago: University of Chicago Press, 1984), 275.

96. Roger Fry, "An Essay in Aesthetics" (1909), in *Vision and Design* (London: Pelican, 1961), 29. Shiff discusses this passage in *Cézanne and the End of Impressionism*, 145–46.

97. Two years later, in his series of lectures at the Grafton Gallery, Fry broadly defended Post-Impressionism in terms of the artist's ability to control form for expressive ends. For the Post-Impressionists, "arrangements of form and color . . . are calculated to stir the imagination." Roger Fry, "Post Impressionism," *Fortnightly Review* 95 (December 1911): 857–58.

In his study "Roger Fry's Formalism," Michael Fried considers Fry's loosely expressionist commitment to the "communication of emotion (or a mental state) from the artist to the viewer." As Fried describes it, Fry's fascination with the mental state of the artist (Rembrandt, for instance) helped him to "determine the expressive content of the picture." This is undoubtedly true, but it also seems Fry believed (in the "Essay on Aesthetics," for instance) that line and color were efficacious "in themselves," which puts the significance of the artist's mental state in some doubt. As I see it, Fry, like other Symbolists, was ambivalent about the nature of expression. See Michael Fried, "Roger Fry's Formalism," *The Tanner Lectures on Human Values* (delivered at University of Michigan, 2001), 24, http://tannerlectures.utah.edu/lectures.

98. Françoise Cachin offers a concise summary of the shared concerns of Gauguin's generation: "Gauguin discussed Neo-Platonic concepts such as the Golden Number or the meaning of lines and colors [at the same moment as] . . . Seurat, and young Symbolist writers such as Gustave Kahn and Félix Fénéon. They were also discussed by the aesthete and physiologist Charles Henry, the author of a scholarly *Introduction à une esthétique scientifique* that was published at the same time that Gauguin was musing about mathematical keys and absolute pictorial solutions in Copenhagen. All these men searching for the means to go beyond Impressionism had a common pictorial and literary source: Eugène Delacroix, or rather, Delacroix as interpreted by Baudelaire." Françoise Cachin, *Gauguin,* trans. Bambi Ballard (Paris: Flammarion, 2003), 35. Signac confirms the close atmosphere of exchange at the time. After his visit to Vuillard's home and studio, he reflected on the surprising proximity of their pictorial concerns: "It did me a great deal of good to discover that Vuillard, though his means are as different as possible from ours, is engaged in the same search for art and involved, like ourselves, in the cruel dilemmas of representation." Paul Signac, "A Visit to Vuillard, 1898," in *Edouard Vuillard,* ed. John Russell (London: Thames & Hudson, 1971), 95. For a useful discussion of the broad ties among the various avant-garde factions, see H. R. Rookmaaker, *Gauguin and Nineteenth Century Art Theory* (Amsterdam: Swets & Zeitlinger, 1972).

99. Charles Henry, "Introduction à une esthétique scientifique," *La Revue contemporaine* 2 (August 1885): 441–69.

100. "Pleasure corresponds with the direction from low to high . . . [while] pain corresponds to the direction high to low." Ibid., 447.

101. Henry, quoted in André Chastel, "Une Source oubliée de Seurat" (1959), in *Fables, formes, figures* (Paris: Flammarion, 1978), 402.

102. Henry, "Introduction," 445. Signac collaborated with Henry on an article that was never completed titled "L'Education du sens des forms."

103. Gustave Kahn, "De l'Esthétique du verre polychrome," *La Vogue* (May 1886): 55; Kahn, "The Aesthetic of Polychrome Glass," trans. Sabine Jaccaud, in Harrison and Wood, *Art in Theory,* 1012.

104. G.-Albert Aurier, *Le Symbolism en peinture: Van Gogh, Gauguin et quelques autres,* ed. Pierre-Louis Mathieu (Paris: L'Échoppe, 1991), 58. I owe a debt of thanks to Charles Palermo for bringing this passage to my attention.

105. Ibid., 26. The "magic irradiation of forms" is quoted in Patricia Townley Mathews, *Aurier's Symbolist Art Criticism and Theory* (Ann Arbor, Mich.: UMI Research Press, 1984), 67.

106. Charles Baudelaire, *Oeuvres complètes,* ed. Claude Pichois (Paris: Bibliothèque de la Pléiade, 1975), 2:747.

107. Aurier, *Le Symbolism en peinture,* 23. Henri Dorra's translation of "Symbolism in Painting: Paul Gauguin" inexplicably translates *épeler* as "read." Dorra, *Symbolist Art Theories,* 199.

108. Baudelaire, *Oeuvres complètes,* 1:11.

109. William Innes Homer observes that Superville was a key source for Seurat's later work. He was "more significant" for Seurat's "ideas about linear directions" than Henry, Homer writes.

William Innes Homer, *Seurat and the Science of Painting* (Cambridge: MIT Press, 1964), 205. We also know that Gauguin's *Manao tupapau* was inspired by Superville's print *Allegory* of 1801. For a useful overview of Superville's work, see Stafford, *Symbol and Myth.*

110. Christine Poggi, *In Defiance of Painting: Cubism, Futurism, and the Invention of Collage* (New Haven, Conn.: Yale University Press, 1992), 169–70.

111. Ibid.

112. According to Superville, signs are "attached not at all to the facial organs as such, but to their directions as aesthetic signs . . . as visible and constant elements of all the non-convulsive action of the physiognomy." By "convulsive action" Superville meant the inner experience of the actor's emotional state. In a seemingly paradoxical move, Superville declared that inner feelings had no bearing on the expressive content of signs that appear on the face. With or without "inner" content, signs in themselves bore expressive meaning. Crucially for Superville the "abstract signs" that happen to appear on a face express themselves outside of any intentional context—that is what makes them "unconditional" and "absolute." See D. P. G. Humbert de Superville, *Essai sur les signes inconditionnels dans l'art* (Leyden: C. C. Van der Hoek, 1827–32), 7.

113. Georges Seurat, "Letter to Maurice Beaubourg" (1890), trans. Akane Kawakami, in Harrison and Wood, *Art in Theory,* 970. See also Seurat's notebook entries on Delacroix, *Notes sur Delacroix* (Caen: L'Échoppe, 1987).

114. Georges Seurat, letter to Félix Fénéon, June 20, 1890, quoted in Homer, *Seurat and the Science of Painting,* 19, 55. Martha Ward brilliantly analyzes Seurat's attempt at "engineering a response" where everything is "staged to *act upon* the viewer" in *Pissarro, Neo-Impressionism, and the Spaces of the Avant-Garde* (Chicago: University of Chicago Press, 1996), 139, 143.

115. Georges Lecomte, "La Société des artistes indépendants: Sixième Exposition," *L'Art moderne* (March 30, 1890): 100, quoted in Homer, *Seurat and the Science of Painting,* 185.

116. Georges Seurat, letter to Félix Fénéon, June 20, 1890, quoted in Robert Herbert, *Seurat: Paintings and Drawings* (New Haven, Conn.: Yale University Press, 2010), 173. It is hard to see why Jonathan Crary makes no mention of Seurat's stated aversion to Henry's aesthetics in his extensive account of the artist. Crary's system is straightforwardly dualist in its claims about the "adjacency" of opposites: conscious versus unconscious, order versus affect, unity versus dispersal, attention versus dissociation. When we read that the "elimination of orthogonals" in Seurat's *Parade* is "decisive," we know it is because "any geometrical semblance of stability is a mask over a more powerful dispersal and circulation of affect." Jonathan Crary, *Suspensions of Perception: Attention, Spectacle, and Modern Culture* (Cambridge: MIT Press, 1999), 214.

117. André Chastel helpfully describes the central concerns of this moment: "In sum, a few years after Gauguin, Seurat formulates the secret of painting in the ability of colors and signs conceived as agents, at the same time physiological and psychological, as the unique and mysterious intermediaries between the unknown of nature and the human spirit." Chastel, "Une Source oubliée de Seurat," 386.

118. Arsène Alexandre, "Le Salon des Indépendants," *Revue de Paris* (March 20, 1891). I owe this reference to Marnin Young.

119. Signac, quoted in Rewald, *Georges Seurat,* 58.

120. Paul Signac, "Les Besoins individuels et la peinture: La Signification du tableau (l'émotion picturale)," in *L'Encyclopédie française,* vol. 16, sec. 84 (Paris: Société nouvelle de l'Encyclopédie française, 1935), 8.

121. Paul Signac, *D'Eugène Delacroix au néo-impressionisme,* ed. Françoise Cachin (Paris: Hermann, 1964), 129; Signac, *From Eugène Delacroix to Neo-Impressionism,* 278.

122. Paul Signac, "Impressionists and Revolutionaries" (1891), trans. Christopher Miller, in Harrison and Wood, *Art in Theory,* 797.

123. Derain, quoted in John Golding, *Visions of the Modern* (Berkeley: University of California Press, 1994), 32–33.

124. Letters from Derain to Matisse, between March 25 and April 15, 1906, "Correspondance André Derain–Henri Matisse," in Rémi Labrusse and Jacqueline Munck, *Matisse–Derain: La Vérité du fauvisme* (Paris: Hazan, 2005), 337–38; "A Selection of André Derain's Letters," 135–36. As Éric Alliez and Jean-Claude Bonne aptly observe, there is a high degree of ambiguity in Derain's use of the word "representation" here. In their words, "on peut le comprendre comme visant un art qui refuse de lier son destin à quelque objet/sujet que ce soit pour s'élever au rang d'un 'art pour l'art' . . . ; mais on voit mal comment la quête d'une 'idée à exprimer en dehors de la peinture' ne lierait pas le dépassement de la conception représentationnelle de l'art au refus de 'l'art pour l'art.'" Alliez and Bonne, *La Pensée-Matisse,* 50–51. Alliez and Bonne opt for the latter reading. More generally, their account is the most consistently antirepresentational of any available (I will consider their claims in chapter 2). See also Rémi Labrusse, "'Ne plus faire rien qui répresente quelque chose' (Matisse, Derain)," in *Matisse: La Condition de l'image,* 50–66.

125. Derain, quoted in Georges Duthuit, *Les Fauves,* ed. Rémi Labrusse (Paris: Michallon, 2006), 114; Duthuit, *Fauvist Painters,* 29.

126. Vlaminck, quoted in Florent Fels, *Vlaminck* (Paris: Marcel Seheur, 1928), 33; Duthuit, *Fauvist Painters,* 27.

127. Matisse, interview by Courthion, 1941, 3.

128. Ibid., 134.

129. Ibid., 132.

130. Matisse, *Matisse on Art,* 156; Matisse, *Écrits et propos sur l'art,* 201.

131. Matisse, *Matisse on Art,* 155; Matisse, *Écrits et propos sur l'art,* 200.

132. Matisse, *Matisse on Art,* 160; Matisse, *Écrits et propos sur l'art,* 300–301. In his memoir of Matisse, Jean Puy described him as "hammering out his surfaces by lines and strokes regulated to produce a maximum resonance on the eye" and observed his use of "every scientific resource" available to produce the most intensive "sensorial shock" on the beholder. Jean Puy, "Souvenirs," *Le Point* 21 (July 1939): 20–22. Despite Puy's mention of "scientific resources," Puy's aim was clearly to capture the intensity of Matisse's expressive concerns.

133. Matisse, *Matisse on Art,* 41; Matisse, *Écrits et propos sur l'art,* 41.

134. Robert Delaunay, "Sonia Delaunay-Terk," in *Du Cubisme à l'art abstrait,* ed. Pierre Francastel (Paris: SEVPEN, 1957), 201; Delaunay, "Sonia Delaunay-Terk," in *The New Art of Color: The Writings of Robert and Sonia Delaunay,* ed. Arthur A. Cohen, trans. David Shapiro and Arthur A. Cohen (New York: Viking Press, 1978), 133; Delaunay, "Guillaume Apollinaire: The Beginnings of Cubism Reality, Pure Painting," in *New Art of Color,* 89.

135. Delaunay, "Sonia Delaunay-Terk," 201/134. Delaunay's *First Disk* (1912), for instance, elaborates a double structure, at once instantaneous, in its initial blast of color, and absorptive, in its suggestion of slow revolving motion. Delaunay imagined that the rounded shape of the disk corresponded to the shape of the human eye and that by mirroring the eye's form he could induce more immediate reactions. I am indebted to Gordon Hughes for allowing me to read his manuscript "Resisting Abstraction: Robert Delaunay and Vision in the Face of Modernism."

136. Robert Delaunay, "Fragments rédigés pour les entretiens" (1938–39), in *Du Cubisme,* 217; Delaunay, "Fragments Drawn Up for the Discussion Groups," in *New Art of Color,* 144. Taking his cue from the designs for shop fronts, Delaunay noted how they "undeniably produce on your retina . . . a new sort of unaccustomed appeal" followed by a state of "intellectual agitation." To produce an "undeniable" result is of course another way to neutralize the significance of the painter's intention. Studying these displays, Sonia Delaunay discovered how "to bring off with the greatest effect and brilliance" new forms of design. Robert Delaunay, "L'Art du mouvement" (1938), in *Du Cubisme,* 209; Delaunay, "The Art of Movement," in *New Art of Color,* 139–40.

137. Gabriel Mourney, quoted in Pascal Rousseau, *Robert Delaunay: De l'Impressionisme à l'abstraction* (Paris: Centre Georges Pompidou, 1999), 185. The whole passage deserves citation: "We insist that vibrating around us, as amplified in tone as possible, are only straightforward and vigorous colors: of the same sonorous reds as the bugle's call, of acid greens that make you, the sick, gnash your teeth, but which give us such exquisite sensations. . . . We cherish the stark oppositions, the audacious contrasts which our decorators specialize in, making use of colors that remind us of the violence of our preferred sports. . . . Because form doesn't exist, form is nothing. There is only the *tache.* Form is a manifestation of intelligence; the *tache* is a manifestation of instinct. We are therefore resolutely for the *tache,* and against form." I thank Gordon Hughes for bringing this passage to my attention.

138. Antonin Artaud, *Selected Writings,* ed. Susan Sontag (Berkeley: University of California Press, 1976), 490, 491.

139. Ibid., 488.

140. Antonin Artaud, "The Theater of Cruelty," in *The Theater and Its Double* (1933), trans. Mary Caroline Richards (New York: Grove, 1958), 89–100; Artaud, "Le Théâtre et la cruauté," in *Le Théâtre et son double* (Paris: Gallimard, 1964), 131–55. Further page references to the English translation of this work, followed by page numbers in the French edition, will appear in the text.

141. "The Futurist Synthetic Theater," trans. Victoria Nes Kirby, in Michael Kirby, *Futurist Performance* (New York: Dutton, 1971), 202.

142. Catherine Dale, "Cruel: Antonin Artaud and Gilles Deleuze," in *A Shock to Thought: Expression after Deleuze and Guattari,* ed. Brian Massumi (London: Routledge, 2002), 92.

143. Deleuze, *Francis Bacon,* 40/33–34. The "body without organs," one of Deleuze's basic ideals, was a concept borrowed from Artaud's writings. See Antonin Artaud, "The Body Is the Body," trans. Roger McKeon, *Semiotext(e)* 2, no. 3 (1977): 38–39.

144. Artaud's suggestion that the techniques of the new theater "must not be divulged" and that they were the privilege of a "small nucleus of men [un noyau d'hommes] capable of imposing this superior notion of the theater, men who will restore to all of us the natural . . . equivalent of the dogmas in which we no longer believe" (32/47) was a notion fully embraced by Bergson. Artaud's "small nucleus of men" is akin to Bergson's "privileged soul" who knows how to organize the flow of the élan vital. Following Bergson and Artaud, Deleuze affirms the existence of "privileged souls" and the "society of creators." Gilles Deleuze, *Bergsonism,* trans. Hugh Tomlinson and Barbara Habberjam (New York: Zone Books, 1988), 117–18. I consider this topic in chapter 2.

145. Artaud, "The Jet of Blood," in *Modern French Theatre: The Avant-Garde, Dada, and Surrealism,* ed. and trans. Michael Benedikt and George E. Wellwarth (New York: Dutton, 1964), 221–26.

146. Stanley Cavell reflects on the fanatical ideal of blood transfer as the inverse and equal of skepticism in his study of Shakespeare's *Macbeth.* Stanley Cavell, "Macbeth Appalled," in *Disowning Knowledge in Seven Plays of Shakespeare,* updated ed. (Cambridge: Cambridge University Press, 2003), 223–32.

2. Freedom and Memory

1. Christopher Green, *Art in France, 1900–1940* (New Haven, Conn.: Yale University Press, 2000), 144.

2. In the hyperbolic words of Thomas Hanna, Bergson's *Creative Evolution* "appeared like a rocket in 1907 and soared cleanly over the walls of the Academy into the camp of the general public. This, the third of Bergson's major works, quickly became one of the rarities of philosophical literature, a smash. If not actually read by everyone, it was, like the Bible, known by everyone and quoted by all." Quoted in Flam, *Matisse: The Man and His Art,* 243.

3. Zeev Sternhell, *Neither Right nor Left: Fascist Ideology in France,* trans. David Maisel (Princeton, N.J.: Princeton University Press, 1986), 269.

4. H. Stuart Hughes, *Consciousness and Society: The Reorientation of European Social Thought, 1890–1930* (New York: Knopf, 1958), 113.

5. Bergson, *Matter and Memory*; Deleuze, *Bergsonism*; Gilles Deleuze, *Le Bergsonisme* (Paris: Presses Universitaires de France, 1966). See also Deleuze's earlier studies of Bergson: "Bergson, 1859–1941," in *Desert Islands, and Other Texts, 1953–1974,* ed. David Lapoujade, trans. Mike Taormina (Cambridge: MIT Press, 2003), 22–31; "Bergson's Conception of Difference," trans. Melissa McMahon, in Mullarkey, *The New Bergson,* 42–65; and "Lecture Course on Chapter Three of Bergson's *Creative Evolution,*" trans. Bryn Loban, in "Henri Bergson's *Creative Evolution* 100 Years Later," ed. Michael Kolkman and Michael Vaughan, special issue, *SubStance,* iss. 114, vol. 36, no. 3 (2007): 72–90.

6. To take a brief measure of the recent success of Bergsonism in the humanities (reserving my discussion here for his reception in English), I would point to the following titles: Frederick Burwick and Paul Douglass, eds., *The Crisis in Modernism: Bergson and the Vitalist Controversy* (Cambridge: Cambridge University Press, 1992); F. C. T. Moore, *Bergson: Thinking Backwards* (Cambridge: Cambridge University Press, 1996); two books by John Mullarkey, *Bergson and Philosophy* (Edinburgh: Edinburgh University Press, 1999) and the edited volume *The New Bergson*; Jonathan Crary's *Suspensions of Perception*; two books by Elizabeth Grosz, *The Nick of Time: Politics, Evolution, and the Untimely* (Durham, N.C.: Duke University Press, 2004) and the edited volume *Becomings: Explorations in Time, Memory, and Futures* (Ithaca, N.Y.: Cornell University Press, 1999); a special 2005 issue of *Modern Language Notes* that includes the proceedings of a conference on Bergson organized by Suzanne Guerlac; Guerlac's *Thinking in Time: An Introduction to Henri Bergson* (Ithaca, N.Y.: Cornell University Press, 2006); Keith Robinson, ed., *Deleuze, Whitehead, Bergson: Rhizomatic Connections* (New York: Palgrave Macmillan, 2009); and Michael R. Kelly, ed., *Bergson and Phenomenology* (New York: Palgrave Macmillan, 2010). These texts are the most recent additions to a rapidly evolving corpus.

7. Mark N. Hansen, *New Philosophy for New Media* (Cambridge: MIT Press, 2004); Keith Ansell Pearson, *Philosophy and the Adventure of the Virtual: Bergson and the Time of Life* (London: Routledge, 2002); Massumi, *Parables for the Virtual*; Manuel DeLanda, *Intensive Science and Virtual Philosophy* (New York: Continuum, 2005); Valentine Moulard-Leonard, *Bergson–Deleuze Encounters: Transcendental Experience and the Thought of the Virtual* (Albany: State University of New York Press, 2008).

8. Sara Danius, *Etienne-Jules Marey, Bergson, and the Crisis of Human Vision: The Senses of Modernism* (Ithaca, N.Y.: Cornell University Press, 2002); Mark N. Hansen, "Seeing with the Body: The Digital Image in Postphotography," *Diacritics* 31, no. 4 (2001): 54–84.

9. See, for example, the work of Deborah Hauptmann, including Hauptmann, ed., *The Body in Architecture* (Rotterdam: 010 Publishers, 2006); Hauptmann, "The Past Which Is, the Present That Was: Benjamin and the Bergson Trajectory," in *Cities in Transition,* ed. Deborah Hauptmann (Rotterdam: 010 Publishers, 2000), 350–61.

10. Christopher Francis Hasty, *Meter as Rhythm* (New York: Oxford University Press, 1997); Salomé Voegelin, "Sonic Memory Material as 'Pathetic Trigger,'" *Organized Sound* 11, no. 1 (2006): 13–18.

11. Hilary L. Fink, *Bergson and Russian Modernism, 1900–1930* (Evanston, Ill.: Northwestern University Press, 1999); Michael Glynn, *Vladimir Nabokov: Bergsonian and Russian Formalist Influences in His Novels* (New York: Palgrave Macmillan, 2007); Mark Antliff, *Inventing Bergson: Cultural Politics and the Parisian Avant-Garde* (Princeton, N.J.: Princeton University Press, 1993); Mark Antliff and Patricia Leighten, *Cubism and Culture* (London: Thames & Hud-

son, 2001); Mary Ann Gillies, *Henri Bergson and British Modernism* (Montreal: McGill-Queen's University Press, 1996); Ariele Freedman, *Death, Memory and Modernism: Trauma and Narrative in British Fiction* (London: Routledge, 2003); Justin Beplate, "Joyce, Bergson, and the Memory of Words," *Modern Language Review* 100, no. 2 (2005): 298–314; Robert Bernard Hass, "(Re)reading Bergson: Frost, Pound and the Legacy of Modern Poetry," *Journal of Modern Literature* 29, no. 1 (2005): 55–75; Tom Quirk, *Bergson and American Culture: The Worlds of Willa Cather and Wallace Stevens* (Chapel Hill: University of North Carolina Press, 1990); Paul Douglass, *Bergson, Eliot, and American Literature* (Lexington: University Press of Kentucky, 1986).

12. Adrian Parr, *Exploring the Work of Leonardo da Vinci within the Context of Contemporary Philosophical Thought and Art: From Bergson to Deleuze* (Lewiston, N.Y.: Edwin Mellen Press, 2003); Suzanne Guerlac, "The Useless Image: Bataille, Bergson, Magritte," *Representations* 97 (Winter 2007): 28–56. In addition, Branden W. Joseph makes wide use of Bergson in *Random Order: Robert Rauschenberg and the Neo-Avant-Garde*, new ed. (Cambridge: MIT Press, 2007).

13. Leroy N. Meyer, "In Search of Native American Aesthetics," *Journal of Aesthetic Education* 35, no. 4 (2001): 25–46; Messay Kebede, "Negritude and Bergsonism," *Journal on African Philosophy* 3 (2003).

14. This is a large topic, much of it focused on Deleuze's studies of cinema. See Gilles Deleuze, *Cinema 1: The Movement-Image*, trans. Hugh Tomlinson and Barbara Habberjam (Minneapolis: University of Minnesota Press, 1986), esp. 1–11, 58–71; Deleuze, *Cinema 2: The Time Image*, trans. Hugh Tomlinson and Robert Galeta (Minneapolis: University of Minnesota Press, 1989), esp. 44–82, 98–123; Paul Douglass, "Bergson and Cinema: Friends or Foes?," in Mullarkey, *The New Bergson*, 209–28; Francois Zourabichvili, "The Eye of Montage: Dziga Vertov and Bergsonian Materialism," in *The Brain Is the Screen: Deleuze and the Philosophy of Cinema*, ed. Gregory Flaxman (Minneapolis: University of Minnesota Press, 2000), 141–52; Melissa Clarke, "The Space-Time Image: The Case of Bergson, Deleuze, and *Memento*," *Journal of Speculative Philosophy* 16, no. 3 (2002): 167–81; Temenuga Trifonova, "A Nonhuman Eye: Deleuze on Cinema," *SubStance*, iss. 104, vol. 33, no. 2 (2004): 134–52.

15. Dorothea Olkowski, "The End of Phenomenology: Bergson's Interval in Irigaray," *Hypatia* 15, no. 3 (2000): 73–91; Elizabeth Grosz, *Time Travels: Feminism, Nature, Power* (Durham, N.C.: Duke University Press, 2005).

16. Bessel van der Kolk and Onno van der Hart, "Pierre Janet and the Breakdown of Adaptation in Psychological Trauma," *American Journal of Psychiatry* 146, no. 12 (1989): 1530–40; Roberta Culbertson, "Embodied Memory, Transcendence, and Telling: Recounting Trauma, Reestablishing the Self," *New Literary History* 26, no. 1 (1995): 169–95; Peter A. Levine, "Memory, Trauma and Loss," *Creations* (November 2000): n.p.; Levine, "Memory, Trauma, and Healing," *Journal of Evidence-Based Complementary and Alternative Medicine* 4, no. 2 (Summer 1998): 115–21; Stephen E. Robbins, "Virtual Action: O'Regan and Noë Meet Bergson," *Behavioral and Brain Sciences* 27, no. 6 (2004): 906–7.

17. Alexandre Lefebvre, *The Image of Law: Deleuze, Bergson, Spinoza* (Stanford, Calif.: Stanford University Press, 2008). See also Christopher S. Jones, "A Lost Tradition: Nishida Kitarō, Henri Bergson and Intuition in Political Philosophy," *Social Science Japan Journal* 5 (2002): 55–70.

18. Pete A. Y. Gunter, "Bergson and the War against Nature," in Mullarkey, *The New Bergson*, 168–82.

19. Gershom Zajicek, "Bergson and Medicine," *Cancer Journal* 9, no. 6 (November/December 1996); Giovanni Stranghellini, "A Dialectical Conception of Autism," *Philosophy, Psychiatry, and Psychology* 8, no. 4 (2001): 295–98; Giovanni Stranghellini and Massimo Ballerini, "Autism: Disembodied Existence," *Philosophy, Psychiatry, and Psychology* 11, no. 3 (2004): 259–68.

20. Pete A. Y. Gunter, "Bergson's Philosophy of Education," *Educational Theory* 45, no. 3 (1995): 379–94.

21. Stephen Linstead, "Organization as Reply: Henri Bergson and Casual Organization Theory," *Organization* 9, no. 1 (2002): 95–111; Martyna Sliwa, "The Implications of Henri Bergson's Philosophy for the Management and Measurement of Service Quality" (paper presented at the Philosophy of Management conference, St. Anne's College, Oxford, July 2004); Alexander Styhre, "How Process Philosophy Can Contribute to Strategic Management," *Systems Research and Behavior Science* 19, no. 6 (2002): 577–87; Styhre, *The Innovative Bureaucracy: Bureaucracy in the Age of Fluidity* (London: Routledge, 2007).

22. Henri Bergson, *Mind-Energy* (1919), trans. H. Wildon Carr (New York: Henry Holt, 1920), 136; Bergson, *Oeuvres*, 898.

23. Bergson, *Mind-Energy*, 134–35; Bergson, *Oeuvres*, 897.

24. Bergson, *Mind-Energy*, 169; Bergson, *Oeuvres*, 919–20.

25. Bergson, *Mind-Energy*, 169; Bergson, *Oeuvres*, 920.

26. Bergson, *Mind-Energy*, 170; Bergson, *Oeuvres*, 920.

27. Bergson, *Matter and Memory*, 155; Bergson, *Oeuvres*, 296.

28. Bergson, *Matter and Memory*, 82; Bergson, *Oeuvres*, 228.

29. Bergson, *Mind-Energy*, 171; Bergson, *Oeuvres*, 921.

30. Bergson, *Mind-Energy*, 157–58; Bergson, *Oeuvres*, 913.

31. Bergson, *Mind-Energy*, 178; Bergson, *Oeuvres*, 925.

32. Bergson, *Creative Evolution*, 53–54; Bergson, *Oeuvres*, 534–35.

33. Bergson, *Creative Evolution*, 194; Bergson, *Oeuvres*, 645.

34. Henri Bergson, *The Creative Mind* (1934), trans. Mabelle Andison (Westport, Conn.: Greenwood Press, 1946), 230; Bergson, *Oeuvres*, 1460. In a recently published lecture course, Deleuze reflects on Bergson's idea that an "assemblage of curves already known can never be equivalent to the pencil-strokes of a great artist." Bergson, *Creative Evolution*, 261; Bergson, *Oeuvres*, 698; Deleuze, "Lecture Course on Chapter Three," 86.

35. Bergson, *Time and Free Will*, 166; Bergson, *Oeuvres*, 109.

36. Henri Bergson, *Laughter: An Essay on the Meaning of the Comic* (1900), trans. Cloudesley Brereton and Fred Rothwell (New York: Macmillan, 1911), 167–68; Bergson, *Oeuvres*, 467.

37. See Pippin, *Modernism as a Philosophical Problem*.

38. On the "true self," see Henri Bergson, *Mélanges*, ed. André Robinet (Paris: Université de France, 1972), 1060, 1061. On "true memory," see Bergson, *Matter and Memory*, 151; Bergson, *Oeuvres*, 292.

39. Bergson, *Mind-Energy*, 116–17; Bergson, *Oeuvres*, 886–87.

40. Bergson, *Creative Evolution*, 219; Bergson, *Oeuvres*, 665.

41. Bergson, *Time and Free Will*, 231–32; Bergson, *Oeuvres*, 151.

42. Bergson, *The Creative Mind*, 128; Bergson, *Oeuvres*, 1365.

43. Bergson, *Creative Evolution*, 7; Bergson, *Oeuvres*, 498. Bergsonian psychologist William Brown noted that when he put a "patient into a deep hypnotic state, [he] can bring up memories from any part of his life. . . . We can make him go back as early as his first year, and can get him to go back again and again and find that the same memories come up on successive occasions." William Brown, *Psychology and Psychotherapy* (London: Edward Arnold, 1922), 185. For Brown, Bergson's theory fully supported psychical research into "survival of bodily death" and mental "telepathy" (ibid., 186–87). Brown pointed to the work of Morton Prince, who hypnotized patients "very deeply in order to try to get back to the original memory which would explain" and perhaps cure traumatic symptoms. "We can bring back memories from the earlier life of a hypnotized subject," Brown concluded, "and such memories are often extremely accurate and bear out Bergson's view" (ibid., 189).

44. Bergson, *Matter and Memory,* 134; Bergson, *Mind-Energy,* 137; Bergson, *Oeuvres,* 276, 899.

45. Deleuze, *Bergsonism,* 57, 98, 111; Deleuze, *Bergsonisme,* 52, 101, 117.

46. Bergson, *Mind-Energy,* 157; Bergson, *Oeuvres,* 913. Brian Massumi makes the contemporaneous doubling of the present a central fact of his philosophy of the virtual. There is a "conversion or unfolding of the body," he writes, "contemporary to its every move. Always accompanying. Fellow-traveling dimension of the same reality. This self-disjunctive coinciding sinks an ontological difference into the heart of the body." Massumi, *Parables for the Virtual,* 5. For a brilliant critique of Massumi and the scientifically oriented claims of Silvan Tomkins and his followers, see Ruth Leys, "The Turn to Affect," *Critical Inquiry* 37, no. 3 (Spring 2011): 434–72.

47. Bergson, *Mind-Energy,* 95; Bergson, *Oeuvres,* 873.

48. Bergson, *The Two Sources of Morality and Religion* (1932), trans. R. Ashley Audra and Cloudesley Brereton with W. Horsfall Carter (New York: Henry Holt, 1935), 253; Bergson, *Oeuvres,* 1190.

49. Bergson, *Two Sources,* 311; Bergson, *Oeuvres,* 1240.

50. Deleuze, *Bergsonism,* 107; Deleuze, *Bergsonisme,* 112. "Without a doubt," Deleuze writes, "this liberation [of mankind], this incarnation of cosmic memory in creative emotions only takes place in privileged souls [âmes privilégiées]." These privileged souls constitute a "society of creators, where we pass from one genius to another" and whose ideas leap "from one soul to another . . . crossing closed deserts." Deleuze also calls them "les grandes âmes." Deleuze, *Bergsonism,* 111; Deleuze, *Bergsonisme,* 117–18. See also Deleuze and Félix Guattari's discussion of the "exceptional individual" and "leader of the pack," in *Mille Plateaux: Capitalisme et schizophrénie* (Paris: Éditions de Minuit, 1980), 293–99; Deleuze and Guattari, *A Thousand Plateaus: Capitalism and Schizophrenia,* trans. Brian Massumi (Minneapolis: University of Minnesota Press, 1987), 243–48. Deleuze's biological elitism is a topic for another discussion, although it is one that has barely been touched upon by his commentators.

51. For a widely different perspective on this topic focused on Bergson's concept of "attachment to life," see David Lapoujade, "The Normal and the Pathological in Bergson," *Modern Language Notes* 120, no. 5 (2005): 1146–55.

52. Bergson, *Matter and Memory,* 170; Bergson, *Oeuvres,* 309.

53. Bergson, *Mind-Energy,* 175; Bergson, *Oeuvres,* 923.

54. Charles Richet, *L'Homme et l'intelligence: Fragments de physiologie et de psychologie* (Paris: Félix Alcan, 1884), 248.

55. Amedee-Marie-Paulin Rouillard, *Essai sur les amnésies: Etiologie des troubles de la mémoire* (Paris: Jules Leclerc, 1885).

56. Henri Bergson, "The Problem of Personality," in *Les Études bergsoniennes* 7 (Paris: Editions Albin Michel, 1966), 78–79. Although the notion of "unconscious memory" recalls the title of Samuel Butler's famous study, Bergson was largely critical of Butler's memory theory. See Bergson's "Letter to Floris Delattre," rpt. in *Henri Bergson: Key Writings,* ed. Keith Ansell-Pearson and John Mullarkey (New York: Continuum, 2002), 369–71. Deleuze follows Bergson closely on these terms: "Useless and inactive, impassive, memory IS, in the full sense of the word: It is identical with being in itself." Deleuze, *Bergsonism,* 55; Deleuze, *Bergsonisme,* 50.

57. Bergson, *Matter and Memory,* 99; Bergson, *Oeuvres,* 234.

58. Bergson, *Matter and Memory,* 139; Bergson, *Oeuvres,* 280.

59. Bergson, *Matter and Memory,* 117; Bergson, *Oeuvres,* 261–62.

60. "If memories are really deposited in the cortical cells," Bergson wondered, then "we should find in sensory aphasia . . . the irreparable loss of certain determined words, the integral conservation of others." Bergson observed that there was no loss of the past, only an apparent one. Bergson, *Matter and Memory,* 119; Bergson, *Oeuvres,* 263.

61. Bergson, *Matter and Memory,* 121; Bergson, *Oeuvres,* 265–66.

62. No matter what happens to the material body, our whole "past psychical life is there: it survives . . . with all the detail of its events localized in time." Bergson, *Matter and Memory,* 95; Bergson, *Oeuvres,* 241.

63. Bergson, *Matter and Memory,* 176; Bergson, *Oeuvres,* 315.

64. Bergson, *Matter and Memory,* 119; Bergson, *Oeuvres,* 264.

65. Jean-Paul Sartre, *Imagination* (1936), trans. Forrest Williams (Ann Arbor: University of Michigan Press, 1962), 48.

66. Ibid., 59.

67. Ibid., 48–49.

68. Jean-Paul Sartre, *Being and Nothingness: A Phenomenological Essay on Ontology* (1943), trans. Hazel E. Barnes (New York: Philosophical Library, 1956), 162.

69. Sartre, *Imagination,* 49.

70. Bergson, *Matter and Memory,* 177; Bergson, *Oeuvres,* 315.

71. Bergson, *Matter and Memory,* 14–15; Bergson, *Oeuvres,* 166.

72. Bergson, *Matter and Memory,* 237; Bergson, *Oeuvres,* 367. Bergson noted that his theory of memory was confirmed among Freudians: "Even my idea of integral conservation of the past has more and more found its empirical verification in the vast collection of experiments instituted by the disciples of Freud." Bergson, *The Creative Mind,* 75; Bergson, *Oeuvres,* 1316. Bergson did not offer any citation in support of the claim, but he was presumably speaking of Carl Jung and his disciples.

73. Bergson, *Mind-Energy,* 35; Bergson, *Oeuvres,* 835.

74. Bergson, *Matter and Memory,* 85–86; Bergson, *Oeuvres,* 231.

75. Sartre, *Imagination,* 55.

76. Bergson, *Matter and Memory,* 14; Bergson, *Oeuvres,* 166.

77. Leonard Lawler defends the most controversial aspects of Bergson's metaphysics of memory and death. "The experience of memory," Lawler writes, "is one that verifies that memories survive brain lesions; only such an experience would allow us to establish an independent reality for spirit." And again: "Only such a pure experience of death can verify that memories survive independent of the body." Leonard Lawler, *The Challenge of Bergsonism: Phenomenology, Ontology, Ethics* (New York: Continuum, 2003), 58, 59.

78. Bergson, *Mind-Energy,* 47; Bergson, *Oeuvres,* 843.

79. Bergson, *Mind-Energy,* 95; Bergson, *Oeuvres,* 873.

80. Rouveyre, quoted in Raymond Escholier, *Matisse from the Life,* trans. Geraldine and H. M. Colvile (London: Faber and Faber, 1960), 163.

81. Bergson, *Matter and Memory,* 154–55; Bergson, *Oeuvres,* 295. For a contrasting view of regressive memory retrieval, see Campbell W. Perry, Jean-Roch Laurence, Joyce D'Eon, and Beverlea Tallant, "Hypnotic Age Regression Techniques in the Elicitation of Memories: Applied Uses and Abuses," in *Hypnosis and Memory,* ed. Helen M. Pettinati (New York: Guilford Press, 1988,) 128–54.

82. Bergson, *Laughter,* 160; Bergson, *Oeuvres,* 464. Édouard Le Roy explicitly identified ontological memory with racial memory: "There is a racial memory by which the past is continually accumulated and preserved." Édouard Le Roy, *The New Philosophy of Henri Bergson,* trans. Vincent Benson (New York: Holt, 1913), 92.

83. Bergson, *Two Sources,* 311; Bergson, *Oeuvres,* 1240.

84. Bergson, *Matter and Memory,* 174; Bergson, *Oeuvres,* 312.

85. Bergson, *Mind-Energy,* 94–95; Bergson, *Oeuvres,* 873.

86. Bergson's fascination with the moment of death was not restricted to his later writings. The conclusion to *Time and Free Will* turned on a similar consideration of what he called the

"decisive moment" that "cannot be expressed in . . . language." Bergson, *Time and Free Will,* 237; Bergson, *Oeuvres,* 154. We must return to "those moments of our life when we made some serious decision [décision grave], moments unique of their kind, which will never be repeated." Bergson, *Time and Free Will,* 239; Bergson, *Oeuvres,* 155. While starvation, hanging, and drowning certainly qualify as decisive moments, it is more difficult to see what the content of the decision is, except to live.

87. Bergson, *Creative Evolution,* 137; Bergson, *Oeuvres,* 600. In support of his claims here, Bergson cited an 1894 article by Russian physiologist Marie de Manacéine, "Quelques observations expérimentales sur l'influence de l'insomnie absolue," and "observations" made by Russian biologists Tarakevitch and Stchasny "on a man who died of inanition after a fast of thirty-five days." Bergson, *Creative Evolution,* 137; Bergson, *Oeuvres,* 600.

88. Bergson, *Matter and Memory,* 257; Bergson, *Oeuvres,* 295.

89. Bergson reviewed Egger's *La Parole intérieure: Essai de psychologie descriptive* (1881) for the journal *Critique Philosophique* in 1885. See Henri Bergson, "Intelligence et conscience," *Critique Philosophique* 2 (1885): 81–93. Robinet argues that Egger's thesis in *La Parole intérieure* "corresponds exactly to that of *Time and Free Will.*" Bergson, *Oeuvres,* 1545.

90. Bergson, *The Creative Mind,* 152–53; Bergson, *Oeuvres,* 1387.

91. Bergson, *Mind-Energy,* 94; Bergson, *Oeuvres,* 872.

92. Bergson, *The Creative Mind,* 193; Bergson, *Oeuvres,* 1425.

93. Bergson, *Creative Evolution,* 259, 210; Bergson, *Oeuvres,* 696–97, 658.

94. Bergson, *The Creative Mind,* 190; Bergson, *Oeuvres,* 1422.

95. Bergson, *The Creative Mind,* 193; Bergson, *Oeuvres,* 1425.

96. Bergson, *Time and Free Will,* 165, 166, 167; Bergson, *Oeuvres,* 109, 110.

97. Bergson, *Time and Free Will,* 166; Bergson, *Oeuvres,* 110.

98. Bergson, *Time and Free Will,* 168; Bergson, *Oeuvres,* 111.

99. Bergson, *Time and Free Will,* 170; Bergson, *Oeuvres,* 112.

100. Bergson, *Time and Free Will,* 172; Bergson, *Oeuvres,* 114.

101. Bergson, *Time and Free Will,* 173; Bergson, *Oeuvres,* 114.

102. Bergson, *Time and Free Will,* 172–73; Bergson, *Oeuvres,* 114. Bergson uses a range of analogies to describe the difference between free and automatic acts. A free act is one that has been blended, assimilated, permeated, or impregnated with our whole personality; a blind act is one that is external, superficial, parasitic, and grafted onto our "phantom self." Bergson, *Time and Free Will,* 165; Bergson, *Oeuvres,* 109.

103. Bergson, *Time and Free Will,* 167; Bergson, *Oeuvres,* 110.

104. Bergson, *Time and Free Will,* 166; Bergson, *Oeuvres,* 110.

105. Bergson, *Time and Free Will,* 170; Bergson, *Oeuvres,* 112.

106. Bergson, *Time and Free Will,* 166; Bergson, *Oeuvres,* 110.

107. Bergson, *Time and Free Will,* 166; Bergson, *Oeuvres,* 110.

108. Henri Bergson, "Simulation inconsciente dans l'état d'hypnotisme," *Revue Philosophique* 12 (1886): 525–31; hereafter cited in the text. This essay was reprinted in Bergson, *Mélanges,* 333–41. Howard Caygill has recently granted this essay some of the attention it deserves. In his unpublished study "Bergson and the Conditions of the Visible," Caygill reviews some of the same material I consider here, but his basic concerns diverge from mine.

109. In contrast to the related phenomenon of telepathy, which works at a distance, thought transference consists in the "direct perception by one mind of what is passing in another, independent of ordinary means of expression or communication. *The Oxford English Dictionary Online,* s.v. "thought-transference," http://dictionary.oed.com. In the occult literature of the time, a crucial distinction was made between thought transference and telepathy. More broadly conceived than thought transference, telepathy involved the "communication of impressions of any

kind from one mind to another, independently of the recognized channels of sense." *The Oxford English Dictionary Online,* s.v. "telepathy," http://dictionary.oed.com. The deeper relevance of this historical distinction will become evident in what follows.

110. As Alan Gauld notes, "Subjects who have been frequently hypnotized may be more susceptible, and may even be affected purely through the imagination." Alan Gauld, *A History of Hypnotism* (Cambridge: Cambridge University Press, 1992), 281.

111. Charles Sauvaire, "Observations hyperesthésie des sens dans l'état hypnotique," *Revue Philosophique* 12, no. 2 (1886): 332–35.

112. Review of the *Proceedings of the English Society for Psychical Research* and *Phantasms of the Living,* by Edward Gurney, Frederick W. H. Meyers, and Frank Podmore, *American Journal of Psychology* 1, no. 1 (1887): 140.

113. Telepathy does not require the face-to-face presence of two actors, whereas thought transference requires such contact. More significant is a distinction between thought transference and hyperesthesia. The latter does not require the communicators to be face-to-face but still offers an empirical basis for occult phenomena. Thought transference is a mode of direct perception, while telepathy accords a role to mediators. Thought transference and hyperesthesia are both modes of direct perception, but the latter is ostensibly available to calculation and observation; it is not strictly "independent of ordinary means of communication."

114. Bergson, "Rapport sur 'La Psychologie inconnue,' d'E. Boirac" (1908), in *Mélanges,* 761.

115. Ibid.

116. Ibid.

117. Bergson, "Le Parallelisme psycho-physique et la métaphysique positive" (1901), in *Mélanges,* 494. As historian R. C. Grogin has noted, "What Bergson was trying to do in large part in the generation following 1889 . . . was validate esoteric ideas through empirical and rational means. This was why he rejected the more extreme forms of the occult in favor of the empirical methods of psychical research." R. C. Grogin, *The Bergsonian Controversy* (Calgary, Alberta: University of Calgary Press, 1988), 43. For Bergson, metaphysics was simply a higher form of physics. As he put it at the end of his life, he sought the "ever-spreading mystic intuition . . . a vision of life beyond attained through the furtherance of scientific experiment." Bergson, *Two Sources,* 317; Bergson, *Oeuvres,* 1245. In the future, science would join hands with metaphysics and bring humankind into closer contact with an expanded sense of reality.

118. In 1913–14 Bergson served as president of the Society for Psychical Research. His presidential address, "'Phantasms of the Living' and Psychical Research," appears as chapter 3 of *Mind-Energy.*

119. Frederic W. H. Myers, "On a Case of Alleged Hypnotic Hyperacuity of Vision," *Mind* 12, no. 45 (1887): 155; rpt. with a new addendum as "Note on Certain Reported Cases of Hypnotic Hyperaesthesia," *Proceedings of the Society for Psychical Research* 11 (1887): 532–39. See also Myers, "Telepathic Hypnotism, and Its Relation to Other Forms of Hypnotic Suggestion," *Proceedings of the Society for Psychical Research* 10 (1886): 127–88. Myers was later chiefly known for his posthumously published study *Human Personality and Its Survival of Bodily Death* (New York: Longmans, Green, 1904), to which Bergson was heavily indebted. Myers discussed the matter of hyperesthenia in "On a Telepathic Explanation of Some So-Called Spiritualistic Phenomena," *Proceedings of the Society for Psychical Research* (November 28, 1884). The central aim of that text was to refute contemporary claims regarding the occurrence of hyperesthenia and to redescribe them in terms of thought transference. Virtually every case of occult phenomena, according to Myers, could be shown to hinge on thought transference. Myers explained: "There seems reason to believe that in many cases of hysteria and similar affections where the subject is said to be *clairvoyante,* the phenomenon is in reality referable to thought-transference only. An interesting case, recently published by Dr. Taguet, of Bordeaux, affords a good instance of

the confusion of thought at present prevalent on such subjects. His hysterical patient manifested during her *accès* an extraordinary hyperaesthesia of smell and hearing. Her eyes, meantime, were shut, or at any rate the eyeballs were completely upturned. But, nevertheless, she manifested what Dr. Taguet rather oddly describes as 'hyperaesthesia of vision,' under the following circumstances. Dr. Taguet stood completely behind her, and fixed his eyes on certain words in a book. A sheet of cardboard was held before her face, in such a position that, had it been a mirror, the book would have been reflected therein. The girl then, in her trance, took the cardboard for a mirror, and spelt out the words reflected in the cardboard before her. Now Dr. Taguet does not attempt to explain this further than by calling it hyperaesthesia of vision. But he can hardly mean that she really saw the words reflected in the cardboard. Perhaps the only other solution which suggested itself to him was that she saw the words clairvoyantly, and this solution he did not like to adopt. And there is in fact no reason, as the facts are reported, for assuming clairvoyance. Thought-transference would amply suffice to explain the phenomenon. If, then, we find telepathy occurring in mesmeric trance and spontaneous trance, we may infer that it is not inseparably linked with the ordinary stream of normal consciousness." Myers, "On a Telepathic Explanation," 219–20. For useful discussion of Myers and Bergson and the debates surrounding telepathy, see Roger Luckhurst, *The Invention of Telepathy: 1870–1901* (Oxford: Oxford University Press, 2002), chap. 7.

120. Myers, "On a Case of Alleged Hypnotic Hyperacuity of Vision," 155.

121. Eduard von Hartmann, *Der Spiritismus*, 2nd ed. (Leipzig: Berlin, Friedrich, 1885), 103, quoted in Andreas Fischer, "'The Reciprocal Adaptation of Optics and Phenomena': The Photographic Recording of Materializations," in *The Perfect Medium: Photography and the Occult* (New Haven, Conn.: Yale University Press, 2005), 175.

122. Paul-Charles Dubois, *The Psychic Treatment of Nervous Disorders*, trans. Smith Ely Jelliffe and William A. White (New York: Funk & Wagnalls, 1907), 116, quoted in Leys, *Trauma*, 87–88. See also Alfred Binet, *Les Idées modernes sur les enfants* (Paris: Flammarion, 1911). Pierre Janet reviewed these debates in *Psychological Healing: A Historical and Clinical Study*, vol. 1, trans. Eden Paul and Cedar Paul (New York: Macmillan, 1925), chap. 3.

123. Freud, *Standard Edition*, 7:288.

124. As recent commentators have shown, early in his career Freud was deeply concerned with the suggestive nature of psychoanalytic treatment. Beginning in 1895, he vigorously tried to dissociate telepathy and thought transference—commonly conceived at the time by both the scientific community and the popular press to be hopelessly bound up with the "suggestive influence" of the analyst—from the "discipline" of psychoanalysis. Nonetheless, the "scientific" foundations of psychoanalysis were haunted by the proposition that patients did not arrive with pathologies; rather, they were "suggested" to them, albeit "unintentionally," by the analyst. To this end, Freud reexamined his early involvement with Bernheim and sought to undermine Bernheim's claim that "all hypnotic manifestations would be mental phenomena, effects of suggestions." Taking sides with Charcot against Bernheim, Freud countered that "the principal points of the symptomatology of hysteria are safe from the suspicion of having originated from suggestion by the physician." "Anyone who has seen" the physiological effects of hysteria, he concluded, "will without hesitation exclude unintentional suggestion as a possible cause." Sigmund Freud, "Preface to the Translation of Bernheim's *Suggestion*" (1888), in *Standard Edition*, 1:78, 81, 82.

125. Sigmund Freud, *Dora: An Analysis of a Case of Hysteria*, trans. James Strachey (New York: Simon & Schuster, 1963), 69.

126. Stanley Cavell, *Philosophy the Day after Tomorrow* (Cambridge, Mass.: Harvard University Press, 2006), 186–87; see also 20.

127. Henri Bergson, "The Metaphysics of Life" (1886–87), trans. Bryn Loban, *SubStance* 114 (2007): 25.

128. Charles Richet, "La Suggestion mentale et le calcul des probabilités," *Revue Philosophique* 18 (1884): 609–74; Pierre Janet, "Les Actes inconscients et le dédoublement de la personnalité pendant le somnambulisme provoqué," *Revue Philosophique* 22 (1886): 577–92.

129. Bergson, *Creative Evolution,* 290; Bergson, *Oeuvres,* 721.

130. Bergson, *Time and Free Will,* 7; Bergson, *Oeuvres,* 9.

131. Bergson, *Time and Free Will,* 12; Bergson, *Oeuvres,* 12. A great artist, Bergson writes, chooses, among the "outward signs of his emotions, those which our body is likely to imitate mechanically [imitera machinalement], though slightly, as soon as it perceives them, so as to transport us all at once into the indefinite psychological state which called them forth." Bergson, *Time and Free Will,* 18; Bergson, *Oeuvres,* 16. Bergson returned to the dancer image in *Laughter.* The artist is someone who can "impose [his work] upon our attention" and "compel us, involuntarily, to be inserted into this music, like passers-by who enter into a dance." Bergson, *Laughter,* 156; Bergson, *Oeuvres,* 462. And again, in his last book, Bergson described the listener's mimetic movements at the symphony: "We feel, while we listen, as though we could not desire anything else but what the music is suggesting to us. . . . Let the music express joy, grief, pity or love, every moment we are what it expresses. We are not only ourselves, but many others, nay, all the others, too. When music weeps, all humanity, all nature, weeps with it. In point of fact it does not introduce these feelings into us; it introduces us into them, as passers-by are forced into a dance." Bergson, *Two Sources,* 40; Bergson, *Oeuvres,* 1008.

Following Bergson's examples of the beholder's "ideo-motor" imitation of the dancer's movements, Hippolyte Bernheim, in his study *L'Hypnotisme et la suggestion* (1897), considered the general role suggestion played in all forms of human interaction. Here is Bernheim: "We have established that all suggestions tend to be carried out, that all ideas tend toward action. Translated into the language of physiology, that means that every brain cell stimulated by an idea stimulates the nervous fibers that have to carry out that idea. . . . Hearing a suggestive waltz causes our body to vibrate in unison with the waltz; and even though we are not waltzing, even though we are making an effort not to waltz, if someone were to register the movements of our body with an instrument, a pattern would be obtained sketching out the unconscious choreographic movements of our machine." Hippolyte Bernheim, *L'Hypnotisme et la suggestion dans leurs rapports avec la médecine légale* (Paris: Doin, 1897), 1–2. Bergson would likely be unsatisfied with Bernheim's description. He would refuse Bernheim's materialist claim that one could actually register the bodily movements before the dance or that those registrations would be meaningful. Which is to say, Bernheim suggests that the *value* of the work resides in its "ideo-motor" effects. As I will show, Bergson rejected this idea.

132. Bergson, *Time and Free Will,* 12–13; Bergson, *Oeuvres,* 12.

133. Bergson, *Time and Free Will,* 14; Bergson, *Oeuvres,* 13.

134. Bergson, *Time and Free Will,* 17; Bergson, *Oeuvres,* 15.

135. Bergson, *Time and Free Will,* 18; Bergson, *Oeuvres,* 16–17.

136. Bergson, *Time and Free Will,* 14; Bergson, *Oeuvres,* 13.

137. Bergson, *Time and Free Will,* 14; Bergson, *Oeuvres,* 14.

138. Bergson, *Time and Free Will,* 125; Bergson, *Oeuvres,* 83.

139. Bergson, *Time and Free Will,* 14–15; Bergson, *Oeuvres,* 14.

140. Bergson, *Time and Free Will,* 15; Bergson, *Oeuvres,* 14.

141. Bergson, *Time and Free Will,* 125; Bergson, *Oeuvres,* 83.

142. Bergson, *Laughter,* 61; Bergson, *Oeuvres,* 416.

143. Bergson, *Time and Free Will,* 15; Bergson, *Oeuvres,* 14.

144. Bergson, *Time and Free Will,* 15; Bergson, *Oeuvres,* 14.

145. Bergson, *Time and Free Will,* 15–16; Bergson, *Oeuvres,* 14.

146. Bergson, *Time and Free Will,* 16; Bergson, *Oeuvres,* 15.

147. Bergson, *Time and Free Will,* 15; Bergson, *Oeuvres,* 14. Unfortunately, the clarity of the idea is compromised when Bergson says that nature, "like art, proceeds by suggestion." Bergson, *Time and Free Will,* 16; Bergson, *Oeuvres,* 14. Bergson does not polarize the distinction between art and nature. In fact, he compares nature's long-term effects, like those of a work of art, to the effects of hypnotic suggestion: "The slightest indication by nature of a feeling arouses sympathy in our minds, just as a mere gesture on the part of the hypnotist is enough to force the intended suggestion upon a subject accustomed to his control." Bergson, *Time and Free Will,* 16; Bergson, *Oeuvres,* 15. For Bergson there is a kind of aesthetic continuum that runs from the natural world through the work of art.

148. Bergson, *Time and Free Will,* 17; Bergson, *Oeuvres,* 15.

149. Bergson, *Time and Free Will,* 17; Bergson, *Oeuvres,* 15.

150. Bergson, *Time and Free Will,* 17; Bergson, *Oeuvres,* 15.

151. Bergson, *Time and Free Will,* 18; Bergson, *Oeuvres,* 16.

152. Bergson, *Laughter,* 167; Bergson, *Oeuvres,* 467.

153. Bergson, *Laughter,* 167–68; Bergson, *Oeuvres,* 467.

154. Bergson, *Time and Free Will,* 128–29, 166–67; Bergson, *Oeuvres,* 85, 111.

155. Bergson, *Time and Free Will,* 12; Bergson, *Oeuvres,* 12–13.

156. Bois, "Bonnard's 'Passivity,'" 53–54.

157. Prichard, quoted in Labrusse, *Matisse: La Condition de l'image,* 278.

158. Ibid., 279.

159. Ibid., 278.

160. Bergson, *Matter and Memory,* 68; Bergson, *Oeuvres,* 215.

161. Jack D. Flam, "Recurrent Themes in the Art of Matisse" (lecture presented at the Baltimore Museum of Art, 1976), 7. See also Flam's discussion in *Matisse: The Man and His Art,* 242–44, 389–92.

162. Matisse, quoted in Escholier, *Matisse from the Life,* 188. Spurling writes of this and related letters that in 1944 Matisse "spent thirty-six hours reading Bergson with concentrated attention for the first time in his life." Spurling, *Matisse the Master,* 423.

163. As Spurling points out, "The nearest Matisse got to reading him [Bergson] was in Tangier, where he kept one of Bergson's books . . . beside the bed for light reading in the mornings after a sleepless night." Spurling, *Matisse the Master,* 151–52.

164. Jack Flam, in *Matisse on Art,* 33. Flam's arguments are largely drawn from his earlier discussion of "Notes of a Painter" in *Matisse: The Man and His Art,* 242–44.

165. In a more recent study, Flam presents a concise summary of his Bergson-inspired claims. See Jack D. Flam, "Matisse's *Dessins: Thèmes et variations*: A Book and a Method," in *Henri Matisse: Zeichnungen und Gouaches Découpées* (Stuttgart: Stuttgarter Galerieverein, 1992). Matisse's *Themes and Variations* (1937) is said to exemplify the artist's practice as a whole: "The *Thèmes et variations* . . . serves as a statement of method in the way it throws light on a phenomenon that may be remarked from his earliest to his last works: the subtle and provocative ways in which he used recurrent themes and motifs throughout his career" (ibid., 121). Flam is surely correct to take Matisse's recurrent and self-reflexive use of themes and motifs as a key to his larger concerns. And as Flam suggests, this set of procedures speaks to Matisse's underlying commitment to a Bergsonian notion of flux. Flam continues: "The way in which Matisse used recurrent themes and variations suggests that his art was based on a concept of reality remarkably close to that of Bergson, in which form is conceived as the outline of movement and reality as a perpetual state of becoming. It also stresses the relativity of all experience and the subjective and arbitrary nature of all imagery" (ibid., 124). But it is hard to say how Bergson authorizes the claim to relativity. Flam elaborates on the idea when he characterizes Matisse's "refusal to fix a single image as the single truth of a person or thing" (ibid., 125). Saying that there are multiple ways

of understanding something is not the same as saying imagery is arbitrary. Nonetheless, Flam's more basic approach, including a range of terms such as *metamorphosis, semiosis, dynamism, flux, becoming, development, fluidity, seriality,* and *process,* well characterizes the multiple nature of Matisse's approach and is loosely compatible with aspects of my account in chapters 3 and 4. Above all, what Flam's account shows is the marked difference of approach between the first wave of Bergsonian interpretations and the more recent set of analyses associated with the New Bergsonism and the renewed focus on beholder response.

166. Catherine Bock-Weiss, "A Vitalist Critique: Decoration and Spirituality," in *Henri Matisse: Modernist against the Grain* (University Park: Pennsylvania State University Press, 2009), 147–68; hereafter cited in the text.

167. Antliff, *Inventing Bergson,* 99–100.

168. Antliff, "Rhythms of Duration," 202; hereafter cited in the text. According to Antliff, Bergson's philosophy of "rhythmic duration" stands in sharp contrast to the "visual model promoted by Greenberg in the 1960s," a model that was "a disembodied one, pared to a temporal experience of 'pure instantaneity, into an abstract condition with no before or after.'" Antliff cites Krauss's "The Im/pulse to See" here, an essay discussed in chapter 1.

169. Matisse, quoted in a letter from M. S. Prichard to M. Warren, November 7, 1913, cited in Flam, *Matisse: The Man and His Art,* 374.

170. According to Bergson, "Our personality shoots, grows and ripens without ceasing." Bergson, *Creative Evolution,* 8; Bergson, *Oeuvres,* 499. But compare Bergson's metaphor of a "ripening" flower with the marks made on the canvas with the blunt end of the brush. Perhaps there is something ironic in the suggestion of growth when viewed against the opaque expression of the sitter and the abrasively treated surface.

171. Bois, "On Matisse"; hereafter cited in the text.

172. Bois, "Matisse," in Foster et al., *Art since 1900,* 1:104. See also Bois's account of Barnett Newman's *Abraham* (1949), which is identical in many particulars to his account of Matisse's *Music.* Yve-Alain Bois, "Perceiving Newman," in *Painting as Model,* 201–4.

173. In "Painting as Trauma" Bois describes the figures in Picasso's *Les Demoiselles d'Avignon*—the painting to which Matisse is said to be responding in *Music*—as "prime indicators" of Freud's "castration complex." Here again Bois refers to Freud's study of the Medusa myth. Sigmund Freud, "Medusa's Head," in *Standard Edition,* 18:273–74. This text is said to contain a "multitude of meanings," all seemingly inscribed in Picasso's and Matisse's works. Here is Bois: "The Medusa's head is the female sex organ—the sight of which arouses castration anxiety in the young male; the image of castration itself (decapitation–castration); and the denial of castration, on the one hand by a multiplication of penises (her hair consists of snakes) and, on the other, by its power to turn the spectator to stone, in other words, into an erect, albeit dead, phallus. . . . [The Medusa myth] functions as a 'return of the repressed.' It thematizes the spectator's petrification (the theoretical basis of Renaissance monocular perspective), and it makes the female sex organ (the Medusa's head) the essential interrupter of narrative, the icon that challenges the (male) spectator by signifying to him that his comfortable position, outside the narrative scene, is not as secure as he might think." In Bois's reading, Picasso's work enacts manifold "petrifactions": the beholder is "petrified" before the work; the work thematizes petrifaction; Matisse was "seized when he saw the picture"; Braque and Derain were plunged into "horrified stupefaction." Yve-Alain Bois, "Painting as Trauma," in *Picasso's Les Demoiselles d'Avignon,* ed. Christopher Green (Cambridge: Cambridge University Press, 2001), 42–44. Once again, "seizure," "stupefaction," and "blinding" are not taken metaphorically; they are the literal effects produced by the work. For further reflections on Freud's text and the "traumatic" nature of Picasso's work, see Rosalind Krauss, "The Trauma of the Gaze," in Foster et al., *Art since 1900,* 1:82–84. A key source for Krauss's and Bois's reflections is Louis Marin's discussion in "The

Medusa Head as Historical Painting," in *To Destroy Painting* (1977), trans. Mette Hjort (Chicago: University of Chicago Press, 1995), 136–44.

174. Sándor Ferenczi, *Final Contributions to the Problems and Methods of Psychoanalysis* (London: H. Karnac, 1994), 360. Freud refers to Ferenczi's earlier reading of the Medusa myth in "Infantile Genital Organization of the Libido" (1923), in *The Collected Papers of Sigmund Freud: Sexuality and the Psychology of Love*, ed. Philip Rieff (New York: Collier, 1963), 174.

175. For a brilliant analysis of Ferenczi's text, see Leys, *Trauma*, 134–38.

176. Ibid., 138.

177. Freud, "Medusa's Head," 273–74.

178. Bois, "1951," in Foster et al., *Art since 1900*, 2:366.

179. Consistent with the logic of his claims, Bois makes no mention of the vandals' intentions. Instead, intention is projected onto the picture that assumes agency. As discussed in chapter 1, for Bois the meaning of the work is conflated with the beholder's actual responses to it. For this reason the slashing of *Who's Afraid of Red, Yellow, and Blue* is said to reveal something about the picture, but not about the vandal.

180. Wright, *Matisse and the Subject of Modernism*, 85–86.

181. Like Bois's account, Wright's affective formalism holds an important place for representation. The affective violence of Matisse's pictures occurs within a representational context (what he calls "ruined mimesis"). The formalism emerges in Wright's dogged emphasis on the "sheer presence of paint" at the expense of what that paint represents. Wright's account is saturated with these formalisms: "Brushwork is just brushwork. Color becomes mere pigment." Or "pigment is all there is" (ibid., 73, 75). For Wright what makes these more than empty formalisms is that they occur within a structural or representational system. Color, line, pigment is encountered within a failed structure of meaning.

Wright's literalism is given even fuller latitude with his discussion of the reactions of Matisse's critics. If for Maurice Denis fauvism was "vertiginous, painful, blinding, if it took vision apart, a more important factor was his inability . . . to compose what he found in front of him. . . . What disturbed Denis was the senseless violence—and I mean this literally: the violence that is without sense, without signification. . . . These signifiers are experienced with all the force of their sheerly physical presence. The viewer is brought to attend to the materiality of paint in itself, which is thus experienced in all its blinding intensity" (ibid., 84). If the effect is without sense, it is also beyond our capacity to evaluate its validity. The reader is forced to accept Wright's claims as fact (here is where affectivity merges with positivism). Nonetheless, a few questions of logic are in order. How can a signifier, if it is actually a signifier and not a shape, be physical? If the signifier is "without sense," then how is it a matter of signification at all? Alternately, if the marks on the canvas are conceived as signifiers, but the violent effect they have on the beholder is senseless, then one still has to interpret it, just like any signifier. But as Wright claims, Matisse's pictures produce *effects*, not sense—the paintings are without signification. And if they are without signification, what differentiates them from the wall they hang on? Neither paintings nor wall solicits interpretation.

182. Éric Alliez and Jean-Claude Bonne, "Matisse with Dewey with Deleuze," trans. Rafael Winkler and rev. by Robin Mackey, in *Gilles Deleuze: Image and Text*, ed. Eugene W. Holland, Daniel W. Smith, and Charles J. Stivale (London: Continuum, 2009), 104–5. This essay is largely drawn from the chapter "Peinture architecturale: Les *Danses* de Merion et de Paris," in *La Pensée-Matisse*, 247–76. Further citations of *La Pensée-Matisse* appear in the text.

183. Éric Alliez and Jean-Claude Bonne, "Matisse and the Becoming-Life of Art," *Polygraph* 18 (2006): 112.

184. Alliez and Bonne, "Matisse with Dewey with Deleuze," 110.

185. J. M. Bernstein, "In Praise of Pure Violence (Matisse's War)," in *The Life and Death of*

Images: Ethics and Aesthetics, ed. Diarmuid Costello and Dominic Willsdon (Ithaca, N.Y.: Cornell University Press, 2008), 37–55; hereafter cited in the text. I am grateful to J. M. Bernstein for allowing me to read the longer version of this talk.

186. This quote appears in Deleuze, *Francis Bacon: The Logic of Sensation*, x.

187. Ibid., 39.

188. Butler, "Response to J. M. Bernstein," 58; hereafter cited in the text.

3. The Influence of Others

1. Louis Aragon, *Henri Matisse: Roman* (Paris: Gallimard, 1971), 1:183. Aragon characteristically described Matisse's power over him as *hypnotic*: "His blue hunter's gaze fixed on me. I immediately grasped the nature of the magnetism he exercised upon me. And to be aware of it meant yielding to it. One is as powerless before genius as before a snake" (ibid., 1:42).

2. Escholier, *Matisse from the Life*, 118. Escholier notes that this view "echoes Delacroix" (ibid.).

3. Aragon, *Henri Matisse*, 1:183.

4. Matisse, *Matisse on Art*, 29; Matisse, *Écrits et propos sur l'art*, 56. Further page references to *Matisse on Art*, followed by corresponding page numbers in the French edition, will be cited in the text. Where a single page number appears, the citation refers to a text originally published in English.

5. Delectorskaya, quoted in Spurling, *Matisse the Master*, 359. Duthuit piously spoke of "a sacred egoism which sometimes threatens" to undo the artist. Duthuit, *Les Fauves*, 269; Duthuit, *Fauvist Painters*, 65.

6. Duthuit, *Les Fauves*, 269; Duthuit, *Fauvist Painters*, 69.

7. Matisse, quoted in Jane Simone Bussy, "A Great Man," *Burlington Magazine* 128, no. 995 (February 1986): 81.

8. Walter Pach, "Why Matisse?" *Century Magazine* 89 (February 1915): 634.

9. The classic account of skepticism and its limitations is J. L. Austin's "Other Minds," in *Philosophical Papers*, 76–116. I am indebted here to Stanley Cavell's analysis of skepticism in *The Claim of Reason: Wittgenstein, Skepticism, Morality, and Tragedy* (Oxford: Oxford University Press, 1999). I take my cue from Cavell's discussion of the relation between art and distance or separateness: "The art of fiction is to teach us distance—that the sources of what is said . . . is for us to discover. . . . Speaking together face to face can seem to deny that distance, to deny that facing one another requires acknowledging the presence of the other, revealing our positions, betraying them if need be. But to deny such things is to deny our separateness. And that makes us fictions to one another." Stanley Cavell, *The Senses of Walden*, expanded ed. (Chicago: University of Chicago Press, 1992), 65.

10. Michel Puy, "Les Fauves," *La Phalange* (November 15, 1907), rpt. in *Matisse: A Retrospective*, ed. Jack Flam (New York: Park Lane, 1988), 70.

11. For an excellent discussion of these matters, see Lisa Siraganian, *Modernism's Other Work: The Art Object's Political Life* (Oxford: Oxford University Press, 2012).

12. Raymond Escholier, *Matisse, ce vivant* (Paris: Floury, 1937), 41. This passage was excised from the English edition of Escholier's text.

13. Sembat, quoted in ibid.

14. Aragon takes the issue of influence to bewildering proportions. It was in Matisse's work of the summer of 1904, he wrote, "where the influence of Seurat" was evident. Then, around 1905, "Seurat's influence disappears . . . under the influence of Gauguin, although I cannot consider as an effect of an 'influence' Matisse's *meditation* on Gauguin or van Gogh, Ingres or Delacroix." Aragon, *Henri Matisse*, 1:300.

15. Marius-Ary Leblond, "La Peinture nouvelle: À propos des 'Indépendants,'" *Les Arts de la vie* 16 (1905): 235.

16. Louis Vauxcelles, "The Salon d'Automne," in Flam, *Matisse: A Retrospective*, 45.

17. *Zhivoe Slovo* 35 (1911), cited in Albert Kostenevich and Natalia Semyonova, *Collecting Matisse* (Paris: Flammarion, 1993), 51.

18. Picasso, *Picasso on Art*, 164.

19. While some of them stress how Matisse's works resist the gaze, authors unanimously see this as a kind of freedom held out for the beholder. Labrusse, for instance, describes how "the risk of being absorbed by the image is averted and the gaze doubly liberated: rhythmical expansion leads the gaze beyond the frame of the painting, the gaze [is held] at a distance." Rémi Labrusse, "'What Remains Belongs to God': Henri Matisse, Alois Riegl and the Arts of Islam," in *Matisse, His Art and His Textiles: The Fabric of Dreams* (London: Royal Academy of Arts, 2004), 57. But to describe the partially closed (what I am calling skeptical) structure of Matisse's work as a form of "liberation" for the viewer would miss the point: that the beholder is potentially in the same position as the artist—closed to the work as well as to others.

20. Michael Fried brilliantly explores issues of specularity, severance, and distantiation as well as immersion and identification in *The Moment of Caravaggio* (Princeton, N.J.: Princeton University Press, 2010).

21. Matisse, in a telegram to the Galerie Maeght in Paris, 1945. Quoted in Dorthe Aagesen and Rebecca Rabinow, "Introduction," in *Matisse: In Search of True Painting*, ed. Dorthe Aagesen and Rebecca Rabinow (New Haven, Conn.: Yale University Press, 2012), 12.

22. The problem of autonomy as self-alienation is the subject of my dissertation, "The Despair of the Physical: Materialism in Henri Matisse and George Santayana" (Ph.D. diss., University of California, Berkeley, 2005). What is missing from that study is a sense of the *limits* of skepticism as a philosophical attitude.

23. Bussy, "A Great Man," 81. Bussy's article is an abridged version of a 1947 lecture she gave at the Bloomsbury Memoirs Club.

24. As Catherine C. Bock notes, this phrase resembles a 1907 entry in Henri-Edmond Cross's notebook. Cross writes: "One cannot take hold of everything. What should be seized? Only what is useful to the expression of what one is painting. To know how to distinguish the necessary elements . . . from the useless. Everything that is not useful is harmful. Exaggerate the useful." Quoted in Bock, *Henri Matisse and Neo-Impressionism*, 102.

25. Aragon states that Matisse "must have known" Diderot's work. See Louis Aragon, *Henri Matisse: A Novel*, trans. Jean Stewart (New York: Harcourt Brace Jovanovich, 1972), 2:46.

26. Denis Diderot, *Essais sur la peinture*, ed. Jean Varloot (Paris: Editions Sociales, 1952), 711, quoted in Michael Fried, *Absorption and Theatricality: Painting and the Beholder in the Age of Diderot* (Berkeley: University of California Press, 1980), 84.

27. Matisse, quoted in Escholier, *Matisse from the Life*, 38; Escholier, *Matisse, ce vivant*, 36.

28. Matisse, quoted in Gilot, *Matisse and Picasso*, 77.

29. Bussy, "A Great Man," 81. Pierre Schneider describes the same episode in *Matisse*, trans. Michael Taylor and Bridget Strevens Romer (New York: Rizzoli, 1984), 34. Spurling has discovered some key facts about Matisse's stage hypnotist, Donato. See Hilary Spurling, *The Unknown Matisse: A Life of Henri Matisse, the Early Years, 1869–1908* (New York: Knopf, 1998), 30–32.

30. When asked what projects he saw in his future, he responded, "God guides my hand." To which he added the proviso, "Of course He doesn't speak directly to me" (163/306).

31. Sigmund Freud, *Group Psychology and the Analysis of the Ego*, rev. ed. (New York: W. W. Norton, 1990), 76. In his study "Freudian Theory and the Pattern of Fascist Propaganda," Theodor W. Adorno followed Freud in assuming the presence of an unmoved actor behind the hypnotic spell. The German masses, according to Adorno, "do not really identify themselves with

him [Hitler] but *act* this identification, *perform* their own enthusiasm, and thus participate in their leader's performance. . . . It is probably the suspicion of this fictitiousness of their own 'group psychology' which makes fascist crowds so merciless and unapproachable. If they would stop for a second, the whole performance would go to pieces, and they would be left to panic." Theodor W. Adorno, "Freudian Theory and the Pattern of Fascist Propaganda" (1951), in *The Essential Frankfurt School Reader,* ed. Andrew Arato and Eike Gebhardt (New York: Continuum, 1982), 136–37, my emphasis. Freud and Adorno assumed the presence of a withdrawn self that can potentially rebuff any hypnotic lures. It is precisely the status of this detached ego that is under inquiry. For a related discussion of Freud's text and the problem of "mass psychology," see Frankfurt Institute for Social Research, "Masses," in *Aspects of Sociology* (1956), trans. John Viertel (Boston: Beacon Press, 1972), 72–88.

32. Borch-Jacobsen describes the import of Freud's break with hypnosis: "What was at stake around 1895, when Freud decided to abandon all hypnosuggestive practices in favor of the method known as 'free association,' was thus nothing other and nothing less than the very identity of psychoanalysis, in its supposedly total difference from all psychotherapy and indeed from all thaumaturgy." Mikkel Borch-Jacobsen, "Hypnosis in Psychoanalysis," in *The Emotional Tie,* 39. Much later, Lacan repeated Freud's gesture. "Now, as everyone knows, it was by distinguishing itself from hypnosis that analysis became established," Lacan explained. "For the fundamental mainspring of the analytic operation is the maintenance of the distance between the I—identification—and the *a*. . . . [The analyst] isolates the *a,* places it at the greatest possible distance from the I that he, the analyst, is called upon by the subject to embody." Jacques Lacan, *Four Fundamental Concepts of Psychoanalysis* (1964), trans. Alan Sheridan (New York: W. W. Norton, 1977), 273. The analyst must break the identification between the subject and the subject's specular object. Only once identification has lapsed can the subject step outside herself to see herself as the "nothing" that she is. Despite the recognition of the "nothing" that *is* the self, Lacan nonetheless insisted on therapeutic forms of narrative detachment that hypnosis had placed in doubt.

33. The wider context of this passage is worth citing in full: *"If I have confidence in my hand* that draws, it is because as I was training it to serve me, I never allowed it to dominate my feeling. I very quickly sense, when it is paraphrasing something, if there is any disaccord between us: between my hand and the 'je ne sais quoi' in myself that seems submissive to it" (172/237).

34. When an interviewer asked the artist whether one should "worry about excess of feeling," Matisse offered a sharp (and unsolicited) retort: "Watch out for the influence of wives" (162–63/304–5). In a 1917 essay on Cézanne, Roger Fry closely followed Matisse's terms. Fry cited Cézanne's "constant attitude of distrust" toward others. According to Cézanne, Fry noted, "all women were *'des veaux et des calculatrices.'"* Fry glosses this as Cézanne's "dread of any possible invasion of his personality, and his sense of impotence in face of the forces of life." Roger Fry, "Paul Cézanne," in *Vision and Design* (London: Chatto and Windus, 1920), 170.

35. Paul Valéry, *Degas, Manet, Morisot,* trans. David Paul (Princeton, N.J.: Princeton University Press, 1971), 37. A copy of Valéry's book was in Matisse's library at the time of his death.

36. Duthuit, *Fauvist Painters,* 65; Duthuit, *Les Fauves,* 270. In "La Panique politique," an essay to which I am broadly indebted here, Philippe Lacoue-Labarthe and Jean-Luc Nancy consider the "theoretical panic" that is induced by Freud's analysis of the ego. "Panic takes place in the withdrawal" from "pre-originary mimesis" in the collapse of the hypnotic "relation without relation (a relation of non-relation)." Philippe Lacoue-Labarthe and Jean-Luc Nancy, "La Panique politique," in *Retreating the Political,* ed. and trans. Simon Sparks (London: Routledge, 1997), 29. By "pre-originary mimesis" they mean the moment prior to the establishment of the self and prior to what Freud called "primary narcissism." According to Lacoue-Labarthe and Nancy,

panic is evoked at the recognition of a primal, presubjective sociality as though the self were invaded, penetrated by others from the start.

37. Duthuit, *Fauvist Painters,* 68; Duthuit, *Les Fauves,* 281. Duthuit cites Jean-Paul Sartre's critique of Bergson's "materialism" (discussed in chapter 2)—"the inert images that the painter sometimes lets subsist, 'like stones in water'"—to describe the static qualities of Matisse's art.

38. Matisse, quoted in Escholier, *Matisse from the Life,* 43. When asked, "Which painter has exerted the most influence on you?" he replied, "Cézanne." "Matisse Answers Twenty Questions," *Look* 27, no. 17 (1953): 71.

39. T. J. Clark, "Freud's Cézanne," in *Farewell to an Idea: Episodes from a History of Modernism* (New Haven, Conn.: Yale University Press, 1999), 158. Clark draws a connection between the intensity of Cézanne's involvement with available modes of representation and his ability to glimpse an alternative to it: "My argument has been that Cézanne's art pursues questions of form and equivalence relentlessly, and does so in a deeply nineteenth-century way. [That is, Cézanne is painting from within an established regime of representation.] . . . if I am also proposing that the ultimate interest of Cézanne's art lies in its happening on the powers and limits of a particular system of representation, then presumably I do not believe that his art lies simply within that system—imprisoned by it, exemplifying it. I should expect the sheer doggedness with which Cézanne tries to exercise the powers in question to lead him continually to their boundaries and insufficiencies. My argument is that glimpses of alternative systems of representation are only thrown up by the most intense and recalcitrant effort to make the ones we have finally deliver the goods" (ibid., 165.)

Although Clark offers one of the most persuasive accounts of Cézanne available, I disagree with the picture of representation presented here. Rather than coming at the end of a representational regime and glimpsing something beyond it, Cézanne and Matisse, I would suggest, tried to make their work meaningful by an "intense and recalcitrant effort" to make their representations *significant,* as though meaning were available for the first time, which required a certain destruction of available modes of making and seeing but not in the effort to move beyond it to somewhere else. For further discussion of these matters, see my introduction.

40. Susan Sidlauskas, *Cézanne's Other: The Portraits of Hortense* (Berkeley: University of California Press, 2010), 82. On the problem of affective merger in Cézanne see also my review of Sidlauskas's book: Todd Cronan, "Mysterious Exchange: On Susan Sidlauskas's *Cézanne's Other: The Portraits of Hortense,*" nonsite.org 1 (2011), http://nonsite.org. In this review I also consider the larger problem of Merleau-Ponty's account of Cézanne. At times Merleau-Ponty suggests that perception itself connects us to the world, as though one just need awaken to this fact to overcome the perceived split between self and world.

41. Paul Cézanne, *Letters,* 5th ed., ed. John Rewald, trans. Marguerite Kay (New York: Da Capo, 1995), 309. Cézanne's advice to Camoin, then repeated by Matisse to his students, was itself drawn from Cézanne's teacher Thomas Couture. In a letter of September 13, 1904, Cézanne cites his teacher: "Couture used to say to his pupils: 'Keep good company, that is: go to the Louvre. But after having seen the great masters who repose there, we must hasten out and by contact with nature revive within ourselves the instincts, the artistic sensations which live in us'" (ibid., 297–98). See also Cézanne's letter of December 9, 1904, to Camoin, where he cites Couture's phrase as his own.

42. Fry, "Paul Cézanne," 168.

43. Ibid., 169, 172.

44. This phrase is drawn from Leo Stein's memoir. Stein relates: "Matisse once pointed to the difference in two plaster casts that I had of heads by Donatello and Michelangelo. In

the Donatello, he said, if one cut away the surface modeling nothing would be left, but the Michelangelo could be rolled down a hill till most of the surface elements were knocked off." Once those "surface elements" were removed, "the form would still remain." Leo Stein, *Appreciations: Painting, Poetry and Prose* (New York: Crown, 1947), 125.

45. Gustave Le Bon, *The Crowd: A Study of the Popular Mind* (1895), trans. E. Andrews (New York: Viking Press, 1960), 31.

46. Borch-Jacobsen, *The Freudian Subject,* 159.

47. Leys, *Trauma,* 46.

48. According to Leys, the hypnotic rapport, as the originary mode of sociality, a state of being before the constitution of the reflective self, is still experienced through a mode of representational mediation, an "originary and affective 'mimesis' or identification that emphasizes notions of nonspecular absorption in a traumatic scenario that is immemorial not because of a constitutive breakdown of all representation but because that scenario is unavailable for a certain *kind* of representation—theatrical self-representation—and hence for conscious memory" (ibid., 275).

49. Michel Puy, "Les Fauves (1907)," in *L'Effort des peintres modernes* (Paris: Messein, 1933), 66–67. Puy's essay first appeared, in slightly different form, in *La Phalange* (November 15, 1907): 450–59.

50. In his study of Roger Fry's formalism, Fried considers the place of the unconscious in the critic's writings. "[Cézanne's work] has that supreme spontaneity as though he had almost made himself the passive, half-conscious instrument of some directing power," Fry said of Cézanne. Fried glosses this idea in terms of Diderot's antitheatrical ideal: "My point is that unconsciousness lines up with antitheatricality, not having a design on an audience; more precisely, under the Diderotian paradigm unconsciousness in the mode of *oubli de soi,* self-forgetting, is the infallible sign of a personage's complete absorption. Fry's harping on the artist's unconsciousness (or half-unconsciousness or almost-unconsciousness) thus amounts to both a displacement and a radicalization of Diderot: to the extent that an artist is imagined as unaware of doing a particular thing, it cannot be claimed that he or she did it in order to make a particular impression on the viewer." Fried, "Roger Fry's Formalism," 21. One difference between Fry and Matisse on this point is that Matisse continually thematized the presence of the beholder in his work and writings. One might say that Fry's unconscious ideal, from Matisse's perspective, risked *nontheatricality,* as though Fry suggested the audience really did not exist. For further discussion of complications with Fry's orientation toward the beholder, see chapter 1.

51. Escholier, *Matisse from the Life,* 22, 70.

52. Prichard letter to Francis Burton-Smith, addendum to *Henri Matisse* (Montross Gallery: New York, 1915), n.p. Matisse also spoke of being "bitten by the demon of painting" (200).

53. Matisse, quoted in Lawrence Gowing, *Matisse* (London: Thames & Hudson, 1979), 32. In an interview conducted late in his life, Matisse reflected back on his career and explained that the only thing that "surpasses my compass" is "my personality" (213/304). But even at the depths of the self, the voice of another rang out—Matisse was citing the words of romantic sculptor François Rude.

54. Matisse, letter to Georges Besson, cited in Dominique Fourcade, "An Interrupted Story," in *Henri Matisse: The Early Years in Nice, 1916–1939,* ed. Jack Cowart and Dominique Fourcade (New York: Abrams, 1986), 57.

55. Matisse, quoted in Escholier, *Matisse from the Life,* 69.

56. Gilot, *Matisse and Picasso,* 178, 137; hereafter cited in the text.

57. Duthuit, *Fauvist Painters,* 85; Duthuit, *Les Fauves,* 335.

58. Gilot spoke directly to Matisse's fascination with pictorial conjuring tricks: "Matisse, like Merlin, threw [all his objects] into the magic carousel of his art. . . . With his brushes he made

them whirl; with his wizardry he bound them together, and they obeyed" (143). And again: "Like a wizard, he came in and out of his own paintings and drawings" (172). And finally: "With the ease of a magician he appears, disappears, and comes back, while at the same time he displays, juggles with, or conjures away the objects he loves or his own models" (175).

59. Guillaume Apollinaire, "Portrait of a Fauve," rpt. in *Apollinaire on Art: Essays and Reviews, 1902–1918,* ed. and trans. LeRoy C. Breunig (New York: Viking Press, 1972), 56.

60. Denis Diderot, *The Paradox of Acting and Masks or Faces?,* ed. Wilson Follett, trans. Walter Herries Pollock (New York: Hill & Wang, 1957), 17. As is well-known, Rousseau, in his *Letter to M. d'Alembert on the Theatre* (1758), offered a retort to Diderot's view of the actor as unaffected in his assumption of roles. Any act of impersonation, Rousseau argued, diminished the strength of one's personality. An actor is someone who in "counterfeiting himself, of putting on another character than his own," deteriorates the integrity of the self. See Jean-Jacques Rousseau, *Politics and the Arts: Letter to M. d'Alembert on the Theatre,* trans. Allan Bloom (Ithaca, N.Y.: Cornell University Press, 1968). On this topic, see Philippe Lacoue-Labarthe, "Diderot: Paradox and *Mimesis,*" trans. Jane Popp, in *Typography: Mimesis, Philosophy, Politics,* ed. Christopher Fynsk (Stanford, Calif.: Stanford University Press, 1998), 248–66. Mikkel Borch-Jacobsen further elaborates Lacoue-Labarthe's analysis in *Remembering Anna O.* (New York: Routledge, 1996), where he compares the hypnotized subject to the ideal actor of Diderot's *Paradox of Acting.* Nonetheless, Borch-Jacobsen's conclusions diverge widely from my claims here as he offers a performative reading of the Diderotian actor. For an incisive critique of Borch-Jacobsen's later interpretation of Freud and Diderot, see Leys, *Trauma,* 162–72.

Moreover, Bertolt Brecht followed Diderot closely in his account of the actor's attitude toward his role. Skeptical of the "hypnotic" relation of the audience to the action, Brecht insisted on a kind of "coldness which comes from the actor's holding himself remote from the character portrayed." When the actor stood aloof from his role, so the audience would maintain the same observational, or nonhypnotic, relation to the action depicted. Bertolt Brecht, "Alienation Effects in Chinese Acting" (1935), in *Brecht on Theatre,* ed. and trans. John Willett (New York: Hill & Wang, 1982), 93.

61. It is worth comparing Matisse's terms here with a related comment by Claude Monet. Dutch critic Willem Byvanck interviewed Monet at the time of his first exhibition of the *Wheatstacks* in 1891. Byvanck recalled that Monet was especially drawn to two earlier portraits of a woman with an umbrella that were shown alongside the *Wheatstacks.* Like the repeating sets of stacks, Monet noted, it was the same woman in both paintings, "but painted under different atmospheric conditions [au milieu d'une atmosphère differente]." He concluded: "For me it is only the surroundings [les alentours] which give true value to the subjects." Monet's claim reverses Matisse's priorities. Monet was primarily concerned with the atmosphere for his objects; it was the setting that gave value to the painting. For Matisse, to allow the setting to shape the work was to abdicate one's pursuit of autonomy.

62. Matisse, quoted in Schneider, *Matisse,* 666.

63. Spurling, *Matisse the Master,* 247.

64. Speaking of *Woman with a Hat,* Francis Carco boldly observed that "nothing about it was physically human. You had the impression that the artist had been much more preoccupied by his own personality than he was with the model's." Quoted in Spurling, *The Unknown Matisse,* 331.

65. Jean Guichard-Meili, *Matisse,* trans. Caroline Moorehead (London: Thames & Hudson, 1967), 209.

66. A far more sophisticated version of this problem emerges with Derrida's analysis of the voice in Husserl. Derrida's critique is focused on the problem of auto-affective self-constitution. See Jacques Derrida, "Meaning as Soliloquy," in *Speech and Phenomena, and Other Essays on*

Husserl's Theory of Signs, trans. David B. Allison (Evanston, Ill.: Northwestern University Press, 1973), 32–47.

67. Maurice Merleau-Ponty brilliantly addresses the role of mirrors in Matisse's work: "Mirrors are instruments of a universal magic that converts things into spectacle, spectacle into things, myself into another, and another into myself. . . . This explains why artists have very often chosen to draw themselves in the act of painting (they still do—witness Matisse's drawings), adding to what *they* could see of things at that moment, what *things* could see of them—as if to attest to there being a total or absolute vision, leaving nothing outside, and which closes itself over them." Merleau-Ponty, "Eye and Mind," 130. Although Merleau-Ponty's language is strongly coded in terms of merger and continuity between painter and world, his analysis of the mirror evokes the fictional or reflective nature of this connection.

Merleau-Ponty's terms contrast sharply with Bois's. According to Bois, mirroring is a marginal phenomenon within Matisse's practice. Matisse, he writes, persistently aimed to defeat the lure of "absolute vision" through the pursuit of a "peripheral" form of artistic production. Despite some early "wholly Albertian views" from around 1900 to 1904, Bois continues, and a small group of "quite exceptional works where he does . . . place himself . . . in the represented space," he "does not 'very often' [he is quoting Merleau-Ponty,] represent himself in his paintings; . . . he does not represent himself." Bois, "On Matisse," 71, 77. As I am arguing, Matisse's investment in mirroring self-presentation is unexceptional. Where Bois and I might agree is that what is "peripheral" in Matisse's practice is the establishment of connection with the beholder. This connection, however, is not at the expense of the artist's mirroring self-involvement, but through it. Autonomy sets the conditions for connection; otherwise, it risks denying both difference and sameness.

68. According to Lydia Delectorskaya, the image recalls a performance Matisse saw at the Folies-Bergère at the turn of the century (cited in Schneider, *Matisse,* 666). For a brief review of the "observer observed" motif, see Jack Cowart, *Henri Matisse: Paper Cut-Outs* (New York: Abrams, 1977), 110–11.

69. Matisse, quoted in Escholier, *Matisse from the Life,* 49.

70. Clement Greenberg, *Henri Matisse* (New York: Abrams, 1953), n.p.

71. For a useful discussion of the standing nude figure type, see the entry on *Standing Nude, Arms on Head* in *Matisse: Painter as Sculptor* (New Haven, Conn.: Yale University Press, 2007), 142–43.

72. It is difficult to establish whether Matisse would have seen Cézanne's *Bather* or his earlier variation on the figure in *The Bathers at Rest* (1875–76), now at the Barnes Foundation, at this time. Nonetheless, as commentators have consistently observed, the studio pictures of 1900 mark Matisse's first serious engagement with Cézanne's example.

73. John Elderfield aptly characterizes *Girl Reading* as "stylistically self-conscious" and marked by "overt technical discontinuity," coining the term "mixed-technique Fauvism" to describe it. John Elderfield, *Matisse in the Collection of the Museum of Modern Art* (New York: Museum of Modern Art, 1978), 44. Elderfield first used the term "mixed-technique Fauvism" in his catalog *The "Wild Beasts": Fauvism and Its Affinities* (New York: Museum of Modern Art, 1976), 56. Elderfield's comments on *Girl Reading* are useful throughout. In *Matisse in the Collection* he describes the picture as torn between the "Bergsonian world of perpetual change" and the girl's "absorption in quite another world [that] serves to insulate her from her surroundings" (44).

74. Yve-Alain Bois, *Matisse and Picasso: A Gentle Rivalry* (Paris: Flammarion, 2001), 36, 244. Discussing Matisse's *Reclining Nude* (1935), he further observes: "One of the things that is amazing about that work is that she looks the beholder in the eye. That's not something that Matisse usually does. And I think that's a kind of direct quote of Picasso, because that's some-

thing that characterized Picasso very much." "An Artistic Exchange," in "Matisse and Picasso: Conversations," 2001, http://www.matisse-picasso.org.

75. For a discussion of Matisse's relation to Manet, see Dominique Fourcade, "Matisse et Manet?," in *Bonjour Monsieur Manet* (Paris: Musée National d'Art Moderne, 1983), 25–36; Schneider, *Matisse,* 39–43; Isabelle Monod-Fontaine, "De Manet à Matisse, ou du noir à l'orange," in *Mélanges en hommage à Françoise Cachin,* ed. Henri Loyrette (Paris: Gallimard, 2002), 132–39.

76. According to Puy, Matisse's preoccupation with Manet at this time coincided with the installation of *Olympia* in the Louvre. Puy, "Souvenirs," 36.

77. As Flam observes, the group constitutes "his first obviously contrived figure compositions." Flam, *Matisse: The Man and His Art,* 89.

78. There are important exceptions to this rule. I have already mentioned the case of *Music,* with its outward-directed figures harkening back to Manet's *The Old Musician.* But thematically Matisse has more in common with Manet's absorptively attuned predecessor Gustave Courbet. Writing of Courbet, Pierre Schneider observes the apparent contradiction between the artist's assertive realism and his equally salient aesthetic of silence: "Despite his aggressive fidelity to subject matter and reality, the garrulous Courbet was irresistibly attracted to silence. The figures in some of his finest works are asleep: *The Sleeping Spinner,* . . . *The Sleeping Blonde,* who seems caught in the lull between the distant beats of a heart slowed down by deep slumber; the sensuously entangled women of *Sleep,* and a half dozen more. And the dark, monumental frieze of *Burial at Ornans* . . . is concerned with the deepest sleep of all, death." Pierre Schneider, *The World of Manet, 1832–1883* (New York: Time-Life Books, 1968), 42–43. There is compelling proof that Matisse was fascinated with these aspects of Courbet's work. He collected more works by Courbet than by any other artist. His collection included several drawings and three paintings by Courbet, two of which feature states of rest: *Sleeping Blonde* (ca. 1849–57) and a large sketch for *Young Ladies on the Banks of the Seine* (1856). The third work, *The Source of the Loue* (ca. 1864), shares a similarly absorptive theme. In Fried's estimation, the latter work, along with a small range of related scenes, represents the ne plus ultra of Courbet's absorptive imagery. See Fried, *Courbet's Realism,* 213.

79. Manet's picture constitutes the lower segment of the larger *Bullfight* (1865–67), which he divided up. Manet reiterates the basic arrangement of the dead toreador in a lithograph depicting a dead soldier in *Civil War (Scene from the Paris Commune)* (1871).

80. I owe this observation to Michael Fried.

81. Another proximate source for Manet's *Dead Toreador* is the *Dead Warrior* (formerly known as *Orlando Muerto*) by an unknown seventeenth-century master, which in Manet's time was thought to be by Velázquez. W. S. Di Piero reflects on the "assembled," "accumulative" quality of *The Dead Christ, after Philippe de Champaigne,* which aptly characterizes the intensity of Matisse's effort to *revive* the fallen figure. See W. S. Di Piero, "Matisse's Broken Circle," in *Out of Eden: Essays on Modern Art* (Berkeley: University of California Press, 1993), 127.

82. Matisse shared the sitter for *The Monk* with his friend Jean Puy, who made two portraits of him, one of which amounts to a virtual pastiche of Manet's *The Reader.* See *Le Moine (or Le Liseur)* of 1903, illustrated in *Catalogue raisonné de l'oeuvre peint de Jean Puy (1876–1960)* (Roanne: Amis de Jean Puy, 2001), 64. More than once Matisse reflected back on *The Monk.* "Do you remember our work sessions in the Boulevard de Clichy?" he asked Puy in a letter of 1949. "That old model dressed as a monk—what charm did he have for us to be so devoted to him? Color, values, a grave expression . . . we avoided words in order to express ourselves, we were looking for a plastic, purely plastic language, without resorting to theories which abounded even in those days. *Drawing, color, values* . . . . Our attitude toward nature was like that of mystics awaiting a *revelation.*" Quoted in Schneider, *Matisse,* 427.

83. Fried observes a similar tension in some key transitional works by Manet, including *The Reader* (1861) and *Monk in Prayer* (1865). As he describes them, "They make use of traditionally absorptive subject matter, though . . . aspects of both mise-en-scène and paint handling are at odds with the ostensibly beholder-denying implications of the theme." Fried further remarks on the "bravura brushwork and seamless, aspatial background" of *Monk in Prayer,* both of which are characteristic of Matisse's pictures, as "somehow inconsistent with the devotional [or generally absorptive] motif." Fried, *Manet's Modernism,* 280–81.

84. Matisse seemed to identify with the monk's intense mood of (performed) inwardness, telling Puy that he "would like to live like a monk in a cell provided that I could paint without care or disturbance." Puy, "Souvenirs," 32.

85. To borrow a phrase from Michael Fried, these works embody "a kind of *forcing* of the issue of absorption—*although* the figures 'face' . . . toward us, they appear wholly absorbed in their worlds . . . as if in simultaneous affirmation of and dialectical response to Manet's liquidation of absorption in the interests of facingness." Fried, "Caillebotte's Impressionism," 13.

86. With the exception of Dürer, this list of "favorite masters" roughly corresponds to Manet's artistic heirs. On the subject of Rembrandt, commentators have noted that Matisse's *Self-Portrait as an Etcher,* made at the same moment as the costume pieces, refers to Rembrandt's *Self-Portrait at the Easel* of 1660. Beginning in 1893 and continuing throughout the decade, Matisse made more than twenty-five copies after works in the Louvre. Most of these are French paintings from the seventeenth and eighteenth centuries, including works by Poussin, Watteau, Fragonard, and Chardin.

87. The specific stakes of the debate surrounding Manet's sources—whether or not they represent an attempt to secure "the natural genius of French painting," which as Fried suggests was to overcome nationality itself—does not concern me here. Nonetheless, I concur with Fried that to treat Manet's or Matisse's sources as equivalent instances of the "arbitrariness of the sign"—that "*all* the images that went into the making of his paintings matter to him in exactly the same way: as *mere* images"—is mistaken. Fried, *Manet's Modernism,* 84, 181.

88. Matisse's guitarists also refer to Auguste Renoir's *Young Standing Guitarist* of around 1897. In addition to contemporary sources, Matisse took Watteau's work as a model in several works. Compare, for instance, Watteau's *Diana at Her Bath* (ca. 1715) and Matisse's *Woman by a Stream* of 1905 and then again Watteau's *Nymph and Faun (Jupiter and Antiope)* (ca. 1715) and Matisse's *Nymph and Satyr* of 1908–9. Flam considers these sources in *Matisse: The Man and His Art,* 166, 246–48. I would also add two further sources for Matisse's guitarist imagery. Jean Puy sees "la femme à la guitare en costume de toréador" as "un peu hollandais," citing Vermeer's *La Brodeuse* (1669–70) as a point of reference. Puy, "Souvenirs," 26. Gowing also sees Pissarro's *Woman Sewing* of 1895 as a further point of reference, although this is more difficult to see. Gowing, *Matisse,* 43.

89. See Schneider, *Matisse,* 286–88.

90. Carol Armstrong, *Manet Manette* (New Haven, Conn.: Yale University Press, 2002), 17–19.

91. Wright, *Matisse and the Subject of Modernism,* 48.

92. Ibid., 47. An important source behind Armstrong's and Wright's claims is Jean Clay's "Ointments, Makeup, Pollen." According to Clay, "The history of art is on sale [for Manet], the past is flattened, desacralized, manipulated, instrumentalized—the end of *aura.*" Jean Clay, "Ointments, Makeup, Pollen," trans. John Shepley, *October* 27 (1983): 3. Wright, in his discussion of Gauguin's *Noa Noa* prints, claims that "all is mere repetition." Alastair Wright, "Paradise Lost: Gauguin and the Melancholy Logic of Reproduction," in *Gauguin's Paradise Remembered: The Noa Noa Prints* (New Haven, Conn.: Yale University Press, 2010), 70. Wright's skeptical

melodrama—ideas about the arbitrary nature of the sign in "all painting" and "all art"—occurs throughout his writings.

93. Emerson, quoted in John Lysaker, *Emerson and Self-Culture* (Indianapolis: Indiana University Press, 2008), 35–36. I thank Lysaker for bringing these quotes (about quotes) to my attention.

94. For a brilliant account of modernism as antifoundationalism, to which I am indebted here, see Pippin, *Modernism as a Philosophical Problem.*

95. Matisse's notion of personality development and its relation to imitation is closely related to a phrase from his friend Charles Morice's 1903 review "Le XIXe Salon des Indépendants," *Mercure de France* 43, no. 161 (1903). Morice stated: "It would be puerile, if it were not so dangerous, to deliberately forbid imitation. It is through imitation that all the truly strong personalities have developed."

96. Matisse repeated the whole of the last paragraph in a 1925 interview with a slight but important alteration in phrasing. The word "development" was dropped, and he suggested that the "artist's personality affirms itself through the struggles it has suffered" (80–81/84–85).

97. In a chapter titled "Painting and the Ready-Made," Wright considers some of the problems I am tracking here. But Wright's aim is to limit Matisse's claims about personality to the fauve years. "Concern about Matisse's *'individualité,'*" he says, "first began to emerge around 1905." "Before this time many critics had described the artist as promising to develop his artistic selfhood under the liberal tutelage of Gustave Moreau, . . . whose teaching methods facilitated the development of [his] students' individual styles." Wright, *Matisse and the Subject of Modernism,* 19. For Wright, Matisse's emphasis on personality in the 1907 interview was a response to the negative criticism he received beginning in 1905. This argument is belied by the fact that Matisse's engagement with the problem of *personnalité* began with his earliest recorded statements and continued to his last. For a useful discussion of the term *personnalité* in Matisse's writings, see Roger Benjamin, *Matisse's "Notes of a Painter": Criticism, Theory, and Context, 1891–1908* (Ann Arbor, Mich.: UMI Research Press, 1987), 70–72, 83–84.

98. Freud used similar language in his confrontation with a parallel instance of influence. In his introduction to *Group Psychology and the Analysis of the Ego* Freud contrasted "the chief subject of psycho-analytic research," what he called "social phenomena," with "narcissistic" processes, wherein "the instincts" are "withdrawn from the influence of others" (69). Freud's intention here, as it is throughout *Group Psychology,* is to reduce social psychology to individual psychology. By turning the problem of social psychology into the problem of *self*-analysis—the former simply repeats the latter in an exponential manner—Freud presupposes the existence of a subject at the foundation.

99. Matisse, *Écrits et propos sur l'art,* 56.

100. Yve-Alain Bois, "Matisse's *Bathers with a Turtle,*" *Saint Louis Art Museum Bulletin* 22, no. 3 (1998): 15.

101. E. Tériade, "Édouard Manet vu par Henri Matisse," *L'Intransigeant* (January 25, 1932), n.p.

102. In Edgar Michel, *Gustave Moreau et ses élèves: Lettres d'Evenepoël à son père* (Paris: Mercure de France, 1923), 19, quoted in Schneider, *Matisse,* 57. Matisse rephrased Moreau's terms of rediscovery of self near the end of his life, only now his masters were his models. "I had to do this parakeet with colored paper," he wrote. "Very well! I became a parakeet. And I rediscovered myself in the work." Quoted in Henri Matisse, M.-A. Couturier, and L.-B. Rayssiguier, *La Chapelle de Vence: Journal d'une création,* ed. Marcel Billot (Paris: Les Editions du Cerf, 1993), 137; Matisse et al., *The Vence Chapel: The Archive of a Creation* (Milan: Skira, 1999), 139.

103. Carrière, quoted in Azar du Marest, *Pitres, mandarins et drôles. Silhouettes contemporaines en un volume* (Paris, n.d.), quoted in Benjamin, *Matisse's "Notes of a Painter,"* 72. Like

Moreau and Carrière, Octave Mirbeau described Monet as "the pupil of no one." According to Mirbeau, despite the profound "influences" of Monet's early mentors—Mirbeau mentions Boudin, Courbet, Manet, and Pissarro—he fully "rid himself of those few external souvenirs that prejudiced the complete development of his personality." Mirbeau's triple pejorative—few, external, and souvenir—includes common terms within the Symbolist discourse on personality. Octave Mirbeau, "Claude Monet," *Le Figaro* (March 10, 1889), rpt. in *Correspondance avec Claude Monet,* ed. Pierre Michel and Jean-François Nivet (Tusson: Du Lérot, 1990), 243.

Remy de Gourmont made an analogous set of claims. Citing a letter from Goethe to Wilhelm von Humboldt, de Gourmont discussed the role of education in artistic creation: "The sooner a man becomes educated, the sooner he learns that there is a technique, an art, which will furnish him the means of achieving the regular development of his natural faculties. What he acquires would never be able to damage, in any way, his original individuality. The supreme genius is he who assimilates and appropriates everything without prejudice to his innate character . . . [while] he who mingles naively in the crowd . . . loses his personality." Remy de Gourmont, "Subconscious Creation" (1900), in *Selected Writings,* ed. and trans. Glenn S. Burne (Ann Arbor: University of Michigan Press, 1966), 145.

104. In the following year, speaking again to students, he said: "I believe in the necessity of museums. But of course one must take everything upon oneself, only asking for support and confirmation from the masters. After all is said and done, everything depends on the individual." Matisse, *Écrits et propos sur l'art,* 316. Picasso reiterated this claim on Matisse's behalf: "Everything depends on oneself. . . . The rest is nothing. It's only for that reason that Matisse is Matisse." Picasso, *Picasso on Art,* 45.

105. Matisse, quoted in Frank Harris, *Contemporary Portraits,* 4th series (New York: Brentano's, 1923), 135.

106. Matisse to Simon Bussy, 1903, in Flam, *Matisse: A Retrospective,* 42. Only after the "purge" of being "a good bourgeois" was over, Matisse went on to say, could he "appear with a calm and smiling face to the crowd of collectors who don't like uneasy or tormented people."

107. In the 1890s the problem of influence was commonly conceived in terms of physical contagion. Although Matisse was "appalled when press and public . . . identified him as a plague-carrier, spreading infection and pollution," he nonetheless solicited that reaction. Spurling, *Matisse the Master,* 35. Speaking of *The Dinner Table* of 1897, Matisse wryly noted that "the public was generally terrified of germs. One had never seen so many cases of typhoid. The public found germs at the bottom of my decanters!" In Flam, *Matisse: A Retrospective,* 30. "All my life I've been in quarantine," he later wrote. "They feared contagion," he explained, but quickly problematized the claim. "The person who *pretends* to have typhoid fever is not dangerous: it's the one who *has it.*" Matisse, interview by Courthion, 1941, 26.

108. Marcel Sembat, "Henri-Matisse," *Cahiers d'aujourd'hui,* April 1913, 189. Similar concerns were raised by de Gourmont: "I have often observed the unconscious process of mental digestion and assimilation," and "I have always refrained from disturbing its course with a premature reflection." De Gourmont, "Subconscious Creation," 147.

109. Although he was the "same man," his "one idea" was "realized by different means," Matisse explained (207/246).

110. Matisse, quoted in Walter Pach, *Queer Thing, Painting: Forty Years in the World of Art* (New York: Harper and Brothers, 1938), 122.

111. Sembat, "Henri-Matisse," 191. Matisse told his students to leave the École des Beaux-Arts and go study at the zoo, where they "could learn the secrets of embryonic life, of quiverings" (213/304). Matisse frequently used such idiosyncratic formulations centered on embryonic fluids and germs.

112. Matisse in an interview with Gotthard Jedlicka, rpt. in "Autres propos de Henri Matisse," ed. Dominique Fourcade, *Macula* 1 (1976): 106.

113. What is the nature and status of the "other" if it is always grasped in terms of a fixed core around which it unfolds? Following a broadly Aristotelian definition of the self, Matisse imagined personality as a seed that contains its own future; it needs sunlight and water ("others") to develop into a mature plant. For a detailed discussion of the Aristotelian grounds of Matisse's theory of the self, see Cronan, "The Despair of the Physical."

114. The French phrasing bears citation here: "On est dans tout ce qu'on fait, dans ses premières toiles aussi bien que dans ses dernières. Mais c'est le développement de la personnalité qui existe déjà dans la première toile qui donne l'existence dans le monde à la personnalité, parce qu'elle s'est développée. Ça existait déjà, mais c'était à l'état de cellule." Matisse, interview by Courthion, 1941, 10.

115. Lacoue-Labarthe and Nancy, "La Panique politique," 13.

116. Moreover, Matisse's view of self stood in sharp relief against aspects of Bergson's philosophy as well as its Deleuzian revision. While for Bergson the self was something that "grows and changes without ceasing," Matisse could deny the very existence of change and becoming. Bergson, *Creative Evolution,* 17; Bergson, *Oeuvres,* 506.

117. Matisse, quoted in Catherine Puget, *V. J. Roux-Champion, 1872–1953* (Pont-Aven: Musée de Pont-Aven, 1991), 8.

118. "The depth [fond] remains the same," he noted on another occasion. Matisse, *Écrits et propos sur l'art,* 242.

119. He later told a puzzled interviewer, who had been celebrating his "courageous individualism," that "I owe my art to all painters" (185). In his conversations with Picasso, Matisse conceded that the artist "must entertain a dialogue with the dead and keep them alive within himself or herself" (90).

120. The artist who "only used his talents would not exist," he went on to say. This last statement subtly conflicts with his earlier view. Matisse scolded Roux-Champion for neglecting his talents, telling him that if he continued to immerse himself in the past "he would not exist."

121. Robert Pippin, "Hegel on Political Philosophy and Political Actuality," *Inquiry* 53, no. 5 (October 2010): 412.

122. The phrase "triangle of interest" suggests René Girard's incisive analysis of the "mimetic triangle" in *Deceit, Desire, and the Novel: Self and Other in Literary Structure,* trans. Yvonne Freccero (Baltimore: Johns Hopkins University Press, 1976).

123. Lawrence Gowing, *Matisse, 1869–1954: A Retrospective Exhibition at the Hayward Gallery* (London: Arts Council of Great Britain, 1968), 28.

124. Freud, *Standard Edition,* 7: 217.

125. Mikkel Borch-Jacobsen, "The Freudian Subject: From Politics to Ethics," in *The Emotional Tie,* 22. Consider too Stanley Cavell's analysis of narcissism in Shakespeare's *Othello.* According to Cavell, *Othello* illustrates "the murderous lengths to which narcissism [defined here as 'a kind of denial of an existence shared with others'] must go in order to maintain its picture of itself as skepticism, in order to maintain its stand of ignorance, its fear or avoidance of knowing [others], under the color of a claim to certainty." Stanley Cavell, "*Coriolanus* and Interpretations of Politics ('Who Does the Wolf Love?')," in *Themes Out of School: Effects and Causes* (Chicago: University of Chicago Press, 1984), 61.

4. Matisse and Mimesis

Epigraph: Hannah Arendt and Martin Heidegger, *Letters: 1925–1975,* ed. Ursula Ludz, trans. Andrew Shields (New York: Harcourt, 2003), 106; translation modified with assistance from Andrew Mitchell. Thanks to Klostermann and the Heidegger estate for permission to reprint the poem.

1. Matisse, *Matisse on Art,* 222; Matisse, *Écrits et propos sur l'art,* 178. Further page

references to *Matisse on Art*, followed by corresponding page numbers in the French edition, will be cited in the text. Where a single page number appears, the citation refers to a text originally published in English.

2. Matisse, quoted in Guichard-Meili, *Matisse*, 222.

3. Leo Tolstoy, *What Is Art?*, trans. Aylmer Maude (London: World's Classics, 1898), 123.

4. A classic version of this idea appears in George Heard Hamilton's textbook on modern art: "Because each work of art originates in the mind and feelings of a human being, it reaches its destination in the mind and feelings of another." George Heard Hamilton, *Painting and Sculpture in Europe, 1880–1940*, 6th ed. (New Haven, Conn.: Yale University Press, 1993), 19.

5. Maurice Denis, "Painting," *L'Ermitage* (November 15, 1905); rpt. in *Pour ou contre: Le fauvisme*, ed. Philippe Dagen (Paris: Editions d'art Somogy, 1994), 60.

6. Gide, "Promenade au Salon d'Automne," 483.

7. Louis Vauxcelles, "The Salon des Indépendants," *Gil Blas* (March 20, 1907): 1; Vauxcelles, "The Salon d'Automne," *Gil Blas* (September 30, 1907); rpt. in Dagen, *Pour ou contre*, 108.

8. Charles Morice, "Modern Art," *Mercure de France* (November 1, 1908); rpt. in Dagen, *Pour ou contre*, 167.

9. Rivière, "Une Exposition de Henri Matisse," 47, 50.

10. See T. J. Clark, "Madame Matisse's Hat," *London Review of Books* 30, no. 16 (August 14, 2008): 29–32. Clark's account of Matisse is largely free of the antirepresentational impulse I considered in my introduction. Nonetheless, Clark consistently describes Matisse as a "materialist," someone who assumed that paint could "put the viewer directly in touch with things." It is on this materialist premise that Clark's deconstructive approach is based. That is to say, Matisse's effort at "direct touch" was bound to fail. See T. J. Clark, "Phenomenality and Materiality in Cézanne," in *Material Events: Paul de Man and the Afterlife of Theory*, ed. Tom Cohen (Minneapolis: University of Minnesota Press, 2001), 93.

11. Clark, "Madame Matisse's Hat," 32.

12. See Lacoue-Labarthe, *Typography*. See also Borch-Jacobsen, *The Freudian Subject*.

13. Freud, *Group Psychology and the Analysis of the Ego*, 47.

14. Ibid.

15. Freud, "Mourning and Melancholia" (1917), in *Standard Edition*, 14:249. Laplanche and Pontalis significantly alter Freud's meaning when they describe "primary identification" as the "primitive mode of the constitution of the subject on the model of the other person—a mode not dependent upon any prior establishment of a relationship in which the object can at first lay claim to an autonomous existence. Primary identification is closely bound up with the relation known as oral incorporation." J. Laplanche and J.-B. Pontalis, *The Language of Psycho-Analysis*, trans. Donald Nicholson-Smith (New York: W. W. Norton, 1973), 202. Laplanche and Pontalis assume the presence of a "model" at the constitution of the subject, whereas Freud suggests there is a mimetic state prior to the differentiation of subject and model.

16. Matisse, quoted in Aragon, *Henri Matisse: A Novel*, 236; see also Matisse, *Écrits et propos sur l'art*, 162.

17. Gilot, *Matisse and Picasso*, 242.

18. Ibid.

19. Letter from Henri Matisse to Pierre Matisse, February 12, 1945, quoted in Spurling, *Matisse the Master*, 425.

20. *Matisse-Rouveyre Correspondance*, ed. Hanne Finsen (Paris: Flammarion, 2001), 302.

21. Leys, *Trauma*, 8–9.

22. Ruth Leys provides a powerful exploration of this subject in *From Guilt to Shame: Auschwitz and After* (Princeton, N.J.: Princeton University Press, 2007).

23. Freud, "Remembering, Repeating and Working-Through" (1914), in *Standard Edition*, 12:147–56.

24. "Fragment d'un lettre de Henri Matisse," *Labyrinthe* 22–23 (1946): 3.

25. Ibid.

26. John Klein considers this passage in "Matisse after Tahiti: The Domestication of Exotic Memory," *Zeitschrift für Kunstgeschichte* 60, no. 1 (1997): 51, 59. Klein's analysis is largely focused on the sociohistorical import of Matisse's encounter with Tahiti. Klein observes that Matisse's Tahitian works were a "surrogate for a larger collective desire, expressing France's unconscious needs in its periodic renewal of the quest for paradise in the face of the relentless advance of the modern world" (ibid., 81).

27. Matisse, *Écrits et propos sur l'art,* 126.

28. Matisse, quoted in Brassaï, *Conversations with Picasso,* trans. Jane Marie Todd (Chicago: University of Chicago Press, 1999), 292.

29. Matisse to Father Couturier, quoted in Schneider, *Matisse,* 45.

30. Matisse et al., *La Chapelle de Vence,* 137; Matisse et al., *The Vence Chapel,* 139.

31. Aragon, quoted in Escholier, *Matisse from the Life,* 159.

32. Matisse et al., *La Chapelle de Vence,* 137; Matisse et al., *The Vence Chapel,* 139.

33. Matisse et al., *La Chapelle de Vence,* 137; Matisse et al., *The Vence Chapel,* 139.

34. Matisse, quoted in Escholier, *Matisse from the Life,* 46.

35. According to Gilot, for Matisse "the natural pulse of the human libido was crossed out in order to be integrated at the sublimized level of artistic creation." Gilot, *Matisse and Picasso,* 175. Gilot unsympathetically suggested that for Matisse the libido was something abstractly situated outside art. Passages such as this led Adrian Stokes to remark that Matisse gained assurance by "reducing the concrete world to terms of his own personal rhythm. . . . He reduces objects to terms of his own calligraphic omnipotence." Adrian Stokes, "Matisse and Picasso" (1931), in *The Critical Writings of Adrian Stokes,* ed. Lawrence Gowing (London: Thames & Hudson, 1978), 1:313. When Clement Greenberg said that Matisse, "full of arrogant purpose," "imposes his temperament too radically and inflexibly" on his subject, he intended it as a compliment. Clement Greenberg, "Review of an Exhibition of Pierre Bonnard, and an Obituary of Arnold Friedman" (1947), in *The Collected Essays and Criticism,* vol. 2, *Arrogant Purpose, 1945–1949,* ed. John O'Brian (Chicago: University of Chicago Press, 1986), 120. Picasso similarly lauded Matisse's pictorial arrogance. "Painting isn't a question of sensibility," he declared, "it's a matter of seizing the power, taking over from nature. . . . That's why I like Matisse. Matisse is always able to make an intellectual choice about colors." Quoted in Françoise Gilot with Carlton Lake, *Life with Picasso* (New York: McGraw-Hill, 1964), 254.

36. Escholier, *Matisse from the Life,* 142.

37. One of Schneider's basic claims is that Matisse's "oeuvre oscillates continually between realistic three-dimensionality and abstract two-dimensionality." Schneider, *Matisse,* 34. As I have been arguing, Schneider's foundationalist claim seems unsustainable.

38. Matisse, *Écrits et propos sur l'art,* 188.

39. Matisse, quoted in A. H. Barr Jr., *Matisse, His Art and His Public* (New York: Museum of Modern Art, 1951), 50. See also Bock, *Henri Matisse and Neo-Impressionism,* 37. Near the end of his life, Matisse reflected back fondly on the two works, noting that he saw them as situated "at a transitional stage between values and colors. . . . The values got the better of it in *The Studio Under the Eaves*—what depths and suppleness in the shadows." Quoted in Schneider, *Matisse,* 446.

40. Cited in Barr, *Matisse, His Art and His Public,* 77.

41. Matisse, quoted in Schneider, *Matisse,* 242.

42. There is some confusion as to what he showed at the Salon. It is unclear, for instance, whether a fourth in the sequence, *Dishes and Fruit on a Red and Black Carpet,* now in the Hermitage, was part of the exhibition. According to Antonina Izerghina, the latter work rather than the Grenoble still life was exhibited. Antonina Izerghina, *Henri Matisse: Paintings and*

Sculptures in Soviet Museums (Leningrad: Aurora Art, 1978). Spurling persuasively shows that the Hermitage picture was unfinished at the time of the exhibition and was only completed in Paris in the fall of 1906. Spurling, *The Unknown Matisse,* 369.

Matisse's critics were largely supportive of his new work, which they construed as a reversion to his pre-fauve approach. As Louis Vauxcelles wrote: "Well, he has gotten a grip on himself, and his trip to the land of the Helots seems to have done him no harm. He is returning to the deep and fleecy shimmering of his canvases of four years ago. No more abstraction, no more painting 'in itself' [en soi], in the absolute, or 'noumenon pictures.' . . . And the large still life [with red rugs], despite certain aspects that are difficult to accept, has a sumptuous harmony. The imprint of objects could be no better seen or rendered. What still shocks me is the disregard for the laws of perspective, the indifference to volume (a lemon [as in *Still Life with Plaster Figure*] is not *flat,* Matisse!). I note for the first time the use of brown—a brown with green earth, or with English green—in M. Matisse's pictures. Only someone with M. Matisse's prodigious qualities could risk that; it would be muddy and sooty in the work of twenty others." Louis Vauxcelles, "Au Grand-Palais, Le Salon d'Automne," *Gil Blas* (October 5, 1906); rpt. in Dagen, *Pour ou contre,* 78–79.

In a characteristic remark, Paul Jamot, writing in *La Chronique des arts et de la curiosité* (1906), noted that Matisse's still life submissions "testify in favor of a rare colorist, one we can all appreciate when he consents, as he does here, to be intelligible."

43. Flam, *Matisse: The Man and His Art,* 179.

44. The presence of *Flowers* at the back of *Still Life with Plaster Figure* was first noted by Françoise Forster-Hahn in *French and School of Paris Paintings in the Yale University Art Gallery* (New Haven, Conn.: Yale University Press, 1968), 17.

45. Earlier in his career Matisse fashioned two explicitly paired works: *Still Life with Oranges I* and *II* of 1899 and *Still Life with a Purro I* and *II* of 1904. It is also possible that Matisse retitled these earlier works in light of his later practice.

46. Matisse, *Écrits et propos sur l'art,* 188.

47. For a discussion of this work, see Jack Flam, "Matisse and the Fauves," in *"Primitivism" in Twentieth Century Art: Affinity of the Tribal and the Modern,* ed. William Rubin (New York: Museum of Modern Art, 1984), 211–39.

48. Bois, "Matisse's *Bathers with a Turtle,*" 1–13.

49. Ibid., 17, 9, 13.

50. Wilhelm Niemeyer, "Henri Matisse—Der Architektonische Rhythmus," in *Denkschrift des Sonderbundes auf die Ausstellung MCMX. Malerisches Impressionen und koloristischer Rhythmus* (1911): 87, quoted in Bois, "Matisse's *Bathers with a Turtle,*" 12.

51. Bois, "Matisse's *Bathers with a Turtle,*" 13.

52. Greenberg offered a brilliant dialectical account of the work in his short volume on Matisse. "The artist tries to 'imbed' the figures by using Cézanne's device of heavy blue shading *outside* their contours in order to make these vibrate backwards into depth," he explained. "But perhaps they remain too stark," he wondered. Greenberg, *Henri Matisse,* n.p.

53. Bois, "Matisse's *Bathers with a Turtle,*" 17.

54. Matisse made shelled creatures a feature of his art training. "Exaggerate according to the definite character for expression," Sally Stein recorded in her class notes. "You may consider this Negro model as a cathedral . . . and as a lobster, because of its shell-like, tense muscular parts. . . . But from time to time it is very necessary for you to remember that he is a man and not lose him and yourself in your construction" (46–47/64–66). The alternates are by now familiar: getting "lost" in one's construction while at the same time maintaining one's reserve, keeping the model in view.

55. Matisse knew the Barnes version of *The Large Bathers* as early as 1904 from a widely

circulated photograph of the artist before the unfinished work. Mary Louise Krumrine suggests that Cézanne's crouching figure refers back to Coysevox's *Crouching Venus* of 1685, although that is an unlikely point of reference for Matisse. Mary Louise Krumrine, *Paul Cézanne: Die Badenden* (Basel: Eidolon/Schweizer Verlagshaus, 1989), 247, 249, 253.

56. Looking further back in time, one powerful precedent for *Small Crouching Torso* is Michelangelo's *Crouching Boy* (ca. 1530–34), designed for the Medici Chapel in Florence, although never included in the ensemble. Hunched over upon himself, the boy clasps both hands to his right foot, his left arm sandwiched between his broadly bent legs. It is an image of precarious balance; the massive weight of the boy's torso is held together, suspended by the clenched hands that grasp his leg, while his backside rests upon an abbreviated stump. The boy's pose repeats the cubic form of the marble block the work was made from and still suggests the constrained nature of that condition. The play of light on the rough marble surface covered with chisel marks accentuates the massive projecting muscles of the bent legs. The body suggests infantile enclosure and withdrawal as well as emphatic bodily potential, as though it could expand to massive proportions if it were to emerge from its compact state. Although there is no obvious iconography for the figure, scholars have seen it as an allegory for the unborn soul. In Matisse's hands Michelangelo's strained and contorted bodies signal the ambivalent condition of self-identification (or narcissism). They express both the ideal of inwardness and the inevitability of bodily exposure. The best discussion of Matisse's lifelong fascination with Michelangelo's work is Pierre Schneider, "Una 'Belva' tra I Donatello," in *Henri Matisse: Matisse et l'Italie* (Milan: Arnoldo Mondadori, 1987), 24–28.

57. Alex Potts, *Flesh and the Ideal: Winckelmann and the Origins of Art History* (New Haven, Conn.: Yale University Press, 1994), 146.

58. John Elderfield, *Matisse in the Collection of the Museum of Modern Art,* 57. Elderfield cites Escholier's *Matisse from the Life,* 73.

59. Jacob Tügenhold, quoted in Elderfield, *Matisse in the Collection of the Museum of Modern Art,* 58.

60. Charles H. Caffin, *The Story of French Painting* (New York: Century, 1911), 216.

61. Danièle Giraudy, "Correspondence Henri Matisse-Charles Camoin," *Revue de l'Art* 12 (1971): 17.

62. Guy de Maupassant, one of the writers Matisse most greatly admired, considers this figure in "La Main d'écorché," in *L'Almanach Lorrain de Pont-à-Mousson* of 1875 (signed under the name Joseph Prunier).

63. Gowing, *Matisse,* 70.

64. Ibid.

65. Elderfield, *Matisse in the Collection of the Museum of Modern Art,* 82.

66. Ibid., 84.

Conclusion

1. Cormac McCarthy, *Blood Meridian or The Evening Redness in the West* (New York: Vintage, 1985), epigraph.

2. McCarthy, quoted in Richard B. Woodward, "Cormac McCarthy's Venomous Fiction," *New York Times,* April 19, 1992, 31.

3. Paul Valéry, "The Yalu," in *History and Politics,* ed. Jackson Mathews, trans. Denise Folliot and Jackson Mathews (Princeton, N.J.: Princeton University Press, 1971), 371–78.

4. Valéry, *History and Politics,* 373; Valéry, *Oeuvres,* vol. 2, ed. Jean Hytier (Paris: Gallimard, 1960), 1017.

5. Valéry, *History and Politics,* 373; Valéry, *Oeuvres,* 2:1018. Valéry puts this same thought

in his own voice and speaking of his own time in a piece titled "Ashes" (1902): "Our age is equally afraid of blood and time. The great majority loathes durability and sees in it only repetition—and death." Paul Valéry, *Analects,* trans. Stuart Gilbert (Princeton, N.J.: Princeton University Press, 1970), 601.

6. Valéry, *History and Politics,* 375; Valéry, *Oeuvres,* 2:1019.

7. Valéry, *History and Politics,* 374; Valéry, *Oeuvres,* 2:1018–19.

8. Valéry, *History and Politics,* 374; Valéry, *Oeuvres,* 2:1018.

9. Valéry, *History and Politics,* 231; Valéry, *Oeuvres,* 2:933.

10. Valéry, *History and Politics,* 249; Valéry, *Oeuvres,* 2:948.

11. Valéry, *History and Politics,* 249; Valéry, *Oeuvres,* 2:948.

12. Valéry, *History and Politics,* 229; Valéry, *Oeuvres,* 2:932.

13. Valéry, *History and Politics,* 229; Valéry, *Oeuvres,* 2:932.

14. Valéry, *History and Politics,* 362; Valéry, *Oeuvres,* vol. 1, ed. Jean Hytier (Paris: Gallimard, 1957), 1146.

15. Valéry, *History and Politics,* 362; Valéry, *Oeuvres,* 1:1146.

16. Valéry, *History and Politics,* 115; Valéry, *Oeuvres,* 2:936.

17. Valéry, *History and Politics,* 69.

18. Valéry, *Degas, Manet, Morisot,* 145; Valéry, *Oeuvres,* 2:1317.

19. *Self-Portraits: The Gide/Valéry Letters, 1890–1942,* ed. Robert Mallet, trans. June Guicharnaud (Chicago: University of Chicago Press, 1966), 57–58.

20. Ibid., 58.

21. Ibid.

22. Ibid., 59.

23. Ibid.

24. Ibid., 220.

25. Valéry may have been referring to an earlier letter in which Gide fondly recalled the "lewd intoxication [that] convulses me with supreme lyricism" after visiting a prostitute. Ibid., 77.

26. Ibid., 224.

27. Ibid., 84, 223.

28. Ibid., 84.

29. For a discussion of Deleuze and McCarthy, see Alan Bourassa, *Deleuze and American Literature: Affect and Virtuality in Faulkner, Wharton, Ellison, and McCarthy* (New York: Palgrave Macmillan, 2009).

30. Francis Bacon, in David Sylvester, *Interviews with Francis Bacon,* 3rd ed. (London: Thames & Hudson, 1993), 65. See Deleuze, *Francis Bacon,* 32; Deleuze, *Francis Bacon: Logique de la sensation,* 28.

31. Deleuze, *Francis Bacon,* 32; Deleuze, *Francis Bacon: Logique de la sensation,* 28.

32. If the artist has a feeling to communicate, he "must express it in such a way as to produce the maximum effect in the soul of a listener." Paul Valéry, "On Literary Technique" (1889), in *The Art of Poetry,* ed. Jackson Mathews, trans. Denise Folliot (Princeton, N.J.: Princeton University Press, 1989), 313 (the editors include a dual-face translation with the French original). Every artistic effect "is entirely calculated by the Artist," Valéry declared. As T. S. Eliot noted of this essay in his introduction to *The Art of Poetry,* Valéry virtually "invents the role which is to make him representative of the twentieth [century]" (xviii). Of course Eliot meant this as an indictment. It was not Valéry's emphatic pursuit of intentional effects that Eliot rejected but rather how those effects were ultimately sought outside of any cognitive framework or intentional setting.

33. Valéry, *The Art of Poetry,* 319. The "poem's only aim is to prepare its climax" and to produce a "final and overwhelming effect," he explained (ibid., 317). Edmund Wilson offered a

wry, but accurate, description of Valéry's aesthetic ideal: "A poem is like a heavy weight which the poet has carried to the roof bit by bit—the reader is the passer-by upon whom the weight is dropped all at once and who consequently receives from it in a moment an overwhelming impression, a complete aesthetic effect." Edmund Wilson, *Axel's Castle: A Study in the Imaginative Literature of 1870–1930* (1931; New York: Farrar, Straus and Giroux, 2004), 65–66.

34. Paul Valéry, "Introduction to the Method of Leonardo da Vinci," in *Leonardo, Poe, Mallarmé,* trans. Malcolm Cowley and James R. Lawler (Princeton, N.J.: Princeton University Press, 1972), 45; Valéry, *Oeuvres,* 1:1185.

35. Teodor de Wyzewa, "Notes sur la peinture wagnérienne," *La Revue wagnérienne* 2 (May 8, 1886): 100, 113; Wyzewa, "Notes on Wagnerian Painting," in *Symbolist Art Theories: A Critical Anthology,* ed. and trans. Henri Dorra (Berkeley: University of California Press, 1994), 148, 149.

36. Valéry, *Degas, Manet, Morisot,* 19; Valéry, *Oeuvres,* 2:1174. Before Degas, Édouard Manet fulfilled this role for Valéry. Manet was "contemptuous of any effects not arrived at by conscious clarity, and the full possession of the resources of [his] craft. . . . [Manet has] no mind to speculate on 'sentiment' or introduce 'ideas,' until the 'sensation' has been knowingly and subtly organized." Valéry, "The Triumph of Manet" (1932), in *Degas, Manet, Morisot,* 108; Valéry, *Oeuvres,* 2:1328–29.

37. Valéry's account is at the furthest remove from existential accounts of the artist as doubter and outsider, prey to anxiety and a failure to realize his ambitions. Maurice Merleau-Ponty questions Valéry on this point in his essay "Cézanne's Doubt." Merleau-Ponty provides an ironic gloss on Valéry's "Method of Leonardo": "He has complete mastery of his means, he does what he wants, going at will from knowledge to life with a superior elegance. Everything he did was done knowingly. . . . He has discovered the 'central attitude,' on the basis of which it is equally possible to know, to act, and to create because action and life, when turned into exercises, are not contrary to detached knowledge." Merleau-Ponty goes on to reject Valéry's claims here, pointing to the essential "enigma" and "secret history" behind Leonardo's (and Cézanne's) "transparent consciousness." Maurice Merleau-Ponty, "Cézanne's Doubt" (1945), in *The Merleau-Ponty Aesthetics Reader,* 72, 73.

38. Monsieur Teste "had been more or less *influenced* . . . by the kind of Degas," Valéry noted. Valéry, *Degas, Manet, Morisot,* 11; Valéry, *Oeuvres,* 2:1168.

39. While Teste's companion noticed how "deeply M. Teste . . . reflected on his own malleability," Teste was more concerned with how he could "handle, combine, transform" others. Paul Valéry, "The Evening with Monsieur Teste," in *Monsieur Teste,* trans. Jackson Mathews (Princeton, N.J.: Princeton University Press, 1989), 12, 13; Valéry, *Oeuvres,* 2:18.

40. Valéry, *Leonardo, Poe, Mallarmé,* 91–92; Valéry, *Oeuvres,* 1:1197–98.

41. Valéry, *History and Politics,* 65; Valéry, *Oeuvres,* 1:987.

42. Valéry, *Monsieur Teste,* 72; Valéry, *Oeuvres,* 2:68.

43. Valéry, *The Art of Poetry,* 169; Valéry, *Oeuvres,* 2:1262.

44. Valéry, *Monsieur Teste,* 4; Valéry, *Oeuvres,* 2:12. Considered more broadly, Valéry's exploration of his inner life marks no essential change in his project. As Derrida contends, Valéry's efforts to break off communication with the reader, to give up the "affirmation of mastery by means of the exercise of style," led to his invention of the "Implex," a pure condition of "potentiality to act." The "Implex," despite its ostensive opening to the "contingent, conditional," is fundamentally driven by the need for "self presence whose dynamic virtuality" secures the inviolability of the self against the impact of an "irreducible difference." Jacques Derrida, "Qual Quelle: Valéry's Sources" (1971), in *Margins of Philosophy,* trans. Alan Bass (Chicago: University of Chicago Press, 1982), 295, 303.

45. Valéry, *Monsieur Teste,* 46; Valéry, *Oeuvres,* 2:45.

46. Valéry, *Leonardo, Poe, Mallarmé,* 266; Valéry, *Oeuvres,* 1:675–76.

47. Valéry, *Degas, Manet, Morisot,* 26–27; Valéry, *Oeuvres,* 2:1220. Theodor W. Adorno considers this passage in his study "The Artist as Deputy" (1953), in *Notes to Literature,* vol. 1, ed. Rolf Tiedemann, trans. Shierry Weber Nicholsen (New York: Columbia University Press, 1991), 106. According to Adorno, Degas and Valéry were faithful to a utopian view of art as the "human being's possible image" (ibid.). For Valéry, Adorno writes, "to construct works of art means to refuse the opiate that great sensuous art has become since Wagner, Baudelaire, and Manet; to fend off the humiliation that makes works of art media and makes consumers victims of psychotechnical manipulation" (ibid., 107). Of course my argument so far has been largely the opposite: Valéry actively sought to master artistic response with the sensuous means of composition. Nonetheless, as I will show, Adorno's remarks capture a central aspect of Valéry's project.

48. Paul Valéry, *Aesthetics,* trans. Ralph Manheim (New York: Pantheon Books, 1964), 229; Valéry, *Oeuvres,* 2:942.

49. Valéry, *Aesthetics,* 229; Valéry, *Oeuvres,* 2:942.

50. Valéry, *Aesthetics,* 229, 230; Valéry, *Oeuvres,* 2:942, 943.

51. Valéry, *Aesthetics,* 232; Valéry, *Oeuvres,* 2:944.

52. Valéry, *Aesthetics,* 232; Valéry, *Oeuvres,* 2:944. Valéry concluded that we are the "the puppet of nonexistent things—things that need not even exist to affect us" (*Aesthetics,* 233; *Oeuvres,* 2:945).

53. Valéry, *History and Politics,* 155; Valéry, *Oeuvres,* 1:1080.

54. Valéry, *History and Politics,* 156; Valéry, *Oeuvres,* 1:1081.

55. Valéry, *History and Politics,* 117; Valéry, *Oeuvres,* 2:937.

56. Valéry, *History and Politics,* 174; Valéry, *Oeuvres,* 2:1066.

57. Valéry, *History and Politics,* 175; Valéry, *Oeuvres,* 2:1068.

58. Stéphane Mallarmé, *Oeuvres complètes,* ed. Henri Mondor and G. Jean-Aubry (Paris: Gallimard, 1945), 388. At times, Mallarmé dreamed of a book beyond every contingency, one with "nothing fortuitous, a place where chance cannot capture the idea" (ibid., 380).

59. Valéry, *History and Politics,* 175–76; Valéry, *Oeuvres,* 2:1068. Valéry relayed an anecdote about the contradictory character of light in the new scientific situation. "Among the many advances made," he wrote, "none is more astonishing than the progress of light." While light was once the "common symbol of full, distinct, and perfect knowledge," now, with the advent of radiation, it was "destroying our previous ideas of empty space and pure time." Light, he concluded, had become a symbol of the "unintelligible against the intelligible" (*History and Politics,* 166; *Oeuvres,* 2:1027).

60. Paul Valéry, *Occasions,* trans. Roger Shattuck and Frederick Brown (Princeton, N.J.: Princeton University Press, 1971), 81; Valéry, *Oeuvres,* 1:1126.

61. Valéry, *History and Politics,* 116; Valéry, *Oeuvres,* 2:937.

62. Valéry, *History and Politics,* 116; Valéry, *Oeuvres,* 2:937.

63. Valéry, "Poetry," in *Cahiers/Notebooks,* 2:176.

64. Valéry, *Leonardo, Poe, Mallarmé,* 290; Valéry, *Oeuvres,* 1:658.

65. Valéry went so far as to define artistic intentionality as a special or inverted form of everyday automatism, one where *"originality"* emerges as though *"automatically"* in the mastery of a medium. Valéry, *Aesthetics,* 160. This lecture, pages 139–79, is not reprinted in *Oeuvres*; see Valéry, "Réflexions sur l'art," *Bulletin de la Société Française de Philosophie* 35 (1935): 61–91.

66. Valéry, *Degas, Manet, Morisot,* 169; Valéry, *Oeuvres,* 2:1241. This essay, "On the Preeminent Dignity of the Arts of Fire," was the first chapter of Valéry's *Pièces sur l'art* for the 1931 and 1934 editions of the book.

67. Valéry, *Degas, Manet, Morisot,* 169; Valéry, *Oeuvres,* 2:1241.

68. Valéry, *Degas, Manet, Morisot,* 169; Valéry, *Oeuvres,* 2:1241.

69. Valéry, *Degas, Manet, Morisot,* 170; Valéry, *Oeuvres,* 2:1241–42.

70. Valéry, *Degas, Manet, Morisot,* 170; Valéry, *Oeuvres,* 2:1242.

71. Valéry, *Degas, Manet, Morisot,* 170; Valéry, *Oeuvres,* 2:1242.

72. Valéry, *Degas, Manet, Morisot,* 170–71; Valéry, *Oeuvres,* 2:1242.

73. Valéry, *Degas, Manet, Morisot,* 172; Valéry, *Oeuvres,* 2:1243.

74. Valéry, *Aesthetics,* 160–61; Valéry, "Réflexions," 77.

75. Valéry, *Aesthetics,* 161; Valéry, "Réflexions," 78.

76. Valéry, *Leonardo, Poe, Mallarmé,* 298; Valéry, *Oeuvres,* 2:710.

77. Valéry, *Degas, Manet, Morisot,* 171; Valéry, *Oeuvres,* 2:1242.

78. Valéry, *The Art of Poetry,* 161; Valéry, *Oeuvres,* 2:1255.

79. Valéry, *Aesthetics,* 143; Valéry, "Réflexions," 64.

80. Valéry, *Aesthetics,* 147; Valéry, "Réflexions," 67.

81. Valéry described the skeptical situation of the writer this way: "There is the author, his act which impresses form on a piece of matter, and there is someone who sees the matter but not the act—only its result—and experiences something: it may amount to zero, or it may be positive or negative." "The whole thing," he concluded, "is a matter of opinion" (*Aesthetics,* 179).

82. Valéry, *Aesthetics,* 225; Valéry, *Oeuvres,* 2:1284.

83. Valéry, *Aesthetics,* 226; Valéry, *Oeuvres,* 2:1284–85.

84. Valéry, *Aesthetics,* 227–28; Valéry, *Oeuvres,* 2:1286.

85. It is worth noting that Benjamin, following Valéry, also saw the increased potential for fuller intentional expression that came with technological reproduction (a thought, needless to say, he did not fully pursue). Technical reproduction, Benjamin wrote, "can . . . place a copy of the original in situations which the original itself cannot attain. Above all, it enables the original to meet the recipient halfway, whether in the form of a photograph or in that of a gramophone record. The cathedral leaves its site to be received in the studio of an art lover; the choral work performed in an auditorium or in the open air is enjoyed in a private room." Walter Benjamin, "The Work of Art in the Age of Its Technological Reproducibility," in *The Work of Art in the Age of Its Technological Reproducibility, and Other Writings on Media,* ed. Michael W. Jennings, Brigid Doherty, and Thomas Y. Levin, trans. Edmund Jephcott, Rodney Livingstone, Howard Eiland, et al. (Cambridge, Mass.: Harvard University Press, 2008), 21–22. Benjamin's indifference to the photographic mechanism here—it is interchangeable with the phonograph—points to a crucial but little-remarked aspect of the essay. As Walter Benn Michaels notes, "The mechanism of the phonograph reproduces performances which exist as works of art independent of that mechanism; [Benjamin's] comparison to the phonograph suggests that photographs too are mechanized by reproduction. In fact, the photograph is constituted by the mechanism." Walter Benn Michaels, "The Photographic Surface," in *James Welling: Photographs 1977–90* (Bern: Kunsthalle, 1990), 103. In other words, nothing about Benjamin's account suggests that the original has actually lost its intentionality in the transfer; the artist's work is just received by a new audience, one that could potentially grasp that intention more fully now that the work has lost its physically limiting context.

86. Valéry, *Degas, Manet, Morisot,* 176; Valéry, *Oeuvres,* 2:1358.

87. Valéry, *Degas, Manet, Morisot,* 179; Valéry, *Oeuvres,* 2:1360.

88. Valéry, *Degas, Manet, Morisot,* 179; Valéry, *Oeuvres,* 2:81360–61.

89. Valéry, *Degas, Manet, Morisot,* 179; Valéry, *Oeuvres,* 2:1361.

90. Valéry, *Degas, Manet, Morisot,* 179; Valéry, *Oeuvres,* 2:1361.

91. Valéry, *Degas, Manet, Morisot,* 180; Valéry, *Oeuvres,* 2:1361.

92. Valéry, *Degas, Manet, Morisot,* 183, 180; Valéry, *Oeuvres,* 2:1364, 1361. One year prior

to the publication of Valéry's text, Henry Moore offered a similar reflection on his medium: "Sculpture fully in the round has no two points of view alike." Henry Moore, *Henry Moore on Sculpture,* ed. Philip James (New York: Viking Press, 1971), 73.

93. Ezra Pound, "Brancusi," in *Literary Essays of Ezra Pound* (New York: New Directions, 1968), 442.

94. Ibid., 443.

95. Valéry, *Leonardo, Poe, Mallarmé,* 252; Valéry, *Oeuvres,* 1:643.

96. Valéry, *Leonardo, Poe, Mallarmé,* 252; Valéry, *Oeuvres,* 1:643.

97. From the *Notebooks,* rpt. in Valéry, *Leonardo, Poe, Mallarmé,* 379–80.

98. G. W. F. Hegel, *Logique,* 2nd ed., vol. 2, trans. Augusto Véra (Paris: G. Baillière, 1874), 120. For Valéry's astringent reaction to Hegel's *Aesthetics,* see the conversation appended to his "Reflections on Art" (*Aesthetics,* 165–67). Also note his rejection in the same conversation of the Kantian distinction between the "agreeable" and the "beautiful" (*Aesthetics,* 174–79). Of course he was required to reject this distinction, as it hinged on the difference between the viewer's affective response and the viewer's sense of the universality of his or her judgment.

99. Hegel, quoted in Odo Marquand, *In Defense of the Accidental: Philosophical Reflections on Man,* trans. Robert M. Wallace (Oxford: Oxford University Press, 1991), 109.

100. Valéry, *Leonardo, Poe, Mallarmé,* 252; Valéry, *Oeuvres,* 1:643.

101. Valéry, *Aesthetics,* 142; Valéry, "Réflexions," 63–64.

102. Valéry, *Leonardo, Poe, Mallarmé,* 253; Valéry, *Oeuvres,* 1:643.

103. Paul Valéry, *Masters and Friends,* trans. Martin Turnell (Princeton, N.J.: Princeton University Press, 1971), 218; Valéry, *Oeuvres,* 1:594.

104. Valéry, *Masters and Friends,* 218; Valéry, *Oeuvres,* 1:594. Valéry made a similar claim as early as 1910: "There's always something *suspect* about literature: the deference towards the public. Hence the . . . ulterior motives from which all the charlatanism arises." Valéry, "Literature," in *Cahiers/Notebooks,* 2:255.

105. Valéry, *Masters and Friends,* 218; Valéry, *Oeuvres,* 1:594.

106. Valéry, *Occasions,* 159 (essay not reprinted in *Oeuvres*).

107. Ibid.

108. Ibid., 160.

109. Ibid., 159.

110. Ibid., 163.

111. Ibid., 164.

112. Ibid.

113. Ibid., 166.

114. Ibid.

115. Ibid.

116. Valéry, *Aesthetics,* 196.

117. Ibid.

118. Valéry, *Degas, Manet, Morisot,* 136–37; Valéry, *Oeuvres,* 2:1309.

119. Valéry, *Occasions,* 198–99; Valéry, *Oeuvres,* 2:1274.

120. Valéry, *Degas, Manet, Morisot,* 141, 144; Valéry, *Oeuvres,* 2:1309, 1313.

121. Valéry, *Degas, Manet, Morisot,* 151; Valéry, *Oeuvres,* 2:1322.

122. Valéry, *Aesthetics,* 142; Valéry, "Réflexions," 63.

123. Valéry, *Degas, Manet, Morisot,* 151; Valéry, *Oeuvres,* 2:1322.

124. Valéry, *History and Politics,* 124; Valéry, *Oeuvres,* 1:1133.

125. Valéry, *Aesthetics,* 143; Valéry, "Réflexions," 64.

126. Valéry, *Aesthetics,* 143; Valéry, "Réflexions," 64.

127. Valéry, *Aesthetics,* 151; Valéry, "Réflexions," 71.

128. "It suffices to prick an animal in a certain spot to produce effects that are infinitely more intense than the initial action," he wrote. Valéry, *Aesthetics,* 144; Valéry, "Réflexions," 65.

129. Valéry, *Aesthetics,* 143; Valéry, "Réflexions," 64.

130. Valéry, *Aesthetics,* 143; Valéry, "Réflexions," 64.

131. Valéry, *Aesthetics,* 148; Valéry, "Réflexions," 68.

132. Valéry, *Aesthetics,* 147; Valéry, "Réflexions," 67.

133. Valéry, *Aesthetics,* 147; Valéry, "Réflexions," 67.

134. Valéry, *Aesthetics,* 147; Valéry, "Réflexions," 67.

135. Valéry, *Degas, Manet, Morisot,* 143; Valéry, *Oeuvres,* 2:1315.

136. Valéry, *Degas, Manet, Morisot,* 143; Valéry, *Oeuvres,* 2:1315.

137. Valéry, *Analects,* 105; Valéry, *Oeuvres,* 2:554. This is what Valéry meant when elsewhere he described poetic language as something that "must preserve itself, through itself, and remain the same" so as *"not to be altered by the act of intelligence that finds or gives it a sense"* (*The Art of Poetry,* 171; *Oeuvres,* 2:1264).

138. Valéry, *Analects,* 109; Valéry, *Oeuvres,* 2:557. Two pages later Valéry offered a prescient account of a key postwar literary theoretical claim: "An active reader makes experiments with books; tries out, perhaps, reshuffling their contents" (*Analects,* 111; *Oeuvres,* 2:559). Valéry was presumably recalling Mallarmé's suggestion about readers of *Le Livre:* "When the reader takes up a book from here or there, with its varied melodies or figured out like an enigma, it is almost remade by them." *Almost* remade by them, because, as he explained in the next sentence: "The folds will perpetuate a mark, intact, inviting one to open or close the page, according to the master." Mallarmé, *Oeuvres complètes,* 381.

139. Valéry, *The Art of Poetry,* 158; Valéry, *Oeuvres,* 1:1511.

140. Valéry, *Occasions,* 213–14; Valéry, "L'Esprit pur," *Les Annales politiques et littéraires* 94 (June 15, 1930): 576.

141. Valéry, *The Art of Poetry,* 155; Valéry, *Oeuvres,* 1:1509.

142. Valéry, *The Art of Poetry,* 155–56; Valéry, *Oeuvres,* 1:1509.

143. Valéry, *The Art of Poetry,* 158; Valéry, *Oeuvres,* 1:1512. As Philip Wheelwright puts it in his introduction to Valéry's *Idée Fixe,* "By bringing the diverse elements together in a special way . . . the poet . . . has engendered a kind of special energy in whoever is susceptible to it, an energy arising from the modification of the normal semantic potentialities of words, and has thereby elicited a real creative act on the reader's (or hearer's) part." Valéry, *Idée Fixe,* trans. David Paul (New York: Pantheon, 1965), xxi.

144. Valéry, *The Art of Poetry,* 157–58; Valéry, *Oeuvres,* 1:1511.

145. Valéry, *Analects,* 223; Valéry, *Oeuvres,* 2:645.

146. Valéry, *The Art of Poetry,* 152; Valéry, *Oeuvres,* 1:1503.

147. Benjamin, *The Work of Art,* 89.

148. W. K. Wimsatt Jr. with Monroe Beardsley, "The Intentional Fallacy," in *The Verbal Icon: Studies in the Meaning of Poetry* (Lexington: University of Kentucky Press, 1954), 5.

149. For a brilliant analysis of this and related problems, see Jennifer Ashton, "Two Problems with a Neuroaesthetic Theory of Interpretation," nonsite.org 2 (2011), http://nonsite.org.

150. Maurice Blanchot, *The Space of Literature,* trans. Ann Smock (Lincoln: University of Nebraska Press, 1982), 87.

151. Ibid., 103.

152. Barthes, "The Death of the Author," 143–44.

153. Ibid., 144.

154. See Hélène Seckel, "Three Portrait-Manifestoes of Poets: André Salmon, Guillaume Apollinaire, and Max Jacob," in *Picasso and Portraiture* (New York: Museum of Modern Art, 1996), 196n8.

155. Gilot, *Life with Picasso*, 252.

156. Valéry, *Aesthetics*, 143. Duchamp followed Valéry closely here: the "creative act is performed half way by the public or the spectator." Duchamp, "The Creative Act," 139.

157. Gilot, *Life with Picasso*, 252.

158. Valéry, *Analects*, 562; Valéry, *Oeuvres*, 1:373–74.

159. Valéry, *History and Politics*, 274; Valéry, *Oeuvres*, 1:1149.

160. Valéry, *The Art of Poetry*, 156–57; Valéry, *Oeuvres*, 1:1510.

161. Valéry, *The Art of Poetry*, 158; Valéry, *Oeuvres*, 1:1512.

162. Adorno, "Valéry's Deviations," in *Notes to Literature*, 166.

163. Ibid., 170.

164. T. W. Adorno, *The Philosophy of Modern Music*, trans. Anne G. Mitchell and Wesley V. Blomster (New York: Continuum, 2003), 37; Adorno, "Valéry's Deviations," 171.

165. Valéry, *The Art of Poetry*, 147–48; Valéry, *Oeuvres*, 1:1503.

166. Valéry, *History and Politics*, 250; Valéry, *Oeuvres*, 2:950.

167. Derrida, *Limited Inc.*, 145.

168. Ibid., 66.

169. Whereas Barthes describes the shift "from work to text," Derrida raises the stakes again by shifting from text to mark. A mark, rather than a text, is constitutively available to every reader's interpretive—or rather affective, as one does not properly *interpret* a mark—account. Nonetheless, Derrida's account fulfills the logic of Barthes's claims.

170. Derrida, *Limited Inc.*, 149. For an account of the implications of Derrida's effort to turn both work and text into marks, one that I am indebted to here, see Walter Benn Michaels, *The Shape of the Signifier* (Princeton, N.J.: Princeton University Press, 2004).

171. Valéry, *History and Politics*, 249; Valéry, *Oeuvres*, 2:948.

172. Valéry, *History and Politics*, 215; Valéry, *Oeuvres*, 1:508.

173. Valéry, *History and Politics*, 275; Valéry, *Oeuvres*, 1:1149.

174. From the *Notebooks*, rpt. in Valéry, *Monsieur Teste*, 144.

175. Valéry, *The Art of Poetry*, 183; Valéry, *Oeuvres*, 1:1456.

176. Paul Valéry, *Cahiers/Notebooks*, vol. 1, ed. Brian Stimpson with Paul Gifford and Robert Pickering, trans. Paul Gifford (Frankfurt: Peter Lang, 2000), 479.

177. Valéry, *Idée Fixe*, 31 (not reprinted in *Oeuvres*).

178. Deleuze, *The Logic of Sense*, 10.

179. Valéry, *Idée Fixe*, 33.

Index

absorption, of figures in paintings/sculptures, 9, 105, 142, 145, 148–49, 175, 203, 206, 211, 295n78, 296n83
abstraction, 6–7
action and agency: artistic, 68–69, 249–50; Bergson and, 15, 67–70, 281n102; of color, 45, 56, 57; déjà vu and, 66–67; memory and, 74; problem of, 16; representation and, 223, 264n6; Valéry and, 223
Adorno, Theodor, 17, 249–50, 289n31, 306n47
affect: the agreeable as, 5–6; Artaud and, 61, 63–64; art's direct transmission of, 14–15, 23–27, 31–33, 101; color's generation of, 15, 27–28, 36, 40–41, 54–56, 59, 270n82; Deleuze and, 263n3; empirical analysis of, 27, 265n17; form's generation of, 25, 47; Freud on, 256n7; lines' generation of, 15, 41, 54–55; Matisse and, 7–8, 23, 27–28, 32; postmodernism and, 14; representation and, 2–6; Valéry and, 226–28. *See also* affective formalism; body
affective analysis, 26–27, 32
Affective Fallacy, 247
affective formalism: Artaud and, 60–61, 63–64; Baudelaire and, 45–46; Bergson and, 70–71; Blanc and, 39–42; Delacroix and, 28–31; Fauvism and, 56–59; Gauguin and, 46–51; Gombrich and, 42; history of, 14–15, 27–31, 38–64; intention and, 34–38; meaninglessness of, 43–44; Neo-Impressionism and, 53–56; Poussin and, 38–40, 43; scientific writings about, 45; Symbolism and, 40, 44–54; tensions in, 39–40, 42, 45–46, 47, 51, 52; Wright and, 287n181
agency. *See* action and agency
agreeable, the, 5–6, 44
Alain (pseudonym of Émile-Auguste Chartier), 246
Alexandre, Arsène, 55
Alliez, Éric, 15, 70, 104–6, 108, 256n8, 274n124
animals, memory of, 77–78
anthropology, 5
anti-intentionalism, 11–13; affective formalism and, 15; agency of beholders in, 108; basis of, 259n39; Baudelaire and, 46; in Bergsonian Matisse interpretations, 96–108; New Bergsonism and, 16; Valéry and, 17, 236, 246–49
antirepresentationalism: affective formalism and, 14–15; Derain and, 56–57; of modernism, 1, 22; neomodalism and, 43–44; New Bergsonism and, 16
Antliff, Mark, 15, 70, 99–100
Apollinaire, Guillaume, 116, 124, 154–58
Aragon, Louis, 109, 172, 288n14
architecture, 94

Aristotle, 299n113
Armstrong, Carol, 152–53
art and artworks: affects generated by, 14–15, 23–27, 31–33, 43, 60–61, 63–64, 101; agency of, 68–69, 249–50; autonomy of, 41–42, 107–8; Bergson on, 92–96, 284n131; causality and, 231; evaluation of, 12, 13, 24, 27, 95, 225, 226–27, 232–34; intention in relation to, 12, 13, 35; likened to music, 28–30, 46; nature compared to, 41, 44, 47, 54, 95, 285n147; objects in relation to, 7, 12, 15, 37, 234–35, 238, 243–44, 246–47, 255n1; in relation to world, 22; and the self, 93–96; Valéry on, 243–44, 306n47; viewers' relationship to, 2–3
Artaud, Antonin, 14, 44–45, 60–61, 63–64, 275n144
Artful Mind, The, 43
artist at work, images of, 2, 128–34
artistic communication, 11–13, 48, 166, 220, 243–44. *See also* intention and intentionality; meaning
artistic effects, actual vs. intended, 34–38, 55, 267n52
artists: agency of, 68–69; art historical and critical emphasis on, 42; as Bergson's model of intentionality, 68–69; and the other, 167; relationship of, to beholder, 10, 243–44 (*see also* beholder/reader response). *See also* control, artistic; death of the author; intention and intentionality
Ashton, Jennifer, 265n19
audience. *See* beholders/readers
Aurier, Albert, 53–54, 57
Austin, J. L., 264n6
automatism, 67
autonomy: of artworks, 41–42, 107–8; of color, 10, 15, 26, 36; of form, 28, 43, 48; of lines, 10, 15, 26; Matisse and, 110, 112–13, 119–20, 157–58, 164; modernism and, 120; of objects, 36, 57; skepticism in relation to, 112
avant-garde, 1, 57
Avignon Pietà, 52

Bacon, Francis, 24, 225, 263n3
Barthes, Roland, 4–5, 14, 17, 105, 248
Barye, Antoine-Louis, 172–74
Bataille, Georges, 20
Baudelaire, Charles, 45–46, 51, 54, 242–43
Beardsley, Monroe, 247
beautiful, the, 5–6
behavior, automatic vs. intentional, 67–68
beholder/reader response: art's material and formal determination of, 23–24, 26–27, 53; to artworks, 7; Baudelaire and, 45–46; Bergson on, 92–95, 284n131; Delacroix on, 30–31; Gauguin and, 48–49; Gombrich and, 42; hypnosis and, 123; Matisse's work and, 97; modernist emphasis on, 4, 24, 37, 44, 269n75; to objects, 7; relevance/irrelevance of, 27, 34, 36; Seurat and, 55; as traumatic, 3, 21, 23–24, 32–34; Valéry and, 223, 225–29, 235, 236, 238–40, 242–51; as the work of art itself, 37. *See also* control, artistic
beholders/readers: artworks' relationship to, 2–3; birth of, 18; as creators, 11, 12–13, 15, 37, 105–6, 108, 235, 242–49; Matisse's relation to, 2, 112, 123–24, 152, 165–66, 175, 289n19; relationship of, to artist, 10; violence of artistic encounters, 32. *See also* beholder/reader response
Benjamin, Walter, 235, 247, 307n85
Berenson, Bernard, 97
Bergson, Henri: and absorption, 258n35; and action, 15, 67–70, 281n102; affective formalism and, 70–71; on art, 92–96, 284n131; *Creative Evolution*, 68, 98; and death, 72, 76–80, 280n86; on déjà vu, 66–67, 71–72; and freedom, 15, 68–72, 74, 79, 80; and habit,

9–10, 71; and hypnosis, 70, 80–96; and intention, 9–11, 15, 67–70, 80, 93–94; and intuition, 2; and materialism, 73–75; Matisse compared to, 2, 9, 96; Matisse influenced by, 98, 285n165; *Matter and Memory,* 16, 66, 71–78, 97; and memory, 15, 70–80, 278n43, 280n72; and perception, 3; popularity of, 65; and representation, 2, 8–9; revival of interest in, 65–66; *Time and Free Will,* 15, 80, 92; "Unconscious Simulation in the State of Hypnosis," 15, 81–85
Bernard, Émile, 51
Bernheim, Hippolyte, 256n7, 283n124, 284n131
Bernheim-Jeune Gallery, 196
Bernstein, J. M., 15, 70, 106
Besson, Georges, 122
Binet, Alfred, 88
Blanc, Charles, 30, 51, 54, 59, 268n60; *Grammaire des arts du dessin,* 39–42
Blanchot, Maurice, 17, 247–48
blinding, as effect of Matisse's work, 23, 32–33, 101, 107
Bock-Weiss, Catherine, 15, 98–99
body: Artaud and, 63; art's determination of affective response of, 23–24, 26–27, 31–34, 43, 60–61, 63–64, 104–7, 270n82, 270n87 (*see also* affective formalism); form in relation to, 51; Gauguin on art's relation to, 46–48; modernist privileging of, 1; without organs, Deleuzian concept of, 105, 107. *See also* affect
Boirac, Émile, 84–85
Bois, Yve-Alain, 2–3, 19–21, 23, 24, 26–27, 31–33, 43, 70, 101–4, 145, 156, 175, 206, 286n173, 287n179, 294n67
Bonnard, Pierre, 26
Bonne, Jean-Claude, 15, 70, 104–6, 108, 256n8
Borch-Jacobsen, Mikkel, 8, 121–22, 164, 256n7, 290n32
brain: Gauguin on role of, in artistic experience, 46–48, 270n82; pathologies of, 72–78
Brancusi, Constantin, 238
Brassaï (pseudonym of Gyula Halász), 171
Brecht, Bertolt, 34–35, 293n60
Brown, William, 278n43
Bussy, Jane, 110, 113–14
Bussy, Simon, 156
Butler, Judith, 15, 24, 70, 107–8
Butler, Samuel, 279n56

Cachin, Françoise 272n98
Caffin, Charles, 214
Camoin, Charles, 119
cannibalism, 167, 203–4
Carrière, Eugène, 156
causality, 223, 231, 243
Cavell, Stanley, 90, 288n9, 299n125
ceramics, 232–34
Cézanne, Paul, 32, 50, 109, 111, 117–20, 136, 153, 196, 291n39, 291n41; *The Bather,* 142, 143; *The Large Bathers,* 117–18, 211; *The Peppermint Bottle,* 197–200; *Plaster Putto,* 196–200, 214, 217; *Standing Nude,* 136, 137, 142; *Still Life with Statuette,* 199; *Stoneware Pitcher,* 199–200
Champaigne, Philippe de : *Dead Christ,* 148
chance: artist's intention in relation to, 232–36, 241; ceramics and, 232–34; literature and, 239–40; Mallarmé and, 231, 239; photography and, 241; sculpture and, 236, 238
change: Bergson and, 16; Matisse and, 42, 110
Chantelou, Paul Fréart de, 38
Chapel of the Rosary, Vence, France, 27, 29
Charcot, Jean-Martin, 88, 89, 283n124
Chardin, Jean-Baptiste-Siméon, 152; *The Ray,* 207
Chavannes, Puvis de, 153
Chevreul, Michel, 59

citation: in costume paintings, 146–47, 152–53; Manet and, 152; Matisse and, 21, 111, 112, 113, 128–34, 146–47, 152–54, 159; self-, 112, 128–34; and subjectivity, 113
Clark, T. J., 22, 117–18, 166–67, 262n80, 263n81, 291n39, 300n10
color: affects generated by, 15, 27–28, 36, 40–41, 54–56, 59, 270n82; agency of, 45, 56, 57; autonomy of, 10, 15, 26, 36; Delaunay and, 59; Fauvist debates about, 56–59; Gauguin and, 46–48, 270n82; Matisse and, 27–28, 58–59, 256n8; meaning of, 39–40, 47, 53–54; as object, 54; as a punch, 59; sensory contact through, 2. *See also* form
communication. *See* artistic communication
contagion, 48
control, artistic: Duchamp on, 11–12; lack or limitations of, 10–13; Matisse and, 42, 58, 116, 126, 301n35; Valéry on, 233–34, 236, 238, 240, 242–43, 305n37. *See also* beholder/reader response
conventions: Valéry on, 229–30
Corot, Jean-Baptiste-Camille, 152, 159, 242–43, 244; *Seated Monk, Reading,* 149, 150
Corra, Bruno, 63
correspondences, 51, 54
Courbet, Gustave, 295n78
Courthion, Pierre, 58, 158
Couture, Thomas, 291n41
Crary, Jonathan, 273n116
Craven, Arthur, 59
crouching figure type, 207–11

Dada, 18
dance, 92–93, 284n131
Darstellung, 8
death: Bergson and, 72, 76–80, 280n86; beyond, 75–79; the European mind and, 221–22; Matisse and, 76, 148; memory and, 72, 75–76, 78; near-death experiences, 78
death of the author, 4, 18, 105, 120, 248
Debord, Guy, 22, 230, 262n80
Degas, Edgar, 226, 228
déjà vu, 66–67, 71–72
Delacroix, Eugène, 28–31, 45–46, 54, 152, 242–43; *The Massacre at Chios,* 29–30, 31; *Young Guitarist in Costume of the Italian Renaissance,* 152
Delaunay, Robert, 59, 274n135, 274n136
Delaunay, Sonia, 274n136
Delectorskaya, Lydia, 110
Deleuze, Gilles, 1, 4, 23, 24, 26–27, 31–34, 43, 63, 66, 71, 72, 104–8, 225, 249, 251, 263n3, 265n17, 270n83, 279n50; *Bergsonism,* 16, 66
Denis, Maurice, 50–52, 166, 271n89
Derain, André, v, 35–36, 56, 59
Derrida, Jacques, 1, 17, 250, 255n3, 305n44, 310n169
Descartes, René, 1, 255n1
detachment/separateness: artist's sense of, 129, 168; Cézanne and, 118; in experience of art, 288n9; in Freudian treatment, 170; in hypnosis, 10; limitations of, 17, 164; in Matisse's artistic approach, 7–8, 17, 110, 112, 124, 165–67; in Matisse's character/personality, 169; realism associated with, 175; between self and other, 288n9. *See also* skepticism
devouring affection, 167–68, 203–4
Dickerman, Leah, 18
Diderot, Denis, 45, 114, 124–26, 292n50, 293n60
difference: between art and world, 7, 22, 37; Cézanne and, 117–19; disagreement vs., 36–37, 106; in hypnotic bond, 122; Matisse and, 165, 167; of the other, 110; representation and, 7, 22
disagreement over meaning and interpretation, 3, 5, 17, 26, 34–37, 64, 97, 99, 102, 106, 235, 245

Matisse and, 9–13, 36, 42, 58; meaning in relation to, 3–4, 11–14, 17, 35–37, 233; medium in relation to, 13, 232–34; Picasso on, 248; Poussin's work and, 39–41; psychology not pertinent to discussions of, 12; relevance/irrelevance of, 4, 10–11, 24, 31, 36, 38, 44, 51, 55, 106; unconscious, 13, 68; Valéry and, 17–18, 228–29, 232–36, 238–41, 244–51, 260n52, 304n32, 305n37, 306n65. *See also* anti-intentionalism; artistic communication; death of the author
interpretation, 34–37; act of, 14; affective analysis vs., 26–27; Brecht on, 34–35; comparisons and evaluations of, 3–6, 12, 17, 26–27, 34–37, 235, 245, 250; force and, 250; perception as locus of, 3–4; persuasion as criterion for, 4, 12; relevance to, of beholder's response, 27. *See also* disagreement over meaning and interpretation; meaning
intuition, 2

Jacques-Dalcroze, Émile, 264n9
Jamot, Paul, 302n42
Janet, Pierre, 91
Joblaud, Caroline, 175–76, 190
judgment, shared quality of, 5
Jung, Carl, 280n72

Kahn, Gustave, 53, 270n82
Kandinsky, Wassily, 25–26, 28–29, 36, 42, 59, 264n9, 265n24
Kant, Immanuel, 5–6, 257n14, 257n16
Klein, John, 301n26
Krauss, Rosalind, 18–20, 258n22, 266n40

Labrusse, Rémi, 98, 263n4
Lacan, Jacques, 170, 290n32
Lacoue-Labarthe, Philippe, 158, 167, 290n36
language: racial memory of, 76–77; as weapon or tool, 251
Laplanche, J., 300n15
Lawler, Leonard, 280n77
Le Bon, Gustave, 121
Lecomte, Georges, 55
Le Corbusier, 34
Leonardo da Vinci, 68–69, 227, 305n37
Leys, Ruth, 103, 121–22, 169–70, 259n38, 292n48
life after death, 75
lines: affects generated by, 15, 41, 54–55; autonomy of, 10, 15, 26; meaning of, 38–41, 53–54; as objects, 54. *See also* form
Lissitzky, El, 20–21, 262n80
literalism, 18
lived experience, 22
Loos, Adolf, 35
Lot and His Daughters (anonymous), 60–61, 62

machine: Baudelaire on artwork as, 45; Matisse on artwork as affective, 2, 58; painting as affective, 23–64, 101; Valéry on artwork as, 226–28, 246–47
Maillol, Aristide: *Woman with Crab,* 211, 212
Malevich, Kazimir, 7
Mallarmé, Stéphane, 4, 51–52, 228, 231, 234, 239–41, 309n138
Manet, Édouard, 110, 113, 145–49, 152, 153, 156, 296n83; *The Dead Toreador,* 147–48; *Déjeuner sur l'herbe,* 152; *The Guitar Player,* 152; *A Matador,* 152; *Monk in Prayer,* 149, 150, 296n83; *The Music Lesson,* 152; *Old Musician,* 152; *Olympia,* 147; *Self-Portrait with Palette,* 152; *The Spanish Singer,* 152; *The Street Singer,* 152; *The Tragic Actor,* 152; *Young Man in the Costume of a Majo,* 152
Marinetti, Filippo, 63
marks, 250, 310n169
Marx, Karl, 70
Massumi, Brian 257n8, 270n81, 279n46

materiality and materialism: Bergson and, 73–75; Derain and, 35–36, 56–57; Freud and, 89, 256n7; Loos and, 35; Matisse and, 300n10; memory and, 73–74; modernist privileging of, 1; Valéry and, 223, 249–51

Matisse, Henri, v; and affect, 7–8, 23, 27–28, 32; artistic practice of, 9, 12, 114, 168, 172; and autonomy, 110, 112–13, 119–20, 157–58, 164; bedroom of, 162; Bergson compared to, 2, 9, 96; Bergson's influence on, 98, 285n165; Cézanne's influence on, 117–20, 196–200; and change, 42, 110; and color, 27–28, 58–59, 256n8; control as theme/issue for, 42, 58, 116, 126, 301n35; copies after works in the Louvre, 296n86; criticisms of, 7, 111, 159, 166–67, 302n42; and daughter's traumatic experiences, 168–69; and death, 76; drama/theater in character and works of, 113–14, 123, 126, 167; "Exactitude Is Not Truth," 124; and expression, 2–3, 36, 101, 110, 123–24, 153, 165–67, 220; on genius, 109; Goldberg's influence on, 41–42; and hypnosis, 16, 113–17, 121–24; influences on, 16, 98, 109, 110–11, 116, 117–20, 155–60, 285n165; and intention, 9–13, 36, 42, 58; interpretations of, 3, 7–8, 70–71, 96–108, 263n4; and materialism, 300n10; and meaning, 110; and mimetic representation, 8, 17; and nature, 117; and nature of signification, 21, 153–54; "Notes of a Painter," 9, 41, 58, 110, 117, 134, 159, 166, 172, 174; and the other, 16, 109–10, 112, 124, 127, 152, 160–67, 220, 299n113; and *personnalité,* 16, 111, 113, 116, 154–60, 297n97, 299n113; and phenomenological mode of representation, 17, 136, 175–220; and phenomenology, 17; Picasso's relationship with, 160–63; "Portraits," 165; Prichard's relationship with, 97; and realism, 17, 116, 174–220; and representation, 2–3, 7–9, 105–6, 128, 136, 174–75, 217, 220; and the self, 16, 109–10, 120, 122–23, 155–60, 163–64, 299n113; skepticism of, 110–13, 124–27, 129, 157, 164, 166–67, 216; and specular representation, 7–8, 17; and the studio, 2, 111–12. *See also* detachment/separateness; identification

Matisse, Henri, works by: *The Alps in Savoy,* 134, 135; *Auguste Pellerin I,* 201; *Auguste Pellerin II,* 144, 145, 201; *Bathers by a River,* 136; *Bathers with a Turtle,* 203, 204, 206–7, 211; *Bevilacqua as Toreador,* 146, 152; *Blue Still Life,* 126; *Blue Tablecloth,* 126; *Le Bonheur de vivre,* 191–92, 201, 207–8, 213; *Bouquet on a Bamboo Table,* Plate 11, 189, 190, 194, 217; *Café Table,* Plate 9, 188, 194; *Carmelina,* Plate 2, 128–30, 136, 152, 187; Chapel of the Rosary, Vence, France, 27–28, 29; *Copy after Puget's Écorché,* 215, 216; costume sequence, 145–54; crouching figure type in, 207–11; *The Dance,* 161; *The Dance I,* 214; *The Dance II,* Plate 1, 24, 32, 37, 213–14; *The Dead Christ, after Philippe de Champaigne,* 148, 149; *Destiny,* 105; *Dishes and Fruit on a Red and Black Carpet,* Plate 18, 192, 194–96, 301n42; *Dishes and Melon,* Plate 14, 192, 194–96; *Female Guitarist,* 146; *Flowers,* Plate 16, 192, 194–95; formal characteristics of, 111–12; *Fruit and Coffee Pot,* Plate 8, 188; *The Geranium,* Plate 12, 189–90, 211; *Goldfish and Palette,* 201; *Goldfish and Sculpture,* 201; *Guitarist,* 146–47; *Harmony in Red,* 23, 25, 37–38, 101, 126; *Interior with a Goldfish,* 201; *Interior with a Top Hat,* 187; *Interior with Aubergines,* Plate 20, 214–17; *Interior with a Young Girl (Girl Reading),*

142, 144, 145; *Interior with Goldfish,* 201; *Italian Man (Bevilacqua),* 149, 151, 152; *Jaguar Devouring a Hare (after Antoine-Louis Barye),* 172–74; *Jazz,* 105, 115, 116, 131; *Lagoons,* 105, 106; landscapes, 134; *Laurette in a Green Robe (Black Background),* 217, 219, 220; *Lorette Reclining,* 201; *Lucien Guitry (as Cyrano),* 146, 152; *Le Luxe I,* 201–3, 207; *Le Luxe II,* Plate 19, 201, 203, 207; *Luxe, calme et volupté,* 152, 153; *Mademoiselle Yvonne Landsberg,* 99–101; *The Model,* 136, 139; *The Monk,* Plate 4, 146, 148–49; *Music,* 32, 33, 101–2, 152; *Music Lesson,* 201; *Nasturtiums with "Dance" I,* 201; *Nasturtiums with "Dance" II,* 201; *Nude Study in Blue,* 136, 139; *The Painter in His Studio,* 217, 219, 220; paired or double, 201–3, 220, 302n45; *Parakeet and Mermaid,* 172; *Piano Lesson,* 201; *Pine Trees,* 134, 135; *Pink Onions,* Plate 13, 190, 195, 217; *Plate with Nude,* 208, 209; *Portrait Medallion (II),* 176, 177; psychological effects and meanings of, 102, 203–4, 206–14; *The Red Blouse,* 130–31, 132; *The Red Rugs,* Plate 17, 192, 194–96; *Red Studio,* 35; *The Red Studio,* 107; *Room at Ajaccio,* 182–83; *The Rose,* 190, 191, 194, 195; *Seated Figure, Right Hand on Ground,* 208; *Self-Portrait,* 124, 125; self-portraiture, 2, 112, 113, 124, 176; self-reference in, 112, 128–34; skepticism of, 206–7; sketch of a film set, 126, 127; *Small Crouching Nude with Arms,* 208; *Small Crouching Nude without an Arm,* 208; *Small Crouching Torso,* 208, 209, 210–11, 302n55, 303n56; *The Snail,* 207, 208; standing figure type in, 113, 134–45; *Standing Guitarist,* 146; *Standing Nude* (ca. 1901), 136, 137; *Standing Nude* (ca. 1905), 136, 138; *Standing Nude* (sculpture), 192, 193, 194, 196; *Standing Nude (Study in Blue),* Plate 3, 136, 142; *Standing Nude, Arm Raised,* 136, 141; *Still Life,* Plate 7, 187–88; *Still Life with a Checked Tablecloth,* 130, 131, 187; *Still Life with African Sculpture,* 203, 204, 205; *Still Life with an Oil Jug,* 185, 186, 187; *Still Life with Apples,* 181–82; *Still Life with a Purro I,* 302n45; *Still Life with a Purro II,* 302n45; *Still Life with Aubergines,* 217, 218; *Still Life with Black Knives,* 183–85; *Still Life with Clay Pitcher and Black Knife,* 178, 179; *Still Life with Crab and Clay Pitcher,* 207; *Still Life with Fruits and Bottles,* 177–78, 179; *Still Life with Geranium,* 126; *Still Life with Oranges I,* 302n45; *Still Life with Oranges II,* 302n45; *Still Life with Pitcher,* 185, 186, 187; *Still Life with Plaster Figure,* Plate 15, 192, 194–95; *Still Life with Self-Portrait,* Plate 6, 176, 190, 194; *Still Life with Two Bottles,* 178, 180–82; *The Studio, quai St.-Michel,* 201; *Studio under the Eaves,* Plate 10, 189; *The Swimmer in the Aquarium,* 131, 133; tensions, conflicts, and dualities in, 8, 58, 109–10, 123, 129, 134, 136, 145, 172–220; *Thorn Extractor,* 189–90, 208, 211; *The Weeper,* 140; *Woman by a Stream,* 208; *Woman Leaning on Her Hands,* 189, 190; *Woman Reading,* Plate 5, 175–76, 187; *Woman with a Hat,* 59, 152, 166–67; *Young Sailor I,* 201; *Young Sailor II,* 201

Matisse, Marguerite, 168–70

Matisse, Pierre, 169

Maury, L. F., 78

McCarthy, Cormac, 221–22, 225, 249

meaning: beholder/reader as locus of, 15, 223, 246–47 (*see also* beholders: as creators); Bergson on, 95–96; of color, 39–40, 47, 53–54; communication confused with, 13; form

in relation to, 44, 45, 48, 50, 51, 52; intention in relation to, 3–4, 11–14, 17, 35–37, 233; of lines, 38–41, 53–54; Matisse's conception of, 110; public, 5, 247–48; relevance to, of beholder's response, 34; Valéry's conceptions of, 17. *See also* artistic communication; interpretation
medium: artist's intention in relation to, 13, 234; Matisse's relation to, 110, 165, 175; Valéry on role of, 232–34
Medusa, 102–3, 286n173
memory: and agency, 74; animal, 77–78; Bergson and, 15, 70–80, 278n43, 280n72; conservation of, 72–78, 278n43, 280n72; death and, 75–76, 78; déjà vu and, 66–67, 71–72; freedom and, 74; Freud and, 73, 280n72; materialist theory of, 73–74; ontological or world, 71–79; perception and, 71–72; unconscious, 77, 279n56
merger. *See* immersion
Merleau-Ponty, Maurice, 260n60, 294n67, 305n37
methods, art historical, 14
Michaels, Walter Benn, 261n77, 307n85
Michaud, Eric, 269n75
Michelangelo: *Crouching Boy,* 303n56
mimetic representation: characterized, 167–68; Matisse and, 8, 17, 168–74; tensions in, 167–68, 172. *See also* imitation
mimicry, 113–15
Mirbeau, Octave, 298n103
mirrors, 128–31, 133–34, 187, 294n67
model/subject: artist's detachment from, 168; artist's identification with, 17, 124, 165, 171–74
modernism: and autonomy, 120; beholder response emphasized in, 4, 24, 37, 44, 269n75; postmodernism derived from, 4, 24, 27; and reality, 1; and representation, 1, 22; and trauma, 104
modernity: Valéry on, 223, 230
Modes, theory of, 38–39, 43
Mondrian, Piet, 1, 255n1, 257n20
Monet, Claude, 110, 111, 293n61
Montesquieu, Charles-Louis Secondat, Baron de La Brède et de, 250
Moreau, Gustave, 111, 156
Morice, Charles, 166
Mourney, Gabriel, 59, 275n137
music: art likened to, 28–30, 46
Myers, Frederic W. H., 87, 282n119
mythmaking, 60

Nabis, 50–51
Nadler, Steven M., 255n1
Nancy, Jean-Luc, 158, 290n36
narration, and trauma, 169–70
nature: art compared to, 41, 44, 47, 54, 95, 285n147; as dictionary, 30, 54; identification with and possession of, 171; Matisse and, 117, 171, 174–75; realism and, 174–75; Valéry and, 222–23
near-death experiences, 78
necessity, déjà vu and, 67
Neo-Impressionism, 53–56
Nerval, Gérard de, 240
neuroarthistory, 43
New Bergsonism, 15–16, 65–66; on beholder response, 93–94; Matisse interpretations in, 96–108; subject areas of, 66
Newman, Barnett: *Who's Afraid of Red, Yellow, and Blue,* 103–4
Niemeyer, William, 206
Nietzsche, Friedrich, 19–20, 70, 105, 153
nudes, 136, 142

objectivity: photography and, 241–42
objects: artworks in relation to, 7, 12, 15, 37, 234–35, 238, 243–44, 246–47, 255n1; autonomy of, 36, 57; Brecht's distinction of, 34–35; colors as, 54; lines as, 54; self in relation to, 164; Valéry on artworks as, 221, 234–35, 238, 243–44, 246–47

October (journal), 19
ontological memory, 15
opticality, 7, 258n22
originary representation, 19–20
O'Sullivan, Simon, 266n34
other, the: artists and, 167; difference, 110; Gide and, 224; identification with, 166, 167, 170, 172; Matisse in relation to, 16, 109–10, 112, 124, 127, 152, 160–67, 220, 299n113; Valéry and, 224
"outside painting," 36, 56–57

Paillot de Montabert, Jacques-Nicolas de, 38
painting: Derain's notion of "outside painting," 36, 56–57; sculpture vs., 41, 236, 268n60
Parayre, Amélie, 182
pathologies of self: Bergson on, 9, 15, 72–78
Péladan, Sâr Joséphin, 159
Pellerin, Auguste, 145
perception: Bergson and, 3, 71–72; as locus of art interpretation, 3–4; Matisse's work and, 101–2; memory and, 71–72
performance: in relation to composition, 239, 242
performatives, 264n6
personnalité, 16, 111, 113, 116, 154–60, 297n97, 299n113. *See also* self, the; subjectivity
perspective, visual, 20–21
persuasion in interpretation, 4, 12
PET scans, 27
phenomenological mode of representation: immersion associated with, 175; Matisse and, 17, 136, 175–220; realist mode compared to, 175–220
photography, 19, 20, 241–42, 307n85
physiology. *See* body
piano, 28
Picasso, Pablo, 12, 13, 32, 111, 134, 156, 160, 206, 248, 301n35; *Les Demoiselles d'Avignon,* 206–7, 213, 286n173; *Winter Landscape,* 160–63
Pippin, Robert, 160, 259n39,
Pissarro, Camille, 51
pleasure, 5–6
Poe, Edgar Allan, 226
Poggi, Christine, 54–55
politics: of the avant-garde, 57; Valéry and, 250–51; visual form and, 20–21, 56, 57
Pollock, Jackson, 12, 260n51
Pontalis, J.-B., 300n15
portraiture, 68–69
postmodernism: and the affective turn, 14; modernism as source for, 4, 24, 27; and risk, 231
Potts, Alex, 211
Pound, Ezra, 238
Poussin, Nicolas, 38–40, 43, 153; *The Testament of Eudamidas,* 39, 40
predictability, 223, 230–31, 235
Prichard, Matthew, 16, 97–98, 99, 101, 108, 122
primary identification, 168, 300n15
Prince, Morton, 278n43
Proust, Marcel, 4
psychological effects and meanings of Matisse's work, 102, 203–4, 206–14
psychological interpretation, 102
public meaning of artworks, 5, 247–48
Puy, Michel, 110, 122

Raphael, 153
readers. *See* beholder/reader response; beholders/readers
realism: defined, 175; detachment and skepticism associated with, 175; Matisse and, 17, 116, 174–220; and nature, 174–75; phenomenological mode compared to, 175–220; as pictorial mode, 17, 175
reality: art in relation to, 22; Krauss on surrealist photography and, 19; modernism and, 1
Redon, Odilon, 111

Rembrandt van Rijn, 152
Renoir, Pierre-Auguste, 111, 165
representation: and action/agency, 223, 264n6; and affect, 2–6; Bergson and, 2, 8–9; Cézanne and, 196–200, 291n39; déjà vu and, 67; limits of, 2; Matisse and, 2–3, 7–9, 105–6, 128, 136, 174–75, 217, 220; meanings of, 6–8; modernism and, 1; *October* aesthetics and, 19; originary, 19–20; in relation to world, 22; Rodchenko on, 6–7; two modes of, 8–9, 17, 136, 175–220; Valéry and, 223; violence of, 225. *See also* antirepresentationalism
rhythm, 29–30, 32, 92–93
rhythmic duration, 93, 96, 99
Ribot, Théodule, 78
Richet, Charles, 73, 91
Ricoeur, Paul, 70
Rivière, Jacques, 7, 166
Robinet, André, 81, 86
Rodchenko, Alexander, 1, 6–7, 255n1
Rodin, Auguste, 44; *The Crouching Woman,* 211, 212
Rouillard, A. M. P., 78
Rousseau, Jean-Jacques, 293n60
Rousseau, Pascal, 59
Rouveyre, André, 41, 76, 169
Roux-Champion, Victor, 158–59

Salon d'Automne, 146, 192, 211, 214, 301n42
Sartre, Jean-Paul, 74, 75
Schneider, Pierre, 16, 98, 115, 152, 295n78, 301n37
Schuffenecker, Émile, 44, 48
sculpture: Bergson on, 94; painting vs., 41, 236, 268n60; Valéry on chance and, 236, 238
Séailles, Gabriel, 41
self, the: abnormal/pathological psychic states and, 9, 15, 72–78; art and, 93–96; Bergson and, 70, 93–94; Freud on, 164, 168, 290n36; hypnosis and, 16, 80–81, 115–16, 121–22; identification as root of, 168; influence and, 109, 116, 119; Matisse and, 16, 109–10, 120, 122–23, 154–60, 163–64, 299n113; objects in relation to, 164; Valéry on, 229–31. *See also* identification; *personnalité*; subjectivity
self-hypnosis, 122–23
self-portraiture, 2, 112, 113, 124, 176
self-reference, painters', 112, 128–34
Sembat, Marcel, 111, 157
semiotics, 18–21
separateness. *See* detachment/separateness
Settimelli, Emilio, 63
Seurat, Georges, 50, 54, 55, 110, 111, 153, 273n116; *Chahut,* 55
Shakespeare, William, 96
shock: produced by color or form, 53, 56, 58
Sidlauskas, Susan, 118
Signac, Paul, 53, 55–56, 111, 153, 265n22
signs: freed from the semantic, 20; literature and, 240; Matisse and, 153–54; mediating function of, 18–19, 21; qualities of, 7
simulation, 85, 88, 90
skepticism: autonomy in relation to, 112; limits of, 112, 156, 164, 204, 216; Matisse and, 110–13, 124–27, 129, 157, 164, 166–67, 206–7, 216; realism associated with, 175; Valéry and, 232, 235, 242, 244, 307n81. *See also* detachment/separateness
social conformity, 91–92
Society for Psychical Research, 78, 87, 91
South Seas, 171
spectacle, 61
specular representation, 7–8, 17, 187. *See also* realism
Spurling, Hilary, 126
standing figure type, 113, 134–45
Stein, Gertrude, 97
Sternhell, Zeev, 65
Stokes, Adrian, 301n35

studio: Matisse's preoccupation with, 2, 111–12, 142, 146–47
subjectivity: déjà vu and, 66–67; in experience of art, 5–6; and freedom, 71; representation and, 8. *See also* identification; *personnalité*; self, the
subject matter, 46–49
subject of art. *See* model/subject
suggestion: Bergson and, 85–88, 90–92; Bernheim on, 284n131; Freud and, 89, 115–16, 283n124, 289n31, 290n32; hypnotic, 80–81, 83, 121, 229; problem of, from scientific perspective, 85–92; in psychoanalytic treatment, 283n124. *See also* hypnosis; influence
Superville, Humbert de, 54–55, 273n112
surrealism, 159
surrealist photography, 19
Sutter, David, 38–39
Swedenborg, Emanuel, 54
symbolism, 14, 30, 40, 44–54, 159, 239
synesthesia, 265n24

Tarde, Gabriel, 121
technology: Benjamin on, 307n85; Valéry on, 235
telepathy, 83–87, 281n109, 282n113
theater. *See* drama and theater
theater of cruelty, 60–61
Thoreau, Henry David, 21
thought transference, 81–88, 281n109, 282n113, 282n119
Tolstoy, Leo, 166
trauma: in beholder's experience of art, 3, 21, 23–24, 32–34, 61, 103; Bergsonian Matisse interpretations and, 96–97, 101–2; defined, 169–70; hypnosis in relation to, 169–70; identification and, 102–3, 169–70; Matisse's daughter and, 168–70; Medusa myth and, 102–3; modernist painting and, 104; Picasso's work and, 286n173
Tügenhold, Jacob, 214
Turner, J. M. W., 111
unconscious, the: Bergson on, 73–74, 84–87, 90; Freud and, 13, 89; hypnosis and, 90; and intention, 13, 68; and representation, 9–10
unconscious memory, 73, 77, 279n56

Valéry, Paul, 4, 221–51; on art as machine, 226, 226–27; on art in general, 243–44, 306n47; and blood, 224, 225, 249, 251; and causality, 223, 231, 243; "Commentaries on *Charmes*," 245, 246; and communicative methods, 225–30; "The Conquest of Ubiquity," 235; on conventions, 229–30; *Degas, danse, dessin,* 116; on Eastern vs. Western cultures, 221–22; on European culture, 221–23; and evaluation of art, 232–34; and hypnosis, 229–30; and intention, 17–18, 228–29, 232–36, 238–41, 244–51, 260n52, 304n32, 305n37, 306n65; "Introduction to the Method of Leonardo da Vinci," 227, 305n37; *La Jeune Parque,* 248; "Letter about Mallarmé," 239; and literature, 223–29, 239–41, 245; "Literature and Politics," 251; and materialism, 223, 249–51; *Monsieur Teste,* 228; "Monsieur Teste's Logbook," 228; "My Bust," 238; "Notes on the Greatness and Decline of Europe," 223; "Odds and Ends," 245; "On History," 223; "On Literary Technique," 225–26; "On Nations," 222–23; "On Political Parties," 250; "The Outlook for Intelligence," 230; "Philosophy of Photography," 241; on poetic affect, 226–28; and reader/beholder response, 223, 225–29, 235, 236, 238–40, 242–51; "Reflections on Art," 243; and representation, 223; and the self, 229–31; skepticism of, 232, 235, 242, 244, 307n81; "The Struggle for Peace," 223; on technology and media, 235; and violence, 223–24; "The Yalu," 221–22, 225

vandalism of art, 104
van Gogh, Vincent, 50, 60, 110, 166, 187, 270n82
Vautier, Renée, 236, 237
Vauxcelles, Louis, 111, 166, 302n42
Velázquez, Diego, 152; *Las Meninas,* 152; *Pablo de Valladolid,* 152
viewers. *See* beholders/readers
violence: Artaud and, 61, 63; of artistic material and form, 23–25, 32; in beholder's experience of art, 61, 63; Deleuze on, 225; Fauvism and, 57–58; in Matisse's artistic practice, 168; in Matisse's work, 106–7; of representation, 225; Valéry and, 223–24
vision: Bergson's privileging of, 69; Freud's privileging of, 103; hierarchies of, 20–22, 24, 32–33
vitalism, 74, 79
Vlaminck, Maurice de, 57–58
Vollard, Ambroise, 120, 211
von Hartmann, Eduard, 87–88
Vorstellung, 8
Vuillard, Édouard, 50, 194

Wagner, Richard, 226, 227, 242–43, 245
Ward, Martha, 55
Watteau, Antoine, 152; *La Finette,* 152; *Mezzetin,* 152
Weston, Edward, 34
Wimsatt, William, 247
Winslow, Forbes, 78
Wittgenstein, Ludwig, 109
world. *See* reality
World War II, 168
Wright, Alastair, 15, 23–24, 70, 104, 153–54, 263n1, 287n181, 297n97
Wyzewa, Teodor de, 226

Yolton, John W., 255n1

Zarlino, Giuseppe, 38
Zone Books, 66

Todd Cronan teaches modern art at Emory University.